CW01021041

A CLASSICAL LEXICON FOR
Finnegans Wake

A Classical Lexicon for
Finnegans Wake

A Glossary of the Greek and Latin
in the major works of Joyce

including
Finnegans Wake, the Poems, *Dubliners*, *Stephen Hero*,
A Portrait of the Artist as a Young Man, *Exiles*, and *Ulysses*

by Brendan O Hehir
and John M. Dillon

University of California Press

BERKELEY   LOS ANGELES   LONDON

UNIVERSITY OF CALIFORNIA PRESS
BERKELEY AND LOS ANGELES, CALIFORNIA
UNIVERSITY OF CALIFORNIA PRESS., LTD.
LONDON, ENGLAND

PRINTED IN THE UNITED STATES OF AMERICA

This book is dedicated to the whisky distillers of Ireland, without whose spiritual comfort it could never have been brought to completion.

PREFACE

This book is designed to be a companion to O Hehir's *A Gaelic Lexicon for Finnegans Wake* and Bonheim's *A Lexicon of the German in Finnegans Wake* (both Berkeley and Los Angeles, 1967). It follows the same tricolumnar format as those earlier works, listing the words or phrases to be glossed not alphabetically but in the order of their occurrence in the text, by page number and line number on the page. The first column lists the item to be glossed, the middle column rectifies the textual appearance into orthodox Greek or Latin, and the third column provides the gloss in the form of a translation or explanatory note. We request purists to forgive us that we have not taken what seems to us the needlessly circuitous course of rendering Greek words in the Greek alphabet. Since perhaps a majority of users of this work will not be conversant with Greek, use of the Greek letters would be a pedantic luxury that would still require transliteration for the sake of intelligibility. Besides, the Greek or Greek-derived words that Joyce uses all appear in roman transliteration in the first place; in the entire corpus of his published books only one three-word phrase occurs in Greek characters (*Finnegans Wake* 269.L3). In transliterating Greek we have followed the established conventions: η and ω we represent respectively by ê and ô; υ we represent variously by u or y, as seems more appropriate or revealing.

Aberrations from the format described above, when they are compelled by the vagaries of Joyce's practice, should occasion no difficulty. Unlike the situation in the *Gaelic Lexicon*, we have felt no necessity to provide a guide to the pronunciation of Latin and Greek. Like the *Gaelic Lexicon*, however, the present work, in order to avoid overloading the glosses, has had recourse to a series of longer notes gathered together at the back of the book. Appendix A and Appendix B, listing respectively proper names and recurrent phrases, are arranged alphabetically; Appendix C, essentially an extended gloss to pages 306–308 of *Finnegans Wake*, treats its materials in the order of their occurrence; the final alphabetic series of Supplementary Notes is a sequence of expanded glosses directly comparable to their counterparts in the *Gaelic Lexicon*.

That the present book is somewhat bulkier than its precursors should occasion no surprise, inasmuch as it deals with two languages, not one, and those two are languages that have contributed immensely to the vocabulary of modern English. This latter fact poses, of course, a very crucial problem for the compilers of a Latin and Greek lexicon to *Finnegans Wake*: manifestly, to gloss every word in the text that derives from a Latin or Greek root could entail glossing every second word. But at what point is the line to be drawn? One potential criterion would be to gloss no word that appears in a standard English dictionary. This, however, we discarded early as too restrictive. Such Latin terms as *nisi prius* and *de facto*, such Greek locutions as *hoi polloi* and **eureka*, appear in every standard English dictionary, but it would be ludicrous for a purported glossary of Latin and Greek on that account to exclude them. On the other hand, many thousands of words in *Finnegans Wake* are not to be found in the standard dictionary of any language, at least verbatim and literatim, so such a rule would admit more than it could exclude. But although many words in Joyce's nightmare are distortions of readily identifiable English words of Latin or Greek derivation that can be easily reconstituted, the very distortion itself is usually significant. When the distortion is in some way a reflex of the etymology of the word in question we have usually felt required to provide a gloss sufficient to illuminate Joyce's apparent intention, or at least the mechanism of his deformation. Nevertheless on occasion an English word of Latin or Greek origin will appear in undistorted dictionary form. In such cases we have examined the word in context to attempt to determine if its resonance is fully perceptible in English alone, or if, as so often, Joyce is etymologizing. Whenever we have suspected that etymologizing is afoot we have conceived it our responsibility to provide a gloss.

This procedure, therefore, must have led us on occasion to redundant glossing. Likewise our glossing of the etymologies of proper names, so far as determinable, may be redundant: we have no persuasive evidence that Joyce knew, cared about, or made use of the possible etymologies of the names of Plato or Aristotle or Caesar. But he *did* know and make use of the fact that the name Leonidas has something to do with lions. This general topic is touched upon in the Preface to *A Gaelic Lexicon* (p. viii) in words more pregnant than their author knew when he wrote them: "Sometimes etymologizing names in *Finnegans Wake* reveals a surprising applicability in the context, often enough it reveals nothing at all that I, at any rate, can see. But perseverance has its rewards. . . . Sometimes a sudden flash will illuminate the use Joyce is making of an underlying meaning; sometimes no flash comes and the etymologizing of names remains a dry pedantic exercise." In the *Gaelic Lexicon* the names Kettle, Griffith, and Moynihan (306.09) are dutifully glossed and etymologized in a dry pedantic exercise from which no flash then came. But in the present work, when those names came together in a classical context, the *Irish* etymologies of the latter two set off a blinding flash: the curious reader is referred to the glosses on 306.09 and to Appendix C. But again to quote that former Preface, "a lexicographer is not called upon to decide the relevance of what he records," and we offer no apology for the possibility that we have overglossed. A comment is in order on a certain class of words which classicists may find unfamiliar, and which our classicist member frequently balked at. This consists of glosses derived from Hesychius' lexicon. These words are frequently bizarre, and often, perhaps, not even Greek, but we are persuaded that Joyce in fact thumbed through his Liddell and Scott, and so that it is hard to exclude anything to be found therein.

It is in the matter of underglossing that we feel somewhat meek and humble; we cannot escape the apprehension that we must have failed to notice or gloss properly material that unquestionably belongs to our province. At the same time we must assert that our province is coterminous with the classical languages and classical culture only, a point we shall return to below. That we should at some point have failed adequately to gloss the classical references in *Finnegans Wake* at least, strikes us as inevitable and condonable in that we have had to deal with a text wherein *Eggs squawfish lean yoe nun feed marecurious* (384.36) can be quite unexceptionable Latin, and "Men, teacan a tea simmering, hamo mavrone kerry o? Teapotty. Teapotty" (247.14-15) can be an intelligible conversation in Greek. We have spotted these two instances; what have we missed? For the captious reader we offer the following instances of what echo like Latin or Greek in our ears, but out of which we have been unable to construe sense:

Tez thelon langlo, walking weary! (202.22)—*is this Greek?*

Oglores, the virtuoser prays, olorum! (286.31-287.01)—*is this a sequential piece of Latin?*

Whet the bee as to deflowret greendy grassies yellowhorse. (360.26-30)—*is this Latin [Ut tibi . . .]?*

Still let stultitiam done in veino condone ineptias made of veritues. (510.05-06)—*is this an entire Latin sentence?*

Lacaus esant taratara. (*Ulysses* p. 370)—*is our explanation of this utterance correct?*

As to the exclusion or inclusion of words of undoubted classical provenance, perhaps the somewhat subjective principle we have tried to adhere to may be made clearer to the reader by a recapitulation of the approach we took to glossing one word— *rhumanasant* (084.05). The word is used in the course of describing some kind of a weapon: "their humoral hurlbat or other uncertain weapon of *lignum vitae,* but so evermore rhumanasant of a toboggan poop . . ." As we read this we hear an underlying straightforward English phrase, "reminiscent of a tobacco pipe," as we assume most English-speaking readers will also. And we take instant note that "reminiscent" derives from Latin *reminiscens,* present participle of the verb *reminiscor.* Shall we therefore gloss "rhumanasant" by reference to *reminiscor?* Lewis and Short tell us that *reminiscor* means "to recall to mind, recollect, remember; to call to mind, imagine, conceive," so that *reminiscens* means "calling to mind, recollecting, remembering, having the power to call to mind, etc." An American college dictionary tells us that the word *reminiscent* means "having the nature of or characterized by reminiscence; remembering; recalling the past; bringing to mind . . ." and defines the noun *reminiscence* invoked in the foregoing definition as "a remembering; recollecting; recalling to mind." So far as we can see, there is (a) no significant difference in meaning between Latin *reminiscens* and English *reminiscent,* and (b) no indication that Joyce is attempting to exploit in any way the microscopic shades of difference. So we avoid wasting space and patronizing the reader by refraining from telling him what "reminiscent" means. Yet the fact still remains that "rhumanasant" is something more than "reminiscent." Our ears also suggest to us the presence of "ruminative" or the verb "ruminate," and this too is a word of Latin derivation. *Ruminatio* means "a chewing over again, chewing the cud, rumination [!]; a thinking over, revolving in the mind." The verb *ruminor* means "to chew over again, chew the cud, to ruminate; to think over, to muse *or* ruminate upon." Our American dictionary gives us: *ruminate,* "to chew (the cud) as a cow does; to turn (something) over in the mind; meditate or reflect (on)," and *rumination,* "the act of chewing the cud; meditation; reflective consideration." It is not our task or purpose to tell the reader what *English* words are contained or reflected in *Finnegans Wake.* He will see (or hear) for himself that "rhumanasant" probably contains both "reminiscent" and "ruminant"; the fact that we have introduced neither of the Latin words *reminiscens* or *ruminans* into our gloss reflects our judgment that to do so would add not an iota of illumination to the reader's understanding of the English words. But it is also evident that both "reminiscent" and "ruminant" together cannot account fully for the word "rhumanasant." "Ruminant" would account for both the -u- of the first syllable and the -a- of the last, as against the -e- and -e- of "reminiscent." But the -h- after the initial r—a distinctively Greek-indicating feature—and the -a- of the second syllable (as against the -i- of both "reminiscent" and "ruminant") both need to be accounted for. Our ventures with Greek *rheuma* and Latin *mano*—which seem to us to yield adequate sense— will be found in the appropriate place (p. 55).

And just as it is not our task or purpose to tell the reader what English words are contained or reflected in *Finnegans Wake*, neither is it our purpose to gloss words or allusions in foreign languages other than Latin or Greek, even when those allusions predominate over classical material at the same locus. Although it seems to us that this restriction should be clear without stating it, our experience with various readers who have seen this work in manuscript requires us to insist upon the point. How can we gloss "Alphos, Burkos and Caramis" (064.23) with a frigid "alpha, beta, gamma," a reader will protest, ignoring the patent allusion to the *noms de guerre* of the Three Musketeers? The response is obvious: neither Dumas nor his characters have any bearing on our classical province. At 071.16-17 we gloss *"Tummer the Lame the Tyrannous"* as a probable allusion to Oedipus, wholly overlooking the reference to Tamerlane (*Timur-i-Leng*, "Lame Timur"!) because both the Central Asian scene and the dates of his career (1336–1405) are far removed from the classical world. He is just none of our present business. If it pleases the reader to condemn our blindness at overlooking some recondite German allusion or fascinating French word-play we are glad of his pleasure but still ask him to consider if it is well-placed. On this particular border of our province, in fact, we feel we might more justifiably be rebuked for our occasional incursions into the romance languages (and in a very few instances even wider afield—as far as Russian at 518.31!) than reprimanded for the timidity of our aggressions against exposed targets. But for our final defense both as to commissions and omissions we invoke Aristotle, who has stated our case better than we can express it ourselves: "In studying this subject we must be content if we attain as high a degree of certainty as the matter of it admits" (*Ethics* I .iii).

At this point it may be in order to speak about what this Lexicon reveals concerning Joyce as a classicist. In sum, the picture conforms to that already discernible in, for example, Ellmann's biography. Joyce's education, while not profound, was heavily Latinate. He knew Latin quite well and could compose in that language with fair fluency and sense of stylistic effect. He saw the classical world, as did most products of the Medieval and Humanist literary tradition, through Latin spectacles. He knew the Olympian pantheon and Greek mythology through the *interpretatio Romana*—typically he invokes Mercurius rather than Hermes and produces such linguistic hybrids as Venus (instead of Aphrodite) Pandemos. He quotes snatches from Latin authors—Vergil, Ovid, Horace, medieval Schoolmen—not from Greek authors. He probably normally pronounced Latin in the medieval Italianate manner formerly used for the Roman liturgy, but he was aware of the reconstructed "classical" pronunciation. In his days at University College Dog-Latin was in fashion; *Stephen Hero* and *A Portrait of the Artist* abound in examples, and sometimes the Latin in *Finnegans Wake* is of the same quality—e.g., *petroperfractus* (041.06) for "stony broke." Joyce's mind was also well furnished with fragments of Church Latin—echoes of the liturgy, devotional works, the writings of the Fathers and better-known scriptural passages. Sometimes his quotation of Latin Scripture is inaccurate, as if he were retranslating into Latin from the English text with the aid of a somewhat faulty memory. An occasional esotericism in vocabulary may derive from these extra-classical sources, though we are also persuaded he must have done a good deal of brute dictionary-browsing in both Latin and Greek. A case in point is Joyce's assurance to Harriet Weaver on 15 November 1926 that "rory" in the first paragraph of *Finnegans Wake* (now the second paragraph: 003.13) " = Latin, roridus = dewy." Had it not been for this gloss explicitly provided by Joyce himself, we should not have noted "rory" as Latin at all. Without his express authority we should never have presumed to promote the stem *rori-* into the full adjective *roridus* (we have not so proceeded in any other instance), and besides it would not have spontaneously occurred to us to see the Latin word for "dewy" even in that stem, for *roridus* is by no means the usual or common Latin word for "dewy." Vergil and the chief classical writers use rather the word *roscidus*; Lewis and Short cite only two instances of the form Joyce uses.

One aspect of Joyce's Latinity piques us, so far in vain. At several places in *Finnegans Wake* occur little mnemonic rhymes enshrining particular cruxes of Latin grammar, a device at one time frequent in Latin texts designed for schools. These rhymes at once struck a nostalgic chord in the mind of the classicist member of our team who, like Joyce, had received his Latin grounding in Dublin. We have been unable to ascertain, however, precisely which primer was used by Joyce in school. Kennedy's *Latin Primer* (in a multiplicity of editions) seemed the most probable, but we have been unable to find an exemplar containing precisely the rhymes quoted in *Finnegans Wake*. To our sorrow, Kevin Sullivan's *Joyce Among the Jesuits* has been of no service in this regard.

On the subject of Greek Joyce was far less masterful than he was with Latin. In effect he knew little or no classical Greek, though he picked up some fluency in Modern Greek from Greek residents of Trieste. The Stephen Daedalus of *Stephen Hero* affects contempt for Greek literature—perhaps as a reflex of his cultural inferiority complex—and readers of *Ulysses* will recall Buck Mulligan's expressed desire to teach Stephen Dedalus Greek (005.07-08). But invidious deduction is needless in the light of Joyce's clear assertion to Miss Weaver in a letter of 24 June 1921: "I don't even know Greek though I am spoken of as erudite. . . . I spoke or used to speak modern Greek not too badly . . . and have spent a great deal of time with Greeks of all kinds . . ." His approach to classical Greek was as it were through the medium of Latin—the Greek surname of his youthful self-projection is Daedalus or Dedalus, not Daidalos. Otherwise, as in *Finnegans Wake*, when he attempts to reproduce the phonetics of Greek, he ascribes modern Greek phonetic values—farther removed from those of the classical age than those of Italian from Cicero's Latin—to the letters of the Greek alphabet. A curious anomaly, arising out of modern phonetic values, occurs in his representation of Greek in *A Portrait of the Artist*. In Chapter IV of that book, Stephen, walking on the Bull Wall, is greeted by his schoolfellows as "Bous Stephaneforos" (168.04-05, etc.). We have rendered the latter word, conventionally, *stephanêphoros*. But Joyce has apparently chosen to render the Greek consonant φ ("phi") as f, which of course accurately represents its modern phonetic value, rather than as the traditional and historically valid ph. In Modern Greek the letter φ is certainly used to render the f of western languages, and Joyce may have considered the ph alternative musty antiquarianism. If so, he reveals his unawareness that the Latin digraph ph was first used to transliterate Greek φ because φ genuinely represented the sound of p + h (see Supplementary Note, *Labials*). And Joyce compounds the anomaly by retaining the -ph- of "Stephan-," transliterating precisely the same Greek letter, where his rather cranky rationalization—if that is what it is—would seem to call for *Stefaneforos. But we have worried some of these matters in the Appendixes and Supplementary Notes (see especially Appendix A, *Daedalus*, and

Supplementary Notes *Digamma, Greek-to-Latin* and *Labials*). Nevertheless, if we correctly ascribe to Joyce's conscious intent a considerable number of the Greek words we find in *Finnegans Wake*, he must have made many lucky dips into Liddell and Scott.

Because of the extensive use of Latin particularly (including Dog-Latin) in Joyce's earlier works, this Lexicon should be of considerable service to the general, unclassical reader of Joyce's entire corpus, even to one who cares not to venture into the wilder torrent of *Finnegans Wake*. Unlike the *Gaelic Lexicon*, the present work has had to gloss *Stephen Hero* as well as the other early works, and so can fairly claim to be a classical vade mecum to all of Joyce, even though glosses to *Finnegans Wake* outnumber those to the entire additional bulk of Joyce's works in the proportion of something like seven to one.

The principal works consulted in compiling this Lexicon are listed separately in the Bibliography, but again it is necessary to acknowledge the indispensable help afforded by Clive Hart's pioneering *Concordance to Finnegans Wake*. We have picked up some valuable hints and insights from, in addition to those works listed below, Robert M. Adams' *James Joyce: Common Sense and Beyond* (New York, 1966).

BIBLIOGRAPHY

The following are the works chiefly consulted in making this Lexicon:

Ellmann, Richard *James Joyce*, New York (1959).

Encyclopedia of the Classical World, The (Elseviers), Englewood Cliffs, N.J. (1965).

Glasheen, Adaline, *A Second Census of Finnegans Wake*, Evanston (1963).

Lewis, Charlton T. and Charles Short, *A Latin Dictionary*, Oxford (1879).

Liddell, Henry George, and Robert Scott, *A Greek-English Lexicon*: new ed. rev. by Sir Henry Stuart Jones, Oxford (1940).

Oxford Classical Dictionary, The, Oxford (1949).

Sullivan, Kevin, *Joyce Among the Jesuits*, New York (1958).

Thomson, J. O., *Everyman's Classical Atlas*, London and New York (1961).

We have also browsed *ad libitum* in the vast field of Joycean scholarship, and have no doubt picked up many an unintentionally unacknowledged gem.

CONTENTS

KEY TO THE GLOSSARIES

All the Glossaries are arranged in three principal columns. On the left, preceded by page and line numbers of Joyce's respective works, occurs *verbatim et literatim* the word or phrase to be glossed. The central column prints in Latin or Greek as the case may be (designated respectively L or G) the original of the word or phrase Joyce has used. The third or right-hand column translates the word or phrase into English, or provides an explanatory comment, or on occasion does both.

Because the contents of the Glossary for *Finnegans Wake* are to be incorporated into a computer-readable "polyglossary" of all the foreign languages in *Finnegans Wake*, a new system of enumeration for entries in that Glossary has been adopted, going beyond the convention established by Clive Hart's *Concordance*. Each word or phrase is now designated not only by page and line, but also by an alphabetical letter indicating the position of the word in the line. Therefore the word "Trinitatis" on page 240, for example, is labeled 240.10 G, indicating it is the seventh word of the tenth line on that page. Words divided at the end of a line are counted only as the last word in that line, and do not enter at all into the word-count of the succeeding line upon which they are concluded—the first complete following word on the next line counts as word "A" of that line. Typographical peculiarities of *Finnegans Wake* produce certain problems in enumeration, which are resolved as follows:

1) The hundred-letter thunderword: Occurrences of this word extend over from two to three lines of text. Each such word has been arbitrarily divided into segments of five letters each, regardless of syllabification, and each such group of five letters counted as a separate word. Thus the Greek word "–bronnton–," composed of letters 35-43 of the first occurrence of the thunderword, is cited as 003.15 I-K. Two words precede the thunderword on line 15, so that the first five letters of the latter constitute 003.15 C; the "–b–" of "–bronnton–" is the last letter of group I, "–ronnt–" is group J, and "–on–" uses the first two letters of group K.

2) The Triv-and-Quad chapter: This chapter presents two kinds of problems, as follows: (a) Right and left marginal, or shoulder, notes: after the page-number each note is first marked L or R to designate Left or Right margin, then by an arabic numeral to indicate the number of the note in

column on its page. Where notes are printed closely in succession, a period (full-stop) is taken to mark the end of any given note. Within each shoulder-note, each word is labeled alphabetically according to its position in the text of the note. Thus "VIRGINIANAE" is captioned 281.R3 B, it being the second word of the third note in the righthand margin of page 281.

(b) Footnotes: (i) words occurring in footnotes no longer than one line are denoted by page-number, footnote-number, and alphabetical position, F signifying "footnote." So the word "lucreasious" occurs as 277.F2 H, being the eighth word in footnote 2 on page 277. (ii) Words occurring in footnotes longer than one line are additionally identified by line-number within the footnote. So "amare" is designated 279.F1.9 G, because it is the seventh complete word in line 9 of footnote 1 on page 279.

3) Hyphenated strings of words: At first it was decided to count each complete hyphenated string as a single word, but this decision was later revoked in favor of counting each component word in a hyphenated string as a separate word.

Because of an editorial decision not to print in column the alphabetical letters indicating the position of each word in its line, much of the foregoing information may appear otiose. The letter-indicators are, however, retained in the computer's memory, and cross-references in the printed text generally cite the letter as well as the page and line number. The value and necessity of the new system will become manifest only when *all* foreign words and phrases come to be glossed in a single "polyglossary."

ABBREVIATIONS AND SYMBOLS

#A	See captioned item alphabetically listed in Appendix A
Acc.	the form of the word denoting the Accusative Case
adj.	adjective
adv.	adverb
#B	See captioned phrase alphabetically listed in Appendix B
#C	See captioned item in Appendix C
C	century
Celt.	Celtic: the language of the continental Celts, e.g., the Gauls
Dat.	the form of the word denoting the Dative Case
eccl. L	ecclesiastical Latin: the form of Latin used in the Roman Church
Eng.	English: the English language
Etr.	Etruscan or Etrurian: the language of the ancient Etruscans
fem.	feminine: the feminine form of a noun or adjective
Fr.	French: the French language
fut.	future: the form of a verb denoting the future tense
G	Greek; the Greek language
G + L	the captioned word is a compound of Greek and Latin elements
Gael.	Gaelic: the Irish language
Gen.	the form of the word denoting the Genitive Case
G L	the word belongs to both the Greek and the Latin languages, either because it occurs spontaneously in identical form in both languages, or because it has been adopted unchanged by Latin from Greek
Heb.	Hebrew: the Hebrew language
L	Latin: the Latin language
LL	Late or Low Latin: the form of Latin spoken from about a.d. 100 to 500.

masc.	masculine: the masculine form of a noun or adjective
MG	Modern Greek: the form of the Greek language spoken in recent times including the present
ML	Middle *or* Medieval Latin: the form of Latin spoken and written in the Middle Ages, from about a.d. 500 to 1500.
Mod.L	Modern Latin: the artificial form of Latin that is used at the present day usually to coin scientific terms
n	noun
neut.	neuter: the neuter form of a noun or adjective
Nom.	the form of the word denoting the Nominative Case
OG	Old Greek: Greek of the pre-classical period, as witnessed in archaic inscriptions, in the Minoan B tablets, and as deductively reconstructed
OL	Old Latin: Latin of the pre-classical period, as witnessed in archaic texts and inscriptions, and as deductively reconstructed
Osc.	Oscan: the Oscan language, an extinct language of Italy related to Latin
part trans.	partly translates, is a partial translation of
pl.	plural: the form of the word that denotes the plural
pp.	past participle, the past-participial form of a verb
pron.	pronounced: the word is pronounced as indicated
Sab.	Sabine: the Sabine language, an extinct language of Italy related to Latin
sing.	singular: the form of the word that denotes the singular
trans.	translates, is a translation of; translation
vb.	verb
Voc.	the form of the word denoting the Vocative Case
*	(preceding a word) indicates the word is not actually attested in the surviving corpus of Greek and Latin. We have used this symbol indifferently in the conventional manner, i.e., to mark words hypothetically reconstructed by scholarship, and to mark words which appear to be Joyce's idiosyncratic constructions out of Greek or Latin elements
#	see indicated Supplementary Note

Glossary for *Finnegans Wake*

003.02	commodius	Commodus L (161–192)	"Convenient": bad Roman emperor
.02	vicus	vicus L	row of houses, street, village
.05	Armorica	Armorica L	"at the sea" (*ar mor* Celt., *ar mare* OL): northern provinces of Gaul; modern Brittany; #*A*
.06	penisolate	paene L paeninsula L	almost almost-island: peninsula
.07	exaggerated	exaggero L	to raise a mound, to heap up ["to mound up"—*Joyce to Harriet Weaver, 15 November 1926*]
.08	gorgios	Gorgias (483–376 BC) G	"Lively[?]": sophist, eponym of Platonic dialogue: taught that nothing knowable exists, language cannot communicate knowledge: advocated development of prose style as pure art

.13	rory	roridus L	dewy [*Joyce to Weaver*, 15 Nov. 1926]
.15	–bronnto–	brontaô G	to thunder
.15	–bronnton–	Brontôn G Bronton L	"Thunderer": epithet of Zeus, #A
.15	–ton–	tono L	to thunder
.24	livvy	Titus Livius L	Roman historian: "Livy"; #A
004.02	Brékkek Kékkek Kékkek Kékkek! Kóax Kóax Kóax!	Brekekekex, ko-ax, ko-ax, Brekekekex ko-ax, ko-ax, G	croaking of Aristophanes' *Frogs* (405 b.c.)
.03	Quauoauh	qua L	on which side? where? how?
.04	mathmaster	mathê *or* mathêsis G	learning, education
.05	camibalistics	ballistra G balista L	war-machine for throwing heavy masses of stone
.07	appalling	appallens L	growing pale
.15	Phall	phallos G	image of erect penis carried in Dionysiac processions
.17	secular	saecularis L saeculum L	pertaining to a *saeculum* generation, century, age; the world
.17	phoenish	phoenix L phoinix G	fabulous bird of Arabia; *see 130.11*
.21	Helviticus	Helveticus L Leviticus L	pertaining to the Helvetii; *mod.* Swiss pertaining to Levi *or* the Levites
.21	deuteronomy	Deuteronomion G	"Second Law" (*5th book of bible*)
.24	eviparated	aevi (*Gen.*) L pario L *aevipario L	of eternity to give birth to, to beget to give birth to eternities
.24	guenneses	Genesis G	Origin, Creation (*1st book of bible*)
.24	exodos	Exodos G	Going Out (*2nd book of bible*)
.25	pentschanjeuchy	Pentateuchos G	Five Volumes (*first 5 books of bible*)

.27	supra	supra L	above; previously; more
.28	liddle	Henry George Liddell G	lexicographer; #A
.28	phifie	#Labials	wifie
.30	balbulous	*balbulus L	somewhat stuttering
		*Balbulus L	Little Balbus
		Balbus L	"Stuttering": Roman cognomen: "*Balbus was building a wall*" in Stephen Dedalus's Latin primer; see Portrait 043.18
.31	habitacularly	habitaculum L	dwelling-place; little [monk's] habit
.32	caligulate	Caligula L	"Little Boots": insane Roman emperor
.36	erigenating	[Joannes Scotus] Erigena L	[John the] Irishborn [Scot]; medieval schoolman; #A
		êrigeneia G	"early-born": epithet of Dawn
		erigo L	to erect
005.01	celescalating	caeli L	the heavens
		escalis L	pertaining to food
		scalae L	staircase, ladder
.01	hierarchitectitiptitoploftical	hierax G	a hawk
		hierarchês G	high-priest
		arch- G	first-, chief-
		architekteô G	to be chief builder
		tektainô G	to frame, design
.05	arms and a name	*echoes* arma virumque L	Arms and the man: *first words of Vergil's* Aeneid
.07	ancillars	ancilla L	maid servant, female slave
		ancillaris L	relating to maid servants; servile
.08	helio	hêlios G	the sun
.13	tragoady	tragôdia G *from*	tragedy; *perhaps* "goat-song"
		tragos G *and*	goat
		ôdê, aoidê G	song
.25	ansars	ansa L	handle
		anser L	goose

.27	collupsus	collapsus L	fallen in, fallen together
		[h]upsos G	height, grandeur
.32	autokinotons	*autokinêton G	self-moving [thing] (*G-L hybrid* automobile *is here pure G*)
.32	hippohobbilies	hippos G	horse
.32	tournintaxes	taxis G	arrangement, order
		tachys G	swift, rapid
.32	megaphoggs	megaphthongos G (-*gg*- *G* = -*ng*- *L*)	great voice
.33	circuses	circus L	circle; race-course
.33	basilikerks	basilikê [stoa] G,	royal [porch], *whence*
		whence basilica L	public building with courtroom and commodity exchange,
		whence basilica LL	*whence* metropolitan church, cathedral
.33	aeropagods	aero- LG	air-
		aero L	wicker basket
		ho Areios pagos G	the hill of Ares ("Areopagus") at Athens
006.01	noobibusses	nubibus (*Dat., Abl. pl.*) L	to, for, by clouds
.05	domecreepers	domus L	house, home
.15	chrissormiss	chrisimos G	used for anointing
		chrisis G	smearing, anointing
		chrisma G	anointing, unction; grace; plaster
.23	Priam	Priamos G	"Patron": king of Troy at its fall
.23	Olim	olim L	at that time; once upon a time
.25	deepbrow fundigs	de profundis L	"from the depths": opening of *Ps. 130*
.25–.26	the dusty fidelios	adeste fideles L	"be present, faithful ones," *i.e.,* "Come all ye faithful" (*carol*)
.26	a bockalips	apokalypsis G	uncovering, revelation; Revelation (*last book of bible*)
.27	guenesis	Genesis G	Creation (*1st book of bible*)

.30	tautaulogically	tau G	letter T
		t'auta G	the same
		tautologeô G	to repeat what has been said
007.01	livvy–	Titus Livius L #A	see 003.24
.03	trochees	trochaios G	running, spinning; metrical foot of one long plus one short syllable
.03	carina ... carina	carina L	keel of a ship
.08	Grampupus	pupus L	boy, child; puppet; pupil of the eye
.16	rubicund	rubicundus L	red, ruddy
		Rubico or Rubicon L	"Red-colored": river separating Italy from Cisalpine Gaul, crossed by Caesar (49 b.c.) to start civil war against Pompey
.16	Salmosalar	salmo L	salmon
		salar L	trout
		sal L	salt; salt sea; wit
		salarium L	salt-money; soldiers' pay
		salio L	to leap
.16	Agapemonides	agapê G	love, charity
		*agapêmon G	loved one
		*agapêmonidês G	sons of a loved one
.18	summan	Summanus L	"Dweller on high": Roman god of nocturnal lightnings
.20	brontoichthyan	brontê G	thunder
		ichthys G	fish
		*brontoichthys G	thunderfish
.22	Bronto	brontê G	thunder
		Bronton G L	Thunderer: see 003.15
.22–.23	Hic cubat edilis. Apud libertinam parvulam.	Hic cubat aedilis apud libertinam parvulam L	Here sleeps the magistrate with [chez] the little freedgirl
.26	unda	unda L	wave, billow
.28	Brontolone	brontê; Brontôn G	see 007.22

.29	cranic	kranion G	skull
		cranium L	
		kranos G	helmet
.29	caster	kastôr G castor	beaver
		L	
.30	verdigrass	ver L	springtime
		viriditas L	greenness, verdure
.31	fellonem	fello L	to suck
.31	mund	mundus L	the universe, the world; *also*, clean, nice; an elegant person; ornaments; feminine finery
008.04	minxt	minxit L	[he, she] urinated
.08	Kathe	kathê G	you sit
		kathairô G	to cleanse
.14	Saloos	salus L	good health
.16	Lipoleum	lipos G	animal fat, lard
		lippus L	blear-eyed
		oleum L	olive-oil
.19	dux	dux L	leader
.20	pulluponeasyan wartrews	ho Peloponnêsiakos polemos G	the Peloponnesian War (431–404 B.C.) between Athens and Sparta
		hê Pelopos nêsos G	"the isle of Pelops": major peninsula of south Greece
		Pelops G	son of Tantalus, Poseidon's lover, ancestor of Atreus
.22	lipoleum	*see 008.16 A, C*	
.23	inimyskilling	inimicus L	enemy, foe
.24	lipoleum	*see 008.16 A, C*	
.25	lipoleum	*see 008.16 A, C*	
.28	arminus–varminus	armi– L	weapon-
		Arminius L	[Herman]: German prince who defeated a Roman army under Varus in the Teutoburg forest, A.D. 9
		varus L	bent, stretched
		P. Quintilius Varus	defeated by Arminius
.28	Delian	Dêlios G Delius L	of the island of Delos, birthplace of Apollo and Diana

		Delia L	Diana
		Delian League	confederacy of G states organized 478 B.C for naval war against Persia
.30	lipoleums	*see 008.16 A, C*	
.32	undisides	unda L	wave, billow
		undique L	from all parts, on all sides
.35	mormorial	mormoros G	baneful, fearful
		Mormô G	bugbear to frighten children
		mormolykeion G	hobgoblin
		marmor L	marble
.35	obscides	ob, obs L	towards; in front of
		occido, obcido (*obscido) L	1. to strike down, beat, smash; destroy; kill. 2. to fall down; to go down; to perish
.36	Sexcaliber	sex L	six
009.01	phillippy	Philippi L	site of Antony's defeat of Brutus and Cassius (42 B.C)
		Philippos G	"Horse-lover": Philip II of Macedon, founded Philippi
.05	Leaper	Liber L	Old Italian god of fruit and wine
		liber L	1. free; 2. child; 3. book
.05	Leaper Orthor	liberatur L	[he, she, it] is freed
.05	Orthor	orthos G	straight
		orthros G	daybreak, dawn
.08	lipoleums	*see 008.16 A, C*	
.22	lipoleums	*see 008.16 A, C*	
.25	their mobbily	Thermopylai G	"Hot Gates": pass
		Thermopylae L	where Persians outflanked Greeks 480 B.C.
.26	Brum! Brum!	bruma L	midwinter
		Cumbrum	cum L	with; while
.33	marathon	Marathôn G	"Overgrown with Fennel": site of G defeat of Persians 490 B.C.

8   GLOSSARY FOR FINNEGANS WAKE

.34	marmorial	marmor L	marble
.34	Sophy–	sophia G	cleverness, skill; wisdom
010.01	lipoleums	see 008.16 A, C	
.03	lipoleums	see 008.16 A, C	
.08	lipoleums	see 008.16 A, C	
.10	lipoleums	see 008.16 A, C	
.13	Culpenhelp	culpa L	fault, crime
.14	lipoleums	see 008.16 A, C	
.14	insoult	insulto L	to leap, bound, jump, spring
.20	lipoleums	see 008.16 A, C	
.26	annaone	annona L	yearly produce; grain; income; prices
011.02	triboos	tribus L	tribe
.04	Nixy	[di] Nixi L	goddesses of childbirth
		nix L	snow
.05	nubo	nubo L	to cover, to veil; to marry
		nubes L	cloud
.05	Neblas	nebula L	mist, vapor, fog
.09	peri	peri G	about, around
.09	potmother	potmos G	lot, destiny, fate; Homer: evil destiny, death
.09	peri potmother	peri potmon G	concerning fate; about death
.12	pacts	pax L	peace
.12	huemeramybows	euhêmerêma G	success, good luck
		euhêmeria G	fine weather
		eumêros G	with beautiful thighs
		-bôs G	adverb ending
		-ibus L	Dat. & Abl. pl. ending
.13	armitides	*Armitidês G	sons of *Arme
.14	militopucos	milito L	to be a soldier
		paucus L	few, a little
		puknos G	close, compact
		puka G	closely
.16	suso	susurro L	to whisper
.20	clavicures	clavicula L	small key
		claviger L	club-bearer (Hercules); key-bearer (Janus)
		clavis L	key
		cura L	care, concern, trouble
		*clavicura L	care of the key, charge of the keys

.20	scampulars	scapula LL	the shoulder
		scapulae L	shoulders, back
.25	pleures	pleura G	rib
.30	historic presents	historic present [tense]	*grammarians' term for L historians' use of present tense to vivify narrative of past actions*
.30	past postpropheticals	*parody of names of certain L tenses,* e.g., "plusquam perfectus" L	"more than finished"
.33	plores	ploro L	to cry aloud, to lament
012.05	Luntum	lentum (*neut.*) L	flexible, viscous; heavy, durable, calm, phlegmatic; at ease; slow
.08	glaubrous	glubo L	to peel off, to strip, to skin (*used in obscene sense by Catullus*)
.09	phace	phasis G	denunciation; utterance, expression; judgment
.09	vesta	Vesta L	goddess of the household; holy fire burned perpetually in her temple
.12	frumpty	frumentum L	corn, grain
.28	bergincellies	caeli LL	the heavens
.34	robolous	*robulus L	*little oaktree, *pole
		robur L	oak or other sturdy tree
		Romulus L	founder and first king of Rome; #A
.34	rebus	rebus L	by things
		remus L	oar
		Remus L	brother of Romulus, slain by him; #A
.35	macroborg	makro- G	long-
.36	Microbirg	mikro-G	small-
013.09	Miry	mirus L	marvelous
.10	gravemure	murus L	wall
.11	Ptollmens	Ptolemaios	"Warlike": name of all kings of the
		[*Macedonian*] G	Macedonian dynasty of Egypt; #A
		Claudius Ptolemaeus (a.d. 121–151)	Alexandrian astronomer and mapmaker, first to mark Dublin (*Eblana*) on a world map

.11	Incabus	incubus L	nightmare
.12	jubalee	Juba	name of two kings of Numidia, subjected by the Romans; Newman character; #A
		juba L	mane
.16	optophone	opto L	to hope
		optos G	visible; *also*, roasted
		phonê G	sound, voice
		optophone (*modern coinage*) G	"Visible Sound": patented device to convert printed letters to musical tones, enabling blind to read
.16	ontophanes	onta Gr	reality, things that actually exist
		phainô G	bring to light, cause to appear
		phanê G	a torch
.20	Lujius	Lucius L	"Of the day": Roman praenomen
		lucius L	the pike (*fish*)
.21	historiorum	historiarum (*Gen. pl.*) L	of histories
.21	Boriorum	*boriorum, *correctly* borearum L	of the north winds
		Boarium L	the Cattle Market in Rome
.24	T.	T[itus] L	Roman praenomen
.24	Totities	totidem L	just as many
		toties L	as many times
		titius L	name of a dance [*cf.* Titus]
.24	*Unum*	unum (*neut.*) L	one
.25	*Duum*	duum L	of two
.26	*Triom*	trium L	of three
.27	*Quodlibus*	quodlibet L	as many as one pleases
.29	innocens	innocens L	harmless
		Innocens L	Innocent: *name of 13 popes*
.30	anaclete	Anacletus L	"Renowned": third
		Anakleitos G	pope (76–88); *also* an anti-pope (died 1138) *opposed to* Innocent III

.34	Ublanium	Eblana G	Dublin; on Ptolemy's map
		uber L	udder; full, plentiful
		lana L	wool
		lanius L	butcher, executioner
		*Ublanium L	place abounding in wool *or* butchers
014.09	Puropeus Pious	*Puropeus L *from* *Pyrops G	Fire-eye
		*Puropeus Pius L	Fire-eye the Dutiful
		Pius L	pious, conscientious, honest; *epithet used of Aeneas by Vergil; title affected by the emperors from Antoninus (a.d. 86-161) onward; name of 12 popes*
.12	Primas	primus L	the first
.13	Primas	*see 014.12 J*	
.16	parently	parens L	appearing
.17	annadominant	anno Domini L	in the year of the Lord (a.d.)
		domina L	lady, mistress
		dominans L	ruling, bearing sway; absolute ruler
.19	excelsissimost	excelsissimus L	the very highest
.19	empyrean	empyreus LL	highest part of heaven, abode of pure fire
		from empyrios G	fiery
.21	scribicide	*scribicida L	slayer of a scribe
.25	gynecure	gynê G	woman
		cura L	care, concern
		gynecura G + L	woman-care
		modeled on sinecura L	without-care
.28	peragrine	per L	through
		ager L	field, countryside
		peregrinus L	foreign, exotic; foreigner, alien
.29	*Liber Lividus*	Liber Lividus L	Blue Book; *or* Livian (*i.e.*, by Livy) Book
.30	eirenical	eirênikos G	peaceful

.32	pastor	pastor L	shepherd
.33	viridities	viriditas L	greenness, verdure
015.05	chiliad	chilias G	a thousand
.05	perihelygangs	*perihêlios G	around-the-sun
.09	paxsealing	pax L	peace
.12	confusium	confusum L	disorderly
		confusim L	confusedly
.15	surssurhummed	susurro L	to hum, buzz, murmur
		sursum L	upwards
.20	floras	Flora L	goddess of flowers
		flores L	flowers
.21	shyfaun	Faunus L	god of agriculture and shepherds
.29	Anem	anemos G	wind
		onoma G	name
.32	pectoral	pectoralis L	of or belonging to the breast
.32	mammamuscles	mamma G L	the breast, esp. female
016.03	Cave!	cave L	beware!
.03	prapsposterus	posterus L	following, next, future
		praeposterus L	back to front
.04	Hirculos	hirculus L	a little goat
		Hercules L	legendary hero and
		Hêraklês G	demigod
.04	Hirculos pillar	Herculis Columnae L	promontories between which lies the Strait of Gibraltar
.07	phonio	phôneô G	to speak, utter
.07	saxo	Saxo L	a Saxon
		Saxo Grammaticus L (1150–1206)	"The Learned Saxon": Danish historian whose *Gesta Danorum* is the source of the *Hamlet* story
		saxum L	rock, large stone
.08	verbs	verba L	words
.18	hauhauhauhaudibble	hau L	oh! ah!
		hau OL	*haud* before consonants
		haud L	not at all, by no means, hardly at all
.20	Aput	apud, aput L	with, at, near, by, amid, among
.20	surd	surdus L	deaf, stone-deaf
017.01	Monomark	monomachos G	fighter in single combat; gladiator

		Constantine IX Monomachos G	Byzantine Emperor (1042–1055), an elderly debauchee, lazy and corrupt
		monarchos G	sole ruler
.03	Taciturn	Tacitus L	"silent"; Roman proper name
		Cornelius Tacitus (a.d. 50–?)	Roman historian
		M. Claudius Tacitus	emperor a.d. 275–276
.09–.10	Rooks roarum rex roome	*schoolboy's attempt to decline a* L *noun through* Nom., Gen., Dat., & Acc., *mixing* res, rex, rôs *and* rûs:	thing, king, dew, countryside (*see below*)
		res, rei, rei, rem; rerum (*Gen. pl.*)	a thing, of a thing, to a thing, thing; of things (in general), of the world
		rex, regis, regi, regem	king, of a king, to a king, king
		rôs, rôris, rôri, rôrem; rôrium (*Gen. pl.*)	dew, of dew, to dew, dew; of dews
		rûs, rûris, rûri, rûs	countryside, of countryside, to countryside, countryside [*N.B.* **rûs** *is cognate with English* "*room*"]
.10	rex roome	rex Romae L	king of Rome
.17	agreem	-mi G (*1st person sing. ending of certain old verbs*)	*I agree
.18	albutisle	albus L	white
		trans.	"almost-island":
		paeninsula L	peninsula
.21	isthmon	isthmos, *Acc.* isthmon G	neck, narrow passage; isthmus

		isthmion G	anything belonging to the neck; necklace
.23	Punct	punctum L	punctuation mark; period; point
.25	surgence	surgens L	rising, growing up
		*surgentia L	a rising
.26	requiesce	requiescens L	reposing, resting (*esp.* the dead)
.32	Fiatfuit	fiat L	let there be
		fuit L	it was
.35	anequal	a- G	not-, un-
		an- G	down-
018.03	thanacestross	thanasimos G	deadly, fatal
		thanatêphoros G	death-bringing
		thanatos G	death
.05	humus	humus L	earth, soil, the earth
.05	roturns	roto L	to turn round like a wheel, to revolve
.11	Forficules	forficula L	a small scissors; small claw of a beetle (*e.g.*) earwig
.11	Amni	amnis L	stream, river
.22	Porsons	Richard Porson (1759–1808)	English classical scholar
.29	terricolous	terricola L	dweller upon earth
		terricula L	fright, scarecrow, bugbear
.29	vivelyonview	vivlion viou MG *for* biblion biou G	book of life
.32	yoxen at the turnpaht	boustrophêdon G	turning like oxen in ploughing (of writing from left to right and right to left in alternate lines)
.33–.34	Here say figurines . . . figurines see here	boustrophêdon	*2nd sentence is 1st sentence read backwards*
.34	effingee	# Digamma	an F *that is a* G [gamma]
.36	⊓ace	san G *numerical symbol*	old letter SS 900
019.01	ptee	pt- OG = p- G, *e.g.* ptolis OG, polis G	city

.01	holos	holos G	whole, entire
		*holFos G =	entire, healthy, whole
		salvus L	
		# *Digamma*,	
		# *G-to-L*	
.02	cued peteet peas	qu- L = p-, t-	
		G, *e.g.*	
		quinque L,	five
		pente G	
		quattuor L,	four
		tettara G	
.03	pecuniar	pecunia L *from*	property, riches, wealth
		pecus L	cattle
.07–.08	mnice . . . mness . . . mnakes	mn- G = m- L, *e.g.*	m-
		mnemosynê G,	memory
		memoria L	
		mn- G, *e.g.*	*pron.* n-
		mnêmonikos G	mnemonic, *pron.* *ni-mon'ik*
.09	alfrids, beatties . . . daltons	alpha, bêta . . . delta G	letters A, B . . . D
.11	epsilene	e psilon G	"short e": letter E
		epicoenus L	"in common": G or L
		from epikoinos G	noun of common gender or having fixed gender regardless of sex of denoted being
.11–.13	oldwolldy wobblewers . . . Sss! See the snake wurrums . . sworming in sneaks	*play with* san *and* # Digamma	*obsolete G letters*
.15	cargon	*kargôn fake-G	cargo
		# *G-to-L* argon	shining; lazy
		(*neut.*) G	
		k'argon G	and shining; and lazy
.15	pomefructs	pomum L	fruit, *esp.* apple
		pomus L	fruit-tree
		fructus L	fruits, produce; use of
.21	nursus	nurus L	daughter-in-law
		versus L	against
.22	idim	idem L	the same
.22	boaboa	boaô G	cry aloud, shout
.24	liberorumqueue	[mulierum]	of [women] and
		liberorumque L	children

		liber L	book
.26	squattor	*squattor fake-L (*as if deponent or passive verb*)	I squat *or* I am squatted
		quattuor, quattor L	four
.26	anntisquattor	ante- L	before
		anti- L	against, counter
.27	postproneauntisquat-tor	post L	behind, after
		pro L	before, in front of
		prone L	bending forward (*adv.*)
		pronus L	prone (*adj.*)
.31	in nillohs dieybos	in illis diebus L	in those days
		in nullis diebus L	in no days
		in nihilo L	in nothing
		bos L	cow, ox, bull
.32–33	mightmountain . . . flee	parturiunt montes, nascetur ridiculus mus (*see Horace*, Ars Poetica, *139*) L	the mountains are in labor, a laughable little mouse is born (*when much is promised, little performed*)
.32	micies	mico L	to move quickly; to quiver, tremble
.34	quizzed	quis L	who
.34	quid	quid L	what
.35	quod	quod L	that, because, though
020.06	terracook	terra cocta L	baked earth (Ital. *terracotta*)
.08	primer	primus L	first
		prime L	especially
.08	omniboss	omnibus (*Dat., Abl. pl.*) L	to *or* for all; for everyone
.08	rubrickredd	rubrica L	red earth, red chalk
.10	papyr	papyros G	papyrus
		papyrikos G	"made of papyrus": paper
.13	Typus	typos G	print, impression; image, model
.13	Tope	topos G	place, passage in a book, occasion
.13	typtopies	typos, topos G	*see previous entries*
.15	toptypsical	*see 020.13H*	

.19	Nondum	nondum L	not yet
.29	noarch	Noa L	Noah
		noa G	stream, fountain
		*noarchos G	fountain-leader (see Genesis 7:11)
		nauarchos G	naval commander, admiral
.29–.30	pomme full grave ... fammy of levity	pomus gravide [or gravis] ... fama levitatis [or levis] L pseudo-aphorism modeled on e.g. [*] gravida ventris, famae levis L	a heavy-laden fruit-tree ... a reputation of lightness [or a light reputation] laden of belly, light of repute
.32	pyrrhique	pyrriche G	war-dance
.34	expectungpelick	expectoro L pelex L	to expel, banish concubine, kept mistress
.34	Veil	vel L	take your choice; or; or else
.34	volantine	volans L volens L	flying wishing, willing
.34	valentine	valens L	being strong
021.01	weenybeenyveeny- teeny	veni L bineô G	I came to have illicit intercourse
		tenui L	I held
.03	corne	cornu L	horn
.11	jiminies	gemini L	twins
.12	Tristopher	Christophoros G tristis L triste L pherô G *Tristophoros L+G	Christ-bearer sad a sad thing to carry "Sadness-bearer"
.12	Hilary	hilaris L "In tristitia hilaris hilaritate tristis" L "oderunt hilarem tristes tristemque jocosi" L	cheerful, gay "In sadness cheerful, [in] gaiety sad"—motto of Giordano Bruno "the sad hate the cheerful man, the joyous the sad"—Horace, Epistle I. 18, 89

.17	perusienne	perusi G	last year
.18	poss	possum, posse L	to be able
.21	jiminy	*see 021.11 J*	
.21	Tristopher	*see 021.12 C*	
.28	jiminy	*see 021.11 J*	
.29	convorted	convorto L	to turn around, change direction
.30	luderman	ludus L	a play, game, diversion
.31	redtom	reddo L	to give back, return
		redeo L	to come back
.32	jiminy	*see 021.11 J*	
.33	pinafrond	pinea frons L	pine branch
.36	jimminy	*see 021.11 J*	
.36	Hilary	*see 021.12 E*	
022.02	histher	*histher fake-G *for* *sister fake-L # *G-to-L*	sister
.05	poss	possum, posse L	to be able
.16	monitrix	monitrix L	monitress, female assistant, instructress
.16	provorted	provorto L	to turn forwards
.17	tristian	tris L *also see 021.12*	three
.18	ter	ter L	thrice
.28	arkway of trihump	arcus triumphalis L	triumphal arch
.28	trihump	triumpus OL	solemn entrance of a general into Rome after an important victory
		tri- L	three-
.29	Tris	tres, tris L *also see 021.12*	three
.29	poss	possum, posse L	to be able
.34	cholar	cholas L	species of emerald
		cholas G	guts
		cholera G	nausea
		cholê G	gall, bile
		cholos G	anger, wrath
023.01	panuncular	panuncula L	thread wound upon a bobbin
		*panuncularis L	of a little swelling *or* tumor
.07	–fait–	fiat L	let there be
.07	–illi–	illi L	in that place, yonder; therein

.13	jimminies	gemini L	twins
.14–.15	the hearsomeness of the burger felicitates the whole of the polis	obedientia civium urbis felicitas L	the obedience of the citizens [is] the city's happiness—*motto of Dublin*
.15	polis	polis G	city
.16	o foenix culprit	O felix culpa [quae talem ac tantum meruit habere Redemptorem] L	O happy sin [that merited such and so great a Redeemer]: hymn on Adam's fall that elicited the Incarnation
.16	Ex nickylow malo comes mickelmassed bonum	ex nihilo malo venit nihilum [*or* multum] bonum L ex nihilo nihil fit L ex malo venit multum bonum L	out of nothing evil comes nothing [*or* much] good nothing is made out of nothing out of evil comes much good
.19	Norronesen	nêsos G	island
.19	Irenean	eirênê G	peace
.19–.20	Quarry silex	quare siles? L	wherefore art thou silent?
.20	silex	silex L	flintstone
.20	Undy gentian festyknees	unde gentium festines? L	whence in the world are you hurrying?
.20	Livia	Livia L	"Bluish"; *name of Augustus's wife*
.21	audiurient	audio L uro L uriens L urina L *audiuriens L	to hear to burn; to fret desiring urine burning to hear
.25	Impalpabunt	*impalpabunt L impalpabilis L	they shall untouch untouchable
.26	abhears	ab L	away from
.30	perpetrified	*perpetrifactus L	thoroughly made of stone
.32–.33	loab, libe	*allusion to* Loeb Classical Library	well-known series of bilingual editions of G and L authors
.33	pudor	pudor L	shame
024.01	Novo	novo (*Abl.*) L	[from, by] new

.05	volant	volans L	flying
		volens L	willing
.06	louse for us	lucifer[us] L	"light-bringer": the morning star
.14	*Usqueadbaugham*	usque ad bacam L	all the way to the berry, all the way to the olive
		instead of usque ad mala L	all the way to the apples; *i.e.*, all the way to the end [of a Roman meal] *see 184.28* [*see Brendan O Hehir, "Whines, Whiskey, Life, Death, in Polyglutteral," AWN V (1968), 74, responding to Godfrey Tanner, "Classical Commentary on Finnegans Wake," AWN III* (1966), 129)
.18	Healiopolis	Hêliopolis G	Sun-city: religious center in Syria; *mod. Baalbek*; Egyptian city; #A
.34	Homin	homin- L	oblique stem of *homo*: man, human being
025.04	Mielodories	mel L meli G	honey
		melos G	song
		mêlon G	apple, fruit
		dory G	plank, oar, spear.
		dôron G	a gift
.07	nectar	nektar G	drink *or* food of the gods
.09	Basilico's	basilikos G	royal, kingly
.16	manument	manu- L	hand-, by hand
		monumentum L	that which preserves the memory (*of something*)
.17	Eirenesians	eirênê G	peace
		nêsos G	island
		eirênonêsiôtai G	peace-islanders
.19	oner	onero L	to lade, to burden
.24	apter	#*Labials*	after
.27	Erinnes	Erinys G	an avenging deity
		erinyes G	avenging deities, upholders of moral order

		Erinna G	poetess of Têlos, 4th century b.c.
.36	Magnus	magnus L	great, large
026.04	Arssia	ars L	art, skill
.04	Arssia Manor	Asia Minor L	"Lesser Asia"
.12	Copricapron	coprea L = koprias G	dung
		capronae L	forelocks
		caper L	he-goat
		kapron (Acc.) G	wild boar
.13	Virgo	virgo L	maiden, virgin
.17	Isid	is L	he
		id L	it
		Isid- G	oblique stem of Isis (Egyptian goddess)
.18	Totumcalmum	totum L	all
.18	metherjar	methê G	strong drink
.36	Allfor	alpha G	letter A
027.02	pathoricks	see 019.02	catholicks (see O Hehir, Gaelic Lexicon, #P/K Split,#L/R Interchange)
		pathos- G	suffering, experience
		pathicus L from pathikos G	sodomite
.02–.03	doublejoynted janitor	Janus geminus or Janus anceps	double Janus or two-headed Janus; old Italian deity, god of beginnings and passages
.08	ide	Idus L	the Ides: 15th or 13th day of month
.08	laus	laus L	praise, glory, fame
.10	encostive inkum	encaustum L from enkauston G	purple-red ink used by later Roman emperors [etymon of "ink"]
		costa L	rib
.13	Felix	felix L	fruitful; lucky, happy
.15	Luna's	luna L	the moon
.16	Pia de Purebelle	pia et pura bella L	pious and pure wars (Vico; #B)
.25	Dimitrius	Dêmêtrios G	"belonging to Dêmêtêr (goddess of corn; also of the dead)": common name
.25	O'Flagonan	flagr- L	root meaning burn, flame

.28	lumbos	lumbus L	loin; genitals
.31	Kate	Kathairô G	to cleanse
.33	murial	muria L	salt liquor, brine, pickle
		muralis L	of *or* belonging to a wall
028.05	lex's salig	lex salica L	Salic law: 5th-century compilation of Germanic laws; law excluding females from the rule of France and Spain
.05–.06	cat's hours	Castor L Kastôr G	"Beaver": son of Leda, brother of Helen and Pollux
.06	Pollockses'	Pollux L Polydeukês G	son of Leda, brother of Helen and Castor
.09	nesters	Nestôr G	aged king of Pylos in Homeric epics
.23	Stilla	stella L	star
		stillare L	to drip
.27	*Viv*	viv- L	*stem meaning* life, live
029.04	ivoeh!	euoi G evoe L	shout of joy at Bacchic festivals
.15	monothoid	monos G	alone, solitary
		monothen G	singly
		eidos G	that which is seen; shape
		*monoeidês G	appearing to be alone; of unique type
.15	theatrocrat	theatrokratia G	rule exercised by the spectators in a theater
		*theatrokratôr G	theater-ruler
.19	Esc	esca L	food
.30	humile	humilis L	("on the ground"): lowly, small
.30	commune	communis L	common to all, universal
030.01	Iris	Iris G L	goddess of the rainbow
.03	agnomen	agnomen L	surname of an individual recognizing a feat or service, as Scipio *Africanus*, from his victories in Africa
.04	prodromarith	prodromê G	sally, sudden attack

		prodromos G	running headlong forward; advance guard; precursor
		arithmos G	number; unit of troops
		*prodromarithmios G	before numbers, pre-numerical
.07	Ankers	Ancus (Marcius)	"Servant (of Mars)": fourth king of Rome
.13	Cincinnatus	Cincinnatus L	"Curly-haired": cognomen of Lucius Quinctus, dictator 458 b.c., who resigned and returned to his farm after defeating the Aequi
.20	ethnarch	ethnarchês G	ruler of a tribe or nation
.23	solascarf	sol L	the sun
031.07	paternoster	pater noster L	our father; the "Our Father"
.19	protosyndic	prôtos G	foremost, first
		syndikos G	advocate, helper in law court
		*prôtosyndikos G	foremost advocate
.21	scholarch	scholarchês G	head of a school
.22	triptychal	triptychos G	consisting of three layers, threefold
.23	puritas	puritas L	1. cleanness, purity; 2. purulency
.23	doctrina	doctrina L	teaching, instruction, science, learning
.24	dilsydulsily	dulce L	sweetly, pleasantly
		dulcis L	sweet, agreeable
.33	ide	Idus L	Ides; see 027.08
.33	nominigentilisation	nomen gentile L	clan (gens) name: second of the three names borne by freeborn Romans
.34	accolated	accola L	neighbor
.35	andrewpaulmurphyc	anthrôpomorphikos G	having to do with the human form
		Andreas L from	Andrew
		Andreios G	Manly, Masculine
		Paulus L altered by the apostle	Little: Paul
		from Saulos G	Mincing, Effeminate

.35	fata	Fata L	The Fates: bad fortune
.36	sibylline	sibyllinus L	pertaining to the Sibyl *whose prophecies were preserved in the Capitol, to be consulted in national emergencies*
		Sibylla G L	a female soothsayer
.36	*fas*	fas L	divine law; lawful; possible
.36	*nefas*	nefas L	impious deed; sinful, criminal thing; impossible
032.03	cumsceptres	cum sceptris L	with staves
		concepta (*fem. pp.*) L	conceived
.06	punical as finikin	Punicus L	Punic, Phoenician
		Phoinikos G	
		# *Labials*	
.12	Miliodorus	milio L	the kite (*bird*)
		miliarius L	having to do with thousands *or* miles
		dôron G	a gift; *see 025.04*
.12	Galathee	gala G	milk
		thea G	goddess
		Galateia G	"Milk-white": a
		Galatea L	sea-nymph
		Galatai G	Celts
.14	sigla	sigla L	signs of abbreviation, abbreviations
.29	Semperkelly's	semper L	always, forever
.31	homedromed	homodromos G	running the same course with
033.03	cecelticommediant	Keltikoi G	Celts
		Celticae L	
		Keltikos G	Celtic, Gallic
		Celticus L	
		coco L	clucking of a hen
		comedo L	to eat up, to waste; a glutton
		commeditor L	to practise, to imitate
		# *Reduplication*	
.27	Hay, hay, hay!	hae L	these, they (*fem.*)
.27	Hoq, hoq, hoq!	hoc L	this, it

.28	Faun	Faunus L	god of wild animals
.28	Flora	Flora L	goddess of flowers
.34	quondam	quondam L	at a certain time, formerly
.34	pfuit! pfuit!	fuit L	[he, she, it] was
.35	interdum	interdum L	sometimes, occasionally
.35	quidam	quidam L	a certain, somebody, something
.36	quoniam	quoniam L	since now, because, whereas
.36	abhout	ab L	from, away from, since, after
.36	stambuling	eis tên polin G	into the city: phrase misunderstood by Turks as name of Constantinople, *whence* "Istanbul," "Stambouli"
034.02	topantically	to pan G	the whole; all things
.02	anonymos	anônymos G	nameless
.05	Ibid	ibidem L	in the same place, just there
.07	pfiat! pfiat!	fiat L	let there be
.08	alicubi	alicubi L	somewhere, anywhere, wherever
.14	homogenius	homo L	man, human being
		genius L	spirit, wit
		genus L	birth, descent; class, sort
		homos G	one and the same, common
		homogenês G	of the same race or family
.18	immodus	*immodus L	*immeasure, unend, illimit
.24	wapt ... wept	#*Labials*	waft ... weft
.31	villa-	villa L	country-house, farm
035.02	calzium	calcium (*Acc.*) L	shoe
.02	chloereydes	chloê G	green shoot, young grass
		*chloeidês G	grass-like
		chlôros G	green
.02	hydrophobe	hydrophobos G	water-fearing; water-fearer
.03	Ides-of-April	Idus Aprilis L	April 13th
.11	luciferant	luciferens L	light-carrying

.11	oriulate	*orilatus L	risen-broad, broad-risen
		*horalatus L	hour-borne
.20	bradys	bradys G	slow
.22	nexally	nex L	murder, slaughter
		nexus L	fastening; obligation
		nexilis L	bound together
.23	noxally	nox L	night
		noxa L	harm, injury
		noxalis L	relating to an injury
.28	communionism	communio L	1. to fortify, to barricade *vb.* 2. mutual participation *n.*
.29	usucapture	usucaptum L	having ownership acquired by long use and possession
		usucapio L	acquisition of ownership by long use or possession
.31	tonuant	tonans L	thundering (*epithet of Jupiter*)
		*tonuans L	stretching, toning
.35	pondus	pondus L	weight
.36	cumfusium	cum L	with
		confusio L	mixture
036.02	compompounded	componderans L	weighing
		pompo L	to do a thing with pomp
		pompê G	solemn procession
		# Reduplication	
.03	vimvital	vim (*Acc.*), vis L	force, energy
		vitalis L	of life
.07	triplehydrad	tripleheaded	Cerberus, underworld-monster, had three heads
		Hydra G	sevenheaded waterserpent
.10	quiritary	Quirites L	Roman citizens
		quiritare L	to shriek, lament (*lit.*, call to the citizens)
.13	Gygas	gigas G L	giant, titan
		Gygês G L	Lydian king who had ring of invisibility
.14	chronometrum	chronometron G; # G-to-L	time-measure

.15	ambijacent	*ambijacens L	lying around
.20	Shsh shake,	# Reduplication	
	co-comeraid		
.22	nonation	nunation;	G grammar: adding
		# Reduplication	letter *nu* to 3rd person
			pl. vb. ending
.23	mewmew mutual	# Reduplication	
.23–.24	woowoo willing	# Reduplication	
.25	ruru	ruro L	to live in the country
.25	ruru redemption	# Reduplication	
.34	fibfib fabrications	# Reduplication	
037.01	postpuberal	*postpuber L	after being adult
.01	hypertituitary	hyper G	over, above
		titeuô G	to pay a fine
		tittheuô G	to be a wetnurse
		titthos G	woman's breast
		*hypertittheuô	to be superlatively a
		G	wetnurse; to be
			supermammalian
.11	monticulus	monticulus L	a small mountain
.13	verbigracious	verbi gratia L	for instance
.15	verbaten	verba L	words
.16	balbly	balbus L	stuttering
.22	aquiassent	aqui- L	water-
.33	senaffed	sinapi G	mustard
038.05	Cur	cur L	wherefore, why
.09	Bareniece	Berenikê,	"Victoria": "carrying
		Macedonian	off victory." Name of
		form of	several queens of
		Pherenikê G	Ptolemaic dynasty
.11	persicks	persicum	peach (*lit.* "persian
		prunum L	plum")
.11	armelians	armeniacum	apricot (*lit.* "armenian
		prunum L	plum")
.11	Pomeranzia	pomum L	apple; tree fruit
		pomus L	appletree; fruit tree
.12	clav	clava L	cudgel, club
		clavis L	key
		clavus L	nail, spike
.14	vhespers	vesper; vespera	evening
		L	
		hesperos;	evening
		hespera G	
		# Digamma	
.16	Hegesippus	Hêgesippos G	"Horse-commander";
			4th C. Athenian orator;
			name also of at least 3
			writers

.20	intra	intra L	on the inside, within
.23	epistolear	epistola L *from*	written communication,
		epistolê G	letter
		epistolaris L	state secretary
.25	in vinars venitas	in vino veritas L	in wine, truth
		vinarius L	wine-dealer; wine-bibber
		vanitas L	emptiness, nullity; falsehood, untruth
		ars L	art, skill, craft
		venustas L	loveliness
.25	volatiles	volatilis L	flying, winged; swift, fleeting, transitory
		*volatiles L	fowls
.25	valetotum	vale L	farewell
		totum L	all
.28	poul	paulus L	small; #*A* Paul
.28	soul	saulos G	mincing, effeminate
.29	Ecclectiastes	Ekklêsiastês G	member of an assembly, synagogue or church
		eklektos G	picked out, chosen, elect
.30	Hippo	Hippo Regius	North African city, St. Augustine's home
		hippos G	horse
.34	rubiend	rubens L	reddish; blushing
.35	aurellum	Aurelium L	"Golden"? belonging to an *Aurelius* (Roman family name)
		*aurilla L	little ear
		*aurellum L	little-ear-thing [earwig?]
.36	orthophonethics	orthos G	correct, proper
		phônos G	sound, noise, voice
		ethika G	customs, habits
		*orthophônethika G	correct voice habits
039.02	hippic runfields	*part trans.*	"horse-running-places":
		hippodromoi G	racecourses
.06	ek	equus L	horse
.14	pisononse	Piso L	"Mortar": Roman surname
		Pisonianus L	of *or* belonging to a *Piso*

		Epistola ad Pisones L	Letter to the Pisos, title of Horace's Ars Poetica
.15	voax	vox L	voice
.32	meth	methê G	strong drink; drunkenness
040.06	nom	nomê GL	ulcer
		nomen L	name
.06	num	num L	interrogative particle: whether?
		Numa L	second king of Rome
		numen L	nod; command; divine will
.07	rusinurbean	rus in urbe L	country in the city
.10	eyots of martas	Idus Martiae L	March 15th (Caesar's assassination)
.11	katya	kathairô G	to cleanse
.11	lavinias	Lavinia L	daughter of Latinus; wife of Aeneas
.11	mens	mens L	mind, disposition, intellect
		mensis L	month
.14	metagonistic	*metagônistikos G	fit to be translated, fit to be conveyed from one place to another
.14	epickthalamorous	epikos G	epic, poetic
		thalamos G	bride chamber
		epithalamios G	bridal song, sung before bride chamber
		amor L	love, lust
.21	Hosty	hostis L	stranger, foreigner, enemy
		Hostius L	epic poet, 2d century b.c.
		Hostius Quadra	licentious voyeur; # A
.27	ifidalicence	fida L	trustworthy, faithful (fem.)
		bona fides L	good faith; # B
.28	parabellum	para G	beside
		bellum L	war
.31	sibicidal	*sibicidalis (sibi Dat. instead of sui Gen.) L	to-the-self killing (instead of of-the-self)
.32	quitybus	*quietibus (for quitis) L	to the dead
		*quitibus (for queuntibus) L	to those who can

041.04	O'Deavis	dea L	goddess
		vis L	force, strength
.05	epipsychidically	epi G	upon
		psychidion G	a little soul
		*epipsychidioni-kos dog-G	upon having a little spirits?
.05-.06	hostis et odor insuper petroperfractus	dog-L	an enemy [Hosty? see 040.21] and a stink besides stony broke
.08	Hosty	hostis; Hostius	see 040.21
.19	superficies	superficies L	surface
.19	linea	linea L	lines
.19	puncta	puncta L	points
.20	maniplumbs	manus L	hand
		plumbo L	to solder with lead, make of lead
		*maniplumbo L	to make by hand out of lead
.30	prothetic	prothetikos G	setting before itself, prefixing; prepositional
.32	Cujas	cujas L	whence? from what place? of what family?
.33	Cecily	Caecilia L	martyr, patroness of music
042.04	phewit	fuit L	he [she, it] was
.15	melomap	melos G	limb; musical phrase; song
		mappa L	napkin, towel
.20	Eleutheriodendron	eleutherios G	free-spirited, liberal
		dendron G	tree
.32	weedulicet	videlicet L	it is easy to see, clearly, evidently
043.06	braxy	branchos G	anthrax or foot-and-mouth disease
		brachys G	short
.11	dianas	Diana L	goddess of the chase, etc.
.20	curiolater	curio L	priest of a curia (ward in Rome)
		latreia G latria L	worship, service
.22	felibrine	felis L	cat
		felix L	fortunate, happy
		febris L	fever
.22	trancoped	trans L	across, beyond

		kopê G	a cutting, blow
		*trankopê L+G	a cutting across
		modeled on	"with-cutting": cutting
		synkopê G	up into small pieces, cutting short; stoppage; sudden weakness, swoon
.30	Scotia Picta	Scotia Picta L	Painted Scotia (Ireland, later Scotland)
		Scotia Pictorum L	Scotia of the Picts (Scotland)
.34	rapsods	rhapsôdos G	reciter of epic poems
.36	sputabout	sputa L	spit, spittle, spits
044.02	Ductor	ductor L	leader, commander, general
.03	signum	signum L	token, sign; banner; password; image
.04	silentium in curia	silentium in curia L	silence in the court
.06	Annona's	annona L	yearly produce; annual income; corn
		Annona L	goddess: personified yearly produce
.08	Hosty	hostis; Hostius	see 040.21
.12	Lex	lex L	law
.15	Hosty	hostis; Hostius	see 040.21
.20	–kak–kak–kak–	kak G	letter K
		kakos G	bad
.20	–klop–	klopaios G	stolen, fraudulent
.22	Ardite	ardite L	be on fire! blaze!
045.25	Hosty	hostis; Hostius	see 040.21
046.14	Eblana	Eblana G	Ptolemy's name for Dublin
.20	Onesine	onêsimos G	useful
.25	Hosty	hostis; Hostius	see 040.21
047.03	crux	crux L	tree, gibbet, cross; rascal; trouble
.08	rotorious	roto L	to turn a thing wheel-wise; to whirl
.09	omnibus	omnibus (Dat. pl.) L	for everybody
.19	Suffoclose	Sophoklês	Athenian tragedian 496–406 b.c.
.19	Seudodanto	pseudo- G	false-
		danta G (Hesychius)	[yoked] pair

.27	corpus	corpus L	body, material object; whole collection (*of laws, an author's works, etc.*)
.29	bis	bis L	twice, in two ways
048.04	liddled	Henry George Liddell (1811–1898)	compiler of Liddell and Scott's *Greek-English Lexicon* (father of Lewis Carroll's *Alice*)
.05	Humidia	Numidia L	"country of the nomads": ancient North African kingdom and Roman province, *in modern* Algeria
.07	Vergobretas	Vergobretus L *from* Bergobretos G	title of the chief magistrate among the Aedui, a tribe of Celtic Gaul
		# *Labials*	
.07	Caraculacticors	Cara[c]tacus L	king of the Silures in Britain who fought the Roman invasion
		caracalla L	hooded great-coat worn by Gauls
.18	antilibellous	*antelibellos L *antilibellos G + L	before books against books
.19	whole wholume	holos G volumen L (*pron.* wol-)	whole, entire roll of writing; book; roll; revolution
		# *Labials*	
.19	Osti–Fosti	ostium L fostis, *form of* hostis L	door, entrance, mouth stranger, enemy
		# *Digamma*	
.23	Tuonisonian	tuor L sonus L	sight, vision noise, sound
.24	Animandovites	anima L	air, breath, breath of life, life, soul
		ovis L	sheep
		ovum L	egg
		vita L	life
049.10	Columbarium	columbarium L	dove-cot, pigeon-house; sepulchre with niches for urns of ashes

.13	Vasileff's	Vasilefs MG *pron. of* Basileus G	king
.13	Cornix	cornix L	crow
.13	inauspiciously	inauspicato L	without consulting the auspices; without observing the flight of birds; of ill omen
.24	ebbrous	ebrius L	full of drink, drunk
.26	atlas	Atlas G	"Very Enduring": Titan who holds the sky up
.33	centuple	centuplex L	hundred-fold
.34	egourge	*egôourgos G *modeled on* dêmiourgos G	worker for the self worker for the people, craftsman
.34	Micholas de Cusack	Nicolaus Cusanus	theologian, wrote *De Docta Ignorantia*; see *163.16,17*
050.11	transmaried	*transmareo *for* mare transeo L	to cross over the sea
.12	tabularasing	tabula rasa L	a clean [erased] writing-tablet
.13	involucrum	involucrum L	wrapper, envelope
.15	redivivus	redivivus L	alive again; renewed, renovated
.17	transtuled	transtulit L	[he] has brought over, transported, transferred
.17	latitat	latitat L *latitat Eng. *modeled on* habitat Eng. *from* habitat L	[he] lies hidden hiding-place dwelling-place [he] dwells
.17	finsterest	finis terrae L	end of the earth
.17	interrimost	in terra L *interrimus *recte* intimus L	on earth inmost, farthest in, farthest inland
.22	rarevalent	rare L valens L	seldom, rarely powerful
.23	Fratomistor	frater L *mistor L	brother a mixer
.24	presspassim	passim L	here and there
.25	enthusiastically	enthousiastikôs G	in a manner inspired by a god
.32	jovesday	*trans.* dies Jovis LL	Thursday

.32	*Fuitfuit*	fuit L	it was
.35	nix	nix L	snow
.36	nebuless	nebula L	fog, mist
.36	autodidact	autodidaktos G	self-taught
051.02	altered its ego	alter ego L	another self, a second self; *Pythagorean definition of* a friend
.02	possing	posse L	to be able [to]
.05–.06	sword of certainty . . . never falls	*possible allusion to* sword of Damocles	the courtier Damocles praised the happiness of Dionysius I (430–367 b.c.), who symbolically feasted him with a sword hung by a hair over his head
.05	indentifide	denti- *oblique stem* L	tooth
		fide (*Abl.*) L	by faith
.18	halfsinster	sinister L	on the left
.20	Mu	mu G	letter M
.23	Juxta–Mare	juxta mare L	beside the sea
.29	Silurian	Silures L	a people of ancient Britain
.29	Ordovices	Ordovices L	a people of ancient Britain
		ordo L	order, arrangement
.31	*regifugium*	regifugium L	"of the king's flight": Roman holiday (February 24) celebrating expulsion of the kings
.31	*regifugium persecutorum*	refugium persecutorum L	refuge of the persecuted
.35	panomancy	*pantomanteia G	divination by all things
		*panimantia LL	divination by bread
052.11	curolent	*curolens L	smelling of care
.14	precoxious	praecox L	ripe before time, premature
.15	Via	via L	way, road
.18	television	têle- G	far off, at a distance
		visio L	sight, vision
.18	telephony	têle- G	far off, at a distance
		phônê G	sound, voice
.31	legomena	legomena G	sayings

.36	solence	solent L	they are accustomed to; they have intercourse with
		*solentia L	opposite of insolence
053.04	odable	odibilis L	hateful, odious
		audibilis L	hearable, audible
.04	os	os L	1. mouth, face; 2. bone
.04	wineless Ere	allusion to [epi] oinopa ponton G	[upon] the winey sea: Homeric tag ["wineless air"?]
.04	œdor	oideô G; # G-to-L	to swell, become swollen
.15	augustan peace	part trans. pax Augustana L	the empire of Augustus
.16	fortitudinous ajaxious	*fortitudines Ajacis L	the brave deeds of Ajax
.16–.17	fortitudinous ajaxious rowdinoisy tenuacity	fortitudo ejus Rhodum tenuit L	his strength has held Rhodes: motto of the knights of St. John of Jerusalem; # B
.18	doerehmoose	adoremus L	let us adore
.19	genuane	[flectamus] genuane? L	shall we kneel?
.20	letate!	laetate L	gladden!
.18–.20	doerehmoose genuane	Adoremus. Flectamus genua. L	Let us adore. Let us kneel.
	. . . letate	Levate. L (liturgical directions)	Rise.
.23	soide	oideô G	swell, become swollen
.23	quoite	quoi OL	to whom
		quo L	where
.26	Sorer	soror L	sister
.34	floruerunts	floruerunt L pl. of	they flourished
		floruit L	"he flourished": formula of ancient historians when birth and death dates are unknown
.35	turrified	turris L	tower
054.03	Farseeingetherich	Vercingetorix	Gallic king who fought against Caesar

.04	Charachthercuss	Cara[c]tacus	British king; see 047.07
.05-.06	Favour with your tongues	Favete linguis L	"Be well-disposed with tongues!" *i.e.* be silent: command to citizens at religious ceremonies
.06	*Intendite!*	Intendite L	Direct your attention! Attention!
.10	Casaconcordia	casa concordiae L	house of harmony *or* agreement
		casa concordis L	harmonious *or* concordant house
.12	–triginta–	triginta L	thirty
.12	Tippoty, kyrie, tippoty	ti pote, kyriê, ti pote G	what on earth, lord, what? Why, lord, why?
.12-.13	kai . . . kai	kai G	and, even
.13	makkar	makar G	blessed, happy
.15	Epi alo	epi allo G	upon another thing
.32	ancestralolosis	lousis G	washing, bathing
.34	conciliabulite	conciliabulum L	a place of assembly, public place
055.01	lobe	*allusion to* Loeb Classical Library?	
.03	Atreox	Atreos G	Atreus, son of Pelops, served the flesh of his brother's children to him, at which the sun recoiled in horror. Hermes cursed the house of Atreus.
		atrox L	gloomy, hideous, savage, fierce, atrocious, harsh
.03	Ilyam	*Iliam *for* Iliadem (*Acc.*)	The Trojan Woman: Helen
.03	Ilyum	Ilium L *for* Ilion G	Troy (*poetic*)
.03	Maeromor	maeror L	mourning, sadness
.04	mundibanks	mundi (*Gen.*) L	of the world, world's
.07	livit	lividus L	bluish, leaden
.09	pretinately	praetenuis L	very thin
.11	the hen	to hen G	the One (*philosophy*)
.11	everintermutuomergent	inter L	between, among
		mutuo L	to borrow

		mergens L	plunging into, sinking, drowning
.16	quopriquos	quid pro quo L	something for something
.19	mastic	mastichê G	odoriferous gum
		masticatio L	a chewing
.22	Cycloptically	kyklôps G	"Round-eyed":
		Cyclops L	one-eyed cannibal encountered by Odysseus
.27	gigantig's	Gigantes G L	earth-giants buried under Aetna
.28	phoenix	Phoenix L	fabulous bird of Arabia
		Phoinix G	
.29	cacuminal	*cacuminalis L	pointed, sharpened, acute
.29	erubescent	erubescens L	blushing; feeling ashamed
.30	Archicadenus	archi- G	chief-
		cadenus (*Swift's* anagram)	decanus
		decanus L	one in charge of ten; dean
		Archidecanus LL	chief dean, archdean
.34	Dyas	dyas G	the number two
.34	Dyas in his machina	deus ex machina L	"god from a machine"; melodramatic method of plot resolution
.35	hypostasised	hypostasis G	foundation; substance
.36	orerotundity	ore rotundo L	with rounded mouth
056.03	*pro tem locums*	pro tem[pore] locum tenens L	holding the place for a time
.06	nonot	necnon L	and also, likewise
.06	plangorpound	plangor L	beating the breast in grief
.13	Molyvdokondylon	*MG pron.* molybdokondyl-on G	lead-knuckle
.16	sillonise	sillos G	"squint-eyed": satirical poem
.23	zooteac	zôdiakos [kyklos] G	animaled [circle]: zodiac
		zôon G	animal
.29	Nous	nous G	mind, intelligence

.31	pragma	pragma G	deed, act, matter, affair
.31	formal cause	causa formalis LL *trans.* aitia [paradeigmati-kê] G	one of Aristotle's four metaphysical "causes"; the others being "material" "efficient" and "final"
.36	regnans	regnans L	reigning
057.02	melos	melos G	musical passage, song
.07	hantitat	*hantitat fake-L *modeled on* habitat L	he haunts: *Eng,* "haunting-place" he dwells: *Eng,* "dwelling-place"
.07	Zoans	zô G zôon G	to live animal, living being
.12	thermites	thermos G	hot
.18	irreperible	irrepertus L *irreperibilis L	not found, undiscovered undiscoverable, unlearnable
.18	adjugers	adjugo L *adjugor L	to yoke, fasten together one who yokes
.19	his judicandees	his judicandis L	for the purpose of judging these things
.21	kudos	kydos G	glory
.22	exegious monument, aerily perennious	exegi monumentum aere perennius (Horat. *Carm. III*.30.1) L	I have completed a monument more enduring than bronze—*opening of last poem in Horace's 3rd book of* Odes
.26	bland sol	sol blandus L	the pleasant sun
.27	corrugitate	corrugo L corrugis L	to wrinkle wrinkled, folded
.32	Dablena Tertia	Eblana G Tertia L	Dublin the Third, the Third Dublin
.32	maladik	maladictus L	accursed
.32	multvult	multi vultus L *nult-vult *for* non vult-vult L multum vult L	many faces, many expressions he will not-he will, willy-nilly he wills much
.33	magnoperous	magnopere L	very much, exceedingly, earnestly
.33	rota	rota L	wheel
.36	pro	pro L	for, in front of

.36	contestimony	con- L con[tra] L	with-, together- against
058.04	bisaacles	bis saeculo L	twice in a generation, twice an age
.05	ulvy	ulva L	sedge
.05–.06	ulvy came, envy saw, ivy conquered	veni, vidi, vici L	I came, I saw, I conquered; #B
.08	uxpiration	uxor L	wife
.08	annuhulation	annullo L	to annihilate
.09	deprofound	de profundis L	"out of the depths": Ps. 130
.09	souspirs	suspiritus, suspirium L	sigh
.11	Ahdostay, feedailyones	Adeste, fideles L	Be present, faithful ones (Come, all ye faithful)
.14	boviality	*bovialitas L	cowlikeness, oxlikeness
.18	Eheu, for gassies	Eheu, fugaces [... labuntur anni]—Horat. Carm. II.14.1-2 L	Alas, the fleeting [... years glide away]—opening of Horace's 14th Ode of the Second book
.32	retro	retro L	backwards
.32	santoys	san G	ancient letter S
059.03	emptors	emptor L	buyer, purchaser
.11	viridable	vireo L *viridibilis L	to be green, to bloom greenable
.13	climatitis	clima L *climatitis Mod.L klêma G *clematitis Mod.L	clime, region, part inflammation of a part twig, branch inflammation of a branch
.15	obitered to his dictaphone	obiter dicta L	things said in passing
.15	entychologist	entychia G tychê G *entychalogistos G	conversation; meeting chance; fortune specialist in conversation
.15	propenomen	*prope-nomen L	almost-name
.16	properismenon	properispômen- on G	word circumflexed on the penultima
.22	propogandering	propaganda L	things which are to be propagated
.30	ave	aves L	birds

		ave L	hail! (*greeting*), hello!
.34	infamatios	infamatio L	calumny, defamation
060.06	merrytricks	meretrix L	prostitute, harlot
.07	revulverher	vulva L	seed-covering; womb
.14–.15	caveman ... canem!	cave canem L	beware the dog
.16	sanit Asitas	sanitas L	health, sanity
.21	torrifried	torris L	brand, firebrand
		torreo L	to roast, scorch
.21	indradiction	*intradictio L	inward speech
.26	Caligula	Caligula L	"Little Boots": Gaius Julius Caesar Germanicus, emperor 37–41; mad; assassinated
.27	Eastralian	australis L	southern
		[Austria *latinized from* Oesterreich *looks as if*]	"Eastern land"
		from austrina L	the southern regions
.31	turridur's	turris dura L	a hard tower
.32	probiverbal	proba verba L	good words, honorable language
		*probeverbalis L	excellently worded
.33	upsiduxit	ipse dixit L	he himself said
.33	*mutatus mutandus*	mutatis mutandis L	the required changes having been made; the things to be changed being changed
061.01	scenities	scaenitae L	actresses
.01	una	ûnâ L	in one and the same place
		una (*fem.*) L	one
.01	mona	monê, mona (*fem.*) G	alone, solitary
		mona (*neut. pl.*) G	unique things
		Mona L	Isle of Man; Anglesea
.01	*Meminerva*	memini L	to remember
		Minerva (*same root as* memini) L	goddess of wisdom, *identified with* G Pallas Athena
.16	Questa	questa (*fem. pp. of* queror) L	complained, lamented, bewailed
.16	Puella	puella L	girl

.24	piscman	piscis L	fish
.25	Puellywally	puella L	girl
		vale L	farewell
		# Labials	
.27	Keysars	Caesaris (Gen.) L	Caesar's
.27	Trite	tritos G	third, the third
.29	rex	rex L	king
.30	leaden age	pun [invented by Alexander Pope?] on Saturnia regna L	"the reign of Saturn," i.e., the golden age. But Saturn in alchemy = lead (whence "Saturnian days of Lead and Gold" Dunciad IV.16)
.36	Urovivla	MG pron. *Ourobybla G	Urine-papyroi; sacred urine-writing on papyrus
062.02	Atreeatic	[mare] Hadriaticus L	[the sea] belonging to Hadria (a city, now Adria, in N.E.Italy): the Adriatic
		Atreus	in G mythology, founder of accursed dynasty, father of Agamemnon and Menelaus
.11	lottuse	lôtos G lotus L	food (flower?) eaten by a people encountered by Odysseus; makes the eater forget his own country
.11	luctuous	luctuosus L luctuose L	sorrowful, lamentable dolefully, mournfully
.12	-illuim	Ilium L illim L	poetical name for Troy from that place, thence
.16	inhabitands	*inhabitanda L	places requiring to be inhabited, inhabitable places
.16	astea	astea (pl. of astu, asty) G asteia G	towns of the town, polite, urbane
.16	agora	agora G	assembly, marketplace
.16	helotsphilots	heilôtês G	Spartan serfs (word may mean "captives")

		philotês G	friendship, love
.21	Humpheres	pheres G	-bearing, -carrying
		*Hump-pheres	Hump-bearing
		Eng. + G	
.21	Exarchas	exarchos G	leader; chorus-leader; commander
		ex archôs G	from the beginning
.21	Humpheres ... Exarchas	*Hump-pheres Exarchos G	hump-bearing leader
		*Hump-pheres ex archas G	hump-bearing from the beginning
.34	Pomona	Pomona L	goddess of fruit and fruit-trees
063.12	Myramy	mira me L	admire me
.30	pseudojocax	pseudo- G	false-
		*jocax L	joker; *pseudo-etymon of Joyce*
		*pseudojocax G+L	false-Joyce[?]
.30–.31	[pseudo joc]ax ax-[planation]	labrys G	two-headed axe
		supposed etymon of labyrinthos G	labyrinth in Crete built by Daidalos (*2-headed axe a common Minoan symbol*)
.30–.31	pseudojocax axplanation	*labyrinthine allusion to*	James Joyce (Sham Shem), Stephen Dedalus
.33	*magnum bonum*	magnum bonum L	the great good
064.03	Delandy is cartager	delenda est Carthago L	Carthage must be destroyed: *Cato's slogan*
.04	mormon	mormô G	bugbear who destroys children
		marmor L	marble
.13	martiallawsey	martialis L	of *or* belonging to Mars
.13	marses	Mars L	Roman god of war; #A
.15	Pompery	Pompeius L	name of a Roman gens
		Pompeii L	"belonging to the gens Pompeius": town buried by Vesuvius a.d. 79
		Cn. Pompeius Magnus	Pompey the Great (106–48 b.c.); #C

.17	liffopotamus	potamos G	river
.17	ploring	ploro L	to cry aloud, to wail
.19	Rejaneyjailey	Regina Coeli LL	Queen of Heaven (*name of a prison in modern Rome*)
.23	Alphos, Burkos and Caramis	Alpha, Bêta, Gamma G	letters A, B, G—*first letters of G alphabet*
.23	Astrelea	astralis L	pertaining to the stars
		australis L	southern
		Astraea L	goddess of justice, lived
		Astraia G	on earth in the golden age
.23	astrolajerries	astrologia GL	knowledge of the stars
		astrologus L	astronomer
.30	nonobli	nono L	ninthly
		non oblitus L	not forgotten
.31	Scapolopolos	scapus L	shaft; cylinder; sheet of paper; newel post; beam of a balance
		Scapula L	Roman surname
		scapula LL	shoulder
.32	machelar's mutton	# *Labials*	bachelor's button
.34	hen	[to] hen G	[the] One (*philosophy*)
065.02	auctumed	auctumno L	to cause autumn
		auctus L	increase
.03	orgibald	orgia G	nocturnal festival in honor of Bacchus; orgies
.04	Colley	chôlê (*fem.*) G	lame, limping
		cholê G	bile
.04	Macairs	machaira G	knife, dagger, sword
.05	Simper	semper L	always, ever
066.05–.06	in ... reeboos publikiss	in rebus publicis L	in states, in commonwealths, in republics; in public affairs
.05	reeboos	reboo L	to bellow back, to resound
.06–.07	secular sequence	saeculorum sequentia L	the sequence *or* continuity of the centuries
.12	Fierceendgiddyex	Vercingetorix	Gallic king who fought Caesar
.18–.19	lappish language	lapsus linguae L	a slip of the tongue
.19	semposed	sym- G *for* com- L	with-

.26	halpbrother	*# Labials*	halfbrother
.26	herm	hermês G	head carved on top of a square pillar, stood in front of private houses
.29	tristinguish	tris- L	thrice-, in three
		for dis- L	twice-, in two
.30	jubabe	Juba L	*see 013.12; #A*
		juba L	mane
.31	invened	invenio L	to come upon, find out, learn
067.01	Nivynubies'	nivalis L	snowy
		nivens L	winking
		nubis L	a cloud
		nubilis L	marriageable
.08	analectralyse	analecta L *from* analektês G	one that picks up crumbs after a meal; a word-gatherer
		analektra (*pl.*) G	shoulder-pads
		!ysis G	loosing, releasing
		*analektralysis G	loosening of shoulder-pads
.08	chymerical	Chimaera L *from*	mythological fire-breathing monster
		chimaira G	she-goat
		chymeia G	art of alloying metals
.10	heliose	hêlios G	the sun
.16	epening	*# Labials*	evening
.19–20	hickicked ... hick	hic L	this, this here; here
.22	appop pie oath	apeipon G	declare, deny, forbid, renounce
.33	Lupita	lupula L	little she-wolf
		lupa L	she-wolf; prostitute
.36	Luperca	Luperca L	goddess: she-wolf that suckled Romulus
068.06	*ad huck*	adhuc L	to this place, hitherto, just now
		ad hoc L	"to this": for a particular purpose
.12	lacessive	lacesso L	to provoke, arouse, excite, stimulate, irritate
.17	tease fido, eh tease fido, eh eh tease fido	*disfido L	to distrust
		fido L	to trust

.18	Angealousmei	Angelus mei L *for*	Angel of me
		Angelus Dei L	The Angel of God
		angelus L *from* aggelos = angelos G	messenger
.19	Arcoforty	Arcus-fortis L	Strong-bow: *Earl of Pembroke, led Anglo-Norman invasion of Ireland*
.19	farfar	farfarus L	colt's-foot (*plant*)
		far L	grain, corn
.29	stele	stêlê G	pillar, column
.29	Phenicia	Phenicia LL *for* Phoenica L *for* Phoinikê G	sea-coast country of the Levant, including mod. Israel, Lebanon, Syria
.29	Little Asia	*trans.* Asia Minor L	lesser Asia
.29	obelise	obelizô G obelos G	to mark with an *obelos* "skewer": horizontal line used as a critical mark to indicate a passage in a text is spurious
.34	Tatcho	taceo L	I am silent
069.09	orts	ortus L	a rising, beginning, origin
.09	oriorts	orior L	to rise, appear; to spring from, to originate
.11	aves	aves L	birds
		ave L	hail
		Eva (ave *backwards*) L	Eve, first woman
.12	lousaforitch	lucifer L	light-bringer: the morning star
.13	shoodov	ovum L	egg
.14	Asterr	astêr G	a star
.14	drema	*drêma (hyper-Ionic) G	drama
.17	prime	primus L	first
070.06	consstated	constat L	it is settled, it is agreed
.12	obuses	*obusus L *modeled on* abusus L	a proper use, a use for a purpose a wasting, consuming, misuse

.14	Titus	Titus L	a Roman praenomen
.28	taxis	taxis G	order, arrangement
.31	atillarery	at illa L	moreover she, but on the other hand she
		Attila (406–453)	king of the Huns; overran eastern Europe and also Italy
.36	ear ... of Dionysius	Ous Dionysiou G	Dionysios's Ear: a cave in which the slightest whisper could be heard
.36	Dionysius	Dionysios G	"Belonging to Dionysos [*the god*]": very common G name
		Dionysos I (430–367 b.c.)	tyrant of Syracuse; deported Plato; wrote bad plays but won first prize in Athenian contest by political influence; *see 307.L25, 307.20-21*
071.03	ripidian	rhipidion G rhipis G	a small bellows a fan
.03	flabel	flabellum L	a fan, fly-whisk
.15	Hoary Hairy	horum (*masc.*) harum (*fem.*) L	of these
.16	Hebdromadary	hebdomatos G hebdomados (*Gen.*) G dromadarios G *hebdomadroma-darios G *hebdomadromi-kos G	seventh week's, of a week runner week-runner, seven-day-runner week-swift, swift as a week
.16–17	*Tummer the Lame the Tyrannous*	*pseudo-trans.* Oidipous ho Tyrannos G	"Swollen-footed" the Monarch: Oedipus Rex
.18	*Pantojoke*	panto- G	all-, everything-
.31	*Facktotem*	factotum LL	"do all": handyman, man of all work
.32	*Lycanthrope*	lykanthrôpos G	werewolf, man-wolf
072.11	*Sickfish Bellyup*	sic fit belua [?] L	thus is made a monster.
.14	*Phallusaphist*	phallos G	processional image of erect penis
		philos G	lover, friend

		saphês G	plain, distinct
		sophistês G	sage, wise man
.16	*Polis*	polis G	city
.33	grumus	grumus L	little heap, hillock
073.01	paleologic	palaios G	ancient
		logos G	word, account
		Palaiologoi G	Paleologues: last dynasty of Byzantine emperors (1261–1453).
		Palaiologikos G	"Traditional"[?]: pertaining to the Palaeologue dynasty
.05	cocoa come	# *Reduplication*	
.09	nobodyatall	*trans.* Outis G	"Nobody": *name Odysseus called himself to the Cyclops*
.09	Wholyphamous	*trans.*	"Much spoken of"[?]:
		Polyphêmos G (Polyphamos, *Doric*)	*Cyclops encountered by Odysseus*
.18	falladelphian	phallos G	*see 072.14*
		philos G	*see 072.14*
		adelphê G	sister
		adelphos G	brother
		delphys G	womb
.19	*Et cur Heli!*	et cur *Heli L modeled on* et tu Brute?	and why *Heli [Healy?] and even you, Brutus?
.23	exetur	*exetur for exitur L	there is an exiting, a going out takes place
.24	archicitadel	arx L	citadel
		archi- G	chief-
.25	Nestor	Nestôr G	aged king of Pylos in Homeric poems
.25	Alexis	Alexis G	"Help": *name of a shepherd in Vergil's 2nd Eclogue*
.30	eolithostroton	êôs G	dawn
		lithos G	stone
		strôsis G	paving
		*strôton G	piece of pavement[?]
		*êôlithostrôton G	piece of dawn-stone-paving
.33	Olivers lambs	Alpha Lambda G	letters A, L

.35	nubilettes	nubilis L	marriageable
		nubila L	clouds
.35	cumule	cumulo L	to form a heap
		cumulus L	a heap, a pile
074.04	Wulverulverlord	ulva L	sedge
.06	deyes	dies L	day
.06	Deyus	Deus L	God
.06	Allprohome	pro L	for
.07	Allprohome	*see 074 .06 J*	
.07	Add some	Adsum L	I am here (*in classics-centered schools* [*e.g., Clongowes Wood*], *schoolboy's response at rollcall:* "Present!")
.08	*Animadiabolum, mene credidisti mortuum?*	Anima ad diabolum mene credidisti mortuum? L	Soul to the devil did you believe me dead?
.09	faustive	faustus L	favorable, lucky
.09	Truiga	Troja L	Troy
.11	pantriarch	pan-, panto- G	all-
		archos G	chief, leader
		archôn G	ruler, commander
		*pantarchos, *pantarchôn G	all-ruler
.11	Comestowntonobble	Constantinopolis L *for* Konstantinou polis G	Constantine's city: Byzantium from 4th to 15th C; *mod.* Istanbul
075.02	Ariuz	Arios G	Mede, Aryan
.02	Arioun	Arion (*Acc.*) G	Mede, Aryan
.04	sigilposted	sigilla (*pl.*) L	little figures; a seal
.05	undeveiled	unde L	whence? from whom?
.07	Fooi, fooi	fui L	I have been, I was
.18	*ex profundis malorum*	ex profundis malorum L	out of the depths of evils
.20	nomened	nomen L	name
076.02	*pace*	pace L	with [*someone's*] leave
.07–.08	*sigarius . . . vindicat urbes terrorum*	sicarius vindicat urbes terrorum [ex terroribus] L	the assassin sets free the cities of terrors · [from terrors]
		securus iudicat orbis terrarum L	untroubled, the world judges; #*B*
.07	sic	sic L	thus [*i.e., misspelling* sigarius *is correctly transcribed*]

.08	sicker	*sic-er *fake*-L	*thuser [*i.e., improbable reading* terrorum *is even more correctly transcribed*]
.08–.09	the obedience of the citizens elp the ealth of the ole	*trans.* obedientia civium urbis felicitas L	the citizens' obedience is the city's happiness: *Dublin's motto;* # *B*
.13	porpus	# *P/K Split*: corpus L	body
.21	protem	pro tem[pore] L	for the time
.22	misonesans	misos G	hatred
		nêsos G	island
		*misonêsiôtai G	island-haters, hate-islanders
.23	limniphobes	limnê G	lake
		phobos G	fear
		*limnêphobos G	lake-fearer
.30	somnolulutent	somnolentus L	sleepy, drowsy
		somnolenter L	sleepily
		lutensis L	mud-living, living in mud
		*somnoleluten-sis L	sleepily living in mud
.34	phallopharos	phallos G	image of a penis
		pharos G	1. piece of cloth; 2. plough; 3. lighthouse
		phallopheros G	bearer of the *phallos* at a Dionysiac festival
		*phallopharos G	phallos-cloth; phallos-plough; phallos-lighthouse (*phallos the size of a lighthouse; lighthouse that is a phallos; phallos to plow with*)
.36	obcaecated	*obcaecatus *for* occaecatus L	made blind; rendered senseless
077.01	petrifake	*petrifacio L	to make stone, to petrify
.04	hydromine	hydro- G	water-
.06	*circiter*	circiter L	round about, near
.07	Auton Dynamon	auto dynamikon (*neut.*) G	self powerful
		*autôn dynamikôn G	of self powerful things

.18	heptarchy	heptarcheia G	magistracy of a seventh part (*of a country, or the like*)
.23	*et*	et L	and, even
.23	a.u.c.	a[nno] u[rbis] c[onditae] L, *or* a[b] u[rbe] c[ondita] L	in the year of the founded city since the city was founded (*designation of Roman-era years [reckoned from 753 b.c.]*)
.25	velediction	vel L	if you will; or else; or; at least; whatever you like; either
		velum L	a sail
		valedictio L	a saying farewell
		*veledictio L	a saying of "take your choice," a saying of "either way"; *or*, a saying farewell at sailing
.34	honophreum	*Honophreum *modeled on* Mausoleum L	the tomb of *Honophreus the tomb of King Mausolus
078.03–.04	*hypnos chilia eonion*	hypnos chilia aiônôn G	a sleep for thousands of ages
.04	lethelulled	Lêthê G	"Forgetfulness": *river from which dead drink to forget past*
.05	megapod	megapous, megapodos G	big foot
.11	Sideria	siderea L	starry, pertaining to constellations
		sidêreia G	iron-mines
.11	Utilitarios	utilitas L	usefulness, profit
.12	propaguting	pro- L pagus L	for- village
.12	plutorpopular	Pluto L Ploutôn G	god of the underworld
		Plutus L Ploutos G	"Wealth": god of riches
.12	progeniem	progeniem (*Acc.*) L	descent, posterity, offspring
.18	septuply	septuplex L	sevenfold

.19	monads	monas G	unit
.21	portrifaction	porterium facio L	to make the fare [for Charon]
.25	Celtiberian	Celtiber L	member of a mixed
		Keltibêr G	Celtic-Iberian people of Middle Spain
.27	Vetera Uladh	Vetera [Uladh] L [+ Gael.]	Old Ulster, Ancient Ulster
.29	cons	con- L	with-
.29	dives	dives L	rich
.31	Bellona's	Bellona L	goddess of war
079.03	whigissimus	[whig]issimus L	whiggest, most whig, superlatively whig
.05	hibernating	hiberno L	to winter, to pass the winter
		Hibernia L	Ireland
.18	Venuses	Venus L	goddess of love; # A
.18	temptatrix	*temptatrix for tentatrix L	[female] assailant, attempter, tempter; eccl. L: temptress
.18	vulcans	Volcanus L	the fire-god; for story of Venus and Volcanus, # A
.19	frockful of fickles	forficula L	pincers [of an earwig]
.28	vidual	vidua L	widow
.32	salmofarious	salmo L	salmon
		fario L	salmon-trout
080.01	nekropolitan	nekros G	corpse
		nekropolis G	city of the dead: cemetery
		*nekropolitikos G	of, for or about dead citizens or citizens of a nekropolis
.06	Phornix	fornix L	arch, vault; brothel
		porneion G	brothel
		porneia G	fornication
.07	tautaubapptossed	tau G	letter T
		t'auta G	the same things
		tauta G	these things
		tautologeô G	to repeat what has been said
.13	castrament	castra L	military camp
		castrametor L	to pitch camp
		castratio L	pruning; castration
		atramentum L	ink

.20–.21	propagana fidies	propaganda fide L	things of the faith to be propagated (*name of a Vatican agency*)
.22	morphyl	Morpheys, Morpheus G	"Shaper": god of dreams
		morphê G	form, shape
.22	pome by pome	pomum L	fruit
		pomus L	fruit-tree
.23	terrine	terrenus L	consisting of earth, earthy
		terrens L	frightening
.24	Agni	agna L	ewe lamb
		agni (*Gen.*) L	lamb's
		ignis L	fire
.24	araflammed	ara L	altar
		flamen L	priest of one particular deity
		aurea flamma L	golden flame: oriflamme, *ancient royal standard of France*
.24	Mithra	Mithras	*Indo-Iranian god, associated with sun; his cult rivaled early Christianity in Rome and Italy*
.24	monished	moneo L	to remind, to advise, to teach
.25	obluvial	*obluvius L *modeled on*	"washed-for"
		alluvius L	"washed-to": land washed to the shore by flowing of water
.25	noarchic	nauarchos G	admiral
		*Noa Nauarchos G	Admiral Noah
.26–.27	torchpriest, flamenfan	flamen L	"he who burns": priest of one particular deity
.27	flamenfan	fanum L	shrine, temple
.28	Jove	Jovis (*Gen.*) L	Jupiter, Roman sky-god; #A
.28	Posidonius	Posidonius L (135–51 b.c.)	historian, philosopher, teacher of Cicero
		Poseidôn G	god of the sea, *equated with Neptune*

.29	O'Fluctuary	fluctuor L	to move in the manner of waves, to undulate, be driven hither and thither, to fluctuate
.29	Lave	lave L	wash!
.30	minx	minxit L	[he, she] has urinated
.36	lucans	Marcus Annaeus Lucanus (a.d. 39–65) L	Lucan: Spanish-born Roman poet, forced by Nero to commit suicide
081.01	vicinals	vicinalis L vicinus L	neighboring neighbor
.03	Fluminian	flumineus L	of, in, or belonging to a river
		[Circus] Flaminius L; [Via] Flaminia L	Flaminian Circus; Flaminian Way; both built by Gaius Flaminius, consul 223 b.c.
.05	mausoleum	Mausoleum L Mausôleion G	tomb of King Mausolus; see 077.34
.05	O Adgigasta, multipopulipater	*O Adgigasta, multipopulipater L	O Adgigastes, many-peoples'-father
.05	Adgigasta	ad, ad- L gigas G	to, towards; to-, towards- a giant
.07	Hermes	Hermês G	1. son of Zeus and Maia, equated with Mercury 2. wooden pillar surmounted by a bust; see 066.26
.07–.08	Per omnibus secular seekalarum	per omnia saecula saeculorum L in saecula saeculorum eccl. L	for all ages of ages in ages of ages phrases signifying forever, to all eternity
.07	omnibus	omnibus L	for all, for everyone
.09	rhedarhoad	r[h]aeda L	four-wheeled carriage (spelling with -h-, though to be found, is false)
		r[h]aeda-r[h]oad L, Eng.	carriage-road (spelling with -h- is false) # B

		rhêdios G	easy to do; easygoing
		rhodon, *pl.*	rose, roses
		rhoda G	
.10	rhinohide	rhino- G	nose-, nasal-
		rhinos G	hide (animal skin)
.12	disoluded	dissolutus L	unloosed, disconnected, lax
		ludus L	game, play, sport
.13	rupestric	rupes L	rock
		rupester L	rocky
.25	hemosphores	haimo- G	blood-
		haemo-, hemo- LL	
		spora G	sowing; origin, birth; procreation, begetting; seed, offspring
		*haimosporai G	blood-births; blood-begettings; blood-seeds
		*haimophoros G	blood-bearing, bearing blood
.28	patrecknocksters	Pater noster L	Our Father
082.03	Servious	Servius L	Roman proper name:
		Marius Servius Honoratus	4th C commentator on Vergil
		Servius Sulpicius Rufus	jurist, contemporary with Cicero
		Servius Tullius	sixth king of Rome
		servus L	slave, servant
.12	vermicular	vermiculus L	worm, grub, maggot
		vermiculor L	to be wormy, full of worms
.15	collidabanter	collidabantur L	they were brought into collision, they used to be brought into collision, they were being rubbed together
.17	illortemporate	illo tempore L	at that time
.25	tenitorial	teneo L	to hold, keep, grasp
.31	excelcism	excelsus L	elevated, lofty
		Excelsus L	the Highest, the Most High
		excelsitas L	loftiness

083.07–.08	lards porsenal	Lars Porsena	*Etruscan figure associated in conflicting legends with the traditional kings of Rome. Both words may be titles rather than names.*
.09	lux	lux L	light
.09	apointlex	apud L	with, at, near
		lex L	law
.11	aprioric	a priori L	from the previous, from the former
.11	aposteriorious	a posteriori L	from the latter; subsequent
.15	coctable	*coctabilis L	cookable
		coctivus L	cookable
.25	lexinction	lex L	law
.31	portlifowlium	porto L	to carry, bring along
		folium L	a leaf
.32	pax	pax L	peace
.33	poghue	[osculum] pacis L	[the kiss] of peace [*etymon of Gael.* póg, "*kiss*"]
084.04	humoral	[h]umerale L	military cape, shoulder-cover
.05	*lignum vitae*	lignum vitae L	wood of life
.05	rhumanasant	rheuma G	stream
		mano L	to flow
.11	contusiums	contusio L *as if* *contusium *from* *kontusion G	contusion, bruise # G-to-L
.11	coccyx	coccyx L kokkyx G	cuckoo "cuckoo": 1. a stammerer; 2. a bone at the base of the spine; 3. the arse-hole
.14	exilicy	exilis L	thin, lank, lean
.15	sitisfactuary	*sitisfactura L	a making thirsty
.15	conclusium	conclusio L *as if* *conclusium *from* *konklusion G	a shutting-up, closing; conclusion *see 084.11* # G-to-L
.16	agripment	Agrippa L	Roman family name; name of two native rulers of Roman Judaea

.16	deinderivative	deinde L	thereafter, next
.27	corso	korsos G	trunk of a tree
.31	olympiading	Olympias G	the Olympic games; space of four years between Olympic games
085.09	umphrobited	#*Labials*	unprohibited[?]
		umbo L	protuberance, boss, nipple
		omphalos G	navel, umbilical cord
.09	semitary	semita L	path, lane
.13	*acta*	acta L	register of public acts, records; journal
.13	*legitima*	legitima L	usages prescribed by law
.13	*plebeia*	plebeius, -a, -um L	belonging to the common people
.13	*acta legitima plebeia*	Acta legitima plebeia L	Daily record of the lawful public acts of the common people. Acta *at Rome included* Acta publica, Acta Senatus, Acta Diurna, Acta Triumphorum, *but no known* Acta L. P.
.20	Phenitia	Phenicia LL *for* Phoenicia L Phoinikê G	country of the coastal Levant in modern Israel, Lebanon, Syria
.27	calends of Mars	Kalendae Martiae L	March 1, *first day of Roman year; feast of married women,* Matronalia, *whence called* femineae Kalendae, "*the feminine calends*"
.28	equinoxious	*equinoxius L	equally harmful
.30	fesses	fessus L	wearied, feeble
		faeces L	dregs, sediments
.32	ambrosiaurealised	ambrosia GL	food of the gods
		aureolus L	golden
		Ambrosius Aurelianus	British leader, organized successful resistance against Saxons 470–480 a.d.; called "last of the Romans" by Gildas

		Ambrosius L	[St.] Ambrose; church-father, 4th C bishop of Milan
		Aurelius [Augustinus] L	[St.] Augustine; disciple and friend of St. Ambrose
.34	fight	# Digamma	white
.36	mamertime	Mamers	Oscan name for Mars
		mamertinus L	of or belonging to the Mamertini ("Sons of Mars"), Umbrian mercenaries
086.01	exution	exutio L	an exclusion
		[a venia] exutio eccl.L	they who are excluded from divine forgivenness, the utterly reprobate [St. Ambrose]
.01	fluors	fluor L	a flowing, flow; flux, diarrhoea
.07	elois	alias L	otherwise
		eleêson G	have mercy
.09	pixes	pix L	pitch, tar
.09	luvial	*luvio L	a washing
.19	matrmatron	mater L	mother
		matri- L	mother-
		matrona L	married woman
.20	Angricultural	angaria L	service to a lord, villanage
		angario L	to compel, constrain (service)
.21	Prepostoral	prae- L	before-
		post L	after
		oralis L	pertaining to the mouth
.29	Qui Sta Troia	trans. Hic Stat Troia	Here Stands Troy
.29	hiss or lick	Hissarlik	site in Turkey identified by Schliemann as Troy
.34	Nullnull	nullus L	not any, none
087.03	bonafides	bona fides L	good faith; # B
.05	Juno	Juno L	goddess, daughter of Saturn, wife of Jupiter, deity of women
.06	the Rainmaker	trans. Pluvius L	epithet of Jupiter
.07	decembs	decem L	ten

		December L	tenth month of the Roman year
.07	ephemerides	ephêmerides G	diaries, journals, daybooks
.11	patrified	*patrifactus (*pp.*) L	made a father
.12	Hyacinth	Hyacinthus L Hyakinthos G	Laconian youth beloved by Apollo who accidentally killed him; the flower sprang from his blood
.14	sivispacem	si vis pacem L	if you want peace
.27–.28	betterwomen with bowstring hair of Carrothagenuine ruddiness	*The women of Carthage, at the final siege by the Romans, 146 b.c., cut off their hair to make bowstrings*	
.34	crossexanimation	exanimatio L	suffocation; terror
.34	testis	testis L	1. a witness; 2. a testicle
.35	treepartied	[Vita] Tripartita L	*The Three-Part Life* [of St. Patrick]: L source for much of Patrick legend; *possible allusion here also to shamrock*
		[Gallia est omnis divisa in] partes tres ... L	[Gaul as a whole is divided into] three parts ... *opening of Caesar's* Gallic War; *we are not persuaded of the reality of this allusion here*
088.02	evervirens	virens L	1. being green; 2. a green plant
		part trans. sempervirens	evergreen
.02	abfalltree	ab L	away from
.06	gnosible	gnôsis G	knowledge
.07	conatively	conatum L	undertaking, attempt, venture, hazard
		*conativus L	*grammar:* of "attempting" verbs *or* tenses

.07	cogitabundantly	cogitabundus L	thoughtful
.09	morphomelosophopan-creates	morphoô G	to shape, form
		melos G	music; limb
		sophos G	skilled
		pan G	all, everything
		kreas G	flesh, meat
		pankreas G	"all-meat": pancreas
		*morphomeloso-phopankreas G	flesh-all-shaped-skillfully-by-music
.13	pediculously	pediculus L	louse
.14	Morbus	Morbus L	"Disease": a deity (*personification*)
.13–.14	pediculously . . . Morbus	morbus pediculosus L	"lousy disease": ancient disease, in which the body swarmed with lice
.17	ares	Arês G	god of war, identified with Mars; #*A*
.17	inquiline	inquilinus L	of foreign birth
.18	nase	nasus L	nose
.22	Maximus	Maximus L	"Greatest": *surname of many persons of antiquity*
.22	Vercingetorix	Vercingetorix	Gallic leader against Caesar
.23	Bentley	Richard Bentley	classical scholar (1662–1742)
.24	phoenix	Phoenix L	fabulous bird of Arabia; *see 130.11*
		Phoinix G	
.28	Cumbilum	cumbalum L	cymbal
		kumbalon G	
		cum- L = syn- G	with-
		*cumbolum L *for* symbolon G; #*G-to-L*	tally, token, contract, treaty, mark of identity
.28	comes	comes L; LL; ML	1. (L) companion; teacher 2. (LL) occupant of a state office 3. (ML) earl, count
.33–.34	Wirrgeling and maries	P. Vergilius Maro L	Roman epic poet
.35	Tem	tem[pus] L	time
089.03	dromium	Dromios G	god of the racecourse

		dromos G	racecourse
.05	coram populo	coram populo L	in the presence of the people
.10	ajaciulations	Ajacis (*Gen.*) L	Ajax's, of Ajax; *see* 306.L13
.11	in cursu	in cursu L	in progress, underway
.16	portavorous	*portavorax L	gate-devouring
		*portovorax L	port[wine?]-swallowing
.19	Harlyadrope	hêliotropion G	sun-dial
.20	Magistra	magistra L	mistress
.22	recipis	recipis L	you (*sing.*) get back, retain, receive
.27	*Quare hircum?*	Quare hircum L	Why the goat?
.27	*Unde gentium fe...*	Unde gentium fe[stines] L	Whence on earth are you hurrying? # *B*
.34	jotalpheson	iota, alpha G	letters I, A
.34	jasons	Jason L Iasôn G	leader of the Argonauts; *see 123.26*
.34	in	in L	on, upon
.34	a pigeegeeses	epexêgêsis G	detailed explanation
		*apexêgêsis G	an explaining-away
.34	pigeegeeses	Pegasus L	winged horse of the Muses
		Pêgasos G	
.35	pontiff's	pontifex L	"bridgemaker": Roman high-priest
090.02	solasistras	sola (*fem.*) L	alone
		solaris L	pertaining to the sun
		sistra L seistra G (*pl.*)	metallic rattles used in worship of Isis
.03	laud	laus L	praise
.03	Labouriter	*laboriter *recte* laboriose L	laboriously, with effort
.03	laud from Labouriter	laus laboris L	praise of the work
.06	pugnaxities	pugnax L	fond of fighting
		*pugnacitas L	fondness of fighting
.06	antepost	ante- L	before
		post- L	after
		*antepost L	beforeafter
.10	soords	surdus L	deaf
.13	Foght	fuit L	there was
.17	Saturn's	Saturnus L	"The Sower": *in myth, the most ancient king of Latium; afterwards god of agriculture and civilization, identified with* Kronos *father of* Zeus

.18–.19	Camellus	camelus L	camel
		kamêlos G	
		Camillus L	*Roman cognomen*
		M. Furius	general, *conguered Veii*
		Camillus	*and saved Rome from*
			the Galls
.18	Gemellus	gemellus L	a twin
.19		Gemellus L	"Twin": *Roman*
			agnomen
.20	Obsolutely	absolute L	completely, perfectly
		obsolete L	poorly, meanly
.26	Thos Thoris,	*garbled*	*Nom., Gen., Dat., Acc.,*
	Thomar's Thom	*paradigm of a*	*Abl. cases*
		3rd declension	
		masc. noun	
		[e.g., flos, floris,	
		flori, florem,	
		flore]: *Thos,	
		Thoris, Thori,	
		Thorem, Thore,	
		mixed with a	
		2nd declension	
		paradigm in	
		which Acc. of	
		Thos would be	
		*Thom	
.26	rudacist	[# *rhotacism*	*the process by which in*
		[*from* rho G]	*oblique cases of nouns,*
			the -s *of the stem passes*
			over, between vowels,
			into -r- *[e.g.,* flos, floris;
			*Thos, *Thoris]
.29	tertianly	tertianus L	of *or* belonging to the
			third, thirdly
.32	–scorta–	scortum, *pl.*	harlot, strumpet
		scorta L	
.32	–porna–	porneia G	prostitution
		pornê G	prostitute
.32	–stippata–	styppeion,	coarse fiber of flax *or*
		stippeion, *pl.*	hemp, tow, oakum
		styppeia,	
		stippeia G	
		stipata L	surrounded, pressed
			together
.36	punic	Punicus L	Carthaginian

091.06	Cliopatrick	Clio L *from* Kleiô G	Muse of History
		patricius L	belonging to the nobility
.13	Markarthy	Mars L	god of war; *see 091.14*
		Marcus Antonius	Roman triumvir; *lover of Cleopatra, with whom he was defeated by Octavian (Augustus)*
.14	Baalastartey	Astarte-Aphrodi-tê G	goddess of love, beauty and fertility partly derived from Semitic goddess Astarte. Arês (Mars) *appears in myth as both her paramour and her husband. See 091.13*
.25	Tyre-	Tyrus	*important Phoenician coastal city*
.36	helic	helice L *from*	winding; constellation Great Bear
		helikê G	convolution of a shell
092.01	exthro	echthro- G	hated-, hostile-
.06	hilariohoot	hilaris L	cheerful, gay, jovial
.06	cumjustled	cum- L	with-, together with
.07	tristitone	tristis L	sad, grieved, depressed
.07	*isce et ille*	isce et ille L	*this (emphatic) and that*
.09	*iste*	iste L	that of yours
.10	symphysis	symphysis G	growing together; joint; structure; organic union
.11	duasdestinies	duas, dyas G	the number two
.12	lunarised	lunaris L	lunar, of the moon
.13	eranthus	êranthos G	spring flower
.13	myrrmyrred	myrris G	sweet cicely; myrtle
.16	thyacinths	thyaktas G	sacrificing priest
		hyakinthos G	*see 087.12*
.25	Gentia Gemma	Gentica Gemma L	national gem
		gentianae gemma L	gentian bud
.35	Untius	unctus L	anointed, oiled; an anointment
.35	Muncius	munitus L	fortified, safe
.36	Punchus and Pylax	Pontius Pilatus L	governor of Judaea, time of Christ

.36	Pylax	phylax G	a guard
		pylaios G	at the gate
		pylaikos G	silly
093.01	Nolans	nolens L	being unwilling
.01	Brumans	bruma L	winter, midwinter
.06	curial	curialis L	1. pertaining to religious services of the districts of Rome; 2. belonging to the imperial court
.06	Commodore	commodo L	seasonably, in time
		quomodo L	how, in what way
.06	valley	vale L	be well, fare well, farewell
.06	valley O	valeo L	I am strong, I am well
.06	Commodore valley O	commodo valeo L	I am seasonably well
		quomodo valeo L	how I am well, how am I well
.07	hairy	heri L	yesterday
.07	Arthre	arthra (pl.) G	joints, connections; articles [Gram.]
		ta arthra G	the genitals
		*Aratre (Voc.) recte Arator L	O Land-holder, O Farmer
.07	jennyrosy	generose L	nobly
.07	Arthre jennyrosy	for Arator generose L[?]	O noble Lord
.06–.07	Commodore valley O hairy, Arthre jennyrosy?	commodo valeo heri, Arator generose L perhaps intended for Quomodo vales hodie, Arator generose? [not classical] L	I am seasonably well yesterday, O noble Sir How fares your health today, noble gentleman?
.09	tumass	tum L	at that time, then
		tumens L	swelling
.09	equinous	equi- L	horse-
		aequus L	equal
		nous G	mind, intelligence
		*equinous L+G	horse-sense[?]
		*aequinous L+G	equal-mind

.13	soccered	socer L	father-in-law
		soccus L	slipper
		succurro L	to aid, come to the help of, be useful
.14	fenemine	fenus, faenus L	profit
		faenum L	hay
		Phainôn G	"Shiner": the planet Saturn
.15	gratiasagam	gratias agamus L	let us give thanks (*nickname for St. Patrick*)
.16	donatrices	donatrices (*pl.*) L	[female] givers, [female] donors
.17	venuson ... dovetimid	*allusion to* Aeneas	*son of Venus (and Anchises). Doves are associated with Venus*
.19	conclaiming	conclamo L	to cry out together; to call to arms
		conclamans L	noisy
.21	Putor	putor L	foul smell, stench; rottenness
		pudor L	shame
.27	Lesbia	Lesbia L	"Woman of *Lesbos*": *name used by* Catullus *for his mistress* Clodia, *sister of* P. Clodius Pulcher *and wife of* Q. Caecilius Metellus Celer
.31	Kathleen	kathairô G	to cleanse
.33	Op.	op[us] L	work, labor, art
.33	Op. 2	opto L	to choose, elect; wish for
.33	Phil Adolphus	philadelphos G	loving *one's* brother *or* sister, brotherly, sisterly; *frequent title of kings*
.33	Op. 2 Phil Adolphus	Ptolemy II Philadelphus (308–246 b.c.)	second Macedonian king of Egypt; *founded Library at Alexandria*
094.07	Hen	[to] hen G	[the] One (*philosophy*)
.10	perlection	perlectio L	a reading through
.12	Una	una L	in one and the same place
		una (*fem.*) L	one (*cp.* Hen *above*)

.12	Ita	ita L	thus, so, in this way; yes
.13	Agrippa	Agrippa I ("Herod Agrippa")	king of Judaea a.d. 41–44
.13	propastored	pro- L	before; on behalf of, for
		pastor L	shepherd, herdsman
		*propastor L	substitute shepherd
		propatôr G L	forefather, ancestor
		praeposterus L	back-to-front, absurd, perverted
.14	timid Danaides	timeo Danaos [et dona ferentes] L	"I fear the Greeks [when they bear gifts]"—Vergil, *Aeneid* II .49
.14	Danaides	Danaides G L	daughters of Danaus: *at their father's order 49 of the 50 killed their husbands*
.14	Ena	hen G	one
		ennea G	nine
.14	milo	Milo L Milôn G	famous athlete of Crotona
		T. Annius Milo	Roman gangster-politician, *murdered P. Clodius, defended in Cicero's* Pro Milone
.14	melomon	melos G	music; limb
		melomai G	to care for
.16	sycopanties	sykophantês G	"fig-informer" (one who informed against illegal exporters of figs from Attica): informer, tale-bearer, backbiter; flatterer
.16	amygdaleine	amygdalon G	almond
.21	A ... O	Alpha, Omega G	letters A, Ô—1st & last of G alphabet
.26	suspices	suspiciose [etc.] L	in a way to raise mistrust
		suspicio L	1. to look up at; to look up to; 2. to mistrust
		instead of auspices L	diviners through the flight of birds; favorable signs

.27	Solans	Solanus L	the east wind
		Solôn G	Athenian poet and legal
		(7th–6th C b.c.)	reformer
.29	bouc	bucca L	the cheek; a bawler; a
			mouthful
.35	monopoleums	mono- G	one-, single-
		polemos G	war
095.01	Minace	minax L	jutting out; threatening
		minaciter L	threateningly
		Minos G	1. king of Crete; 2.
			underworld judge
.09	Minxy	minxi L	I have urinated
.15	sayman's	semen L	seed
.16	effluvium	effluvium L	a flowing-out; outlet
.27	unguam	unguentum L	ointment, perfume
		unguis L	fingernail, claw
		unquam L	at any time, ever
.28	nunguam	nunquam L	at no time, never
.28	lunguam	linguam (*Acc.*)	tongue
		L	
096.02	rhinoceritis	rhino- G	nose-
		rhinos G	skin
		keras G	horn (*of an animal*)
		*rhinoceritis	inflammation of a
		Mod.L	nose-horn
.03	contradrinking	contra L	against
.06	marcus	marcus L	large hammer
		Marcus L	Roman praenomen
.20	Lolly	Lollius L	name of a Roman gens
			(*cp. Eng.* Tully *for*
			Tullius)
.30	foliated	foliatus L	leaved, leafy
.33	*securus iudicat orbis*	securus iudicat	free from care, the
	terrarum	orbis terrarum L	circle of the lands
			judges; *i.e.,* untroubled,
			the world judges—*St.*
			Augustine; #*B*
.34	possum	possum L	I can
.34	hagious	hagios G	sacred, holy
.36	urbiandorbic	urbi et orbi eccl.	to the city and the
		L	world: *a papal blessing*
			or pronouncement
097.05	Urse's	ursa L	bear
.14	volponism	vulpes L	fox
.15	onasum	ona G	she-ass

		onasis (*Doric*) G.	profit
		sum L	I am
.15	abomasum	ab L	from, away from
		abomino L	to deprecate as an ill omen, to detest
		sum L	I am
.21	protown	pro- L	in front of, before, for
		prôton (*neut.*) G	destined
		prôton G	first
.22	attax	attakos G	locust
		atrox L	savage, cruel, fierce
.23	depontify	*depontifacio L	to unbuild a bridge
.24	unhume	humus L	the earth
.27	Winceywencky	veni, vidi, vici L	I came, I saw, I conquered
		vinco L	to conquer, to defeat
.30	Eruct	eructo L	to belch
		eructus L	a belch
.33	triduum	triduum L	the duration of three days, a period of three days
.33	Saturnalia	Saturnalia L	general festival in honor of Saturn, *beginning December 17 and lasting several days*
.34	goatservant	satyr (?)	goat-footed creature, servant of Dionysus
.34	Forum	forum L	public place, market place
.36	epheus	ephu G	it was, it happened
		eheu L	alas
098.02	Fama	Fama L, *personification of:*	goddess, daughter of *Terra*, swiftfooted, all-seeing, growing as she runs
		fama L	that which people say, rumor, common talk, gossip
.03	ether	ether LL, aether L *from* aithêr G	heaven; air; the divine element in the human soul
.05	*via*	via L	way, road
.07	*hod*	haud L	not at all, by no means

.09	Cornelius	Cornelius L	*Roman gens celebrated as embracing the most distinguished Roman men and women*
.10	Asia Major	*Asia Major L	Greater Asia, *as distinguished from*
		Asia Minor L	Lesser Asia—*but originally meant lesser regions around town Asia in Lydia*
.12	omnibox	omnibus L	for all, for everyone
.18	vulgovarioveneral	vulgo L	universally, everywhere, publicly
		varius L	diverse, different, varying, changeable
		varus L	pimple
		venereus L	of *or* belonging to sexual love
		*vulgivarivenere- us L	having to do with universally changeable sexual love
		*vulgivarovener- eus L	having to do with universally pimpled sexual love
.26	fas	fas L	divine law; a court day; lawful, proper
.27	auchnomes	auc- L	fruit-, increase-
		nomos G	habitation; usage, custom
.27	*acnomina*	acnomen, *pl.* acnomina L	surname, name acquired by a person to signalize some accomplishment, *e.g.*, Scipio *Africanus*, Fabius *Cunctator*
.27	*ecnumina*	ec- L	outside-, out-
		numen L	divine power
		ecnumina L	outside of the divine will, outside the power of the gods
.31	rome	Roma [urbs] L	Rome: *actual city traditionally founded by and named after* Romulus, *who killed his brother* Remus

.32	reme	*Rema [urbs] L	Reme: *potential city that might have been founded by and named after* Remus *had he killed his brother* Romulus
.33	immor	immoror L	to tarry in, to stay at, to linger near
		immo L	on the contrary
.34	Toties testies quoties questies	toties testes quoties questus *or* quoties questus toties testes	how often complaints, so often witnesses [a witness will appear each time a complaint is made]
099.02	lowquacks	loquax L	talkative
.02	tacit turn	tacet L	[he] keeps silent
		taciturnus L	untalkative
.03	ruining	ruina L	a falling down [*Milton uses this same etymologization:* "Hell saw Heav'n *ruining* from Heav'n" *PL*, VII . 867–68]
.04	*Estout pourporteral*	esto perpetua L	it is to be permanent! let it be permanent
.09	Carpulenta	corpulentus, -a L	fat
.09	Gygasta	gigas G	giant
.11	oertax	ortyx G	the quail
.19	filiform	*filiforma L	thread-shape
.23	fortitudo	fortitudo L	strength; durability; steadfastness
.23	prudentiaproven	prudentia L	skill; sagacity; discretion
.30	dexter	dexter L	the right hand
.33	fervxamplus	fervidus L	glowing hot, burning
		examplexor L	to clasp, embrace
		exemplum L	imitation, example
.36	quasicontribusodalitarian's	quasi cum tribus sodaliciarius L	as it were comrade with three [*like D'Artagnan?*]
100.02	atalaclamoured ... The latter! The latter!	Thalatta! Thalatta! G	Sea! Sea! *shout of Xenophon's men when they at last sighted the Black Sea on the retreat from Persia (the* Anabasis)

.11	sliduant	-ans L	*suffix of certain participles equivalent to* -ing *in English*
.13	Parteen-a-lax	Parthenos G	"Virgin": the goddess Athena; *also* Artemis; *the constellation* Virgo
		partheno- G	maiden-
		lax G	with the foot, under foot
.14	Abies Magnifica	abies magnifica L	noble fir
.15	resipiency	resipio L	to have a flavor of, to smack of
		resipiscentia eccl. L	a change of mind, reformation, repentance
.16	Quintus	Quintus L	"Fifth": Roman praenomen
.16	Centimachus'	centum L	hundred
		machê G	battle
.16	Quintus Centimachus'	*trans.* Conn Céadcathach	Conn Hundred-fighter, "Conn of the Hundred Battles"
.17	porphyroid	porphyroeidês G	purply, purplish
.18	*En caecos harauspices!*	En caecos harauspices! L	Behold the blind soothsayers!
.18	*Annos longos patimur*	Annos longos patimur L	We endure long years
.27	venter	venter L	belly
.28	tristurned	tris L	thrice, three times
		tristor L	to be sad
.34	authenticitatem	*authenticitatem (*Acc.*) L	authenticity
.34	aliquitudinis	*aliquitudinis (*Gen.*) L	of somethingness
.35	tesseract	tessera L	die (*for gaming*); watchword; square table; tile
.36	fronds	frons L	leafy branch, bough, foliage
.36	Ulma	ulmus L	elm-tree
101.02	tellus	tellus L	the earth; land
.02	tellas	#R/L *interchange:*	
		terra L	dry land, ground

.08	Varina	Varina Mod.L	[Jane] Waring: *coinage by Swift*
.09	Quarta Quaedam	quarta quaedam L	some fourth woman
.12–.13	Homo Capite Erectus	homo capite erectus L	1. erect man with a head; 2. man erect as to the head
		homo capite erecto L	man with head erect
.15	cainozoic	*kainozôikos G *opposite*	proper to recent animals
		to *palaiozôikos G	proper to old animals (paleozoic)
.35	prim	primus L	first
102.03	arche	archê G	beginning, origin
.03	noes	Nôe G Noe L	Noah
.05	okeamic [*misprint?*]	ôkeaneios G	of, in, from the ocean
.07	ur, uri, uria	ouris G	chamber-pot
		ouria G	wards, watches
		ouria G	for urine
.07	gorgony	gorgonia L gorgoneia G	coral
		Gorgô, Gorgonê G	"Grim One": Medusa, whose face turned beholder to stone
.11	curlicornies	cornu L	a [*generally crooked*] horn [*e.g., of a ram*]
.14	Egon	egô G ego L	I (*1st pers. sing. pronoun*)
.15	Steploajazzyma	Septuagesima L	the seventieth (*fem.*)
.15	Sola	sola L	only, single (*fem.*)
		sol L	the sun
.18	Wery weeny wight	veni vidi vici L	I came I saw I conquered—*Julius Caesar*, #B
		#*Labials*	
.19	herbata	herba L	grass
		herbacea L	grassy, grass-colored (*fem.*)
		*herbatica L	grass-eating creatures
		herpeta G	creeping things, serpents
.26	Chlora	Chlôris G	"Greenness": goddess of flowers
		Flora L	goddess of flowers

.27	huemoures	[h]umores L	liquids, fluids
103.02	*Attabom attabom, attabombomboom*	atta G & L	"dad": salutation to old man surname for persons who walk upon the tips of their toes
.04	*Attabom, attabom, attabombomboom*	*see 103.02 A–C*	
104.02	Plurabilities	*plorabilitas L pleura G	weepable-ness rib
.04	mamafesta	mamma L festa (*fem.*) L	breast, pap merry; holiday-
.06	*Augusta*	Augusta L	1. "Highness": *title of emperor's wife, mother, daughter, sister* 2. [city of] Augustus: *name of several towns*
.06	*Angustissimost*	angustissimus L augustissimus L	narrowest, closest most majestic, most venerable
.06	*Augusta Angustissimost*	Augusta Angustissima L Augustus Augustissimus L	Closest Augusta (*the empress?*) Most August Majesty
.06	*Seabeastius*	Sebastos G	Venerable, Reverend, August: *G equivalent of L* Augustus
.08	*Anna Stessa's*	anastasis G	rising again; raising up [*from the dead*]; resurrection
.11	*dik*	dico L	I say
.11	*et tu*	et tu [Brute] L	and even you, [Brutus]: *dying utterance of Julius Caesar;* # B
.11	*mihimihi*	mihi L	to me
.12	*Hesterdays*	hesternus L	yesterday's, of yesterday
.13	*Arcs*	arx L arcus L	citadel bow, arch
.14	*Rebus de Hibernicis*	*Collectanea de Rebus Hibernicis* L	"Collected [Works] on Irish Matters": *collection of Irish historical documents published 1770 by Vallancey*

.17	plutherplethoric	*plusquampleth-oricus ML	more than excessive
.20	*Cleopater's*	Cleopatra L	"Paternal Glory":
		Kleopatra G	*famous queen of Egypt, 1st C b.c.*
		*Cleopater L	Glory-father
		*Kleopatêr G	
		kleos G	rumor, fame, glory
		Kleiô G Clio L	Muse of History
.22	*Placeat Vestrae*	placeat vestrae [majestati] LL *or* ML	may it please Your [Majesty]
.23	*Portentos*	portentum L	sign, omen; monster
		portentosus L	full of monsters; unnatural
.24–.01	*When the Myrtles of Venice Played to Bloccus's Line*	When the myrtle of Venus joins with Bacchus's vine	*line from song* "To Anacreon in Heaven" (*air of* Star-Spangled Banner)[*supplied to us by an anonymous reader*]
105.01	*Venice*	Venus L	goddess of love; # A
	Bloccus's	Bacchus L	name for Dionysos, god
		Bakchos G	of passionate religion, vegetation and wine
		# *Labials*:	
		floccus L	straw
.02	*Oremunds*	ore L	by mouth, with the mouth
.04	*Ceteroom*	ceterum L	the rest, for the rest; otherwise
.10	*Notylytl*	notylos G	"moist"[?]: *medical term describing a pulse*
.11	*Extorreor*	extorreo L	to parch, to scorch
		extorreor L	to be parched, to be scorched
.16–.17	*Huskvy Admortal*	[Anima mea tristis] usque ad mortem (*Matt. 26:38*) L	[My soul *is* sorrowful] even unto death (*Christ's words in Gethsemane*)
.18	*Ophelia's*	ôpheleia, ôphelia G	help, aid, succor
.18	*Culpreints*	culus L	the posteriors, the fundament

.18	*Ophelia's Culpreints*	O felix culpa L	"O happy sin"—*medieval hymn on Adam's "fortunate fall" that resulted in the Incarnation;* #B
.18	*Hubty Hublin*	hubris G	wanton violence, insolence
.20	*Ventriliquorst*	ventriloquor L	to speak in *or* by means of the belly
		*ventriliquor L	1. to be liquid, to dissolve, to melt away in *or* by means of the belly 2. belly-liquid, belly fluid
.23	*Pupublick*	pubes publica L	the public men *or* public signs of manhood *or* public private parts
		instead of res publica L	the public matter, the public thing, the commonwealth, the republic
		pupa L	doll
.26	*Galasia*	gala G	milk
		Galatai G	Celts
		Galatia G, L	"Celt-land"—*country in* Asia Minor *inhabited by the* Galatai
.28	*Horuscoup*	Horus	*god of lower Egypt widely worshipped by Greeks and Romans; son of* Isis
		hauris L	you (*sing.*) drink up, drain
.30	*Esperations*	aspiratio L	blowing on; enunciating a word with an *h* sound
		speratus L	that is hoped *or* longed for
.32	*Columbkisses*	columba L	dove, pigeon
.33	*Trion*	Triones L	the constellation of the Wain, *i.e.,* Ursa Major and Ursa Minor
.34	*Totties*	toties L	so often, as many times
106.09	*Polynesional*	poly- G	many-

		nêsos G	island
		*polynêsiôtês G	many-insular; many-islander
.13	*Pessim*	pessimus L	worst
		passim L	at different places, at random
.19	*Miction*	mictio, minctio L	urination
.26	*Exat*	exeat L	let him go out, let him depart
.32	*Abbrace*	ab- L	from, away, away from
		bracchium L	the arm
		*abbrachiare L	to push away from the arms [?]
		instead of	
		*imbrachiare L	to hold in the arms, to embrace
.32	*Umbellas*	umbella L	umbrella, parasol
		umbo L	knob, boss, swelling; elbow
107.02	*L.S.D.*	L[ibrae] S[olidi] D[enarii] L	Pounds, Shillings, Pence
		libra L	Roman pound (weight)
		solidus L	gold coin of the Roman emperors
		denarius L	Roman silver (*later* copper) coin
		L[aus] S[emper] D[eo] L	Praise ever to God; *#B*
.08	proteiform	prôto- G	first-
		prôteios G	of the first quality
		Prôteus G	minor sea-god; a shapechanger in *Odyssey* 4.
.08	graph	graphê G	representation by lines; drawing; writing; Holy Scripture
.13	entomophilust	entomos (*sing.*) G	[a thing] cut in pieces
		entoma (*pl.*) G	insects
		entomias G	eunuch
		philos G	friend, lover
		*entomophilos G	lover of something cut into pieces; insect-lover; eunuch-lover

.13	nymphosis	nympheusis G	bridal, marriage
		*nymphôsis G	bride-pushing
.14	Oriolopos	Ôriôn G, L	mythical hunter transformed to a constellation
		lopas L	limpet (shellfish)
		lopas G	dish, plate
		lupus L	wolf
.16	goods trooth	*trans.*	perfect, admirable,
		kalokagathos G	splendid
		= kalos	beautiful and good
		k'agathos G	
.18	persequestellates	persequor L	to follow perseveringly, to pursue
		stella L	star
		stellatus L	starry
		*persequestello L	to follow a star
.19	madernacerution	*keroution G	horn
.34	semper	semper L	always, forever
108.12	Carprimustimus	karpos G	fruit; corn; profit
		primus L	first
		timos L	fear
.19	barbar	barbar G	sound, *to Greeks*, of all languages other than G
		barbaros G	non-Greek, foreigner; one whose language sounds like *bar-bar*; a barbarian
.24	epiepistle	epi G	upon, about
		epistolê G	message; letter
		epi epistolês G	about a message; upon a letter
.27	glorisol	sol L	the sun
.27–.28	glorisol ... in this Aludin's Cove of our cagacity	*probable allusion to Plato's comparison of this world to imprisonment in a cave in which only the shadows cast by real things can be seen* (*Republic*, Book 7).	

.30	odia	odia (*pl.*) L	hatreds, grudges
109.01	questy	questio, questus L	complaint
.19	antecistral	ante- L	before, prior to
		cista L	wooden box, basket
110.08	lutran	lutra L	otter
		lutron, *pl.* lutra G	ransom
.09	ult aut nult	ultio aut nullum L	revenge or nothing
		ultimum aut nullum L	last or nothing
		vult aut *nult (*for* non vult) L	he wills or he does not will
.10	Phaiton	*Phaitôn *false G for* Phaethôn G L; # G-to-L*	"Shining One": son of the sun destroyed by Zeus
.11	Drainophilias	drainô G	to be ready to do, to have strength
		philia G	friendship, fondness
.15	improbable possibles	Aristotelian formulation (*Poetics*, ch. 25)	in a tragic plot Aristotle prefers a sequence of probable impossibles to one of improbable possibles
.17	Harrystotalies	Aristotelês G	famous philosopher; #A
		telêeis G	total
.17	vivle	*MG pron.*; # Labials	bible
.22	that original hen	to hen G	the One (*philosophy*)
.22	kuur?	cur L	why?
.23	Premver	premo L	to press
		verum L	the truth
		primo vere L	at the beginning of spring
.26	copsjute	kopron G	dung
.28	limon	limen L	threshold
.31	*illico*	illico L	in that place
111.06	quinquegintarian	quinquagenarius L	1. a fifty-year-old 2. captain of fifty men (Old Test.)
		Quinquegentiani L	"Of Five Cities": a people in Cyrenaica [of the "Five Towns"—English pottery center?]

		quinque L	five
		quinquaginta L	fifty
.06	Terziis	Tertius L	"Third": Roman proper name
.31	turb	turba L	turmoil, brawl; mob
.33	hen	to hen G	*see 110.22*
112.02	the hen	to hen G	*see 110.22*
.12	volucrine	volucer L	flying, winged
		volucris L	bird
.16	genesic	genesis G	origin, race; generation; species
		*genesikos G	having to do with generation; having to do with the Creator
.18	auspice	auspicium L	divination by observing the flight of birds
.28	marcella	Marcella L	*fem. of* Marcellus (*dim. of* Marcus, "Hammer"), Roman family name
.29	Arths	arthron G	joint
.29	anomorous	anomos G	lawless, impious
.30	Toga Girilis	toga virilis L	toga of manhood: *ordinary peacetime outer garment of a Roman citizen*
.31	nosibos	nasibus (*Dat., Abl. pl.*) L	to, for *or* by noses
.35	rudess	rudis L	stick, rod, staff
.35	robur	robur L	oak, oakwood
113.02	postmantuam	post- L	after-
		Mantua L	city; *birthplace of Vergil*
		Mantuanus L	Vergilian
		mantum L	a Spanish cloak
.02	lapins	Latini L	the Latins
.02	grigs	Graeci L	the Greeks
.04	Dariaumaurius	Dareus, Darius L Dareios G	*name of several Persian kings; also of a gold coin*
		Marius L	name of a Roman gens
		C. Marius	conqueror of Jugurtha, seven times consul
		Maurus L	Moorish
		aureus L	standard Roman gold coin

.05	plate	platys G	wide; flat
		platysma G	a flat object
.06	sine	sine L	without
.07	anakars	anakar G	to the head, upward
		anax G	lord, master
		[w]anakas OG	
		Anakes G	"The Lords": Castor and Pollux
		Anacharsis G	Scythian sage c. 600 b.c.; *one of the Seven Sages*
.08–.09	tutus . . . tutus	tutus L	guarded; safe, secure
.09	–exin–	exin L	from there, thence
.11	Silvapais	silva L	woodland, forest
.16	Spissially	spisse L	thickly, closely; rapidly
.17	camelia	camilla L	maiden unblemished in birth and character
.19	Treestone	*see 216.03J–.04A*	
.19	Mons	mons L	mountain
.19–.21	Mons + Venis	mons Veneris L	"Mound of Venus": prominence above the public bones in women
.21	Venis	#*Labials*	penis
.21	Kate	kathairô G	to cleanse
.28	nolensed	nolens L	unwilling
.29–.30	*Habes aures et num videbis?*	Habes aures et num videbis? L	You have ears and you will not see?
.30	*Habes oculos ac mannepalpabuat?* [*emending probable errata:* . . . nonne palpabant?]	Habes oculos ac *manipalpabat?* L . . . nonne palpabant [palpabas?]? L	You have eyes and [he/she] *touched by hand [*felt his/her way(?)] . . . have they [you?] not seen?]
114.06	incunabula	incunabula L	swaddling-clothes; the cradle; childhood; a beginning
.11	antechristian	ante- L	before-
.15	domestic	domesticus L	pertaining to the house (*domus*)
.15	economical	oikonomikos G	pertaining to the house (*oikos*)
.16–.17	writing thithaways . . . hithaways writing	*description and imitation of* boustrephodon G	"ox-turning": writing alternate lines in opposite directions

.18	semetomyplace	sêma G	sign, mark, omen, token
		tomê G	cut place, cut; a cutting
.19	Hum. Lit.	Hum[aniores] Lit[erae] L	Humane Letters: the Humanities
.25	voos	MG *pron.* *boos	booze?
.33	complexus	complexus L	1. twined around; 2. embrace, an encircling
115.11	Tiberias	Tiberias L	city on Lake Galilee
		Tiberius L	emperor a.d. 14–37
.12	gerontophils	*gerontophilos G	old-man lover, lover of old men
.15	*prostituta in herba*	prostituta in herba L	exposed on the grass; a prostitute on the grass [on the turf?]
		prostituta in verba L	unchaste in words, foul-spoken
.21	Sykos	sykon G	fig
		psychos G	cold, coldness
		psycho- G	life-, soul-
.25	*in camera*	in camera L	in the chamber: secretly, privately
.26	virgated	virgatus L	made of twigs, wickerwork; striped
.30	pudendascope	pudenda [membra] L	"the shameful parts": the privy parts
		skopos G	watcher; object of sight
.30	neurasthene	*neurastheneia G	sinew-weakness, nerve-weakness
.30	nympholept	nympholêptos G	caught by nymphs: raptured, frenzied
.31	typus	typus L typos G	figure, image; a kind of fever
.32	drauma	drama G	deed, action; stage play
		trauma G	wound, hurt
.33	agnates	agnatus L	blood-relative on the father's side
.33	cognates	cognatus L	blood-relative on either side
.34	lubricitous	lubricitas LL	slipperiness; lewdness
		lubricus L	slippery
.34	meiôsis	meiêsis G	diminution, lessening, waning
116.02	meeter	mêtêr G	mother
.03	meeter's	*see 116.02 I*	

.03	half better	alpha bêta G	letters A, B
.04	meeter's	*see 116.02 I*	
.04	half better's	*see 116.03 I–J*	
.04	meeter	*see 116.02 I*	
.11	Spartacus	Spartacus L	Thracian gladiator who led a revolt at Capua in 73 b.c., defeated seven Roman armies
.16	*Est modest in verbos*	Est modus in verbis L	There is a proper measure in words; there is just so much to say
		Est modus in rebus, sunt certi denique fines—*Horat.* Sat. *I. i.106*	There is a proper measure in things, there are definite limits—Horace, *Satire* I, i.106
.18	fornix	fornix L	arch, vault; brothel
.22	kates	kathairô G	to cleanse
.25	lingo	lingo L	to lick, lick up
.30	sesquipedalia	sesquipedalis L	of a foot and a half; one foot and a half (*in length*); excessively long
.31	panepistemion	panepistêmôn G	all-knowing
		*panepistêmion G	body of all knowledge; encyclopedia?
.31	apically	apex L, *pl.* apices	long mark over a vowel; point of a single letter; shape of a letter
		apicula L	a little bee
.33	hapaxle, gomenon	hapax legomenon G	[a thing] once said, said only once; unique example of a word
117.10	olold	ololygê G	a loud cry
.11	stoliolum	stolo L	branch, twig, shoot
		stola L	long upper garment worn by women
.11	quiqui	qui-qui L	whosoever
.11	quinet	quin L	why not?
		quin etiam L	indeed, rather, not even if
.14	sordomutics	sordeo L	to be filthy
		surdus L	deaf
		mutus L	dumb
.14	florilingua	*florilingua L	flower language

.19	Sitys	sitos G	grain, bread, food
.22	milliums	*millium *backformed pseudo-sing.of* millia (*correctly* mille) L	a thousand; a Roman mile
.22	millenions	*millenion *backformed fake-G sing. of* millenia ML (*sing.* millenium)	a thousand years
.27	epistola	epistola L epistolê G	written message, letter
.33	kapnimancy	*kapnimanteia G	divination by smoke
118.04	holusbolus	holos G	whole, entire
		bolus L bolos G	a throw, cast; a haul
.13	Coccolanius	*coccolanius L	scarlet butcher
		*coccolana L	scarlet wool ["though your sins be as scarlet ... they shall be as wool" *Isaiah 1:18*]
.13	Gallotaurus	*Gallotaurus L	Gaul-bull
		*gallotaurus L	cock-bull [cock and bull?]
.16	baccbuccus	bacca L	berry
		bucca L	cheek
.21	chaosmos	chaos G	unformed matter: primordial state of the universe
		kosmos G	order, universe: brought into being out of, and contrary to, *chaos*
.24	possibly pot	possibiliter L *from*	possibly
		possum; posse L *from*	I can; to be able
		potis sum; potis esse L	I can; to be able, to be possible
.28	whyacinthinous	hyakinthos G	blue flower from blood of youth, Hyakinthos; the color blue
119.02	Terracussa	terra L	earth, land, ground
		concussa L	shaken

		terra concussa L	shaken earth
.03	homoplate	homo L	man, mankind
		homos, homo- G	same, common, joint
		platys G	flat
		*homoplatys G	equally flat all over
.04	philophosy	*philophôseia G	love of light
.11	calamite's	calamus L	reed, cane; reed-pen
.11	columitas	columis L	unhurt, safe
		*columitas L	safety
.15	glorioles	gloriola L	a small glory, little glory
.16	tiberiously	Tiberius L	of *or* belonging to the emperor Tiberius
.16	ambiembellishing	ambi- L	on both sides
.16	majuscule	majusculus L	"somewhat larger": large letter in medieval MSS
.17	chrismon	chrisma G [*chrismon *pseudo-sing.* of *chrisma, *neut. pl.*]	anointing, unction; grace
.17	trilithon	*trilithon G	a thing consisting of three stones
.17	ꟺ	san [?] G	archaic letter representing -ss-
.19	sigla	sigla L	signs of abbreviation; abbreviations
.19	Δ	delta G	letter D
.20	alp	alpha G	letter A
.21	delta	delta G	letter D; rivermouth; female pudenda
.23	the hen	*parttrans.* to hen G	the One (*philosophy*)
.32	Mors	mors L	death
		Mors L	goddess of death
.32	monologuy	*monologeus G	single *or* sole speaker
		*monologeia G	one collection, one speech
120.02	pristopher	pristos G	sawn
		*pristophoros G	bearer of something sawn
		Christophoros G #*P/K Split*	Christ-bearer

.02	polombos	palumbes L	wood-pigeon, ring-dove
		columba L	pigeon, dove
		# *P/K Split*	
.02	pristopher polombos	# *P/K Split:*	christopher colombos
.02	Kat Kresbyterians	# *P/K Split*	Pat Presbyterians
.07–.09	dummpshow ... mpe mporn	*MG represents the sound* b *by* mp, *because the letter* b *is pronounced* v. # *Labials*	dumbshow ... be born
.14	obeli	obeli L	critical marks shaped like spits placed opposite spurious passages in texts
		obelos G	a spit, skewer
.18	superciliouslooking	supercilium L	eyebrow; a projecting moulding; a circumflex accent mark (ˆ)
.19	Greek ees	epsilon G	small letter E: made rounded but with top loop open (ε)
.18–.19	superciliouslooking Greek ees	êta G	long G vowel E transliterated (*as in this book*) by a circumflexed e: ê
.20	owls ... to Athens	glauk' Athênaze; glauk' eis Athênas G	owls to Athens—*adage:* "coals to Newcastle"
.21	genuflected	genu flectere L	to bend the knee
.22	aggrily	-gg- G = -ng-	angrily
.22	kakography	*kakographê, kakographia G	bad writing, bad handwriting, bad drawing
.27	iota	iota G	letter I
.27	sinistrogyric	sinistrogyro L	to turn around to the left
.29	muddy terranean	mediterraneus L	midland, inland, remote from the sea
		mediterranea L	interior parts of a country
.33	eff, the hornful digamma	# *Digamma;* # *Labials;*	F = W
.34	digamma	ϝ OG	letter W

.34	bornabarbar	barbar G	see 108.19
.35	lipsus	lapsus L	a fall, slide, slip
		Lips L	1. Libyan 2. west-south-west wind
.35	hetarosexual	hetaros, hetairos G	comrade, companion, messmate
121.01	Claudian	Claudianus L	1. of *or* pertaining to the Emperor Claudius ["Lame"](a.d. 41–54), historian and linguist (*studied Etruscan; attempted to develop more phonetic alphabet*) 2. Claudian, *G-born L poet (d. AD 404)*
.03	Ⅎ	# *Digamma*	letter W
.07	Ⅎ	# *Digamma*	letter W
.08–.13	the curious warning sign ... indicating that the words which follow may be taken in any order desired	Ɔ (antisigma) G L	[letter] S reversed: *a critical mark placed in a MS before a verse which is to be transposed*
.08	protoparent's	prôto- G	first-
.09	*ipsissima verba*	ipsissima verba L	the very same words
.16	disdotted aiches	rough breathing (?) G	letter H: *represented by a tick preceding or over the next letter*
.18	principial	principialis L	original; that is from the beginning
.24	lacertinelazily	lacerta L	lizard
		lacertinus ML	arm
.27	*podatus*	pedatus L	1. footed; 2. an attack
.34	Cod	cod[ex] L	book made of bound pages (*not a scroll*): *abbreviation used in scholarly textual studies*
.34	Pap	pap[yrus] L	a papyrus MS: *abbreviation used in scholarly textual studies*
.34–.35	Brek, Lun, Dinn, Sup, Fullup	brek[fast], lun[ch], dinn[er], sup[per]	imitation of abbreviations used in scholarly textual studies
122.01	glypse	glyphô (*fut. tense* glypsô) G	to carve, cut out with a knife

		glyphê G	a carving, cut-out inscription
.07	ars ... bellical	ars bellica L	the art of war
.07	highpriest's hieroglyph	hiereus G	priest
		hieroglyphikos G	"priestly carving": hieroglyphic
.09	*O'Remus pro Romulo*	oremus pro Romulo L	let us pray for Romulus
		Remus, Romulus L	legendary twins, founded Rome, then Romulus killed Remus
.17	Villain Rufus	William Rufus L	Red William: William II of England
.21	*basia*	basia L	kisses (*of a passionate sort*)
.21	*oscula*	oscula L	pretty mouths: kisses
.23	*Tunc*	tunc L	then
.23	*Tunc* page	Tunc crucifixerant XPI cum eo duos latrones L	Then were crucified CHRI with him two thieves [*Mark 27:38*]: *wording of the* Tunc *page of the Book of Kells*
		XPI[CTOC] = CHRI[STOS] G	"Anointed": Christ
.25	crucian	cruciarius L	pertaining to the cross
.26	Columkiller	columba L	pigeon, dove
.32	labiolingual	*labiolingualis L	pertaining to the lips and tongue
.32	*basium*	basium L	a [passionate] kiss
.32	*suavium*	suavium L	a kiss
123.03	eighteenthly or twentyfourthly	*allusion to G alphabet*	classically: 18 simple letters plus 6 compound additional letters: *th, ph, ch, ks, ps* and *ô* (= *oo*)
.04	penelopean	Pênelopeia G	wife of Odysseus; # *A*
.08	libido	libido L	pleasure, desire, longing, fancy
.08	sex	sex L	six
.12	dectroscophonious	dektêr G	a receiver (*an official*)
		skopeô G	to watch
		phôneêis G	vocal, sounding
		*dektroskopoph-ôneis G	receiver-sight-sounding; receiving sight and sound(?)

.12	photosensition	phôto- G	light-
		sensatio ML	power of feeling
		*phôtosensatio G + ML	power of feeling light
.13	logged	-gg- G = -ng-	longed
.14	Chromophilomos	*chrômophilos G	color-lover
.16	ulykkhean	Odysseus G, Uluxe Etr., Ulixes L	Ulysses; *mod. spelling contaminates L and G, using G -yss- for L -ix-. Joyce hypercorrects, treating x as G chi and transliterating kh.*
.16	tetrachiric	*tetracheirikos G	four-handed
		tetracheir G	four-handed (*epithet of* Apollo)
.16	quadrumane	*quadrumanibus L	with four hands
		*quadrumane L (*as if* manus, "hand," *were an adj.*)	fourhandedly
.18	*Studium*	studium L	assiduity, zeal, study
.18	*Sexophonologistic*	sex L	six
		sexo- L	sex-
		phôno- G	sound-
		logistikos G	skilled in calculating
		*sexophônologistikos LG	skilled in calculating sex sounds
.18	*Schizophrenesis*	schizo- G	split-, cleft-
		phrenôsis G	instruction
		*schizophrenôsis G	split instruction
		phrenitis G	inflammation of the brain
		*schizophrenitis G	split inflammation of the brain
.22	*passim*	passim L	here and there, all over, at random
.22	periplic	periploos G	circumnavigation; account of a coasting voyage

.25	a Punic admiralty report	*allusion to* Victor Bérard, *Les Phéniciens et l'Odyssée* (1902–03)	*Bérard's thesis is that the Odyssey is based on a Phoenician* periploos *of the western Mediterranean, in Homer's time unknown to the Greeks*
.26	*Jason's Cruise*	Argonautica G L	story of Jason's voyage in the Argo to the Black Sea in quest of the Golden Fleece
.27	dodecanesian	Dôdekanêsoi G	Twelve Islands; archipelago off Asia Minor
.30	Tiberiast	Tiberias L Tiberius L	city on Lake Galilee emperor a.d. 14–37
.30	duplex	duplex L	twofold, double
.32	Hanno O'Nonhanno's	Hanno	1. Carthaginian explorer of West Africa c. 480 b.c.; *left a written report that survives in G trans.* 2. the Great: Carthaginian commander in First Punic War
		non L	not
124.02	foliated	foliatus L	leaved, leafy
.06	circumflexuous	circumflexus L	1. bent *or* turned around; *in grammar* pronounced [*a vowel or syllable*] as long 2. a vault, arch
.12	sic	sic L	thus
.16	pneuma	pneuma G	wind, air, breath
.16	rheuma	rheuma G	that which flows, current, stream
.27	bisses	bis L	twice
.35	Jeromesolem	sol L	the sun
.36	Andycox	anticus L	in front, foremost
.36	Olecasandrum	Alexandros G	"Defending-men": Alexander ; *name for Paris of Troy*
		Kassandra G	"Sister-of-men": daughter of Priam, *also known as* Alexandra *(false etym.?).*

125.07	juxtajunctor	*juxtajunctor L	a harnesser-together
.11	Formelly	formella L	a little mould for baking in
.22	kak	kak G	letter K
		kakos G	bad, evil
		kakkê G	human ordure, shit
.22	pfooi	fui L	I have been, I was
126.06	quisquiquock	qui, quae, quod L	who, which (*masc., fem., neut.*)
		quis L	who?
		quisquis L	whoever
.06	apostrophes	apostrophai G	turnings away from, escapes
.10	myther	mythêria G	traditions
.10	maximost bridgesmaker	*part-trans.* pontifex maximus L	"greatest bridgemaker": *title of* chief Roman high-priest
.12	–boa–	boaô G	to shout
.13	nudiboots	[pedibus] nudis L	with bare [feet]
.14	claud	claudeo L	to limp, be lame
.16	epulence	epulae L	feast, banquet
127.01	rotables	rotabilis L	whirling, rotary; practicable
.04	induments	indumenta L	garments
.05	inundered	inundo L	to overflow
.10	F.E.R.T.	F[ortitudo] E[ius] R[hodum] T[enuit] L	His Strength has held Rhodes: #B
		fert L	he carries
.13	zoomorphology	*zôomorphologia G	the study of the shape of animals
.14	omnianimalism	omne animal L	"every living creature":
.22	etcetera, etcetera	et cetera L	and other things, and so forth
.26	Iren	eirênê G	peace
.27	lited	litem ago L	to dispute, quarrel, litigate
.35	myrioscope	*myriaskopos G	ten-thousand-watcher
.35	piscines	piscina L	fish pond
128.01	fuit	fuit L	there was, he [she, it] was
.01	isst	est L	there is, he [she, it] is
.02	herit	erit L	there will be, he [she, it] will be

		heri L	yesterday
.02	quercuss	quercus L	oak, oak-tree
.03	Megalopolis	Megalopolis G	Great City: *capital of Arcadia*
.04	faunonfleetfoot	Faunus L	deity of agriculture and shepherds
.05	carucates	carruca L	four-wheeled coach
.12	puder	pudor L	shame
.13	mundyfoot	mundi- L	clean-
		mundifico L	to cleanse
		mundi (*Gen.*) L	world's, of the world
.13	Miserius	misereo L	to feel pity
		miseria L	wretchedness
		*Miserius L	male embodiment of Misery
.14	Anna Livia	Amnis Livia (?) L	River Liffey
		amnis livia L	blue-grey river
.14	Cerisia	ceresia LL	cherry
		kerasion G	
.14	Cerosia	kêros G	beeswax, sealing-wax
.14–.15	quid rides	Quid rides? [Mutato nomine de te / fabula narratur]—Horat. *Sat.* I.i.69 L	"What are you laughing at? [The name changed, the story is told about you]"—Horace, *Satire* I.i.69; *see also* Sat. II.v.3 (*Ulysses the speaker*)
.15	Titius	Titius L	1. name of a Roman gens; 2. dance named after *Sextus Titius*, tribune of the people
.15	Caius	Gaius (*less correctly* Caius) L	Roman praenomen; *personal name of Julius Caesar, also of Caligula*
.15	Sempronius	Sempronius L	name of a Roman gens; most famous members were the Gracchi
.15	Titius, Caius and Sempronius	Tiberius Sempronius Gracchus (*tribune 133 b.c.*) Gaius Sempronius Gracchus (*tribune 123–122 b.c.*)	brothers, leaders of the *Populares* (reform and agrarian party); both were assassinated

.22	quies	quies L	rest, quiet
.22	metro . . . polis	mêtropolis G	mother-city, mother-country
.25–.26	dance . . . orchistruss	orchis G	testicle
		orchêstra G	"dancing-place" in theater
.28	endonational	endo OL	in, within, on, upon
.29	delictuous	delictum L	crime, transgression
		delictus L	failed, offended
.35	phoenix	phoenix L	"phoenician": *fabulous*
		phoinix G	*bird in Arabia, lived 500 years; from its ashes a new phoenix arose*
.35	pyre	pyr G	fire
.35	cineres	cineres L	ashes
.35	pelium	Pêlion G L	high mountain in Thessaly, *a continuation of* Ossa
.36	ossas	Ossa G L	high mountain in Thessaly
.35–.36	pelium . . . ossas	imponere Pelio Ossam L	to pile Ossa on Pelion: *audacious attempt to scale heaven*
.36	pilluls	pilula L	globule, little ball, pill
.36	hirculeads	hircus L	he-goat
		Hercules L	demigod, son of Zeus and Alkmênê
		Hêraklês G	
		*Herculeis L	*The Herculead*: hypothetical epic poem about Hercules
.36	eatupus	Oidipous G	"Swollen-foot":
		Oedipus L	*legendary tragic king of Thebes*
129.10	ejoculated	ejaculor L	to shoot out, to hurl out
		jocus L	jest, joke
		*ejoculator L	to joke out
.13	holoday	holos G	whole, entire
.14	homoheatherous	homo L	man
		homo- G	same-
.16	emilian via	Aemilia Via L	Aemilian Way: *name of three different Roman roads, built by* M. Aemilius Lepidus *and* M. Aemilius Scaurus

.17	allphannd	alpha G	letter A
.18	patricius	patricius L	a patrician, member of the Roman nobility
		Patricius L	[St.] Patrick
.19	plebmatically	plebeius L	a plebeian, commoner, member of the Roman lower classes
		phlegmatikos G	full of phlegm (*a clammy "humor" of the body in ancient medicine*)
.19	centuries	centuria L	one of the 193 orders into which Servius Tullius divided the Roman people according to their property, and through which they voted
.21	demisfairs	*dêmisphairai G	people-balls, people-globes (worlds?)
.22–.23	seven dovecotes cooclaim to have been pigeonheim to this homer	*seven cities of the ancient world claimed to be the birthplace of Homer; Chios and Smyrna are best supported*	
.23	Smerrnion	Smyrna, Zmyrna G	city on the west coast of Asia Minor; *one of the contenders for Homer's birthplace*
.23	Rhoebok	Rhodos G	Rhodes, island off Asia Minor; *contender for Homer's birthplace*
.24	Kolonsreagh	Kolophôn G	"Summit": Kolophon, Colophon, city in Ionia; *contender for Homer's birthplace*
.24	Seapoint	Salamis G	Salamis, town in Cyprus; *contender for Homer's birthplace; Joyce etymologizes from* hals [*sals], "*sea*"
.24	Quayhowth	Chios G	Ionian island; *contender for Homer's birthplace*

.24	Ashtown	Argos G	"Unworked, Fallow": city in southern Peloponnesus; *contender for Homer's birthplace*
.24	Ratheny	Athênai G	*from* Athênê, Athêna, *the goddess,* chief city of Attica; *contender for Homer's birthplace*
.27	quot	quot L	how many, as many
.28	tot	tot L	so many [*usually with* quot]
130.01	futuerism	futuo L	to fuck
		erisma G	cause of quarrel
.09	pentecostitis	*pentêkostitis G	inflammatory disease of fifty
		costa L	rib
.11	comminxed	comminxit L	he [she, it] polluted, defiled, pissed on
		comminctus L	polluted, defiled
.11	phoenished	Phoenix L	"Phoenician": fabulous
		Phoinix G	bird in Arabia, lived 500 years; from its ashes a new phoenix arose
.16	ads	ad L	to, toward
.16	das	das L	you (*sing.*) give
.20	hickheckhocks	hic haec hoc L	this, this here (*masc., fem., neut.*)
131.08	outpriams	Priamos G	Priam, king of Troy at
		Priamus L	its fall
.09	parisites	Paris G L	son of Priam; *carried off Helen to Troy, occasioning the Trojan War*
.11	saulely	Saulos G Saulus L	St. Paul's Hebrew name; *changed probably to avoid ridicule from its G meaning;* #A
		saulos G	mincing, effeminate in gait

.12	appauling	Paulus L	Roman surname ("Little, Small"): *L name of St. Paul possibly chosen out of respect for* Sergius Paulus, *proconsul in Cyprus* [Acts 13, 7]
		paulus L	little, small
.20	arbuties	arbuteus L	of the strawberry-tree [arbutus]
.22	vikelegal	# *G-to-L*; # *L/R Interchange*	vicelegal, viceregal
.23	Mora	mora L	a delay
.24	Lora	lora L	1. thin wine made of the husks of grapes 2. leather sack
.26	Lego	lego L	1. to send with a commission, to send as ambassador; to depute; to appoint 2. to collect, to extract, to steal, to choose, to view, to read out
.30	*hereditatis columna erecta*	hereditatis columna erecta L	the lofty column of inheritance
.30	*hagion chiton eraphon*	hagios chitôn eripheios G	holy garment of a kid
.32	elimbinated	limbus L	border, hem; the zodiac
		e limbo L	out of the zodiac
.32	integras	integras L	you (*sing.*) make whole, heal, repair, refresh
		integritas L	completeness, soundness, chastity
.36	lithium	# *G-to-L*	lithion
		lithion G	a little stone
.36	anular	anularis L	relating to a signet-ring; a white color made from chalk
132.01	Circos	circos L	precious stone mentioned by Pliny; unidentified
		circus L	circle: *Circus Maximus* ("Greatest Circle"): oval in Rome accommodating 100,000 spectators

		kirkos G	hawk; wolf; circle
.03	apparoxemete	apparo L	to prepare, to make ready beforehand
		approximo L	to be near to, to approach
		paroxys G	pointed, sharp
.03	atlast's	Atlas G L	1. high mountain in Mauretania, on which heaven was fabled to rest 2. king of Mauretania changed into the mountain
.06	hunnibal	Hannibal, Annibal	Punic surname: Hannibal *son of* Hamilcar (247–182) *greatest Carthaginian general against Rome in Punic Wars*
.06	otho	Otho L [Othôn G]	Roman surname; M. Salvius Otho, *ineffectual emperor a.d. 69, committed suicide; a by-word for softness of character*
.07	aiger	aeger L	ill, sick, diseased
		aigeiros G	black poplar
.15	Miraculone	miraculum L	a wonder, marvel, miracle
.15	Monstrucceleen	monstrum L	evil omen, prodigy, monster
		monstruosus L	strange, preternatural
.17	Olaph	alpha G	letter A
.18	Vespasian	Vespasianus L	[*from* Vespasius, *name of a Roman gens; from* Vespa, "*wasp*"] Roman emperor a.d. 69–79; *overthrew* Vitellius *who had overthrown* Otho (*see* 132.06)
.19	Aurelius	Aurelius, Auselius L	Roman nomen; M. Aurelius Antoninus, *emperor a.d. 161–180, author of* Meditations
.19	tradertory	traditor L	traitor
.19	socianist	socius L	fellow, sharer, partner, comrade

		sociennus L	comrade
		socia L	female relative, wife
.27	Colossus	Colossus L	gigantic statue; statue;
		Kolossos G	*esp.* giant statue at Rhodes, dedicated to the sun
.32	quary	quare L	by what means? how? why?
.33	cur	cur L	why?
.34	methyr	methy G	wine
133.09	aquascutum	*aquascutum L	water-shield
.15	Sylviacola	silvicola L	inhabiting woods, sylvan
.18	polemypolity's	*polemopoliteia G	war-citizenship
		polemos G	war
		polis G	city
		politeia G	citizenship
.18–.19	aldays open ... closed for the love of Janus	Janus L	old Italian deity, with face on both front and back of head; the god of all beginnings; *the doors of his temple at Rome were kept open in time of war and shut in peace-time*
.19	eleaxir	Eleaticus L	Eleatic [philosophy]: *founded by Parmenides and Zeno, both of* Elea
		elixus L	thoroughly boiled
.23	judex	judex L	a judge
.30	entumuled	*entumulatus L	put into a burial mound, buried
.30	threeplexes	triplex L	threefold
.35	Eachovos	ovo L	to exult, rejoice
		ovum L	egg
.36	basidens [*misprint for* basideus?]	*basideus L *for* basileus G (*cp.* Odysseus / Ulixes)	king
.36	rexregulorum	rex regulorum L	king of princes, king of kinglings
134.01–.02	ultimate thole	Ultima Thulê L	Farthest Thule
		Thylê G Thule L	island in extreme north; *variously conjectured to be Iceland or Shetland*

.04–.05	threw pebblets for luck over one sodden shoulder	*ref. to* Deukaliôn G Deucalion L *and* Pyrrha	classical Noah and wife; *survived flood in an ark; afterwards threw stones over their shoulders, which became men and women*
.06	Gaudio Gambrinus	gaudeo L gaudium L	to rejoice joy [*this non-classical person is identified in Glasheen,* A Second Census]
.08	cumbrum, cumbrum	cum L bruma L	with midwinter
.12	Mars	Mars L Martius L	god of war March (*named for* Mars)
.13	Virgintiquinque	vigintiquinque L virgineus L	twenty-five maidenly
.14	Hapapoosiesobjibway	hapax G	once, one time, once for all
.14	arithmosophy	*arithmosophia G	skill in counting; number-wisdom
.18	Equadocta	equa docta L *aequa docta L	learned mare, skilled mare experienced female friend
.18	Therecocta	thêr G cocta L	beast, animal cooked, baked
.22	Apostolopolos	apostolos G polos G	messenger, envoy, one sent on a mission, apostle axis, pivot, *thing on which anything turns*
.28	nepos	nepos L	grandson
.35	recensors	recensor L	reviewer, reviser
135.06	annacrwatter	Anakreôn G	lyric poet, *fl.* 540 b.c.
.08	Pimploco	Pimpleus L Pimpla G L locus L	Sacred to the Muses place and fountain in Pieria sacred to the Muses place
.15	a bird of Arabia	Phoenix L Phoinix G	*see 130.11-12*
.16	cryptoconchoidsiphon- ostomata	kryptos G	hidden, secret

		kogchê = konchê G	mussel, mussel-shell
		kogchoeidês = konchoeidês G	mussel-like, shell-like
		siphôn G	tube, pipe
		stomata G	mouths
		*kryptokonchoe-idêsiphônostom-ata G	hidden-shell-like-tube-mouths
.17	herospont	Hellêspontos G	Sea of Hellê (*legendary girl drowned there*): strait between Europe and Asia, the Dardanelles
		Hêrô G	priestess *beloved by Leander who repeatedly swam to her across the Hellespont, but at length drowned*
		hêrôs G	a hero
		*Hêrôspontos G	Sea of Hero; Sea of Heroes
.18	pleninsula	*pleninsula [plena insula] L *modeled on*	full island
		paeninsula L	almost-island: peninsula
.19	unguest	angustus L	narrow, close
.26	locative	locativus [casus] L	case of nouns denoting location at place named [*e.g.*, Romae, "*at Rome*"]
.27	upright one	*trans.* hê orthê [ptôsis]G [casus] rectus L	Nominative Case (*grammar*)
.27	vehicule	vehiculum L	vehicle
.28	celiculation	caelicola L	dweller in heaven; deity
.28	ebblanes	Eblana G	Dublin
.31	Rhoda Dundrums	rhododendron G	"rose-tree": rose-laurel
.32	leguminiferous	*leguminiferax L	vegetable-bearing
136.01	mursque	musque L	and a mouse
		murusque L	and a wall
.03	laud	laus L	praise
.08	Inferus	Inferus L	Below; the netherworld

.14	Boaro	[Forum] Boarium L	cattlemarket at Rome
.14	Toaro	taurus L tauros G	bull
.17	pro homo	pro homine L *prohomo L	for man, for a person vice-man, substitute-man, one who stands in place of a person
.17	dapifer	dapifer L	feast-bearer: waiter at table
.17	pancircensor	panis et circenses L pan- G *pancircumcens- or G L	bread and circus-contests all- all-around-censor
.18	hortifex magnus	hortus L magnus L *hortifex magnus L	garden big, great great gardenmaker
.18	topes	topos G	place; [Rhetoric] commonplace
.18	types	typos G	blow, impression, mould, engraving, model, form
.21	Timour	timor L	fear, dread
.21	Tortur	tortura L	torture
.32	tronf of the rep	triumphus reipublicae L	triumph of the State [imitation of L inscriptional abbreviations]
.32–.33	prosp of the pub	prosperitas publica L	the public prosperity
.34	vaguum	vagus L vacuum L	rambling, wandering empty space, open space
.35	phoenix	Phoenix L Phoinix G	"Phoenician": bird of Arabia, see 130.11-12
.36	lumin	lumen L	light; lamp
137.09	sadurn's	Saturnus L	Saturn; most ancient king of Latium; god of agriculture and civilization; identified with Kronos, father of Zeus

.12	in camera	in camera LL	in the room, in the chamber, privately
.13	excruciated	excruciatus L	torment, torture
.14	chaosfoedted	chaos G	unformed matter, infinite space; precreation state of the universe
		foedatus L	defiled, filthied, befouled
.14	earthborn	*trans.* autochthones G	people sprung from the land itself; natives; *said of the Titans*
.17	Megacene	*megacaenus L *for* *megakainos G	big-new, great-recent
		caenum L	mud
		*Megacaenum G.+L	Big-mud
.24	lymphamphyre	lympha L	spring-water, clear river water
		amphora L amphoreus G	two-handled vessel for liquids
		pyr G	fire
.26	pectorals	pectorale L	breast-plate
.30	corn o'copious	Cornucopiae L	Horn of Plenty: horn of the goat *Amalthea* placed in heaven, *emblem of fruitfulness and abundance*
.31	retrospector	*retrospector L	one who looks back
.33	jugoslaves	jugum L	yoke, horse-collar, ox-collar
		subjugo L	"to bring under the yoke": to enslave
		Sklabos MG Sclavus ML	Slav; slave (*etymon of Eng. "slave"*)
.34	gorgon	Gorgô G	Medusa: *her hair was snakes; she turned all she looked upon to stone*
138.02	qwaternions	quaternio L	the number four; a body of four soldiers
.08	prural	prurio L	to itch; to feel sexual arousal
		#*L/R* *Interchange*	plural

.10	themise	Themis G L	goddess of justice and prophecy
.11	hiberniad	Hibernia L	Ireland
		hibernum L	the winter
		*Hiberneis L	*The Hiberniad: hypothetical epic poem about Ireland or about winter
		*Hibernias G	*the Irish Games (cp. Olympias); *the interval of time between Irish games
.17	Taurrible	taurus L	bull
.23	Ebblannah	Eblana G	Dublin
.25	chrysmed	chrysos G	gold
		chrisma G	anointing, unction
.27	predikants	praedico L	1. to cry in public; to preach 2. to mention beforehand; to warn; to announce; to predict
.27	Darius	Dareus, Darius L Dareios G	name of several Persian kings
.28	infurioted	furiosus L	full of madness or rage
.34	convultures	convoluto L	to whirl, roll around rapidly
		convulsio L	cramp, convulsion
139.05	Cincinnatus	Cincinnatus L	"Ringleted, Curly": cognomen of Lucius Quinctius, called from his farm and made dictator during attack by the Aequi. He defeated the Aequi, resigned his dictatorship and returned to his farm, all in 16 days (458 b.c.)
.06	villas	villa L	country-house, farm
.16	meoptics	*meioptikos G	seeing less
.17	filial's	filialis L	filial
		filius L	son
		filia L	daughter
.17	pontificator	*pontificator L	one who acts as pontifex
		pontifex L	"bridgemaker": Roman high-priest

.18	circumvallator	*circumvallator L	one who surrounds [e.g., a town] with a wall; blockader, besieger
.21	spondees	spondê G	drink-offering (wine poured out to the gods); treaty, truce; fee, tip
.21	ondenees	undeni L	eleven each
		undanter L	like waves, wavily
.26	Clesiastes	*klêsiastês G	member of a vocation
		*kleisiastês G	member of an inn
.32	magda	magdalia G	breadcrust; dogs' meat
.34	Vatandcan	Vaticanus L	1. Vatican Hill in Rome on west bank of Tiber 2. wine from the Vatican (very inferior)
.35	O'Faynix	phoenix L	"Punic, Phoenician":
		phoinix G	fabulous bird, see 130.11-12
		nix L	snow
.35	O'Faynix Coalprince	O felix culpa L	"O happy sin"—medieval hymn on Adam's fall, which elicited the Incarnation
.36	Ebblawn	Eblana G	Dublin
140.02	Musca	musca L	a fly
.03	Uval	uva L	grape; vine
.04	Erat	erat L	there was, he [she, it] was
.04	Est	est L	there is, he [she, it] is
.05	Erit	erit L	there will be, he [she, it] will be
.05	Non michi sed luciphro	non mihi sed lucifero L	not to me but to the light-bringer (lucifer)
.06–.07	Thine obesity, O civilian, hits the felicitude of our orb	Obedientia Civium Urbis Felicitas L	The obedience of the citizens is the happiness of the city (motto of Dublin)
.08	a dea o dea	dea L	goddess
.09	deltic	delta G	letter D; anything shaped like the letter delta, e.g., a rivermouth, the female pudenda
.09	nuinous	nu G	letter N

		nun G	now, at present
.13	phillohippuc	*philohippikos G	fond of horses
		philippikos G	of *or* against Philip (*king of Macedon*)
		Philippos G	Fond-of-horses: Philip
.13	theobibbous	theos, theo- G	god, god-
		bibosus L	given to drinking, fond of drink
		*theobibosus G + L	god-drinking, god-drunken
.15	Delfas	fas L	divine law; lawful, permitted
.33	erroriboose	erroribus L	to *or* for wanderings, meanderings, uncertainties, follies
		Erebus G L	god of darkness, *son of* Chaos, *brother of Night*; the Lower World
141.04	aequal	aequalis L	equal, the same, comparable, uniform
.05	pristmoss	pristinus L #*P/K Split*	former, early, original cristmoss (Christmas?)
.07	non Aequalllllll	non aequalis L	not equal, not the same, not comparable, not uniform
.13	malafides	mala L	jaw
		*malefides L	bad faith
		malefidus L	unfaithful, faithless
.36	Climate	#*P/K Split*, #*L/R Interchange*	Primate
142.08	societate	societate (*Abl.*) L	from *or* by a *societas*
		societas L	fellowship, association, community
.10	curman	cur L	why?
.12	prater	pratum L	meadow
		pratens L	grassy
.12	campos	campus L	plain, field
		campos (*Acc. pl.*) L	fields
.13	Ager	ager L	territory, district; field, improved land

.17	retroratiocination	*retroratiocinatio L	backward reasoning
.18	conflingent	confligens L	striking one thing against another, opposing, contrasting, conflicting
.19	voxes	vox L	voice
.19	vaticination	vaticinatio L	a prediction, a soothsaying
.23	numen	numen L	nod of the head; divine will; might, authority; deity, spirit
.23	daimons	daimôn G	god, goddess; divine power; fortune; good *or* evil genius
.24	consternation	1. consternatio L	confusion, dismay, alarm
		2. *consternatio L	a covering, a stretching on the ground
		3. *consternatio Mod L	a putting of chests *or* breasts together (copulation?)
		from sternum Mod L sternon G	breastbone
.25	miserecordation	misericordia L	pity, compassion, mercy
.25	omniannual	*omniannualis L	every-year-old, all years old
		*omniannuale L	every-yearly
.29	Morphios	Morphios, pseudo-G, *backformation as if from L* Morpheus; # *G-to-L*	Morpheus
		Morpheus G	god of dreams, *named for the* shapes *he calls up before the dreamer*
		morphai G	shapes, forms
143.07	auctual	auctus L	increase, growth
.08	futule	futuo L	to fuck
.08	preteriting	praetereo L	to pass by; to be lost, perish, pass away; to escape

.08	exanimation	exanimatio L	suffocation, depriving of breath; terror, fright
.10	ingredient	ingredior L	to enter
		ingrediens L	entering, engaging in
		ingredientur L	they enter, they go in
.11	egregiunt	egregius L	out of the herd: distinguished, eminent, illustrious
		egredior L	to go or come out, to step forth, to leave
		egredientur L	they step out, they leave
.16	intempestuous	intempestus L	unseasonable
.17	Nox	nox L	night
.16–.17	intempestuous Nox	intempesta nox L	the dead of night
		intempesta . . . Nox L (Vergil, *Aen.* XII .846)	dismal Night (*mother of the Furies*)
.17	gallicry	gallicinium L	cock-crowing: break of day, early dawn
.17	lucan's	lucinus L	light-bringing, bringing to the light
		lux L	light
		Lucanus L	Lucan, *surname of poet* M. Annaeus Lucanus (*a.d. 39–65*), *author of* Pharsalia, *epic on Roman Civil War*
.19	foles	folium L	a leaf
.20	nimb	nimbus L	rain-storm, cloud; bright cloud, cloud-shaped splendor *that envelops gods*; aureole, halo
.20	nihilant	nihil L	nothing
		[ad-, an-]nihilans L	bringing to nothing
		[ad-, an-]nihilant L	they bring to nothing
.28	collideorscape	collido L	to clash, beat *or* press together; to bring into conflict
		*kaloeidoskopos G	beautiful-shape-watcher

.33	angiol	angi- L	narrow-
		aggelos =	messenger
		angelos G	
		olea L	olive
144.05	sociationist	sociatio L	union
.10	ovally	ovalis L	of *or* belonging to an ovation
		ovatio L	ovation, *i.e.*, lesser triumph: *celebration of a lesser* or *easy victory*
		ovum L	egg
		ovatus L	egg-shaped
.20	miser	miser L	wretched, miserable, pitiable
.30	quonian	quoniam L	since now, seeing that, because, whereas
		quondam L	at one time, formerly; at times
.35	fingey	fingo L	to touch, handle, stroke; to arrange
145.04	stomewhere	stoma G	mouth
.05	Tay	te L	thee
.10	acquointance	quoi OL cui L	to whom? to which?
.12	pillale	pilula L	little ball, globule, pill
.21	Transname	transnomino L	to name over again, to change the name *of a person or thing* to *something else*
.25	a jaculation	Ajacis L	Ajax's, of Ajax; *see 306.L13*
		jaculatio L	a throwing, casting, hurling
146.21	encho	egchos = enchos G	spear, sword
.21	tencho	teggô = tengô G	to wet, to moisten; to shed tears; to soak
.24	eroes	êrôes, hêrôes (*pl.*) G	heroes: *semi-historical demigods*
		eros, erôs G	love, desire
147.06	*Aves*	aves (*pl.*) L	birds
.07	*Selvae*	silvae (*Gen. sing.*) L	of a wood, wood's
		silvae (*pl.*) L	woods
.07	*Acquae*	aquae (*Gen. sing.*) L	of water, water's

		aquae (*pl.*) L	waters
.07	*Valles*	valles (*sing.* & *pl.*) L	valley, vallies
.06–.07	*Aves Selvae Acquae Valles!*	aves silvae aquae vallis L	birds of the wood, waters of the valley, *etc. etc.*
		Ave, Salve, atque Vale L	Hail, Good Health, and also Farewell
		Ave, Salve, Vale L	"Hail," "Good Health," "Farewell": *titles of parts of George Moore's memoirs,* Hail and Farewell
		"Frater, ave atque vale" L	"Brother, hail and farewell"—Catullus, *ci.10*
.08	eurhythmytic	eurhythmia G	gracefulness
		eurhythmistikos G	easily shaped
		arithmêtikos G	for reckoning; skilled in reckoning
.11	Celia	Caelia L	"Heavenly[?]"; *fem. of* Caelius, *name of a Roman gens*
.11	Delia	Delia L	Diana, *from her birth on* Delos
.12	Ita	ita L	thus, yes
.12	Katty	kathairô G	to cleanse
.13	Mina	mina L	smooth
.14	Trix	tris L	three
		trixos *Ionic for* trissos, trittos G	threefold
.14	Una	una L	in one place, at the same time
		una (*fem.*) L	one
.14	Vela	vela (*pl.*) L	sails
.14	Xenia	xenia (*pl.*) G L	gifts to guests
		Xenia L G	"Gifts for Guests": *13th book of Martial's epigrams*
.14	Phoebe	Phoebe L	moon-goddess;
		Phoibê G	*identified with* Diana
		phi G	letter PH (*expanding alphabetic series* Ada—Zulma *to 28 members*)

.15	Thelma	theta G	letter TH (*extending series* Ada - Zulma + Phoebe)
.17	Anty	anti- L	against-
.17	Pravidance	pravis L	crooked, deformed, perverse, evil
		pravitas L	crookedness, deformity, perverseness
		providens L	foreseeing, prudent
.21	nomanclatter	nemo L *trans.*	no man, nobody; *name*
		outis G	Odysseus *gave himself to the Cyclops*
		nomenclator L	one who calls [*a person or thing*] by name; a slave employed to tell his master the names of passers-by in the street
		nomenclatura L	a calling by name; list of names
.24	chasta dieva	casta diva L	chaste *or* pure goddess
.29	notmust	trans. oude, ou de G	"notmust, not must": must not
.30	lipsabuss	-abus OL	"by means of" (*Abl. pl. suffix*)
		*labiabus OL	with lips, by means of lips
.32	pouder	pudor L	shame
.34	linguo	lingua L	tongue
		lingo L	to lick
148.02	*Misi, misi!*	misi L	I sent
.05	sweetissest	-issimus L	-est (*superlative suffix*)
.10	chare	charis G	grace, beauty; kindness; gratitude
.17	aucthor	auctor L	creator, maker, author, inventor, father, founder, causer, leader, *etc.*
.17	significat	significat L	he [she, it] shows by signs, points out, publishes, notifies, signifies
.18	nivulon	niveus L	snowy
.31	amor	amor L	love
.35	rugilant	rugio L	to roar
.35	pugilant	pugilor L	to fight with the fists, to box

149.03	Domb Nostrums	domus nostra L	our house
		Dominum Nostrum (*Acc.*) L	Our Lord
.07	immartial	*immartialis L	not belonging to Mars
.20	sophology	*sophologia G	study of wisdom, study of skill
.26	homoid	homo L	man
		homos G	same, common, joint
		*homoeidês G	looking-the-same
		*homo-eidês L+G	man-appearing, man-shaped
.28	theorics	theôrika [chrêmata] G	fund for festivals
		theôrikos G	of *or* for *theôria*
		theôria G	1. embassy to oracles *or* games 2. being a spectator at theater *or* games
.29	plumbsily	plumbum L	lead
		# *P/K Split*	clumsily
.29–.30	quality and tality	qualitas L	property, nature, condition
		qualis ... talis L	as ... so; whatever ... such
.34	Talis	talis L	such, of such a kind, such like
.34	passims	passim L	at different places, in every direction, at random
.35	quantum	quantum L	as much as; as much [*of something*] as
.35	tantumising	tantum L	so much, so many; so greatly, to such a degree
.36	pessim	passim L	*see 149.34* I
		pessimus L	worst
150.01	Talis and Talis	*see 149.34*	Such and Such
.01	optimately	optimas L	belonging to the best *or* noblest, aristocratic
		optimates L	the aristocratic (political) party
.04	Talis	talis L	*see 149.34* A
.04	Craterium	*craterium L *for* kratêrion G	little bowl, little mixing vessel

.05	Talis	talis L	*see 149.34* A
.07	postvortex	post L	after, backwards
		vortex, vertex L	whirl, eddy, whirlwind; top of the head; summit
		Postvorta L	"Turned-backwards": goddess presiding over childbirth, invoked at breech deliveries
.07	infustigation	fustigo L	to cudgel to death
		*fustigatio L	a cudgeling to death
		*infustigo L	to cudgel upon to death
		*infustigatio L	a cudgeling upon to death
.08	spinosis	spinosus L	thorny, prickly
.10	*talis qualis*	talis ... qualis L	as ... so, whatever ... such
.13	Talis	talis L	*see 149.34A*
.14	Qualis	qualis L	how constituted, of what sort, what kind of; of such a sort, as for instance
.18	*toto coelo*	toto coelo [toto caelo]L	by the whole heaven; very much, entirely
.28	A.M.	A[nno] M[undi] L	in the Year of the World
.32	faroscope	*part trans.* têleskopos G	far-seeing; far-seen, conspicuous
		pharos G	lighthouse
.33	television	têle- G	to a distance, afar
		visio L	act of seeing, sight; thing seen, appearance, image
.32	faroscope of	far[o]-scope Eng. + G	television
.33	television	tête-vision G + L	faroscope
151.01	microbemost cosm	*mikrokosmos G	small world, little universe
.06	feracity	feracitas L	fruitfulness
.07	anthrapologise	*anthrôpolog-[e]ia G	study of man
		apologia G	speech in defence
.08	obintentional	ob L	towards; about, before; for, instead of

		intentio L	straining, tension; application
		*obintentio L	straining for
.08	neoitalian	neo- G	new-
.09	paleoparisian	palaio- G	old-, ancient-
.09	schola	schola L scholê G	learned leisure, learned conversation dissertation; place of learning; disciples *or* followers of a teacher
.10	revolscian	Volsci L	powerful people of Latium, hostile to Rome
.10	romanitis	Romanitas L	Romanism: the Roman way *or* manner
.20	Mortadarthella	Morta L Mortê G	Roman name for Atropos, the Fate who ends life
.23	bolo	bolos G	a throw, cast
.23	Tyro	Tyro L Tyrô G	daughter of Salmoneus, king of Elis; mother by Poseidon of Neleus and Pelias
		tyros G	cheese
		[Marcus Tullius] Tiro	secretary and friend of Cicero, invented a system of shorthand
.28	deglutables	deglutio L	to swallow down
.28–.29	lapses lequou	lapsus linguae L	a slip of the tongue
.29	lequou	loquor L	to speak, talk, say
		liqueo L	to be fluid *or* liquid; to be clear
.30	hydrostatics	hydrostatikos G	causing water to rest, bringing water to a standstill
.30	pneumodipsics	*pneumatodipsê-sis G	air-thirst, spirit-thirst [thirst for spirits?]
.31	Marsellas	Martialis L	of *or* belonging to Mars
		Massilianus L	of *or* belonging to Massilia [Marseilles]
.32	Cambriannus	Cambrensis L	of *or* belonging to Wales; Welsh
		Giraldus Cambrensis L	"Gerald the Welshman" (1147–1233), historian

.34	melodeontic	melôdikos G	by means of melody
		*melôdêonta G	musical realities
.35	*quandour*	quando L	when? at what time?
		candor L	whiteness, radiance; fairness, splendor; simplicity
152.07	sermo	sermo L	talk, conversation; ordinary speech
.10	etsitaraw	et cetera L	and other things
.10	etcicero	et Cicero L	and Cicero
.13	Allaboy	alla G	but.
		allos G	other
		alibi L	elsewhere, somewhere else
.13	Minor	minor L	the lesser [*British public schools*: surname for younger of two brothers in the school, *e.g., Smith Minor: the younger Smith boy*]
.14	*Audi*	audi L	listen! pay attention!
.14	Joe Peters	Juppiter, Jupiter L	Jove, chief god of the Romans
.14	*Exaudi*	exaudi L	hear clearly! understand!
.14	facts	fax L	torch; light; that which illuminates
		vox [?] L	voice, a voice ; *see 159.24*
.19	archunsitslike	archôn G	ruler, commander, chief magistrate
.23	flabelled	flabello L	to fan
.23	pilleoled	pilleolus L	a small felt skull-cap
		pilleo L	to place the *pilleus* (cap of freedom) on a *person's* head: *token of manumission of a slave*
.23	vacticanated	vaco L	to be empty
		vaticinatio L	soothsaying, prophesying
		Vaticanus L	Vatican hill on west bank of Tiber; an inferior wine
.24	palliumed	pallium L	coverlet, pall, curtain; Greek cloak, *dress of philosophers*; a philosophic career

.24	impugnable	impugno L	to fight against, to attack, to oppose
		impugnatus L	1. attacked, assailed; 2. not attacked, unassailed
.26	*De Rure Albo*	de rure albo L	from *or* concerning a white countryside *or* country estate
.27	pintacostecas	pentêkostos G	fiftieth
.28	horthoducts	hortus L	garden
		ductus L	a leading, conducting, connection; aquaduct
		orthodoxos G	having correct beliefs in religion
.33	veetoes	veto L	not to permit, to oppose, forbid
.35	pentiadpair	pentas G	group of five, the number five
.36	azylium	asylum L asylon G	sanctuary, place of safety
.36	Shinshone Lanteran	Lateranus L	god of the hearth
		Lateranus L	Roman family name; *family mansion on* Mons Caelius *in Rome given to Popes by emperor Constantine; became seat of the popes; now* the Lateran
153.01	secunding	secundum L	in accordance with, according to
.02	propecies	prope L	near, near by
		propinatio L	a drink to one's health, a toast
.02	*Amnis Limina Permanent*	amnis limina permanent L	the bounds of the river remain
.04	Ninon	ni L	not, that not
		non L	not
.10	olum	olim L	once upon a time, once
		ulmus L	elm-tree
.15	frons	frons L	branch, bough, foliage
.17–.18	Optimus Maximus	Optimus Maximus L	Best [and] Greatest, *epithet of* Jupiter
.20	assumptinome	*assumptinomen L	taken-name
.21	accessit	accessit L	he [she, it] approached
.22	austereways	auster L	the south wind, the south

		austerus L	harsh, strict
.23	Hic	hic L	this, this here
.23	sor	soror [?] L	sister
.24	illud	illud (*neut.*) L	it, that one
.24	hoc	hoc L	this one, this thing
.24	huc	huc L	to this place, hither
.25	poposterously	praepostere L	back-to-front, irregularly
.25	acclammitation	*acclamitatio L	a violent crying at
.26	justotoryum	justitium L	court vacation, legal holiday
		justus L	upright, righteous
.26	encyclicling	encyclius L	belonging to a circle;
		enkyklios G	course of studies; for general circulation: *letter from pope to clergy on a church matter*
.27	diupetriark	diu L	1. by day; 2. a long time
		petreus L	of rock; pertaining to
		petraios G	St. Peter
		patriarchês G	father of a race
		arca L	chest, box, coffer
.27	athemyst-	athemis G	lawless
.28	pederect	*pederecte L	foot-boldly
		*pederectus L	foot-erected
.28	*Deusdedit*	Deusdedit L	"God has given": name of two popes
.29	*Bellua Triumphanes*	Belua Triumphans L	The Triumphing Beast: *part trans.* Spaccio della bestia trionfante, *Bruno's book*
		Belua *Triumphanes L + G*	Three-appearing Beast [Papacy? Cerberus?]
		Bella Triumphantia L	Triumphing Wars
.30	collectium	collectio L	a collecting together
		*collectium pseudo-L *as if from* *kollektion G*	# *G-to-L*
.32	laicness	laicus L *for*	pertaining to the
		laïkos G	people; not pertaining to the priesthood

.32	Quartus	Quartus L	"Fourth": proper name
.33	Quintus	Quintus L	"Fifth": a Roman praenomen
.33	Sixtus	Sextus L	"Sixth": proper name
		Sixtus L *for*	*name of five popes*
		Xystos G	
.34	Lio	lio L leioô G	to make smooth, to plaster over
		leo L	lion
		Leo L	"Lion": *name of thirteen popes*
154.02	rarumominum	rarum (*neut.*) L	loose textured, thin, far apart, scattered, few
		ominosum (*neut.*) L	full of foreboding, portentous, ominous
.04	lithial	lithia G	fine stone, marble
		lithiaô G	to suffer from stone
		lithos G	stone
.06	miserendissimest	miserissimus	most wretched
	retempter	*retentator L	re-assailant, most miserable tempter-again
		misericordissim- us redemptor	most merciful redeemer
.07	telesphorously	telesphoros G	bringing fulfillment, bearing fruit in season
		Telesphorus	pope 125–136
.07	concionator	concionator LL	haranguer of the
		contionator L	people, demagogue, political agitator
.08	sissymusses	-issimus L	-est, most- (*superlative suffix*)
		sisys G	coarse garment
		Sisinnius L	pope 708
.08	zozzymusses	zôsimos G	viable, likely to survive; pertaining to this life
		Zosimus	pope 417–418
.10	nouse	nous G	mind, intelligence
.11	anathomy	anathema G	devoted to evil, accursed; curse
		anathêma G	votive offering
		anatomê G	dissection
.11	infairioriboos	inferioribus L	to the lower regions; from *or* by the dead
.11	anathomy infairioriboos	anathema inferioribus G, L	cursed to hell, curse to hell

.11	animal rurale	animal rurale L	country animal, rustic brute
.12	superbly	superbus L	proud
.12	supremest poncif	supremus pontifex L	highest high-priest (*pontifex,* "*bridgemaker*")
.16	pace	pace L	by [*someone's*] leave
.18	index	index L	pointer, indicator, guide; table, list, summary; the index finger
.18	achilles	Achilles L Achilleus G	Greek hero in Trojan War; a tendon in the heel
		Achille Ratti (1857–1939)	Pius XI, pope 1922–1939
.18	obolum	obolus L obolos G	small Greek coin
.19	nase	nasus L	nose
.19	serene	serene L	clearly, brightly
.20	clement	Clemens LL	"Mild": *name of fourteen popes*
.20	urban	Urbanus L	"Civil": *name of eight popes*
.20	eugenious	Eugenius L *for* eugenês G	"Well-born": *name of four popes*
.20	celestian	Celestinus LL Caelestinus L	"Heavenly": *name of five popes*
.20	formose	Formosus L	"Handsome": pope 891–896
.21	grogory	Gregorius L	"Shepherdly[?]": *name of sixteen popes*
.22	*laudibiliter*	laudabiliter L	in a praiseworthy manner, laudably
		Laudabiliter L	opening word (and hence title) of a Bull *issued in 1155 by the English Pope Adrian IV (1154–1159), sanctioning King Henry II's civilizing mission in conquering Ireland; it is not extant*

.23	Pauline	Paulinus L		of *or* belonging to a *Paulus* ("Small"): 1. saint (353–431), bishop of Nola, writer 2. first Archbishop of York (d.644)
.23	Irene	Irenaeus L *for* Eirênaios G		"Peaceful": saint (140–202), bishop of Lyons, *attempted to prevent rupture of Eastern from Western Church*
		Irene, Eirênê G		"Peace": (752–803), Eastern Roman empress, *canonized by the Greek Church*
.27	*Fuert it?*	fue L		fie! foh!
		fuerit L		[it] may have been; [it] will have been
.28	*Sancta Patientia!*	sancta patientia L		holy patience
.33–.34	loudy bullocker	Laudabiliter L		"Laudably": *see 154.22*
.34	velicity	vel L		or else; take your choice; what you will
		velocitas L		swiftness, speed
.35	inexshellsis	in excelsis L		in the highest
.35	ab ove	ab ovo L		from the egg (*egg was first course at Roman dinner*), from the beginning
		ab ovo usque ad mala L		from the egg to the apples: from the beginning to the end; *see 184.28*
.36	Honoriousness	Honorius L		"Honorable": late Roman emperor; *name of four popes*
155.04	*sus in cribro*	sus in cribro L		pig in a sieve
.04	Semperexcommunic-ambiambisumers	semper L		ever, always
		excommunico L		to put out of the community, to excommunicate
		ambi- L		around-, round about-
		sum L		I am

		sumus L	we are
.05	Tugurios	tugurium L	hut, cottage
.05	Novarome	Nova Roma L	New Rome; *name given by Constantine to Byzantium* (a.d. *330*); *soon became Constantinopolis*
.06–.07	lyonine ... leonlike	leoninus L	belonging to a lion; a lion's
		Lugdunum	city in Gaul: Lyons; *Irenaeus* (see *154.23*) *was bishop 177–202*
		leôn G leo L	a lion
		Leo	"Lion": *name of thirteen popes and six Byzantine emperors*
.07	consistorous	consistorium L	place of assembly; place where the emperor's council met
.08	allocution	alloquor L	to speak to, to address; to exhort; to console
.09	constantinently	Constantinus L	"Steadfast": 1. Roman emperor (306–336); *christianized the Empire; moved the capital to Byzantium* (see *155.05–06, 19–20*); *allegedly granted temporal power in Rome to the pope* 2. an anti-pope (767–769)
.13	sowsieved	*trans.* sus in cribro L	see *155.04* C–E
.14	decretals	decretalis L	depending on a decree
.16	Parysis	parisos G	evenly balanced, equaled
		parousia, paroysia G	presence; the Advent; substance
.17	crucycrooks	*crucicrux L	a criss-cross
.19	momentum	momentum L	a movement; a short time; a cause
.19	Cospol's	Constantinopolis L	Constantine's city: *name for Byzantium after a.d. 330*
		Konstantinou polis G	
		*Kosmopolis G	World-City, Cosmopolis

		kosmopolis G	title of a magistrate in several cities
		kosmopolitês G	world-citizen
.20	foluminous	folium L	leaf
		voluminosus L	full of windings *or* folds
		volumen L	roll of writing, book
.21	*Quas primas*	qua L	on which side, where, how
		prima L	the beginning; first in rank
		qua prima L	which first
		Arma virumque cano, Troiae *qui primus* ab oris—Vergil. Aen. I.1	Arms and the man I sing, the *first who* from the shores of Troy—*line 1, Vergil's* Aeneid
.22	fructus	fructus L	fruit; effect, result
.23	pederect	*pederecte L *pederectus	*see 153.28*
.24	cielung	caelum, coelum L	sky, heaven
.25	lucciolys	Lucceius L	a Roman name
		luceo L	to be light, to shine
.27	docence	docens L	teaching, instructing, telling
.27	gresk	grex L	flock, herd
		Graecus L	a Greek
.27	letton	Latinus L	a Latin
		lingua Latina L	Latin
.28	russicruxian	crux L	cross, gallows
.28	prolegs	prolexis G	foretelling
		prolegomenon G	that which is said beforehand, a foreword
.31	Niklaus ... Niklaus	Nicholaus LL *for* Nikolaos G	"Victory-army": *name of five popes and one anti-pope*
.31	Alopysius	alôpêx G	fox
.32	nimbum	nimbus L	rainstorm; thunder-cloud; saint's aureole
.32	Neuclidius	nucleus L	little nut, kernel
		Euclides L	"Honored": Euclid, G
		Eukleidês G	mathematician, *fl. 300 b.c.*
.32	Inexagoras	in- L = a- G	un-, not-

		Anaxagoras G	"Market-lord": G philosopher (500–428 b.c.)
.33	Mumfsen	Theodor Mommsen (1817–1903)	German classical historian and editor
.33	Orasmus	oremus L	let us pray
		Desiderius L	"Desirable Desirable"
		Erasmus [*for* Erasmios G] (1466–1536)	*or* "Lovable Lovable" [*the L & G names are synonymous*]: Dutch humanist, born Gerrit Gerritszoon
.34	Amenius	Arminius L	"Herman": German prince who defeated a Roman army a.d. 9; *see 008.28*
		Jacobus Arminius (1560–1609)	Jacob Harmensen, Dutch protestant theologian; *opposed Calvinist doctrine of predestination*
.34	Anacletus	Anacletus L Anakleitos G	"Renowned": third pope, 76–78
.34	Augurer	Augur L	member of a college of priests at Rome, who predicted the future by observing lightning, birds and unusual occurrences
156.01	alter	alter L	the other, one of two
.02	binomial	binominis L	having two names
.02	dioram	*diorama G dioraô G	a clear view through to see clearly, to distinguish
.03	penic	peniculus L	little tail, little penis; brush
.03	penic walls	Punic Wars	three wars (264–241; 218–201; 149–146 b.c.) *in which Rome gradually superseded Carthage as dominant power in the western Mediterranean*
.03	the rure	de rure L	concerning the countryside

.04	jus	jus L	right, justice, duty
.05	jugicants	jugis L	1. yoked together; 2. continual, perpetual
		judicans L	judging
		judicanda L	things to be judged
.05	Pontius Pilax	Pontius Pilatus L	governor of Judaea and Samaria 26–36
		phylax G	sentinel
.08	Mooksius	*muccius L	snotty
.08	preprocession	*praeprocessio L	a pre-advance
.08	proprecession	*propraecessio L	*something* for *or* to take the place of a going-before *or* a preceding
.09	duplicitly	dupliciter L *from* duplex L	doubly, in a twofold manner twofold, double
.09	diplussedly	diplous G	twofold, double
.09	ipsofacts	ipso facto L	by that same fact
.10	sadcontras	sed contra L	but on the contrary, but against [that]
.10	Gripos	griphus L *from* griphos G	a riddle, enigma
		griphos G	fishing basket, net
		gripos G	a haul of fish
.11	monophysicking	monophysikos G	of one nature: sectarian belief that Jesus had only one nature, not two (human, divine)
.11	illsobordunates	suborior L	to spring up
.12	semenoyous	sêmeion G	mark *by which a thing is known*; sign from the gods
		sêmeiôsis G	sign, indication
		nous G	mind, intelligence
.12	sarchnaktiers	sarx G	flesh
.12	combuccinate	*combuccino L	to blow a trumpet with
.13	silipses	solus ipse L	self alone
.13	aspillouts	aspello L	to drive away, to remove
		aspilatês G	a precious stone of Arabia
.13–.14	haggyown pneumax	to hagion pneuma G	the holy spirit, the Holy Ghost

.14	synerethetise	syn- G	with-
		erethizô G	to challenge, to provoke
		*synerethizô G	to with-challenge, to with-provoke, to *comprovoke, to challenge along with
.15	sweetovular	ovum L	egg
.15	sakellaries	saccularius L	cut-purse, pickpocket
.16	synodals	synodalis L	of *or* belonging to a synod
		synodus L	a college of priests, an
		synodos G	ecclesiastical assembly
.16	somepooliom	sympôleô G	to sell together; to confirm a sale
		*sympylion G	a set of little gate-halves, a little gateway
		pôlion G	a pony
		*sympôlion G	a with-pony, a pony in a set or team
.17	nepogreasymost	nepos L	grandson
.17	philioquus	philequus L *part trans.* philippos G	horse-lover
		Filioque L	and from the Son (*phrase in Creed disputed between Western and Eastern Churches*: does the Holy Spirit proceed from the Father only, or from the Father *and from the Son*)
.19	con	con- L	with-
.20	pius	Pius L	"Dutiful": *name of twelve popes; also epithet for Vergil's Aeneas*
.21	gregary	gregarius L	belonging to a flock *or* herd
		Gregorius L	"Herdsmanly[?]": *name of sixteen popes*
.25	Vale	vale L	farewell
.25	obselved	#L/R *Interchange*	observed

.25	par	par L	equal
.25	unicum	unicum (*neut.*) L	unparalleled, unique, alone of its kind
.26	Elelijiacks	elegiacus L	elegiac, *i.e.*, written in
		elegiakos G	the elegiac meter
.27	blissim	passim L	here and there, at random
.34	Elissabed	Elissa L G	poetic name for Dido
.36	Hourihaleine	halê G	salt works
		halia G	1. assembly; 2. salt-cellar
		halieinê G	sea-blue
157.01	viterberated	vitiosus L	faulty, bad, corrupt
		verberare (*infinitive*) L	to beat
.01	*canis et coluber*	canis et coluber L	dog and serpent
.02	Tarriestinus	Tarracina L	a town in Latium
		Tarracinensis L	Tarracinian
		tarrion G	small hurdle
.02	Pissasphaltium	*Pissasphaltium L	Pisasphalt-town
		pissasphaltus L	earth-pitch, soft
		pissasphaltos G	bitumen
.03	Unuchorn	unicornis L	one-horned
		unicornuus L	the unicorn
		eunouchos G	"bed-keeper": eunuch
.04	Ungulant	ungulatus L	having claws *or* hoofs
.05	Uvuloid	*uvaeidês L + G	grape-shaped, like a grape
		ovalis L	of *or* belonging to an ovation
.06	Uskybeak	usque L	all the way
.13	nubied	nubo L	to be married
		nubis L	a cloud
.19	constellatria	constellatio L	collection of stars
		constellatus L	star-studded
		latreia G	service, worship
		*constellalatria L	constellation-worship
.21	adiaptotously	adiaptôtos G	infallible
.22	schystimatically	schismatôdês G	of the nature of a cleft, division, *or* schism
		systêmatikos G	like an organized whole
.22	auricular	auricula L	the ear

		auricularius L	a counsellor
.23	*ens*	ens L	a being, a thing
.25	gnoses	gnôsis G	knowledge
.25	intrepifide	intrepidus L	unshaken
		intrepide L	undauntedly, without trembling
		fide (*Abl.*) L	by faith
		*intrepidefide L	with undaunted faith
.26	conclaved	conclave L	*room, hall, cage, stall that may be locked up*
		conclavo L	to nail together
.26	Heliogobbleus	Heliogabalus	*properly* Elagabalus (*a Syrian sungod*): name adopted by emperor M. Aurelius Antoninus (218–222), *notorious for debauchery and perversion of the state religion*
		hêlio- G	sun-
.26	Commodus	Commodus L	"Opportune": Lucius Aelius Aurelius Commodus *alias* Marcus Commodus Antoninus, emperor 180–192; *a megalomaniac, he renamed Rome* Colonia Commodiana
.27	Enobarbarus	Aenobarbus, Ahenobarbus L	Red-beard: a family name of the Domitian gens; *several* Domitii Ahenobarbi *became prominent during the Republic*
		*Aenobarbaros L	brazen barbarian
.28	papyrs	papyrus L	the paper-reed,
		papyros G	papyrus; paper made from the reed
.29	spiration	spiratio L	a breathing; the breath
.29	duiparate	*duiparatus L	twice-prepared
		*duipario L	to two-bear, to give two-birth [to bear twins?]

158.01	Tristis Tristior Tristissimus	tristis, tristior, tristissimus L	sad, sadder, saddest
.03	Accanite	accano L canis L	to sing to *or* with dog
.04	obliviscent	obliviscens L	forgetting
.07	arundo	[h]arundo L	reed, cane
.07	in midias reeds	in medias res L	into the middle of things: *manner of beginning epic narration in the middle of the action (with subsequent flashbacks)*
		Midas, reeds	*his barber whispered to the reeds that King Midas had ass's ears*
.10	Metamnisia	*metamnêsia G amnis L	beyond forgetfulness river
		*Metamnisia G + L	Land beyond the River, Beyond-the-river-land
.11	citherior spiane	Hispania citerior L	Hither Spain, the near part of Spain
.11	innemorous	nemorosus L *inemorosus L	full of woods, wooded 1. not full of woods, unwooded 2. in-the-woody
.19	Vallee	valles L vale L	valley farewell
.19	Maraia	maria (*pl.*) L Maria L	seas Mary
.19	Vallee Maraia	Vale Maria L Ave Maria L	Farewell Mary Hail Mary
.19	Grasyaplaina	gratia plena L	full of grace
.20	dormimust	dormimus L	we sleep
.20	dormimust echo	Dominus tecum L	the Lord with thee
.19–.20	Vallee ... echo	Ave Maria, gratia plena, Dominus tecum L	Hail Mary, full of grace, the Lord [is] with thee
.27	motamourfully	mota- L metamorphôsis G	moving-, motion-transformation
.29	*Aquila Rapax*	aquila rapax L	ravenous [rapacious, snatching] eagle
.29	solem	solus L	single, lone

.35	autotone	auto- G	self-
		tono L	to thunder
		tonos G	stretching
		*autono G + L	to self-thunder
		*autotonos G	self-stretching
.36	cariad	Caria L Karia G	province in Asia Minor
		Caryatides L	representations of
		Karyatidês G	maidens of *Karyai* (town in Laconia) used instead of columns in buildings
.36	beotitubes	beo L	to make happy, to bless
		beatitudo L	the condition of happiness, felicity, blessedness
159.01	*De Rore Coeli*	de rore coeli L	from the dew of heaven
.04	pietrous	petreus eccl. L	of rock *or* of Peter
.05	saule	Saulos G	"Mincing, Effeminate": G form of St. Paul's Hebrew name *Saul* (*possible motive for altering to* paulus)
.11	eon	aiôn G	lifetime, age
.13	singult	singultus L	a sobbing
.20	*diu dursus*	diu durus L	long hard
		dorsus L	the back
.21	Allaboy	alla G	otherwise
		allos G	other
		alibi L	elsewhere, somewhere else
.21	Major	major L	greater [*British public schools*: surname for elder of two brothers in the school, *e.g., Smith Major*: *the elder Smith boy*]
.22–.23	Joe Peters	Juppiter, Jupiter L	Jove, chief god of the Romans
.23	Fox	vox L	voice, a voice; *see 152.14*
.27	symbathos	*symbathos G	together-depth; low together with
.28	Gnaccus	Gnaeus, Gneus L	a Roman praenomen
		Gracchus L	Roman family name

.28	Gnaccus Gnoccovitch	Gaius Sempronius Gracchus	Roman reformer, killed 122 b.c.; son of Tiberius Sempronius Gracchus, consul and censor
.29	ambo	ambo L	both
		ambôn G	rim of a cup; female pudenda
		umbo L	boss of a shield; shield; elbow
.30	curilass	Kyrillos G	"Belonging to the Lord": Cyril (827–69), apostle to the Slavs, *deviser of the Cyrillic alphabet, adapted from the G*
.31	methodiousness	Methodios G	"Following the Way": Methodius (826–85), brother of Cyril, fellow-apostle to the Slavs
.31	theabild	thea G	goddess
.34	rementious	remensus L	re-measured, re-traveled, reimbursed
		rememini L	to recall to mind
160.01	Picea	picea L	the pitch-pine
.01	Tillia	tilia L	the linden, lime-tree
.03	genus	genus L	birth, origin, race, species, kind
.05	redcedera	et cetera L	and the rest, and others
		cedrus L	cedar, juniper-tree
		rhododendron G	rose-tree *or* red-tree
.08	Verney	verni- L	spring-, springtime-
.08	Rubeus	rubeus L	1. reddish; 2. of *or* belonging to the bramble-bush
.08	Verney Rubeus	*vernirubeus L	1. spring-reddish; 2. spring-brambly
.08	deodarty	Adeodatus L	"Given from God": Augustine's son
.09	habitat	habitat L	[he, she, it] dwells
.11	olivetion	olivetum L	olive-grove
		-tion G *for* -tum L	#G-to-L

.12	accaccians	acacia L akakia G	an Egyptian tree
		Acacius L Akakios G [*alias* Arakios]	bear-master of the green faction in Byzantium a.d.508, father of the Empress Theodora [*see Gibbon*]
.13	*Vux*	buxus L [# *Labials*]	the evergreen box-tree
.13	*Populus*	populus L	the poplar-tree
.13	*Vux Populus*	vox populi L	the voice of the people
.13	hickoryhockery	hic, haec, hoc L	this, this here (*masc., fem., neut.*)
		hic-haec-hoc-ery	the L language
.14	*arbor vitae*	arbor vitae L	tree of life
		aqua vitae L	water of life (akvavit, whiskey, etc.)
.21	laetification	laetificatio L	a cheering, rejoicing, gladdening
.21	sideredromites	sidereus L	pertaining to constellations, starry
		sidêro- G	iron-
		dromeus G	runner
		*sidêrodromeus G	iron-runner [railroad? train?]
		*sideredromeus L + G	starry-runner
		*sidêrodromitês G	son[s] of an iron-runner, etc., etc.
.22	irony of the stars	sidêros G	made of iron
		sidereus L	starry, of the stars
161.02	quickquid	quicquid L	whoever, whatever
.08	dogmarks	dogmata G	opinions, judgments
.08	origen	Origenês G (a.d.185–254)	church father, author of *Dogmata* (*Commentaries* [on Scripture])
.09	spurios	spurios (*Acc. pl.*) L	bastards
.12	Burrus	Burrus OL Pyrrhos G	"Red": Achilles' son
		Sextus Afranius Burrus L	Nero's tutor; # *A*
		butyrum L boutyron G	butter

		Marcus Junius Brutus	assassin of Caesar; #A
.12	Caseous	caseus L	cheese
		Gaius Cassius Longinus L	assassin of Caesar
.13	sysentangled	sys- G *instead of*	with-, together-
		dis- L	twice-, un-
.15	Burrus	*see 161.12B*	
.17	risicide	risus L	laugh
		*risicida L	laugh-killer
.18	Caseous	*see 161.12 D*	
.25	Acetius	*acetius L	vinegary
.25	Oleosus	oleosus L	oily
.25	Sellius	selinon G	celery, parsley
		*salius L	salty
		sallius L	jumpy
.26	Volatilis	volatilis L	flying, winged
.25–.26	Sellius Volatilis	sal volatile Mod L	volatile salt
.26	Petrus	Petrus L	Peter; stone, rock
.26	Papricus	peperi G piper L	pepper
		peperizô G	to taste of pepper
		piperatus L	peppered, peppery
.27	Salamoss	Salamis L Salamina G	island, site of Athenian naval victory over Persians
		sal L	salt
		salmo L	salmon
.30	Lettucia	lactuca L	"milky": lettuce
		laetitia L	joy
.36	Caesar outnullused	aut Caesar aut nullus L	"either Caesar or no one": *motto of Cesare Borgia*
162.01	sisar	Caesar L	"Hairy" *or* "Bluish": cognomen in the gens *Julia*, esp. of C. Julius Caesar (102–44 b.c.); #A
.01	Tyrants	tyrannos G	monarch, absolute ruler
.01	regicide	*regicaedes L	king-killing

.01	regicide is too good for you	*among the motives for assassinating Caesar was his apparent desire to become king* (rex); *he was already* tyrannos, *so his murder was* tyrannicide *to forestall the necessity for it to be* regicide	
.13	propper numen	*propenomen L	almost-name
.13	numen	numen L	divine will, power of the gods; deity
.13	colluction	colluctatio L	wrestling, contest; the death struggle
.14	cannasure	Cannae	battle in which Hannibal destroyed the Roman army
		canis L	dog
		kynosoura G	dog's tail: the constellation *Ursa Major*
.15	kuk	#*P/K Split*	pup
.19	inessive	in esse L	in being
.19	impossive	in posse L	in possibility; possible
.19	interlocative	inter locos, inter loca L	between places, between parts
.20	conprovocative	*comprovocativ- us L	called forth together, elicited together
.21	Caseous	caseus L	cheese
		Cassius L	*see 161.12*
.22	Burrus	burrus L	red
		Burrus L	*see 161.12*
		Brutus L	*see 161.12*
.23	fideism	fides L	faith
.23	lac	lac L	milk
.28	semagen	sêma G	sign, mark, token
.28	corrigidly	corrigo L	to make straight, to correct
.29	*ex ungue Leonem*	ex ungue leonis L	out of the lion's claw

.33	Burrus	*see 162.22D*	
.36	me Deus v Deus	mediusfidius OL [me deus fidius L]	by the god of truth!
163.01	arinam	[h]arenam (*Acc.*) L	sand
.03–.04	*Butyrum et mel comedet ut sciat reprobare malum et eligere bonum*	butyrum et mel comedet ut sciat reprobare malum et eligere bonum L	he eats butter and honey so that he may know to reject the bad and to choose the good
.08	Caseous	caseus L	cheese
		Cassius L	*see 161.12*
.09	tyron	tyros G	cheese
.15	*Nex*	nex L	murder
.15	*Nex quovis burro num fit mercaseus?*	Ex quovis burrus [butyrum] num fit merus caseus? L	From any red [butter] there is not made pure cheese?
		ex quovis ligno non fit Mercurius L	a Mercury is not made out of just any piece of wood; not any log you like can be made into a herm; #*B*
.16	learned ignorants	*trans.* docta ignorantia L	learned ignorance
.17	Cusanus ... Nicholas	Nicholas Cusanus L	Nicholas of Cusa (1401–64), *author of* De docta ignorantia
.21	primomobilisk	primum mobile L	first movable [thing]: the outer sphere of the universe, causing the heavenly bodies to move
		obeliskos G	a little skewer; a mark in a book against a spurious passage
.23	sinequam	sine quam L	without as much as
		sine qua L	without which
.23	furibouts	furia L	madness
.24	Nolanus	Nolanus L	the Nolan, the man from Nola: Giordano Bruno (1548–1600)

.25	Theophil	Theophilos G	God-loved: 1. patriarch of Alexandria (385–412); 2. bishop of Antioch (169–177), wrote an *Apology of Christianity*
.25	on principial	in principio L	in the beginning (*first words both of* Genesis *and of* John)
.26	odiose	odiosus L	hateful
		odiose L	hatefully
.30	tyrondynamon	tyros G	cheese
		dynamis G	power
		*dynamon G	powerful thing
		*tyrodynamon G	cheese-powerful thing
.31	helixtrolysis	helix G	spiral, curl
		lysis G	a loosening
		*helikolysis K	loosening of a curl *or* spiral
.31	amboadipates	ambo L	both
		adipes L	fats
164.01	princeps	princeps L	first, first man, first member of the Senate; prince
.04	pictor	pictor L	painter
.05	omber	umbra L	shade, shadow
		Umber L	an Umbrian
.05	*Skotia*	skotia G	darkness, gloom
		Scotia L	Ireland (*Scotia Minor*: Scotland)
.11	platinism	Platônismos G	Plato's philosophical system
		platea L plateia G	open space in a city; plaza
.24	Caseous	caseus L	cheese
		Cassius	*see 161.12*
.24	Burrus	burrus L	red
		Burrus L	*see 161.12*
		Brutus	*see 161.12*
.25	Criniculture	*crinicultura L	hair-care, cultivation of the hair
.26	on (not in)	in L	on, in
.30	Cuticura	*cuticura L	skin-care
.34–.35	*ill tempor*	illo tempore L	at that time

165.06	cantatrickee	cantatrix L	songstress, female singer
.09	orchidectural	orchis G	testicle
		dekteos G	to be received
		dektikos G	fit for receiving, capable of receiving
		*orchidecturalis G + L	of *or* pertaining to receiving testicles
.11	argon	argos G	1. shining; 2. idle
.12	Burrus	burrus L	red
		Burrus	*see 161.12*
		Brutus	*see 161.12*
.12	Caseus	caseus L	cheese
		Cassius	*see 161.12*
.13	isocelating	isokeleuthos G	walking alike, keeping up with
		isoskelês G	with equal legs
.13	biangle	bi- L	two-
		aggkalê = angkalê G	bent arm; angle
.22	Rhomba	rhombos G	bull-roarer; kettledrum; male sex organ; lozenge-shaped figure
		Roma L Rhômê G	Rome
.22	Trabezond	trapeza G	table
		Trapezous G	city in Pontus (*now* Trabzon *in N. E. Turkey*), *medieval* Trebizond
		trapezoidês G	table-shaped geometrical figure
.22	in her *excelsis*	in excelsis L	in the highest
.23	climactogram	klimax G	ladder, staircase
		*klimakogramma G	ladder-picture, ladder-diagram; ladder-writing
.26	eocene	êôs kainê G	new dawn
.26	pleastoseen	pleistokainos G	most-new
.27	morphological	*morphologikos G	having to do with the study of shapes
.28	Philadespoinis	philadespoinis (*fem.*) G philadespoineus (*masc.*)	mistress-loving; Empress-loving

.34	*deductio ad domonum*	deductio ad dominum L	a leading away to the lord *or* master
		deductio ad domum L	a leading away to the house
		reductio ad absurdum L	(*Rhetoric*) a leading back to the absurd
		argumentum ad hominem L	(*Rhetoric*) an argument invoking personalities
.34	*de tacto*	de tactu L	from a touch, from touch
		de facto L	from the fact; in fact, actually
.34	detect	detego L	to unroof, to uncover, to lay bare
.35	*movibile tectu*	mobile [movibile] tectu L	moveable by means of a roof; by a moveable roof
		mirabile dictu L	wonderful to say
166.01	Margees	margê (*fem.*) G	mad, wanton, lustful
.11	ovidently	ovi- L	egg-
		ovis L	sheep
.22	Infantulus	infantulus L	a little baby boy
.23	*seducente infanta*	seducens	misleading
		infantia L	speechlessness
		seducens infanta L	misleading infant girl
.26	totamulier	tota mulier L	all woman
.26	musculink	muscula L	a little fly
		musculosus L	muscular
		musculus L	a little mouse; a muscle
.26	verumvirum	verum L	reality, truth
		virum (*Gen. pl.*) L	of men, men's
		verus vir L	a real man
.27	matres	matres (*Acc. pl.*) L	mothers
.28	micturious	mictorius L	urinative
		micturio L	to go to urinate
.29	uttentions	ut L	as, so as, so that
.30	Burrus	burrus L	red
		Burrus	*see 161.12 B*
		Brutus	*see 161.12 B*

.32	eastasian import	butyrum L boutyron G	butter: *said to be a Scythian word, but probably G* [bous + tyros]. *Butter was an exotic to the classical world, but common to Asian nomads*
.34	cleopatrician	Cleopatra L Kleopatra G patricius L	"Paternal Renown": *queen of Egypt, #A* patrician, member of Roman nobility
.35	Burrus	*see 166.30 F*	
.36	Caseous	caseus L Cassius	cheese *see 161.12D*
167.01	Antonius	Antonius L Marcus Antonius	name of a Roman gens Mark Antony; *opponent of Brutus and Cassius; lover of Cleopatra*
.03	antomine	Antoninus L	of *or* belonging to Antonius; *name of several Roman emperors*
.03	rude ... boor	burrus L	red
.04	Antonius	*see 167.01 D*	
.04	Burrus	burrus L Burrus Brutus	red *see 161.12 B* *see 161.12 B*
.04	Caseous	caseus L Cassius	cheese *see 161.12 D*
.04	grouptriad	tria G *trans.* triumviri, triumviratus L	three three men holding an office together, a board of three, triumvirate: *e.g., Antony, Octavian and Lepidus*
.05	*qualis*	qualis L	of what sort, what kind of a; of such a kind, such as, as
.05	*talis* on *talis*	talis L	such, such like
.06	quantly	quantum L quanto L	as much as, so much as by how much, by as much as
.06	economantarchy	oikonomos G	steward, manager of a household

		archê G	rule, command
		*oikonomarchê G	government by a steward *or* house-keeper
.06–.07	tantum ergons	tantum ergo L	so great, therefore (*opening of a Benediction hymn*)
		tantum L	so great, so much
		ergon G	work
.07	irruminate	rumino L	to chew over, to chew the cud
		*irrumino L	1. not to chew the cud; 2. to chew the cud thoroughly
		irrumo L	1. to give suck to; 2. to abuse, deceive (make a sucker of, *sensus obscaenus*)
.07	quantum	quantum L	as much as, so much as
.09	philadolphus	philadelphos G	brother-loving
.10	athemisthued	athemis G	lawless
.10	exlegged	exlex L	lawless
.10	phatrisight	parricida, patricida L	father-killer
		fratricida L	brother-killer
		phatricida, phratricida G+L	brotherhood-killer
.13	acropoll	akropolis G	upper city, citadel
.14	blasphorus	*blasphoros G	harm-bearing
.14	blesphorous	phoros G	bearing, carrying
.16	gregational	*gregatio L	a gathering into a flock *or* herd
.18	Tarpeia	Tarpeia L	Roman maiden who treacherously opened the citadel to the Sabines
		Tarpeius mons L	Tarpeian rock *in Rome, from which criminals were thrown headlong*
.19	nefand	nefandus L	"unspeakable": impious, abominable

.22	the thundering legion	Legio XII . Fulminata L	Twelfth Legion bore Jove's thunderbolt on its shields; mauled by the Jews in the Jewish War, it took part in the siege of Jerusalem, then was posted in disgrace to a remote Syrian frontier
.22	Olymp	Olympos G	mountain in N. Greece, home of the gods
.23	Twelve tabular	lex duodecim tabularum L	law of the twelve tables: *earliest Roman code, on tablets of bronze or wood in the Forum (450 b.c.)*
.23	edicted	edictus (*pp.*) L	declared, published, established
.23–.24	Merus Genius	merus genius L	pure genius
		genius L	tutelary deity; fondness for good living; wit, talents
		Marcus Junius [Brutus]	*see 161.12 B*
.24	Careous Caseous	cariosus caseus L	dried-out cheese
		Gaius Cassius [Longinus]	*see 161.12 D*
.24	*Moriture, te salutat*	moriture te salutat L	O you about to die, he salutes you
		morituri te salutamus L	we, about to die, salute you: *so gladiators saluted the emperor*
.24	phemous	phêmis G	speech, talk
		Phêmios G	name of a minstrel in the *Odyssey*
.25	themis	themis G	law, custom
.25	Demoncracy	dêmokratia G	government by the people
		*daimonokratia G	government by spirits *or* demons
.29	exponse	*exspondeo L	to take one's self out of a vow, to unpromise, to divorce
.30	velnerate	vel L	or, or else, what you will

		vulnero L	to wound
		vulneratio L	a wounding, a wound
.30	nuptias	nuptias (*Acc.*) L	marriage, wedding, nuptials
.33–.34	*Ubi lingua nuncupassit, ibi fas!*	Ubi lingua nuncupavit, ibi fas L	Where tongue has named, there [is] lawful
		... uti lingua nuncupassit ita ius esto L	... as the tongue has named so let the law be: *fragment from the Twelve Tables*
.34	*Adversus hostem semper sac!*	adversus hostem semper sacer L	against the enemy ever sacred
		adversus hostem semper sic L	against the enemy ever thus
.34	fulmoon	fulmen L	lightning, thunderbolt
168.10	homogallant	homo L	man
		homo- G	same-
		gala G	milk
.11	hemycapnoise	hêmikapnos G	half-smoke
		hêmikapnoeidês G	half-smoke-like
.13	*Sacer esto?*	sacer esto L	let him be sacred; let him be accursed
.14	*Semus sumus!*	semusti sumus L	we are half-burned
		semis sumus L	we are a half
169.01	joky	Jocosa L *from*	"Merry": *fem. name* Joyce
		jocus L	joke, jest
.01	Jacob	Jacobus LL	James
.03	outlex	*part trans.* exlex L	lawless
.14	megageg	mega-G	great-
.20	tristended	tris- L *instead of*	thrice, in three
		dis- L	twice, in two, apart [tristended is fifty percent more than *distended*]
.21	protohistory	prôtohistoria G	first inquiry, first knowledge, first story, first history
170.01	annas and annas	annus L	a year
		Anna Perenna L	goddess of the returning year

		annona L	yearly produce; means of subsistence; prices; dearness
.03	dinar	denarius L	Roman silver coin
.03	dictited	dictito L	to say often, to declare *or* assert repeatedly
.11	a gnawstick	agnôstos G	unknown, unknowable
		gnôstikos G	1. of *or* having knowledge; 2. a believer in Gnosticism, *a hybrid Christian-pagan heresy of the lst and 2nd C*
.19	semisized	semi-; semis L	half-; half
.22	doctator	doctus L	learned, skilled
		dictator L	"orderer, prescriber": magistrate given full power by the Romans for six months in national emergencies
.34	Grex's	grex L	flock, herd
171.03	somatophage	*sômatophagos G	body-devourer, corpse-eater
.03	virgitarian	virga L	twig, switch, rod
		virgetum L	thicket of rods
.08	piscivore	*piscivorus L	fish-eating; fish-eater
.09	hibat	[in]hibet L	he keeps back, he restrains
.10	kukkakould	kukaô G *#Reduplication*	to stir, to mix
.11	kcedron	cedrus L kedros G *#G-to-L*	cedar, juniper-tree
.11	scedar	-ce L *phonetically =* -ce- Eng., Fr. =	-ke- -se-
.16	rhubarbarous	rha L, G rhàon G	plant growing near river *Rha* (*mod. Volga*): rhubarb
		barbaron G	foreign, barbarian
		barbarum L	
		rhabarbarum LL	foreign *rha*: rhubarb
.17	diodying	diodos G	way through; passing through
.20	withswillers	*trans.*	"withdrinkers":
		compotores L	drinking companions, pot companions

		trans. sympotai G	"withdrinkers": fellow-drinkers, boon companions
.27	artstouchups	Artax, Dux [Arostolym, Momfumbres & variants]	apocryphal stars whence Adam's name acronymically derives
.28	Urinia	urina L	urine
		Urania L Ourania G	"Heavenly": Muse of astronomy
.32	unremuneranded	*inremunerand-us L	not to be repaid, not to be rewarded
.35	vias	via L	way, road; by way [of]
.36	exeunt	exeunt L	they leave, they go out
172.01	Patatapapaveri's	papaver L	poppy
.08	Ex!	ex L	out of, out from, from
.09	Exex!	ex L	*as above*
.10	Exexex! COMMUNICATED	excommunicatus L	put out of the community
.17	debit	debitum L	owed
.17	antinomian	antinomianus eccl. L	believer that faith, not law, is the means of salvation
		antinomia G L	conflict of laws
.18	cerebrum	cerebrum L	the brain
.19	explaud	explaudo L	to clap off [the stage]; to drive out, to disapprove
.20	pneumantics	pneumatikos G	of wind; inflated; breathing; spiritual
		*pneumantikos G	prophetic by means of wind *or* spirit
.23	Nearapoblican	Nea polis G	"New city": Naples
		Neapolitanus L	of Naples; Neapolitan
.25	Fireless	#*Digamma*	wireless
.31	Munda	Munda	Caesar's last and most costly victory; #*A*
.35	kidos	kudos, kydos G	glory, renown
		kydos G	reproach, abuse
.35–.36	men ... dem	men ... de G	indeed ... so; on the one hand ... on the other hand: *correlative particles in successive clauses*
173.02	acrux	crux L	cross

.02	transpiciously	transpicio L	to look *or* see through
		*transpiciose L	in a way to see through
.10	pensile	pensilis L	hanging, hanging down; hung up
.12	Chrest	Chrestus L	mutilated form of *Christos* (Christ) used by some early Roman writers
		chrêstos G	useful, serviceable; good, wholesome
.13	Albiogenselman	albi- L	white-
		bios G	life
		gens L	race *or* clan; group of related families
.16	pollititians	polliceor L	to promise
		pollicitum L	a promise
.16	agricolous	agricola L	farmer
.17	manufraudurers	manu- L	hand-, by hand
		fraudo L	to cheat, to embezzle
		uro L	to burn up, to oppress
.17	sacrestanes	sacer L	sacred, holy, set apart; accursed
.18	philanthropicks	philanthrôpikos G	loving mankind, humane
.18	panesthetic	*panaisthêtikos G	all-sensitive, all-perceptive; fully vigorous in the senses
.25	visanvrerssas	visa (*fem.*)	seen
		vice versa L	turned alternately
174.12	gratias	gratia L	favor, grace, courtesy
.14	quiso	quaeso OL	please
.16	focuss	focus L	fireplace, hearth
.19	*hemoptysia*	*haimoptysia G	a state of blood-spitting
.19	*diadumenos*	diadymenos G	slipping through
		diadoumenos G	wearing a diadem
		Antoninus Diadumenus	co-emperor a.d. 218
.19	*hemoptysia*	*haimoptysma	evading bloody sputum
	diadumenos	diadyomenon G	
.26	bis	bis L	twice
.29	laetich	laetitia L	joyfulness, gladness
175.01	contemp	contem[p]no L	to despise, disdain, contemn
.03	pleb	plebs L	the common people, the mass

		plebeius L	one of the mass
.05	Nichil	nichil LL nihil L	nothing
.14	*Witchywithcy of Wench*	Veni Vidi Vici L	I came I saw I conquered: *Caesar's message to Rome after his defeat of Pharnaces II, king of Pontus (47 b.c.)*
.16	*Arcobaleine*	arcus L	bow, rainbow, arch
		balaena L	whale
.16	*forespoken*	*trans.* praedictus L	previously named, before mentioned; *also,* foretold
.29	O fortunous casualitas	O fortuna casualis L	O accidental fate
		O fortunata causalitas L	O lucky causality
		O Fortunatus Casus L	O Fortunate Fall (*continuation of hymn below*)
		O felix culpa L	O happy sin: *hymn celebrating Adam's fall because it elicited the Incarnation*
.31	misoxenetic	misoxenos G	hostile to strangers, hating foreigners
.33	Niscemus	nescimus L	we do not know
.33	Nemon	nemo L	nobody
.33	Niscemus Nemon	nescimus neminem L	we do not know nobody
176.07	*Expolled*	expolio L	to smooth off, to polish
.12	*Heali*	hêlios G	the sun
.13	*futilears*	futio L	a pouring out
		futilis, futtilis L	incontinent; worthless
.36	telemac	Têlemachos G	"Fighting-from-afar": son of Odysseus and Penelope
.36	somnbomnet	somnus L	sleep
		somnium L	dream
177.01	wottle	#*Labials*	bottle
.02	monotheme	monothema G	sole treasure, horoscope, prize, topic for discussion
		monothêma G	solitary tomb

.03	ampullar	ampulla L	flask, bottle, pot
.05	hemiparalysed	hêmiparalytos G	half secretly undone; half paralyzed
.10	revolted	revolsae (*fem. pl.*) L	plucked-away; violated
		revolutae (*fem. pl.*) L	returned; revolved; turned-around
.10	stellas	stellae L	stars
.11	vespertine	vespertinae (*fem. pl.*) L	of the evening
.10–.11	revolted stellas vespertine	revolsae stellae vespertinae L	violated stars of the evening, *etc.*
.14	Nero	Nero L	"Strong": Roman family name
		C. Claudius Nero	notorious emperor
.19	*a latere*	a latere L	1. from the side, aside; in intimate association with; 2. from a brick
.21	heavenlaid twin	Castor and Pollux	twin sons of Leda and Jove, hatched out of one egg
.21	pseudoed	pseudô G	to cheat by lies, to beguile
.24	congregant	congregant L	they assemble together, associate
.25	nexmouth	nex L	murder
.33	andthisishis	antithesis G	opposition
178.01	lapsis	lapis L	a stone
.01–.02	lapsis linquo	lapsus linguae L	a slip of the tongue
.02	linquo	linquo L	to leave, quit, depart from
.03	bear	# *Labials*	fair; fear
.03	prepestered	praepes L	1. nimble, fleet; 2. a bird
.04	postposition	postpositio L	a setting behind, postponement, neglect
.06	multaphoniaksically	multa L	much, many things
		phônêtikos G	vocal, endowed with speech
		phônikos G	a declaimer
		phônê G	sound, voice
.13	baalamb	Barlaam and Joasaph	disguised life of Buddha by John of Damascus
.17	Paltryattic	psaltria G	female harpist

		Attikos, Attikê G	Attic, of Attica
.17	*pura*	pura (*fem. sing. or neut. pl.*) L	clean, pure, unstained
.17	*pia*	pia (*fem. sing. or neut. pl.*) L	dutiful, reverent, pious
.17	*bella*	bella (*fem. sing. or neut. pl.*) L	nice, pretty, beautiful
		bella (*neut. pl. n.*) L	wars
.17	*pura e pia bella*	pia et pura bella L	pious and pure wars (Vico; #*B*)
.17–.18	in junk et sampam or in secular sinkalarum	et nunc et semper et in saecula saeculorum L	both now and always and for all eternity [ages of ages]
.18	bonafide	bona fides L	good faith
		bona fide L	in good faith
.24	*dei colori*	*dei colori L	to the color of a god
.26	dia dose	dia G	through
		diadôma G	girdle, drawers
.30	porcoghastly	porcus L	pig
.33	oving	ovo L	to exult, rejoice
		ovans L	exulting, joyful
		ovum L	egg
		ovis L	sheep
.35	celestious	caelestius L	coming from heaven, heavenly
179.02	*hic sunt lennones*	hic sunt lenones L	here are pimps
		hic sunt leones L	here are lions, there are lions here (*frequent inscription on old maps of Africa*)
		hic sunt Lennones L	there are Lennons here (*Lennon: Irish family name [e.g., of the present senior lexicographer's maternal family]; Joyce's bête noir was Judge Michael Lennon; see Glasheen, Second Census and Ellmann, James Joyce, p. 655*)

.09–.10	Deucalion and Pyrrha	Deucalion and Pyrrha	the classical Noah and wife; *see 134.04–05*
.10	privy ... gods	Lares L	tutelary spirits of the Roman household, hearth and slaves' quarters
.10	pantry gods	*trans.* di Penates L	guardian spirits of the larder in Roman households
.11	Stator	Stator L	Stayer, Supporter: *epithet of* Jupiter
.11	Victor	Victor L	the Conquering: *epithet of* Jupiter
.13	Calumnious	calumniosus L	full of tricks, swindling
.14	Cloaxity	cloaca L	a sewer
.14	Biloxity	bilis L	bile; anger, choler, ire
		*bilox L	bilious; angry
.14	Aper	aper L	wild boar
.15	Atroxity	atrox L	dark, horrible, gloomy, savage, cruel, atrocious
		atrocitas L	horribleness, hideousness
.15	quarify	quare L	how? why?
		# *L/R Interchange*	qualify
.17	dedal	daedalus L daidalos G	artificial, skilful
.19	navico	navigo L	to sail, to set sail, to go by sea
.21	megalomane	megalomanês G	very frantic
.22	septuncial	septunx L	seven-twelfths, seven ounces, seven inches
		*septuncialis L	seven-inch
.23	manuscribe	manuscribo L	to write by hand
.25	inspissated	inspissatus L	thickened
.26	glaucous	glaukos G	gleaming, bluish-green, grey, light blue (*the Greeks disliked this color*)
.26	usylessly	Ulysses *erroneously for* Ulixes L	Odysseus, hero of the *Odyssey*
180.01	queque	que ... que L	and ... and; both ... and
.03	probscenium	proboskis G	snout, trunk

		proscaenium L	the place before the
		proskênion G	scene (*in theater*) where the actors appeared, the stage
		obscenus L	unfavorable, repulsive, filthy
		obscenum L	the private parts
		obscene L	indecently, lewdly
.04	pantheomime	pantheos G	common to all gods; all-embracing divinity
		pantomimos G	imitating everything, acting out everything; an actor who acts out everything
		*pantheomimos G	acting out all the gods; an actor who acts all-embracing divinity, *etc.*
.12	*Alfaiate*	alpha G	letter A
		alphainô G	to bring in, to yield, to incur
.12	*punxit*	punxit L	[he] has punctured, has stung
		pinxit L	[he] has painted
.15	Occidentaccia	occidens L	setting [of the sun]; the west
		taceo L	to say nothing, be silent
.36	lexical	lex L	legislation, law
		lexikos G	pertaining to words, diction
181.06	Barbaropolis	Barbarou polis G	Barbarian's city
.07	hebdomodary	hebdomadikos G	weekly, for a week
.07	metropoliarchialisation	mêtropolis G	mother-city
		archi- G	chief-
		-alis [-ili] L	*suffix indicating Passive Capacity*
		-izô [-iz-] G	*suffix indicating action as*
		*mêtropoliarchializatio G + L	the act of making a mother-city a capital [?]
.07	hebdomodary metropoliarchialisation	*allusion to* the Easter Week Rebellion of 1916	for-a-week making-the-mother-city--a-capital

.13	Nigerian	niger L	black
		Nigera	country in Africa, on *Nigir* river (*Ptolemy's map*)
.14	Vulgariano	*Vulgarius L	Commoner, Mass-Man
.18	Sorority	sororitas L	sisterhood
.34	statuesque ante	status quo ante L	the position in which [affairs were] before [some event]
.35	Drumcondriac	-chondriacus ML *from* chondros G	-cartilaged cartilage
.36	nate	nates L	the buttocks
		natus L	born, *né*; a son
.36	pseudostylic	*pseudostylikos G	made with a false pillar (*architecture*)
		*pseudostilicus G + L	made with a false pen *or* in a false style
182.02	palimpsests	palimpsêston G	"rubbed again; scraped again": a writing-tablet which has been erased and re-used but on which the previous writing is discernible
.03	pelagiarist	Pelagius L Pelagios G	"Of the Sea": British or Irish-born heretic (360–420), his name being a G trans. of Celtic *Morgan* ("Sea-born") *denied original sin; banished from Rome by Pope Zosimus* (*see 154.08*)
		pelagos G	the sea
		plagiarius L	thief, kidnapper
.04	gnose's	gnôsis G	knowledge, investigation
.05	lucifericiously	*luciferaciter L	in a light-bringing manner
.07	mathness	mathêsis G	act of learning; information; education
		mathêtês G	learner, pupil, student
.08	educandees	educandi L	those to be educated *or* reared
		educandis L	to those to be educated

		educandus L	pupil, student
.12	simulchronic	simul L	at the same time, together, at once
		chronikos G	of *or* concerning time
.18	Sardanapalus	Sardanapalus L	Assur-bani-pal
		Sardanapalos G	(669–640 b.c.), king of Assyria; *burned himself with all his possessions; used by Roman poet Martial to designate a weak, effeminate person*
.20	Nichiabelli's	nichil LL nihil L	nothing
		belli- L	war-
		bellum L	war
		bellus L	handsome
.20	monolook	mono- G	sole-, only-
.20	*Hanno, o Nonanno*	Hanno	1. Carthaginian explorer of west Africa 2. Carthaginian commander in the first Punic War
		non L	not
		Nonnus	G epic poet of 5th C a.d. from Egypt
.21	q.e.d.	q[uod] e[rat] d[emonstrandum] L	what was to be demonstrated
.24	dranchmas	drachmê G	"as much as one can hold in the hand": a weight, a silver coin
183.12	amygdaloid	amygdaloeidês G	like an almond *or* almond-tree
.13	alphybettyformed	alpha, bêta G	letters A, B
		alphabêtos G	alphabet
.13	verbage	verba L	words
.13	vivlical viasses	MG *pron.*; # *Labials*	biblical biasses
.13	ompiter	MG *spelling*: -mp- *for* -b-	obiter
.13–.14	ompiter dictas	obiter dicta L	things said in passing
.14	visus umbique	visus undique L	seen from all sides, seen from everywhere, seen completely
		visus ambigue L	seen doubtfully

		umbo L	boss of a shield; shield; elbow
		-que L	and
.16	lucifers	lucifer L	light-bringing; the morning star (Venus)
.16	vestas	Vesta L	goddess of flocks, herds, and the household; goddess of the fireplace *or* hearth
.18	scapulars	scapula LL	the shoulder
		scapulae L	the shoulder-blades; the shoulders
.20	latten tintacks		Latin syntax
.22	quotatoes	# *P/K Split*	potatoes
.29	cintrum	centrum L	the middle of a circle
		kentron G	
		kentron G	a sharp point (*of a compass*), a prickle
.31	antipodes	antipodes G	"with the feet opposite": legendary inhabitants of the other side of the earth
184.13	lithargogalenu	lithargyros G	monoxide of lead
		galena L	lead ore; dross left after smelting lead
.15	moromelodious	morosus L	peevish, slow
		môro- G	foolish-, silly-
		melôdos G	musical
		*môromelôdos G	foolishly musical, musical in a silly way
.18	athanor	athanês G	undying, immortal
		*athanôr G	an undie-er, an immortaler
.22	Asther's	astêr G	star
		asthêma G	weakness
.22	Huster's	hustera, hystera G	1. womb 2. the next, second *or* following woman
.22	micture	micturio L	to go to urinate, to make water
.23	acuredent	akurês G	unfortunate
		akoureutos G	unshaven
		akouros G	childless
.26	calubra	kaluptra G	veil, head-dress, bride's veil

.26	culorum	culorum (*Gen. pl.*) L	of the posteriors
		culus L	the fundament
.28	Usquadmala	usque ad mala L	until the apples [*dessert at meals*]
		ab ovo usque ad mala L	from the egg to the apples: from the beginning to the end [*of a Roman feast; see 154.35*]
		usque ad mala L	even as far as evils
.29	oves	oves (*pl.*) L	sheep (*pl.*)
		ovum, *pl.* ova L	egg, eggs
.29	uves	uva, *pl.* uvae L	grape, grapes
.34–.35	Pastor Lucas	Pastor Lucas L [Loukas G]	the Shepherd Luke
.36	antimonian	antimonium ML	antimony
		antinomianus eccl. L	believer in Faith, not Law
		antinomia G	contradiction between laws
.36	manganese	magnesia L	stone of Magnesia
		Magnêsia lithos G	(*district in Asia Minor*)
.36	limolitmious	limos G	hunger, famine
		limo- G	-hunger, hunger-
		litos G	simple, inexpensive
		*limolitos G	hungrily frugal
185.03	Codex	codex L	book with bound pages (*not a scroll*)
		#P/K Split	Podex
.03	Podex	podex L	fundament, anus
		#P/K Split	Codex
.04	pastor	pastor L	shepherd, herdsman
.04	Flammeus	flammeus L	flaming, fiery
.06	kathartic	kathartikos G	fit for cleansing; laxative
.07	synthetic	synthetikos G	skilled in putting together, constructive; a component
.10	porporates	purpuratus L	clad in purple [a Cardinal]
		#PLK Split	corporates
		corporatus L	member of a corporation

GLOSSARY FOR FINNEGANS WAKE

.10	ordinal	ordinalis L	that denotes an order of succession ["*Apostolic Succession*" *of Anglican orders disputed by Rome*]
.14	*Primum opifex, altus prosator,*	Primum opifex, altus prosator L	In the beginning the maker, the high ancestor,
.14	*altus prosator*	Altus Prosator L	"The High Ancestor," Hymn by St. Colmcille (died 597); alludes to a second fall of the angels
.14	*ad terram viviparam et cunctipotentem*	ad terram viviparam et cunctipotentem L	to the lifebearing and all-powerful earth
.15	*sine ullo pudore nec venia,*	sine ullo pudore nec venia L	without any shame or mercy,
.15–.16	*suscepto pluviali atque discinctis perizomatis,*	suscepto pluviali atque discinctis perizomatis L	having raised his rain-gear and likewise having unfastened his underclothes,
.16	*natibus nudis ut nati fuissent,*	natibus nudis ut nati fuissent L	with buttocks naked as they were born,
.16	*sese adpropinquans,*	sese adpropinquans L	drawing himself nigh,
.17	*flens et gemens, in manum suam evacuavit,*	flens et gemens, in manum suam evacuavit L	weeping and sighing, evacuated into his hand,
.18	*postea, animale nigro exoneratus,*	postea, animale nigro exoneratus L	afterwards, disburdened of the black brute,
.18	*classicum pulsans,*	classicum pulsans L	sounding a trumpet-call,
.19	*stercus proprium, quod appellavit deiectiones suas,*	stercus proprium, quod appellavit dejectiones suas L	his own dung, that he called his purgings,
.19	[*deiectiones*	dejectio L	1. a throwing down, casting down; 2. a purging; 3. an eviction]
.19–.20	*in vas olim honorabile tristitiae posuit,*	in vas olim honorabile tristitiae posuit L	he placed in a once-honorable vessel of sadness,

.20	*eodem sub invocatione*	eodem sub invocatione	in the same place, under invocation
.20–.21	*fratrorum geminorum Medardi et Godardi*	fratrorum geminorum Medardi et Godardi L	of the twin brothers Medard and Godard
.21	*laete et melliflue minxit,*	laete et melliflue minxit L	joyfully and mellifluously ["honey-flowingly"] he pissed,
.21–.23	*psalmum qui incipit: Lingua mea calamus scribae velociter scribentes: magna voce cantitans,*	magna voce cantitans psalmum qui incipit: Lingua mea calamus scribae velociter scribentis L	chanting in a loud voice the psalm that begins: "My tongue the pen of a scribe writing swiftly"[AV:*Ps. 45:1*, "my tongue *is* the pen of a ready writer"; Rheims-Vulgate: *Ps. 44:2*, "my tongue *is* the pen of a scrivener that writeth swiftly"]
.24	*demum ex stercore turpi*	demum ex stercore turpi L	finally out of the foul dung
.24	*cum divi Orionis iucunditate mixto,*	cum divi Orionis jucunditate mixto L	mixed with the good offices of divine Orion,
.24	*Orionis*	Oriôn G	Orion, mythological hunter after whom constellation is named; *according to myth his name was originally* Ouriôn *because he was generated from* ouron, "urine"
.24–.25	*cocto, frigorique exposito,*	cocto, frigorique exposito L	cooked, and exposed to the cold,
.25	*encaustum sibi fecit indelibile*	encaustum sibi fecit indelibile L	he made indelible ink for himself
.27	pious Eneas	pius Aeneas L	dutiful Aeneas: *frequent formula in Vergil's* Aeneid
.27	fulminant	fulminans L	hurling lightning
.28	tremylose	tremulus L *as if* tremylos G	quaking, trembling, quivering

.28	terrian	terrenus L	of the earth
		terreo L	to frighten
.29	nichthemerically	nychthêmeros G	lasting a night and a day
		nychthêmerêsios G	nightly and daily
.30	copriright	kopros G	dung
.31	Ourania	Ourania G	"Heavenly": Muse of
		Urania L	astronomy
		ouranê G	chamber-pot
		ourêma G	urine
		ouron G	urine
		urina L	urine
186.03	transaccidentated	*transaccidentio L *transaccido L	to alter the accidental or inessential parts of
		opposed to transsubsto L	to alter the essence of
.04	a dividual	a- G for in- L	not- [individual]
.10	agglaggagglomerative-ly	agglomero L	to wind string on a ball, to join to
		# Reduplication	
.11	arklyst	arca L arkê G	chest, box
		lysis G	dissolution, emptying
		*arkêlysis G	emptying a chest
.14	sexth	sextus L	sixth
.15	stylo	stylos G	pillar, pole (bad G: stile for writing on waxed tablets)
.22	stoties	toties L	so many times, as often
.22	quemquem	quemquem (Acc.) L	whoever, whatsoever
.22	quum	quum OL cum L	when, as, while
.27	protoprostitute	proto- G	first-
		prostituta L	prostitute
.28	arch	archê G	first
		trans. fornix L	arch, vault, archway; brothel
.28	Arcoiris	arcus L	bow, rainbow; arch
		Iris G L	goddess of the rainbow; rainbow
.31	grazious	gratiosus L	in favor, beloved, agreeable
		gratias L	thanks

.31	oras	ora L	border, brim, edge; sea-coast
		ora L	pray!
		hora L	hour
.33	selfevitant	evitans L	shunning, avoiding
187.11	dominical	*dominicalis L	of *or* belonging to Sunday
.15	-hoploits	hoplitês G	heavy-armed foot-soldier
.17	plutherotested	plutor eccl. L	he who sends rain
		plousiôteros, ploutiôteros G	richer, more wealthy
.20	sept okt nov dec	septem octo novem decem L	seven eight nine ten
.21	labaryntos	laba G	drop
		labyrinthos G	maze, labyrinth, large building consisting of numerous halls connected by intricate passages
.24	JUSTIUS	justus L	just, upright, righteous
.28	Nayman	Nemo L *for* Outis G	No one, no man: *name Odysseus gave himself to the Cyclops; #A*
.28–.30	follow . . . the deponent	[verbum] deponens L	a laying-aside [verb]: *one that* lays aside *its proper passive significance: Grammar,* a deponent, *a verb in passive form with active meaning*
		sequor L	to follow: *standard*
		hepomai G	*instance of a* deponent verb
.31	empirative	imperativus [modus] L	[the mood] of command; *Grammar:* the imperative
		empeiria G	experience
		empeirikos G	experienced, empiric
.36	uterim	*uterim L modeled on*	in whichsoever place here and there, in
		passim L	different places
		uterus L	the womb
		uterim as above	in the womb

188.04	confiteor	confiteor L	I confess, I acknowledge
.08	*cur*	cur L	why?
.08	*quicquid*	quicquid L	whoever, whatever
.08	*ubi*	ubi L	where
.09	*quando*	quando L	when
.09	*quomodo*	quomodo L	in what manner, how
.09	*quoties*	quoties L	how often, how many times
.09	*quibus auxiliis*	quibus auxiliis L	with whose helps, with the helps of what persons
.08–.09	*cur . . . auxiliis?*	*standard questions to be answered in Confession to establish the circumstances and the gravity of each sin*	
.16	anarch	*anarchês G	unleader, one not qualified to be a leader
.16	egoarch	*egôarchês G	I-leader, self-leader, ego-leader
.16	hiresiarch	hairesiarchês G	leader of a school, heresiarch (leader of a heresy)
		hierarchês G	presider over sacred rites, high-priest
.25	Solemonities	sol L	the sun
		sollenis L	yearly, solemn
.27	caldor	caldor L	warmth, heat
.27	opprobo	opprobro L	I reproach, I upbraid
189.01	wious pish	# *Labials*	pious wish
.01	soph	sophia G	cleverness, skill, intelligence, wisdom
.02	elenchate	elegchô = elenchô G	disgrace, put to shame; cross-examine; convict, prove
.04	morosity	môros G	dull, sluggish, stupid
		morosus L	1. peevish, fretful 2. lingering, slow
.06	sponsibility	*sponsibilis L	able to promise, able to engage solemnly
.07	prostability	*prostabilis L	able to stand forth, able to project; able to offer wares for sale; able to prostitute one's self

.08	strabismal	strabismos G	squinting
.08	apologia	apologia G	speech in defence
.13	fluctuant	fluctuans L	moving in the manner of waves, undulating, being driven here and there; swelling, wavering
.14	educanded	educandus L	fit to be educated
.19	*solus cum sola sive cuncties cum omnibobs*	solus cum sola sive cuncti cum omnibus L	[a man] alone with [a woman] alone or else the whole lot with everybody
		solus cum sola sive cunctim cum omnibus L	[a man] alone with [a woman] alone or else collectively with everybody
		*cuncties (*made up word*) L	at all times
.21	debituary	*debituarius L *from*	a debt-notice
		debit L *modeled on*	he [she, it] owes
		obituarius ML *from*	a death-notice
		obit L	he [she, it] dies
.32	impetiginous	impetiginosus L	one who has impetigo
		impetigo L	a skin disease
.33	auspices	auspicia L	divination by observing the flight of birds
.34	auguries	auguria L	divination; signs, omens
190.02	obtundity	obtundo L	to beat, thump, belabor; to blunt, dull; to stun, to deafen
		*obtunditas, obtusio L	bluntness, dulness
.17	*pro anno*	pro anno L	for the year
.30	alibi	alibi L	elsewhere, somewhere else
.31	metamorphoseous	metamorphôsis G	transformation
		phôs G	light
.32	parapangle	parapan G	altogether, absolutely
		pangeloios G	thoroughly ridiculous
		panglykeros G	sweetest of all
.32	preposters	praeposteritas L	inversion

		praeposterus L	reversed, inverted, perverted
		*praeposteriora L	before the posteriors
.33	antinos	antinoos G	opposite in character
		*antinous G	against intelligence, against mind
		Antinous G	1. chief of the suitors of Penelope, slain by Odysseus 2. youth (a.d. 112–130) beloved by Hadrian; drowned in the Nile; deified by the emperor
.34	scatchophily	scateo L	to bubble, gush, well, flow forth
		*skatophilia G	love of dung
.35	prosodite	prosôdia G	song sung to instrumental music; differences of pronunciation
		prosôdos G	singing in accord, harmonious
		prosôdês G	stinking
		prosêlytos G	stranger; convert; proselyte
.36	mus	mus L	mouse
191.04	Afferyank	Afer L	African
		affero L	to bring to, carry to; to bring upon, to cause
.10	Novena	novena ML	nines each
.10	Novara	nova (fem.) L	new
.10	Patripodium	patri- L G	father-
		podium L	foot, base
		podion G	
		Patris podex L	Father's arse, Father's bum
.12	possum	possum L	I can
.13	Immaculatus	immaculatus L	unstained
.14	Altrues	*alterui LL	to or by others
.15	celestine	caelestinus L	heavenly
.17	celebesty	caelebs L	unmarried
.32	frontispecs	frontispex L	one who sees or inspects foreheads
192.01	Marcon	Marcion (100-165 a.d.)	heretic of Sinope who claimed to be Christ

.02	scissymaidies	schisma G	cleft, division; vulva
		schismatikos G	separatist, schismatic
.03	gunorrhal	gunê G	woman
		gonorhoia G	semen-flow, gonorrhea
.03	lupo	lupus L	wolf
		lupa L	she-wolf, prostitute
.03	monkax	monachus eccl. L *from*	monk
		monachos G	unique, solitary, sole instance; monk
.06	hamilkcars	Hamilcar	1. Carthaginian general, 5th C b.c. 2. Hamilcar Barca ["Lightning"] (270–228 b.c.), Carthaginian general, First Punic War; father of Hannibal
.16	hastroubles	Hasdrubal	1. son-in-law of Hamilcar Barca, Carthaginian governor of Spain 2. Hasdrubal Barca, son of Hamilcar Barca, Carthaginian general, brother of Hannibal, killed in battle against the Romans (207 b.c.)
.18	excruciated	excruciatus L	torment, torture
.21	Paraskivee	*MG pron.* Paraskeuê G	the Jewish day of *Preparation* before the sabbath of Passover; the day Christ was crucified; Good Friday
.27	hornmade ivory dreams	keratinos G	horn, made of horn
		krainô, kraiainô G	to accomplish, fulfill
		elephantos G	ivory
		elephairomai G	to cheat, overreach, delude *these four words, with obvious wordplay, occur in* Odyssey *19.562–567*

		Sunt geminae Somni portae, quarum altera fertur / cornea, qua veris facilis datur exitur umbris; / alter candenti perfecta nitens elephanto, / sed falsa ad caelum mittunt insomnia Manes L	There are two gates of Sleep, of which one is said to be / horn, which gives passage to genuine reflections; / the other is made of brightly shining ivory / but through it the shades send false dreams to the earth. —*Vergil*, Aeneid *VI.893–896; modeled* *on* Odyssey *19.562–567*
.30	selene	selênê G # L/R *Interchange*	the moon serene
.36	-jesusalem	# *Rhotacism* (*reversed*)	jerusalem
.36	balbettised	balbutio L	to stammer, to stutter
193.04	holifer	*holoverus G + L	quite real
		holos G -pheros G -fer L	whole, entire -bearer, -bringer
.04	Leon	leôn G leo L	lion
.05	mux	muxa G	discharge from the nose, snot; lamp-wick, soot
		mox L	soon, next
.13	Studiosus	studiosus L	eager, zealous, assiduous
.17	a stigmy	stigma G stigmê G	tattoo-mark, mark spot on [*a bird's*] plumage; brand; mathematical point; anything very small
		*astigma G *astigmatias G	no-mark one who is unmarked
.21	Thacolicus	catholicus L katholikos G	universal, relating to all
.29–.30	*Insomnia, somnia* *somniorum*	insomnia, somnia somniorum L in omnia saecula saeculorum L	sleeplessness, dreams of dreams in all ages of ages: for eternity

.31	MERCIUS	merces L	hire, pay, wages, salary
		*Misericordius L	Merciful One
.31	*Domine*	Domine (*Voc.*) L	O Lord
.31	*vopiscus*	vopiscus L	survivor of a pair of twins when other has been aborted
		L. Julius Vopiscus Flavius Vopiscus	person mentioned by Livy historian *temp.* Constantine; wrote lives of several emperors
.31	*Domine vopiscus*	Dominus vobiscum L	the Lord [be] with you
194.03	attrite	attritus L	rubbed off, worn away; shameless
.04	youyouth ... mimine	# *Reduplication*	
.04	mimine	memini L	to remember
.06	spiritus	spiritus L	breeze, breath, life; spirit
.16	metuor	metuor L	I am feared
.16	horescens	horrescens L	beginning to tremble, growing afraid
.16	astroglodynamonolog-os	astro- G	star-, starry-
		trôglodytês G	one who creeps into holes; caveman
		dynamo- G	power-
		mono- G	sole-, solitary-
		logos G	word, study, wisdom, reasoning
		*monologos G	soliloquy; play for one actor
		*astrotrôglodytê-dynamomonolog-os G	star-creeper-into-holes monologue; play for one actor about starry caveman power
.17	Nilfit's	nil [nihil] fit L	nothing is made
.18	cubilibum	cubilibus L	to *or* by beds
		cubile L	a bed
.22–.23	alpilla, beltilla ... deltilla	alpha, bêta, delta G	letters A, B, D
.32	inuendation	innuendo (*Abl.*) L	by nodding, by intimating

		inundatio L	an overflowing, a flood
195.02	deloothering	diluvium L	flood, deluge
		dilutum L	liquid in which something is dissolved, a solution
		lutum L	mud
.04	Anna Livia	Amnis Livia L	the River Liffey
		amnis livis L	bluish river
		Livia L #A	wife of Augustus, mother of Tiberius
196.03	Anna Livia	see 195.04 D–E	
.04	Anna Livia	see 195.04 D–E	
.04	Anna Livia	see 195.04 D–E	
.05	Anna Livia	see 195.04 D–E	
.21	nicies and priers	nisi prius L	unless before: legal warrant to bring a case to trial at central court unless before that date it shall have been tried locally
.21	fierceas	versus L	turned toward, facing
.21	illysus	Ilisos G Ilissus L	river at Athens
		illusio L	mocking, jeering
		Ulixes, Ulysses L #A	Odysseus, hero of the Odyssey
.22	Temp	Tempea, Tempê G	valley of the river Peneus between Olympos and Ossa
		tempus L	time
.24	Minxing	minxi L	I have urinated
197.01	sinistrous	sinistrorsus L	toward the left
		sinistrum L	the left side: awkward, unlucky, bad; also, lucky, favorable, auspicious
.03	duke alien	Deucalion	classical Noah; see 179.09
.06	Lictor Hackett	lictor L	attendant on a magistrate; bore a bundle of rods from which an axe projected
.06	Lector Reade	lector L	a reader; a slave who read aloud to his master

.08	Caput	caput L	the head
.15	isthmass	isthmos G	strip of land between two seas
		Isthmia G	games held every five years at the Isthmus of Corinth
.17	oxus	Oxos G	river in Asia flowing into the Aral Sea; *now the* Amu Darya (*Afghanistan-U.S.S.R.*)
.18	follyo	folium L	a leaf
.21	raped ... Sabrine	Rape of the Sabine Women	legendary abduction by the founders of Rome of the women of the neighboring Sabines; *invented to account for the large Sabine element in the Roman population*
		Sabrina L	river in Britain, now the Severn
.22	devious	devius L	out of the way, retired, sequestered, shy, inaccessible
		Deva L	river in Caledonia in Britain, now the Dee in Scotland
		Deva Castra L	city in Roman Britain, now Chester
.22	delts	delta G	letter D; anything in the shape of the letter *delta, e.g.,* a rivermouth, the female pudenda
.29	Ivernikan	Iverna L	Ireland
		Ivernicus L	Irish
.29	Okean	Okeanos G	the great sea that encompasses the land; the ocean
.33	timoneer	Timôn G	celebrated misanthrope of Athens
198.02	ptellomey	Ptolemaios G	"Warlike": name of all the kings of Egypt after Alexander until absorption by the Romans (323–30 b.c.)

		Claudius Ptolemaeus (a.d.90–168)	produced (c.a.d.150) atlas of maps with earliest known identification of Dublin (*Eblana*)
.02	escumo	esco L	to eat
.04	salomon	Salomon L Salômôn G salmo L	Solomon salmon
.08	Havemmarea	[H]ave L Ave Maria L Marea G L	hail; fare well Hail Mary lake in lower Egypt near Alexandria
.10	Anna Livia	Amnis Livia L	*see 195.04 D–E*
.11	sals	sal L hals G #G-to-L	salt the sea ("the briny")
.12	pontiff	pontifex L	"bridgemaker": Roman high-priest
.15	a laddery dextro	a latere dextro L	on the right side, on the right flank
.16	me absantee	me absente L	in my absence
.17	proxenete! Proxenete	proxenêtês G proxenos G	broker, agent public guest: *honor conferred on a distinguished foreigner*; a position like that of honorary consul in modern diplomacy; a protector, patron
.20	antiabecedarian	*antiabecedarius G+ML *anteabecedarius ML	person opposed to learning the alphabet pre-elementary
.21	par examplum	*par exemplum L per exemplum L	equal example through an example
.21	telekinesis	têlekinêsis G	movement from afar, motion from afar, far-motion
.22	proxenete	proxenêtês, proxenos G	*see 198.17 D–E*
.22	coxyt	coxa L coxim L kochydeô G	the hip on the hips to stream forth copiously, to gush

.25	cunniform	*cuneiformatus L	wedge-shaped, cuneiform
		cunnus (*called obscene word by Cicero*) L	cunt
		*cunniformatus L	cunt-shaped
.25	cunniform letters	delta G	letter D; *see 197.22* G
.29	glommen	glomus L	ball of yarn
.29	grampus	crassus pisces L	fat fish: *a species of whale*
.30	buboes	bubo L	owl, horned owl
		boubôn G	the groin; a swollen gland
.31	nera	nera (*fem.*) Sabine	strong (*masc.*: nero)
.34	occumule	occumbo L	to set (*of heavenly bodies*); to fall dying, to die
		*occumulo L	to heap up towards, to heap up in front of
.36	obsequies	obsequiae L	funeral rites, carrying out a will
199.11	Anna Livia	Amnis Livia	*see 195.04 D–E*
.21	pyrraknees	Pyrrha	"Red": wife of *Deucalion; see 197.03 and 179.09I-.10A*
		Pyrenes L	the Pyrenees; Spain
.23	vivers	vivo L *MG pron.*	to live, to be alive [im]bibers
.23	metauwero	Metaurus L Metauros G	name of several rivers, *esp. one in Umbria, now* Meturo, *site of defeat of Hannibal's brother Hasdrubal* (207 b.c.)
.24	Hek	haec (*fem.*) L	this, this here
.30	the hen	to hen G	the One (*philosophy*)
.31	turrace	turris L	a tower
.34	Annona	Annona L	goddess of the yearly produce
		annona L	yearly produce; corn, grain; prices; provisions, rations
.34	aroostokrat	*arostokratês G	profit-ruler, ruler by profit

.34	Nivia	nivea (*fem.*) L	snowy
		*Nivea L	"Snowy": *Joyce coinage for the* Neva?
.35	pirryphlickathims	Pyriphlegethôn G	"Fiery-burning": river in the Infernal Regions
.36	virevlies	# *Labials*	fireflies
200.04	porpor	purpura L porphyra G	purple
.06	poother	pudor L	shame
.07	*Wickerymandy*	*vicarimandatarius L	substitute agent
.10	Phoebe	Phoebe L Phoibê G	"Brightness": the moon-goddess, sister of *Phoebus* (the sun)
.15	stult	stultus L	a fool
.16	Anna Liv	Amnis Livia	*see 195.04D–E*
.20	Milucre	mille L lucrum L	a thousand profit
.33	Odet! Odet!	odit L audet L audit L	he [she, it] hates he [she, it] dares he [she, it] hears, listens, learns
.36	Anna Livia's	Amnis Livia	*see 195.04 D–E*
201.04	ore ouse	auris L	ear
.21	Onon! Onon!	ôn, oun G	certainly, really, so then (*particle confirming what is being said*)
.22	single ingul	singultus L	a sobbing, speech interrupted by sobbing
.30	meanacuminamoyas	cum L cuminum L kuminon G	with; while cumin (*a spice plant*)
.30	Olaph lamm	alpha lamda G	letters A, L
.30	et, all	et alii L	and others
.35	Pluhurabelle	pluor L *plorabilis L pluralis L	rain lamentable, bewailable, weepable consisting of many, plural
202.05	flewmen	flumen L	river, stream, flood
.06	so aimai moe, that's agapo	zôe mou, sas agapô G, MG haima G	my life, I love thee blood
.06	aimai	-mai G	1st pers. sing. deponent *or* passive verb suffix

		*aimai Fr.+G	j'aime
.06–.07	aimai ... that's agapo	*aimai = agapô	I love
.09	Fonte-in-Monte	fons in monte L	the spring on the mountain: Hippokrênê, *fountain near Mt. Helikôn, sacred to the Muses*
.15	Polistaman	polis G	city
		politeia G	*derivation of* police
		politia L	
.18	Arc	arx L	citadel
		arcus L	bow, rainbow, arch
.18	Fidaris	fidamen L	trust, confidence
.19	Nieman	Nemo L *for*	"No one": name
		Outis G	Odysseus gave himself to the Cyclops
.19	Nihil	nihil L	nothing
.20	Anser	anser L	a goose
.20	Untie the gemman's fistiknots	unde gentium festines? L	from what country are you hurrying? whence on earth are you hastening? *see 089.27*
.21	Qvic	quic L	combining form of *quis*, relative pronoun
		e.q. quicquid L	whatever
		v L	u *or* w; #*Labials*
.22	Tez thelon langlo	G ?	?
.22	thelon	thelô G	to wish, to be willing
.28	silvamoonlake	silva L	woodland, forest
.33	nymphant	nymphê G	bride; demi-goddess
		nympha L	
		*nymphans L	being a bride, being a nymph
.34	tigris	tigris L	tiger, tigerskin
		Tigris	"Arrowy" (Persian): the more easterly of the two rivers of Mesopotamia ("Between rivers"); still so-named
.34	O happy fault!	*trans.* O felix culpa L	medieval hymn celebrating Adam's sin for eliciting the Incarnation
.35	corribly	corruptibilis L	susceptible to decay

.35	anacheronistic	Acherôn (ho achea rheôn) G	Acheron (the stream of woe): a river in the Underworld; the Underworld
		anacheirizomai G	to delay, to hinder
		*anacherôn G	up the Acheron
		*anacheronteios G	not of the Acheron
.36	nullahs	nulla (*fem.*) L	not any, none
203.12	Neptune	Neptunus L	god of the sea and waters
.13	Tritonville	Tritôn G L	son of Neptune
.13	leandros	Leiandros G	"Plunder of men":
		Leander L	youth of Abydos who nightly swam the Hellespont to visit Hero until he drowned
.13	heroines	Hêrô G L	priestess of Aphrodite in Sestos on the Hellespont, beloved by Leander
.14	nonni	non L	not
		ni L	not
		nonne L	not?
.14	nos	nos L	we
.19	aspersed	aspersus (*pp.*) L	sprinkled
.19	lavabibs	lavabrum L	bath-tub
		lavabo L	I was washing
.20	venersderg	dies Veneris LL	Venus's day: Friday
.20	junojuly	Juno L	chief Roman goddess, wife of Jupiter; *guardian of women and marriage; protectress of childbirth; see 203.21*
		Junius L	"Belonging to Juno": name of a Roman gens; a month (June)
		M. Junius Brutus (85–42 b.c.)	leader of Caesar's assassins
		Julius L	"Belonging to *Iulus*": name of a Roman gens that claimed descent from Venus; a month (July; *formerly* Quinctilis) Named *for* C. *Julius Caesar*

		Iulus L = Ioulos G	"Down," "Fuzz" (boy's facial hair): son of Aeneas, grandson of Venus, eponymous ancestor of the gens Julia
		C. Julius Caesar (102–44 b.c.)	eminent Julian, *assassinated by eminent Junian* M. Junius Brutus
.21	Nixie	Nixi [Di] L	the three guardian deities of women in labor; *see 203.20*: Juno
.26	Vale	vale L	farewell
.26	lucydlac	lucidum lac L	shining-white milk
.28	galbs	galbus L galbinus L	1. yellow; 2. bald greenish-yellow
.29	Mavro	mavro MG mauros G	dark
.30	daphdaph	daphnê G	sweet bay, *Laurus nobilis*
.31	petrock	petra G L	rock
204.02	aestumation	aestus L	undulating, boiling; fire, heat; tide
		aestuatio L	boiling up; agitation of the mind
		aestuarium L	a tidal marsh, a tidal creek or inlet; an estuary
		aestimatio L	valuation *or* appraisal of the money value *of a thing*
.03	bantur	-abantur (*3rd pl. imperfect passive vb suffix*)	they were being ——ed
.05	Livvy	Titus Livius (59 b.c.–a.d. 17)	Roman historian; *wrote a history of Rome in 142 books*
.05	Nautic	nauticus L nautikos G	of *or* belonging to ships *or* sailors
.19	innocefree	innox L	harmless, innocent
205.07	nubilee	nubilis L	marriageable
.08	caloured	calor L	heat
.09	Annan	Anna Perenna L	goddess of the returning year

		annon L	that not?
		Annona L	goddess of the yearly produce
.16	Mericy Cordial	misericordia L	pity, mercy
.27	Porta Lateen	Porta Latina L	The Latin Gate: *gate at Rome to* Via Latina, *oldest Roman road, running* south-east
.27	ikom	eikôn G icon L	an image, figure
.29	turgos	turgeo L	to swell; to be enraged; to be bombastic
.29	Evropeahahn	*imitation MG pron.*	European
.33	rotundarinking	rotunda (*fem.*) L	round, circular
.36	hennad	to hen G henas G *modeled on* monas G	the One (*philosophy*) unit, monad, *henad
.36	Egg	ho Chronos egennêsen ôon G	*Chronos* (Time) produced an egg— *Orphic fragment.* Orphic cosmogony held that out of Chronos were born Aither, Chaos and Erebus; Chronos formed an egg in Aither from which sprang Phanes, creator of the gods
206.01	areopage	Areios pagos G	the Hill of Ares at Athens; a court held there
.02–.03	timpan ... Ma	tympanon G	kettledrum, *used esp. in worship of the Mother Goddess,* Kybelê
.03	Ma	Ma	Cappadocian war-goddess identified with Bellona
.03	hangnomen	agnomen L	surname acquired by an individual not transferred to his posterity, *e.g., Africanus, Cunctator*

204.04	croststyx	Styx G	"Hateful": 1. fountain in Arcadia *the icy waters of which caused death* 2. river in the Infernal Regions
206.04–.05	nyne wyndabouts	nine rivers	*there are nine rivers in the classical Underworld*
.13	Euclid	Eukleidês G (*fl.* 300 b.c.)	"Famous": G mathematician, inventor of geometry
.15	rizo	rideo L	to laugh
.31	galawater	gala G	milk
.31	lauar	lauo, lavo L lauatus, lavatus, lautus L	to wash washed
.33	butterscatch	skato- G	dung-
.35	quincecunct	quincunx L	five-twelfths; the arrangement of the five spots on dice
		cunctus L	all in a body, all together, the whole
		cunnus L	cunt
207.07	rhunerhinestones	rhoia G	flux, flow
		rhinos G	skin, hide
		rhino- G	nose-
.08	Lutetiavich	Lutetia	city in Gaul; now Paris
		luteus L	muddy, yellow
.12	Ciliegia	chiliastys G	group of a thousand people
		Kilikia G Cilicia L	province in Asia Minor
		cilia L	the eyelids
.12	chirsines	chersenus L chersinos G	living on dry land
		Chersonêsos G	"Dry island" (*i.e.,* Peninsula): peninsula of Thrace that runs along the Hellespont; *also,* the Crimea
.19	Anna Livia	Amnis Livia	*see 195.04 D-E*
.21	iern	Iernê G L Ierna L	Ireland
.23	Gaud	gaudeo L gaudium L	to rejoice joy

.24	presta	praesta (*fem.*) LL	at hand, ready
.25	caratimaney	*karatimania G	head-madness, face-madness
.25	Duodecimoroon	duodecimo L	for the twelfth time
.26	Bon a ventura	Bonaventura L (1221–1274)	"Good Event": Franciscan cardinal and ascetic, called "The Seraphic Doctor"; wrote *Biblia Pauperum*, "The Poor Man's Bible"; canonized 1482
.26	liddel	Henry George Liddell (1811–1898)	co-compiler of *A Greek Lexicon*, standard Eng. G dictionary; father of Lewis Carroll's Alice
.28	Amnisty	amnis L	river
.29	angin	angina L	a suffocating disease; distress of mind
.34	moma	mômar G (mômos)	blame, reproach
.36	aues	aues, aves L	birds
208.02	tagus	Tagus L	river in Lusitania famous for golden sands; now Tajo (Tagus) in Portugal
.04	epte	*backformed from* inepte L *correctly* apte L	fitly, suitably
.05	Liviam	Liviam (*Acc.*) L	Livia, wife of Augustus; *see 196.03*
.05	Liddle ... Long	Liddell and Scott Lewis and Short	standard Eng. G dictionary standard Eng. L dictionary
.07	gaudyquiviry	gaude, qui vir ... L	rejoice, whatever man ...
.11	hydeaspects	hydat-, hydato- G	water-
.12	laudsnarers	laus L	praise
.12	cuba	Cuba L	goddess who protects the lying-down of children
.12	salmospotspeckled	salmo L	salmon
.13	galligo	gallus L	cock

		Gallus L	Gaul
		gallina L	hen
.14	rivals	rivales L	those who use the same brook *or* river, neighbors; those who share the same mistress
.17	sequansewn	Sequana L	river in Gaul: the Seine
.20	alpheubett	alpha bêta G	letters A, B
		pheu G	alas!
.25	fluve	fluvius L	river
.26	lungarhodes	lungios G	of a lynx
		langazô G	to slacken
		langôn G	a merchant
		Rhodos G	"Rose(?)": Rhodes, island and city
.29	delia	Delia L	Diana, *from her birth on the island of* Dêlos
.33	chariton	Charitôn (*Gen. pl.*) G	of the Graces
.36	koros	koros G	1. satiety, surfeit; 2. boy, lad
209.02	undification	*undificatio L	making of waves
.03	filimentation	filum L	a thread
.02–.03	undification of her filimentation	Dog-L	waving her hair
.05	meander	Maeander L	"True Mother of Men": the Meander, a river of Caria; *now the* Menderes *in Turkey*
		Maiandros G	
.12	specis	specis L	you (*sing.*) look at
		species L	sight, view; outward appearance, form; pretext
.18	arundgirond	[h]arundo L	reed, cane; fishing-rod; hobby-horse
		gyros G	ring, circle
.25	Romas and Reims	Roma L	Rome
		[Civitas] Remorum L	[State] of the *Remi* (*a people of Gaul*): Reims
		Romulus and Remus	legendary brothers; Romulus slew Remus and founded Rome, named for himself
.31	pollynooties	polynautês G	with many sailors *or* ships

.31	pyre	pyr G	fire
.32	ingenuinas	ingenuina (*fem.*) L	belonging to an *ingenuus* (free born man) or an *ingenua* (free born woman)
.35	susuria	susurrus L	a whisper
.35	Ausone	Ausone (*Voc.*) L	O Ausonus, O Italian
		Ausones G	primitive inhabitants of southern Italy; *in Roman poetry*: Italians, Latins, Romans
		Ausone voce L	*poetic*: in Latin
.35	Ausone sidulcis	Ausonia si dulcis L	Italy so pleasant!
.35	sidulcis	si dulcis L	so sweet
.36	chir	cheir G	the hand
210.09	deltoïd	*deltoeidês (*actually* deltôtos) G	in the shape of the letter *delta*; triangular
.14	O'Dea	dea L	goddess
.27	vaticanned	Vaticanus L	Vatican: hill in Rome, west of Tiber; a very inferior wine
.27	Presbys	presbys G	old man; ambassador; president
.30	Eva Mobbely	aeva mobilia L	moveable ages, moving eternities
		aevum mobile L	moving age, moveable generation
.35	apotamus	*apotamos G	not-river; unrivered, riverless
		apotamia G	larder
.36	dynamight	dynamis G	might, power
211.01	collera morbous	cholera morbus L	jaundice disease
.01	collera	collum L	neck
.01	morbous	bous G	ox, cow
.01	Cloack	cloaca L	sewer
.05	tibertine	Tiburtinus L	of *Tibur*, a town in Latium [Tivoli]
		Tiberis [flumen] L	the Tiber river
.07	penteplenty	pente G	five
.07	lubilashings	lub- L	*stem meaning* desire

.08	Lena	lena L	procuress, bawd
.08	Magdalena	magdalia G	bread-crust, dogs' meat
		magna lena L	great bawd
		Magdalênê G	from Magdala, *town on Sea of Galilee*
.08	Camilla	Camilla L	Volscian heroine in the *Aeneid*
		camilla L	a girl of unspotted character
.08	Dromilla	*Dromilla L	*fem. of* Dromo *or* Dromôn ("running"), *name of a slave in comedy*
.08	Mamilla	mamilla L	breast, nipple
.10	Dora	Dôra (*fem.*) G	gift
		Dôra (*pl.*) G	gifts
.10	Riparia	riparia (*fem.*) L	frequenting river-banks
.14	*Missa*	Missa eccl. L	"sent," "dismissed": the Mass
.14	*pro Messa*	pro messa L	for the things reaped; for harvest
.14	*Missa pro Messa*	Missa pro Messa eccl. L	Mass for the Harvest
.16	Caducus Angelus	Caducus Angelus eccl. L	Fallen Angel
.16	Rubiconstein	Rubico *or* Rubicon L	"Ruddy": river-border between Italy and Cisalpine Gaul, crossed by Caesar (49 b.c.) to start civil war
.17	revery	revera L	in fact, really, in reality
.19	Kate	kathairô G	to cleanse
.20	Hosty	hostis L	stranger, foreigner, enemy
		Hostius L	epic poet, 2d C. b.c.
		Hostius Quadra L	lecher and voyeur of Augustus's time; #*A*
.24	symposium's	symposium L	"a drinking-together":
		symposion G	banquet
.25	naves	naves L	ships
.26	Armoricus	Armoricus L	an Armorican, *person from* Armorica (ar+mor Celtic, at+mare OL, "on the sea"), *i.e., North Gaul* (*Brittany*)

.28	Conditor	conditor L	founder, author, builder
.29	peduncle	pedunculus L	louse
.33	Merreytrickx	meretrix L	harlot, prostitute
.35	Ida Ida	Ida G L	high mountain in Crete, *where Jupiter (Zeus) was reared*
.36	silvier	[Rhea] Silvia L	mother of Romulus and Remus
212.01	Niger	niger L	black
		Nigir, Niger G L	river in Africa, *probably the Niger*
.01	Festus	festus L	solemn, festive, merry
.03	Sully the Thug	Lucius Cornelius Sulla (138–78 b.c.)	Roman general and statesman; successful in wars of defense, became jealous of greater success of Gaius Marius and elevated hatred into civil war; after Marius's death became dictator and instituted a reign of terror; retired in 79 b.c. and died in thorough dissipation
.04	Nerone	Nerone (*Abl.*) L	from *or* by Nero
.04	Macpacem	pacem (*Acc.*) L	peace
.06	Selina	selinas L selinon, *pl.* selina G	kind of cabbage celery
.06	stakelum	stacula L	kind of vine
.06	Pruda	prudentia L	good sense, intelligence, discretion
.07	Katty	kathairô G	to cleanse
.09	Melissa	Melissa G	"Bee": name of a nymph who invented beekeeping
.09	Flora	Flora L	goddess of flowers
.09	Fauna	Fauna L	sister of *Faunus*, god of agriculture, shepherds and oracles; she was also called *Bona Dea* ("Good Goddess")
.10	Penelope	Pênelopeia G	"Webster": faithful wife of Odysseus

.10	Lezba	Lesbia G L	"[woman] of *Lesbos* [home of school of erotic poetry]": Catullus's name for his mistress (probably Clodia)
.11	Leytha	Lêthaia G Lethaea L	"Causing Forgetfulness": woman who was turned into stone because of her pride
.11	Roxana	Rhôxanê	wife of Alexander the Great
.12	Una	una L	in one and the same place
		una (*fem.*) L	one
.12	Bina	bina L	two at a time, a pair
.12	Laterza	latericia (*fem.*) L	made of bricks
		tertia L	third
.12	Trina	trina L	three each; triple
.12	Philomena	Philomênê G	moon-lover
.21	Hibernonian	hiberno L	to pass the winter
		hibernus L	winter
		Hibernia L	Ireland
.21–.22	Hibernonian market	Nonae L	Nones: the 5th of every month except March, May, July and October, when it was the 7th; marketdays were forbidden to fall on the Nones because of royalist associations with the day
.32	narcissus	Narcissus L Narkissos G	youth who fell in love with his own reflection; wasted away into the flower
213.04	suda	suda- L	sweat-
		sudor L	sweat, perspiration
		Suidas	Byzantine lexicon and encyclopedia compiled c.a.d. 975
.07	Aimihi!	ai mihi L	alas to me! woe is me!
.19	Concepta	Concepta (*fem.*) L	conceived

.19	de Send-us-	descensus L	fallen down, having come down, being descended
.20	vert	verto L	to turn, to turn around; to take to
.30	Mutter	Muta L	"Silent": talkative nymph, Lara (*see* *228.21, 618.31*) had her tongue torn out, became Muta (*see* *609.24 & sqq.*)
.30	Deataceas	Dea taceas L	Goddess, be silent
		Dea Tacita L	Goddess *Tacita*, personification of silence, identified with Muta
.31	gloria	gloria L	fame, renown, honor
.32	Allalivial	alla G	but
		Livia L	1. Liffey; 2. Augustus's wife; #*A*
.32	allalluvial	*alluvialis L	washed to shore; land washed to shore by flowing of water
.33	alla	alla G	but
214.01	histereve	hesternus L	yesterday's
		hister Etr. histrio L	stage-player, actor
		Hister L Istros G	the lower Danube
.06	Orara por Orbe	ora pro orbe L	pray for the world
		ara L	altar
.06	Animas	animas (*Acc. pl.*) L	souls, lives
.07	umbas	umbra L	shade, shadow
		umbo L	knob; shield; elbow
.08	spond	spondeo L	to promise solemnly, to pledge
		spendô G	to pour out wine for the gods, to vow
		spondai G	league, alliance
.10	lethest	Lêthê G L	"Forgetfulness": river from which Shades drink to forget the past
.22	creakorheuman	*Graecoroman- us L	Greek-Roman

		rheuma G	a flowing, stream, current
.28	lavandier	lavandaria L	things to be washed; laundry
.30	Scamander	Scamander L	river near Troy: Little
		Skamandros G	Menderes, Turkey
.31	Icis	icis L	you strike; you have struck
		Isis	Egyptian goddess; #A
.34	Tarpey	Tarpeius (masc.)	Roman proper name
		Tarpeia (fem.) L	
		mons Tarpeius	Tarpeian Rock, from
		L	which criminals were hurled to death
215.01	pharphar	pharos G	island, lighthouse; #A
.12	Anna Livia	Amnis Livia L	River Liffey
.12	Livia	Livia L	"Bluish": Liffey; wife of Augustus #A
.19	Bifur	bi- L	two-
		fur L	thief
		*bifur L	twice-thief, double thief
.20	Etrurian	*Etrurianus L	Etruscan
.23	Ordovico	Ordovices L	a people of Roman Britain (N. Wales)
.23	viricordo	*viricorde L	with a manly heart
.24	Livia	Livia L	see 215.12 above
.24	Plurabelle's	plura- L	many-
		pleura G	rib
		*plorabilis L	lamentable, weepable
.25	howmulty	part trans.	how many: quam multi
		quam multi =	for quot is schoolboy
		quot L	redundant inelegancy
.25	howmulty plurators	quam multi [quot]	how many multipliers
		*pluratores L	
		quam multi	how many lamenters
		[quot]	
		ploratores L	
.27	Hircus Civis	hircus civis	the goat citizen of
	Eblanensis	Eblanensis L	Dublin
.35	Livia's	Livia L	see 215.12 above
216.03–	Telmetale of	alla ti ê moi	But why all this about
.04	stem or stone	tauta peri dryn	tree or stone?
		ê peri petrên? G	—Hesiod, Theogony 35
		(Hes. Theog.	(proverb meaning "why
		35)	enlarge on irrelevancies?")

219.05	Somndoze	somnus L	sleep
		somnium L	dream
.09	Genesius	Genesios G	"Creator": *epithet of* Poseidon
		Genesius, Saint L	patron saint of actors
.09	Archimimius	archimimos G	chief comedian, chief actor
.11	Murias	muria L	brine, pickle
.13	Caesar-in-chief	Caesar L	"Hairy" or "Bluish"; cognomen in gens *Julia*; # *A*
.14	Adelphi	adelphoi (*pl.*) G	brothers
.14	Hyrcan	Hyrcanus	"From Hyrcania [*country on Caspian Sea*]": name of two Jewish high priests:
		John Hyrcanus (135–104 b.c.)	son of Simon Maccabeus
		Hyrcanus II (*d.* 30 b.c.)	grandson of John; *struggled for power with his brother* Aristobulus *whom he poisoned; his ears were cut off by A's son, and he was executed by Herod*
.14	Haristobulus	Aristobulus L Aristoboulos G	"Best in Council": 1) Alexandrian Jew, peripatetic philosopher (*fl.* 170 b.c.); 2) son of John Hyrcanus, *ruled as king of Judaea*; 3) brother of Hyrcanus II, *by whom he was poisoned*
.17	–ellene–	[H]ellênê G	Greek
.17	–teuto–	Teutoni L	a people of Germany
.18	cald us	caldus L	warm, hot
220.03	FLORAS	Flora L	goddess of flowers
.07	Butys	boutis G	kind of bowl *or* vase
		boutyron G butyrum L	butter
		buttos G	female pudenda
.11	sanguine	sanguis L	blood

		sanguineus L	bloody
.14	geminally	geminus L	a twin
		gemini L	twins
.15	adumbrace	adumbro L	to cast a shadow on; to shade; to outline
		adumbratio L	a sketch or draft
		*imbracchio L	to take into the arms, to embrace
.20	mandamus	mandamus L	we command; writ from a higher to a lower court requiring a specific action to be taken
.21	hendrud	hen G	one
.30	proconverted	*proconversus L	*for-with-turned
		conversus L	turned with, converted
.32	membrance	membra L	members, limbs, parts of the body
.32	umbrance	umbra L	shade, shadow
.33	quemdam	quemadmodum L	in what manner
		quondam L	at one time, formerly
.34	Poopinheavin	#P/K Split	Coopinheavin: Copenhagen
221.02	Patricius	patricius L	member of the Roman nobility; Patrick
.02	annuary	*annuarium L modeled on	yearly allowance of food or pay; a yearbook [from annus, "year"]
		diarium L	daily allowance of food or pay; a daybook, diary [from dies, "day"]
.04	locomotive	loco moti [motivi] L	moved from [their] place
.12	KATE	kathairô G	to cleanse
.13	d'Elta	delta G	letter D; rivermouth, female pudenda
.23	Incubone	incubus L	nightmare
.27	R.I.C.	#P/K Split: R[equiescat] I[n] P[ace] L	R.I.P.: May he/she rest in peace
.31	Heteroditheroe's	hetero- G	one or the other of two; other-, different-
		heterodidaktos G	taught by another

.32	Phenecian	Phoenicius L	from Phoenice, *a coastal country of Syria*
.32	Sourdanian	Sardinianus L	Sardinian, from the
		Sardonios G	island Sardinia
		sordes L	dirt, filth
		sardanios G	bitter, scornful
222.02	Melodiotiosities	melôdeô G	to chant, to sing
		otiosus L	at leisure, idle
.05	exodus	exodos G	a going out; military expedition; way out
.07	ambiamphions	ambi- L	around-, round about-
		amphi- G	on both sides
		Amphiôn G	son of Antiope by Zeus; king of Thebes; *renowned for his music by which he magically built the walls*
.07	Annapolis	polis G	city
.12	Polymop	polymorphos G	multiform, manifold; versatile; irregular
.13	Undiform	undi, unde L	from which place, whence
.18	Neid	Nêïth G L	Egyptian name for Pallas/ Minerva
		Naïas G L	Naiad, water-nymph
.23	defendy nous	defende nos L	defend us
.26	Punct	punctum L	a point, a period (*in writing*)
.26	sputing	sputo L	to spit
.26	tussing	tussio L	to cough
.26	anisine	anison G	anise
		anisum L	
		sine L	without
.27	brividies	brevis dies L	[our] brief day: human life
.32	Aminxt	minxi L	I have urinated
.36	Sammy, call on	semi- L	half-
223.01		kôlon G	member, limb, part of a verse
.02	Arck	arx L	citadel
		arcus L	bow, rainbow; arch
		arch- G	chief-
.03	agnols	agnus L	lamb
		agnellus L	lambkin
.04	signics	signum L	mark, token, sign, indication

.04	helpabit	alphabêtos G	alphabet
.07	Pervinca	pervinca L	the periwinkle (flower)
.08	melmelode	mel L meli G	honey
		melôdia G	singing; song; music
.19	evangelion	euaggelion =	reward of good tidings
		euangelion G	(*given to the messenger*); good news; the gospel
.21	Et	et L	and, even
.25	prehend	prehendo L	to lay hold of, to grasp, to snatch
.28	kunning	cunnus L	cunt
.28	O theoperil	ho theos G	the god; God
		theopisros G	faithful to God
.30–.31	ne . . . ne	ne L	not, that not
.35	Item	item L	just so, in like manner; likewise, also
.36	Utem	ut L	that, so that
		utinam L	if only! would that!
224.01	Otem	[h]otan G	whenever
		[h]ote G	when, now and then
		[h]oti G	that
		otium L	leisure, repose
.03	Etem	et L	and, even
		etenim L	for, because that, since
		etiam L	and also, and furthermore, likewise, besides
.07	Atem	at L	moreover, yet, and
		atar G	but, nevertheless
.10	deplurable	deplorabilis L	weepable, lamentable
		depluo L	to rain down
		pluralis L	belonging *or* relating to more than one
.11	inhebited	hebeo L	to be blunt; to be dull, torpid
		*inhebeo L	to lounge about in
.14	noces	noceo L	to harm, to hurt
		noces L	you (*sing.*) harm
		nuces L	nuts
.14	interregnation	interregnum L	1. time between king's death and election of another; 2. time between departure of consuls and election of new consuls

.17	subnesciousness	sub- L	under-, below-, beneath-
		nescientia L	the state of not knowing
		*subnescientia L for	below not-knowing
		*subconscientia L	below knowing-with; below consciousness
.19	tynpan	tympanum L	tambourine, used in
		tympanon G	worship of Kybele, the Great Mother
.23	florileague	florilegium L	collection of flowers, bouquet; anthology
.23	consociately	*consociate L	unitedly, harmoniously
.28	Quanty	quantus; quanti (*masc. pl.*) L	how great
.28	bellas	bella L	1. wars; 2. (*fem. sing.*) pretty
.28	Quanty ... bellas	quanta bella L	1. such great wars; 2. how very nice
.36	pricoxity	praecox L	prematurely ripe, precocious
225.05	ulstramarines	ultramarinus L	that is beyond the sea
.06	Ni	ni L	not, that not; if not
.32	mater	mater L	mother
.34	Alabye	alibi L	elsewhere, somewhere else
226.06	Hey, lass	Hellas G	Greece
.06	pooripathete	peripathêsis G	intensity of emotion
		peripatos G	walkway; discussion; lecture; Aristotle's school
.07	symperise	symperaioô G	to conclude together with
		symperaô G	to cross together
		symperieimi G	to go round with
.15	Minuscoline's	minusculus L	rather less, rather small
.17	dulcydamble	dulcis L	sweet
		ambulo L	to go about, to walk
		*dulcitambulo L	to walk about sweetly, to go for a sweet walk
.27	nuptious	nuptia L	wedding, nuptials
.35	before the Luvium	*part trans.* antediluvium L	before the flood
.36	Eons	aiôn G	age, lifetime

.36–.01	Dies of Eirae	Dies Irae L	Day of Wrath: Judgment Day—*title of a medieval hymn*
227.05	casuaway	casus L	a falling down, a fall
.10	rickissime	rectissime L	most righteously, most virtuously
.16	papavere's	papaver L	the poppy
.18	ancelle's	ancilla L	maid servant
.21	virid	viridis L	green
.30	plexus	plexus L	involved, intricate, ambiguous; a braid
.32	excremuncted	excrementum L	refuse, excrement
		mungo L	to blow the nose
		munctum (*pp.*) L	nose-blown, wiped away
.35	vestimentivorous	*vestimentivorus L	garment-eating, clothes-eater
.36	chlamydophagian	chlamydophagos G	cloak-eater
.36	imbretellated	imber L	rain, rainstorm
		imbrex L	a gutter-tile; gutter; mode of applauding with hollowed hands
228.01	Machonochie	machomai G	to fight, to fight against
.03	mungy	mungo L	to blow the nose
.07	petriote's	*petriotês G	rock-dweller
.07	absolation	absolutio L	an absolving, acquittal; completion, perfection
		*solatio L	a comforting, solace
		ab L	away from
		*absolatio L *modeled on*	a comforting away from
		consolatio L	a comforting with
.10	crookolevante	crucilevante L	cross-raising
.11	coriolano	Gaius Marcius Coriolanus (early 5th C b.c.)	Roman patrician, surnamed for destroying Koriola, Volscian town; *in political exile led Volsci against Rome but dissuaded by his mother; a Shakespeare hero*
.12	Brassolis	brassica L	cabbage
		solis (*Gen.*) L	the sun's, of the sun

.14	schlucefinis	*lucefinis L	light-limit, light-end; death of light
.15	eon	aiôn G	an age, lifetime
.15	Era	era L	mistress of a house, lady
		aera LL	"brasses" [see 228.12]: number basic to a reckoning; point in time from which time is measured
.16	Dora	Dôra G	Gifts
.19	Pencylmania	pensilis L	hanging, pendent
		kyla G	the parts about the eyes
		mania G	madness
.19	Armerica	Armorica L	[ar mor Celt., at mare OL, "at the sea"]: northern provinces of Gaul; Brittany
.20	Gloria	gloria L	fame, renown, honor
.20	meteoromancy	*meteôromant- eia G	divination by things in the air
.21	linguified	*linguifactus L	tongue-made, made by the tongue
.21	laracor	Lara L	talkative nymph, her tongue torn out she became Muta (see 213.30, etc.)
		cor L	the heart
.22	Turricum	*turricum L	with a tower, in company with a tower
.24	Roder	rodo L	to gnaw
.25	Libera, nostalgia	libera nos L	free us
		algia G	a state of pain
.25–.26	Beate Laurentie O'Tuli, Euro pra nobis	Beate Laurentie O'Tulie ora pro nobis L	Blessed Laurence O'Toole, pray for us
.26	Euro	eurus, euro- G L	the southeast wind
.26	Euro pra	Europa L Eurôpê G	1. sister of Cadmus, carried to Crete by Zeus in form of a bull 2. the continent of Europe, named for Eurôpê
.28	pronaose	pronaos G	"fore-temple": porch or vestibule of a temple

.28	Fuisfinister	fuit L	he [she, it] has been
		fuisti L	you (*sing.*) have been
		finis L	limit, border, end
		finis terrae L	the extremity of the dry land
		fuit finis terrae L	it was the end of the land
		fenestra L	a window
.33	epistol	epistolê G	message, written communication, letter
.34	Cernilius	cerno L	to separate, to distinguish, to see
		Cornelius L	"Horned [?]": name of a Roman gens celebrated as embracing the most distinguished Romans
		Cornelius	Roman centurion at Caesarea, converted by St. Peter; the first Gentile Christian
.34	prepositus	praepositus L	prefect, commander
.34	Toumaria	tomaria (*pl.*) G	snippets: tracts, booklets
		tu Maria L	thou Mary
		Tomis G L	town on the Black Sea to which Ovid was exiled (*now Constantsa, Romania*)
.35	Anteach	Antiocheia G	"Belonging to Antiochos" Antioch, capital of Seleucid Syria, *named by Seleucus, one of Alexander's generals, after his own father*
.35	Salvo	Salve L	Hail! Good health!
.36	ebribadies	ebrio LL	to make drunk
229.07	S.P.Q.R.ish	S[enatus] P[opulus]q[ue] R[omanus] L	the Roman Senate and People
.10	malodi	malus L	bad, evil, wicked
		odi L	I hate
.10	lalage	lalagê G	prattle
		Lalagê	name of a girl mentioned by Horace in several poems

.13	Ukalepe	Eukalyptos G	"Well-hidden": Eucalyptus tree
		Kalypsô G	"She that conceals": *nymph with whom Odysseus spent several years, and who bore him a son*
		*Eukalypsô G	"She that conceals well"
		Kalpê G	"Pitcher": Gibraltar, *identified by some as Kalypsô's home*
		*Eukalpê G	"Fine pitcher"
.13	Loathers' leave	Lôtophagoi G	"Lotus-eaters": fabled African people famed for hospitality; *visited by Odysseus, whose men were loath to leave*
		lôtos G	the edible nettle-tree *Celtis australis*
.13	Had Days	Hadês G	"Unseen": lord of the lower world, *which Odysseus visited*
.13	Nemo	Nemo L *trans.* Outis G	No one: *name Odysseus called himself to the Cyclops*
.13	Nemo in Patria	Nemo in patria L	No one in the fatherland: *i.e.,* Odysseus in the land of Aiolos (*god of winds*), father of twelve. *Aiolos gave Odysseus a bag of winds that took him safely to Ithaca, his own fatherland, but his crew opened the bag and storms swept them away again*
.13–.14	The Luncher Out	Laistrygones G Laestrygones L	a savage people in southern Italy and Sicily, fabled to have been cannibals; *encountered by Odysseus*

.14	Skilly and Carubdish	Skylla G Scylla L	[*skylax* G, "puppy"; *skylaô* G, "to plunder"]: rock between Sicily and Italy, personified as a sea-monster; *opposite to Charybdis*
		Charybdis G L	[*charypos* G "fierce"]: dangerous whirlpool between Sicily and Italy, opposite to Skylla; personified as a monster; *both encountered by Odysseus*
.14	A Wondering Wreck	Planktai petrai G	Wandering [*perhaps* "Clashing"] Rocks: rocks near Skylla and Charybdis [*the volcanic islands of Lipari*] *that Odysseus is cautioned against, and avoids*
.14–.15	From the Mermaids' Tavern	Seirênes G Sirenes L	[*seira* G, "rape"; *seiroô* G, "to drain dry"]: birds with virgins' faces, *dwelt on the south coast of Italy, with their sweet voices enticed passing mariners ashore and killed them; passed safely by Odysseus*
.15	Bullyfamous	Polyphêmos G	"Much spoken of," "Famous": *name of Cyclops encountered by Odysseus*
.15	Naughtsycalves	Nausikaa G Nausicaa L	"Ship-burner [?]": daughter of Alkinous king of Phaiakia, *encountered bathing by Odysseus*
.15	Mother of Misery	*trans.* Mater Misericordiae	Mother of Mercy: *name of a Dublin hospital, not the one where Bloom endured Mrs. Purefoy's* accouchement

		mater misera L	wretched mother: *Mrs. Purefoy*
.16	Walpurgas Nackt	purgatio L	a cleansing, purging
.20	a great big oh	*trans.* ômega, ô mega G	"great O": letter Ô
.21	megafundum	mega G	great, big
		fundus L	a bottom
		*megafundus G + L	big-bottom
.23–.24	delt her	delta G	letter D; female pudenda
.24	microchasm	mikro- G	small, little
		chasma G	gulf, gaping mouth, wide opening
.26	thea	thea G	goddess
.26	jused	jus L	right, duty, law, justice
.27	jused	jus L	see 229.26F
.31	Caxton and Pollock	Castor L Kastôr G	"Beaver"
		Pollux L	"Offering"
		Polydeukês G	"Very sweet": twin brothers, sons of Leda, now the constellation Gemini
.31	moraculous	mora L	a delay
.35	ottorly	Marcus Salvius Otho (died a.d. 69)	emperor a.d. 69; previously a supporter of Nero, who took his wife from him; committed suicide after defeat by Vitellius. A byword for weakness of character
230.01	yoeureeke	heurêka G	I have found; I have it!: *said by Archimedes when he discovered how to determine specific gravity*
.01	spectrescope	spectro-skopos L + G	apparition-watcher, appearance-watcher
.02	ambothed	ambo L	both
.05	dometry	domus L dôma G	home, house
		domo L	to tame
		*dômametrêsis G	house-measuring

.06	domum	domum (*Acc.*) L	home, house
.07	ark	arx L	citadel
		arcus L	bow, rainbow; arch
.07	finis orbe	finis orbis L	the end of the earth
.08		finis orbe L	a limit by means of a circle
.09	cecialism	Caecilius L	"Blind": name of a Roman gens
		Caecilia L (died a.d. 230)	woman of the gens Caecilia: saint, convert and martyr; patroness of [church] music
.11	sorrors	soror L	sister
.13	trist	tristis L	sad, sorrowful
.13	Parisise	parisos G	evenly balanced
		Paris	lover of Helen, to whom she was granted by Aphrodite
		paradysis G	creeping in beside
		paradeisos G	enclosed park *or* pleasure-garden
.14	mutuurity	mutuus L	borrowed, lent
.15	Neblonovi's	nebula L	mist, fog, cloud
		nebulo L	a worthless rascal
		nebulonis novi (*Gen.*)	a new scoundrel's
		novi L	I have known
		nebulonem novi L	I have known the scoundrel
.16	Nivonovio	niv- L	snow-
		nivosus L	snowy
		Nivomagus *or* Noviomagus	city on the Rhine in Gallia Belgica; *now* Nijmegen *or* Neumagen
.16	Nuby	nubes L	a cloud
		nubo L	to cover, to veil, to be married
.16	ennoviacion	Novia (*fem.*) L	"Newcomer": fem. name
		ennea G novem L	nine
.16	Occitantitempoli	occidens L	1. falling, perishing, going down 2. where the sun sets: the west
		tanti L	so much, of such value, worth as much as

		templi (*Gen.*) L	of a temple
		tempori [#*R/L*	at the right time,
		Interchange] L	timely, seasonably
		polis G	city
.20	Ipsey Secumbe	ipse secum L	himself with himself
.21	M	san G	archaic letter S
		M L	1,000
.22	herslF	# *Digamma*	
.21–.22	M ... herslF	M[onumentum]	made [this]
		F[ecit] L	monument—*ascriptive inscription on Roman tombs, etc.*
.28	Sators	sator L	sower, planter, begetter; *epithet of both* Jupiter *and* Janus
.29	nutritius	nutritius L	1. that suckles, that nurses 2. a tutor
.29	genitricksling	genetrix L	a mother, she that produces
.29	Avus	avus L	grandfather
.30	Avia	avia L	grandmother
.30	Veloutypads	veluti L	even as, just as, like as
		vel L	or else, what you will
		aut L	or, either
		outi G	nothing
.30–.31	a vuncular	avunculus L	maternal uncle
.31	Nurus	nurus L	daughter-in-law
.31	Noverca	noverca L	stepmother
.31	nepotists	nepos L	grandson; nephew
.32	circumpictified	circumpictus L	painted around
		*circumpictifact-us L	made painted around
.32	sobrine	sobrinus (*masc.*) sobrina (*fem.*) L	maternal cousin
.32	census	census L	1. taxed, rated; 2. a census
		sensus L	the power of perceiving, sensation, sense
.32	patriss	patris G	fatherland
		patris (*Gen.*) L	father's
.33	glos	glos L	sister-in-law
.33	germane	germanus L	full brother
		germana L	full sister
		germane L	faithfully, truly

.33	socerine	socer L	father-in-law
.34	vitricus	vitricus L	stepfather
		vitreus L	of glass, glassy
.34	patruuts	patruus L	paternal uncle
.34	archimade	Archimêdês G	"Chief-in-Counsel":
		(287–212 b.c.)	mathematician, discoverer of several mechanical principles, including that of the lever; *see 230.01*
.34	levirs	levir L	husband's brother, brother-in-law
.34	ekonome	oikoumenê G	the inhabited world
		oikonomos G	steward, manager
231.07	*verdigrassy*	viridis L	green
		ver L	the spring
.13	freytherem	fratrem (*Acc.*) L	a brother
.16	sanguish	sanguis L	blood
.16	disconvulsing	*disconvello L	to wrench in two
.18	Sillayass	Tiberius Catius Silius Italicus (a.d. 26-101)	Roman epic poet; starved himself to death to end an incurable disease
.18	Croesus	Croesus L	king of Lydia famous
		Kroisos G (*fl.* 560–546 b.c.)	for his wealth
.18	Nunn	nun G	now
.21	Pugases	puga L pygê G	the rump, buttocks
		Pêgasos G	winged horse
		Pegasus L	
.23	Jove	Jovis-pater L	"Shining-father": etymology of Jupiter, chief god of the Romans
.23	Chronides	Chronidês G *by [ancient] error for*	son of *Chronos* ("Time")
		Kronidês G	son of Kronos: patronymic of Zeus
		Kronos G	a god, *identified with Saturn; father of Zeus*
.28	Malthos	maltho L	to cement, to varnish
		malthôn G	a weakling
		maltha G	mixture of wax and pitch *for caulking ships; see 232.01*

.28	Moramor	mora L	a delay
.30	aers	aêr G	mist, air
		aes (*Nom.*), aeris (*Gen.*) L	copper, bronze; money
.30	poligone	polygonia G	fecundity
		polygonos G	producing much offspring
		polygônon G	many-sided figure
.32	locofoco	locus L	place, spot
		focus L	fireplace, hearth, household
.34	readyos	radius L	spoke of a wheel, staff, rod
232.01	tarpitch	*trans.* maltha G	mixture of wax and pitch; *see 231.28*
.02	chromitis	chrôma G	1. skin; 2. color
		*chrômitis	inflammation of the skin; inflammation of color
.03	Carbo	carbo L	coal, charcoal
		Carbo L	"Coal": Roman surname in the gens Papiria
.03	inflammabilis	inflammabilis L	that may be set on fire
.03	comburenda	comburenda (*neut. pl.*) L	things requiring to be burned
		comburenda (*fem. sing.*) L	woman requiring to be burned
.07	Sousymoust	zôsimos G	viable, likely to survive
		Zosimus	pope 417–418
.08	inculmination	inculminatio L	a placing on the highest point
.11	a stell	stella L	a star
.12	dove astarted	Astartê G L	Syro-Phoenician goddess, identified with Venus; *hence with Venus's dove*
.15	Tot	tot L	so many
.24	mavrone	mavros MG [a]mauros G	dark
.32	glaciator	glacies L	ice
		*glaciator L	ice-man, icer, one who freezes
		gladiator L	swordsman, fighter in the public games

.32	Atlangthis	Atlantis G L	"[island] of Atlas": large island in Atlantic fabled by Plato to have sunk into the Ocean
233.05	Angelinas	*angelina L *from*	little angel
		aggelos = angelos G	messenger
.13	can for dog	canis L	dog
.16	sinistrant	sinistra L	the left hand
		*sinistrans L	lefthanding
.17	server of servants	*trans.* servus servorum [Christi] L	slave of the slaves [of Christ]: title of the popes
.17	rex of regums	rex regum L	king of kings
.25	per causes nunsibellies	per causas nuntiatas belli L	through the declared causes of the war
.34	melanmoon	melas G	black
		melanos G	black pigment
.36	Gelagala	gelo L	to freeze
		gala G	milk
		*gelagala L + G	icecream (?)
.36	nausy is	naus G navis, nauis L	a ship
		nausia G L	seasickness
234.01	Hovobovo	ovum L	egg
		ab ovo L	from the egg; from the beginning; *see 154.35*
		ovis L	sheep
		bovis OL	ox, bull, cow
.02	griposly	griphos G	fishing-basket; enigma, riddle; anything dark and obscure
.03	tristiast	tristis L	sad, mournful
.08	Candidatus	candidatus L	clothed in white; a candidate for office
.08	viridosus	viridis L	green
		*viridosus L	greened, clothed in green
.08	aurilucens	*aurilucens L	ear-shining
		*aurolucens L	gold-shining, shining goldly
.08	Candidatus, viridosus, aurilucens	viridis, candidus, aurosus L	green, white, golden: *colors of the Irish national flag*

.08	sinelab	sine labore L	without effort, without work
.10	mookst	muxa G	snot
.11	anterevolitionary	*anterevolitiona-rius L	one who is before willing again
.11	tonsor's	tonsor L	a barber
.12	haggiography	hagiographia G	holy-writing, writing about holy things, writing saints' lives
.12	duotrigesumy	triginta duo L	thirty-two
		tricesimus secundus L	thirty-second
		duodetriginta L	twenty-eight
.13	soptimost	optimus L	best
.13	sign osure	kynos oura G	dog's tail: the constellation *Ursa Minor*
.15	zvestals	vestalis L	priestess of Vesta, goddess of flocks and of the hearth
.19	lusspillerindernees	lussa G	rage, fury
.19	ripidarapidarpad	ripa L	river bank
		riparius L	frequenting riverbanks
		rapidus L	seizing, tearing away; hurrying, swift
.20	prinkips	princeps L	first, first man, first member of the Senate; prince
.20	neuchoristic	eucharistikos G	of gratitude
		*euchoros G	good dance
		naus G	ship
		neura G	cord, string
		neuron G	sinew, tendon, nerve
.21	allauding	allaudo L	to extol, to praise much
.30	liber	liber L	1. free, unlimited; 2. a child; 3. old Italian deity of planting and fructification; 4. a book
.31	arrahbeejee	alpha, bêta, gamma G	letters A, B, G: *first 3 of the G alphabet*
.35	-cums	-cum L	with, in company with
.35	adolphted ... Adelphus	adelphos G	brother
.36	hopops	epops G	the hoopoe (*bird*): major character in Aristophanes' *The Birds*

235.01	Nabis	Nabis G (*fl.* 200 b.c.)	usurping king of Sparta; assassinated in a coup d'état
.02	prostitating	prostituo L	to place before, to expose publicly, to offer for sale, to prostitute
		prostratio L	an overthrowing, a subverting
.05	holiodrops	hêliotropion G	sun-dial; flower that turns to the sun
.09	Xanthos! Xanthos! Xanthos!	Xanthos G	"Tawny": name the gods call Scamander, river of Troy; *see 214.30*
		sanctus L	sacred, inviolable, holy
.10	fuitefuite	fuit L	he [she, it] has been
.17	edcedras	et cetera L	and the rest
		cedrus L	the cedar, juniper-tree
.17	hypsometers	*hypsometron G	a height-measurer
.18	arthataxis	arthron G	joint
		*orthotaxis G	correct order
.19	Larix	larix G L	the larch-tree
.21	palypeachum	poly- G	much, many
		palai- G	old
.26	Fyat-Fyat	fiat L	let there be
.27	autokinaton	*autokinêton G	self-moving thing
.28	antries	antron G	cave, grotto; closet
		antrum L	
.30	-nomers	nomen L	name
236.01	chloes	Chloê G	"Green corn": girl mentioned by Horace in *Odes* III. 9
.02	glycering	Glycera L *for* Glykera G	"Sweet" girl mentioned by Horace in three odes
.02	lydialight	Lydia G L	country in Asia Minor; girl mentioned by Horace in *Odes* III. 9
.02	cynarettes	kynara G	artichoke
		kynarion G	little puppy
		Cinara, Cynara	girl mentioned by Horace in his *Ode to Venus* (*Odes* IV .1)
.03	Monade	monas G	the number one, a unity, a monad

.08	Niomon	Nemo L *for*	Nobody: *alias*
		Outis G	Odysseus; #*A*
		nimium L	too much
.09	Momor's	mors L	death
		mômos G	blame, disgrace
.17	Anneliuia	Amnis Livia L	River Liffey, bluish river, etc.
		u = v L	
.19	Roamaloose and Remus	Romulus and Remus	legendary twins, founded Rome; *Romulus killed Remus*; *Rome named for Romulus*
.19	pavanos	pava L	peahen
		pavo, pavus L	peacock
		pavoninus L	of *or* belonging to a peacock
.30	taeorns	aiôn G	age, lifetime
.30	obcecity	*obcaecitas L	blindness *about something*
.31	teapucs	# *P/K Split*	teacups
		epocha LL	stoppage; pause;
		epochê G	position; fixed point in time
.31	momie	mômos G	blame, disgrace
		Mômos G	personification of Disgrace
.33	stylled	stilus, stylus L	pen, literary style
.33	nattes	nates L	buttocks
.34	tot	tot L	so many
.35	understamen	stamen L	warp (*in a loom*); thread, thread of life
237.01	heliolatry	hêliolatreia G	sun-worship
.02	calyzettes	kalyx G	seed-pod; cup *of a flower*
		kalykes (*pl. of* kalyx) G	women's ornaments (*precise kind unknown*; *perhaps earrings*)
.03	muscalone	musca L	a fly
.12	O coelicola, thee salutamt	O coelicola te salutamus/salutant	O inhabitant of heaven we/they salute thee
.25	puerity	pueritia L	boyhood, childhood; innocence
.29	Aruc-Ituc	*reversed* cuticura L	skin-care

.30	Demani	demano L	to flow down, to descend
.36	philomelas	philomêlos G Philomêla L Philomêlê G	fond of apples *or* fruit "Apple-lover": girl violated by her brother-in-law, Tereus, and changed into a nightingale; the nightingale (*or else*, the swallow)
238.02	posthastem	*post hastam L	after a spear, after a lance
.04	of	Gen. L	the case of complement, expresses the relationship of *of* in Eng.
.04	on	Acc. L	the case (*inter alia*) of the object affected, expressing the relationship of *on* in Eng.
.04	to and for	Dat. L	the case of the indirect object, expresses the relationship *to* or *for* in Eng.
.04	by and with, from	Abl. L	the adverbial case, expresses the relationship of *by*, *with*, *from* in Eng.
.09	sensitivas	sensitivitas ML *sensitiva (*fem.*) ML	sensitivity one who is sensitive
.20	myriadth	myrias G	ten thousand
.21	May he colp, may he colp her, may he mixandmass colp her	Mea culpa, mea culpa, mea maxima culpa L	Through my fault, through my fault, through my very great fault—*line from* Confiteor (*prayer of confession*)
.22	mus	mus L	mouse
.23	pervergined	*pervergo L *pervirgo L pervinca L	to bend thoroughly to beat thoroughly with rods periwinkle (flower)

.24	conversa	conversa (*fem.*) L	1. turned around, returned; a woman who is turned around *or* who has returned; 2. swept away; a woman who has been brushed away
.25	Vellentam	vello L	to pluck, pull out
		vellens L	plucking, pulling out
		vel L	or else, take your choice, what you will
		tam L	so, so much, as
.31	Sur Soord	surdus L	deaf
.32	iris	Iris G L	goddess of the rainbow; the rainbow
.33	Caro caressimus	caro carissimus L	dearest flesh, most precious body
.34	mellisponds	*mellispondeo L	to honey-swear, to honey-promise, to honey-pledge
		Hellêspontos G	Sea of Hellê (*who was drowned in it*): modern *Dardanelles* (*Leander also drowned here while swimming to his love, Hero: see 135.17*)
.35	Teomeo	timeo L	I fear, I am afraid
		Teôs G	birthplace of the poet Anacreon; *see 135.06, 279.Fl/32, 559.10*
		theos G	god
		Deo meo L	by my God
239.03	milliems	mille L	a thousand
.03	centiments	centum L	a hundred
.06	questuan	questus L	a complaint
.07	lutean	luteus L	1. yellow; 2. muddy
.09	Upsome cauda	sursum corda L	hearts upward: lift up [your] hearts (*adjuration to congregation by priest during Mass*)
		sursum cauda L	tail up!
.14–.15	Vania, Vania Vaniorum, Domne Vanias	vanitas L	emptiness, nothingness
		Vanitas, vanitas vanitatum,	Vanity, vanity of vanities, all [is] vanity

		omne vanitas L	(*Ecclesiastes 1:2*)
		Domine L	O Lord
.18	Klitty	kleitoris G	clitoris
.24	Connie	cunnus L	cunt
.24	Carminia	carmina L	songs, poems
.27	gyrogyrorondo	gyro L	to turn around in a circle
		roro L	to drop dew
		rotundus L	circular, round
.30	wherebus	Erebus L	god of darkness; the lower world
.33	bediabbled	diabolos G	slanderer, enemy; devil
		diabolus L	devil
.34	arimaining	Areimanios G	G version of *angrô mainyus* [Ahriman], the Avestan Spirit of Evil
.34	lucisphere	lucis (*Gen.*) L	of light
		sphaira G	ball, globe, sphere
		*lucisphaira L + G	globe of light, ball of light [*to which Areimanios is opposed*]
.36	rorosily	roro L	to drop dew, to bedew
240.04	ay he	ah L ai G	alas
.06	Cisamis	cis L	on this side
		sisamum L	sesame, *an oily plant*
		sêsamon G	
.06	Examen	examen L	a swarm, multitude; a consideration *or* examination
.08	tumescinquinance	tumescens L	swelling up
		inquinans L	befouling, staining, defiling
.10	Trinitatis	Trinitatis (*Gen.*) L	of the Trinity
.11	peccat	peccat L	he [she, it] offends, sins
.11	pent	pente G	five
.11	Hymserf	#L/R Interchange	Himself
.13	redecant	*redicans L	reconsecrating
		redicens L	repeating
		decanus L	leader of ten; a dean
		recantans L	re-echoing; singing again; charming away by singing; recanting
.13	allbigenesis	bi- L	two-, twice-

		genesis G	origin, coming into being, generation nativity
		*bigenesis L + G	twice-birth
.13	henesies	hen G	one
.14	proforhim	pro- L	for-
		pro forma L	for form, for the sake of form
.15	eggscumuddher	ex L	out of
		cum L	with
		excommunico L	to put out of the community
.16	lavabad	lavabat L	he [she, it] was washing
.16	polentay	polenta L	pearl barley
.16	polentay rossum	pollenter L	powerfully
		ossum L	a bone
		sum L	I am
.19	Terracuta	terra L	land, earth
		terra acuta L	sharp *or* pointed land
.21	Calembaurnus	cale- L	hot-
		Columbanus LL (543–615)	"Of *Columba* ['Dove']": Irish missionary, *founded 3 monasteries in France, also Bobbio in Italy, where he died*
.26	wolkenic	Volcanalis L	of *or* belonging to Vulcan, *the firegod*
		# *Labials*	
.27	Anaks Andrum	anax andrôn G	lord of men: *epithet of Agamemnon in Homer's* Iliad
.30	A. A.	A[nax] A[ndrôn] G	Lord of Men
		A[ulus] A[gerius] L	Conventional name of litigant in Roman Law, "John Doe"
.33	pious alios	pius Aeneas L	Aeneas the dutiful: Vergilian formula
.33	alios	alios (*Acc. pl.*) L	others
		alias L	otherwise
.36	priamed	Priamos G	"Buyer [*possibly not really a G name*]?": king of Troy at its fall
		Priamus L	
241.02	coaxyorum	coxarum (*Gen. pl.*) L	the hips', of the hips

		-orum L	Gen. masc. pl. suffix
		coccorum (*Gen. pl.*) L	of scarlet berries
.05	pruriest	prurio L	to itch
		pruriosus L	excited by sexual desire
.08	Collosul rhodomantic	Colossus Rhodius L ho Kolossos tês Rhodou G	the Colossus at Rhodes: giant statue-lighthouse dedicated to the sun
.08	rhodomantic	*rhodomantikos G	oracular by means of roses
		Rhadamanthus G L	one of the judges of the dead
.10	timentrousnest	timent L	they fear, they dread
		timiditas L	timidity, cowardice
.12	auroholes	auris L	the ear
		aureolus L	golden
		aurora L	the dawn
.14	cupric	cupressus L kuparissos G	the cypress
		cupreus L	made of copper, copper
		Cupria L Kupria G	the Cyprian: Aphroditê (Venus) *because born at Cyprus*
.14–.15	formwhite foaminine	aphros G	foam
		Aphroditê G	goddess of beauty and sexual love
.14–.15	formwhite foaminine, the ambersandalled	foamwhite feminine, the ambersandalled	the birth of Aphrodite/Venus from the sea-foam at Cyprus (see Botticelli's *Nate di Venere*)
.15	Talop's	talôs G (*Hesychius*)	the sun
		ops G	eye, face
		Talôs *or* Talos G	mythological guardian of Crete; made of bronze by Hephaestus; kept strangers off by throwing stones, or burned them, or heated himself redhot and clasped them in his arms; killed by Medea
.21	ignomen	ignominia L	deprivation of one's name: disgrace, dishonor

		agnomen L	surname given to an individual and not transmitted to posterity,*e.g.*, *Africanus, Cunctator*
.21	prima signation	prima signatio L	first signing
.25	rhomatism	rho G	letter R
		rheumatismos G	humor *or* discharge from the body, flux
.30	Calumdonia	callum L	hard skin
		calumnia L	trickery, artifice, evasion; false accusation
		Caledonia L	the highlands of Scotland
.33	sempry	semper L	always, ever
.34–.35	jom petter	Jupiter L	chief Roman god; # *A*
.35	sodalites	sodales (*pl.*) L	companions, comrades
		sodalitas L	fellowship, friendship, society
.36	*Fication*	*ficatio L	a making
242.02	Adenoiks	adên G	gland
		adenoeidês G	glandular
		adênês G	ignorant
.07	autonaut	autonautês G	self-sailor
.11	ecrazyaztecs	ekklêsiastês G	member of a congregation
.12	praverbs	prava verba L	crooked words; improper, vicious words
.13	persona erecta	persona erecta (*Nom.*) L	an upright person, upright character
		personâ erectâ (*Abl.*) L	his character elevated, his form erect
.13	glycorawman	glykys G	sweet
		Graeco-Romanus L	Greek-Roman
.14	julias	Julias L	name of a town in Galilee
		Julia (*fem.*)	a woman of the gens Julia ("belonging to Julus")
.15	theopot	theos G	god
.16	biss	bis L	twice
.16	sympoly	sympolloi G	many together
		sympolizô G	to unite into one city

		*sympolis G	a united-together city
.17	rhainodaisies	rhainô G	to sprinkle, to bestrew
.19	poetographies	poiêtographos G	poet
		*poiêtographia G	poetry, poetry-writing
.24	Strate	strata [via] LL	levelled [road]: street
.25	contrasta toga	contrastâ ML [*contrastatâ L] togâ L	with toga contrasted, in a contrasted toga
		toga *contrastata L	a contrasted toga: *kinds of togas included* pura, praetexta, virilis, candida, pulla, *and* libera, *but not* contrastata
		toga contrastata L	a put-on-instead-of toga: *toga* was slang for "prostitute," prostitutes not being permitted the proper female *stola;* a prostitute's dress would be *de facto* a *toga contrastata*
.28	Avenlith	lithos H	stone
.29	fulgar	fulgur L	flashing lightning
.30	apocryphul	apokryphos G	hidden; underhand; obscure
.31	allaph	alpha G	letter A
.34	iern	Iernê G L	Ireland
.34	flamen	flamen L	1. priest of one particular deity; 2. a blast of wind
.34	vestacoat	Vesta L	goddess of crops and of the hearth
.34	fibule	fibula L	clasp, buckle, pin
.35	pointefox	pontifex L	"bridgemaker": Roman high-priest
243.02	annams	annus L	year
		anima L	air, breeze, breath, breath of life, life; soul
.04	Ani Mama	anima L	*see 243.02*
.05	furibound	furibundus L	raging, mad, furious
.07	pignpugn	pignus L	pawn, security, pledge, mortgage, assurance; children

		pugna L	fistfight, combat; battle
.07	pialabellars	pia (*fem.*) L	dutiful
		bella L	1. wars; 2. beautiful
		ars L	art
.08	jackticktating	jactitatio LL	1. *Law*: false boasting to another's harm; 2. *Medicine*: tossing, twitching
.09	pannellism	Panellênismos G	"All-Greeks-ism": the idea that all the Greeks should unite into one nation or confederation
.15	nutre	nutrio L	to suckle, feed, foster, rear
.15	jacent	jacens L	lying dead
.24	Ulo	ulula L	the screech-owl
.24	Bubo	bubo L	the horned owl
.25	dinars	denarius L	small Roman coin
.26	cloack	cloaca L	sewer
.26	Berenice	Berenikê *Macedonian form of* Pherenikê G	"Victoria": "Carrying off victory": Name of several queens of the Ptolemaic dynasty in Egypt
.27	mulierage	mulier L	woman
.29	baselgia	*basanalgia G	tormenting ache
		*basanalgos G	tormenting pain, racking pain
		basanos G	torments of hell (*Luke 16:23*)
.29	clamast	clam L	secretly, privately
		clamas L	you (*sing.*) cry out
.29	apotria	a patria L	from the fatherland
		apo G	away from
		tria G	three
		apo triôn G	away from three
		apotriazô G	to be victorious in wrestling *or* in the pentathlon
.31	Vatucum	viaticum L	travelling-money, provision for a journey; Charon's fare; money to pay for study abroad; *eccl.* the Last Sacrament

		Vaticanus L	Vatican: hill west of Tiber at Rome; an inferior wine
.31	Crucis	crucis (*Gen.*) L	cross's, of the cross
.33	quaqueduxed	quaqua, quaque L	wheresoever, whithersoever
		dux L	leader, chief, guide, general
		aquaeductus, aquarum ductus L	a conveyance of water: an aquaduct
.33	Hrom	Hrômê, hRômê G	Roma, Rome [Rhômê *is conventional transliteration, but* hrômê *is really more accurate*]
.35	missas	missa L	sent; the Mass
244.03	pire	pyr G	fire
.05	Neomenie	neomênia G	the new moon (a festal day)
.07	syngagyng	syn- G	with-
.14	Alvemmarea	alveus L	hold of a ship; boat; riverbed
		alvus L	belly
		alvum maris L	the basin of the "sea" *in the courtyard of the Temple at Jerusalem*
		Ave Maria L	Hail Mary
.15	circumveiloped	circumvallatus L	walled-around, besieged, beset
.17	Zoo	zôon G	living being, animal
242.17	deff, coal lay on	*MG pron.* Deucalion	the classical Noah; *see 135.04-05*
244.18	pyrress	pyr G	fire
		Pyrrha G	wife of Deucalion; *see 135.04-05*
.25	era's	era L	mistress
		aera L	point from which time is measured; *see 228.15*
.26	Selene	selênê G	the moon
.26	Amune	*amounoô G	to make unsolitary
.26	Ark!?	arx L	citadel
		arcus L	bow, rainbow
		arca L	ark
.31	conticinium	conticinium L	the first part of the night (when all becomes still)

.33	aubens	albens L	white
		albente caelo L	"at the whitening of heaven": at daybreak, at dawn
.33	aubens Aurore	albente Aurorâ L	at the whitening of the Dawn
.33	Aurore	Aurora L	Dawn
.34	panther	panthêr G	"all-beast": name of various *felidae*
		panther L	net for catching wild beasts
.34	monster	monstrum L	divine omen indicating misfortune
.34	panther monster	pater noster L	our father
.35	triump	triumpe L	exclamation (*meaning uncertain*) used in solemn processions of the Arval brothers (*Roman priestly order*)
		triumpho L	to hold a triumphal procession
.35	*Eliphas*	elephas G L	an elephant
.35	*Magistrodontos*	magister, magistro- L	master, master-
		odous, odont- G	tooth
		*magistrodontos L + G	of the master-tooth
		megodontos G	of the enormous teeth
245.01	Rhinohorn	rhinos G	skin, hide
		rhino- G	nose-
		part trans. rhinokerôs	"nose-horn": the rhinoceros
.02	Hopopodorme	hippodromos G	horse racecourse
		epops G upupa L	the hoopoe: leading character in Aristophanes' *The Birds*
		dormio L	to sleep
.10	antargumends	*anteargumentum L	prior argument
		integumentum L	covering
.11	pesciolines	pisciculi L	little fishes
.12	Junoh	Juno L	chief Roman goddess, guardian deity of women; wife of Jupiter

.12	feriaquintaism	feria quinta L	fifth holiday
.23	Hesperons	Hesperos G L	the evening star
.34	omiss	omissus L	negligent, heedless
.34	Kate	kathairô G	to cleanse
.35	A's ... the number	alpha G	letter A; *as a numeral*: one, first
246.01	Whoopee	epops, upupa	hoopoe; *see 245,02*
.07	arthre	arthron G	a limb
.18	Thaddeus	deus L	god
.19	And lead raptivity captive	Graecia capta ferum victorem cepit—Horat. *Ep.* II.i.157	Captive Greece captured her fierce subduer—Horace, *Epistle to Augustus,* 157 [*but see Ephesians IV*:8]
.19	raptivity	*raptivitas L	tendency to rape
.21	campus	campus L	field
.24	Educande	educande L	O one to be educated
.31	felixed ... culpas	felix culpa L	happy sin: Adam's fall because it elicited the Incarnation
.32	d'Anno	de anno L	from the year
.36	Postreintroducing	post- L	after-, afterwards-
247.02	mutualiter	*mutualiter L	interchangeably
.02	velos	velox L	swift
.02–.03	velos ambos	veloces ambos L	both swift
		vel ambos L	or both if you wish
.05	sics	sic L	thus
.06	secs	sex L	six
.09	nobit	nobis L	to *or* by us
		obit L	he [she, it] passes over, dies
.10	Eat	eat L	let him go, he should go
.10	larto	lardo L	with lard
.10	altruis	*altruis LL.	to *or* by others
.14	Men, teacan a tea simmering, hamo mavrone kerry O?	Men, ti kanete sêmeron, ho emou mauro kyrio? MG G	Well, how do you do today, my dark gentleman?
.15	Teapotty. Teapotty	Ti pote. Ti pote G	Why? (Coll.) 'Not too bad' MG.
.17	indeiterum	inde L	from that place, thence
		iterum L	again, a second time

		deuteron G	second
.18	momourning	mômar G	blame, disgrace
		mômaomai G	to find fault with
.19	melained	melainô G	to blacken
.27	moramor	mora L	a delay
.29	skirtaskortas	scorta (*pl.*) L	harlots, prostitutes
		curta (*fem.*) L	shortened
.29	must change her tunics	toga L	prostitute (slang): *a prostitute was not allowed to wear the normal feminine* stola; *had to* change *her dress; see 242.25*
.29	tunics	tunica L	Roman undergarment of both sexes; *a prostitute's was no different from anyone else's*
.34	clearobscure	clarus obscurus L	clear dark (trans. Italian *chiaroscuro*)
.35	bacchante	bacchantes L	celebrants of the festival of Bacchus
.35	hematite	haimatitês G	blood-like
248.01	quasimodo	quasi modo L	as if in the manner; almost in the manner
.02	philomel	philomêlê G	fruit-lover: the swallow *or* the nightingale
		phi G	letter PH
.02	theerose	thêta G	letter TH
.07	asters	astêr G	star
.08	lingua	lingua L	tongue
.11	Achill's	Achilles L	hero of Homer's *Iliad*
		Achilleus G	
.12	a vulser	avulsus L	torn away; withdrawn
		vulsus L	plucked; shorn, smooth, beardless, hairless
.16	Cucullus	cucullus L	1. hood, covering; wrapper; 2. the cuckoo
.20	hys	hys G	pig
.20	hyphen	hyphen G	in one, in a single word
.21	mys	mys G	mouse, rat
.30	benedixed	benedixit L	[he] has spoken well of, has blessed
.31	intimast	intimus L	innermost
.34	Magnus	magnus; Magnus L	big, great; the Great

.34	Max	maximus; Maximus L	biggest, greatest; the Greatest
249.01	adolls	adoleo L	1. to magnify, to worship; 2. to smell, to emit an odor
.02	infuxes	*infuco L	1. to paint; 2. not to paint
		infusco L	to darken, to obscure
		infusus L	a pouring in, an injection
.08	massicious	Massicum L	a highly-regarded wine from *Massicus*, a mountain in Campania [now *Monte Massico*]
.08	Tyrian	tyrianthinus L thyrianthinos G	of a color between purple and violet
.12	uniomargrits	unio L	1. (*masc.*) a single large pearl 2. (*fem.*) a kind of single onion
		margarita L margaritês [lithos] G	a pearl
		una [margarita] pretiosa L	one pearl of great price (*Matt. 13:46*)
		*uniomargarita L	pearl onion?
.13	consonantia	consonantia L	agreement, harmony
.15	vibroverberates	vibro L	to shake, to quiver, to tremble, to move rapidly back and forth
		verbero L	to lash, beat, whip, flog
.15	tegmen	tegmen L	a covering, cover
.15	prosplodes	*prosplodo G + L	to clap for; to approve, to applaud
		instead of explodo L	to clap (*an actor*) off (*the stage*), to drive out by clapping, to hiss off; to disapprove
.16	pomoeria	pomoeria (*pl.*) L	open spaces left free from buildings inside and outside the walls of a town, limiting the city auspices; bounds, limits
.17	augur	augur L	diviner, soothsayer, interpreter of dreams

.17	paypaypay	P[ater] P[atriae]; P[rae] p[ositus]; P[rimi]p[ilus]; P[ro] P[arte] L	Father of his Country; Prefect; Chief Centurion; For the share of (*in Roman inscriptions*)
250.01	Avis	avis L	a bird
.04	simules	simulo L	to imitate, copy, assume the form, feign
.04	rumpffkorpff	corpus L	body
.08	finges	fingo L	to fashion, form, make into, feign
.19	libelman libling	libella L	small silver coin
		libellus L	little book, journal, diary; libel, lampoon
		libelli L	bookshop
.20	Libnius	Libanus L	the Lebanon
.20	Liber	Liber L	old Italian deity who presided over planting and fructification; *identified with Bacchus*
		liber L	1. a freeman; 2. a child; 3. a book
.23	vox	vox L	voice
.27	Aghatharept	agathos G	good; the good
.27	Nebnos	nebros G	fawn, young deer
		nos L	we
.34	Lignifer	lignifer L	one who carries wood *or* a tree
.35	incoronate	incoronatus L	uncrowned
		incarnatus eccl. L	made into the flesh, incarnate
251.01	jocubus	jocus L	jest, joke
		*jocubus L	joke-nightmare, joke-dream
.01	Attilad! Attattilad	Attila (406–453)	king of the Huns; ravished eastern Europe and overran Italy; spared Rome through the Pope's mediation
		Atta L	surname: person who walks on the tips of his toes
		Atta G	Daddy
		attillo L	to tickle, to please

		ad L	to, at
		Thalatta!	Sea! Sea! *cry of*
		Thalatta! G	*Xenophon's men when the leading ranks sighted the Black Sea from the hills above Trebizond, on the retreat from Persia;* # B
.02	impluvium	impluvium L	skylight, opening in roof of Roman house; the square basin beneath that caught rainwater
.04	oblious	obliuius L	forgotten, obsolete
.04	autamnesically	*autoamnêsia G	self-forgetfulness
.05	proprium	proprium L	personal property
.07	apophotorejected	apo phôtos G	away from light
		rejectus L	thrown back, flung back
.13	cuperation	[re]cuperatio L	a getting back, a regaining
		*cupratio L	a coppering
.28	monitorology	monitor L	a reminder; one who reminds a lawyer of legal points; an assistant
		*monitorologia L + G	the wisdom *or* science of being a reminder
.29	*in omnibus moribus et temporibus*	in omnibus moribus et temporibus L	in all customs and times
.31	exaspirated	*exaspiratus L	blown-out-upon
252.13	Grassy ass ago	gratias ago L	I give thanks
.15	bivitellines	*bivitellina L	double-veal
		*bivitellus L	double-calf
		*bivitellum L	double-eggyolk (*Castor and Pollux hatched from one egg*)
		Vitelliani L	Vitellians, supporters of Vitellius (emperor a.d. 69); *see 307.L34*, # C
.15	Metellus	Metellus L	"Hired" *or* "Mercenary": name of a Roman family in the gens Caecilia
		Q. Metellus Celer	husband of the notorious Clodia,

		(died 59 b.c.)	Catullus's *Lesbia*
.15	Ametallikos	ametallikos G	unmetallic
.16	obscindgemeinded	*obscindo L *instead of*	to tear to, to rip toward
		abscindo L	to tear off, to tear away
.16	uruseye	urus L	a wild ox
.17	superfetated	superfeto L	to conceive while pregnant
.20	artthoudux	Artus dux, Arturus dux L	Art the leader, General Arthur: *obscure historical figure who seems to underlie the legendary King Arthur*
.21	heterotropic	*heterotropikos G	turning to another
		heterotropos G	of different fashion
.26	waterstichystuff	stichos G	row, file, line (*of poetry*)
.34	Braglodyte	*bragos, *brachos G	a shallow
		*braglodytês G *modeled on*	one who creeps into *or* lives in shallows; shallowsman
		troglodytês G	one who creeps into *or* lives in caves; caveman
.34	katadupe	katadoupeô G	to fall with a crash
		hoi katadoupoi G Catadupa L	"The Crashing-Falls": the first Cataract of the Nile
.34–.35	condamn quondam	quondam L	at one time, once
253.05	mappamund	mappa L	table-napkin
		mundus L	clean, nice, elegant; toilette
		mappa mundi ML	map of the world
.09	Sol	sol L	the sun
.24	duad	duas, dyas G	the number two
.27	aurinos	auri- L	gold
		Aurininus L	old name for inhabitant of the former town of Saturnia, on the Capitoline Hill
		*aurinasus L	gold-nose

.29	gigantesquesque	gigantes G L	giants: *fabled sons of Earth and Tartarus; stormed the heavens but were smitten by Jupiter with lightning and buried under Aetna*
		quicumque, quique (*pl.*) L	whoever, whoever they be
		-que L	and
.34	mortisection	mortisectio L	dead-cutting, cutting up (*something that is*) dead
.34	vivisuture	*vivisutura L	live sewing-together, sewing together (*something that is*) alive
.35	mauromormo	mauros G	dark
		mormô G	a she-monster that frightens children, a bugbear
		*mauromormô G	dark bugbear
.35	milesian	miles L	soldier
		Milesiae [fabulae] L	Milesians, Milesian [tales]: obscene stories (from Miletus, city in Asia Minor famous for luxury and wantonness)
.36	accountibus	-ibus L	to *or* by: Dat. and Abl. pl. suffix
254.03	Orion	Oriôn G	mythical hunter transformed into a constellation; *according to some, name derives from* ouron G, "urine"
.03	Orgiasts	orgiastês G	one who celebrates *orgia* (secret worship, secret rites)
.04	Ipse	ipse L	himself, he in person
.04	quotidients	quotidie, cottidie L	daily
.05–.06	brutest layaman	Layamon's *Brut*	Middle English epic about Brutus, eponymous founder of Britain, a refugee from Troy (modeled on *Aeneid*)

.07	Clio's	Clio L Kleiô G	"Fame": the Muse of history
.07	chroncher ... sulpicious	Sulpicius Severus (362–425)	Latin monk, wrote *Chronica* from Creation to a.d. 403
.09	Polycarp	Polykarpos (a.d. 69–155) G	"Fruitful": bishop of Smyrna, follower of St. John, lived "in familiar intercourse with many that had seen Christ"; taught Irenaeus
.10	Irenews	Irênaios (a.d. 140–202) G	"Peaceful": pupil of Polycarp; G. church father, became bishop of Lyons
.13	extorreor	extorreo L	to parch up, to be scorched
.16	*dulcisamica*	dulcis amica L	sweet girlfriend
.16	A ... ab ad	a, ab L ad L	from, away from to, at
.18	mar of murmury	*Mare Marmoris ML	"Sea of Marble": the Sea of Marmara (classic name: *Propontis*)
.20	Hocus Crocus	Hocus Pocus *mock-L for* hoc est corpus [meum] L	this is [my] body ... *words of consecration at Mass*
		crocus L krokos G	saffron
		Crocus L	youth metamorphosed into saffron-flower
.20	Esquilocus	Esquiliae L	"Oaks": largest of the seven hills of Rome
		es qui L	you are who?
		locus L	place, spot
.22	Potollomuck Sotyr	Ptolemaios I Sôtêr (367–282 b.c.)	"Warlike" (the Saviour): companion and biographer of Alexander; *founder of the Ptolemaic dynasty in Egypt*
.23	Sourdanapplous	Sardanapalus (669–640 b.c.)	Assur-bani-pal, king of Assyria; *according to G legend burned himself and all his possessions; became a byword for luxurious weakness of character*

.29–.30	say is soft	C L	3rd letter of L alphabet, equivalent to K; did not become S ("soft") until middle ages; some traditional styles of school L pron. C soft (S) in certain combinations (*e.g.* *Caesar* as "Seezer" instead of Kaisar)
.30	ee has a cute angle	ê *or* é	letter E with circumflex or acute accent
.30	hissarlik	Hissarlik	Turkish name for the site of Troy
.31	hennin's	Hennensis L	of Henna or Enna (city in Sicily)
		hen (*neut.*) G	one
		Helenê G	lady whose beauty burned Troy (Helen of Troy)
.31	aspire	pyr G	fire
.36	Artho	Artus	Arthur: *see 252.20*
255.10	Aquileyria	aquila L	eagle
		Aquila L	"Eagle": Roman proper name
		aquilo L	the north wind
		Aquilaria L	town in Zeugitania (mod. Tunisia)
.13	quarantee	quare L	how? why?
.14	Veritotem	veritatem (*Acc.*) L	truth, reality
		vanitatem (Acc.) L	emptiness, vanity
.15	Bearara Tolearis	tolero L	to bear
		Aurora Borealis L	The Northern Dawn: the northern lights
.15	*procul abeat*!	procul abeat L	may he be away far off
.16	Hector	Hektôr G	"Protector": Trojan hero of the *Iliad*
.18	Pliny the Younger	C. Plinius Caecilius Junior (a.d. 62–114)	nephew of Pliny the Elder; author of a panegyric on Trajan and letters

.18–.19	Pliny the Elder	C. Plinius Secundus Major (a.d. 23–79)	uncle of Pliny the Younger; historian and encyclopedist, left 37-volume *Historia Naturalis* to his nephew Lost his life in the eruption of Vesuvius
.19	calamolumen	calamus L	reed pen
		kalamos G	
		lumen L	light, lamp; life
		*calamolumen L	pen-light; reed-torch; life of writing?
.19	contumellas	contumelia L	abuse, insult
		L. Junius Moderatus Columella (*fl.* a.d. 60)	Spanish born writer on agriculture; wrote *De Re Rustica* in 12 books; *#A*
.19	Aulus Gellius	Aulus Gellius (a.d. 135– ?)	Roman author; wrote *Noctes Atticae*, full of extracts from now lost authors
.20	Micmacrobius	*Mikrobios G	"Living short"
		Makrobios G	"Living long"
		Aurelius Macrobius Ambrosius Theodosius (*fl.* a.d. 500)	Roman grammarian; wrote commentary on Cicero's *Somnium Scipionis* and a series of dialogues, much admired in the later middle ages
.20	Vitruvius	Marcus Vitruvius Pollio (1st C b.c.—late)	Roman architect and engineer, wrote *De Architectura*
.21	Cassiodorus	Magnus Aurelius Cassiodorus (a.d. 490–583)	secretary to Theodoric, Ostrogothic king of Italy, wrote history of the Goths and collection of letters
.21	Lukan	M. Annaeus Lucanus (a.d. 39–65)	poet, nephew of Seneca, author of *Pharsalia*, epic poem about Roman Civil War. Suicide at Nero's orders

.28	abuliousness	aboulia G	ill-advisedness, thoughtlessness; irresolution
		aboulios G	inconsiderate, ill-advised, unfeeling
.35	quis separabits	quis separabit L	who shall separate?
256.02	Gallus's	Gallus L	a Gaul; also Roman poet, friend of Vergil
		gallus L	a cock
.03	owreglias	Aurelius L	a Roman name
		Marcus Aurelius Antoninus (a.d. 121–180)	Roman emperor and Stoic philosopher; *author of* Meditations
.04	Prestissima	praestissima (*fem.*) L	closest to hand, readiest
.08	Mas	mas L	male, masculine
.13	yeassymgnays	sym- G	with-
.21	Marusias	Marus L	river in Germany (now the March); tributary of the Danube
.21	Lucanias	Lucania L	district in southern Italy
.21	Jokinias	jocinor L	the liver
.22	Valgur	valgus L	bow-legged
.24	Amnist	amnis L	river
.24	anguished	anguis L	snake
.25	axes	axis L	axle
.25	Collis	collis L	hill
.24–.25	Amnist anguished axes Collis	amnis, anguis, axis, collis L	list of masc. nouns ending -*is* from a L grammar book (alphabetical order)
.33	nibulissa	*nebulissa L	a little mist *or* cloud
257.02	stella's vispirine	stella vesperina L	evening star
.04	rhimba	*rhimba G	large pomegranate
.04	rhomba	rhombos G	bull-roarer; magic wheel; tambourine; male sex organ; lozenge-shaped figure
.04	trappaza	trapeza G	table, counter, bench
.05	Geamatron	Gaia mêtêr G	Mother Earth
		Geômetria G	"land-measuring": geometry

.06	leppers	lepus L	a hare
.11	plattonem	Platôn G	"Broad-shouldered": philosopher
.20	panto's	panto- G	all-, every-
.25	deispiration	*deispiratio L	a god-breathing, god-breath
.25	diasporation	diaspora G	scattering, dispersion
.26	diesparation	*diesparatio L	a day-preparing, day-procuring
.28	–zoo–	zôon G	animal, living being
.28	–sphalna–	sphalma G	a stumble, false step; failure
.35	Orbiter	orbatur L	he is bereaved of
		orbita L	track, rut, orbit
		obiter L	in passing, incidentally, on the way
		T. [or C.] Petronius Arbiter	*arbiter elegantiae* at Nero's court, author of *Satyricon.*
258.02	exeomnosunt	exeunt omnes L	all leave, they all go out
		exeo L	to go out, to depart
		omnis L	all, every
		sunt L	they are, there are
.04	fert	fert L	he carries
.04	Fulgitudes ejist rowdownan tonuout	*fulgitudo ejus retonans tonuit* L	his brightness, resounding, thundered
		fortitudo ejus Rhodum tenuit L	his strength has held Rhodes; # *B*
.04	Quoq	quoque L	also
.05	Kidoosh	kydos G	1. glory, renown; 2. reproach, abuse
.10	Nekulon	*nekulon G nichil ML nihil L	little corpse, corpslet nothing
.13	laud	laus L	praise
.14	Nekulon	*see 258.10D*	
.20	tumbuldum	tumulum LL	mound, hillock; burial mound
		tumultuor L	to be in an uproar
		dum L	while; until
.21	moguphonoised	*megaphônês G	big-sounding; loud-sounder

		*megaphônêeis G	endowed with loud speech
.22	phonemanon	phônê G	sound, tone, voice
		phônêma G	utterance, speech, language
.23	terrerumbled	terra L	the earth, land
		terreo L	to frighten, to terrify
.23	fimament	fimus or fimum L	manure, dung, excrement
.23	fundament	fundamentum L	foundation; bottom; arse
.30	Didymus	Didymos G (St. John's trans. of Aramaic Thomas)	Twin: *name of one of the Twelve* [Thomas] (*John 11:16, 20:24, 21:2*)
		Didymos (80–10 b.c.)	nicknamed Brass-bowels; editor and lexicographer, wrote between 3,500 and 4,000 works
		Claudius Didymus (1st C a.d.)	lexicographer, wrote a comparison of L with G
.31	Domas	*trans.* Didymos G	Thomas: Twin; *see 258.30*
		dôma G	house, household
.35	Timothy	Timotheos G	"Honoring God": companion of St. Paul, co-author of six epistles and recipient of two; *see 274.11*
259.05	ming	mingo L	to urinate
.05	merder	merda L	dung, ordure, excrement
.06	madhowiatrees	iatreia G	healing; medical treatment
.07	miseries	misereo L	to feel pity, to have compassion
		misericordia L	mercy, pity
260.R1	UNDE ET UBI	unde et ubi L	whence and where
.02–.03	Tea tea	ti G	what? why?
.03	oo	ou G	not
.R2	SIC	sic L	thus
.09	Livius	Titus Livius L	historian; #A
.13	Gadeway	Gades (*Phoenician* Gaddir, "the walled place")	port in Spain just beyond Pillars of Hercules; *mod.* Cadiz

.F2	Mater ... Mercerycordial	Mater Misericordiae L	Mother of Mercy (*a Dublin hospital*) # *A*
261.01	chinkaminx	minxi L	I have urinated
.09	cones	kônos G	pine-cone; anything with an apex, *e.g.*, a pyramid
.09	conned the cones	*allusion to pyramids of Egypt*	*one of the seven wonders of the world*
.10	mured	murus L	a wall; *the walls and hanging gardens of Babylon were together one of the seven wonders of the world*
		miro L	to wonder
.10	pensils	pensilis L	hanging; *the hanging gardens and the walls of Babylon were together one of the seven wonders of the world*
.11	olymp	Olympia G	sacred region in the west Peloponnessus where the Olympian games were held; *a statue of Zeus by Phidias, at Olympia, was one of the seven wonders of the world*
.11	delighted in her dianaphous	*allusion to* the lighthouse at Pharos	*one of the seven wonders of the world*
		phôs G	light
.11	dianaphous	Diana L	Italian deity associated with the moon and identified with Artemis; *the temple of Artemis [Diana] at Ephesus was one of the seven wonders of the world*
		*Dianaphôs L + G	moonlight
		diaphanôs G	transparently, distinctly
.12	cacchinated	cacchino L	to laugh aloud, to laugh immoderately

.12	culosses	Colossus L	giant statue-lighthouse
		Kolossos G	at Rhodes; *one of the seven wonders of the world*
		culus L	the posteriors, arse
.13	mosoleum	mos L	manner, custom
		Mausoleum L	magnificent tomb of
		Mausôleion G	king Mausôlos of Caria; *one of the seven wonders of the world*
		*mos- = maus- L	*lower-class* L *pronounced* -au- *as* -o-
.L1	*Daimon*	daimôn G	deity, spirit, demon
.L1	Barbar	Barbaros G	foreigner, stranger,
		Barbarus L	non-G-speaker (*also* non-L-speaker)
.14	evums	aevum L	never-ending time, eternity
.15	stupor	stupor L	numbness, dullness, insensibility
		stuô G	to have an erection
.15	sopor	sopor L	sleep
.15	Cave	cave L	beware! watch out! ("to keep *cave*": *schoolboy slang*, "to act as look-out")
.15	Cave of Kids	*allusion to childhood of Zeus*	the infant Zeus was hidden in a cave on Mount Ida in Crete, and suckled by the she-goat Amaltheia
.15	Hymanian	hymenaios G	bridal song; wedding
.16	denary	denarius L	"containing ten": small silver coin
.17	domm	domus L	house, household, home
.18	chthonic	chthonios G	in *or* under the earth; sprung from the soil; native
.19	antisipiences	*antecipiens L	receiving beforehand, preoccupying
		*anticipiens G + L	against receiving, against taking
		antesapiens L	wise beforehand, shrewd beforehand
		*antisapiens G + L	against being knowing, against being sensible

.20	Dominic	Dominus; Domine (*Voc.*) L	Lord; O Lord
.21	Directus	directus L	straight
.23	Ainsoph	aiens L	affirming, affirmative
		ain- G	terrible, dire
		ainos G	1. tale, story; 2. horrible
		sophos G	skilled, ciever, wise
		*ainsophos G	*terriblewise, skilled in the dire
.25	mehrkurios	Mercurius L	messenger of the gods, god of dexterity; identified with Hermes
		curiosus L	assiduous, careful
		kurios G	lord (*MG*: *Mr.* [*Mister*])
.27	cryptogam	kryptogamos G	secret marriage, clandestine wedding
.28	heaventalk	*allusion to* Homer	topographical names in *Iliad* and *Odyssey* are frequently dual, *e.q.* the stream Xanthos "so called by gods, by men Skamander"
.31	decans	decanus L	one in charge of ten; a dean; the chief of ten parts in a zodiacal sign
.F1.1	ludo	ludo L	to play
.F2.2	Terra Firma	terra firma L	steadfast *or* immoveable earth
262.01	decemt	decem L	ten
.15	requiestress, wakeem	requiescat in pace L	may he [she] rest in peace
.16	let luck's puresplutterall lucy at ease	et lux perpetua luceat eis L	and may perpetual light shine upon them
.R2	GNOSIS	gnôsis G	Knowledge
.L3	*Quartandwds*	quartanus L	of *or* belonging to the fourth; occurring on the fourth day
.R3	AGNOSIS	agnôsia G	ignorance, lack of knowledge; obscurity
.26	Bacchus	Bacchus L Bakchos G	name of Dionysus, god of emotional religion; later thought of as god of wine

.29	pubblicam	[rem] publicam (*Acc.*) L	the state, the commonwealth, the republic
.F4	Apis	Apis	sacred bull worshipped in Memphis in Egypt; widely known in the classical world
.F4	Apis amat aram.	Apis amat aram L	the bee loves the altar
.F4	Luna legit librum	Luna legit librum L	the moon reads a book
.F4	Pulla	pulla L	chick, foal, young animal
		puella L	girl
.F4	Pulla petit pascua	Pulla petit pascua L	the foal seeks the pastures
263.03	Ignotus Loquor	ignotus loquor L	unknown I speak
.05	theobalder	theos G	god
		Theobaldus (*d.* 1161)	archbishop of Canterbury 1138–1161
.06	Egyptus	Aegyptus L Aigyptos G	1. Egypt; 2. legendary king of Egypt, brother of Danaüs; had fifty sons espoused to the fifty daughters of Danaüs
.L1	*Mars*	Mars L	god of war
.07	Cyrus	Cyrus L Kyros G	1. founder of the Persian empire, died 529 b.c.; 2. rebel brother of Artaxerxes, killed at Cunaxa 401 b.c., whence Xenophon led the retreat of 10,000 G mercenaries
.11	Pandemia's	pandêmia G	the whole people
		Pandêmos G	"of the whole people": *epithet of Zeus at Athens; also of Aphrodite and Eros*
.13	Euxine	Euxeinos G Euxinus L	"Hospitable": ancient name for the Black Sea
.14	Emeratic	[h]êmera G	a day
.15	Helleniky	Hellenikê G	the G language

.20	primal ... alter	primus; alter L	the first; the second of two
.21	Idem	idem L	the same
.22	saith the emerald canticle of Hermes	*allusion to* Hermês Trismegistos G	Hermes the Thricegreat: rendering of Egyptian "Thoth the very great": reputed author of philosophical-religious-astrological-magical-alchemical treatises; late product of decadent Greek-Egyptian culture
.22	Hermes	Hermês G	god of flocks, commerce, invention, roads; messenger of the gods; identified with Roman Mercurius (*see* 261.25)
.L3	*Non quod sed quiat*	non quod sed quia L	not because but wherefore (*quod* and *quia* are virtual synonyms)
.27–.28	Securely judges orb terrestrial	*trans.* securus iudicat orbis terrarum L	free from care the circle of the lands judges; *i.e.*, untroubled, the world judges—*St. Augustine; #B (see 096.33, 306.R2, 593.13-14, etc.)*
.28	*Haud certo ergo*	haud certo ergo L	not at all certainly therefore
.29	O felicitous culpability	O felix culpa L	O happy sin: *medieval hymn celebrating Adam's fall because it elicited the Incarnation*
.30	archetypt	*archêtyptô G	to begin to beat, begin to smite
.F1.2	aab	a L *abbreviation for* ab L	away from, from
.F1.2	zoo	-oo = -ô G	*ômega*, last letter in G alphabet
		zôon G	animal, living thing
.F2.2	meditarenias	meditor L	to think upon, to consider

		mediterraneus L	midland, inland, remote from the sea
		[h]arena L	sand
.F4.1	Lutharius	lutarius L	muddy, living in mud; mud-dweller
		Lutherius Mod L	Lutheran
.F4.1	Sinobiled	sino L	to let, allow, permit
		s[ine] nob[ilitas] L	without nobility; *fanciful etymology for "snob"*
264.01	commercio's	commercio (*Abl.*) L	by trade
.02	plurable	*plorabilis L	lamentable, weepable
		pleura G	rib
.R1	ZELOTYPIA	zêlotypia G	jealousy, envy
.R1	ODIUM TELEOLOGICUM	odium theologicum LL	theological hatred
		otium philosophicum L	philosophical leisure
		odium *teleologicum ML	teleological hatred: hatred having to do with the study of final things
.05	saturnine	Saturninus L	"Belonging to Saturn": Roman surname
.07	Amnios amnium	amnis amnium L	river of rivers
.07	fluminiculum flaminulinorum	*fluminiculum *flaminulorum L	streamlet of priestlings
.09	–cum–	cum L	with
.12	Petra	petra G	a rock
.12	Ulma	ulma L	elm-tree
.13	Ulma	ulma L	elm-tree
.14	Petra	petra G	a rock
.15	sojournemus	*subdiurnemus LL	let us sojourn, let us stay
.15	Eblinn	Eblana G	Dublin
.19	phaked	fecit L	[he/she] has made
.19–.20	phaked ... philim pholk	#*Labials*	faked ... film folk
.R2	LATIFUNDISM	latifundium L	ranch, estate, hacienda
.27	marrons	marron G	an iron spade
.F1	vivvy	vivi- L	life-, alive-

264.F3.1	Porphyrious	Porphyrios G Porphyrius L (a.d. 232–305)	"Purple": G neoplatonic philosopher; opposed Christianity
.F3.1	Olbion	olbios G Albion G L	rich, happy, prosperous "White[?]": ancient name for Britain
.F3.1	rose marines	ros marinus L	"sea dew": the herb rosemary
265.08	phoenix	phoenix L phoinix G	fabulous bird of Arabia, lived 500 years; from its ashes the new phoenix arose
.09	pyre	pyr G	fire
.11	turrises	turris L	tower
.11	sabines	Sabini L	ancient Italian people adjoining the Latins, part of whom were early united with the Romans
.11	televisible	têle- G	afar, from far off
.21	Tytonyhands	Tithônos G	husband of Êôs (Dawn); immensely old man granted immortality but not eternal youth
		tytthos G	small, young
.21	Vlossyhair	*trans.* euplokamos G	"with goodly locks, fair-haired": *Homeric epithet for* Êôs
.22	metromyriams	metron G myrias G *metromyrias G	a measure ten thousand measure of 10,000
.22	Presepeprosapia	praesaepe L	stable, manger; hut, dwelling, tavern
		prosapia L praesaepe prosapiae L	stock, race, family the family's manger, hut *or* tavern
.27	radiolumin	radius L	spoke of a wheel, beam, ray
		lumen L radius luminis L *radiolumino L	light, lamp, torch a ray of light to light up with a ray *or* beam

.F5.1	butcher	Samuel Henry Butcher (1850–1910)	Dublin-born British classical scholar. With Andrew Lang made well-known prose trans. of *Odyssey* (1879)
.F5.2	braches	bracae, *braces L	trousers, breeches
266.01–.02	boxomeness of the bedelias makes hobbyhodge happy in his hole	*trans.* obedientia civium urbis felicitas L	the obedience of the citizens is the city's happiness: *motto of Dublin*
.01	bedelias	bdellium L bdellion G (*pl.* bdellia) L G bdella G	aromatic gum of the balsam a leech; a lamprey
.06	peripateting	peripateô G	to walk up and down; to walk about, to discourse (*in the manner of Aristotle and his students*)
.09	mythelated	mythos G	word, speech; thing said
		methy G	wine
		methysos G	drunk
.13	studiorium	*studiorium L	place where studying is done; a study
.16	rifocillation	*refocillatio L	reheating, rewarming
.R1	PREAUSTERIC	prae L	before, prior
		austêros G	rough, bitter, harsh
		*praeaustericus LL	one who is austere *or* rough beforehand
		Auster L	the South Wind
.L1	*anythesious*	anathesis G	setting up in public, dedicating; adjournment; imposition
		Athanasius (a.d. 296–373)	Christian leader against Arian heresy
.21–.22	wranglers ... wringwrowdy wready ... Fꟻ	# *Digamma*	F = W
.R1	PANHYSTERIC	panhysterikos G	allwomb-suffering; all belonging to the womb
.24	catalaunic	Catalaunicus	"of the *Catalauni* [a Gallic tribe]": Châlons-sur-Marne, *site of Aêtius's defeat of Attila*

		katelaunô G	drive down, push down; fuck, screw (*as obscene colloquialism*)
.25	Aetius	Aëtius (a.d. 390–454)	Roman general; *successfully withstood barbarians for 20 years; defeated Attila at Châlons (451)*
.25	Attil's	Attila (a.d. 406–453)	king of the Huns, *ravaged eastern Europe, stopped at Châlons by Aëtius, ravaged Italy, sparing Rome at the Pope's intercession*
267.02	Mimosa	mimos G	mimic, actor
.02	Multimimetica	multi- L mimêtikê (*fem.*) G	many- imitative
		*multimimetica (*fem.*) L	imitative of many
.04	Elpis	elpis G	hope, expectation
.04	speer	spero L	to look for, expect, hope
		spes L	hope
.06	Ausonius	Ausonius L	of Ausonia (lower Italy); Italian, Latin, Roman
		Decimus Magnus Ausonius (a.d. 309–392)	poet, rhetorician and grammarian of Burdigala (*Bordeaux*); *probably a Christian*
.06	Audacior	audacior L	more daring, bolder
.09	plutonically	Pluto L Ploutôn G	king of the lower world, husband of Proserpine; see 267.11
.L1	*Cis*	cis L	on this side
		Dis L	a name for Pluto; see 267.09-11
.11	Proserpronette	Proserpina L	daughter of Ceres, wife of Pluto, *who seized her as she was gathering flowers and carried her off to the infernal regions*; see 267.09, L1
.15	domisole	domus L	house, home

		domicilium L	habitation, dwelling
		solus L	alone
.20	Uwayoei!	euai! G	a cry of joy
		euoi! G	exclamation used in the cult of Dionysus
.22	Vetus	vetus L	old
		Venus L	goddess of beauty and sexual love
.23	Veto	veto L	to forbid
.23	Nova	nova (fem.) L	new
.24	Nereids	Nereidês G L	daughters of Nereus (a seagod): sea-nymphs
.25	Una Unica	una unica (fem.) L	one only, the only one, one-and-only
.F4	Anama anamaba anamabapa	anima L	breeze, breath, life, soul
268.02	sex	sex L	six
.L1	*annaryllies*	Amaryllis G L	"Twinkling": shepherdess in Vergil's *Eclogue* 1
.08	a rhythmatick	rhythmikos G	set to a tempo, rhythmical
		*arythmikos G	not set to a tempo
		arithmêtikos G	skilled in reckoning, arithmetical; arithmetic
.10	novence	novenus L	nine each, nine
.10	charily	hai Charites G	the Graces: attendants on Aphrodite [Venus]
.10	cupid	Cupido L	"Desire": god of love, son of Venus [Aphrodite]
.L3	*Allma Mathers*	alma mater L	nourishing mother
.17	gramma's	gramma G	a writing, a drawing, a letter (*of the alphabet*)
.19	prosodes	prosôdia G	song sung to instrumental music; variation in pitch of the voice; pronunciation, accentuation
.22	dative	[casus] dativus LL	[the case] relating to giving (*Grammar*)
.22	oblative	[casus] ablativus LL	[the case] relating to removal from (*Grammar*)

		*[casus] oblativus LL	[the case] relating to carrying forward *or* offering (*no such case, but it seems identical with the Dative*)
.24	gramma	gramma G	*see 268.17*
.27	hedon	hêdonê G	enjoyment, pleasure
.28	analectual	analecta L	slave who picked up food crumbs
		analektês G	
		analektos G	choice
.29	pygmyhop	*allusion to* pygê G	"buttocks": Spartan dance in which girls kicked up their heels so as to strike the buttocks
		pygmê G	fist
		Pygmaioi G	"Fistlings": fabulous dwarf race *preyed upon by cranes*; *see 269.10*
269.03	subjunctions	subjunctiones L	"joinings-below": additions, subjoinings, subduings
.04	pruriel	prurio L	to itch; to feel sexual desire
.05	aoriest	aoristos G	indeterminate, indefinite: *a tense in G verbs*
.05	plaudered	plaudo L	to clap, to stamp, to applaud
.06	*haec genua omnia*	haec genua omnia L	all these knees
		haec genera omnia L	all these kinds of things
.10	gerandiums	geranion G	a plant: crane's bill
		geranos G	a crane (bird): *preyed on pygmies*; *see 268.29*
		gerundium L	"that which is to act": a gerund, *i.e.*, verbal noun (*Grammar*)
.17	Ares	Arês G	god of war; *identified with Roman Mars*
.18	Boreas	Boreas G L	the north wind
.18	Ganymede	Ganymêdês G	"Bright, Joyful": beautiful youth carried off to heaven to be cupbearer to Zeus

.17–.18	Ares . . . Boreas . . . Ganymede	alpha, bêta, gamma G	letters A, B, G: *first 3 letters of* G alphabet
.18	Zeus	Zeus G	chief god of the Greeks, *identified with Roman Jupiter*
		zêta G	letter Z: *last letter of Roman alphabet*
.19	O'Meghisthest	ho megistos G	the very great
		ô mega, ômega G	letter Ō, *last letter of G alphabet*
.20	Satis	satis L	enough
.20	Satis . . . Werbungsap	verbum sat sapienti [est] L	a word is enough to the wise man
.20	vos	vos L	you (*pl.*)
.L2	οὐκ ἔλαβον πόλιν·	ouk elabon polin; G	they did not capture a city;
.24	patrarc	patrarchos G	tutelary god
		patriarchês G	chief of a family
.27	plutous	ploutos G	wealth, riches
		Ploutos G	"Wealth": god of riches
		Plutus L	(=Pluto)
		Ploutôn G	god of the netherworld [*Christianized: the devil*]
.27	paupe	pauper L	poor; poor man
		-au- *pron.* -o- *in lowerclass* L	pope
		papa L pappas G	bishop, pope
.29	Lindley's	Lindsay [?] (1858–1937)	modern Scottish Latinist, produced *Latin Language* and *Short Historical Latin Grammar*
.29	Murrey's	G. G. A. Murray (1866–1957)	Australian-born British Hellenist of considerable popular renown
		[Lindley Murray (1745–1826)	was a grammarian of *English*]
.31	hortatrixy	hortatrix L	a female inciter, encourager, exhorter
.F3	mens uration	mens L	the mind, understanding

		mensuratio L	a measuring
.F4	Llong and Shortts	Lewis and Short	compilers of major English-language *Latin Dictionary*
		Liddell and Scott	compilers of major English-language *Greek-English Lexicon*
270.02	Quantity counts though accents falter	Allusion to classical metrics	G and L verse scans as patterns of long and short syllables (quantity), not of stressed and unstressed syllables (accent) as in Eng.
.03	Yoking	*trans.* zeugma G	*Grammar:* two subjects with same predicate, strictly belonging to only one ("doth sometimes Counsel take, and sometimes Tea")
.03	oblique orations	oratio obliqua L	indirect discourse (*Grammar*)
.05	sollicitor's	*sollicitor L	annoyer, disturber; seducer
		sollicitor L	I am disturbed; I am being seduced
.14	queckqueck	quisquis, quicquid L	whoever, whatever
		quisque, quicque L	each, all
.21	Liddell	Henry George Liddell (1811–1898)	co-compiler of *Greek-English Lexicon* (*see 269.F4*); father of Lewis Carroll's Alice
.24	Nike	Nikê G	"Victory": goddess of victory
.L2	*O'Mara*	*anagram of* Maro	Vergil's cognomen (with Omar?)
.L2	*Farrell*	Fearghail Mod. I. = Fergil O.I. = Vergilios Celt. = Vergilius L	"Supervalor": ancient Celtic name [see *Gaelic Lexicon*]; Vergil's birthplace, Mantua, was in Gallia Transpadana, his origin Celtic

.L2	*O'Mara Farrell*	Publius Vergilius Maro	greatest L poet, author of *Eclogues, Georgics, Aeneid*
.25	volve	volvo L	to turn, to open (*a book*)
.25–.26	virgil	Publius Vergilius Maro	from 3d C through Middle Ages his works were regularly used for divination; *see 281.R3*
.25	the O of woman is long	*allusion to* quantitative scansion; *see 270.02-03*	assertion that the first syllable of "woman" should scan as long
.25–26	O . . . long	ô mega, ômega G	letter ô
.27	sequent her	sequentur L	they follow
.27	from Nebob see you never stray who'll nimm you nice and nehm the day	*From* nemo *let you never say /* neminis *or* nemine	mnemonic from a L textbook: *nemo* ("no one") substitutes *nullius hominis* (Gen.) and *nullo homine* (Abl.) for **neminis* and **nemine*, although *nemini* (Dat.) and *neminem* (Acc.) both regularly occur
.30	memoiries	moira G Moira G	part, lot, share, fate goddess of Fate
.30–.31	puny wars	Punica Bella L	Punic Wars: three wars between Rome and Carthage for control of the Mediterranean; ended with destruction of Carthage and Roman supremacy
271.L1	*Monastir*	Mona L	1. Anglesea island; 2. Isle of Man
.03	Jeallyous Seizer	C. Julius Caesar (102–44 b.c.)	well-known Roman general, statesman, orator, dictator; assassinated
.L2	*Cliopatria*	Clio L Kleiô G	"Fame": muse of history
		patria L	fatherland

		Cleopatra L	"Paternal Renown":
		Kleopatra G	famous queen of Egypt;
		(69–30 b.c.)	bore Julius Caesar a
			son, later became Mark
			Antony's mistress #*A*
.05	tryonforit of	triumvirate of	held joint power in the
	Oxthievious, Lapidous	Octavianus,	Roman world after the
	and Malthouse	Lepidus and	death of Caesar and
	Anthemy	Marcus	defeat of Brutus and
		Antonius	Cassius at Philippi,
			until Antony's defeat
			by Octavian at Actium
			(31 b.c.)
.06	Lapidous	lapideus L	consisting of stone
.06	Anthemy	anthemoeis G	flowery
.R2	OMEN	omen L	a presage: Octavian
			went on to become
			Augustus, the first
			emperor
.R2	ONUS	onus L	a burden: Lepidus was
			the make-weight in the
			triumvirate
.R2	OBIT	obit L	he opposes; he comes
			to (*a place*); he
			perishes: Antony's
			subsequent career:
			opposed Octavian, went
			to Egypt, was defeated
			and killed himself
.07	Suetonia	Suetonia L	female member of the
			gens named *Suetonius*,
			"Customary"
		C. Suetonius	Roman biographer,
		Tranquillus (a.d.	secretary to emperor
		75–160)	Hadrian; wrote *Lives of*
			the First Twelve Caesars
.10	Mutua	mutua (*fem.*) L	borrowed, lent; a loan;
			in return
		per mutua L	mutually, from one to
			another
.13	trigemelimen	trigemino L	to treble
		trigeminus L	three born at a birth,
			set of triplets
		gemellus L	born at the same time,
			twin-born

		limen L	threshold, lintel, sill
.20	*nolens volens*	nolens volens L	unwilling [or] willing, willing or not, willy-nilly
.21	brume	bruma L	midwinter
.24	Coax	Koax G (?)	croaking of a frog in Aristophanes' *Frogs* (in *Paradise Lost* Milton has Satan "like a Toad" prior to his appearance as a snake)
.25	Hail, Heva	[H]eva L	Eve, first woman
		Ave L	Hail (*Eva* spelled backwards: *a medieval pietistic contrast between Eve and Mary*)
.L4	*hyperape*	hyperapo- G	more-, above-, excessive[ly]-
.F4.2	gymnufleshed	gymnos G	naked
		genu flecto L	to bend the knees, kneel
272.02	Leda	Lêda G	bore by Zeus in the form of a swan two eggs, from which came Pollux, Castor, Helen and Clytemnestra (*different combinations in different versions*) and an immense amount of G literature ("Who would dream there lay there / All that Trojan slaughter / Agamemnon murdered / And the Twins?"—O. St. J. Gogarty [Buck Mulligan])
.05	Pappapassos	pappa L pappas G	word with which infants call for food; a father
		passus L	a step, pace; footstep, track, trace
.05	Mammamanet	mamma manet L	1. a breast remains 2. mamma [mother] remains

.07	totties	toties L	so often, as often
.10	Minnowaurs	Minôtauros G	(*Minos* + *tauros*, "bull"): monster with bull's head and man's body, shut in the Cretan labyrinth and fed human flesh; #*A*, *Daedalus*
		Metaurus	river in Umbria *where Romans defeated Hasdrubal, Hannibal's brother; now* Meturo
.11	actiums	Actium L	promontory in west Greece off which Octavian defeated Antony and Cleopatra in a naval battle (31 b.c.)
.14	A.D.	a[nno] D[omini] L	in the year of the Lord
.16	Janus	Janus	old Italian deity, god of beginnings; his temple at Rome was kept open during war, closed in peace
.20	trace	treis G tres L	three
.21	stirrup	tessara G	four
.24	Murph	Morpheus G	god of dreams
.24	pace	pace (*Abl.*) L	with [*someone's*] leave
.26	Leon	leôn G leo L	lion
.L4	*Hoploits*	hoplitês G	heavy-armed foot-soldier
.L4	*atthems*	Athênai G	Athens
.F3	lethemuse	lêthê G	forgetfulness
		Lêthê G	river in underworld which shades drank of to forget the past
		*lêthês Mousa G	the Muse of forgetfulness
273.02	Opprimor's	opprimor L	I am oppressed
		*opprimor (*correctly* oppresor) L	a crusher, oppresser
.02	Opima	opima (*neut. pl.*) L	honorable spoils

.04	heptarched	heptarchê G	magistracy of one-seventh (*of a country, etc.*)
		hepta G	seven
.04–.05	heptarched span of peace	seven-arched span of peace	the rainbow
		Iris G L	Rainbow
		Eirênê G *Irene L	Peace
.05	lex	lex L	law, a proposed law (bill)
.05	nex	nex L	murder, slaughter
.05	mores	mores L	customs
.06	Fas est	fas est L	it is lawful, it is proper, it is fit; it is possible
.L3	*Cowdung Forks*	Furculae Caudinae L	Caudine Forks, Forks of *Caudium* (*a town*): mountain-pass where Roman army was trapped by the Samnites and forced to pass under the yoke (321 b.c.); *a national humiliation never forgotten by the Romans* [now *Casale di Forchia* near *Benevento*]
.L3	*our pick of the basketfild. Old Kine's Meat Meal*	Cannae L Kannai G	"Reeds, Canes": village in Apulia where Hannibal destroyed a Roman army (216 b.c.); some reports put Roman losses as high as 50,000; afterwards the Carthaginians filled baskets with the rings of Roman knights who had fallen on the battlefield; 50,000 corpses made excellent fertilizer
.17	hectoendecate	hekatoendeka G	one hundred and eleven
		hekta G	six

		hendeka G	eleven
.L4	*nappotondus*	tondeo L	to shear, clip, crop, shave
		tondus (correctly tonsus) L	shaved, clipped
.24–.25	Hell o' your troop	hêliotropion G	heliotrope, sundial
.28	tricuspidal	tricuspis L	having three points *or* tines, threepointed
274.07	Paulus	Paulus L	"Little": Roman surname of the Aemilian family
		L. Aemilius Paulus (*d.* 216 b.c.)	consul, commanded Roman army at Cannae; killed there; *see 273.L3*
		Paulus L	L name of St. Paul, born Saul; *see 274.11*
.09	Hannibal mac Hamiltan	Hannibal son of Hamilcar (246–182 b.c.)	Carthaginian commander in Second Punic War; defeated Romans at Cannae (216 b.c.); *see 273.L3*
.11	Timothy	Timotheos G	"Honoring God": companion of St. Paul, co-author of six of Paul's epistles and recipient of two; *see 274.07*
.14	sempereternal	semper L	always, ever, forever
		sempiternus L	everlasting, perpetual
.15	doloriferous	*dolorifer L	pain-bearing, grief-bearing
.L3	*calends*	kalendae L	the first day of the month
.25	a nemone	anemônê G	anemone, windflower
		a *nemine L	away from no one (*but see 270.27-28*)
.25	windstill	*trans.* Anemôtis G	"She that stills the wind": Athena
.30	prepueratory	*praepueritia L	before boyhood, before childhood
.F2	gnows	gnôsis G	knowledge
		gn- G	kn- Eng (knows)
.F2	gneesgnobs	genua L	knees

		gn- L	kn- Eng (kneesknobs)
.F2	gnatives	gnatus OL natus L	a son
		gnativus OL nativus L	that has arisen by birth
.F2	Genuas	genua L	knees
		gn-, gen- L	kn-
.F2	gnows ... gnees-gnobs ... gnatives ... Genuas	Indo-European correspondences	original Indo-European g- altered variously in daughter languages; L and G retained g-, all Germanic languages (including Eng) replaced with k-
275.01	hircohaired	hirco- L	goat-
.03-.04	these things being so ... those things having done	*trans. of* toutôn d'houtôs echontôn G tauta poiêsas G his factis L	these things being so

these things being done *common G and L beginnings of paragraphs in historical works* |
| .R1 | CENOGENETIC | kainos G *kainogenetikos G | new, fresh newly genitive; newly generative; newly engendered |
| .04 | Pacata | pacatum L | "pacified": any country friendly to Rome |
| .04-.05 | Pacata Auburnia | Pacata *Auburnia L

Pacata Hibernia L | Pacified *Auburnia [loveliest village of the plain?]

Pacified Ireland |
.R1	DIAGONISTIC	*diagônistikos G	thoroughly fit for contest, very contentious, completely disposed to fight
.L2	*macroscope*	*makroskopos G	one that sees [*things*] large
.L2	*telluspeep*	tellus L	the earth, the dry land, the planet Earth
.13	hen's	hen G	one
.18	velivole	velivolus L	sail-flying, winged with sails: *poetic of a ship*

.L4	*Quick quake quokes*	hic, haec, hoc L	this, this here (*masc., fem., neut.*)
		qui, quae, quod L	who, what (*masc., fem., neut.*)
.F5.1	hairyoddities	Hêrodotos G (484–425 b.c.)	earliest G historian, called "father of history" by Cicero
.F6	for the nusances of dolphins born	ad usum Delphini[s] L	"for the use of the Dauphin": the Delphin classics: *series of texts for school use edited by Pierre Daniel Huet (1630–1721), tutor to the Dauphin, published in France 1670–1680*
276.L1	*pulfers*	pulver L	dust, powder
.L2	*Omnitudes*	omnis L	all, every
		*omnitudo L	allness
.09	Hiccupper ... Hagaba	Hecuba L Hekabê G	wife of Priam (*king of Troy at its fall*): *destined as Penelope's slave, she changed to a dog through rage*
.11	Vespertiliabitur	vespertilio L *vespertilio (*invented verb*) L	a bat to be a bat
		*vespertiliabitur L	he will be *bat-ed, he will be *made into* a bat
.13	Becchus	beccus L Bacchus L Bakchos G	beak, bill (*of a cock*) a name for Dionysus; came to be regarded as god of wine
.15	fruminy	frumen L	gruel *or* porridge used in sacrifices
.L3	*aegis*	aegis L aigis G	goatskin: the skin shield of Zeus, lent by him to Athena; *later*, with snake-fringe and Medusa's head, an emblem of power and terror
.R3	OFFRANDES	*offrandi L (*correctly offerendi*)	those fit to be offered

.19	Diana	Diana L	Roman goddess, sister of Apollo, identified with Artemis; of the moon, of hunting, of chastity
.23	noctules	Noctulius	a god of the Brixians (Gauls of *Brixia*, now Brescia)
		noctiluca L	"that shines by night": the moon
.F4.1	Ida	Ida G L	mountain in Crete where Zeus was reared by a she-goat, Amaltheia
.F5.2	capritious	*capritius L	one having to do with goats, a goatish person
277.L1	*Fluminian road*	Via Flaminia L	the great northern highway of Roman Italy, built 220 b.c. by C. Flaminius; extended 209 miles to *Ariminum* (*mod.* Rimini); it was lined with tombs to a proverbial extent
		flumineus L	of, in *or* belonging to a river
.07	To	to (*neut.*) G	the
.07	To obedient of civity in urbanious at felicity	obedientia civium urbis felicitas L	the citizens' obedience [is] the city's happiness—*motto of Dublin*
.08	at	at L	moreover, but, yet
.L5	*deossiphysing*	deus sive natura L	"god or else nature": Spinozan formula
		deus si[ve] L physis G	god or else nature
		*theosophizô G	to theosophize, to act the part of one wise in the ways of God
		*deossifaciens L	de-boning
.L5	*Theas*	thea; theos G	goddess; god
.L6	*pondus*	pondus L	a weight

.F2	rape … lucreasious	the rape of Lucretia	Lucretia, wife of L. Tarquinius Collatinus, was raped by Sextus Tarquinius, son of Lucius Tarquinius Superbus, seventh and last king of Rome; she killed herself, precipitating the expulsion of the Tarquins and abolition of the kingship (6th C b.c.)
.F2	lucreasious	Lucretius L	"Profitable": name of a Roman gens
		Titus Lucretius Carus (99–55 b.c.)	Epicurean philosopher and atomist, author epic poem *De rerum natura* ("On Nature")
.F2	togery	toga L	normal peacetime dress of a Roman citizen
278.04	circuminiuminluminat- ed	circum L	around
		minium L	red-lead, cinnabar; *at a triumph the* triumphator's *face was painted red with* minium
		inluminatus (*pp.*) L	lighted up, illuminated
		*circumminioill- uminatus L	lit up all around with minium
.04	encuoniams	encomia L egkomia = enkomia G	praises, eulogies
		quoniam L	since now, seeing that, whereas
.05	improperies	improperium eccl. L	a reproach, taunt
		improperia (*pl.*) eccl. L	1. the taunts to which Christ was subjected; 2. his reproaches to the scribes and Pharisees and Jerusalem (*Matt. 23*)

.L1	*tinctunc*	tinctus L	a dipping into, a dyeing; baptized
		tunc L	then, at that time
.R1	INCIPIT	incipit	the intermission begins
	INTERMISSIO	intermissio L	
.L2	*Flabbius*	flabilis L	airy; spiritual
		Fabius L	"Skilled": name of a Roman gens
		Flavius L	"Blond": name of a Roman gens
.L2	*Flabbius Muximus*	Quintus Fabius Maximus Cunctator (*d.* 203 b.c.)	dictator in Second Punic War; called *Cunctator* ("Delayer") because relied on guerrilla tactics against Hannibal to conserve Roman strength after Trasimene and Cannae
		Quintus Fabius Maximus Rullianus (*fl.* 300 b.c.)	three other Q. Fabii Maximi notable enough in their lives to have acquired agnomina for significant
		Quintus Fabius Maximus Aemilianus (186–130 b.c.)	accomplishments and to have their names preserved in history books
		Quintus Fabius Maximus Allobrigicus (*fl.* 121–108 b.c.)	
		*Flavius Maximus L	*Flavius the Greatest (*no such specific person*)
		could be Cnaeus Flavius (5th C b.c.)	secretary to Appius Claudius, *pontifex maximus*, published legal proceedings to the people
		or Titus Flavius Sabinus Vespasianus (a.d. 9–79)	Vespasian; emperor a.d. 69–79; restored order after Nero's excesses

		Titus Flavius Vespasianus (a.d. 39–81)	Titus; emperor a.d. 79–81; son of Vespasian; a big spender and lenient toward opponents, he was universally loved in his short reign
		Titus Flavius Domitianus (a.d. 51–96)	Domitian; emperor a.d. 81–96; son of Vespasian and brother of Titus, he began well but became suspicious and repressive, was at last murdered; the last of the Flavian emperors
.L2	*Muximus*	maximus L	the greatest
		muxa G mucus L	snot
		*muximus L	the snottiest
.L2	*Niecia*	Nicaea L	"Victorious": name of
		Nikaia G	several cities
		nica! L nika! G	conquer! *cry by which circus fans encouraged their favorite gladiators*
.L2	*Flappia*	Fabia L	woman of the gens *Fabia*
		Flavia L	"Blonde": woman of the gens *Flavia*
.L2	*Minnimiss*	minimis L	to *or* by the least
		minima (*fem.*) minimus (*masc.*) L	very small, smallest (opp. *maximus*)
.14	a letters	litterae L	"letters [*of the alphabet*]": a letter, epistle, missive
.L3	*Brotus*	Broteas G L	one of the *Lapithae*, slain by the Centaur Gryneus
		L. Junius Brutus (*fl.* 510 b.c.)	semi-legendary leader of revolt against the kings of Rome; founder of the Republic
		M. Junius Brutus (85–42 b.c.)	descendant of L. Junius Brutus; assassin of Caesar

.16	a letters, A letters	*see 278.14 E–F*	
.18	a letters	*see 278.14 E–F*	
.18	Ten men L	*trans.* decemviri	a college or commission of ten men; *of several such in Roman history and the Roman constitution the most noteworthy was the* Decemviri legibus scribundis *that took over the government at the expulsion of the kings; overthrown after Appius Claudius's attempt to seize Virginia was frustrated when her father killed her; see 281.R3, 282.26*
.19	ton	ton (*Acc.*) G	the [man]
.19	men	men G	*particle, expresses* 1. *certainty;* 2. *that its clause or word is correlative to another clause or word to follow*
.20	den men	men ... de G	*correlative particles:* on the one hand ... on the other hand
.21	hen	hen (*neut.*) G	one
		to hen G	the One (*Philosophy*)
.F2.2	culious	culus L	arse
		# *L/R Interchange*	curious
.F3.1	Enastella	stella L	star
.F4.1	Heavenly twinges	Castor and Pollux	twin sons of Leda and of Zeus; the constellation Gemini
.F7.1	proud ... turquin	Lucius Tarquinius Superbus (*fl.* 534–510 b.c.)	L. Tarquin the Proud: traditional last king of Rome; an Etruscan, probably historical; *his son raped Lucretia, precipitating revolt led by L. Junius Brutus that ended the kingship; see 277.F2 and 278.L3*

279.03	Erigureen	Johannes Scotus Erigena (a.d. 813–880)	John the Irish-born Scot [Scot = Irishman]: Irish monist, prominent at court of Charles the Bald in France and as Abbot of Malmesbury in England, where the monks murdered him; *the Church of Rome fell into heresy by disagreeing with his doctrines*
		Erigôn	a river in Macedonia
.04	osseletion	osse- L	bone-
		[de]letio L	an annihilating, destroying
		*osseletio L	a destroying of the bones
.05	omen nome	nomen est omen L	the name is the omen; *i.e.*, the name fits (*e.g.* a *Paulus* might be small, a *Calvus* bald, etc.)
.05	nome	nomê G nome L	an ulcer
.04–.05	osseletion ... omen nome	*symptomatic syphilis*	softening of the bones, ominous ulceration
.F1.4	malody	malo L	to prefer, to choose above (*something else*)
		malus L	bad, evil
		melôdia G	chant, song, music
.F1.8	Quick erit faciofacey	quod erat faciendum feci L	what had to be done I did
		*quid erit facio L	what will be I do
		*quid erit feci L	what will be I did
.F1.8	conjugate	conjungo L	to connect, join, unite; join in marriage; copulate
		conjuga L	spouse, wife
.F1.9	amare	amare (*infinitive*) L	to love
.F1.12	likon	eikôn G icon L	image, likeness
.F1.12	pettigo	petigo L	a scab, eruption

.F1.15	octette and viginty	octo et viginti L	twenty-eight
.F1.24	Bina	bini L	two each
.F1.24	Bisse	bis L	twice
.F1.24	Trestrine	tres L	three
		trini L	three each
.F1.32	anegreon	Anakreôn G (*fl.* 540 b.c.)	lyric poet, born at Teos, Asia Minor, lived at Athens
280.03	annalykeses	*analexis G	a picking up, gathering, selecting, reading through
		analektos G	choice, select
		lykos G	a wolf
.L1	*hicstory*	hic L	this, this here
.L1	*Barbarassa*	barba rasa L	a shaved-off beard
		barbarus L	foreign, strange, non-G
		barbaros G	(*and* non-Roman)
.L1	*harestary*	hairesis G	a taking, acquisition; election; purpose; system of principles; religious party *or* sect
.07	lex	lex L	law
.09	A.N.	A[mati] N[omen] L	name of the beloved
.13	F.M.	F[ecit] M[onumentum] L	has erected [this] monument
.L4	*hélos*	hêlos G	nailhead, stud; nail
.32	fount Bandusian	fons Bandusia L	Bandusia the fountain: a rockspring near Horace's birthplace at *Venusia; see 281.L1*
.32	fount Bandusian shall play liquick music	O fons Bandusiae ... loquaces / Lymphae desiliunt tuae L	O fountain Bandusia ... your chattering clear waters leap down—*opening and close of Horace*, Odes *III .13*
.32	liquick	loquaces (*pl.*) L	chattering
281.L1	*venuse*	Venus L	goddess of beauty and sexual love
		Venusia L	town in southern Italy, birthplace of Horace; *now* Venosa; *see 280.32*
.04	*Pline*	C. Plinius Secundus Major (a.d. 23–79)	Pliny the Elder, encyclopaedist; died in eruption of Vesuvius

		C. Plinius Caecilius Minor (a.d. 62–114)	Pliny the Younger, nephew of the Elder; author of *Letters*
.05	*Columelle*	L. Junius Moderatus Columella (1st C a.d.)	Spanish-born writer on husbandry, wrote *De re rustica* ("About Rural Matters") and *De arboribus* ("On Trees")
.05	*Gaules*	Galli L	the Gauls: Celtic nation occupying the territory of *mod.* France, north Italy, Switzerland, the Low Countries the Rhine valley, and also part of Asia Minor (Galatia)
.06	*Illyrie*	Illyria L	a country on the Adriatic, *mod.* Jugoslavia and Albania
.07	*Numance*	Numantia L	city in *Hispania Tarraconensis*; *destroyed by Scipio Africanus the Younger (133 b.c.); now* Soria on the Duero in the north of Spain
.R1	BELLUM-PAX-BEL-LUM	bellum L	war
		pax L	peace
.R2	MUTUOMORPHOM-UTATION	mutuo L	in return, by turns, reciprocally
		morphês	shape, form
		mutatio L	changing, alteration, exchange
		*mutuomorpho-mutatio L + G	a reciprocal exchange of shape
.14	Margaritomancy	margaritomant-eia G	divination by means of pearls
.14	Hyacinthinous	Hyakinthos G Hyacinthus L	beautiful youth beloved but accidentally killed by Apollo; from his blood sprang the flower
.14	pervinciveness	pervinca L	periwinkle (*flower*)

.R3	SORTES VIRGINIANAE	sortes Vergilianae L	the Vergilian lots: divination by opening a copy of Vergil at random and seeking oracular guidance from whatever line one hits upon
		sortes *Virginianae L	*the Virginian lots: lots having to do with *Virginia*, danghter of *Lucius Virginius*, who stabbed her to death to save her honor from *Appius Claudius* (c. 450 b.c.). *See 278.18; 270.25*
.15	Bruto	M. Junius Brutus (85–42 b.c.)	assassin of Caesar
.16	Cassio	G. Cassius Longinus (*d.* 42 b.c.)	assassin of Caesar
.16	trifid	trifidus L	cleft into three parts; three-forked
.L4	*saxum*	saxum L	a rock, large stone
.L4	*sextum*	sextum (*adv.*) L	for the sixth time
		sextum (*neut.*) L	the sixth (*thing*)
.19	totients	totiens L	so often, so many times, as often
.20	quotients	quotiens L	how often, how many times, as often as
.21	aerger	aeger L	sick, unwell, diseased
		aêr G L	the air
.24	oxyggent	oxys G	sharp
		*oxyggent G = *oxyngent:	
		ingens L	mighty, vast
.F1.1	Valsinggiddyrex	Vercingetorix (*d.* 46 b.c.)	Gallic prince led revolt against Caesar (52 b.c.); *ultimately defeated and captured, he was killed at Caesar's triumph*
		rex L [rix Celt]	king
.F1.2	arks	arx L	citadel

		arcus L	bow, rainbow; arch
.F1.2	triump	triumphus L	ceremonial procession by a victorious Roman general through the streets of Rome with soldiers, the Senate, and chief captives, who were often then killed, as Vercingetorix was at Caesar's Gallic triumph
		triumpe	exclamation used in solemn procession by the Arval brothers (a Roman order of priesthood)
.F1.2	arks day triump	arcus triumphalis L	at a triumph the army entered through a gate which was often later replaced by a commemorative arch
.F2.2	nateswipe	nates L	the rump, buttocks
282.R3	AUSPICIUM	auspicium L	divination by observing the flight of birds
.06	At maturing daily gloryaims	Ad majorem Dei gloriam L	To the greater glory of God: *motto of the Society of Jesus*
.R4	AUGURIA	augura (*pl.*) L	observations and interpretations of omens
.09	arith	arithmeô G	to count, to number
.11	fingures	fingo L	to touch, handle; fashion, make
.L2	*Truckeys'*	trochaios G trochaeus L	running, spinning; *in meter,* a foot consisting of a long syllable followed by a short (*named for its brisk tempo*)
.L2	*dactyl*	daktylos G dactylus L	a finger; *in meter,* a long syllable followed by two short (*like the bones of a finger*)

.L2	*spondee*	spondeion G spondeum L	vessel used in pouring libations; *in meter*, a foot consisting of two long syllables (*because of its slow solemn cadence, as in pouring libations and making vows*)
.21	numen	numen L	a nod of the head: the divine will, divine sway; divinity; a god
.L3	*Panoplous*	panoplos G	in full armor, fully armed
.L3	*peregrine*	peregrinus L	foreign, exotic, strange
.24	hoojahs	hujus L	of this
.24	koojahs	cujus L	whose
.25	catachysm	katachysma G	that which is poured over: *e.g.*, sauce, confetti
.26	quickmarch to decemvers	March to December	the original Old Roman calendar of ten months; seemingly had an uncounted gap in the winter
.26	decemvers	Decemviri	"Ten-men": a college or commission of ten men; *several such occurred in Roman history and in the Roman constitution*
		Decemviri legibus scribundis L	The ten-man board "for writing the laws": commission that composed the laws of the Twelve Tables; governed Rome absolutely after the expulsion of the kings; overthrown after the scandal of Appius Claudius and Virginia; *see 281.R3*
		ver L	the spring
.26–.27	the tenners	*trans.* decemviri	[board of] ten men

.27	thumbs down	sign for a kill in gladiatorial contests	when a gladiator had been forced to the ground his victorious opponent looked to the emperor, or to the crowd, who signalled whether the loser should be finished off or spared by a thumbs down or a thumbs up gesture
.29	caiuscounting	Caius *old spelling for* Gaius	a Roman praenomen
		Gaius Julius Caesar (102–44 b.c.)	reformed the Roman republican calendar into essentially the calendar used today (modified by Pope Gregory)
.F2	Lawdy Dawdy Simpers	Laus Deo Semper L	praise to God forever
		*Lauda Deum semper L	praise God forever
283.L1	*Non plus ulstra*	non plus ultra (*also* ne plus ultra) L	not any farther, no farther; *L trans. Job 38:11: "Hitherto shalt thou come, but* no further"; *also used for* "no longer possible," *and* "unsurpassed"
		non plus *Ulstria L	no more Ulster
.03	borus	Boreas G L	the north wind
.03	notus	Notos G Notus L	the south wind
.03	eurus	euros G eurus L	the southeast wind
.L1	*Elba*	Ilva L	island off west coast of Italy
.L1	*nec*	nex L	murder
.L1	*nec, cashellum tuum*	nec castellum tuum L	nor your castle
		nec *Cashellum tuum L	nor your Cashel (*town with ruined ecclesiastical acropolis in Co. Tipperary*)

.04	zipher	Zephyros G	the western breeze
		Zephyrus L	
.04	tricks	tris L	three
		tertius L	the third
		trixos (Ionic) G	threefold
.04	quarts	quartus L	the fourth
.04	quims	quintus L	the fifth
.08	aloquent	aliquanto L	somewhat, considerably
		aliquot L	some, several, a few
		eloquens L	speaking, endowed with speech
.08	sexes	sex L	six
		sexies L	six times
		sexus L	sex
.08	suppers	septem L	seven
.09	oglers	octo L	eight
.09	novels	novem L	nine
.09	dice	decem L	ten
		dikê G	custom, usage, justice
.13	fullmin	fulmen L	lightning that strikes, thunderbolt
.15	ad libs	ad libitum L	at pleasure, at will
.L2	*Kyboshicksal*	kybos G	dice
.24	nucleuds	nucleus L	a little nut, a kernel
		Eukleidês G (*fl.* 300 b.c.)	inventor of geometry
.24	alegobrew	alegô G	to mind, heed, be careful
.27	agnomes	agnomen L	surname acquired by an individual, not passed on to progeny; *e.g.* *Africanus, Cunctator*
.27	incognits	incognitus L	unexamined, not known, unknown, unclaimed
.28	dororhea	*dôrorhea G	streams of gifts
		Dôrothea (*fem.*) G	gift of God
284.02	parilegs	paralegô G	pluck out superfluous hair; sail along beside; speak beside the point, wander in speech, rave
		paralêgô G	to be next to the end
		paralêxis G	penultima
.08	rivisible	rivus L	small stream, brook

.09	nighttim	*noctim L	in the night, at times in the night
.09	involted	involo L	to fly into, rush upon
		*involtus (*correctly* involatus) L	flown into, rushed upon
.10	heventh	# G-to-L	seventh
.L2	*oxygon*	oxygonon G	kind of poppy: corn poppy, *Papaver Rhoeas* or *Papaver hybridum*
		*oxygônon G	a sharp-sided figure
.12	permutandies	permutandis L	things requiring to be changed
.15	extructed	exstructus (*pp.*) L	built up, filled with buildings
		intended as opposite of instructus (*pp.*) L ?	furnished, provided; versed in
.17	see, ex and three	CXIII L	113
	icky totchty ones	CXI L	111
.19	deaferended	deferendum L	that which is to be carried away
.20	contonuation	*contonatio L	a heavy thundering
.21	urutteration	uro L	to burn up
		# *Reduplication*	complete *utteration
.22	antesedents	antesedens L	sitting in front of
.23	bissyclitties	bis L	twice
		kleitoris G	clitoris
		Clytie L Klytiê G	daughter of Oceanus turned into the heliotrope
.27	tandem	tandem L	at length, at last, finally
.27	ottomantic	mantikê G	science of prophecy
.30	viridorefulvid	viridis L	green
		refulgeo L	to flash back, reflect light; shine
		fulvus L	reddish-yellow, gold-colored, orange
		*viridifulvus L	green-orange (*Irish colors*)
.F4.3	V for wadlock	v- L (# *Labials*)	w-
285.01	lenz	lens L	1. louse's egg, nit; 2. lentil
.03–.04	zitas	*MG pron.* zêta G	letter Z

.03	zitas runnind hare and dart	Zeno's paradoxes	1. Achilles (the hare is a replacement) can never catch the tortoise 2. a flying arrow at any single moment is motionless
.L1	*Finnfinnotus*	notus (*pp.*) L	known; an acquaintance
.L1	*Finnfinnotus of Cincinnati*	Cincinnatus L *cognomen of* Lucius Quinctius Cincinnatus *(519–438 b.c.)*	"Ringleted" favorite hero of the Roman republic; was dictator (458 b.c.) for 16 days in which he defeated the Aequi, resigned, and returned to his farm whence he had been summoned
.09	exarx	exarchês *more correctly* ex archês G	from the beginning
		exarchos G	leader, beginner; the one who goes first, chief
		arx L	citadel
.10	himmulteemiously	# G-to-L	*simmulteemiously
.15	pamtomomiom	panto- G	all-
		mômos G	blame, reproach
		*pantomômion G	place of all reproaches
		Pandaemonium Mod L	place of all demons or devils: Pandemonium
		*Pandaimônion G	(Milton's invention)
.16	aqualavant	*aqualavans L	washing with water, water-washing
.L3	*balbearians*	balbus L	stuttering, stammering
		barbaroi G	foreigners, non-Greeks
		barbari L	(*also* non-Romans)
.27	Iris	iris G L	goddess of the rainbow; the rainbow
.27	Binomeans	binomis L	having two names: *e.g.* Ascanius (also called Iulus), Troy (also called Ilium), the United States (also called America)

.29	aximones	axi- G	worth-, value-, -worthy
		*aximonê G	a worth-stopping at
		*aximonos G	worth being alone
.29	prostalutes	prostas G	porch, vestibule
		lutum L	mud
286.02	aosch	chaos [anagram] G	the first state of the universe, unformed matter; space; infinite darkness
.R1	HEPTAGRAMMAT-ON	*to heptagrammat-on G	the seven-lettered word
		modeled on to tetragrammaton G	the four-lettered word YHWH, the ineffable Hebrew name of God (Yahweh) [the heptagrammaton may be JEHOVAH or JUPITER]
.07	nettus	netus L	1. spun; 2. thread, yarn
268.08	exerxeses	Xerxes (519–465 b.c.)	king of Persia, led vast army against Greece; delayed by defence of Thermopylae, he occupied Athens; his fleet was destroyed at Salamis and his army at Plataia (479 b.c.)
		exercitus L	an organized army; the Army
286.R2	LUSTRAL	lustralis L	relating to purification from guilt or to the appeasing of the gods
		lustrum, pl. lustra L	1. a bog; a house of ill repute; debauchery 2. a purificatory sacrifice performed every five years; a period of five years
.R2	PRINCIPIUM	principium L	a beginning, commencement
.R2	LUSTRAL PRINCIPIUM	lustri principium L	the beginning of a lustrum (five-year period)
		lustrale principium L	a lustral beginning: a beginning relating to purification or to a lustrum

.19	aquilittoral	*aquilitoralis L	of or belonging to the water-seashore
.21	salivarium	*salivarium L	a place to salivate in; a place for mouth-watering in; a place for having an appetite
.21	equoangular	*equoangularis L	horse-angled, having horse corners
.22	trilitter	*trilitteris L	having three letters
.R3	INGENUOUS	ingenuus L	free[born] man
.R3	LIBERTINE	libertinus L	freed man
.25	nei	nei OL ne L	not
.25	numb ... suspecting the answer know	num L	*interrogative particle implying a negative answer is expected:*
		e.g., num barbarorum Romulus rex fuit? L	Was Romulus a king of the barbarians? *(obviously expects answer "no")*
.25	Dolph	adelphos G	a brother
.R4	PROPE	prope L	near, nearby
.26-28	Oikkont ... ninny? ... expecting the answer guess	oukoun G	is it not so? *(expecting the answer "yes")*
		nonne L	not? *(expecting the answer "yes")*
.R4	PROCUL	procul L	far off, afar
.F1	Rhombulus	rhombos G	bull-roarer; magic wheel; tambourine; male sex organ; whirling motion; lozenge-shaped figure
		Romulus L	legendary founder of Rome; twin brother of Remus whom he slew
.F1	Rhebus	rebus (*Abl. pl.*) L	by means of things
		Remus L	legendary co-founder of Rome; slain by his twin brother, Romulus
.F1	rhomes	rhômê G	bodily strength
		Rhômê G	Rome
		Roma L	Rome
.F5	choucolout	lutum L	mud

287.01	olorum	olorum (*Gen. pl.*) L	of swans, swans'
.01	D.V.	Deo volente L	God [being] willing
		Deus vult ML	God wills [it]
.04	Deva	Deva L	river in Caledonia in Britain; *now* Dee *in Scotland*
.08	*Amnium instar*	amnium instar L	1. according to the likeness of rivers; 2. a sketch *or* image of rivers
.09	locus	locus L	a place, spot
.13	Mux	muxa G	mucus, snot
		mox L	soon
.14–.15	*a* but pronounced olfa	alpha G	letter A
.16	*Bene*	bene L	well; good, fine
.18	Dolph	adelphos G	brother
.19	balbose	balbus L	stammering, stuttering
.20	*venite, preteriti, sine more*	venite, praeteriti, sine mora L	come, departed ones, without delay
.20	*dumque de entibus nascituris decentius in lingua romana mortuorum parva chartula liviana ostenditur,*	dumque parva chartula Liviana de entibus nascituris ostenditur, decentius in lingua Romana mortuorum L	and while a little "Livian" paper about beings about to be born is shown, more fitly in the Roman language of the dead,
.21	[*chartula*	chartula L	little writing, piece of paper, bill]
.21	[*chartula liviana*	charta liviana L	"Livian paper": 2nd of 5 grades of papyrus in Imperial Rome, a high quality, used for literary texts; named for Livia wife of Augustus; # *A*]
.21–.22	*sedentes in letitiae super ollas carnium,*	sedentes in laetitia super ollas carnium	sitting in joy above the pots of meat
.22	*spectantes immo situm lutetiae*	spectantes immo situm Lutetiae L	beholding in fact the site of Paris

.22	*unde auspiciis secundis tantae consurgent humanae stirpes,*	unde auspiciis secundis tantae consurgent humanae stirpes L	whence in accordance with the auspices so many human lineages will arise,
.23–.25	*antiquissimam flaminum amborium Jordani et Jambaptistae mentibus revolvamus sapientiam:*	mentibus revolvamus antiquissimam sapientiam flaminum amborum Jordani et Joannis Baptistae L	let us turn over in our minds the most ancient wisdom of both the priests Jordan and John the Baptist:
.24	[*Jordani*	Jordani (Gen.) L	of *Jordan* = Giordano (Bruno)]
.24	[*Jambaptistae*	*Jambaptistae (Gen.) L *recte* Joannis Baptistae L	of *John Baptist* = Giambattista (Vico)]
.25	*totum tute fluvii*	totum tute fluvii L	all safely the rivers
.25	*modo mundo fluere,*	modo mundo fluere L	just now flowed in the world
.25–.26	*eadem quae ex aggere fututa fuere,*	eadem quae ex aggere fututa fuere L	the same which had been fucked from the embankment
.25	[*eadem quae ex aggere fututa fuere,*	eadem quae ex aggere *futura* fuere L	the same which had been *about to be* out of the embankment]
.26	*iterum inter alveum fore futura,*	iterum inter alveum fore futura L	again will be about to be among the riverbed,
.26	[*iterum inter alveum fore fututa,*	iterum inter alveum fore *fututa* L	again will be *fucked* among the riverbed,]
.26	*quodlibet sese ipsum per aliudpiam agnoscere contrarium,*	quodlibet sese ipsum per aliudpiam agnoscere contrarium L	whatever you like recognizes its own self through any other contrary thing,
.27–.28	*omnem demun amnem ripis rivalibus amplecti*	demum amplecti omnem amnem ripis rivalibus L	at last embracing each river with rival [lit. "river-sharing"] banks

.29	rebelliumtending	rebellio L	1. renewal of war; revolt; 2. a rebel
.F3	Canorian	canorus L	melodious, harmonious
288.02	tropadores	tropa- tropê G	turn-, turning-
		tropos G	turn, direction, way
.04	cunctant	cunctans L	delaying
.06	ungles	ungula L	hoof, claw, talon
.09	ficts	ficta (pl.) L	deceptions, untruths
.11	barroccidents	*baroxytonos G	"deep-sharp-sounding": having a grave-acute [circumflex?] accent
		occidens L	falling down, setting
.12	accidence	*accidence*	*the part of G & L grammar dealing with inflection of words*
.14	solomnones	solum L	alone, only, merely, barely
		Nonae L	Nones; the 5th day of every month but March, May, July, October, when it was the 7th
.17	P. T.	P[otestas] T[ribunicia] L	the Tribunicial power, the power lodged in a Tribune
.17	Publikums	publicum L	possessions of the state, public property; the state; a public place
.17	P. T. Publikums	*intended as* Potestas *Tribuni Publici ? [recte Tribuni Plebis] L	the power lodged in a Tribune of the People
.18	sotiric	sôtêr G	savior, deliverer
		sôtêrika G	festival of deliverance
.19	peccaminous	peccamina	fleshly sins, corporeal
	corpulums	corpulenta LL	sins
.21	celestine	caelestinus L	heavenly
.23	nostrums	nostrum (neut.) L	ours, our own
.24	galloroman	Galloromanus L	a Gaul living under Rome
.24	galloroman cultous	cultus Galloromanus L	refinement [culture] of the L-speaking Romanized Gauls, 44 b.c.–a.d. 500.

.24	cultous	cultus L	refinement; care; veneration [of a deity]
.F6.1	petery parley	Peter Parley *penname of* Samuel Griswold Goodrich, *Am. publisher* (1793–1860)	young Stephen Dedalus read "Peter Parley's Tales about Greece and Rome" *see* Portrait *54.12, M 58*
289.02	Propagandi	propagandi L	persons fit to be preserved or propagated
.03	chrism	chrisma G	anointing, unction; grace
.05	esoupcans	Aisôpikos G Aesopicus L	an Aesopic: a beast fable
		Aisôpos G Aesopus L	Phrygian creator of beast-fables
.07	ophis	ophis G	serpent
.09	Pales	Pales L	god and goddess, patrons of flocks; their feastday (21 April) was Rome's birthday
.10	th'Empyre	empyrios G	"in fire": pure light beyond the world; heaven
.14	*hoc*	hoc L	this thing here
.17	coal on:	colon L kôlon G	limb, bodily member; clause
.20	medeoturanian	medeor L	to heal, cure, remedy, mend
		Turan	Etruscan goddess identified with Aphrodite
		*medeoturanius L	pertaining to healing-Turan, to Turan the healer
		mediterraneus L	inland, far from the sea
.22	*disparito*	disparo L	to part, separate
		disparatus L	separated, divided
.27	Ides	Idus L	the thirteenth day of each month except March, May, July and October, when it was the fifteenth

.29	Comes	comes L	companion, comrade; courtier
		comes LL	occupant of any office of state
		comes ML	count, earl
290.04	semicupiose	*semicupidus L	half-desirous
.06	Auliffe	alpha G [aleph Heb.]	letter A
.07	Beth	bêta G [beth Heb.]	letter B
.07	MacGhimley	gamma G [ghimel Heb.]	letter G
.08	sincuries	sine cura L	without care: sinecure
.09	MacDollett	delta G [daleth Heb.]	letter D
.06	Auliffe ... MacDollett	alpha, bêta, gamma, delta G	letters A, B, G, D: first four letters in order of the G alphabet; *but not of the Heb.* [*aleph, beth, veth, ghimel*]
.19	Multalusi	multa lusi L	I have played much
.21–.22	tubatubtub and his diagonoser's lampblick	Diogenês G (412–323 b.c.)	"Born of Zeus": Cynic philosopher, ascetic, lived like a dog in a tub; fabled to have carried a lantern looking for an honest man
.23	*jure*	jure (*abl.*) L	from *or* by justice, with justice
.23.3	F nuncandtunc	nunc L	now
		tunc L	then
.23	simper	semper L	ever, always
.24	plurible	plorabilis L	lamentable, deplorable
		*pluribilis L	multipliable
.27	Lagrima	lacrima L	a tear
.27	Gemiti	gemitus L	a sigh, groan
.F3	Mamalujorum	mamma L	1. a breast; 2. a mother
.F3	Mamalujorum and Rawrogerum	-orum, -um L	*Gen. pl. suffixes for nouns of different declensions*
291.01	Unic	unicus L	one and no more, only, sole, single
.03	mavrue	mavroô MG	to blind; make
		mauroô G	powerless; make dim

.03	synamite	dynamis G	power, might
		syn- G	with-
.08	subsequious	subsequus LL	following, succeeding
.08	timocracy	timokratia G	worth-rule: 1. state in which love of honor is the ruling principle (Plato); 2. state in which power is proportionate to property (Aristotle)
.13	finis	finis L	the end, the finish
.14	nelliza	Elissa	a name for Dido; *see 291.F3*
.17–.18	through, for or from a foe	*trans.* inimico (*Abl.*) L	for *or* from an enemy (*but not* through)
		per inimico L	through a foe
.18	by with as on a friend	*trans.* amico (Abl.) L	by, with, as (*but not* on) a friend
		in amico L	on a friend
.21	ambo's	ambo, ambos (*Acc. pl.*) L	both
.22	amarm	amare (*infinitive*) L	to love
.24	*que*	quei OL	who?
.24–.25	*tu es pitre*	tu es Petrus L	thou art Peter [Rock]
.28	neonovene	neo- G	new-
		novenus L	nine each; nine
		neonymphos G	newly married
.F3	dido	Dido L Didô G	"The Wanderer": legendary foundress of Carthage; according to Vergil became paramour of Aeneas and killed herself upon his departure
.F6	cuticatura	cuticura L	skin-care
.F6	Fennella	faeniculum L	"little hay": fennel
292.01	*Vae Vinctis*	vae vinctis L	woe to the fettered, woe to those tied up
		vae victis L	woe to the defeated: *said by Brennus, Gallic leader who sacked Rome 390 b.c.*
.05	diorems	diôria G	fixed space, appointed time

		theôrêma G	sight, spectacle; object of contemplation; speculation, theory
.12	*gonna*	gynê G	woman
.12	ut	ut L	that, so that
.16	convolvuli	convolvulus, *pl.* convolvuli L	a caterpillar that wraps itself up in a leaf; bind-weed
		*convulvula L	with a little vulva, with a little womb
.17	longa	longa (*fem.*) L	long
.17	yamsayore	jam L	now, at present
.17	longa yamsayore	longaeva L	an old woman
.19	pharahead	pharos G	plough; lighthouse
.19	faturity	fatuor L	1. to talk foolishly; 2. to be inspired
.19	convolvulis	convolvulus, *etc.*	*see 292.16*
.20	the novo	de novo L	newly, as a new thing, once more
.25	symibellically	syn G	with
		semi- L	half-
		bellicus L	of *or* pertaining to war, military
.28	gyrographically	*gyrographikôs G	roundly written; written in circles
.29	gogoing	# *Reduplication*	
.30	Plutonic	*Ploutônikos G	a follower of Ploutôn/Pluto, "the wealth-giver"; god of the underworld
.30	Platonic	Platônikos G	follower of the philosophy of Plato
.F2	brut	Brutus	legendary refugee from Troy, like Aeneas; eponymous settler of Britain
293.07	somnione sciupiones	Somnium Scipionis L	"The Dream of Scipio": *final part of Cicero's* De republica, *a vision of the cosmos widely known in the Middle Ages through preservation with the* Commentary *by* Macrobius

.09	murphy ... murphy ... murphy ... murphy	morphê G Morpheus G	form, shape god of dreams
.10	maryamyriameliamurp-hies	myrias G	ten thousand
		milia (*pl.*) L mille [passus] L	thousand[s] a thousand [paces], a mile
		morphê G Morpheus G	form, shape god of dreams
.11	lazily eye ... lapis	lapis lazuli Mod L lapis L	blue stone stone
.diag-ram	π	pi G	letter P
.diag-ram	ä ... λ	alpha, lambda G	letters A, L
.L1	*Uteralterance*	uter L	1. skin-bag, bottle; 2. which of two
		uterus L alter L alteruter L	womb the other of two one or the other, either
.14	Ulm	ulmus L	elm-tree
.L2	*Vortex*	vortex OL vertex L	whirl, eddy; top of the head; highest point
.18	aristmystic	aristos G mystikos G	best connected with the mysteries; private, secret
		*aristomystikos G	connected with the best mysteries
.19	Ante	ante L	before, prior to
.19	Ante Ann	ante annum L	before the year
.L4	*Vertex*	vertex L	*see* Vortex, *293.L2 B above*
.22	leaves alass! Aiaiaiai	*allusion to* Hyakinthos G Hyacinthus L	youth beloved by Apollo, accidentally killed by him; from his blood sprang the flower, marked on leaves or petals AI
.22	Aiaiaiai	ai G L	alas
.22	Antiann	anti G anti OL ante L	against before, prior to

		ante annum L	before the year
		Antianus L	of *or* pertaining to *Antium, coastal town in Latium, now* Anzio
.F2.1	Pantifox	panti- G	all-
		pontifex L	"bridgemaker": Roman high priest
294.01	presbyoperian	presbys G	old man; ambassador; president
		ôpê G	view, sight
		ôps G	eye, face
		*presbyôpê G	an old sight, a first sight
		*presbyôps G	old-face, old-eye
		opera (*pl.*) L	works, the works
.04	ait	ait L	he says, he affirms
.04	Lambday	lambda G	letter L
.05	anchore	anc[h]ora L	"bend": anchor
		ankyra G	
.L1	*Sarga*	sargos G sargus L	a kind of fish
		sarx G	flesh, meat; the physical order
		surgo L	to lift, raise up; rise, arise, stand up
.08	Olaf	alpha G	letter A
.09	centrum	centrum L	a sharp point: the
		kentron G	stationary foot of compasses; *hence,* middle of a circle
.09	Olaf's lambtail	alpha lambda G	letters A, L
.10	circumscript	circumscribo L	to draw a line around, to enclose in a circle
		circumscriptus L	(*Rhetoric*) rounded into periods, periodic
		circumscripte L	summarily
.10	cyclone	kyklon (*Acc.*) G	ring, circle
.10	ter	ter L	three times, thrice
.11	the calf of an egg	*trans.* vitellus L	1. little calf; 2. yolk of an egg
.12	me now	Menôn G	*Meno*: Plato dialogue featuring a geometry lesson
.12-13	discobely	diskobolia G	discus-throwing
.14	Quok	quo L	where, wherefore; whither

		quoque L	also
.L2	*Docetism*	*Dokêtismos G	"Apparitionism": doctrine that Christ had no physical body
		docet L	[he, she] teaches
.L2	*Didicism*	didachê G	teaching
		didici L	I have learned
.L2	*Maya-Thaya*	mea-tua L	mine-thine [possessions]
.L2	*Thaya*	thea G	goddess
.20	lydias	Lydia	country in Asia Minor, *fabled original home of Etruscans*
.23	auriscenting	auris L	the ear
.24	Abraham Bradley King	ABC L	first letters of L alphabet (C = K)
.26	lavas	lavas L	you (*sing.*) wash
.26	*Bene*	bene L	well; good, fine
.27	Byzantium	Byzantium L Byzantion G	ancient city on Bosporus; renamed New Rome 330, later Constantinople; now Istanbul
.29	Gaudyanna	gaudeo L	to rejoice, be glad
		gaudens L	rejoicing
		gaudienda L	things worth delighting in
.31	consinuously	*consinuose L	very intricately, wound roundabout
		sinus L	a bay
.F1.1	Ex	ex L	out of, out from, from
.F5	anmal matter	alma mater L	nourishing mother
295.01	homolocous	homo- G	same-
		homo L	human being, man
		locus L	place, spot
		*homolocus G + L	in-the-same-place; one who is in the same place
.01	hesterdie	hesterno [die] L	yesterday, on yesterday
.01	istherdie	isto die L	on that day
		[H]ister L	the lower Danube
.02	Vanissas Vanistatums	vanitas vanitatum L	vanity of vanities, emptiness of emptinesses
.13	dromed	dromaô G	to run

		dromeus G	a runner
.13	dromed ... Dairy	dromedarios G	running [camel]:
		dromedarius L	dromedary
.17	*Bene*	bene L	well; good, fine
.19	Loosh	lutum L	mud
		luteus L	muddy
.20	tetra-	tetra- G	four-
.23–.24	Gyro O, gyre O,	gyros G	ring, circle
	gyrotundo	gyro- G	round in a circle
		rotundo L	to make round, to round off
		rotundus L	wheel-shaped, circular
.25	herum	[h]erum (*Acc.*)	master of a house, proprietor
		horum, harum L	of these
.33	Lucihere	luci- L	light-
296.01	mea	mea (*fem.*)	my own, my darling
.01	Nun	nun G	now
.01	lemmas	lêmma G	anything received; gain, credit, profit; (*Logic*): premise; title *or* argument of an epigram; burden
.02	quatsch	quatio L	to shake, to agitate
		quassus L	shaken, shattered
.02	vide	vide L	see!
.02	akstiom	axion (*neut.*) G	of equal value, worth as much as; of value, worthy, worth
		axiôma G	an honor; a decree; self-evident principle
		Aktion G	"Seashore":
		Actium L	promontory in Greece off which Octavian defeated the fleet of Antony and Cleopatra, 31 b.c.
.03	limon	limen L	sill, lintel, threshold
		leimôn G	meadow
.03	stickme	stigmê G	spot, mathematical point
.03	punctum	punctum L	that which is pricked, small hole, puncture, point; punctuation mark

.04	semenal	seminalis L	of *or* belonging to seed *or* semen
.04	Araxes	Araxês G L	river in Armenia flowing into the Caspian; *now the* Aras
.08	Airmienious	Armenius L	an Armenian
		Arminius L (18 b.c.–a.d. 19)	"Herman": German prince who defeated Varus a.d. 9, thus saving Germany from Roman domination
		Jacobus Arminius (1560–1609)	Jacob Harmensen, Dutch theologian, countered Calvinist predestination
.10	apexojesus	apex L	extreme end, point, summit
		apo G	away, away from
		exêgêsis G	explanation, interpretation
		*apexêgêsis G	an explaining away
.16	angelous	angelus L	an angel
.20	arrahquinonthiance	qui non L	who not?
.24	alfa pea	alpha pi G	letters A, P
.26	logoical	logoeidês G	prose-like, prosaic; command of language; resembling reason; reasonable
		logikos G	for speaking; speech; suited for prose; reasonable; argumentative; logical
.28	Nike	Nikê G	"Victory": goddess of victory
.30	*aqua in buccat*	aqua in buccam L	water into the mouth
		aqua in bucca L	water in the mouth, in the cheek
.F3	Suksumkale	sursum corda L	hearts on high; lift up [your] hearts
		sursum caelo L	upwards to heaven
297.01	geomater	*geômêtêr G	earth-mother, mother of land
		geômetrês G	land-measurer, geometer
		Gê mêtêr, Gaia matêr G	mother Earth

.03	hexengown	hexagônos G	six-sided
.05	Sibernia	*Sibernia *pseudo-L for* *Hibernia *pseudo-G*	Ireland # G-to-L
.06	me now	Menôn G	*Meno: see 294.12*
.06	Pisk	piscis L	a fish
295.07	serpumstances	serptum (*pp.*) L	crept, crawled
297.09	trickkikant	tragakantha G	"goat thorn": tragacanth
.10	fillies calpered	felix culpa	happy sin: Adam's Fall; # B
.10	calpered	Calpe L Kalpê G	the Rock of Gibraltar
.12	vortically	vortex L	the highest point; *see 293.L2*
.L2	*Prometheus*	Promêtheus G	"Forethinker": formed men of clay animated with fire stolen from heaven
.14	napex	apex L	extreme end, point, summit
		napê, napos G	grove, thicket; ravine
.L2	*Provision*	provisio L *trans.*	foresight, forethought
		promêtheia G	ditto, *cf. Promêtheus*
.21	discinct	discinctus L	unbuckled; negligent; voluptuous
.21	isoplural	isopleuros G	equilateral
.22	flument	flumen L	river, flood, stream
.22	fluvey	fluvius L	river
.23	fluteus	fluo L	to flow
		luteus L	muddy
.24	triagonal	triagônos G	three-sided
.24	delta	delta G	letter D; anything shaped like letter *delta*, *e.g.*, rivermouth, female pudenda
.25	appia	Appia (*fem.*) L	1. Roman praenomen, esp. of the gens Claudia 2. [Via]: the Appian Way; *road from Rome to Brundisium* (*Brindisì*)
.25	lippia	lippa (*fem.*) L	blear-eyed, dim-sighted

.25	pluvaville	pluvia L	fain
		pluvialis L	rainy
.27	vulve	volva, vulva L	wrapper; womb
.27	usquiluteral	usque L	all the way to, as far as
		lutarius L	muddy, living in mud
		lutum L	mud
		luter L	wash-basin
		usque ad luterem L	as far as the wash-basin
		usque ad lutum L	all the way to the mud
.32	Afrantic	Afer L	African
		Publius Terentius Afer (190–159 b.c.)	Roman comic poet
		Afranius L	name of a Roman gens
		Lucius Afranius (2nd C b.c.)	Roman comic poet, contemporary with Terence
.32	allaph	alpha G	letter A
.32	bett	bêta G	letter B
298.11	*Ambages*	ambages L	a roundabout way; the passages of a labyrinth; circumlocution; ambiguity; puzzle
.04–.05	Quicks herit rossyending	quid erit faciendum L	what will need to be done?
.05	Quef	Qu[id] e[rit] f[aciendum] L	*as above 298.04F–.05A*
.07	tunc's	tunc L	then
.07	tunc's dimissage	nunc dimittis L	now you release ["now lettest thou *thy servant* depart *in peace*" Luke 2:29]
.12	empthood	emptum L	a purchase
		emptus (*pp.*) L	bought
.L2	*Ecclasiastical ... Hierarchies*	Peri tês ekklêsiastikês hierarchias G	*On the Ecclesiastical Hierarchies*: work falsely attributed to Dionysius the Areopagite, *Athenian converted by St. Paul*
.L2	*Celestial Hierarchies*	Peri tês ouranias hierarchias G	*On the Heavenly Hierarchies*: work also falsely attributed to Dionysius the Areopagite

.14	vectorious	vectorius L	of *or* for transport; transport-
.15	circumflicksrent	*circumflictus L	dashed together all around; a collision around
.16	elipsities	elleipsis G	falling short, defect; *conic section* ellipse; omission *in writing*
.16	gyribouts	gyrios G	circular, round
.17	reprodictive	reprodictus L	deferred again, readjourned
.18	unpassible	impassibilis L	not subject to passions *or* emotions
.19	logos	logos G	computation, account, tally, value, proportion; explanation, statement, principle, narrative, word, tradition, language, *etc., etc., etc.*
.20	mantissa	mantissa Etr. L	a worthless addition, makeweight; gain
		mantida (*Acc.*) G	prophetess
.21	minus	minus L	less
.21	nullum	nullum L	nothing
.21	orso	*trans.* velut L	even as, just as, like as; as, for instance
.26	abscissan	abscissa (*neut. pl.*) L	things torn away, separated, divided
.27	Sexuagesima	sexagesima (*fem.*) L	the sixtieth
		sexagesima L	a sixtieth part
		*sexuagesima L	the *sex-tieth
.28	paradismic	paradeisos G	a park, orchard, pleasure-garden; Paradise
		paradeigma G	model, example,
		paradigma L	pattern
.28	perimutter	peri G	around, about
		perimotoô G	to put lint around, to bandage
		perimetron G	circumference
		perimetros G	very large
.L3	*Allothesis*	*allothesis G	a putting somewhere else

.31	calicolum	caelicolum (*Gen. pl.*) L	of the dwellers in heaven
299.01	scholium	scholium L *for* scholion G	interpretation, comment, short note
.02	euchs	euchê G	prayer
.03	Qued	Qu[od] e[rat] d[emonstrandum] L	which was to be proved
.08	Quoint	quoi (*Dat.*) OL	to whom?
.08	quincidence	quin- L	five-, fif-
.08	O.K.	O[mnes] K[alendae] L	all Calends, every first of the month
.L1	*Canine*	Canis L	"The Dog": worst throw with dice (1 on a single die, 2 on a pair, *etc.*)
.L1	*Venus*	Venus L	"The Beauty": highest or best throw with dice
.09	*Omnius Kollidimus*	omnes collidimus L	we all clash together, we all collide
.L1	*Aulidic*	Aulidikê G	belonging to Aulis (*small port in Boeotia from which the G fleet sailed to Troy*)
		aulêtikê G	having to do with a flute
.L1	*Aphrodite*	Aphroditê G	goddess of sensual love, identified with Venus. *Neither an* Aphroditê Aulidikê *nor* Aphroditê Aulêtikê *is on record*
.13	mooxed	muxa G	snot
.L2	*Ors*	orsa L	beginnings; an attempt; words, speech
.L2	*Sors*	sors L	lot, fate, chance
.22	Simperspreach	semper L	ever, always
.L2	*Fors*	fors L	chance, luck
		Fors L	goddess of chance
.24	ars	ars L	art
.28	lozenge	*trans.* rhombos G	lozenge; male sex organ
.F4.1	⊓	san G *numerical symbol* G	archaic letter: SS (?) 900
.F4.1	Δ	delta G	letter D

		numerical symbol G	10
.F4.1	⊣	*part of* ê G	old letter = h; *when H became used for sound ê [êta],* ⊢ *was reduced in size and written over a letter to indicate h-sound [ȧ = ha];* ⊣ *was also reduced and written over initial vowels to indicate* no *h-sound [ȧ = a]*
		numerical symbol G	900 (variant of ⊓)
.F4.1	X	chi G	letter CH
		numerical symbol G	1,000
.F4.1	Λ	lambda G	letter L
		numerical symbol G	30
.F4.1	Ϲ	wau G [# *Digamma*]	letter W (common variant form)
		numerical symbol G	6; *also* 5 (as variant of *gamma*)
300.04	aequal	aequalis L	that can be put on an equality with; equal
.07	invernal	infernalis L	nether, lower, belonging to the lower regions
		vernalis L	of *or* belonging to spring
		*invernalis L	1. in-spring-ish 2. unspringlike 3. very springlike
.L1	*Primanouriture*	primanuritura LL	first-suckling
.L1	*Ultimogeniture*	*ultimagenitura LL	last generated, last created
.16	*leo*	leo L	lion
.16	*leo* I read	lego L	I read [*leo*: Spanish]
.17	escribibis	bibis L	you (*sing.*) drink
		*scribebis (correctly scribes) L	you (*sing.*) will write [*as if 1st or 2nd conjugation rather than 3rd*]

.17	mycoscoups	mykês G	mushroom
.18	ravenostonnoriously	tonans L	thundering
.18	ihs	IHS[OUS] = Iês[ous] G	Jesus
.24	curructive	ructatus (pp.) L *corructatus L	belched belched together
.24	mund	mundus L	elegant person; the world
.25	grafficking	graphikos G	capable of drawing, suitable for writing, skilled in writing
.26	sinister	sinister L	left, on the left
.26	cyclopes	kyklôpes G	"round-eyed": one-eyed giant savages
.26	trigamies	*trigamos G	three-marriage, marriage of three spouses
.30	thur	thus, thuris L thuos G	incense
.30	quartos	quarto L	for the fourth time
.32	tamquam	tamquam L	as much as, so as, just as, as if
301.08	moultylousy	*multilucidus L multa lusi L	many-lighted I have played much
.15	animal	anima L	soul
.19	mysterion	mysterion G	mystery, secret rite
.19	purate	#P/K split	curate
.23	quisquis	quisquis L	whosoever, whoever, whatsoever
		quisquiliae L	sweepings, droppings, refuse
		allusion to Odysseus?	outis or quisquis with the Cyclops
.25	the Cartesian spring	Pierius L	Pierian: sacred to the Muses (daughters of Pieros); poetic ["Drink deep, or taste not the Pierian spring"—Pope, Essay on Criticism, 216]
.26	diesmal	dies mali L	evil days
.F3.1	profused	profusus (pp.) L	poured forth
.F5.1	Dear old Erosmas	Desiderius Erasmus (1466–1536)	Dutch humanist né Gerrit Gerritszoon

		desiderius L	dear, lovable
		erasmios G	dear, lovable
.F5.1	Erosmas	Erôs G	sexual love; the god of sexual love
302.03	pascol's	pasco L	to pasture, to drive to pasture
		paschalis L	pertaining to Easter *or* Passover
.03	kondyl	kondylos G	a knuckle
.06	bistris-	bis L	twice, two times
		tris L	thrice, three times
.12	elementator joyclid	Eukleidês (*fl.* 300 b.c.)	"Of good fame": wrote textbook *Elements* (*of mathematics*)
.12	joy-	*trans.* eu-	happily-, well-
.R1	LEMAN	Lemannus L	lake in Gaul; *now* Lake Geneva
.13	jure	jure (*Abl.*) L	by *or* with justice
.16	calamum	calamum (*Acc.*) L	reed pen
.22–.23	ad lib	ad libitum L	at will, as one pleases
.24	Orbison	orbis L	the world
.27	dies	dies L	a day; days
.31	ook, ook, ook	ouk G	not, no
.32	holypolypools	holos G	the whole, all
		poly- G	many-
303.11	parparaparnelligoes	par L	equal
		para G	beside, along, from
		ligo L	to tie, bind together
.18	puppadums	puppa L	girl, lass
.19	paraboles	parabolê G	comparison, illustration, analogy
.19	famellicurbs	famelicus L	suffering from hunger
.23	pergaman	Pergamon G L	City-State in Asia Minor. fl. 3rd-2nd cent. b.c.
		pergamena L	parchment, orig. from Pergamon
.26	quare	quare L	by what means? how? why?
.32	misocain	miso- G	hating-
		*misokainos G	hating the new
.F1.1	eelyotripes	hêliotropos G	sun-dial; a flower (heliotrope)
304.R2	PIX	pix L	pitch, tar

		pyx (adv.) G	with the fist
		pyx G	buttocks
		pyxis G	a box, a pyx
.R3	EUCHRE	eucheiria G	sleight of hand
.R3	EUCHRE RISK	eucharistos G	agreeable, grateful, beneficient
		Eucharistia G LL	"Thanks-giving": the Eucharist
.17	toxis	toxon G	a bow
		toxikon G	poison (for arrows)
.18	Saxon Chromaticus	Saxo Grammaticus L	"The Learned Saxon"—Danish chronicler, source of the Hamlet-story
.18	Chromaticus	chrômatikos G	relating to color; chromatic (music)
.19	Nubilina	*nubilina L	1. little marriageable girl (sing.); 2. cloudlets (pl.)
.25	Virginia's	Virginia L	her dishonor by Appius Claudius led to downfall of Decemvirs; see 281.R2
.L2	Catastrophe	katastrophê G	a down-turning (cf. 298.L2 The Descending): an overthrow, ruin
.26	delph	adelphos G	a brother
.L2	Anabasis	anabasis G	going up, ascent (cf. 298.L2 The Ascending)
		hê Anabasis	The March Up: Xenophon's account of Cyrus' march up into Persia
.28	ambows	ambos L	both
.L3	processus	processus L	a going forward, advance, progress
.29	crambs	krambê G	cabbage
		krambis G	cabbage-caterpillar
.31	allaloserem	alla G	but
		alalos G	speechless, dumb
		alalai G	a cry of joy
		allos G	other, another
		allêlôn G	of one another
.31	cog it out, here goes a sum	cogito, ergo sum L	I think, therefore I am: Descartes' famous axiom

305.03	salubrated	saluber; salubris L	health-giving, healthful; advantageous, beneficial
.R1	COMPITA	compita L	crossroads
.R1	CUNCTITITITILAT-IO	cuncti L	all in a body, all together, all
		titillatio L	a tickling
.09	hiscitendency	hisco L	to open, gape, yawn
.13	energument	energos G	at work, active, busy
.L1	*Orexes*	orexis G L	longing, appetite
.19	jubalee	Juba	*name of 2 Numidian kings; #* A
		juba L	mane
.R2	IOIOMISS	io io L	ho ho!
		Iô G L	girl turned into a heifer by Jove
.L2	*Trishagion*	to Trishagion G	the Thrice-holy [Trinity]
.23–.24	shanty ... scanty shanty ... slanty scanty shanty	sanctus, sanctus, sanctus L	holy, holy, holy
.27	Ave	ave L	hail!
.28	Vale	vale L	farewell
.28	Ovocation	ovum L	egg
		ovatio L	lesser triumph, *after a minor* victory
		Oboca L Oboka G	river in Hibernia on Ptolemy's map; *mod.* Avoca
.29	salvy	salve L	fare well, be well; hello; goodbye
.31	book ... lobe	*allusion to*	Loeb Classical Library
306.05	loud ability	Laudabiliter L	"Laudably": Pope Adrian's bull; #*A*
.06	singulfied	singultus L	a sobbing
.09	Oikey	oikoi (*pl.*) G	houses, homes, habitations
		ouki, ouchi G	no, not
.10	Impostolopulos	impostor L	one who *puts upon*: deceiver, imposter
		apostolos G	messenger, ambassador, apostle
.R2	SECURES GUBERNANT URBIS TERROREM	secures gubernant urbis terrorem L	axes govern the city's terror
		securus iudicat orbis terrarum	unconcerned, the world judges; #*B*

.11	studiavimus	*studiavimus, *correctly* studuimus *or* studivimus L	we have studied
.12	manducabimus	manducabimus L	we shall chew
.12	triv	trivium L	1. road fork; place where three roads meet 2. *ML*: lower division of seven liberal arts in educational curriculum: *grammar, logic, rhetoric*
.13	quad	quadrivium L	1. crossroads; place where four roads meet 2. *ML*: upper division of seven liberal arts in educational curriculum: *arithmetic, geometry astronomy, music*
.L2	*Cato*	Cato L	"Cunning": Roman cognomen
		Cato L	*name of a 4th C a.d. collection of moral precepts popular in the Middle Ages; see next entry*
		Marcus Porcius Cato (234–149 b.c.)	the Elder: nicknamed "Censor" because of his advocacy of a strict and simple social life
		Marcus Porcius Cato (95–46 b.c.)	the Younger: reformer and Stoic, in the spirit of his ancestor
.15	Duty, the daughter of discipline	*allusion to* Cato	*see Appendix C:* "Manducanda at Triv and Quad"
.L3	*Nero*	C. Claudius Nero	notorious depraved emperor
.15–.16	the Great Fire at the South City Markets	*allusion to* Nero	# C
.15	*Aristotle*	Aristotelês	# A
.17–.18	A Place for Everything and Everything in its Place	*allusion to* Aristotle	# C

.L6	*Julius Caesar*	Gaius Julius Caesar	#A
.18–.19	Is the Pen Mightier than the Sword?	*allusion to* Julius Caesar	#C
.L7	*Pericles*	Periklês G (490–429 b.c.)	"Far-Famed": Athenian statesman, orator, and general
.19	A Successful Career in the Civil Service	*allusion to* Pericles	#C
.L8	*Ovid*	Publius Ovidius Naso	#A
.20–.21	The Voice of Nature in the Forest	*allusion to* Ovid	#C
.L10	*Domitian*	Domitianus L	belonging to a *Domitius*, "domestic" (*name of a Roman gens*)
		Titus Flavius Domitianus (a.d. 51–96)	emperor 81–96; began as good emperor, but had to be murdered to end the reign of terror at his end
.22	On the Benefits of Recreation	*allusion to* Domitian	#C
.L11	*Edipus*	Oidipous G Oedipus L	tragic king who married his mother
.22–.23	If Standing Stones Could Speak	*allusion to* Oedipus	#C
.L12	*Socrates*	Sôkratês G (469-399 b.c.)	G philosopher, *wrote no books but taught both Xenophon and Plato; used dialectical technique of investigation*
.23	Devotion to the Feast of the Indulgence of Portiuncula	*allusion to* Socrates	#C
.24	Portiuncula	portioncula L Porcioncula ML	a small part *or* portion the "Little Portion" of Our Lady
.L13	*Ajax*	Aias G Ajax L	son of Telamon, king of Salamis; in the *Iliad* he leads the Salaminian contingent against Troy; *of enormous size, a byword for physical strength*

.24–.25	The Dublin Metropolitan Police Sports at Ballsbridge	*allusion to* Ajax	# C
.L14	*Homer*	Homêros G	poet believed by the Greeks to have written the *Iliad* and the *Odyssey; nothing indisputable is known of his life*
.25–.27	Describe in Homely Anglian Monosyllables the Wreck of the Hesperus	*allusion to* Homer	# C
.27	Hesperus	Hesperos G	at evening; the evening
		Hesperus L	star; evening; western, the west
.L15	*Marcus Aurelius*	Marcus L	"Hammer": a Roman praenomen
		Aurelius L	a Roman nomen
		Marcus Annius Verus Aurelius (a.d. 121–180)	emperor 161–180; Stoic philosopher
.27–.28	What Morals, if any, can be drawn from Diarmuid and Grania?	*allusion to* Marcus Aurelius	# C
.L16	*Alcibiades*	Alkibiadês G (450–404 b.c.)	"Strong-Force": Athenian statesman and general in the Peloponnesian War
.28–.30	Do you Approve of our Existing Parliamentary System?	*allusion to* Alcibiades	# C
.L17	*Lucretius*	Lucretius L	"Profitable": name of a Roman gens
		Titus Lucretius Carus (94–55 b.c.)	Epicurean philosopher and poet, expounded the atomist-materialist philosophy in *De rerum natura*
.30	The Uses and Abuses of Insects	*allusion to* Lucretius	# C
.30	Insects	*trans.* insecta L = entoma G *but as if*	cut-into, notched, segmented: insects

		*insecta L =	uncut, uncuttable:
		atoma G	atoms
307.L1	*Plato*	Platôn G	"Broad": major
		(429–347 b.c.)	philosopher, pupil of
			Socrates, teacher of
			Aristotle; developed the
			Idealist philosophy
.01	Clubs	*allusion to* Plato	#C
.L3	*Horace*	Horatius L	"Belonging to *Hora*
			['*Lady': goddess, wife*
			of Romulus]": name of
			a Roman gens
		Quintius	Roman poet and
		Horatius	satirist, friend of Vergil
		Flaccus (65–8	and Augustus
		b.c.)	
.01–.02	Advantages of the	*allusion to*	#C
	Penny Post	Horace	
.L5	*Tiresias*	Teiresias G	legendary blind Theban
			seer so wise his ghost
			still has its wits and is
			not a mere shadow
.03–.04	Is the Co-Education	*allusion to*	#C
	of Animus and Anima	Tiresias	
	Wholly Desirable?		
.03	Animus	animus L	the rational soul in
			man, the mind, the
			reason; sensibility;
			courage
.04	Anima	anima L	air, breeze; breath,
			breath of life, life, soul;
			the vital principle
.L6	*Marius*	Marius L	"Of the sea": name of
			a Roman gens
		Gaius Marius	Roman general, seven
		(157–86 b.c.)	times consul
.04–.05	What Happened at	*allusion to*	#C
	Clontarf?	Marius	
.L7	*Diogenes*	Diogenês	Cynic philosopher; *see*
			290.21-22
.05–.06	Since our Brother	*allusion to*	#C
	Johnathan Signed the	Diogenes	
	Pledge		

.L8	*Procne, Philomela*	Proknê, Philomêla G	sisters, of whom P. was married to Tereus king of Thrace; pretending P. was dead, T. sent for Ph., raped her, and cut out her tongue. P. found Ph. and took vengeance by serving T. his child for dinner. T. pursued both women but the gods changed him to a hoopoe, P. to a nightingale and Ph. to a swallow (*L authors reverse the last two*)
.06–.07	the Meditations of Two Young Spinsters	*allusion to* Procne *and* Philomela	# C
.L10	*Nestor*	Nestôr G	king of Pylos in the Homeric poens; *noted for old age and wisdom*
.08	Hengler's Circus Entertainment	*allusion to* Nestor	# C
.L11	*Cincinnatus*	Lucius Quinctius Cincinnatus	Roman farmer-dictator-farmer; *see 285.L1*
.08–.09	On Thrift	*allusion to* Cincinnatus	# C
.L12	*Leonidas*	Leônidas G (d. 480 b.c.)	"Lionlike": king of Sparta, defended the pass at Thermopylae with 300 Spartans against the invading Persians; he and all his men fell fighting
.09–.10	The Kettle-Griffith-Moyni-han Scheme for a New Electricity Supply	*allusion to* Leonidas	# C
.09	Kettle	*pseudo-trans.* Thermopylai G	"Hot Gates": because of boiling springs there
.09	Griffith	*pseudo-trans.* Leônidas G	"Lionlike"
.L14	*Theocritus*	Theokritos G #(310–250 b.c.)	"God-chosen": poet of Syracuse (Sicily), inventor of the *Idyll*

.11	American Lake Poetry	*allusion to* Theocritus	# C
.L16	*Fabius*	Fabius L	"Skilled": name of a Roman gens
		Quintus Fabius Maximus Cunctator (died 203 b.c.)	dictator in Second Punic War; called *Cunctator* ("Delayer") because relied on guerrilla tactics against Hannibal to conserve Roman strength after Trasimene and Cannae
.13	Circumspection	*allusion to* Fabius Cunctator	# C
.L19	*Esop*	Aisôpos G Aesopus L (6th C b.c.)	G fabulist of Phrygia, creator of beast-fables
.14–.16	Tell a Friend in a Chatty Letter the Fable of the Grasshopper and the Ant	*allusion to* Aesop	# C
.L20	*Prometheus*	Prometheus G	"Forethinker": formed men of clay and animated them with fire stolen from heaven
.16	Santa Claus	*allusion to* Prometheus	# C
.L22	*Pompeius Magnus*	Pompejus L Gnaeus Pompeius Magnus (106–48 b.c.)	name of a Roman gens Pompey the Great: Roman general and politician; fought for Sulla against Marius (*see 307.L6*), fought pirates, extended Roman sway in the East; took part in triumvirate with Caesar and Crassus, fought Caesar in the Civil War, was murdered in Egypt
.17–.18	The Roman Pontiffs and the Orthodox Churches	*allusion to* Pompey	# C

.17	Pontiffs	pontifex L		"bridgemaker": Roman high-priest
.L22	*Miltiades Strategos*	Miltiadês G (550–489 b.c.)		Athenian viceroy and Persian vassal in the Thracian Chersonese, he took part in the Ionian Revolt and fled to Athens. Commanding during the Persian invasion, he defeated the Persians at Marathon.
.L22	*Strategos*	stratêgos G		general, military commander
.17–.18	The Roman Pontiffs and the Orthodox Churches	*allusion to* Miltiades		# C
.L23	*Solon*	Solôn G (640–559 b.c.)		Athenian statesman and poet; reformed the constitution of Athens, establishing the basis of democracy
.18–.19	The Thirty Hour Week	*allusion to* Solon		# C
.L24	*Castor, Pollux*	Castor L Kastôr G Pollux L Polydeukês G		# A
.19–.20	Compare the Fistic Styles of Jimmy Wilde and Jack Sharkey	*allusion to* Castor and Pollux		# C
.L25	*Dionysius*	Dionysios G Dionysos I (430–367 b.c.)		"Belonging to Dionysos [*the god*]" tyrant of Syracuse; deported Plato; wrote bad plays but won first prize in Athenian contest by political influence; *see 070.36*
.20–.21	How to Understand the Deaf	*allusion to* Dionysus		# C

.L26	*Sappho*	Sapphô (*fl.* c. 600 b.c.)	poetess, born in Lesbos, leader of a religious guild of girls; wrote 7 books of poems, most amatory, some homosexual (*whence* "*Lesbian*"), most not; allegedly killed herself for love (of Phaon, a man) but this is an invention. Only fragments of her poems survive
.21–.22	Should Ladies learn Music or Mathematics?	*allusion to* *Sappho*	# C
.L29	*Catilina*	Catilina L Lucius Sergius Catilina (108–62 b.c.)	Roman family name Roman conspirator; active adherent of Sulla in the Civil War and subsequent thuggery; schemed to murder the consuls in 65 b.c., was tried and acquitted. Lost election for Consul to Cicero and organized another conspiracy; this broken, he was killed at head of a rebel force
.24	The Value of Circumstantial Evidence	*allusion to* Catiline	# C
.L30	*Cadmus*	Kadmos G	legendary founder of Thebes; sowed dragon's teeth to get a crop of armed men. Introduced alphabet into Greece
.25	Should Spelling?	*allusion to* Cadmus	# C

.L33	*Themistocles*	Themistoklês G (523–458 b.c.)	"Famous for Justice": Athenian general and statesman; built up the navy; a national hero for the naval victory over the Persians at Salamis (480), postwar anti-Spartanism led to his exile. He fled to Persia and became satrap of Magnesia, where he died peacefully
.26	Eu	eu G *allusion to* Themistocles	well; fine, good #C
.L34	*Vitellius*	Vitellius L	"Calf-like": name of a Roman gens
		Aulus Vitellius (a.d. 15–69)	emperor in 69, the "Year of the Three [or Four] Emperors"—he being second last; caught and murdered
.26–.27	Proper and Regular Diet Necessity For	*allusion to* Vitellius	#C
.L35	*Darius*	Darius	name of three kings of Persia
		Darius I (521–486 b.c.)	after revolt of the six cities of Ionia (*see 307.L33 above*) he invaded Greece, was defeated at Marathon (490 b.c.)
.27	If You Do It Do It Now	*allusion to* Darius I	#C
.F3	Paris	Paris G	son of Priam king of Troy; asked to judge a beauty contest among Hera, Athena, Aphrodite, he picked the latter, who bribed him with Helen. This precipitated both the Trojan War and the participation in it of the gods

.F7.2	hippofoxphiz	hippos G	horse
.F8	Où	ou G	no, not
.F8	Eu	eu G	well; fine, good
.F8	Nenni No	nonne L	not so? (*expecting affirmative answer*)
		Nennius (*fl.* 796)	Welsh annalist: *his Historia Britonum records Arthur's victories*
308.L1	*Xenophon*	Xenophôn G (430–354 b.c.)	Athenian soldier and author, a disciple of Socrates; served abroad as a mercenary, was banished from Athens, lived in Sparta and Corinth
.01	Delays are Dangerous	*allusion to* Xenophon	# C
.01	Vitavite	vita L	life
.02	Mox	mox L	soon
.L2	*Pantocracy*	*pantokratia G	universal rule, almightiness
.L3	*Bimutualism*	bi- L	two-, twice-
		mutualis LL	in return, mutually
		*bimutualis LL	twice in return
.L6	*Superfetation*	*superfetatio L	conception while pregnant
.L7	*Stabimobilism*	stabilis L	that stands firm; firm, steadfast, steady
		mobilis L	easy to be moved, movable; loose, not firm
		*stabilimobilis L	firmly loose
.R2	KAKAOPOETIC	kakopoiêtikos G	prone to do evil
		*kakkapoiêtikos G	prone to make shit
.R2	LIPPUDENIES	lippus L	blear-eyed, dim-sighted, purblind
		lipôdês G	fatty, oily
.L12	*theoric*	theôrikon G	fund at Athens for providing free seats at the theater and public spectacles
.L12	*Amallagamated*	amalla G	a sheaf, bundle of wheat

290 GLOSSARY FOR FINNEGANS WAKE

		gameô G	to marry
		gamos G	a wedding
		*amallagamos G	a *sheaf-wedding
.F1	anticheirst	anti- G	against, opposite
		cheir G	a hand
		anticheir G	thumb
309.02	tribalbutience	tribas G L	female homosexual, lesbian
		alba L	pearl
		albus L	white
		balbutiens L	stuttering, stammering
.05	lymph	lympha L	clear water
.08	allatheses	*allothesis G	placed somewhere else
.09	Etheria	aether L aithêr G	the bright upper air
		Aetheria	*5th or 6th C abbess who left a description of the Holy Land in colloquial L*
.09	Etheria Deserta	Arabia Deserta L	Empty Arabia: *one of the 3 ancient divisions of Arabia: the interior*
.10	ruric	ruro L	to live in the country
		ruris (*Gen.*) L	of the countryside
.10	cospolite	kosmopolitês G	citizen of the world
.11	Hiberio-	Hibêria G L	1. Spain; 2. Caucasian Georgia
.11	Miletians	Milesii L	inhabitants of Miletus, *G city in Asia Minor*
		Milesii ML	descendants of *Miles, legendary colonizer of Ireland from Spain*
.11	Hiberio-Miletians	*Hiberii-Milesii L, ML	Spanish-Irish, Georgian-Miletians, *any combination*
.12	otion	ôtion G	little ear, auricle; little handle
		otium L	leisure, ease, vacation
.21	vaticum	*vaticum L	with a soothsayer, with a poet
		viaticum L	travelling-money, provisions for a journey; Charon's fare; (*eccl L*) the last Sacrament of the dying

.21–.22	woman ... mobile ... man ... static	[*Mozartean?*] *reversal of Pythagorean Table of Opposites*	the *male* column lists "Motion" (*kinêsis*), the female "Rest" (*stasis*)
.23	eliminium	elimino L	to turn out of doors
		*eliminium L	the right to remain outcast, the right to be deprived; being in exile
		modeled on postliminium L	the right of reprisal *or* recovery (*legal term pertaining to prisoners of-war in enemy hands*)
.24	eclectrically	eklektikos G	capable of moral choice; selective
		êlektron G	amber
		êlektôr G	the beaming sun
310.01	enginium	ingenium L	innate quality, nature; temper, peculiarity; talent, genius
.04	twintriodic	triodos G *modeled on*	a three-way
		diodos G, *actually from*	way-through, passage, pass
		dia + hodos G, *as if*	through + way, road
		*diodos G *from*	a two-way
		dis + hodos G	two + way, road
.04	singul-	singultus L	a sobbing
.06	howdrocephalous	hydrokephalon G	water in the head
.07	megacycles	megakykloi G	the Great Cycles in which all the heavenly bodies return to their original position (*apokatastasis*)
.08	serostaatarean	sero L	late, at a late hour
.09	pinnatrate	pinna L	feather, wing
.10	auricular forfickle	forficula auricularia Mod.L	"small shears pertaining to the ear": the European earwig
.12	meatous	mea, tua L	mine, thine [possessions]
		meatus L	a going, way, path, passage

		ous G	ear
.12	conch	concha L	mussel-shell, seashell
		konchê G	
		concha Mod L	the outer ear
.12	meatous conch	ous Aphroditês G	"Aphrodite's ear": a shellfish
.12	meatous ... culpable	mea culpa L	by my fault (*phrase from prayer of confession*)
.14	concertiums	concerto L	to contend, dispute, debate
.20	Iren	eirênê G	peace
.20	Curlymane	*trans.* Cincinnatus	Roman farmer-dictator
		Carolus Magnus L	Charles the Great: Charlemagne
.21	otological	*ôtologikos G	pertaining to the study *or* design of the ear; auricular
.22	cartomance	chartomanteia G	divination by little bits of paper (*mod.*, by playing-cards)
.36	bulletaction	*bulletactio; bulla tactio L	a touching by a *bulla*
		bulla L; eccl L	a knob, amulet; a papal bull [*Laudabiliter?*]
.36	catharic	katharizô G	to cleanse
		kathartikos G catharticus LL	fit for cleansing *or* purifying; purgative
.36	emulsipotion	*emulsipotio L	a drinking of dregs
		emulsipotio Mod L	a drinking of an emulsion
.36	catharic emulsipotion	catharticae emulsionis potio Mod. L	a drinking of a purgative emulsion
311.10	propencil	*propensilis L	hanging down in front
.12	O, Ana	ô Ana G	O Lady, O Mistress
.18	O Connibell	O cunne belle L	O pretty cunt
.18	Connibell	konnos G	1. a trinket; 2. a beard
.26	finixed	phoenix L phoinix G	fabulous bird; *see* 265.08
.26	finixed coulpure	felix culpa L	happy sin; #*B*
.33	tog	toga L	ordinary peacetime urban dress of a Roman citizen

.33	tog his fringe	*part-trans.* toga praetexta L	purple-fringed garment worn by freeborn boys until they assumed the adult toga
312.10	maremen	mare L	sea
.33	plebs	plebs L	the common people
.35	quorum	quorum (*Gen. pl.*) L	of whom
313.08	ructified	*ructifactus (*pp.*) L	made a belch, made into a belch
.11	sagasfide	fide (*Abl.*) L	with faith, in faith
.12	pnomoneya	pneumata (*pl.*) G	blasts, winds
		pleumonia G	pneumonia
.18	sottovoxed	vox L	voice
.20	ind	indu OL in L	in, within, on, upon, into
.20	ast	ast OL at L	moreover, but, yet
.20	velut	velut L	even as, just as, like as
.25	Nummers	nummus L	a coin, piece of money
.25	summus	summus L	the top
.27	Heres	heres L	heir
.33	peripulator	peri G	around
		ambulator L	one who walks about, idler, lounger
		peripatêtês G	one who walks about
314.08	–choractors–	choros G	dance; group of dancers in a play
		chorêgos, choragetas G	leader of a *choros*
.08	–sum–	sum L	I am
.08	–sumum–	summum L	the top
.08	–arum–	-arum L	*fem. Gen. pl. suffix*
.11	Propellopalombarouter	propello L	to drive, push, urge forward; impel, incite, urge
		palumba L	wood-pigeon, ring-dove
.16	arboriginally	arbor L	a tree
		ab origine L	from the beginning
.17	sartor's risorted	sartor resartus L	the tailor retailored: *title of a book by Carlyle*
.19	gibbous	gibbus L	hunched, humped; a hump
.19	pushpull, qq	quisquilia L	waste, rubbish, sweepings

.20	pp	p[ater] p[atriae]; p[rae]- p[ositus]; p[rimi] p[ilus]; p[ro] p[arte] L	father of [his] country; prefect; chief centurion; for the share [*of* *so-and-so*]; *L* *inscriptional* *abbreviations*
.20	intervulve	inter vulvam L	in the middle of the vulva, in the middle of the womb
.21	Paradoxmutose	paradoxos G paradoxotês G mutus L mutuus L	contrary to expectation marvellousness dumb, mute borrowed
.34	*ros in sola velnere*	ros in solo vulnere L	dew in the only wound
.34	*velnere*	volo L	to will, wish for
.34	sicckumed	sic L siccum L	thus dry land, a dry place
.34	homnis	hominis (*Gen.*) L omnis L	a man's, a person's all, every
.34	terrars	terras (*Acc. pl.*) L	lands, countries
.34	sicckumed of homni's terrars	circum omnes terras L	around all the lands
.34		circum Hominis terras L	around the countries of Mankind
.36	famalgia	fama L fames L *famalgia L + G	rumor, fame hunger, greed fame-sickness; hunger-sickness
.36	famas	fama L fames L	talk, rumor, what is said, fame hunger, greed
315.05	liddle	Henry George Liddell	G lexicographer; # *A*
.09	Burniface	Bonifacius L	"Handsome-face"; # *A*
.10	hostily	hostile L hostiliter L	the enemy's territory hostilely
.13	diluv's	diluvies; diluvium L	flood, deluge
316.02	ulstravoliance	*Ulstria Mod L ultra L	Ulster on the other side, beyond, farther, more, besides

		volens L	willing, intending
		volans L	flying
.15	Mitropolitos	Mêtropolitês G	citizen of a mother-city; citizen of *Mêtropolis, capital of Arcadia*
		*Mitrapolitês G	citizen of [Bishop's] Miter-city
.15	hiberniating	Hibernia L	Ireland
		hibernans L	wintering, staying in winter-quarters
		*Hibernians L	Irelanding, staying in Ireland
.19	locquor	loquor L	I speak
.21	Mortimor	timor mortis L	the fear of death
.28	furt	furtum L	theft, robbery
.34	posthumour's expletion	postuma expletio L	a final satisfying
		posthumata expletio L	a satisfying after burial
317.02	relogion's	logion G	an oracle; one of the sayings of Jesus
.02-.03	out of tiempor	*part trans.* ex tempore L	"out of the time": simultaneously, forthwith, on the spur of the moment; according to circumstances
.04	tomtartarum	Tartarum (*Acc.*) L	the infernal regions
.08	cater	quattuor L	four
.12	osturs	ostreon G	oyster
.29	unium	*unium bad L for* unionem (*Acc.*) L *or as if from* *onion G; # G-to-L	a unity, union; a single large pearl; an onion
.32	rosed	ros L	dew
318.04	anerous	anêr G	male person, man [= *vir* L, *fear* Gaelic]
		anêros G	grievous, troublesome, annoying
.05	enthropoise	anthrôpos G	human being, man [= *homo* L, *duine* Gaelic]
		entropê G	"turning towards": respect, modesty; humiliation

.05	homovirtue	homo L	human being, man [= anthrôpos G, duine Gaelic]
		vir L	male person, man [= anêr G, fear Gaelic]
		virtus L	manliness, strength, courage; capacity, worth
.06	Obsit nemon	absit omen L	may an omen be away, i.e., may there be no omen [in it]
		obsit nemo L	may no man be against; may no one injure
.09	panoromacron	pan G	all
		horama G	that which is seen, a sight
		makron G	a long time, a long way
		*panoramamakron G	all that which is seen a long way or a long time
.10	wandercursus	cursus L	a running, course, march, journey
.11	Annexandreian	annexus L	a tying-to, connection
		Anax Andrôn G	Lord of Men: epithet of Agamemnon in Iliad
		Alexandrinus L	a citizen of Alexandria; a luxurious life
.11	Annexandreian captive conquest	Graecia capta ferum victorem cepit L —Horat. Ep. II .i.157	captive Greece captured her savage subduer—Horace, Epistle to Augustus, 157; see 246.19
.12	Ethna	Aetna L Aitnê G	"Burner[?]": Sicilian volcano with multiple legendary associations
		ethnos G	band of men; tribe; nation; sex
.13	deltas	delta G	letter D; rivermouth; female pudenda
.15	amilikan	miliacus L	fed with millet
		meli G	honey
.18	Mina	mina L	smooth
.18	nepertheloss	nêpenthes G	"banishing pain and sorrow"; "free from sorrow": epithet of Apollo; name of a drug

		nepos L	grandson
.22	aurowoch	auro L	to gild, cover with gold
		urus L	a wild ox
.23	Taif	fiat L	let there be
.24	Alif	fila L	a thread
.24	Annapolis	polis G	city
.25	Mussabotomia	Mesopotamia G	"Between Rivers": area between Tigris and Euphrates; *mod.* Iraq
.32	nihilnulls	nihil L	nothing
		nullus L	none, not anyone
.32	Memoland	memor L	mindful, remembering
.33	ulvertones	ulva L	sedge, swamp-grass
.33	spectrem	spectrum L	appearance, form, image, spectre
.34	irised	Iris G L	goddess of the rainbow; the rainbow
.34	calvitousness	calvitium L	baldness
319.01	valleylow	vale L	farewell
.05	Demetrius	Dêmêtrios G	"Belonging to *Dêmêter* ('Earth-mother' *or* 'People-mother')[goddess]": name of 19 persons listed in *Oxford Classical Dictionary*
		Dêmêtrios I Poliorkêtês (336–283 b.c.)	"The Besieger": king of Macedonia, inventor of scientific siegecraft
.06	stircus	stercus L	dung, excrement
		hircus L	he-goat
.06	hesteries	hesternus L	of yesterday, yesterday's
		hystera G	womb
.08	collemullas	colles (*pl.*) L	hills
		columella L	pillar, small column
		L. Junius Moderatus Columella	agricultural writer; #*A*
.12	pangeant	pangens L	fastening, fixing, driving in, composing, contracting, agreeing
.17	rheumaniscences	rheuma G	current, stream
.21	Horace's	Quintus Horatius Flaccus	Roman poet and satirist; *see 307.L3*

.24	dyode	*dyodos G	two-way, a double-way
.28	fornicular	fornacula L	little furnace, oven
		fornicatio L	1. vault, arch; 2. whoredom, fornication (*in the vaults, under the arches*)
.34	fierifornax	fieri L	to be made
		fornax L	furnace, oven, kiln
.34	thurst	thura G	door
		thur- L	incense-
.34	motophosically	moto L	to keep moving, to move about
		phôs G	1. man, male person; 2. light
.36	empty	emptus (*pp.*) L	bought
.36	dempty	demptus (*pp.*) L	removed
320.01	dyply	dy- G	two-
		diplous G	double
.04	nosestorsiums	nasturtium L	"nose-twisting": a kind of cress
		torsio L	a wringing, twisting
		tortio LL	torment, torture
.19	hised his bungle oar his shourter	*allusion to* Odysseus	to end Poseidon's wrath O. must carry his oar so far inland it will be taken for a winnowing-fan
.20	Fellagulphia	fella- L	sucking-
		Philadelphia G	city in Egypt named for Ptolemy Philadelphos
		Philadelphos G	Brother-loving, Brotherly
.25	flating	flatus L	blowing, snorting
.28	Afferik	Afer L	African
		affero L	to carry [*a thing*] to [*a place*]
.28	Arena	[h]arena L	sand
321.05	corollas	corolla L	a garland
.06	virus	virus L	slime, poison
.15	Hircups	hircus L	he-goat
.16	Phoenix	phoenix L	fabulous bird; *see*
		phoinix G	*265.08*
.17	Irinwakes	eirênê G	peace
		Iernê G	Ireland

.23	Odorozone	odor L	a smell
		ozô G	to smell, to give off an odor
.26	digit	digitus L	a finger
322.09	confiteor	confiteor L	I acknowledge, I confess (*confession prayer*)
.23	pyre	pyr G	fire
.30	mhos for mhos	mos L	custom, manner
.30	for mhos	formosus L	handsome
.31	dielectrick	dialektikos G	pertaining to
		dialecticus L	disputation
.32	obsoletion	obsoleto L	to degrade, soil, stain; *eccl. L*, to defile
.33	millestones	mille L	a thousand
		mille [passus] L	a mile [thousand paces]
.34	libitate nos, Domnial	libera nos Domine L	free us, O Lord
		libita L	the things that please, one's will, pleasure, humor
.33–.34	from the millestones of Ovlergroamlius, libitate nos, Domnial	de militibus Oliveri Cromwelli libera nos, Domine [?] L	from the soldiers of Oliver Cromwell free us, O Lord
.35	culp	culpa L	fault, sin, blame, failure
323.15	fumbelums	fumus L	smoke
		funambulus L	rope-walker, rope-dancer
.16	faus	faustus L	fortunate, favorable
.23	Fadgestfudgist	fiat L	let there be
		fuit L	there was
.25	selenium	selenium Mod L	"moon-stuff ": an element
		selênion G	the peony
		selênê G	moon
.29	ambilaterally	*ambilateralis L	belonging to both sides
324.01	first foetotype	prôtotypos G	first-impression: original, principle, archetype
.01	foetotype	*phôtotypos G	light-impression, impression by light

.07	sphinxish	Sphinx G	"Binding, Constricting": mythological monster; symbol of death; asked the famous riddle of the three ages of man
.07	Ede	Oidi[pous] G Oedi[pus] L	"Swollen[foot]":solved the Sphinx's riddle; *see 306.L11*
.09	Thallasee	thalassa G	sea; #*B*
.18	missage	missa (*pp.*) L Missa eccl. L	sent the Mass
.23	Am. Dg.	A[d] m[ajorem] D[ei] g[loriam] L	For the greater glory of God: *Jesuit motto*; #*B*
.32	lucal	lux L lucus L	light sacred grove
.36	Birdflights	auspicium L	divination by observing birdflights
.36	abbroaching	*abpropinquo L *instead of* adpropinquo, appropinquo L	to draw nearly away from to draw near to, to approach
.36	nubtials	nubes L nubilis L	clouds marriageable
325.01	R.I.D.	R[equiescat] I[n] D[eo] L requiescans in Deo L	may he rest in God resting in God: *in Ireland a markedly Protestant locution*
.03	Ls. De.	L[aus] s[emper] De[o] L L[ibrae] s[olidi] De[narii] L	praise to God always (*Jesuit slogan*) Pounds shillings Pence #*B*
.04	gainous sense uncompetite	genus sensibus competit L	the genus accords with sense-perception
.06	auspicable	*auspicabilis L	divinable by observing the flight of birds
.10	Kalastus	kallistos G	most beautiful
.11	Lavantaj	lavandaria L	things to be washed, laundry
.11–.12	christianismus ... christianismus	*Christianismos G Christianissimus L	Christianism, Christianity most Christian

.11–.12	christianismus	Christê eleêson,	Christ have mercy,
	kirjallisuus, kirjallisuus	Kyriê eleêson,	Lord have mercy, Lord
	christianismus	Kyriê eleêson,	have mercy, Christ
		Christê eleêson	have mercy
		G	
.13	ahorace	Quintus	Roman poet
		Horatius	
		Flaccus	
.20	pacts	pax L	peace
.22	Aestmand	aes L	copper, bronze
		aestimans L	determining the value of
.25	Idyall	Idyllium L	Little Idea, Little
		Eidyllion G	Shape, Little Poem: an Idyll: short, highly wrought descriptive poem
.30	marelupe	mare L	the sea
		lupus L	a wolf
		maris lupus L	"wolf of the sea": the pike
.35	ultitude	ultio L	revenge
326.03	Paddeus	deus L	god
.04	crux	crux L	cross, gallows
.07–.08	*intra trifum triforium trifoliorum*	intra tribum trifariam trifoliorum L	within the threefold tribe of shamrocks; *or,* within the tribe of shamrocks triply *or* in three places
.08	forfor	forfor OL furfur L	bran; dandruff
.08	furst	fur L	a thief
.14	Tera	ter L	three times, thrice
		terra L	land, earth
.15	ternatrine	ternarius L	consisting of three
		terni, trini L	three each, three
.15–.16	chrisan athems	chrysanthemon G	"golden flower": garden ranunculus
.16	athems	athemis G	lawless
.18	osion	[h]osion (*neut.*) G	hallowed, holy, sanctioned by God
.19	Anomyn	anomos G	lawless, impious
		anonymos G	nameless, unnamed
.27	sutor	sutor L	shoemaker, cobbler
.30	eurekason	hêurêka G	I have found; I have it

.33	crismion	krismion G *glossed as* = phylakion G	1. a watch: party of four soldiers; 2. a sanitary napkin
327.02	Brandonius	*Brandonus L (a.d. 484–577)	Brendan, Irish saint
.02	*filius*	filius L	son
.02	Cara	cara (*fem.*) L	dear, precious
.05	tesura	*thesaura (*fem.*) L	treasure, loved one
		thesaurus L thêsauros G	hoard, treasure, provision, store
		tessera L	square, square piece of wood; slogan, die
.06	livving	Livia L Titus Livius L *Livia L	wife of Augustus; #*A* Roman historian; #*A* "Bluish": Liffey; #*A*
.06	plusquebell	plus quam belle L	more than beautifully
.07	lippeyear's	lippus L	blear-eyed
.08	tramity	tramite (*Abl.*) L	by a by-path
.10	Hyderow	hydro- G	water-
.10	Hyderow Jenny	*hydrogenês G	"born of water": hydrogen (*mod. coinage*)
.11	rheadoromanscing	rhêa G r[h]aeda L	easily four-wheeled carriage; #*B*
		Rhaeti L	mountain people between Rhine and Danube
		RhaetoRomanic	language, descended from L, spoken in parts of Switzerland, N. Italy, and Austria
.12	Lavinias	Lavinia	daughter of Latinus, wife of Aeneas
.13	periglus	peri G glus L *periglus G + L periculosus L periplus L periplous G	around glue glue-around dangerous a sailing-around, circumnavigation; navigational record
.15	mallaura's	malus L	1. bad; 2. apple-tree

		aura L	the air
		*malaura L	bad air; malaria
		laurus L	laurel
		*mallaurus L	apple-tree-laurel
.17	glowru	u L = y G	glowry; glory
.19	ladins	Ladin (*RhaetoRomanic*)	"Latin": the RhaetoRomanic language
.20	calding	caldus L	hot, warm
.21	Combria	Cambria ML	Wales
.23	wishtas	v- L *pron.* w-	vishtas; vistas
.26	Fortunatus	Fortunatus L Venantius Honorius Clementianus Fortunatus (a.d. 530–600)	Lucky writer of many poems and hymns; the last L poet of Gaul
.32	roaryboaryellas	Aurora Borealis L	the Northern Dawn: the northern lights
.33	Humpopolamus	polemos G	war
		potamos G	river
		hippopotamos G	river-horse: hippopotamus
		*hippopolemos G	war-horse
.36	cawcaws	caucus L kaukos G	a kind of cup
328.01	pullar	pullarius L	1. pertaining to young animals; 2. a chicken-keeper
.12	Slavocrates	*Slabokratês G	Slav-ruler
.13	onerable	*onerabilis L	loadable, fillable
.17	pravacy	pravitas L	crookedness, inequality, deformity; perversity, viciousness
.19	Hullespond	Hellêspontos G	Sea of Helle (*who drowned in it*): mod. Dardanelles
.20	mallymedears	mallos G	woolen fleece
.25	Heri	heri L	yesterday
.25	Concorant	*conchorans L + G	dancing together with
		concordans L	agreeing with, agreeing together
.28	raptist	raptim (*adv.*) L	by snatching away

		rapta (*fem. pp.*) L	snatched, raped
.29	tha lassy! tha lassy!	Thalatta! Thalatta! G	Sea! Sea!: *cry of Xenophon's men*; #B
.34	Horuse	Horus	Egyptian god worshipped by Greeks & Romans
329.04	horatia	Horatia L	fem. member of gens *Horatia* ("*belonging to* Hora ['*Lady*'] [*wife of Romulus; goddess*]"); "*Horace*"
.05	Magnus	Magnus L	"the Great": Roman surname, *as of* Cn. Pompeius Magnus; *see 329.25*
.06	*Ulivengrene*	oliva L	olive; *see note at 550.18*
.13	Cawcaught. Coocaged.	# *Reduplication*	
.20	Holyryssia	y G = u L	Holyrussia
.25	Pompei	Pompeius L Gnaeus Pompeius Magnus	name of a Roman gens Roman soldier & statesman; *see 329.05, 307.L22*
		Pompeii L	"Belonging to [a] *Pompeius*": city in Campania overwhelmed by Vesuvius a.d. 79
.34	enfysis	en G	in
		physis G	nature
		emphysêsis G	inflation, flatulence
.36	conspectrum	*conspectrum L	the visibility of a thing
330.09	Tyrrhanees	Tyrrheni L Tyrrênoi G	Tyrrhenians: Pelasgian people who migrated to Italy and formed the parent stock of the Etruscans
.22	augurs	augur L	diviner, soothsayer
.25	Nova	nova (*fem.*) L	new
.29	mundom	mundum L	1. in readiness; 2. toilette
		mundum (*Acc.*) L	the world, the universe
.35	kathareen	*katharinos G	pure

331.02–.03	phaymix cupplerts	felix culpa L	happy sin; #B
.06	tellusit	tellus L	the earth, dry land, planet earth
.14	sol	sol L	the sun
.15	trisexnone	tri- L G	three-
		sex L	six
		nonus L	ninth
.22	mensuring	mensuro L	to measure
.22	megnominous	mega- G	great-
		nomen L	name
		nominatus (pp.) L	named
		*magnominatus L	great-named
		nous G	mind, intelligence
.23	myrioheartzed	myrias G	ten thousand
.23	toroidal	*toroeidês G	drill-shaped, looking like a drill
.25	velican	veli- L	sail-
		vel L	or else, or, as you will
.28	capriole	capreolus L	wild goat, chamois; weeding-hoe
.31	laetification	laetificatio L	a making glad
.31	neuhumorisation	euêmereô G	to spend the days cheerfully
		euhêmerizô G	to euhemerize, to follow the doctrines of Euhêmeros
		Euhêmeros G (fl. 300 b.c.)	wrote Sacred Scripture proposing that gods were originally merely great men to whom grateful memory attributed divinity
332.07	anruly	an- G	un-
.12	testies	testes (pl.) L	1. witnesses; 2. testicles
.14	gaauspices	auspicia L	divinations by observing birdflights
		auspices L	bird-inspectors
.19	ribbeunuch	eunouchos G	bed-keeper; eunuch
.24	theogamyjig	theogamia G	marriage of gods
.28	pontine	Pontinus, Pomptinus L	marshy district in Latium; the Pontine Marshes
.29	nilly	nihili L	of no value, worthless

.31	phoenix	phoenix L	fabulous bird
		phoinix G	
.31–.31	phoenix his calipers	felix culpa L	happy sin; # B
.32	psourdonome	pseudônymos G	under a false name
		*pseudonômêsis G	a false observation
		*pseudonomos G	a false custom
		surdus L	deaf
.34	suburbiaurealis	aurora borealis L	the northern dawn: the northern lights
		*suburbiaureus L	*gold coin of a town near Rome
.34	suburbiaurealis ... rure	rus in urbe L	the country in the city
.34	rure	rure (Abl.) L	from the country
333.06	nummifeed	nummus L	coin, piece of money
		nummi (Gen.) L	coin's, of a coin
		nummi (pl.) L	coins
.27	amnest	amnis L	river
.30	reformication	formicatio L	an irritation of the skin resembling the crawling of ants
		formica L	ant
.35	licture	*lictura; correctly ligatura	binding, twisting
		lictor L	"Binder, Tier-up": attendant on a Roman magistrate
.35	caudal	cauda L	tail
.36	noviny	novani L	immigrants, new residents
		noveni (Gen.) L	nine's, of nine each
334.01	lethurgies	lêthê G	forgetfulness
		ergon G	work
		*lêthourgon G	work for forgetfulness
		*lêthourgos G	worker for forgetfulness
		modeled on	
		dêmiourgos G	worker for the public
		leitourgia G	public service
.03	ensallycopodium	*insalicipodium L	a balcony made of willow, a balcony in a willow-tree, a platform in a willow-tree

		lycopodium	wolf-foot: a kind of
		Mod L *for*	creeping plant:
		*lykopodion G	club moss
.03	melost	melos G	limb; piece of music; melody, song
.07	choractoristic	choros G	dance; group of dancers in a play leader of a
		choragetas Doric G,	*choros*
		chorêgos G	
.09	vulcanite	Vulcanus L	god of fire
.10	natecup	nates L	the buttocks
.18	Prosim	prosim L	may I be of use, may I profit
.18	prosit	prosit L	may it be of use, may it be profitable
.26	canins ... canins	canis L	a dog
		caninus L	pertaining to a dog, canine
.28	katey's	kathairô G	to cleanse
.30	Duras	duras L	you (*sing.*) harden, you last out
335.07	Holispolis	holos G	whole, all, entire
		polis G	city
		*Holopolis G	Whole-City
.20	generand	generans L	begetting, procreating
		generandus L	fit to be begotten, apt to be generated
.26	hibernian	Hibernianus L	Irish
.27	it sint barbaras	ut sint barbari L	that they may be barbarians, let them be barbarians
.30	Arthurduke	Artus dux L	original of King Arthur; *see 252.20*
		Arthox, Dux, *etc.*	stars for which Adam was named
.36	pioupious	pius L	dutiful
		Pyrôpeus Pius G + L	Fire-eyed the Dutiful; *see 014.09*
336.01	cyclums cyclorums	saeculum saeculorum L	an age of ages; eternity
.02–.03	enterellbo add all taller Danis	introibo ad altare Dei L	I will go in to God's altar
		Danis (*Dat., Abl. pl.*) L	to *or* by the Danes
.04	sorracer	Soracte L	mountain in Etruria with temple of Apollo

.12	A (tillalaric)	at illa L	moreover she, but on the other hand she
		Attila	king of the Huns
		Alaric I (a.d. 370–410)	leader of the Goths; sacked Rome a.d. 410
.15	awebrume	bruma L	midwinter
.21	*qua*	qua L	where, by what way; as far as, in so far as; to what degree
.21	golden meddlist	Auream quisquis mediocritatem / Diligit ... Horat. *Carm.* II .x.5–6 L	Whoever esteems a golden middle state ... Horace, *Odes* II .x, 5–6
.22	Publius	Publius L	"Of the People": Roman praenomen
.22	Manlius	Manlius L	"Handy": name of a Roman gens
		T. Manlius Torquatus (*fl.* 361 b.c.)	won a golden torque (collar) in duel with a giant Celt; model of *public* virtue: while consul he condemned his own son to death
.24	liberaloider	liberalis L	pertaining to the free-born condition; gentlemanly, noble-minded, generous
		*liberaleidês L + G	looking like a gentleman, seeming generous
.27	atalantic's	Atalanta L Atalentê G	mythological maiden who will marry no one who cannot beat her in a footrace
.30	candidacy	candidatus L	clothed in white
.31	illicterate	illic L	he/she yonder
		illicitus L	forbidden, not allowed
		illectus (*pp.*) L	allured, enticed, misled, led astray
.32	nullatinenties	nullatenus L	by no means, in no wise
		nulla tenens L	holding nothing
		ens, entis L	being

.34	photognomist	phôtognômos G	one who knows light
.36	panegoric	panêgyrikos G	pertaining to a public assembly; a speech made on such an occasion
		parêgorikos G	encouraging, consoling; soothing
337.04	alaterelly	a latere L	on or at the side or flank
.06	bonafacies	bona facies L	good or handsome face or shape; # A
.06	solafides	sola fides L	only faith
.06	bonafacies ... solafides	bona fides L	good faith
.08	vanished consinent	vanished continent	Atlantis, in Plato's myth
		vanished consonant	# Digamma
.08	annapal	[H]annibal	Carthaginian leader
.09	lude	ludus L	play, game, diversion, pastime
.09	semeliminal	semel L	once, a single time, once for all
		*liminalis L	pertaining to a threshold
.17	sylvias	Rhea Silvia	mother of Romulus
.17	sub	sub L	under
.19	Omnibil	omnibus L	for all
.24	paltipsypote	paltos G	brandished, hurled
.28	Faunagon	Faunus L	"Favorable": rural deity
		faunus L	generic type of sylvan deity
		agôn G	struggle, contest
.34	Gereland	gero L	to bear, to wear, to carry, to produce; to entertain, cherish; to behave; to perform
.36	Artaxerxes	Artaxerxes	name of three kings of Persia in 5th and 4th centuries b.c.
.36	Flavin	Flavina L	a small Etrurian city
		Flavius L	"Blond": name of a Roman gens
		flamen L	priest of a particular deity

338.03	Germanon	germanus L	full brother
.07	*umberolum*	umbraculum L	shady place, bower; school; sunshade, parasol, umbrella
.14	Sea vaast a pool	Sebastêpolis G	city of Augustus; G settlement in Tauric Chersonesus; *now* Sevastopol *in the Crimea*
.17	jubalant	juba L	mane
		Juba	name of two kings of Numidia; Shem-character in Newman's *Callista*; #*A*
.19	gubernier	gubernator L	governor; steersman, pilot
.19	gerenal	gero L	to bear, to act; *see 337.34*
.20	amaltheouse	Amaltheia G	she-goat who suckled Zeus
.20	leporty	lepus L	a hare
.24	monowards	monos G	one
.25	manosymples	mano L	to flow, distil, spread; proceed, emanate
		manu L	by hand
		sym G	with
.27	Ajaculate	Ajas L Aias G	Ajax: G hero at Troy
		jaculatio L	a throwing, casting, hurling
		ejaculatio L	a throwing out
.34	*meditabound*	meditabundus L	earnestly meditating
.36	*Aerin*	aes, aeris L	copper, bronze; a copper coin
339.03	Icon	eikôn G	an image
.08	dos	dos L	dowry; gift, endowment
.08	ros	ros L	dew
.09	Chromean	chrôma G	skin; complexion; color; style
		chromê G	a crashing sound
.11	roscians	Roscianus L	belonging to a *Roscius*
		Roscius L	"Dewy": name of a Roman gens
		Lucius Roscius Otho	passed a law reserving seats in the theater for Roman knights; Cicero defended the law

		Quintus Roscius Gallus	famous actor, his name came to mean "supreme actor"; Cicero defended him in a private lawsuit
		Sextus Roscius	accused on political grounds of parricide, successfully defended by Cicero
.13	perikopendolous	periculosus L	dangerous
		perikopê G	cutting all around, mutilation; diminution; outline; section; section of a work
		pendulus L	hanging down
.14	pulchers	pulcher L	beautiful, fair, handsome
.18	*Perssiasterssias*	Persis	mid-East country, original home of the Persians; *mod.* Fars *in Iran*
		astêr G	a star
		tertius, tertia (*masc., fem.*) L	the third
.24	*nate*	nates L	the buttocks
.24	*farused*	Pharos G	island lighthouse; #*A*
.25	*florahs*	Flora L	goddess of flowers
.28	consomation	con- L	with-
		sôma G	body
.29	voluant	voluans, volvans L	turning around, tumbling
		volans L	flying
.29	Erminia's	Arminius L	"Herman": German prince: *see 008.28*
		Jacobus Arminius	theologian; *see 155.34*
		Armenia	country of Asia
.32	*Attahilloupa*	Attila	king of the Huns
		lupa L	she-wolf; prostitute
.35	*vatercan*	Vaticanus L	hill outside Rome; an inferior wine
.35	*holypolygon*	holos G	whole, entire
		polygônos G	many-sided, a many-sided figure
		*holopolygônos G	a whole polygon

.36	*letteracettera*	littera L	letter (*of the alphabet*)
		cetera L	the rest, the other things
340.06	*Djublian Alps*	Alpes Juliae L	the Julian Alps: eastern range, extending into Illyria (Jugoslavia).
.13	*regulect*	regula L	straight piece of wood, ruler
		lectus L	a reading
.15	*faminy*	femina L	woman
		*famina LL	hunger
.15	*relix*	relictus (*pp.*) L	left behind
.22	lelias	Laelia L (lst C b.c.)	intellectual mother-in-law of Lucius Crassus the triumvir
.24	narse	Narses	1. Persian king c. a.d. 298; 2. Byzantine general
.25	*psychophannies*	*psychophanês G	one who shows the soul
.26	*psuckofumbers*	psuchê, psychê G	soul
.26	*bulchritudes*	pulchritudo L	beauty
.28	*pollex*	pollex L	the thumb; the big toe
.31	pan	pan G	all
.32	soll	sol L	the sun
.32	luna	luna L	the moon
341.01	aureolies	aureolus L	golden; a gold coin
.04	*menody*	*menôdê G	a mighty song
		*mênôdê G	a moon-song
		Menôn G	*Meno*: title-character of Plato dialog
.08	*sumphoty*	sumphôtia G	a giving of light together with
.09	balacleivka	kleis G clavis L	bolt, key; collarbone
.11	*cholaroguled*	cholas G	bowels, guts
		cholera G	a disease of the bowels
		gula L	the throat; palate, appetite
.12	*olfact*	olfactum (*pp.*) L	smelled, scented
		olfacto L	to smell at, to snuff
.13	monad	monas G	the number one, unity

.15–.16	star and . . . moon	*attributes of* Artemis-Hecate-Selene	Byzantium, saved from plague by Hecate (340 b.c.), placed her crescent and star on coins and symbols of the city; the conquering Turks adopted the city's emblem, whence it has spread through Islam
.18	*verbivocovisual*	verbum L	a word
		vox L	the voice
		visum L	a thing seen
		visualis LL	attained by sight
		visualia LL	sight, the power of seeing
.22	*Hippo-*	hippos G	horse
.23	*helioscope*	hêlios G	sun
		skopos G	a watcher
		*hêlioskopos G	a sun-watcher
.24	*Meusdeus*	meus Deus L	my God
		medius L	by God!
.25	*satisfunction*	satis L	enough
		functio L	performance
.26	*Epiphanes*	epiphanês G	coming to light; present to aid; manifest; notable
		Ptolemy V Epiphanes (210–180 b.c.)	king of Egypt 205–180 b.c.; reign marked by rebellions and invasions
.28	*assuary*	assuesco L	to accustom, to habituate; to be accustomed to
		ossuarium LL	container for bones (*of the dead*)
.28	*bonum*	bonum (*neut.*)	good
.28	*osstheology*	os; ossis L	bone; of a bone
		osteon G	bone
		*osteologia G	study of bones
		theos G	god
		theologia G	study of God; theology
.30	*nupersaturals*	nuper L	newly, lately
		satura L	"well-filled": dish filled with a mixture of various ingredients: mixed salad, mixed stew

		*nupersatura L	a recent mixture
.30	*metanoic*	metanoêtikos G	given to repentance
.30	*excomologosis*	ekkômazô G	to rush wildly about
		logos G	word, idea, reason
		*logôsis G	an abnormal state of language
		*ekkômalogôsis G	an abnormal state of wildly-rushing language
.33	*damas*	dama L	deer, antelope, chamois
342.05	*Timoth*	Timotheus G	"Honoring God": companion of Paul
.08	*semperal*	semper L	ever, always
.10	*causas es quostas?*	causa es; quo stas? L	you (*sing.*) are the cause; where do you stand?
.11	*Da Valorem's*	da valorem L	give value
		ad valorem L	to the value, at the value, at value
.11	*Dominical*	Dominicalis LL	pertaining to Sunday
.14	*Jumpiter*	Juppiter L	chief Roman god; #*A*
.18	*Xristos*	X (chi) G	letter CH
		Christos G	Anointed; Christ
.18	*Holophullopopulace*	holos G	whole, entire
		phullon G	leaf; plant
		holophulos G	entire, perfect, uncastrated
.23	*Homo*	homo L	human being, man
.26	*Immensipater*	*immensipater L	immeasurable father
.28	*Proformly*	pro forma L	for form, as a matter of form
.28	*annuysed*	annus L	year
.34	*colliberated*	*colliberatus (*pp.*) L	freed at the same time
.35	*tiomor*	timor L	fear
343.01	*orangultonia*	*Ultonia Mod L	Ulster
.01	*orients*	oriens L	rising
.01	*Sagittarius*	Sagittarius L	the Archer: the constellation
.02	*Draco*	Draco L	the Serpent, the Dragon: a constellation; (*eccl. L*: the Devil)
.04	*cerberating*	Cerberus L	three-(*or* hundred-)headed monster in the Underworld
		Kerberos G	

.09	Perfedes Albionias	Perfida Albion, Perfidiosa Albion L	Treacherous *Albion* (*old name for Britain*)
		Perfidens Albion L	Very-Trusting Britain
.11	micramacrees	mikros G	small, little
		makros G	big, great
.11	Miles	miles L	soldier
.15	anggreget	aggreget L *as if* *angreget G	let him add to the flock; let him ally himself
		-gg- G	-ng-
.16	*aposteriorly*	a posteriori L	from what follows after
.17	*greak*	Graecus L	Greek
.17	*esthate*	aisthêtês G	one who perceives, a perceiver
.17	*phophiar*	phôs G	1. light; 2. a man
		phiaros G	gleaming, shining
		*phôtophiaros G	light-gleaming
.18	*erixtion*	erexi L	to have set up, to have erected
		rixor L	to quarrel, brawl, disagree
.18	*soseptuple*	septuplum L	a group of seven
.18	*apriori*	a priori L	from the previous
.21	Schtschuptar	Juppiter L	chief Roman god
.22	quirasses	Quirites L	the Roman people in a civil capacity
.22	tragedoes	tragôdos G	an actor in tragedy
		tragôdia G	"goat-song": tragedy
.26	egondoom	ego L egô G	I (*lst pers. sing. pronoun*)
		agôn G	a struggle, contest
.27	pulversporochs	pulver L	dust, powder
.28	nemesisplotsch	nemesis G	retribution; righteous anger over injustice
		Nemesis G	goddess of divine retribution for injustice
		nemêsis G	[equal] distribution
.28	salubrate	salubris L	health-giving, wholesome
.29	ultradungs	ultra L	on the other side, beyond, farther
.30	chorams	coram L	in the presence of, in the face of; in the very act; in person

		choros G	dance; group of dancers in a play
344.02	*ligious*	*ligiosus L	disposed to be tied up
.09	*cumulikick*	cumulus L	a heap, pile
.10	*changecors*	cor L	heart
.10	*induniforms*	indu OL	in, within, on, upon
		induo L	to put on, to don, to assume, to clothe
.15	cathargic	*kathargikos G (katharos + argos) *modeled on* lêthargikos G	idle from cleanliness, pure lazy / drowsy, lethargic (forgetfulness-idle)
.16	Messar	messa (*pl.*) L	things that are reaped, harvest
.17	renewmurature	muraturus L	about to be walled, about to be provided with walls
.26	aurals	aura L	air, breeze, wind; vapor, mist, odor
.27	altipaltar	altus L	high
		paltos G	brandished
		*altipaltus L + G	brandished on high
.31	meac Coolp, Arram	mea culpa L	by my fault, through my sin
		aram (*Acc.*) L	altar
		arram (*Acc.*) L	earnest-money, money to ratify a contract, security-money
.33	Saur	saura, sauros G	lizard
.34	arge	argia G	idleness, laziness
345.02	Gospolis	polis G	city
.04	*prepensing*	praepensus L	hanging down in front
.12	pepeace	# *Reduplication*	
.21	*nonobstaclant*	nihil obstat L	nothing stands in the way: *form of approval by Church censor*
		non obstans L	not standing in the way
		non *obstaculans L	not hindering
.24	oukosouso	ou, ouk, ouch G	no, not
		oukoun G	certainly not; then, in that case
		sous G	upward motion

		souson G	lily
.26	*phot*	phôs G	1. a man; 2. light
		phôt- G	light-
.28	*centelinnates*	centum L	a hundred
		centeni L	a hundred each
		nates L	the buttocks
.29	*potifex*	*potifex L	an able-maker, an enabler
		*potiofex L	a drink-maker
.29	*potifex miximhost*	Pontifex Maximus L	"Greatest Bridgemaker": chief Roman high-priest
.29	*haruspical*	haruspicalis L	pertaining to a soothsayer *or* inspector of entrails
.29	*hospedariaty*	hospes L	a host, one who entertains a stranger a visitor, guest; stranger, foreigner
		hospitalitas L	being a guest; living in a foreign country
.34	*abbosed*	*abpositus L *modeled on*	placed away from
		obpositus, oppositus L	placed against
346.04	*Hebeneros*	Hêbê G	"Youthful Prime": goddess of youth
		Nero	notorious emperor
		Erôs G	"Love, Lust": god of love
.05	*Bella*	bella (*pl.*) L	wars
		bella (*fem.*) L	pretty, pleasant
		bellum quod res *bella* non sit L	*war*: because it would not be a *nice* thing: *ancient etymology* kat' antiphrasin; # *B*
.13	*phumeral's*	phuma G	growth
.13	*roselixion*	*rosalectio L	a gathering of roses
		lix L	ashes, lye
.15	*Colliguchuna*	collis L	a hill
		colligatio L	a binding together, a connection
.19	*versingrhetorish*	Vercingetorix	Gallic chieftain; *see* 281.F1
		rhêtoreia G	oratory

.19	Buccleuch	bucca L	cheek
.24	soculums	socii L	fellows, comrades, companions, allies
		saeculum L	an age, century, lifetime
.35	Colporal	corporalis L	bodily, corporeal
.35	Phailinx	phalagx = phalanx G	line of battle, battle-array
.35	Colporal Phailinx	culpa felix L	happy sin; #B
347.02	equinarx	equina arx L	castle belonging to horses, equine citadel
.02	cholonder	cholos G	gall, bile; bitter anger, wrath
.04	Nemorn	Nemo L	"No one": Ulixes' *nom de guerre*; #A
.09	Krzerszonese	Chersonesus L Chersonêsos G	"Peninsula": the Chersonese: 1. the Thracian peninsula at the west of the Hellespont (*mod.* Gallipoli); 2. the Tauric peninsula (*mod.* Crimea)
.09	Milesia	miles L	soldier
		Milesia L Milêtos G	city in Asia Minor
		Milesiae [fabulae] L Milesioi [logoi] G	filthy stories [*from Miletos*]
.19	heptahundread	hepta G	seven
.19	annam dammias	anni Domini L	years of the Lord
		animae damnatae eccl.L	damned souls
.22	Icantenue	tenue (neut.) L	subtle; thin, fine; weak, trifling
.22	incommixtion	*incommixtio L	1. an unmixing, an unmingling 2. a mixing-in, a mingling-in
.26	longa	longa (*fem.*) L	long, spacious; long-lasting, tedious
.26	villa	villa L	countryhouse, farm
.26	longa villa	longa villa L	a spacious country house
.28	stissas me aunties	antistita L	a female overseer; chief priestess

.29	coxerusing	coxa L	hip
.30	exercitise	exercitus L	trained organized army; the Army
.35	*durblinly obasiant to the felicias of the skivis*	obedientia civium urbis felicitas L	Dublin's motto; # B
.35	*obasiant*	basia L	kisses
.35	*felicias*	felices L	lucky *or* happy persons
.35	*skivis*	skeuê G skivi MG	equipment, attire, apparel
.36	*fulvurite*	fulvus L	deep yellow, tawny
		fulgur L	flashing lightning
348.05	awlphul omegrims	alpha, ômega G	letters A, Ô; *first and last of the G alphabet*
.06	futules	futilis, futtilis L	worthless
		futuo L	to fuck
.08	platoonic leave	Platonic love	ideal *or* spiritual love, *in accordance with Plato's doctrines concerning the soul*
.09	misenary	misênerôs G	maddened by love
		misêtês G	a hater
.11	alma marthyrs	alma mater L	nurturing mother
.11	marthyrs	martyr G	a witness
		thyra G	a door
.18	said	sed L	but, yet
.22	khakireinettes	kakos G	bad, evil
		eirênê G	peace
.24	palposes	palpo L	to stroke, touch softly, pat
		palpus L	the palm of the hand
.26	lispia	Lesbia L G	woman of Lesbos; amorous woman: *name used by Catullus for his mistress*
.28	Anathem	anathema G	devoted to evil, accursed
.30	*sinuorivals*	*sinuorivales L	1. sharers of the same river by a bay; 2. bosom-rivals; 3. purse-neighbors; 4. any combination of the foregoing
.33	*infructuosities*	infructuositas LL	unfruitfulness, unproductiveness, uselessness

.35	Rhoda	Rhoda G	"Roses": ceremony at which graves were decked with roses
		rhoda (*pl.*) G	roses: female pudenda
349.01	pene	penes L	in possession of, in the house of
		poena L	punishment, penalty
.05	chorias	choreia G	dance, choral dance with music
.05	ethur	aithêr G aether L	air, pure air, the fifth element
		thus, thuris L	incense
.06	*heliotropical*	*hêliotropikos G	having to do with the sun turning: tropic of Capricorn, *where the sun turns back*
.07	*viseversion*	*viseversio L	a turning around in appearance
.07	*metenergic*	*metenergêtikos G	active with; active after; changeactive, active for change
.09	*teleframe*	têle- G	far-, from afar
.10	*photoslope*	phôto- G	light-
.10	*syncopanc*	syn- G	with-
		synkopê G	a cutting up into small pieces; conciseness; stopping
		pan G	all
.12	*glitteraglatteraglutt*	glutto L	a glutton
		gluttus, glittus L	tenacious, well-tempered, soft
		glut glut L	sound of water running through a hole
		later L	brick, tile
.12	*carnier*	carnis L	flesh, meat
.14	*alextronite*	alex- G	defending-, averting-
		alexô G	to ward off, turn aside
		alektôr, alektryon G	a cock
.14	*nichilite*	nichil ML nihil L	nothing
.15	*rutilanced*	rutilans L	glowing redly; shining
.16	*caeseine*	caesius L	bluish-grey (color of eyes)
		caseus L	cheese

.17	*mephiticism*	mephiticus L	pestilential
.17	*caoculates*	caecus L	blind
		oculatus L	having eyes, seeing
		*caecoculatus L	having blind eyes
.18	*inconoscope*	in L	in, within, on, upon
		con- L	with-
		skôpos G	watcher
.20	*idolon*	eidôlon G	phantom, reflected image
.22	*Michelides*	*Michaelidês (pl.) G	Michaels
.22	*Apaleogus*	Palaiologos G	"Traditional": name of
		Palaeologus L	the last Byzantine dynasty
.22	*Michelides Apaleogus*	Michael VIII Palaeologus (reigned a.d. 1259–1282)	recaptured Constantinople from the Venetians (1261) and established new dynasty
		Michael IX Paleologus (reigned a.d. 1293–1320)	an ineffective successor of above
.28	*nosoes*	nasus L	nose
		[P. Ovidius] Naso	the Roman poet Ovid, #A
.31	*opten, ... obening*	#Labials	often ... opening
.32	*manucupes*	*manucupido L	desire by hand, lust by hand
		mancupium L	a taking by hand; formal acceptance; formal purchase
		mancupo L	to transfer property, to give title to
.33	*pedarrests*	pedarius L	belonging to the foot
		paiderastês G	a boy-lover, pederast
.34	*comfoderacies*	confodio L	to dig thoroughly; to stab, pierce; to damage seriously; to cross out
		confoedo L	to pollute, defile
350.01	*caudant*	cauda L	tail
.05	*in pontofert*	in ponto fert L	he [she, it] carries in the sea
		in pontone fert L	he [she, it] carries in a punt *or* on a pontoon

.05	*pontofert*	*pontifer* L	bridge-carrier
		pontifex L	"bridgebuilder": Roman high-priest
		ponto L	punt; pontoon
		pontos G	sea
		pontus L	
.05	*jusfuggading*	jus L	law, right, justice
		fuga L	flight, a fleeing, running away
		*jusfugitans, jure fugitans L	fleeing the law, fleeing from justice
.05	*amoret*	amor L	love
		amaret L	he [she, it] might love
.08	*avensung*	aves L	birds
.12	*mundaynism*	mundanus L	pertaining to the world
		*mundanismos L + G	worldliness
		Munda	site of Caesar's last battle; #A
.13	*melovelance*	melos G	song, music
		vel L	as you wish, or if you like
		vela L	sails of a ship
.15	Prostatates	prostatês G	president; leader, chief man (*in a democracy*)
		prostatus (*pp.*) L	stood in a public place, offered for sale, prostituted
.16	circumstancias	circumstantia (*fem.*) L	a standing around; a surrounding circle, a troop; state, condition
		circumstantia (*neut. pl.*) L	details, circumstances
.22	pukny	puknos, pyknos G	compact, firm, frequent
.25	th'osirian	Osiris	Egyptian deity; #A
.31	sand us	sanctus L	holy
.33	komnate	com- L	with-, fellow-
		nates L	buttocks
.34	rugiments	rugio L	to roar, to rumble; to bray
		ruginosus L	wrinkled
351.05	Arcdesedo	arx L	citadel
		arcus L	bow, rainbow; arch
		arca L	chest, box

		desideo L	to remain inactive; to go to stool
		sedo L	to allay, to calm, to lull
.05	hellsyown	alkyôn G	kingfisher
		*halskyôn G	"sea-conceived" [*false etymology for* alkyôn]: the halycon: mythical bird that nests on the sea
		hai alkyonides [hêmerai] G	the halcyon days: calm winter days when the halcyon can nest; *proverbial*: undisturbed tranquility
.14	Bissbasses	bis L	twice
		basium L	a kiss
.16	vives	vives L	you (*sing.*) will live
		vivet L	[he] will live
.17	Togatogtug	toga L	ordinary dress of a Roman citizen
.17	droomodose	dromos G	race, a running
.23	movemens	movens L	movable
		mens L	mind, disposition, soul, conscience
.24	sunpictorsbosk	sumpêktos G	fitted together, welded
		pictor L	painter
		boskô G	to feed, nourish
		boskos G	herdsman
.26	cominations	comminatio L	a threatening, menacing
		comminus L	in close contest, hand to hand
.31	Heriness	heri L	yesterday
		herus L	master of a house, proprietor
.35	Jova	Jovis-pater L	Jupiter; *chief Roman god*; #A
352.01	urssian	ursus L	a bear
.01	gemenal	gemens L	sighing, groaning
		*gemenalis L	sigh-provoking, mournful
		geminus L	twin
.02	nemcon	nemo L	no one
.02	enchelonce	enchelys G	eel
.09	sord	sordeo L	to be filthy
.11	Almagnian	Alemanni L	confederation of German tribes on the upper Rhine

		alma (*fem.*) L	nourishing
		magni- L	great-, big-, loud-
.11	Gothabobus	Gothi L	powerful north-German tribe
		ab L	from, away from
		ob L	for, in front of
		bobus (*Dat., Abl. pl.*) L	to, for, by, with *or* from cows
		*Gothabobus fake-L	to, for, by, with *or* from Goths
.13	synnots	synodos G	assembly, meeting, get-together
.14	pullyirragun	polyergon G	a thing highly wrought, elaborate
.14	parrylewis	parilis L	equal, like
.19	*autosotorisation*	autosôtêr G	self-saver, self-savior
		*autosôtêrizô G	to act as self-saver
.19	*idiology*	idiologia G	subjective theorizing; private conversation
.20	*homosodalism*	homo L	human being, man
		homos G	one and the same, common, joint
		sodalis L	mate, comrade
		*homosodalism-os L + G	comradeship with mankind
		*homosodalism-os G + L + G	comradeship with one's self *or* one's own kind; joint-comradeship
.25	shutter reshottus	sartor resartus L	the tailor retailored
.28	*trigitty*	triginta L	thirty
.28	*shittery*	tettares G	four
.28	*pet*	pente G	five
.30	umbozzle	umbo L	boss (*of a shield*); shield; elbow; promontory; boundary-stone; full part of a garment; toga
.32	Cumbulent	cumulus L	a pile, heap
		comminus L	in close contest, hand to hand
.33	Embulence	emboleus G	anything put in: piston, peg, etc.
		embolimos G	intercalary month
		embolion G	missile; interlude; episode

		eminus L	at [spear-throwing] distance, at a distance [*opposite to* comminus]
.33	Russkakruscam	*rosicrucianus Mod L	of a rose-cross, of Rosenkreuz (the founder): rosicrucian
.36	*pungataries*	pungo L *pungatorius (*adj.*) L	to prick, puncture pricking, puncturing, *puncturative
353.01	*praktice*	praktikê (*fem.*) G	practical, fit for action; effective
.01	*theogonies*	theogonia G	generation *or* birth of gods
		Hê Theogonia G	*The Genealogy of the Gods*, poem by Hesiod
.02	Trisseme	trisêmos G	of three times; (*Prosody*) equivalent to three short syllables, *i.e.*, one long and one short
.02	Marsiful	Mars L	god of war; #*A*
		Marsi L	people in Latium celebrated as wizards and snakecharmers; hostile to the Romans
.03	Gragious	grex L	herd, flock
		gregalis L	belonging to the herd
.03	in souber	insuper L	above, overhead; in addition
.04	civiles	civilis L	pertaining to citizens, civil, civic
		civile L	courtesy
.06	*maomant*	maomai G	to seek for
.06	*apoxyomenously*	apoxy- G	sharp-, pointed-, intense-, shrill-,
		ominose L	forebodingly, ominously
		*apoxyominose G + L	sharply-forebodingly
.08	*euphorious*	euphoros G	well *or* patiently borne; easy to bear; manageable; graceful;patient
.08	*hagiohygiecynicism*	*hagiohygiêkyni- kismos G	holy-healthy-doglike- ism; holy-healthy- cynicism

			kynikismos G	Doglike-ism: the philosophy of Diogenes *ho Kynikos,* "the Doglike" (*from his personal habits*)
.12	Ussur Ursussen	ursus L	a bear
.12	viktaurious	taureus L	of a bull, bullish
		Tauricus L	the Crimea
.13	arctic	arktikos G	near the Bear; northern
.18	exitous	exitus L	a going out, departure; a way out, conclusion
.18	*Deo Jupto*	Deo Jove (*Abl.*) L	by *or* with the God Jupiter
		Deo juncto L	God having been joined [to]; if God be joined
.18	instullt	stultus L	foolish, silly
.21	Sparro	spero L	I hope
.22	*abnihilisation*	ab nihilo L	away from nothing
		*abnihilatio L	a bringing away from nothing
.22	*etym*	etymos G	true
		etymon G	true sense of a word
.24	*Parsuralia*	Pars *Uraliae L	a portion of Uralia; *imitation of inscription identifying peripheral countries on old maps: e.g.* Italiae pars
		Uralia (*made-up word*) L	Land of the Urals: Russia
.25	*fragoromboassity*	fragor L	a breaking to pieces; crashing noise
		rhombos G	bull-roarer; lozenge; male sex organs
		boaô G	to shout
.26	*moletons*	moles L	a mass, bulk
		molecula Mod L	a little mass
		*molêton G	something that is coming
.26	*mulicules*	mulierculae L	little women, mere women, girls
		moleculae L	little masses, molecules
.28	scenatas	scaenaticus L	stage-player
		skênêtês G	tent-maker
.29	*empyreal*	empyrealis L *from*	belonging to the realm of pure fire

		empyrios G	outside the world; heavenly
.29	*empyreal Raum*	imperialis Roma L	Rome of the emperor[s]
.29	*mordren*	mors L	death
.29	*Atems*	atomon G	that which cannot be cut; an atom
		Athênai G	"Belonging to Athena": Athens
354.01	uptheaires	thea G	goddess
.05	*vility of vilities*	vilitas L	cheapness
.09	*umbraged*	umbra L	shade, shadow
.10	*Erssia's*	*Ursia L	Bear-land
.10	*magisquammythical*	magis quam L	more than, greater than
.14	*circuminsistence*	*circuminsisto L	to press in upon in a circle
.14	*Cicilian*	Caecilia L	saint of music
.18	*sophsterliness*	sophistês G	master of a skill, expert
.19	*pugnate*	pugna L	a fistfight
.20	*astoutsalliesemoution*	outi G	by no means, not at all
		oun G	certainly, in fact
.21	*cococancancacacanoti-oun*	coco, cocococo L	clucking (*of a hen*)
		canis L	a dog
		cacabo L	to cackle
		caco L kakaô G	to go to stool, to defecate
		cano L	to sing
		otior L	to be at leisure
		hotioun G	anything
		hoti G	what, why
.22	Anthea	Antheia G	"Blooming," "Flowery": epithet of Hera; of the Hôrai; of Aphrodite
		thea G	goddess
.23	opter	opto L	to choose, select
.25	murdhering idies	Idus Martiae L	the Ides of March: March 15, the day Caesar was murdered (44 b.c.)
.25	idies	Idus L	the 13th of each month but March, May, July, October, when it was the 15th

		idea G	semblance, appearance
		dies L	a day
.25	iries	Iris G L	goddess of the rainbow; the rainbow
.25	idies ... iries	dies irae L	day of wrath: Judgment Day
.26	plinnyflowers	Gaius Plinius Secundus Major; Gaius Plinius Caecilius Secundus Junior	Pliny the Elder; Pliny the Younger; see 255.18-19, 281.04
.26	Calomella's	kalos G	beautiful
		melas G	black
		mella L	honey-water
		L. Junius Moderatus Columella	agricultural writer; #A
.28	sex	sex L	six
.29	seep	septem L	seven
.30	soord	surdus L	deaf
.31	flossim	*flosim, *florim L	in accordance with the flower, flower-wise
.32	lancifer	lancifer L	a plate-bearer, dish-bearer
		*lanceafer L	a lance-bearer
.32	lucifug	lucifuga L	light-fleeing, light-shunning; one who uses night as day
.33	cosyn	co- L	with-
		syn G	with
.33	corollanes'	corolla L	a garland
		*corollanus L	one who is garlanded
		Coriolanus L	legendary Roman hero
355.06	*ex*	ex L	out of
.06	*ad*	ad L	to, at
.10	Vociferagitant	vociferor L	to cry out, cry aloud, scream, bawl
		agitans L	reproving, deriding, insulting
.10	Viceversounding	vice versa L	turned around instead
.12	Hercushiccups'	hircus L	he-goat
.12	educe	educo L	to lead out
.22	Amelakins	Amelas	town in Lycia, Asia Minor
		#L/R Interchange	Amerakins

.36	in venuvarities	in vino veritas L	in wine [there is] truth
		in Venere varietas L	in Venus [Loveliness][there is] variety
356.01	iota	iota G	letter I
.01	faust	faustus L	fortunate, lucky
.05	sollecited	sollicito L	to disturb, distress, vex, tempt
.07	encloded	*inclaudo, *inclodo OL	to shut in, confine, enclose, imprison
		includo L	prison
.08	Jura	Jura L	chain of mountains from the Rhine to the Rhone
		*jura *correctly* jussa L	laws
		jure L	with justice, justly
.09	Messafissi	*messa L	things that are reaped
		Messia L	goddess of reaping
		fissum L	a cleft, slit, fissure
.11	primeum nobilees	Praemium *Nobelium L	the Nobel Prize
		nobilis L	well-known, renowned; noble
		primum mobile L	"the first movable": outer sphere of the heavens, imparts motion to all the inner spheres
.12	notomise	noto L	to mark, to summarize, to note
		trans. a- G	not-
		part-trans. *atomizô G	to atomize; to be an Atomist
.12	ubivence	ubi L	where
		ubivis L	where you will, be it where it may
		venio L	to come
.15	sicsecs	sic L	thus
		sex L	six
.24	pastureuration	pasturae *uratio L	the burning up of a pasture
.30	ambullished	ambulo L	to go about, to walk
		ampulla L	two-handled vessel for liquids

		bullitus (*pp.*) L	boiled, bubbled
		bulla L	1. amulet worn upon the neck; 2. a papal bull
.32	passiom	passim L	here and there, far and wide, at random
		passio L	an enduring, a suffering
.33	venerections	Venere (*Abl.*) L	by means of Venus
		veneratio L	highest respect, reverence
		erectio L	a setting up, erecting; pride, insolence
357.04	Bismillafoulties	bis L	twice
		mille L	a thousand
.06	aurorbean	aurora L	the dawn
		orbe (*Abl.*) L	by means of a circle; by means of the world
.09	realisinus	sinus L	curve, hollow; the bosom; the purse, money; intimacy; interior; bay, gulf; valley; drinking bowl
.10	pene	paene L	almost
		poena L	punishment, penalty
.13	catatheristic	*katathêristikos G	downwards beastly, beastly below
.15	sangnificant	*sanguinifaciens L	bloody-making
.15	*Culpo*	culpa L	fault, sin
.15	*Dido*	Dido G L	Aeneas's paramour
.15	Ars	ars L	art
.20	cawcaw	caco L	to shit
.22	lamatory	lama L	bog, fen ("bog," *Irish slang* = toilet)
		*lamatorium L	a place for a bog
		lavatorium L	a place for washing
.30	Eonochs	êôs G	the dawn
		aiôn G	an age, lifetime
		nox L	night
		eunouchos G	chamberlain, bedkeeper, eunuch
.30	Cunstuntonopolies	Constantinopolis L	Constantine's city, Constantinople
		Konstantinou polis G	

.30	Eonochs	eunouchos	a eunuch *or*
	Cunstuntonopolies	Konstantinoupol- eôs G	chamberlain of Constantinople
.34	virvir	vir L	man, male person
.34	vergitable	vergo L	to bend, to twist
		*veritabilis L	true
		virga L	branch, twig, rod
		virgo L	a maid, virgin
358.03	murmurrandoms	murmurandum L	[something] to be murmured
.03	renations	rena-, renes L	kidney-, kidneys
		*renatio L	a being reborn
.08–.09	happy burgages	*trans.*	Dublin's motto; #B
	abeyance would make	obedientia	
	homesweetstown	civium urbis	
	hopeygoalucrey	felicitas L	
.09	hopeygoalucrey	lucrum L	profit
.09	mottu propprior	motu proprio L	by his own motion: executive document on minor disciplinary matters issued by the Pope in his own name
.10	pelaged	pelagos G	sea
		pelagus L	
		Pelagius	*Morgan,* "Seaborn", heretic; *see 182.03*
.10	gluttened	gluten L	glue
.12	colombophile	columbus L	male dove, cock-pigeon
		*columbophilos L + G	pigeon-lover
		M̄ L	1,000,000
.12	corvinophobe	corvinus L	raven
		*corvinophobos L + G	raven-fearer
.19	win a gain was in again	*win OG = *in G	#*Digamma*
.20	padar	pater L	father
.20	madar	mater L	mother
.20	hal	hals G	salt
.20	sal	sal L	salt
.21	Amick amack amock	*echo of* hic, haec, hoc L	this, this here (*masc., fem., neut.*) #B
.24	lauds	laus L	praise
.27	plultibust	pluribus L	to *or* by many
.27	preaggravated	*praeaggravatus L	burdened beforehand

.28	thaurity	taurus L	bull
.29	arthouducks	Artus dux L	Duke Art, original of King Arthur
		Arthox, Dux, *etc.*	stars from which Adam named; #*252.20*
		arktos G	bear
.30	ducomans	duco L	to lead, conduct, draw, bring forward
		manus L	the hand
		maneo L	to stay, remain
.31	cara	cara (*fem.*)	dear, precious
.32	Gemuas	geminus L	twin
		gemulus L	moaning, complaining
		genua L	the knees
.35	frons	frons L	1. leafy branch; 2. the forehead
.35	fesces	fascis L	a bundle
		Fescennini L	Fescennine verses: jeering verse dialogues
359.02	toork	taurikos G	concerning bulls
.03	outhired	outhar G	udder
.03	taratoryism	taurus L	bull
.04	lumbojumbo	lumbo- L	loin-
.09	diamoned	diamonê G	permanence
.09	penceloid	pensilis L	hanging, pendent
		pensilia L	fruit hung up to dry
		*pensiloeidês L+G	pendent-looking; looking like fruit hung up to be preserved
.17	layaman's brutstrenth	Layamon's *Brut*	Middle English epic based on *Aeneid*
.27	Tintinued	tintinno L	to clink, clank, jingle
.28	In Lucan	in luce L	in the light
.28	Lucan	M. Annaeus Lucanus	Roman poet; #*A*
.28	Lhirondella ... lhirondella	hirundo L	the swallow
.32	Alys!	alys G	agitation; ennui, boredom
.33	Alysaloe	alôê G	threshing-floor; garden, orchard, vineyard
		aloê G	aloes
.36	Oiboe	oiboiboi G	alas! woe's me!
360.02	floflo	flos L	a blossom, flower
.02	floreflorence	florea florens L	flowery garland, garland of flowers

.04	prime	primus L	first
.04	secund	secundus L	second
.04	terce	tertius L	third
.05	theorbe	theos G	god
		orbe L	for the world
.05	dulcifair	dulcifer L	containing sweetness, very sweet
.10	duol	duo L	two
.13	Carmen Sylvae	carmen silvae L	a song of the woodland
.13	Sylvae	Silvae L	"Woodlands": collection of poems by Statius; also one by Dryden
.17	samph	samphoros G	horse branded with the letter *san*
.21	ventruquulence	venter L	the belly
		truculentia L	savageness, ferocity
		loquentia L	fluency of speech
		*ventritruculentia L	belly-ferocity
		*ventriloquentia L	belly-talking, ventriloquism
.24	hypnot	hypnos H	sleep
.27	salms	psalma G	tune played on a stringed instrument
.27	Carolus	Carolus ML	Charles, Karl
.29	Whet the bee as to deflowret greendy grassies yellowhorse	L [?]	?
.30	Kematitis	*kematitis G	inflammation of a fawn
		kêmatitis G	inflammation of the muzzle
.30	cele	celo L	to hide, to conceal
		caelum	heaven
.33	enormanous	manus L	the hand
.36	Panchomaster	panto- G	all-
361.02	nil	nil L	nothing
.02	nix	nix L	snow
.04	a pace	a pace L	away from peace
.11	Eustache	eustachys G	rich in corn; blooming, youthful
.11	mingen	mingo L	to urinate
.13	ovful	ovum L	egg
.20	immutant	immutans L	unchanging
.21	onangonamed	gonos G	offspring, procreation, seed, semen

.27	folliagenous	*folleagenus L	bellows-born, produced by a bellows
		*foliagenus L	leaf-born
.30	Hilarion	Hilarion (290–372) G	"Joyful": saint
.32	gestare romanoverum	res gestae Romanorum L	the deeds of the Romans
		gestare Romanum verum L	to bear Roman truth, to tell Roman truth
		gesta rerum novarum L	deeds of the revolution
362.01	sixdigitarian	Sedigitus L	Six-fingered: cognomen of Roman poet C. Volcatius Sedigitus (fl. 100 b.c.)
.03	condomnation	*condomatio L	a complete taming
		*condominatio L	joint-lordship, joint-rule
.04	totomptation	totum L	all, whole
.04	repepulation	*re-pepulisse L	to have beaten again
.16	generose	generose L	nobly
.17	umbrasive	umbra sive L	a shadow or if
.17	corpsus	corpus L	body, substance
.25	evacuan	evacuo L	to empty out
.31	Amodicum	modicum L	a little way, a little
.34	aspectable	aspectabilis L	visible; worthy of being seen
.35	perspectable	*perspectabilis L	that may be seen through; perceptible
		perspicibilis L	clearly visible, bright
363.03	coras	cora L	the pupil of the eye
		coram L	in the presence of
.09	exexive	XXIV ; XXV L	24; 25
		exesus L	eaten up; preyed upon
.17	bis	bis L	twice
.18	palam	palam L	openly, publicly, plainly
.18	calam	calamus L	reed pen
		clam L	secretly
.20	fellows culpows	felix culpa L	happy sin; #B
.26	trisspass	trispastos G	hoisting-tackle with three pulleys
		tristis L	sad
.26	minxmingled	minxi L	I have pissed
		mingo L	I piss

.28	theactrisscalls	thea G	goddess
.28	imprecurious	*impraecuriosus L	not bestowing care on beforehand
.36	Missaunderstain	Missa L	"Sent": the Mass
364.04	perambulatrix	perambulatrix L	[she who is] a rambler-through, a traverser, a visitor, a conductor of herself
.11	bisextine	bisextilis	containing a double sixth [day before the Kalends of March]: containing an intercalary day: *i.e.*, a leap-year
.17	avragetopeace	avrektos MG *for* aurêktos (Aeolic) G, arrhêktos G	unbroken
.18	apoclogypst	apokalypsis G	uncovering, disclosing, revelation
		apologistês G	accountant, bookkeeper
.20	abwaited	ab L	away from
.21	intectis	intectus L	uncovered, unclad; open, frank
		intactus L	untouched
		in tectis L	on the roofs
.21	Registower	Regis L	of the King, the King's
.22	Analbe	analbus G+L	not-white
		Eblana (*backwards*) G	Dublin; #*A*
.24	perensempry	perenne L	constantly, perpetually
		semper L	always, ever
.24	sex	sex L	six
.29	lyst	lyssoô G	to enrage, madden
		lyst G (spelling) =	lust (*spelling*)
.29	turpidump	turpiter L	in an ugly *or* foul manner
.29	arkens	arcens L	enclosing, keeping off, defending
.29	litigimate	litigo L	to dispute, quarrel
.33	mundamanu	munda manu L	with a clean hand
		Munda	Caesar's last battle; #*A*
.33	victuum	victuum (*Gen. pl.*) L	of sustenances, of nourishments

365.02	caves	caves L	you (*sing.*) are on your guard
.03	sacreligion	sacra religio L	holy religion
		sacrilegium L	temple-robbery, sacrilege
.04	daimond ... daimond	daimôn G	spirit, genius, demon
.05	panthoposopher	*pantôposophos G	one who is wise through seeing all
.06	Bacchulus	Bacchulus L	a little Bacchus
		baculus L	stick, staff, walking-stick
.09	sebaiscopal	Sebastou polis, Sebastes polis G	Augustus's city, Augusta's city: Sevastopol (*Crimea*)
		episcopalis eccl. L	pertaining to a bishop
		episkopos G	overseer, inspector; bishop
.10	biasement	Bias of Priene	one of the seven sages
.17	prostatution	prostas G	porch, vestibule
		prostata (*pp.*) L	offered for sale; prostituted
.19	nompos mentis	non compos mentis L	not in control of the mind; insane
.19	Novus	novus (*masc.*) L	new, young
.19	Elector	elector L	elector, chooser, selecter
		êlektôr G	shining sun
.28	Nixies	Nixi [Di] L	three deities of women in labor
366.02	nexistence	nex L	murder
		*nexsistensia L *modeled on*	unemergence, unmanifestation, nonexistence
		*exsistensia L	emergence, becoming, manifestation, existence
.03	vividence	vividus L	lively, animated
		vivide L	vigorously
		vivide evidens L	vigorously visible, vigorously manifest, vigorously evident
.03	Panto	panto- G	all-
.03	suppline	suppleta (*fem. pp.*) L *based on* completa L	filled up, made complete filled, full; *compline*

.09	sodalists	sodalis L	mate, comrade, companion
.12	perthanow	parthenos G	maiden, girl
		hê Parthenos G	The Virgin: Athena; Artemis; the constellation *Virgo*
.14–.15	deepseep daughter which was borne up pridely out of medstreams unclouthed when I was pillowing in my brime	[deepsleep/deep-sea]daughter which was [born/borne] up [proudly/bright-ly] out of [my dreams/Mediter-ranean][encloud-ed/unclothed] when I was [pillowing/billo-wing] in my [prime/brine]	1. birth of Athena: she sprang fully armed from the forehead of Zeus; 2. birth of Aphrodite: she was borne up naked out of the seafoam at Cyprus
.17	*in re*	in re L	in the matter
.20	defecalties	defaeco L	to cleanse, purify, wash
.21	Terry	terra L	land, earth
.21–.22	grace for the grass	gratia L	grace
.23	catasthmatic	*katasthmatikos G	suffering from panting-against
.23	improctor	*emprôktos G	in-the-anus
.23	seducint	seducens L	leading away, misleading, seducing
.26	humand	humandus L	requiring to be buried
.27	Torrenation	torreo L	to dry up; to nip, to pinch
.36	nun	nun G	now
367.04	chinchinatibus	Cincinnatus L	Roman farmer-dictator
.13	lymphing	lympha L	clear water
.14	avunculusts	avunculus L	maternal uncle
.17	Synopticked	synoptikos G	seeing the whole together
.20	Jukoleon	Deucalion	the classical Noah; # *A*
		leôn G leo L	lion
.25	thalassocrats	thalassokratôr G	master of the sea
.28	numbulous	nummulus L	some money
		nebula L	mist, fog, smoke, cloud
		cumulus L	a heap, pile
.35	anononously	anemos G	wind

		anomos G	lawless
		anonêtos G	unprofitable
368.10	belloky	bello L	to wage war
.12	Monabella	Mona bella L	1. pretty Isle of Man; 2. pretty Anglesea
.12	culculpuration	culus L	the arse
		culpo L	to reproach, to blame
		culpa L	crime, fault, defect
		cuculus L	the cuckoo
.13	perperusual	perperus L	faulty, defective, wrong
		perperos G	vainglorious
.14	*sic*	sic L	thus
.14	*suc*	succus L	juice, sap
.15	bellock	bellax L	warlike, martial
.16	caving	caveo L	to be on guard, to take care, beware
.17	quicely	qui L	who? which?; how? why?
.17	quicely rebustly	quis rebus L	by what matters? by what affair?
.17	rebustly	rebus L	by things
.21	consients	consient OL	they be coexisting, they may coexist
.26	quaram	quarum (*Gen. pl. fem.*) L	whose, of whom; of what women?
.33	Leonocopolos	leontocephalos G	lion-headed
369.06	sublation	sublatio L	a lifting up; removal; annulling
.06	radification	*radificatio L	a root-making
.12	Fert	fert L	he bears, he carries
.12	Fort	fortis L	strong, powerful, brave
.12	Fert Fort	*Fortitudo Ejus Rhodum Tenuit*	His Strength has held Rhodes; #*B*
.12	ontowhom	ontôs G	really, actually
		onta G	reality, things that actually exist
.17	Fidelisat	fidelis L	trusty, faithful, reliable
		Fideli sat L	[it] suffices for the faithful one
.24	decumans	decumanus L	1. of tithes; 2. tithes-collector
		decumanus [limes] L	boundary line drawn east-to-west
		Decima L	one of the Fates = *Lachesis* G; goddess of accouchements

.25	Pandoria	Pandôra G	1. Giver of All: the Earth; 2. All-Endowed: let evils out of a jar
.26	Paullabucca	paula bucca L	little cheek, little mouth
.33	ephumeral	pheu G	alas! oh!
		ephêmerios G	during the day; for a day only
		[h]umerale L	covering for the shoulders, cape
		[h]umerus L	the upper arm
.36	cubital	cubital L	elbow-cushion, for leaning on
		cubitalis L	pertaining to the elbow
370.06	Mather Caray's	mater cara L	beloved mother
.06	*pante*	panto- G	all-
		pente G	five
.13	Aletheometry	*alêtheometreia G	truth-measuring; truth-measurement
.15	Onamassofmancy-naves	onomasia G	name
		onomastos G	named, to be named
		*onomatomant-eia G	divination from names
		naves (*pl.*) L	ships
.24	rumpumplikun	rem publicam (*Acc.*) L	the State, Commonweal, Republic
.30	polisignstunter	polis G	city
.32	knootvindict	vindicta L	liberating rod: with which a slave was touched to be freed; protection
.34	onem	omen L	a prognostic
		nemo L	no one
.35	Nomo	nemo L	no one; #*A Odysseus*
		nomen L	name
.36	glutany	gluten L	glue, beeswax
371.09	Ostia ... Ostia	Ostia L	"Mouths": seaport at Tiber mouth
.09	Ostia! From the say! Away from the say!	*allusion to history of Ostia*	in Caesar's time silting at Ostia required new port 3 miles north. After 300 new harbor became town, Portus; Ostia, away from the sea, declined

.15	cupturing	cupio, *pp.*	to desire
		cupitus L	
		capio, *pp.*	to seize
		captus L	
.15	dropes	*drôps G	person, man
.17	sture	sturioô G	to guarantee with an oath
.22	Benefice	benefice L	beneficently
		Bonifacius L	"Handsome": anti-Irish English saint; #A
.23	recolcitrantament	recolo L	to cultivate again; to revisit
.24	probenopubblicoes	pro bono publico L	for the public good
.24	clamatising	clam L	secretly, privately
		clamator L	bawler, noisy declaimer; shouter
372.01	hircomed	hirco L	to howl
		hircus L	he-goat
.12	The scenictutors	De Senectute L	*On Old Age*: essay by Cicero
.16	labious	labeosus L	having large lips, blubber-lipped
.18	duoly	duo L	two
.23	hosty	hostis L	stranger, foreigner, enemy
		Hostius L	epic poet of 2d C b.c.
		Hostius Quadra L	lecher and voyeur; #A
.23	mirification	*mirificatio L	a making wonderful, causing wonder
		*mirror-ficatio Eng+L	making of mirrors [Hostius Quadra devised mirrors for gratification]
.24	lutification	*lutificatio L	a making of mud
.24	paludination	*paludinatio L	state of being a swamp
373.12	Horkus	horkos G	that by which one swears; an oath
		Horkos G	divinity who punishes perjury
		Orcus L	the god of the Underworld; Hades
.12	ebblynuncies	Eblana G	Dublin
		*Eblanensis L	*Dublinean, of Dublin

		nunc L	now
		nuntius L	messenger
.12	Horkus chiefest ebblynuncies	Hircus Civis Eblanensis L	Goat Citizen of Dublin
.16	Lanno's	lanosus L	woolly
.21	methylogical	*methylogikos G	a student of wine *or* drunkeness
.21	imberillas	imber L	rain, rainstorm, pouring rain
.23	lemans	[Lacus] Lemanus L	Lake Geneva
.24	Ericus	erikos G	woolen
		ericius L	the hedgehog
.24	Vericus	verus L	true
		veritus (*pp.*) L	awed, made to feel reverence
		veridicus L	truth-telling, veracious
374.07	Anonymay's	anônymei (*adv.*) G	without name, namelessly
.07	palinode	palinôdia G	a recantation, revocation; repetition of an ode; repetition
		hê Palinôdia G	*The Palinode*: ode in which Stesichorus recanted a previous attack upon Helen
.10	gommas	gamma G	letter G
		komma G	clause in a sentence
.12	dueluct	due- L	two-
		luctamen, luctatio L	a wrestling, struggle, contest
		luctus L	sorrow, mourning
		*dueluctamen L	a struggle for two, duel
		*dueluctus L	lamentation for two
.17	postoral	post L	after, afterwards
		os, oris L	the mouth
		*postoralis Mod L	after by mouth
.17	lector	lector L	a reader
.17	Epistlemadethemology	epistolê G	written communication, letter
		epistula L	letter
		epistêmê G	knowledge, understanding, skill
		epistêmologia G	science of knowing how, science of knowledge

		thema G	that which is laid down; deposit; cemetery; case proposed for discussion
		*epistolothemal-ogia G	the science of that which is discussed in letters
.20	vendoror	vendo L	to sell
		vendor L	I am sold
		venditor L	a seller
.21	hic	hic L	this, this here
.22	Numah	Numa Pompilius L	second king of Rome
.23	Nomon	nomos G	1. district, province; 2. law, custom
		Nemo L	No one: Ulixes' name; #A
		gnômôn G	one that knows, an interpreter; carpenter's square; determining mark
		gnomon L	the pointer on a sundial
.23	Ecclesiast	Ekklêsiastês G	Member of a congregation; Qoheleth
.31	Basil	basileus G	king
		Basilios G	"Kingly": saint
		Basilios I Makedonikos	Byzantine emperor, murdered his predecessor
.33	sinus	sinus L	bent surface, fold, hollow, bay
375.05	jurors' cruces	juror cruce L	I swear by the cross
.08	anarthur	anarthros G	unarticulated, without joints, strengthless, inarticulate
.10	myrds	myrias G	ten thousand
		merda L	dung
.13	haemicycles	haimakyklos G	blood-circle, blood-cycle; menses
.14	in cameras	in camera L	in the chamber: secretly, confidentially
.15	extra	extra L	outside, in the open [opp. of in camera]
.18	Nazi Priers	nisi prius L	unless before; legal phrase

.28	Magnes	magnês G	a magnet, loadstone
		magnes L	
		magnus L	great, big
		Magnus L	the Great
.28	cirrchus	circus L	circular line, circle
		cirrus L	curl, ringlet, tuft
.29	Fummuccumul	fumus L	smoke, steam
		cumulus L	a heap, pile
.31	nimb	nimbus L	rainstorm, raincloud; glory that envelopes gods (and saints)
376.03	minx	minxi L	I have urinated
.09	cucconut	cucubo L	the screech-owl
		cucullus L	1. the cuckoo; 2. a kind of hood
.11	Delphin	delphis, delphin G delphinus, delphin L	the dolphin; the Dolphin, a constellation
		delphinus ML	the Dauphin
.13	dos	dos L	dowry
.15	corpus entis	corpus entis L	body of being; body of a thing
.16	Nichtia	nychth- G	night-
		nychia G	nightly watch
.34	Fisht!	I[êsos] CH[ristos] TH[eou] [h]Y[ios] S[ôtêr] G	Jesus Christ, God's Son, Savior
		ichthys G	fish
377.01	Angus! Angus! Angus!	agnus L	lamb
		sanctus! sanctus! sanctus! L	holy! holy! holy!
.04	helo	hêlos G	nailhead, stud, nail
.08	gibbous	gibbus L	hump
.09	Postumus	Postumus L	"Last-born": Roman surname; friend of Horace's, addressed in Odes II.9
		posthumus LL	"after-burial": erroneous ancient etymology for postumus
.12–.13	mouldem imparvious	multum in parvo L	much in little

.21	gallus	gallus L	a cock
		Gallus L	1. a Gaul; 2. castrated priest of Cybele
378.03	Buccas	bucca L	cheek, mouth
.04	lac	lac L	milk
.09	rattillary	Attila	king of the Huns
		at illa L	and she also
.09	–traum–	trauma G	wound
.09	-conductor	conductor L	tenant; contractor
.13	O'Cunnuc	cunnus L	cunt
.13	Rix	rix Celt. = rex L	king
.13	Adversed ord	adverso ordine L	in reversed order
.15	Motometusolum	motus metu solo L	moved by fear only
.20	Tiemore moretis	timor mortis	the fear of death
	tisturb badday	conturbat me L	disquiets me
		timor mortis	the fear of death
		disturbat te L	throws you into disorder
.26	os	os L	1. mouth; 2. bone
.31	vulsyvolsy	vulsus, volsus L	shorn, smooth, plucked, hairless; effeminate; spasmodic, suffering from convulsions
		vice versa L	turned around opposite
.33	nocense	nocentia L	guilt, transgression
.36	foul a delfian	Philadelphia G	"Love of brothers," "Brother-love": *name of two cities*
379.08	Saxolooter	Saxo L	a Saxon
.11	Aerian's Wall	aerios G aerius L	aerial, airy (*poetic*)
		Vallum Hadriani L	Hadrian's Wall: wall begun a.d. 122 across northern Britain to fend off the Picts
		Vallum Aureliani L	Aurelian's Wall: the city wall of Rome constructed a.d. 271–275
.14	hores	hora L	hour
		Hora L	goddess, wife of Romulus

.15	Idas	Ida G L	mountain in Crete where Zeus was reared
.16	Nessies	nêsos G	an island
.17	delysiums	delusus (pp.) L	mocked, deceived, made sport of
		Êlysion G	the abode of the blest
		Elysium L	
.21	sord	sordeo L	to be filthy
.29	augur	augur L	diviner, soothsayer
.31	adceterus	ad L	to, at
		*ceterus L	the other, that which exists beside; the other part
		et cetera L	and the rest
.31	adsaturas	ad L	to, at
		satura L	dish of various kinds of food; mixed salad; stew; kind of didactic poetry (satire)
.31	Megantic	mega G	big, great
		gigas G	a giant
		*megagigantikos G	hugely mountainous
.34	Timmotty	Timotheus G	"Honoring God": companion of Paul
380.01	Katey	kathairô G	to cleanse
.02	Katey	see 380.01 L	
.03	bonnefacies	bona facies L	handsome face
		Bonifacius	saint; #A
		bona fides L	good faith; #B
.03	Aquasancta	aqua sancta L	holy water
.05	Malincurred	*malincurro L	to fall in with evilly, to attack wickedly
.07	melumps	melos G	tune, air, song
.12	polemarch	polemarchos G	war-lord, chieftain
.17	equilines	equus, equi L	horse
		equile L	a stable
.33	Rex	rex L	king
381.04	Hauburnea's	Hibernia L	Ireland
.09	faix	faex L	dregs, lees, sediment
.14	panprestuberian	*panpresbyteri- on G	council of all elders
		pan G	all
		praesto L	at hand, ready
		uber L	1. an udder; 2. rich, fruitful

		*panpraestuberi-us L + G	all-at hand-fruitful
.18	allocutioning	allocutio L	a speaking to, an address; a consoling, a comforting
.19	*Ergen*	ergon G	work
.23	*todie*	hodie L	today
382.02	cheeriubicundenances	rubicundus L	ruddy
		Rubico L	"Ruddy": river Caesar crossed to start Civil War
		ubi L	where
.18	folkenfather of familyans	*part trans.* paterfamilias L	father of a family, head of a house-hold, patriarch: exercised sovereign authority over all members of the family
.20	composs	compos L	having mastery, control *or* power over
383.11	*Tristy's*	tristis L	sad, mournful
.24	vuoxens	vox L	voice
384.01	solans	solanus L	the east wind
		sol L	the sun
		Solôn G	Athenian legislator
.03	auspices	auspicium L	divination by observing the flight of birds
.08	Marcus	Marcus L	"Hammer": Roman praenomen; #A
.11	Marcus	*see 384.11 E*	
.15	fish for Christ	I[êsous] CH[ristos] TH[eou] [h]Y[ios] S[ôtêr] G	Jesus Christ God's Son Savior
.16	fish	ICHTHYS G	FISH
.17	Augusburgh	Augusta Vindelicorum L	Augusta [*city of Augustus*] of the Vindelici [*a German people*]:Augsburg
.18	pulchrum's proculs	pulchrum procul L	beauty far off
.23	cubin	cubo L	to lie down
.26	sinister	sinister L	on the left; ill-omened
		sinistra L	the left hand

.26	dexterity	dexteritas L	aptness, readiness; prosperity
		dextera L	the right hand
.27	vicemversem	vicem versam (*Acc.*) L	turned around reciprocally
.27	et	et L	and
.27	assaucyetiams	*assauciatio L	a wounding-to, wounding-at, an assassination
		associatus (*pp.*) L	joined to, united with
		socii L	comrades, associates, allies
		etiam L	and also, furthermore, likewise
.28	sexfutter	sex L	six
.29	palpably	palpabilis L	that may be touched *or* felt
.29	bulbubly	bulbulus L	a small bulb
		balbus L	stammering
.32	Trisolanisans	*trisolani L	three-eastwinds
		*trisolinêsitês L + G	three-sun-islander
.36	vulgar ear	aera vulgaris L	the common reckoning of time
385.12	vellicar	vellico L	to pluck, twitch, pinch
.13	Ultonian	*Ultonianus bogus-L	of Ulster
.14	Totius	toties L	so often, so many times
.14	Quotius	quoties L	how often, how many times
.14	tribluts	tribulo L	to press; to oppress, to afflict
		tribulus L	iron-pronged device thrown on the ground to impede cavalry
.19	Marcus	Marcus L	"Hammer": Roman praenomen
.20	moves and senses	*allusion to* Syntax of the Moods and Tenses of the Greek Verb	*by W. W. Goodwin,* new ed. 1889: *monument of American classical scholarship*
386.05	pantometer	pantomêtêr G	all-mother, mother of all

		pantometron G	an all-measure, that by which everything is measured
		pentametros G	consisting of five measures; pentameter
.06	duckasaloppics	*dekasyllabikos G	having ten syllables, decasyllabic
.13	pater familias	paterfamilias OL	father of an extended family
.18–.19	*quiescents in brage*	quiescens in pace L	reposing in peace
		bracae L	britches, trousers
.22	prostituent	prostituens L	placing in front, exposing publicly to prostitution
.24	prumisceous	pru[riginosus] L	itchy, scabby; lecherous, lascivious
		promiscuus L	mixed, without distinction, indiscriminate
		promiscue L	in common
.26	jaypee	J[uppiter] p[luvius] L	Jupiter who dispenses Rain
.35	deeseesee	DCC L	700
.35	erumping	erumpo L	to cause to burst forth, to burst, to break out
.35	oround	oro L	to argue, plead; pray
.36	Judgity	jugiter L	perpetually
.36	Yaman	jam L	now, at present
387.02	Aferican	Afer L	African
.05	parapilagian	*parapelagios (*adj.*) G	along-the-sea
		trans.	*ar-mor* Celt, *at-mare*
		Armoricus L	OL: tribes of north Gaul (Brittany)
.06	jaypee	J[uppiter] p[luvius] L	Jupiter the Rain-bringer; #*A*
.06	Elevato	elevo L	to lift up, raise
		elevator L	one who raises up, a deliverer
		elevatio LL	a lifting up, raising
.12	exestuance	exaestuans L	boiling up, foaming up, fermenting; effervescing; glowing; exhaling

.13	explutor	ex L	out, out of
		plutor eccl L	the rainer, he who sends rain
		*explutor eccl L	the outrainer, he who sends rain out
.14	manausteriums	manus L	the hand
		auster L	the south wind
		austerus L	harsh, sour, tart; severe,
		austêros G	rigid, strict
		monasterium eccl. L monastêrion G	a monastery
.14	Marcus	Marcus L	Roman praenomen
.18	Momonian	Momonianus bogus-L	of Munster
388.01	Exeunc	exeunt L	they go out, they leave, they depart
.10	Marcus	Marcus L	Roman praenomen
.14	lacustrian	lacus L	tank, vat, lake, pond; basin, cistern
		lacustrinus Mod L	found in or on a lake
.15	Dona	dona (pl.) L	gifts
.16	marents	mare L	sea
		parens L	procreator, father or mother, parent
		*marens L	ditto: as if parens from pater, *marens from mater [parens is from pario, "to bring forth, to bear"]
.26	silvestrious	silvestris L	pertaining to a wood, overgrown with woods, wooded
.28	gloriaspanquost	gloriae panis quo est L	where is the bread of glory?
.29	anarxaquy	anarchia G	lack of a leader, lawlessness
		exsequiae L	funeral procession
		arx L	citadel
.29	doxarchology	*doxarchologia G	the science or art of being a leader of opinion
.30	Hibernia	Hibernia L	Ireland
.31	sexon grimmacticals	Saxo Grammaticus L (1140–1206)	The Learned Saxon: Danish chronicler; source of the Hamlet-story

.34	regnumrockery	regnum L	Kingship, royalty; dominion, rule; a kingdom
.34	Marcus	*see 388.10 A*	
389.03	twelve tables	lex duodecim tabularum L	law of the twelve tables; *see 167.23,*
.03–.04	per pioja at pulga bollas	per pia et pura bella L	through dutiful and undefiled wars
		pia, pulchra, bella (*fem.*) L	dutiful, beautiful, pretty
.06	supper	super L	above, on top, upon
.06	matther	mater L	mother
.09	gynecollege	gynê G	woman
		collegium L	colleagueship; association, guild, society
		gynaikologia G	the science of women, gynecology
.10	Andersdaughter	andros (*Gen.*) G	man's, of a man
.13	bis	bis L	twice
.15	Fatimiliafamilias	fati (*Gen.*) L	of an utterance; of a prediction, of an oracle, of destiny, destiny's
		milia [passus] L	a mile
		familias OL	family's, of a family
.17	psadatepholomy	psadyros G	crumbling, friable
		psadda G	cinnabar
		tephra G	ashes
		pholis G	horny scale
.19	*arma virumque romano*	Arma virumque cano L	Arms and the man I sing: *opening of Vergil's* Aeneid
		Arma virumque Romano L	Arms and the man by a Roman
		Arma virumque *romano L	Arms and the man I roman
.22	gagagniagnian	agnus L	lamb
.24	troad	Trôas G L	Troad: district in which Troy was situated
.28	Cornelius Nepos	Cornelius Nepos L	Roman historian (99–25 b.c.)
.28	Mnepos	nepos L	grandson
		Mnêmôn G	"Having a good Memory": surname of Artaxerxes; *also,* a Roman surname

.28	Anumque	anumque (*Acc.*) L	1. and the old woman 2. and the anus; and a hemorrhoid
.29	umque	umque L	and -*um* (*suffix*)
		umquam L	at any time, ever
.30	Queh? Quos?	queo L	to be able to
		quei OL	to whom?
		quo L	where?
.32	gamen	gamos G	a wedding
390.07	croniony	Kronidês, Kroniôn G	son of Kronos, *i.e.*, Zeus
.11	confarreation	confarreatio L	solemn Roman wedding by offering bread (*far*)
.11	per	per L	through; during; for; by
.17-.18	Roman hat, with an ancient Greek gloss on it	glôssai G	1. words or expressions not belonging to the spoken language familiar to the critic, but to a dialect of another region or time [G] 2. marginal or interlinear interpretations of difficult or obsolete words [L]
.22	per	per L	*see 390.11*
.22	Nupiter	*Nupiter [Nubis-pater *modeled on* Jovis-Pater: Jupiter] L	"Cloud-father," "Veil-father"
		nubo L	to cover, to veil; to be married
.22	Nupiter Privius	Jupiter Pluvius L	Jupiter dispenser of Rain
.23		Nupiter *Privius L	Veil-father dispenser of one's own
.23	terpary	ter L	three times, thrice
391.01	Erminia	Armenia G L	Armenia: country in Asia
		mus Armenius L	Armenian mouse: ermine
.01	Reginia	regina L	queen
.05	Hohannes	Johannes, Iohannes LL	John

.07	attraxity	atrox L	horrible, frightful, dreadful
		atrocitas L	harshness, horribleness, hideousness
		attractio L	a drawing together
.08	chors	choros G	dance; troop of dancers in a tragedy; the chorus
.10	materfamilias	materfamilias L	mother of a family, matriarch
.13	missoccurs	missus L	a sending away, a despatching
		occurso L	to run to meet, to meet
		occursus L	a meeting, encounter
.14	Marcus	Marcus L	Roman praenomen
.15	chronometer	chronometron G	time-measurer
		*chronomêtêr G	time-mother, mother of time
		*Chronomêter, *Kronomêtêr G	Mother of Chronos/Kronos: Gaia, the Earth
.18	Neptune's	Neptunus L	Roman god of the sea and waters
.20	hersute	hirsutus L	rough, shaggy, bristly, prickly
.21	bronnanoleum	brontaô G	to thunder
		brontê G	thunder
		oleum L	oil, olive oil
.23	Dion Cassius	Dion *or* Dio Cassius G	historian
392.08	Martyr Mrs MacCawley's	Mater Misericordiae L	Mother of Mercy (*a Dublin hospital*)
.14	Emeritus	emeritus L	soldier who has served his time, veteran exempt from further duty
		emeritus (*adj.*) L	worn out, unfit for service
.18	Mnepos	nepos L	grandson
		Nepos L	surname in the gens Cornelia: Cornelius Nepos: *see 389.28*
		Mnêmôn G	"Having a good Memory": *see 389.28*
.19	perigrime	peregrinus L	foreign, strange, exotic

.23	Caucuses	caucus L	drinking vessel, kind of
		kaukos G	cup
		Kaukasos G	chain of mountains in
		Caucasus L	Asia between the Black
			and the Caspian Seas
.24	Themistletocles	Themistoklês G	"Famous for Justice":
			Athenian statesman;
			#C
.27	Iren	eirêne G	peace
		Ierne L	Ireland
.27	auspices	auspicia L	divinations by
			observing the flight of
			birds
.28	kalospintheochromato-	kalos G	beautiful
	kreening		
		spinthêr G	spark
		spinthêro- G	spark-
		theos G	god
		chrômato- G	color-
		krênê G	well, fountain, spring
		*kalospinthêro-	beautiful-spark-color-
		chrômatakrênê	fountain
		G	
.36	laudabiliter	Laudabiliter L	"Laudably": John
			Bull's bull; #B
393.08	Soteric	Sôtêr G	Savior
		Sôtêrika G	festival in honor of
			Ptolemy Sôtêr
		sôtêrikos G	pertaining to a saver or
			savior
.13	boccat	bucca L	cheek, mouth
.23–24	from alum	malum L	1. an apple; 2. an evil,
			calamity
.24	alum	alum L	a kind of garlic
.24	oves	oves (pl.) L	sheep
		ovum L	egg
.23–.24	from alum and oves	reverse of ab	from the egg all the
		ovo usque ad	way to the apples; from
		mala L	the beginning to the
			end [of a Roman feast];
			#B
394.14	panementically	*panemmenetik-	disposed to abide by
		os G	all, disposed to endure
			all
		*pan-ementitus	all-forged, all-fabricated
		G + L	

.19	arthroposophia	arthropedê G	fetter, band for the limbs
		*arthropous (*mod. coinage*) G	joint-foot: insect, arachnid, crustacean
		*arthroposophia G	wisdom concerning arthropods
		*anthrôposophia G	wisdom concerning mankind
.21	gutterful	guttur L	gullet, throat
.23	palpabrows	palpebra L	eyelid
		palpebro L	to blink
.29	Huber	hubris G	wanton violence, insolence
		uber L	teat, pap, udder; fruitful, fertile, abundant
.30	binnoculises	bineô G	to fornicate
		oculus L	an eye
.30	memostinmust	*memorrimus L	most mindful
.30	egotum	ego tum L	I, then; I, at that time
.31	upers	[h]uper G super L	over, above; beyond
.31	deprofundity	de profundis L	out of the depths (*Ps.* 129/130)
.32	pancosmic	pankosmikos G	belonging to the whole world
.36	pugnoplangent	*pugnoplangens L	beating with fists, fist-striking; fist-lamenting
395.01	higherdimissional	dimissio L	a sending in different directions; a sending out, sending forth
.06	how long tandem	*part trans.* Quo usque tandem [abutere nostra patientia, Catilina?] L	How long at length (*i.e.,* How far, then) [will you abuse our patience, Catiline?]: *opening of Cicero's 1st Oration against Catiline*
.08	narcolepts	narkôlêptos G	seized by numbness
.08	Coma	kôma G	deep sleep
		coma L	hair of the head, tresses
		*Coma *pl. of* Comum L	town in Gallia Transpadina, *now* Como

.10	Fumadory	fumus, fuma- L dory G *fumadory L + G	smoke, smoke- oar, mast, ship; spear steamship
.11	catara	katara G	a curse
.12	*qua*	qua L	on which side, where; how, how much
.19	delightafellay	fellatio L	sucking
.20	perfidly	perfide L	faithlessly, treacherously
.33	lepes	lepas G L	limpet, clinging shellfish
		lepus L	hare
.33	lopes	lupus L	wolf
.35	Amoricas	amor L	love
		Armoricus L	"Sea-side": Armorican, belonging to north Gaul; Breton
.35	Champius	campus L *campius L	field, flat plain belonging to a field
.36	virilvigtoury	virilis L vigoro L	manly to animate, to gain strength
396.01	Eburnea's	eburnea (*adj. fem.*) L Hibernia L	ivory, of ivory Ireland
.08	prisscess	priscus L	of former times, ancient, of yore
.19	Hagakhroustioun	aga- G chrusos G oun G Hagios Christos G hagios Christianos G	very- gold certainly, in fact, really Holy Christ a holy Christian
.24	pulpous	pulposus L	fleshy
.24	mhost phassionable wheathers	# *Labials*	
.25 .29	volupty	voluptas L	satisfaction, pleasure, delight
.36	peributts	periboêtos G peri G	celebrated, famous around, about, all around
397.02	owneirist	*oneiristês G	a dreamer
.16	ovasleep	ova (*pl.*) L	eggs

		ovatus L	1. egg-shaped; 2. a shouting, rejoicing
.21	Marcus	Marcus L	Roman praenomen
.26	caschal pandle	# *P/K Split*	paschal candle
.27		paschalis L	pertaining to Passover *or* Easter
.27	magnegnousioum	magnês G	a magnet
		magnêsion G	name of several different ores and metallic amalgams
		gnôsis G	research, knowledge
.32–.33	*totam in tutu*	totam (*fem. Acc.*) in	the whole [woman?] in safekeeping
		tutu L	*or* security
.34	orther	orthos G	straight, upright
		orthros G	dawn
.34	regul	regula L	straight piece of wood, ruler
		regulo L	to direct, regulate
.34	incubation	incubatio L	a sleeping in *or* on; illegal possession; sleeping in a temple to obtain a prophetic dream
398.02	Marcus	Marcus L	Roman praenomen
.02	Podex	podex L	the fundament, anus
.08	in medios loquos	in medias res L	into the middle of the plot: *conventional beginning for epic*
		in medios locos L	into the middle of places
.08	loquos	loquor L	to speak, discourse
.12	oremus	oremus L	let us pray
.14	meter	mêtêr G	mother
.14	peter	patêr G	father
		petra G	rock
		Petros G	Rock; Peter
.15	peregrine ... peregrine	peregrinus L	strange, foreign, exotic; a stranger, foreigner
		peregrinus ML	pilgrim
.15	for navigants et peregrinantibus	pro navigantibus et peregrinantibus ML	for sailors and for pilgrims, for travelers by sea and travelers to remote places (*a prayer*)

.18	Iovasteamadorion	adoro L	to accost; to beseech; to adore; to respect
		*adorion L+G	a little thing that is adored
		dôrion (*neut.*) G	Dorian
		*adôrion (*neut.*) G	non-Dorian
.29	Tristan	tristis L	sad
.31	*Anno Domini nostri sancti Jesu Christi*	anno Domini nostri sancti Jesu Christi L	in the year of our blessed Lord Jesus Christ
399.04	*Sybil*	*Sibylla G L*	a female soothsayer, prophetess
.04–.07	*queen ... surfriding ... brine on her brow*	description of the birth of Aphrodite from the seashore foam at Cyprus	see Botticelli's *Nate di Venere*
403.02	kater	quattuor L	four
.02	sax	saxum L	a stone
		sex L	six
.03	Hork	horkos G	that by which one swears; an oath
.07	nasoes	nasus L	the nose
		Naso L	"Largenosed": Roman family name in four gentes
		Publius Ovidius Naso	Roman poet; #A
.09	Titubante	titubans L	tottering, staggering, reeling
		titubanter L	loosely, totteringly, drunkenly
.09	Titubante of Tegmine-sub-Fagi	Tityre, tu patulae recubans sub tegmine fagi L: Vergil. *Ec.*I.l	Tityrus, thou reclining beneath the shelter of the spreading beech-tree: *opening of Vergil's first* Eclogue
.11	Anastashie	anastasis G	raising up [*the dead*]; resurrection
.12–.13	Gugurtha! Gugurtha!	Jugurtha	king of Numidia, defeated by Rome
.17	Apagemonite	apagô G	to carry off, lead away, take away
		apage G	carry off! go away!

404.01	affluvial	*affluvialis L	pertaining to flowing towards
.07	vociferated	vociferatio L	a loud calling, clamor
		vociferor L	to cry out, cry aloud, exclaim
.26	Tamagnum	tam magnum L	so big, so great
.35	Haggispatrick ...	hagios (*masc.*)	holy; saint
	Huggisbrigid	hagia (*fem.*) G	
405.01	multiply	multiplico L	to increase, to become *much* (*multum*)
.01	plultiply	*pluriplico L	to increase more, to become *more* (*plus*)
.32	pranzipal	prandium L	lunch
.32	*plus*	plus L	more
406.01	merendally	merenda L	afternoon luncheon
.07	onion (Margareter,	unio margarita	pearl onion; *see 249.12*
	Margaretar	L margaritarius	pearl-fisher female
	Margarasticandeatar)	L margaritaria	pearl-dealer goddess
		L dea L	
.14	vitellusit	videlicet L	it is easy to see, clearly, of course
		vitellus L	a little calf; veal; egg-yolk
		Aulus Vitellius	dissolute emperor a.d. 69; murdered
.15	carusal	carus L	dear, precious, beloved
		Marcus	emperor 282–283,
		Aurelius Carus	struck by lightning
.20	pax cum Spiritututu	pax cum spiritu tuo L	peace with thy spirit
		tutus L	safe
.25	Mabhrodaphne	mavrodaphnê MG	dark bay; type of sweet red wine
		maurodaphnê G	
.28	Ayternitay	aeternitas L	eternity
407.04	biss	bis L	twice
.13	voce	vox L	voice
.14	puer	puer L	boy, child
.14	palestrine	palaestra L	wrestling-school,
		palaistra G	gymnasium, school
		Praenestinus L	pertaining to Praeneste (*ancient city of Latium*) *now* Palestrina
.15	panangelical	panangelikos G	conveying information to all, conveying all information; pertaining to all angels

		panis angelicus L	angelic bread [the Sacred Host]: *a hymn*
.15	Tu es Petrus	Tu es Petrus L	Thou art Peter
.17	numerose Italicuss	numerus Italicus L	an Italic number
.21	Nova Scotia's	Nova Scotia Mod L	New Scotland; New Ireland
.27	Alo, alass, aladdin,	amo, amas, amat, amamus L	I love, you love, he loves, we love
	amobus	amabis L	you shall love
.29	anteprepreviousdays'	ante L	before
		pro L	for, in front of
		praevius L	going before, leading the way
		*antepraevius dies L	before the day before
.32	hicnuncs	hic et nunc L	here and now
.33	*ex alto*	ex alto L	from on high
.36	hesternmost	hesternus L	yesterday's, of yesterday
408.02	manducators	manducator eccl. L	a chewer
.13	postoomany	postumo L; eccl. L	to come after; to be inferior
.19	os	os L	1. mouth; 2. bone
.26	Elien	alienus L	that belongs to another person *or* place
.35	helotwashipper	heilôtês G	Spartan serfs
		hêlios G	sun
.36	Piscisvendolor	piscis L	a fish
		vendor L	a seller
		dolor L	pain, ache, grief
409.01	Gemini	Gemini L	the Twins (*constellation*): Castor and Pollux
.15	columbuses	columbus L	a pigeon, dove
.18	crux	crux L	cross, gallows
.24	Clump	-mp- MG = -b-	Club
.26	day o'gratises	Deo gratias L	thanks to God
.27	Hagios	Hagios G	Saint
.29	*Solvitur*	solvitur L	he [she, it] is loosened, is set free, is released; is acquitted, absolved
.29	*palumballando*	palumbes L	ring-dove, wood-pigeon

		ballando L	by dancing
.30	Adie	*adie L	from the day
		hodie L	today
.31	salve a tour	salvator LL	savior, preserver; the Savior
.31	ambly andy	ambulando L	in passing, lit. while walking
.35	Hireark	hierarchês G	high-priest
		Hieroklês G	Stoic philosopher
.36	Eusebian	Eusebius	church historian, wrote against Hieroklês
410.04	orologium	[h]orologium L	clock, sundial, waterclock
.04	oloss	[h]olus L	kitchen vegetables, cabbage
.04	olorium	*olorium L	1. place where swans are kept; swannery; 2. place where odors are kept; smellery
.14	wineupon ponteen	epi oinopa ponton G	upon the wine-colored sea (*Homeric formula*)
.17	umniverse	universum L	"turned-into-one": the whole world
		*omniversum L	"turned-into-all": the disparate elements of the world
.23	Emailia	[regio] Aemilia L	[region of the] Aemilian [Road]: between Ariminium [Rimini] and Placentia [Piacenza]: Gallia Cispadana: Italy just south of the Po
411.05	Excelsior	excelsior L	higher
.12	Eironesia	eirôn G	ironist, dissembler
		*eirônnêsia G	ironist-island-land
		eirênênêsia G	peace-island-land
.14	declaret	declaret L	may [he, she] make clear
.15	Geity's	Gê G	Earth
.15	Pantokreator	panto-creator G + L	all-begetter, all-creator
		Pantokratôr G	Almighty
.15	epizzles	epi G	on, upon
		epistolê G	written message, letter

.16	apossels	apo G	away, away from
		apostolos G	messenger, envoy; apostle
		posse L	to be able; ability
.17	muthar	Muta L	nymph silent because her tongue was torn out
.21	Greedo	Credo L	"I believe": the Creed
.29	diogneses	Diogenês	Cynic philosopher: sought an honest man
.32	focoal . . . focoal	focus L	fireplace, hearth
.33	Impregnable	*impraegnabilis L	1. capable of being made pregnant 2. incapable of being made pregnant
412.03	scotographically	skotos G	darkness
		*skotographikos	pertaining to darkness-writing
		opposite of	
		phôtographikos G	pertaining to light-writing
.07	mielodorous	*melodorus L	smelling of honey
.08–.09	*Buccinate in Emenia tuba insigni volumnitatis tuae*	Buccinate in neomenia tuba in insigni die solemnitatis vestrae L	Blow up the trumpet on the new moon, on the noted day of your solemnity (*Douai-Vulgate Ps. 80:4*); Blow up the trumpet on the new moon, in the time appointed, on our solemn feast day (*AV Ps. 81:3*)
.09	*volumnitatis*	Volumni L	The Well-wishers: tutelary deities of new-born infants
.10	Pontoffbellek	pontifex L	"bridgemaker": Roman high-priest
		bellicus L	pertaining to war, martial
.16	physiog	physiognômôn G	judging character by the features
.24	Scotic	Scoticus L	Scottish; Irish
.26	poss	posse (*infinitive*) L	to be able to

.33	capri	capri (*Gen.*) L	goat's, of a goat
.36	Nickil Hopstout	Nihil Obstat L	Nothing stands in the way: certificate by *censor librorum* that no religious or moral consideration prohibits publication of a book
.36	Christcross	Imprimatur. ✠ N.N., episcopus L	Let it be printed. ✠ [*signature,*], Bishop: *bishop's warrant to print a book,* contingent on the Nihil Obstat
413.04–.05	Salutem dicint	[N.] salutem dicit L	[So-and-so] speaks a greeting: *usual beginning of a Roman letter: e.g., Cicero tibi salutem dicit,* "Cicero greets you" 2 .05
		[N. & N.] salutem dicunt L	[So-and-so and so-and-so] speak a greeting
.10	tottydean verbish	totidem verbis L	in so many words, in as many words
.18	assauciations	*assauciatio L	wounding-to, wounding-at, assassination
.20	sophykussens	sophia G	wisdom
.22	mund	mundus L	clean, elegant, arranged; toilette; the world
.23	quad	quoad, quaad L	how long? how far? as long, as far
.27	cadenus	decanus (*anagram*) L	chief of ten; dean
.29	venusstas	Venus L	goddess of sexual love; #A
		venustas L	loveliness, beauty
.31	fumiform	*fumiformus L	smoke-shaped
.32	Hooraymost	oremus L	let us pray
.36	ex-voto	ex voto L	out of a vow, as a result of a vow
414.01	rhino	rhis, rhinos G	nose
		rhinos G	skin, hide
.01	spondaneously	spondeo L	to promise solemnly, to bind

		spondê G	drink-offering (*to the gods*)
		spondai G	solemn treaty *or* truce
.03	ligname	lignum L	wood
.08	spont	sponte L	of free will, of one's own accord
.08	innation	*innatio L	1. a not-being-born, a being unborn 2. a being born in, a being inborn, a being native 3. a swimming upon
.10	Quoniam	quoniam L	since now, since then, seeing that, whereas
.13	Quick take um whiffat andrainit	Qui tecum vivat et regnit L	Who with thee may live and reign
		Qui tecum vivit et regnat L	Who with thee lives and reigns
.14	vi et	vi (*Abl.*) et L	with force and
.17	Esaup	Aisôpos G	G fabulist
		Aesopus L	
.18	casus	casus L	falling, overthrow; error; event, accident; occasion; case *in grammar*
		kasis G	brother
.18	cousis	kasis G	brother
		kasioi G	brothers, cousins (*in the same boys' training company at Sparta*)
.19	–tussem–	tussem (*Acc.*) L	a cough
.19	–mandam–	mandamus L	we command; *legal term*
.19	–damna–	damna (*pl.*) L	losses, injuries; fines.
.20	–bix–	bêx G	a cough
.20	–carcar–	carcer L	prison
		karkaron G	
.25	Vespatilla	*vespatilla L	little wasp
.25	pupa-pupa	pupa L	girl, damsel, lass; doll, puppet
.26	pulicy-pulicy	pulex, pulicis L	flea, of a flea
.26	pushpygyddyum	*pygidium L *for* pygidion G	a little rump, little buttocks
.30	melissciously	melissa G	bee
.32	fourmish	formica L	ant
.34	cald	caldus L	warm, hot

.34	fourmillierly	formicalis L	resembling the crawling of ants
.35	Besterfather	*trans.* Pater Optimus	Best Father: *title of Jupiter*
.36	Zeuts	Zeus G	"Sky," "Day": chief god of the Greeks; #*A*
.36	corollas	corolla L	garland
.36	albedinous	albedo L	white color, whiteness
		nous G	mind, intellect
415.01	elytrical	elytron G	covering; shard of a beetle's wing
.02	Dehlia	Dêlia G L	Diana, *from her birth on* Delos
.02	Peonia	paiônia G paeonia L	"belonging to Paiôn/Paeon [*god of medicine*]": the peony
.02	druping	drupa L druppa G drupepês G	shriveled-up olive olive tree-ripened, quite ripe
.02	nymphs	nymphê G	bride, marriageable maiden, daughter-in-law, young girl; goddess of lower rank, *esp.* of springs *or* water; soul seeking birth; young bee *or* wasp in pupa stage; winged male ant
.04	cacumen	cacumen L	extreme end, extremity, point
.04	tramsitus	transitus L	a going over, passing over, passage
		trames L	side-path, by-way
.04	diva	diva L	goddess
.05	sapo	sapo L	soap
.09	cantoridettes	cantor L cantharis, *pl.* cantharides L kantharis, *pl.* kantharides G	singer, poet a genus of beetles
.10	retrophoebia	*retrophoebia L + G	a backward[ness] of Phoebus [Apollo: the sun]; reversal of the sun
.12	toesis	tussis L	a cough

.13	myrmidins	Myrmidones G	a people of Thessaly; in *Iliad*, followers of Achilles
		myrmêdôn G	ants' nest
		myrmêx G	ant
.14	*Satyr's*	Satyros G	the god Dionysos; spirit of wildlife in the woods, bestial and goatlike; lewd person; kind of ape
.16	sciencium	*scientium *as if sing. of* *scientia (*neut. pl.*) scientia (*fem. sing.*) L	knowledge, skill, expertness, science
.17	Omniboss	omnibus L	for everyone, for everything
.20	day as gratiis	Deo gratias L	thanks to God
		Deus gratiis L	God, out of kindness; God, for nothing; God gratuitously; God into the bargain
.21	O'Cronione	Kroniôn G	son of Kronos: Zeus
.22	his sunsunsuns	sons, son's, suns	original sungod was Hêlios; his son Phaitôn, drove the sun with disastrous results; Hêlios became identified with Apollo, whose father Zeus was the son of Kronos son of Ouranos/Uranus (the sky)
.26	Libelulous	libellulus L	a very little book
.26	Inzanzarity	Zan (*Doric-Ionic*) G	Zeus: chief G god
.28	hisphex	sphêx G	wasp
.29	antitopically	anti G	against, in return
		topikos G	in respect to place; local
		*antitopikos G	contrary to local
.29	Nixnixundnix	nix L	snow
.32	khul	culus L	arse
.33	ovipository	*ovipositor L	egg-placer
.34	me no	Menôn G	*Meno*: Platonic dialogue on learning

.34	Seekit Hatup	sicut habet L	just as he has
.35	May no	Menôn G	*as at 415.34*
.35	pig shed on	pygidion G	little rump
416.06	psyche	psychê G	life, soul; butterfly, moth
.06	laus	laus L	praise
.06	ikey	eikôn G	likeness, image
.06	his ikey	psychê G	as above
.11	nautonects	nauta L	sailor, mariner, seafarer
		nex L	murder
		*autonex G+L	self-murder, suicide
		nectar L nektar G	drink, food, of the gods
		necto L	to tie, fasten together
.12	*ichnehmon*	ichneumôn G	Egyptian rat, destroys crocodiles' eggs
.12	*diagelegenaitoikon*	diagelaô G	to laugh at, mock, deride
		aiteô G	to ask for, beg, demand
		aitios G	culpable, responsible; the cause
		oikon (*Acc.*) G	house
.13	tantoo	tantus L	of such size, so great in amount
		tanto L	by how much, so much the . . .
.13	quant	quantus L	how great, so great
		quanto L	by how much, by as much as
.14	hemsylph	sylphes Mod L *from*	immortal, soulless being of alchemy
		silvestris	nymphs of the woods
		nympha L	
.15	corapusse	corpus L	body
.15	hospes	hospes L	he who entertains a stranger: host, guest, friend
.16	osa	os, *pl.* ora L	mouth, face
		ossum, *pl.* ossa L	bone
.16	volomundo	volo L	1. I wish, want, will ; 2. I fly
		mundo L	I make clean, I cleanse
.16	osi	Osi L	a people of Germany
.16	videvide	vide L	see!

.17	muscowmoney	musca L	a fly
.18	Iomio! Iomio!	io! L	ho! hurrah! look!
		Iô G	paramour of Zeus turned into a cow
.19	corbicule	corbicula L	little basket
		corviculus L	little raven
.19	melanctholy	*melanchthôn G	black earth
		*melanotholos G	black mud
.22	styearcases	stear G	suet, lard
		sterus L	dung
		caseus L	cheese
.22	mensas	mensa L	a table
		menses (pl.) L	months
.23	seccles	saecula (pl.) L	centuries, ages, lifetimes
.23	mundballs	mundus L	cleanliness; toilette; the universe
.23	ephemerids	ephemeris pl.	day-book, diary,
		ephemerides G	account-book, journal
		ephemeridon G	short-lived insect; mayfly
.24	glutinously	gluten L	glue
.25	ternitary	terni L	three each; three
.26	Chrysalmas	chrysallis G	1. chrysalis; 2. cockroach
.27	Tingsomingenting	mingo L	to urinate
		ingens L	vast
.29	grillies	gryllos G	grasshopper, cricket
		gryllus L	
.30	Tossmania	mania G	madness
.33	millipeeds	mille pedes L	a thousand feet
.34	myriopoods	myrioi podes G	ten thousand feet
.34	Boraborayellers	Bora	mountain in Macedonia
		Boreas G L	the northwind
		borealis L	northern
		[Forum]	the cattlemarket in
		Boarium L	Rome
417.01	siphonopterous	siphôn G	tube, pipe; mosquito
		*siphônopteros G	tube-winged, pipe-winged; mosquito-winged
.01	Graussssssss	graus G	old woman
.02	Graussssssss	see 417.01 D	

.04	entymology	*entomologia G	the science *or* study of insects
		etymologia G	the science *or* study of truths, of true derivations of words
.04	nissunitimost	unitas L	oneness, unity
		*unissimus L	onliest
.06	vico	vico (*Abl.*)	by, with *or* from a village
.06	phthin	phthinô G	to decay, waste away, wane, perish
.06	phthir	phtheir G	a louse
.08	aquinatance	Aquinates L	inhabitants of Aquinium, *town in Latium, now Aquino* [*St. Thomas's birthplace*]
.11	prostrandvorous	prostrandus L	[one] to be overthrown, to be subverted
		*prostrandivor-us L	feeding on those to be overthrown
.12	Papylonian	papilio L	butterfly, moth
.15	plate o'monkynous	Platôn G	idealist philosopher
.15	o'monkynous	nous G	mind, intellect
.16	aceticist	acetum L	vinegar
.16	aristotaller	aristos G	best
		Aristoteles	materialist philosopher; #*A*
.17	Libido	libido L	pleasure, desire, eagerness, fancy
.17	Floh	flos L	blossom, flower
.19	Vespatilla	*vespatilla L	little wasp
.20	entomate	entoma (*pl.*) G	insects
.27	formicolation	formico L	to crawl like an ant
		formicula L	little ant
.32	veripatetic	peripatêtikos G	given to walking about, *esp.* while teaching *or* disputing: Aristotle's school of philosophy
		*veripatêtikos L+G	true-walking
.32	imago	imago L	imitation, copy; phantom; image; echo; imagination; similitude
.33–34	ephemeral	ephêmera G	things that live but a day; short-lived insects

.34	mantis	mantis G	diviner, prophet; kind of grasshopper (*mantis religiosa*, the praying mantis); green garden-frog
.35	animule	animula L	a little soul
		animulus L	darling
.36	chorous	choros G	dance; body of dancers; place for dancing
418.01	gravitates	gravitates (*pl.*) L	weights; severities; dignities, importances, powers
.03	Conte	compte L	elegantly
.03	Carme	carmen L	tune, song; poem
.04	*Ad majorem ... Divi gloriam*	Ad majorem Dei gloriam L	To the greater glory of God: *Jesuit motto*, #*B*
.04	*l.s.d.*	L[ibri] S[olidi] D[enarii] L	Pounds, Shillings, Pence
		L[aus] S[emper] D[eo] *recte* L[aus] D[eo] S[emper] L	Praise to God forever: *Jesuit slogan*, #*B*
.04	*Divi*	Divi OL Dei (*Gen.*) L	of God, God's
		D[eo] V[olente] L	God willing, if God wills
.05	Orimis	oremus L	let us pray
.10	*merd*	merda L	dung, shit
.10	*nauses*	nausea L nausia G	seasickness
		nosos G	sickness, disease
.11	*fauces*	fauces L	throat, gullet
.14	*Floh*	flos L	flower, blossom
.15	*Vespatilla*	*vespatilla L	little wasp
.22	*castwhores*	Castor L Kastôr G	one of the Twins; #*A*
.22	*pulladeftkiss*	Polydeukês G Polydefkis MG	one of the Twins; #*A*
.22	*oldpollocks*	Pollux L	Polydeukês; #*A*
.23	*Culex*	Culex L	"The Gnat": youthful poem by Vergil
.23	*Pulex*	pulex L	flea
.24	*locus*	locus L	a place, spot
.25	Homo Vulgaris	homo vulgaris L	ordinary man
.26	*Aquileone*	Aquilonia L	town in Italy, *now* Lacedogna

		aquilonius L	northern
		aquilo L	the northwind
.29	*longsephyring*	zephyrus L	a gentle west wind,
		Zephyros G	western breeze
.31	*Nolans go volants*	nolens volens L	unwilling or willing,
			willy-nilly
.31	*volants*	volans L	flying
.34	*tectucs*	tectum L	a roof
419.02	*whercabroads*	hircus L	he-goat
.03	*haud*	haud L	not at all, by no means
.12	volupkabulary	voluptas L	satisfaction, enjoyment,
			pleasure
.19	anaglyptics	*anaglyptikos G	pertaining to carving-up
.21	quistoquill	quisquiliae L	rubbish
.21	acoustrolobe	*akoustolabos G	instrument for taking
		modeled on	hearing *or* sounds
		astrolabos G	armillary sphere:
			instrument for taking
			the altitude of stars
.24	Oscan	Oscan	Italic language, related
			to L
.24	transluding	*transludens L	playing across
.27	hellas	Hellas G	Greece
.29	theodicy	*theodikêia G	[the study of] God's
			justice
		The *Odyssey*	*Odysseia* G: Homeric
			epic
.29	*re*	[in] re L	in the matter [of]
.34	*et omnibus*	et omnibus L	and for all
.36	Lucan's	M. Annaeus	Roman poet; # *A*
		Lucanus	
420.11	ecotaph	*oikotaphos G	a house-tomb
.17	Hek	hic, haec, hoc L	this, this here (*masc.,*
			fem., neut.)
.18	Hek	*see 420.17* G	
.20	Laonum	leonem (*Acc.*) L	a lion
.21	Loco	loco (Abl.) L	by *or* from a place
.23	noa's	Noa L	Noah
		noa G	fountain
.24	Noon sic parson	non sic possum	not thus can I
		L	
.25	Ave	ave L	hail
.25	Vale	vale L	farewell
.25	Exbelled	ex bello L	from the war
.26	sextiffits	sextus L	sixth

.28	Q.V.	Q[ui] V[ixit] L	Who Lived, Who was alive
.33	Traumcondraws	trauma G	injury, wound
		con- L	with-
421.02	Lemmas	lemma G	that which is peeled off, rind, husk
		lêmma G	anything received; assumption, premise; title, argument, commission
.03	Ediles	aedilis L	Roman magistrate in charge of buildings and works
.04	kate's	kathairô G	to cleanse
.05–.06	Abraham Badly's King	A, B, C[=K] L	first 3 letters of L alphabet
.06	Salved	Salve L	Be well (*greeting*)
.10	A.B.	A[rtium] B[accalaureus] Mod L	Bachelor of Arts
.10	ab	ab L	away from, away
.23	ares	Arês G	god of war, identified with Mars; #*A*
		ars L	art
.26	dieoguinnsis	Diogenês	Cynic philosopher; *see 290.21-22*
.34	clergimanths	*klêrikomantha-nô G	to learn by study about inheritances *or* about the clergy
.35	mammy far	mammifer L	breast-bearing, a breast-bearer
422.07	dalickey cyphalos	*dolichokephal-os G	having a long head
.07	brach	brachys G	short
		bracchium L	forearm
.11	Homo	homo L	person, man
		homos, homo- G	the same, same-
.12	criniman	crinis L	the hair
		krinô G	to judge
.14	Obnoximost	*obnoximus L	most punishable, most liable, most submissive
.14	posthumust	postumus L	the last
		posthumus LL (*false etymon of* postumus)	"after burial": child born after its father's death

.22	esiop's	Aisôpos G	G fabulist
		Aesopus L	
.26	Melosedible	*meledibilis L	honey-eatable
		*melosedibilis G+L	music-edible
.27	honorey causes	honoris causa L	on account of esteem, honorary
.28	thelemontary	thelêmôn G	willing
		voluntarius L	willing
		*thelêmontarius G+L	willingwilling
.30	trifulgurayous	*trifulgureus LL	thrice-charged with lightning
.36	noisy priors	nisi prius L	unless before; *legal term*
423.02	Ananymus	ananios G	without pain
		anonymos G	nameless
.03	parawag	para G	along, beside
.04	feraxiously	ferax L	fruit-bearing, fertile
		feraciter L	fruitfully
.04	ovas	ova (*pl.*) L	eggs
.06	ambitrickster	ambi- L	around, round about
		ambestrix L	a female waster
.06	decan's	decanus L	one in charge of ten; dean
.09	idioglossary	idioglôssa G	distinct, particular *or* private language
		*idioglossarium LL	a vocabulary of private *or* peculiar words that need explanation
.10	hicks hyssop! Hock!	hic, haec, hoc L	this, this here (*masc., fem., neut.*)
.12	kates	kathairô G	to cleanse
.16	prhose	prosa L	straightforward speech
.17	beogrefright	beo L	to gladden, make happy
.18	in muddyass ribalds	in medias res L	in the middle of the plot: *place to begin epic narration*
		[est] modus in rebus—Horat. *Sat.* I.l.106 L	[there is] a moderation in things—Horace, Satires I.1.106
.21	*ante mortem*	ante mortem L	before death
.21	sygnus	cygnus L	swan
.28	vegetable soul	*trans.* vegetabilis anima *or* vegetamen L	the animating power, vivifying principle

.33	*Negas*	negas L	you (*sing.*) deny
.33	*negasti*	negasti L	you (*sing.*) have denied
.33	negertop, negertoe	negator L	a denier
.33	negrunter	negarentur L	they might be denied
		nigrantur L	they are made black
.35	itching	*trans.* pruriens L	itching, feeling sexual desire
.35	europicolas	*Europicola L	inhabitant of Europe
424.01	temp	tempus L	time
.05	vitandist	vitandus L	to be avoided
.07	Cecilia's	Caecilia L	patron saint of music
.07	Galen	Galen	Graeco-Roman physician
.07	Asbestopoulos	asbestos G	unquenchable, inextinguishable
.07	Inkupot	incubus L	nightmare
.08	encaust	encaustum LL	ink
		enkauston G	"burnt-in": picture made with heated pigments
.09	Tiberia	Tiberia (*fem.*) L	Tiber-land; pertaining to *Tiberius*
.09	Prost	prosit L	may it be of use
		pro L	for
.09	Conshy	con- L	with-
		con[tra] L	against
.10	arestocrank	arestos G	acceptable, pleasing, satisfactory
		aristos G	best
.11	libber	liber L	1. free; 2. a child; 3. tree-bark, book
		Liber L	old Italian deity of planting and fructification
.11–.13	libber ... Ex. Ex. Ex. Ex.	ex libris L	from the books [of so-and-so]; *conventional bookplate formula*
.13	Ex. Ex. Ex. Ex.	ex L	out of, from
		XXXX L	40
.26	Peax! Peax!	pax L	peace
		koax! koax! G	croaking of Aristophanes' *Frogs*
.26	vealar	velaris L	pertaining to a veil *or* curtain
.26	penultimatum	paenultima L	the second-last syllable

		*penultimatum	the next-to-last
		Mod L	proposal *or* offer
.34	monothong	monophthongos G	sounded as a single vowel
425.15	soroquise	soror L	sister
.17	ingenuous	ingenuus L	free-born
.18	arrah	ara G	interrogative particle
.20	trifolium	trifolium L	three-leaved grass, trefoil, shamrock
.20	librotto	libro L	to balance, make even
.20	authordux	Artus dux L	King Arthur; *see* 252.20
		dux L	leader
.24	Outragedy	ou G	not
.24	Acomedy	a- G	not-, un-
.30	ops	ôps G	eye
		ops L	power, might; property, wealth
.32	*spaciaman spaciosum*	specimen speciosum L	handsome example, plausible model
		specimen spatiosum L	ample token
		spatium spatiosum L	ample space
.35	infradig	infra dignitatem L	beneath [one's] dignity
.35	ultravirulence	*ultravirulentia L	an excessive stench
		ultra virulentiam L	beyond a stink, more than a stench
		ultra vires L	beyond one's powers, outside one's competence
426.03	annyma	anima L	breath, vital principle
.13	sickself	sic L	thus
.17	Fu Li's gulpa	felix culpa L	happy sin; #*B*
.18	orthough	orthos G	straight, correct
.21	joepeter's	Juppiter L	chief god of the Romans; #*A*
.21	gaseytotum	chaos G	original state of the universe
		totum L	the whole, the all; the universe
.22	scruting	scrutor L	to examine closely
.24	sirious	seirios G	the dog-star Sirius; the hot season

.26	lacteal	lacteus L	the Milky Way
		lacteolus L	milk-white
.28	lusosing	lusis G	a loosing, releasing, ransoming
		lusus L	a playing, play
		lussoô G	to enrage, madden
.32	asterisks	asteriskos G	a little star
.33	postlude	post ludum L	after play, after a game
.35	*via*	via (*Abl.*) L	by way [of]
427.02	lapes	lapis L	stone
.04	crucethouse	cruciet L	may he crucify, let him afflict
.07–.08	circular circulatio	circularis circulatio L	a round revolution
		saeculum saeculorum L	age of ages: eternity
.10	stellas	stella L	star
.11	aromatose	arômatôdês G	spicy
.13	dulcid	dulcis L	sweet
.13	languidous	languidus L	faint, weak, dull, sluggish
.25	manomano	mano L	to flow, trickle, drop, spread, pour
		manu (*Abl.*) L	by hand
.25	myriamilia	myrias G	ten thousand
		milia (*pl.*) L	thousands, thousand
.25	mulimuli	mulier L	a woman
.29	salus	salus L	health, safety
.31	propredicted	prodictus (*pp.*) L	appointed beforehand; deferred, adjourned
		praedictus (*pp.*) L	published, proclaimed; preached, foretold
428.01	Suasusupo	sua sus L	his *or* her sow
		suasus L	a persuading
		supo L	I throw, I scatter
		*suasusupo L	I scatter persuadingly
		suavis L	sweet
.02	Samoanesia	Samos G	name of several islands
		nêsos G	island
		*Samonêsia G	the condition of the island Samos, the country of the island Samos
		*Samoanêsia G	the condition of the island Samoa, the country of the island Samoa

.10	vale	vale L	farewell
.19	Quartos	quarto L	for the fourth time, the fourth time
.25	timus	timos OL timor L	fear, dread
		timous G	high-priced
		timeo L	to fear
		timê G	value, honor
.25	tenant	tenens L	holding, keeping
		teneant L	let them hold, they may keep
429.02	cothurminous	cothurnus L	buskin, high boot worn
		kothornos G	by tragic actors; Tragedy; time-server, trimmer (kothornos *could be worn on either foot*)
.16	januarious	Januarius L	"Belonging to *Janus:*" January: Christian martyr
		Janus L	god of beginnings
.17	buskin	*trans.* cothurnus L	see *429.02*
		kothornos G	
.17	halluxes	[h]allex L	the big toe
		aluxis G	escape
		lux L	light
.23	equilebriated	equile L	stable for horses
		ebriatus (*pp.*) L	intoxicated, made drunk, drunk
430.05	brinkspondy	spondeion G	1. vessel used in
		spondeum L	pouring libations 2. metrical foot of two long syllables
.06	the rarerust	de re rustica L	*Of Rural Affairs*: book by Columella #*A*
.11	typtap	typtô G	to beat, strike, smite
.11	dactylogram	daktylos G	1. a finger; 2. metrical foot of one long and two short syllables
		*daktylogramma G	a finger-picture, finger-drawing
.30	tactily	tactilis L	tangible, that can be touched
.31	sixtine	*Sixtinus L	pertaining to one named *Sixtus*

		Xystos G	Sixtus, name of five popes
		Sextus L	"Sixth": Sixtus
.35	Agatha's	Agatha G	"good": martyr [Agatha's lamb: one born in early February]
.36	columbillas	columbus L	dove, pigeon
		L. Junius Moderatus Columella	author of de re rustica; # A; see 430.06
.36	Juliennaw's	Julianus L	"pertaining to Julius [Caesar] or to July": Roman proper name
		M. Didius Severus Julianus Augustus	emperor for 66 days (a.d. 193)
		Flavius Claudius Julianus Apostata	"Julian the Apostate": emperor 360–363
.36	Eulalina's	Eulalia G	"Sweet-spoken": fem. name
431.06	lavariant	lavans L	washing
.07	hum	humerus L	shoulder
.13	infuseries	infusio L	a pouring in, watering, wetting
.14	eroscope	erôs G	sexual love
		skopos G	a watcher
		*erôskopos G	love-watcher, voyeur
.18	benedict	benedictus L	blessed
.23	scolastica	scholastica L	school-exercises
		Scholastica (d. 550)	saint; sister of St. Benedict
.30	anun	nun G	now
.32	dieobscure	dies obscura L	dark day, dusky day
		Dioskouroi G	"Sons of Zeus": Kastôr and Polydeukês
.35	erigenal	*Erigenalis LL	pertaining to Erigena; pertaining to being Irish-born
		Joannes Scotus Erigena	Irish schoolman; # A
.36	Phoebus	Phoebus L	"Radiant": the Sun, Apollo
		Phoibos G	
.36	Pollux	Pollux L	one of the Dioskouroi; # A
		Polydeukês G	

432.01	Castor's	Castor L Kastôr G	one of the Dioskouroi; #*A*
.01	Parrish's	Paris	Helen's lover
.04	Andcommincio	commingo L	to pollute, defile
		*cominitio L	to begin with, to originate along with
.05	introit	introit L	he enters
		introitus L	entrance, beginning; first variable part of the Mass
.05	exordium	exordium L	beginning, commencement, introduction
.05	*quiproquo*	quid pro quo L	something for something, something in exchange for something else
		qui pro quo L	who for something? how for something?
.07	orational dominican	orationes Dominicae eccl. L	Sunday prayers
.10	nuncupiscent	nunc cupiscens LL	now desiring
		nuncupatativus LL	so-called, nominal
.11	confarreating	confarreatio L	very solemn manner of marriage
.11	viragos	virago L	manlike maiden, female warrior
.11	viragos intactas	virgo intacta L	an untouched virgin
.14	manny	Manes L	benevolent spirits of the dead
.15	larries	Lares L	tutelary deities of the hearth
.15	pignatties	pignus L	pledge, security, mortgage
		Penates L	tutelary deities of the larder
		*Pignates L	tutelary deities of the mortgage
.14–.15	the manny larries ate pignatties	Di Manes, Lares et Penates [*Pignates]	the Ancestral Ghosts, the Hearth-Gods and the Larder-Gods [*Mortgage-Gods]: protectors of the home: the home

.17	offertory	offertorium L	place to which offerings were brought
.19	verbs	verba (*pl.*) L	words
.20	bishop titular ... purtybusses	episcopus titulus ... in partibus [infidelium] eccl. L	bishop titled [of X] in the parts of the unbelievers: nominal bishopric of a former diocese (usually in the now-Islamic parts of the Roman empire): *given to assistant bishops and merely administrative bishops*
.20	to all his purtybusses	in omnibus partibus L	in all parts
.25	apsence	ab[sentia] L	away from, away
		apo G	away from, away
.30	rubrics	rubrica L	title of a law (*written in red*); a law
.30	mandarimus	mandamus L	we command: *legal term*
		mandaremus L	we might command, were we commanding
.30	pasqualines	pascua (*pl.*) L	pastures
		pascua LL	a pasture
.31	indecores	indecoris L	unbecoming, unseemly, disgraceful, shameful
		indecore L	unbecomingly, indecently
.32	lithurgy	lithourgia G	sculpture in marble, working in stone
433.01	ignitious	ignitus L	fiery, glowing
		Ignatius L	"Fiery": man's name: Ignatius Loyola, founder of the Jesuits
.01	Purpalume	purpura L	purple
		palum L	stake, prop
		lumen L	light
.01	Ultramare	ultra mare L	beyond the sea
.02	in terrorgammons howdydos	interrogemus auditos L	let us interrogate those who have been heard
.03	Undetrigesima	undetriginta L	twenty-nine
		undetricesima (*fem.*) L	twenty-ninth
.04	vikissy manona	vicesima nona (*fem.*) L	twenty-ninth

.04	Doremon's	adoremus L	let us adore
		dôron G	gift, present
.06	Manducare	manducare (*infinitive*) L	to chew, to eat
.07	in china dominos	in cena Domini L	to the Lord's supper
.08	jocosus	jocosus L	full of jesting, humorous, droll, facetious [*etymon of Joyce?*]
.19	*Minxy*	minxi L	I have urinated
.20	bisbuiting	bis L	twice
.24	compunction	compunctio L	a puncture
		*compunctio L	a severe pricking, a pricking
.27	usemake	*trans.* usufacio L	to have intercourse with
.28	sacral	sacralis Mod L	relating to the sacrum
		[os] sacrum L	the sacred [bone]: bone at the bottom of the spinal column
.30	O foolish cuppled	O felix culpa L	O happy sin, #B
.30	dice's	dikê G	justice
		Dis L	god of the infernal regions; Satan
.30	error	error L	a wandering
.34	circumspicious	circumspicio L	to look around, to observe
.36	despyneedis	de spinetis L	from the thorn-bushes
434.07	Rhidarhoda	rheda L	four-wheeled carriage, #B
		rhoda (*p.*) G	roses, #B
.07	Daradora	dare (*infinitive*) L	to give
		dôra (*pl.*) G	gifts
.09	pantos	panto- G	all-, every-
		pantose G	every way, in all directions
.11	Femorafamilla	femur L	thigh
		femorale L	covering for the thigh
		feminalia L	thigh-bandages
		famula L	maid-servant
.25	Diobell	diabolos G	slanderer, enemy; Satan
		diôbelia G	daily allowance of two obols to the Athenian poor

.29	Ulikah's	uligo L	moisture
		Ulixes L	Odysseus
.30	cupiosity	cupio L	to long for, desire
.32	martimorphysed	Marti- L	Mars-, martial-
		timor L	fear
		morphê G	form, shape
		physaô G	to blow, puff
		physis G	origin, growth, appearance; nature
.33	skorth	scortum L	harlot, prostitute
.35	Autist	*autistos G	*self-ist
.35	Algy	algeô G	to feel pain
		algeo L	to be cold
		algidus L	cold
.35	pulcherman	pulcher (*masc.*) L	beautiful, handsome
		P. Clodius Pulcher	dissolute gangster-politician
.36	*oleas*	olea L	an olive
		oleum L	oil, olive-oil
		alias L	otherwise
435.03	*Venus*	Venus L	goddess of sexual love, #*A*
.09	dowdycameramen	dôdekaêmeron G	of twelve days
		camera L	chamber, room
.10	phyllisophies	phyllis G	foliage; salad
		Phyllis G	girl turned into an almond-tree
		sophia G	cleverness, skill; wisdom
.18	paravis	para G	along, beside, athwart
.19	Prunella	*prunela L	a little burning coal
		prunula (*pl.*) L	little plums
.35	lowcusses	locus L	place, spot
436.01	interstipital	stipes L	log, post, tree-trunk; blockhead
		*interstipitalis L	between trunks, among branches
.05	triching	trich- G	hair-
		trichokosmêtês G	hairdresser
		trichôsis G	coiffure, *etc.*
.09	disgenically	*disgenikos G	twice belonging to the race

.15	generable	generabilis L	that has power of generating, generative, creative; that may be produced
		gener L	son-in-law
.24	2bis	bis L	twice
437.01	gastricks	gastêr G	belly; womb
		gastris G	pot-bellied; a glutton
.02	gym	gymnos G	naked
.04	acclivisciously	acclivis L	uphill, ascending, steep
.09	ptossis	ptôsis G	1. calamity; 2. inflection, case, mood (*Grammar*)
		ptôssô G	to shrink from, cringe, skulk
		tussis L	a cough
.13	twelfinger	*trans.*	[*that which is*] of
		duodenum L	twelve [*fingers' breadth*]: first section of the small intestine
.14	inhibitating	inhabito L	to dwell in
		inhibeo L	to keep back, restrain
.14	lict your	lictor L	"binder, tier-up": *attendant on a Roman magistrate*
.15	lector	lector L	reader
.15	ostiary	ostiarius L	doorkeeper, porter
.25	hippopotamians	*hippopotamitai G	*horse-riverers, *river-horsers; inhabitants of hippopotamus-country
.28	stuprifying	stupro L	to debauch, ravish, rape, defile
.30	Pannonia	Pannonia G L	country between Dacia, Noricum and Illyria (*mod.* Hungary, Slovenia and eastern Austria)
.31	femurl	femur L	thigh
.33	Melosiosus	melos G	tune, air, song
		*melosiosus LL	he who is full of song
438.06	idiot	idiotês G	peculiarity, particular characteristic; individuality; private trait; personal existence; relationship

.19	Paulus	Paulus L	"Little," #A
.22	pulexes	pulex L	flea
.27	*qua*	qua L	to what degree, in what manner
.29	subpenas	sub poena L	under penalty
439.04	cocottch	coc L	clucking
.07	Lousyfear	Lucifer L	light-bringing: the morning star
.09	trumpadour	MG *spelling*	*trubadour
.14	Amene	mênê G	moon
.19	Theo	theos G	god
.26	rogister	rogus L	funeral-pile
		rogo L	to question, interrogate
		rogito L	to inquire eagerly
.31	nostrums	nostrum L	ours, our own
.32	belave	lavo L	to wash
.34	allasundrian bompyre	*allusion to* burning of the Alexandrian Library	Plutarch says the Library at Alexandria was burned when Caesar was besieged in the city; other sources attest that only a book-storehouse was burned
.36	verile	verus L	true
440.01	verilatest	verum latet L	the truth lies hidden
.01	Arsdiken's	ars L	art
		dikê G	justice
.02	*Miracula*	miracula (*pl.*) L	wonders, marvels; *eccl. L,* miracles
.04	cathalogue	kata logon G	according to plan
		katharos G	pure
.05	labronry	labros G	furious, boisterous, turbulent
		labrus L	greedy
		labrônios G	large wide cup
		labrum L	lip
.06	Denti	denti (*Dat.*) L	to a tooth
.06	Alligator	alligator L	one who binds [*something*] to [*something*]; *word found only in Columella*
.07	index	index L	pointer, indicator, index finger

.07	arisus	arrisus (*pp.*) L	smiled upon, favored
.09	Carnival	carni vale ML	farewell to meat, goodbye to the flesh
.12	Hibernites	hiberno L	to winter, to pass the winter
.12	*licet ut lebanus*	licet ut Libanus L	it is permitted that Lebanon
.13		licet ad libitum L	it is permitted as much as you like
.15	disimally	dies mali L	evil days
.18	nates maximum	nates maximae L	biggest buttocks
.18	Liddlelambe's	Henry George Liddell G	lexicographer, #A
.22	saucerdotes	sacerdotes (*pl.*) L	priests
.25	Contrabally	contra L	over against, opposite
.28–.29	Cog that out	cogito L	I think
		cogitat L	[he, she] thinks
.32	vestalite	Vesta L	goddess of flocks and the hearth
		Vestalis L	priestess of Vesta, Vestal virgin
.35	ekumene	oikoumenê G	inhabited region; the inhabited world
441.02	Faminy	femina L	woman
.09	ad libidinum	ad libidinem L	at fancy, at caprice, at passion, as one lusts
		ad libitum L	as one wishes
.11	Cantilene	cantilena L	old hackneyed song; trite trivial gossip ("*that* old song")
.16	rose marine	ros marinus L	"sea dew": rosemary
.26	voixehumanar	vox humana L	human voice
.28	kinantics	kineô G	to move
		kinêtikos G	motor, stimulating, turbulent
.29	curname	cur L	why?
.33	saxopeeler	Saxo L	a Saxon
442.05	constantineal	*Constantinealis L	pertaining to Constantine; *see 155.09*
.08	Remus	Remus L	brother of Romulus; #A
.08	Eboracum	Eboracum L	city in Britain, *mod.* York

.09	Ulissabon	Olisipo, Ulysippo L	city in Lusitania, *mod.* Lisbon
.19	Quary	quare L	by what means? wherefore?
.21	ignoratis	ignoratis L *modeled on*	you (*pl.*) misunderstand, do not know, make a mistake; ignore
		ignoramus L	we misunderstand, do not know, etc.
.27	Ohibow	oiboiboi G	ah me! alas! woe!
443.01	quoram	quorum (*Gen. pl.*) L	of whom
		quonam L	where to, please?
.12	magistrafes	magis L	in a higher degree, more completely, more
.12–.13	*Filius nullius per fas et nefas*	filius nullius per fas et nefas L	a son of no one through right and wrong
.23	pithecoid	pithêkoeidês G	ape-like
.26	*alias*	alias L	otherwise
.31	hebdomedaries	hebdomades (*pl.*) G	weeks
		hebdomadikos G	weekly
.32	Buinness's	bineô G	to fornicate, fuck
444.02	omnibus	omnibus L	for all
.03	claudication	claudicatio L	a limping
.11	Forstowelsy	Fors L	Chance; goddess of chance
.27	tangotricks	tango L	to touch
		tactrix L	female toucher
.28	lupitally	lupula L	little she-wolf; witch, hag
.36	Luperca	Luperca L	"She-wolf": Roman goddess, wolf that suckled Romulus and Remus
445.01	Bios	bios G	life
.10	lecit	licet L	it is permitted
		lectum L	bed, couch
.13	*Aveh*	ave L	hail
.13	*Roma*	Roma L	Rome
.13	*Aveh Tiger Roma*	Amor Regit Heva[m] L	Love guides Eve

.17	papapardon	papaver L	poppy
.17	rhodatantarums	rhoda (*pl.*) G	roses
		rhododendron G	"rose-tree": a plant
.18	calorrubordolor	calor L	warmth, heat
		rubor L	redness, blush
		robur L	oak; hard wood
		dolor L	pain, ache
.23	greedypuss	gradibus L	by degrees, by steps
.23	greedypuss beautibus	gradibus	by degrees to
		*[beaut]ibus L	beauties[*parody of old classical textbook titles*]
.26	nuncio	nuntio L	to announce, declare, inform
		nuntio (*Abl.*) L	by means of a messenger
.32	homerole	Homêros G	the epic poet
446.01	multipede	multipeda L	insect with many feet
.04	Hyphen	hyp' hen, hyphen G	in one, as a single word
.06	Armor	amor L	love
.07	isabellis	bellis L	to, for *or* by, with, from wars
.18	stade	stadion G	measure of length, 606.75 feet
.23	suant	suens L	sewing, stitching
.26	Knowme	gnômê G	means of knowing, judgment, opinion
.30	Euphonia	euphônia G	goodness of voice, excellence of tone
.35	circumcivicise	circum L	around
		civis L	citizen
		*circumcivesizô L + G	to make citizens all around
447.06	Anglia's	Anglia ML	England
.06	Armouricans	Armorica L	north Gaul, Brittany; #A
.06	core	cor L	heart
.08	mortinatality	mors, mortis L	death
		natalis L	pertaining to birth, birthday
		*mortinatalicius L	pertaining to a death-birthday, pertaining to a death-anniversary

.22	Citizen	*trans.* civis L	city-dweller, member of a city
.22	Pagan	*trans.* paganus L	villager, rustic
.28	perdrix	perdix G L	partridge
.29	Oralmus	oramus L	we argue, plead; pray
		oremus L	let us pray
.29	autointaxication	autotaxis G	self-arrangement
.34	ecclastics	ekklazô G	to cry aloud
		ekklaô G	to break off
448.07	kakes	kakos G	evil, bad
		kakê kakia G	wickedness, vice
.10	kateclean	katherinê (*fem.*) G	clean, pure
.11	Troia	Trôia G L	Troy
.12	Carmen	carmen L	song, poem
.13	wellbelavered	lavo L	to wash
.18	Opian	ops L	wealth, power
		ôps G	eye, face
.18	Opian Way	Via Appia L	Appian Way: road south from Rome to Brundisium
.28	temse	tempus L	time
.30	discalced	discalceatus L	unshod, barefoot
.33	plexus	plexus L	a turning, plaiting; braid
.33	sanguine	sanguineus L	bloody
.35	luting	lutum L	mud
		lûtum L	yellow-weed; yellow (dye)
.35	dorse	dorsum L	the back
449.01	phonoscopically	*phônoskopikos G	pertaining to sound-watching *or* to a watcher of sound
.01	incuriosited	incuriosus L	careless, negligent
.02	fulmament	fulmen L	lightning that strikes, thunderbolt
.03	stellar	stella L	star
.07	tristys	tristis L	sad
.10	Mona	Mona L	Anglesea; the Isle of Man
		monê (*fem.*) G	alone, solitary
.10	Vera	vera (*fem.*) L	true, real
.10	Toutou	toutou (*Gen.*) G	of this
		tute L	you (*sing.*), you yourself

.11	Ipostila	hypostellô G	to draw in, contract, shrink
		hypostylion G	lowest level of a building
.15	lapidated	lapidatus (*pp.*) L	stoned, had stones thrown at
.15	Jacobus	Jacobus L	James
.15	intercissous	intercessus L	intervention
		intercisus (*pp.*) L	cut to pieces, divided
.15	thurifex	*thurifex L	incense-maker
		thurifer L	incense-bearing, incense-bearer
		thura G	door
.16	Peter	Petros G Petrus L	Rock
.17	cubits	cubitum L	elbow
.32	philopotamus	*philopotamos G	river-lover
.32	crekking	brekekekek G	croaking of Aristophanes' *Frogs*
.35	cumuliously	cumulus L	a heap, pile
450.07	antis	anti G	opposite
.13	humely	humilis L	low, close to the earth
.18	chthonic	chthonios G	in *or* under the earth; sprung from the earth; native
.18	solphia	sophia G	skill, wisdom
		sol-fa	*system of syllables to represent the tones of a musical scale; the 5th and 4th ascending tones*
		*from Sol*ve L *and*	Cleanse
		*Fa*muli L	Servant's
.19	fairyaciodes	feriae L	holidays
.20	I give	*trans.* do L [It.] *recte*	*first tonic sol-fa note*
		ut L	so that
.20	a king	*trans.* re [It.], *1st syllable of*	*2nd ascending sol-fa note*
		resonare L	to resound
.20	to me	*trans.* mi [It.], *1st syllable of*	*3rd ascending sol-fa note*

		mira L	the wonders
.20	she does	*trans.* fa [It.], *1st syllable of* famuli L	*4th ascending sol-fa note* servant's
.20	alone	*trans.* sol [It.], *1st syllable of* solve L	*5th ascending sol-fa note* cleanse
.20	up there	*trans.* la [It.], *1st syllable of* labii L	*6th ascending sol-fa note* lip's
.20	yes [see]	*trans.* si [It.], *acronym of* Sancte Iohannes L	*7th ascending sol-fa note* O Saint John
.20	I give ... yes see	*trans. as if from* It. *of syllables basic to sol-fa:* Ut queant laxis Resonare fibris, Mira gestorum Famuli tuorum, Solve polluti Labii reatum, Sancte Iohannes L	That the loose strings may be able to resound the wonders of your deeds, of your servant cleanse the guilt of a defiled lip, O Saint John
.22	I give ... alone	*trans. as if* do, mi, sol It. *for* Ut, Mira, Solve L	So that, Wonders, Cleanse (*as above*)
.23	forte	forte L	by chance, accidentally
.27	funantics	funis L funambulus L	rope rope-walker
.31	heimlocked ... death-cup	*allusion to* death of Socrates	*executed by being made to drink hemlock*
451.01	subdominal	*subdominalis L	pertaining to the *subdomen
		*subdomen L	*the part of the belly that is subdued *or* appended
		from subdo L	to lay under, to append, to subject
		and modeled on abdomen L	the lower part of the belly
		from abdo L	to hide

.07	hydromel	hydromeli G	honey-water, mead
.11	Annadromus	anadromos G	running-up: *of a fish entering a river from the sea*
.11	pescies	pisces (*pl.*) L	fishes
.13	Milice	miles L	soldier
.19	ignitial's	ignitulus L	somewhat fiery
		initialis L	original, initial
.21	sponse	sponsa L	betrothed woman, bride
.32	sybarate	Sybarita L	inhabitant of Sybaris, *town noted for luxury and debauchery*
.35	famiksed	famescens L	suffering hunger, hungering
		famex L	bruise, contusion
.36	shoepisser pluvious	Juppiter Pluvius L	Jupiter the Rain-dispenser; #*A*
.36	assideration	*assideratio L	a looking at the stars
452.01	hedrolics	hedra G	seat, chair; backside
		*hedroaulikos, hedrôlikos G	concerning a tube in the backside; concerning the anus
.03	atramental	atramentum L	ink; blacking, black pigment
.08	Sissibis	Sisipus OL	robber punished in hell
		Sisyphus L	by rolling uphill a stone that rolls back again
		bis L	twice
.10	tripos	tripous G tripus L	three-footed stool; tripod
.11	focus	focus L	fireplace, hearth
.12	phono	phôno- G	sound-
		phonos G	murder, slaughter
.18	profund	profundus L	deep, vast
.19	livy	Titus Livius	Roman historian; #*A*; #Livia
.20	pharoph	pharos G	plow; lighthouse; #*A*
.27	nenni	ne L ni OL	no, not
		nonne L	not? not so?
		Nennius (*fl.* 796)	Welsh annalist; *his Historia Britonum mentions Arthur*
.29	Lucan	M. Annaeus Lucanus L	Roman poet, #*A*
.34	Annanmeses	anamnêsis G	calling to mind, reminiscence

.34	wholeabuelish	aboulia G	ill-advisedness, thoughtlessness, irresolution
453.07	lemoncholic	*part trans.* xanthêcholikos G	dominated by yellow bile (*xanthê cholê*)
		part anagram melancholikos G	dominated by black bile (*melancholê*)
.14	ossicles	ossiculum L	a small bone
.17	voiceyversy	vice versa L	turned reciprocally
.18	gala	gala G	milk
.18	bene fit	bene fit L	it becomes well, it is made well
.19	tunc	tunc L	then
.26	Sussumcordiales	sursum corda L	hearts upward! [lift] up [your] hearts!
.26	alloyiss	aliis L	for others
.26	and ominies	dominis L	for *or* by lords
.26	ominies	omnis L	all
		hominis (*Gen.*) L	of a person, a man's
.32	fieldnights eliceam	*part trans.* Elysii campi L	the Elysean fields, *abode of the blest*
.32	eliceam	eliciam L	I may draw out, entice out, elicit
.36	postilium	post Ilium L	after Troy
		post illud L	after that
		*postilium pseudo-L for *postilion pseudo G	postilion
454.01	myopper	myôps G	shortsighted; horse-fly, gadfly; goad, spur; stimulant, incentive; the little finger
.07	Huck	huc L	to this place, hither
.09	stenorious	stenos G	narrow, close, confined; narrowminded
		stenorrumê G	narrow alley
.13	missammen	missa (*fem. pp.*) L	sent
		Missa eccl. L	the Mass
		*Missamen L	Massness
.15	hicky hecky hock	hic haec hoc L	this, this here (*masc.,fem.,neut.*) # B

.15	huges huges huges	hujus hujus hujus L	of this (Gen. of *hic, haec, hoc*)
.15–.16	hughy hughy hughy	huïc huïc huïc L	to this (Dat. of *hic, haec, hoc*)
.20	mercury	Mercurius L	deity, messenger of the gods; conductor of the dead to the nether world; #*A*
.29	gloria's	gloria L	praise, honor
.30	doxologers	doxologia G	laudation, praising (saying "*gloria*")
.30	suburrs	Subura L	quarter in Rome, of provision markets and prostitutes; the "redlight" district of ancient Rome
.33	Shunt us! shunt us! shunt us	Sanctus, sanctus, sanctus L	Holy, holy, holy
.34	If you want to be felixed come and be parked	*part trans.* Si vis esse felix, sequi pacem L	If you wish to be happy, follow peace
.35	seanad and pobbel queue's remainder	Senatus Populusque Romanus L	the Roman Senate and People
.35	Seekit	sicut L	so as, just as
455.01	Cohortyard	cohors L	1. enclosure, court, yard; 2. unit of the Roman army, about 600 men
.01	apuckalips	apokalypsis G	uncovering of the head; disclosure, revelation, manifestation; Revelation (*biblical book*)
.06	experdition	ex perditione L	out of ruin, out of perdition
.06	horrus	Horus	Egyptian deity worshipped by Greeks and Romans
.08	Iereny	eirênê G	peace
.11	Joe Hanny's	Johannes L Johannis (*Gen.*) L	John John's
.11	Postmartem	post Martem L	after Mars, *i.e.*, after the war, post-war

		post mortem L	after death
.13	crass	cras L	tomorrow
.13	hairy	heri L	yesterday
.14	howdiedow	hodie L	today
.23	Hyam Hyam's	jamjam L	already, now, right now
.27	chrisman's	chrisma G	anointing, unction
.27	pandemon	*pandaimôn G	an all-demon
.28	SPQueaRking	S[enatus]	the Roman Senate and
		P[opulus]q[ue]	People
		R[omanus] L	
456.04	psalty	psaltêrion G	harp, stringed instrument
.07	Oh Kosmos	Ho Kosmos G	The Universe
.08	Cincinnatis	Cincinnatus L	"Curly," name of Roman statesman
.09	quid	quid L	what? which? something
.10	recipimus	recipimus L	we get back, we recover; we receive
.10	recipe	recipe L	take back! receive!
.15	aigrydoucks	aegritudo L	illness
.16	albies	albus L	white
.18	Eat a missal lest	Ite, missa est L	Go, it is sent (concluding words of the Ordinary of the Mass; whence Missa, "Mass")
.22	kates	kathairô G	to cleanse
.22	erics	ereikion G	flaky pastry
.23	oinnos	oinos G	wine
.24	fustfed	fustis L	club, cudgel
.26	Terminus	terminus L	boundary, limit, end
		Terminus L	god of boundaries
.27	Littorananima	litoralis L	belonging to the seashore
		littera L	a single letter of the alphabet
		anima L	breath, breath of life, vital principle
.30	Thaddeus	deus L	god
.30	Kellyesque	[silvae]	[woods] and
		callesque L	mountain-paths
457.12	onus	onus L	load, burden
.13	tethera	tettara G	four
.13	methera	methê G	strong drink

		mêtheteros G	neither of the two
.28	tactilifully	tactilis L	that may be touched, tangible
.28	corrispondee	spondeo L	to promise solemnly, to pledge one's self, to vow
.32	tacitempust	tacitum tempus L	time not spoken of, secret time, time passed over in silence
458.03	X.X.X.X.	XXXX L	40
.14	floralora	Flora L	goddess of flowers
		Floralia L	festival of Flora
		lora L	thin wine made from grape husks
.21	pneu	pneuma G	blast, wind; breath
.22	curiose	curiose L	with care, carefully
.27	stringamejip	gameô G	to marry
.29	ans	ansa L	handle; occasion, opportunity
.35	praxis	praxis G	doing, transaction, business
459.03	solve	solve L	loosen!
.27	Obealbe	ob L	towards, about, in front of, for
		albeo L	to be white
.35	passioflower	passio L	a suffering, enduring; event, occurrence
460.12	immutating	immuto L	to change, alter, use metonymy
.12	aperybally	aperio L	to uncover, lay bare, open
		aperibilis (adj.) L	opening, aperient
		peribolê G	garment
.16	ulmost	ulmus L	elm-tree
.17	stele	stêlê G	block of stone
.17	A'Mara	amara (fem.) L	bitter
		amara G	trench, conduit, ditch; hollow of the ear
		amara (Doric) G	day
.18	O'Morum	morem (Acc.) L	manner, custom
		amorem (Acc.) L	love
.22	mort	mors, mortis L	death

.22	libans	Libanus L	1. Lebanon; 2. frankincense
		libanios G L	kind of vine
.23	cyprissis	Cypris L Kypris G	the Cyprian: Venus/Aphrodite
		cyprus L kypros G	a tree growing in Cyprus
.26	Quaidy	qua L	on which side, where; as far as
		Q[uod] E[rat] D[emonstrandum] L	What was to be proved or demonstrated
.27	Flavin	flavus L	golden yellow, reddish yellow
.27	boysforus	Bosphoros G	Heifer's Ford: strait between Europe and Asia at Byzantium; #A
.29	Sarterday	sartor L	a tailor
.29	lex	lex L	law, legislation
461.02	fesces	Fescennini L	kind of jeering verse-dialogue
		fascis L	bundle (of wood, straw, etc.)
.19	lidlylac	lac L	milk
.30	tu	tu L	thou, you (sing.)
.33	sororal	*sororalis L	sisterly
462.01	eucherised	eucheir G	handy, dexterous
		euchereia G	licentiousness, unscrupulous conduct, irresponsibility
		eucharizô G	to give thanks, to thank
.04	Amingst	mingo L	to urinate
.16	monophone	monophônos G	with only one tone (describing utterance of deafmutes)
		*monophônê G	a single voice or tone
.21	penumbrella	*paenumbrella L	an almost-little shadow, an almost-umbrella
.34	aether	aether L aithêr G	pure air, the bright air, the heaven
.34	quinquisecular	*quinquisaecular- is L	of five centuries, five-centuries'
463.02	sinister	sinister L	on the left
.03	annis	annis L	to, for or by, with, from years

		amnis L	river
.05–.06	Figura Porca	figura porca L	sow-shape
.06	Lictor	lictor L	"binder, tier-up": attendant on a Roman magistrate
.06	Lictor Magnaffica	lictor magnificus L	noble lictor
.06	Magnaffica	adfixa, affixa L	appendages belonging to a possession (*Law*)
.07	altar's ego	alter ego L	other I, other self
.07	Auxonian	auxô G	to increase
		Ausonius L	south-Italian; Italian
.15	suckled by the same nanna	*allusion to* childhood of Zeus	Zeus was suckled by the she-goat Amaltheia
.19	nasturtium	nasturtium L	nose-twisting, nose-torturing: a kind of cress
.21	diasporation	diaspora G	a scattering, dispersion
.21	quinconcentrum	quincunx L	five-twelfths; trees planted in form of a five on dice
		concentus L	symphony, harmony, harmonious music
		centrum L	prickle, point,
		kentron G	compass-point; center of a circle
.22	Basilius	basileus G	king
.24	Alba	alba (*fem.*) L	white
		Alba L	"White": mother-city of Rome; *destroyed, never rebuilt*
.31	Columbsisle	columbus L	pigeon, dove
464.04	cog	cognatus L	blood-relative, kinsman
.07	*Shervos*	servus L	slave, servant
.07	*Shervos ... Shervorum*	Servus Servorum L	Servant of Servants, Slave of Slaves: *title of the popes*
.09	Nuntius'	nuntius L	bearer of news, reporter, messenger
.14	cruxader	crux L	cross, gallows
.16	Intelligentius	*intellegentius L	pertaining to understanding *or* perception
.22	phoney	phônê G	speech, voice

.23	dextremity	dextra L	the right hand
		extremitas L	the outer end
.24	frother	frater L	brother
		# *Labials*	
.26	moppamound	mundo L	to make clean, to cleanse
		mappamundi ML	map of the world
.32	Tower Geesyhus	Turgesius (died a.d. 844) ML	Latinized name of a Viking invader of Ireland [*see* Gaelic Lexicon, *p. 398*]
.32	Mona	Mona L	Isle of Man; Anglesea
		monê (*fem.*) G	alone, solitary
465.03	delltangle	delta G	letter D; rivermouth; female pudenda
.05	*Shervorum*	servorum (*Gen. pl.*) L	of servants, of slaves; *see 464.07 I*
.06	spinister	sinister L	on the left
.07	husbandmanvir	vir L	man, human male
.09	bothsforus	Bosphoros G	Heifer's Ford: strait between Asia and Europe; #*A*
.10	thurily	thuri- L	incense-
		thura G	door
.13	Idos	eidos G	form, shape, appearance
		Idus L	the Ides; 13th of most months, 15th of four months
.18	tertius quiddus	tertium quid L	a third something
.21	Loona	Luna L	the Moon
.25	leberally	leber OL	free, unrestrained
.26	bilabials	*bilabialis L	pertaining to two lips
466.01	Momie	mômai G	to seek after, covet; meditate, purpose, intend
		mômeuô G	to blame, criticize
		Mômos G	god of faultfinding
.01–.02	To pan! To pan!	to pan G	the all
.06	Leos	leo L	lion
		leôs G	people
.09	pyre	pyr G	fire
.10	tropeful	tropos G	a turn, direction, way
.14	hero and lander	Hêrô, Leandros G	heroine and hero of tragic love affair on the Hellespont

.19–.21	Rota rota … Rota	rota L	a wheel
.23	deas	dea L	goddess
.30	Poss	posse (*infinitive*) L	to be able to
		posse ML	power, might
.30	myster	mystês G	one initiated
.31	*Taurus periculosus*	taurus periculosus L	dangerous bull
.31	*morbus pedeiculosus*	morbus pediculosus L	lousy disease, phthiriasis.
.32	*Miserere mei in miseribilibus*	miserere mei in *miserabilibus L	pity me in [my] wretchednesses
.32	uval	uva L	grape
.34	in misery with his billyboots	in miserabilibus L	in wretchednesses
.35	ovocal	ovum L	egg
		Oboca L Oboka G	river in Hibernia; *mod.* Avoca
467.01	The misery billyboots	de miserabilibus L	concerning the pitiable
.06	Bissing	bis L	twice
.07	Triss	tris OL	three
		tris G	thrice, three times
.08	megalogue	*megalogos G	big in speech
.08	octavium	*octavium L	a thing belonging to the eighth
		Octavius L	name of a Roman gens; *youthful name* of Augustus Octavianus
.13	Caius	Caius OL Gaius L	a Roman praenomen
.08	octavium … Caius	Caius/Gaius Octavius (died 58 b.c.)	father of the emperor Augustus
.16	Balbus	Balbus L	"Stammering": a Roman cognomen
.19	by his diarrhio	diario (*Abl.*) L	by [his] daybook
.19	diarrhio	diarroia G	flowing through; diarrhea
.29	auracles	auricula L [forficula] auricularia L	the external ear the earwig
.30	quadra	quadra L [Hostius] Quadra L	a square Roman voyeur and lecher; #*A*

.32	prisckly	prisce L	in the oldfashioned way, strictly
		priscus L	ancient, antique, primitive, olden
		Tarquinius Priscus	"Ancient Tarquin": fifth king of Rome
.33	*p.p.*	p[ro] p[arte] L	for the share [of]; to the best of [one's] ability
.33	mimograph	mimographos G	writer of mimes
.33	numan	Numa L	Roman proper name
		Numa Pompilius	second king of Rome; added two months to calendar
		numen L	divine power
.33	ancomartins	Ancus Marcius L	"Servant of Mars": 4th king of Rome
.34	steps ad Pernicious	*part trans.* Gradus ad Parnassum L	"Stairway to Parnassus": *Renaissance text-book*
.35	rhearsilvar	Rhea Silvia L	mother of Romulus and Remus
.35	ormolus	Romulus L #*A*	founder and 1st king of Rome
.35	torquinions superbers	Tarquinius Superbus L	"Proud Tarquin": 7th and last king of Rome
		torquis L	twisted collar; wreath
.36	tullying	Tullius L	name of a Roman gens
		Servius Tullius	sixth king of Rome
		Marcus Tullius Cicero	Roman statesman, *called "Tully" in older English*
.36– 468.01	tullying my hostilious	Tullus Hostilius	third king of Rome; destroyed Alba
.01	hostilious	Hostilius L	"Pertaining to the Enemy": name of a Roman gens
.01	recitatandas	recitanda L	things worth reading aloud
.03	P? F?	P[ater]? F[ilius]? L	Father? Son?
.04	soboostius	sebastios G	pertaining to *Sebastos*, (G for *Augustus*)
.04	augustan	*trans.* Augustalis L	pertaining to *Augustus*

.04	cesarella	Caesarina (*fem.*) L	pertaining to Caesar; # *A*; imperial
.05	gest	gesta L	acts, deeds
.04–.05	augustan ... gest	Res Gestae Divi Augusti L	*The Accomplishments of the Divine Augustus*; Augustus's autobiography
.08	verg	P. Vergilius Maro	Roman augustan poet
		virga L	rod, switch
.10	Hammisandivis	amnis L	river
		[?] ignis L	fire
.11	axes	axis, *pl.* axes L	axle
.11	colles	collis, *pl.* colles L	hill
.11	waxes	vectis, *pl.* vectes L	lever
.11	warmas	vermis, *pl.* vermes L	worm
.11	sodullas	sodalis, *pl.* sodales L	mate, comrade, crony, fellow
.10–.11	Hammisandivis axes colles waxes warmas like sodullas	Amnis *and* [?] ignis, axis, collis, / vectis, vermis, *like* sodalis L	mnemonic rhyme from a L schoolbook; *cp.*: Many Nouns in *is* we find / to the Masculine assigned: / amnis, axis, caulis, collis, / clunis, crinis, fascis, follis ... *etc. for 10 lines* (*Kennedy's* Latin Primer, *App. IV , p. 223*)
.16	dactylise	daktylizô G	to finger
.18–.19	Fond namer, let me never see thee blame a kiss for shame a knee	*For* nemo *let me never say* neminis *or* nemine L	mnemonic rhyme from a L schoolbook; *see* 270.27-28
.21	nikrokosmikon	nikê G	victory
		eikôn G	image, picture, statue
		*mikrokosmiki-on G	a little small world
.29	Tempos fidgets	tempus fugit L	time flees
.29	manoark	manu L	by hand
		arcus L	bow, rainbow
		arca L	chest, box

		monarchos G	sole ruler
.30	hoodies	hodie L	today
.31	corthage	Carthago L	Carthage: Rome's chief rival for Mediterranean supremacy
.32–.33	Andrew Clays	Androklês G	slave who cured a lion's foot to be later spared from death by the lion
.35	sistra	sistra (*pl.*) L	metallic rattles used in worship of Isis
.36	Orcotron	Orcus L	god of the dead; the nether world; death
		Horkos G	god who punishes perjury
469.03–.04	earth's . . . sun's . . . air's . . . water's	the four elements	classical physics held the world to be constructed of four elements: earth, water, air, fire
.04–.05	Seven oldy oldy hills	*allusion to* Rome	traditionally built on seven hills: Aventinus, Caelius, Capitolinus, Esquilinus, Palatinus, Quirinalis, Viminalis
.18	Jerne	Ierne L	Ireland
.18	valing	vale L	farewell
.23	nunc	nunc L	now
.23–.24	Bennydick hotfoots onimpudent stayers	Benedicat vos omnipotens Deus . . . L	May the almighty God bless you . . . *last blessing at Mass*
.29	postludium	*postludum L	afterplay, aftergame
.34	biga	biga L	1. pair of horses; 2. two-horse chariot
.34	triga	triga L	1. three-horse team; 2. three-horse chariot
.34	rheda	rhaeda L	four-wheeled travelling carriage; # *B*
470.02	hermetic	Hermêtikos G	pertaining to Hermês, messenger of the gods, identified with Mercury; # *A*
.02	hermetic prod	*allusion to* Hermês Psychopompos G	Hermes Conductor of Souls: *prods the dead along with his staff*

.07	dorckaness	dorkas G dorcas L	gazelle
.09	pollylogue	polylogos G	loquacious
.13	dosiriously	dos L	dowry
		Osiris	Egyptian deity worshipped by Greeks and Romans, #A
		Sirius L Seirios G	the dog-star; the hot season
.13	psalmodied	psalmôdia G	singing to the harp
.14	to-maronite	Maro L	"Thoughtful": family name of the poet Vergil
.16	Oisis	Isis	Egyptian mother-goddess worshipped by Greeks and Romans, #A
		Osiris	Egyptian god, husband of Isis, #A
.16	coolpressus	cupressus L kuparissos G	cypress, evergreen tree sacred to Zeus/Jupiter, used at funerals
		Cupris L Kupris G	Cyprian: name for Venus/Aphrodite, #A
.17	Gladdays	gladius L	sword
.18	oisis	see 470.16 A	
.20	oisis	see 470.16 A	
.20	playtennis	platanus L	plain-tree
.30	agnelows	agnellus L	little lamb
.33	*hastaluego*	[?] hasta L	spear
471.01	Irine	eirênê G	peace
.03	Damadomina	domina L	lady, mistress
.08	estellos	stella L	star
.08	venoussas	venustas L	charm, beauty, sex-appeal
		Venus L	goddess of sexual love, #A
.16	stadion	stadion G	measure of distance: 606.75 feet
.17	herm	hermês G	pillar surmounted by a bust, representing Hermês; placed at doorways in Athens
.23	posse	posse (*infinitive*) L	to be able to
		posse ML	power, ability

.28	statuemen	statumen L	that upon which anything rests, a support, stay, prop
472.17	photophoric	*phôtophorikos G	pertaining to light-bearing _or_ to shining
.19	mansuetudinous	mansuetudo L	tameness, gentleness
.20	manipulator	*manipulator Mod L _from_	handler
		manipulus L	handful
		manipulatim L	by handfuls
.21	adie	*adie L	from the day
		hodie L	today
.22	lampaddyfair	*lampadafer L _for_ lampadaphoros G	torch-bearer
.23	lucerne	lucerna L	lamp
.30	indivisibles	*indivisibilia L	things not divisible:
		trans. atoma G	atoms
		individua L	things not divided, individuals
473.01	decennia	decennia L	periods of ten years, decades
.03	Sylvester	Silvestris L	"Forester": name of two popes and an anti-pope
		Silvestris I (pope a.d. 314–335)	saint; is asserted to have baptized Constantine and received the Donation of temporal power at Rome (_a fiction_)
		Silvestris II (pope a.d. 999–1003)	scientist; reputed in league with the devil; introduced arabic numerals and clocks
.04	murmurand	murmurans L	murmuring, muttering, rustling
		murmuranda L	things worth muttering, things requiring to be grumbled
.06	avicuum's	avis L	bird
		vicus L	street, quarter, village
		vacuum L	empty space

.16	phaynix ... Erebia	phoenix of Arabia	fabulous bird
.16	Erebia	Erebus L Erebos G	god of darkness, son of Chaos; the lower world; death
.18	spyre	pyr G	fire
.24	fost	fostis [= hostis] L	stranger, foreigner, enemy
474.05	parapolylogic	*parapolylogi-kos G	very loquacious, illogically loquacious
.07	lucan	lucens L	shining
		Marcus Annaeus Lucanus	Roman poet; #A
.12	phew	pheu G	alas! oh!
475.01	phopho	phobos G phôs G	panic flight, panic fear light
.10	narcosis	narkôsis G	a benumbing
.11	epicures	Epikouros G	"Ally": Athenian philosopher
.11	gardenfillers	*allusion to* hoi apo tôn kêpôn G	"those from the gardens": followers of Epicurus, whose school was in a garden (*kêpos*) and so named *Kêpos*
.12	Phopho	phobos; phôs G	*see 475.01*
.14	nebulose	nebulosus L	misty, foggy, cloudy
.15	melanite	melanizô G	to be black
.15	phosphor	phôsphoros G	bringing light, giving light
.17	electrolatiginous	*êlektro-lati-gen-ês G + L + G	amber-flank-born
.19	quiry	quare L queror L	how? why? to complain
.28	caperchasing	caper L	he-goat
.31	quorum	quorum (*Gen. pl.*) L	whose, of whom
.35	kapr	kapros G caper L	wild boar he goat
476.01	dianablowing	Diana L	goddess of hunting, the moon, etc.
.03	proto	prôtos, prôto- G	first, first-
.07	proxtended	*proextendo L proximo L proxenos G	to stretch out for to draw near agent, protector

.08	Manuum	manuum (*Gen. pl.*) L	hands', of hands
.13	personer	persona L	mask; character
.13	quatyouare	quattuor L	four
.14	stenoggers	stenos G	narrow
.14	solons	Solôn G	G statesman
.14	psychomorers	psychomôros G	soul-fool
		moror L	1. to delay; 2. to be a fool
.15	daimons	daimôn G	deity, spirit, demon
.22	oscasleep	Osca L	town in Hispania, *mod.* Huesca, Spain
		Osci L	the Oscans: primitive Italic people, neighbors of the Romans
.24	Lumen	lumen L	light
.26	Marcus	Marcus L	"Hammer": Roman praenomen
.26	Lucas	Lucas L	Luke (*evangelist*)
.29	ensorcelled	sors L	lot, chance, fate
.35	pnum	pneuma G	wind, breeze; breath; spirit
477.01	tetrahedrally	tetraedros G	having four faces
.11	octopuds	oktôpodes (*pl.*) G	eight feet
.12	chromous	chrôma G	1. skin; 2. color
.16	hospices	auspices (*pl.*) L	bird-inspectors, diviners from bird-flight
.19	quadriliberal	quadrilibris L	weighing four pounds
.21	thurrible	thuribulum L	vessel to burn incense in, censer
.21	mystagogue	mystagôgos G	guide into the mysteries, teacher, priest
.22	crucifer's	crucifer L	cross-carrying; a cross-bearer
.22	cauda	cauda L	tail
.23	backslibris	ex libris L	from the books [of ...]
		lubricus L	slippery
.26	chromes	chrôma G	1. skin; 2. color
.28	thripthongue	thrips G	wood-worm
		triphthongos G	three-vowel sound; having three voices
		triptychos G	consisting of three layers, threefold

.30	mellifond	*mellifons L	honey-fountain
.33	Ecko	ecce L	look! behold!
478.07	deuterous	deuteros G	second
.08	Esellus	asellus L	little ass, ass's colt
.09	Magis	magis L	in a higher degree, more completely
		magis G L	dish, platter; kneading-trough
.12	vallums	vallum L	rampart, palisaded earthwork
.12	majestate	majestate (*Abl.*) L	with grandeur
.13	rheda	rhaeda L	four-wheeled travelling carriage; #*B*
.13	rhoda	rhoda (*pl.*) G	roses; female pudenda; #*B*
.13–.14	hallucinian via	Eleusinia Via L	the Sacred Way at Eleusis through which celebrants of the mysteries passed to the hall of initiation
.14	via nor aurellian	Via Aurelia L	Aurelian Way: road north from Rome to Arelate (mod. Arles)
.14	aurellian gape	Porta Aurelia L	Aurelian Gate; westernmost gate of Rome, across the Tiber
.15	cruxway	*part trans.* Via Crucis L	The Way of the Cross
		crux L	cross, gallows
.16	*unde derivatur*	unde derivatur L	whence [it] is derived
.17–.18	*Magis megis enerretur mynus hoc intelligow*	[quo] magis enarratur [eo] minus hoc intellego L	the more completely it is explained the less I understand this
.17	*megis*	megistô G	greatness
.17	*enerretur*	inerretur L	it may be rambled about
.31	ultramontane	*ultramontanus L	beyond the mountain[s]
.32	doraphobian	*dôraphobia G	fear of gifts
.32	primafairy	primo vere L	at the beginning of spring

479.01	on the fourth day	tetradistês, tetradi gegonas G	one born on the fourth day: a Wednesday's child: proverbially, one born to hard work; *epithet of* Herakles/Hercules
		allusion to Hermes?	honored on the fourth of each month
.08	zoedone	zôê G	living, livelihood, life
		zôdion G	small figure; sign of the Zodiac
.08	zephyros	zephyros G	the west wind; the west
.21	austers	auster L	the south wind
.36	Nautsen	nauta L nautês G	sailor, seaman
480.09	bonofide	bona fide L	in good faith; # *B*
.10	oxeyed	*trans.* boôpis G	having large, full eyes; *epithet of* Hêra *and of* beautiful women
.12	Magnus	Magnus L	the Great: *Roman surname*
.12	perfyddye	perfide L	faithlessly, treacherously
		perfidia L	faithlessness, dishonesty
.14	Ecce	ecce L	look! behold!
.14	Hagios	hagios G	sacred, holy
.15	Chrisman	chrisma G	anointing, unction; grace
.20	Hunkalus	avunculus L	uncle
.21	Emania	emano L	to spring out of, to arise, to emanate from
.24	circuls	circulus L	circular figure, circle
.25	pancercrucer	pan G	all
		crucio L	to torture, torment
.27	lyceum	Lyceum L	"Of a Wolf" *or* "Of Lycia [*country in Asia Minor*]": gymnasium at Athens where Aristotle set up his school
		Lykeion G	
.28	volp volp	volpes *or* vulpes L	fox
.35	lupus	lupus L	wolf
481.04	A cataleptic	*akatalêptikos G	incomprehensible

		akatalêktikos G	1. incessant; 2. *Prosody* (*L: acatalecticus*): verse in which the last foot contains its full number of syllables
.04	cataleptic	katalêptikos G	able to check; conveying direct apprehension, manifestly
.04	mithyphallic	mythos G	word, speech, message; fiction
		ithyphallikos G	"pertaining to an erect phallos": meter of poems used in Bacchic festivals: consisting of three trochees
.04	*Totum Fulcrum Est*	totum fulcrum est L	all is a bed, it is all a bed-post
.05	*Dies Eirae*	Dies Irae L	Day of Wrath
.06	*Anno Mundi*	anno mundi L	in the year of the world
.10	tristich	tristichia G	group of three verses; three-line verse
.11	fui fui	fui L	I have been, I was
.13	occeanyclived	Oceanus L	great sea that surrounds the land, Ocean
		Ôkeanos G	
		clivus L	declivity, slope, ascent, eminence
.14	vulganized	vulgus L	the multitude, the public
		Vulcanus L	god of fire; #A
.15	lavast	lavas L	you (*sing.*) wash
.16	*Ad Horam*	ad horam L	at the hour, on time
		Hora L	"Lady": wife of Romulus
.17	ob	ob L	for, in front of
.17	by, with or from an urb	urbe (*Abl.*) L	by, with *or* from a city
.18	differenciabus	differentiabus LL	to, for *or* with, by differences, diversities, species
.19	locative	locativus [casus] Mod L	case of L & G nouns expressing place at *or* in which; *e.g.*, *Romae*, "at Rome"

.20	assertant	*assertant pseudo-L *as if from* *asserto; *recte* asserunt *from* assero L	[they] declare, set free, claim
.21	re	re (*Abl.*) L	with *or* by a thing, matter, affair
.21	of Chivitats Ei	De Civitate Dei L	*Concerning the City of God*: famous work by St. Augustine
.21	Chivitats	civitas L	citizenship; city *or* state
.21	Ei	ei (*Dat.*) L	to him, to her, to that
.21	Kaledon	Kalydôn G	city in Aetolia with temple of Artemis; Meleager killed a boar there
		Caledonia L	district in north Britain: the highlands of Scotland
.22	Argos	Argos G L	capital of Argolis in the Peloponnessus; *Poetic*: Greece
.28	Noctuber	noctu L	at night, by night
		uber L	udder, breast; fertile, abundant, copious
		*noctuber L	copious by night, abundant at night
.35	in Ranelagh ... Petries and violet ice	in nomine Patris et Filii et Spiritus Sancti L	in the name of the Father and of the Son and of the Holy Spirit
.35	fué! fué!	fui L	I was, I have been
.35	Petries	Petrus L	Rock; Peter
.35	I am yam	iamiam, jamjam L	already
482.01	Eddy's Christy	Aedes Christi L	Dwellingplace of Christ
.01–.02	and spiriduous sanction	et Spiritus Sancti L	and the Holy Spirit
.03	Aures	aures (*pl.*) L	ears
.03	aureas	aureus L	golden
.04	Me das	Midas	legendary king of Phrygia, had ass's *ears* and a *golden* touch
.05	White eyeluscious	videlicet L	it is easy to see, plainly, evidently

.07	Lucas	Lucas L	Luke (*evangelist*)
.07–.08	Vulva! Vulva! Vulva! Vulva!	vulva L	wrapper; womb
.09	onagrass	onagros G onagrus L	wild ass
.10	stavrotides	*stavrotidês MG *staurotidês G	descendant of a cross
.12	O'mulanchonry	mulax G melanchros G	millstone swarthy, sunburnt
.12	plucher	pulcher L plochmos G	beautiful, handsome lock, braid (*of hair*)
.17	psychical	psychikos G	spiritual
.17	chirography	cheirographia G	report in writing, written testimony, *handwriting
.27	farfar	farfarus L	a plant: colt's-foot
.31	prouts	prout L	according as, in proportion, just as
.31	invent	invenio L	to come upon, to find
.32	poeta	poeta L	maker, contriver, poet
.35	decorded	de corde L	from the heart
483.01	altereffects	alter L	the other (*of two*), other
.04	Sameas	*trans.* prout L	*see 482.31*
.10	anteproresurrectionism	ante L	before, prior to
		anti G pro L	against for, in front of
.17	Marcantonio	Marcus Antonius L	triumvir
.18	initiumwise	initium L	a going in, entrance; beginning; element, constituent part
.19	alpybecca's	alpha, bêta G beccus L	letters A, B cock's bill
.20	ikeson ... ikeson	eikôn G eikos G	likeness, image likely, probable
.20	imprincipially	in principio L	in the beginning (*Vulgate*: first words both of Genesis and John)
.21	Puer	puer L	boy, child
.21	ens	ens L	a thing, a being
.21	innocens	innocens L	harmless, guiltless

.21	Puer, ens innocens	Puer, ens innocens L	A boy, a harmless being
.24	parallaling	parallassô G	to cause to alternate; to interchange; to deviate
.24	buttyr	butyrum L boutyron G	butter
.24	altermobile	*alteromobilis L	moveable by another
.26	habitand	habitans L habitandus L	residing, dwelling appropriate to be inhabited
.30	impostulance	impostus (pp.) L	placed upon, set, put upon; deceived
.32	Mezienius	Mezentius	Etruscan king killed by Aeneas
.32	Mezosius	Methodios	apostle to the Slavs
.33	verted	vertus (pp.) L	turned
.34	laud	laus L	praise
.34	patristic	*patristikos G *patristicus L	pertaining to the [Church] fathers
.35	meas minimas culpads	mea minima culpa L	through my least fault
.35	icoocoon	eikôn G	likeness, image
484.02	octopods	oktôpodes (pl) G	eight-feet
.03	mansuetude	mansuetudo L	accustomed to the hand; tameness, mildness, clemency
		Mansuetudo L	Clemency, Grace: *mode of address to emperors*
.03	Audeon's	audeo L audio L to Ôideion G	to dare to hear the Odeum: hall for musical performances built at Athens by Pericles
.04	tropps	tropos G	a turn
.07	he all locutey sunt	hi allocuti sunt L	these have spoken to, these have consoled
.07	sexth	sex L	six
.08	delated	delatus (pp.) L	accused, denounced
.11	Momoluius	Mômos G	"Fault-finding": pseudo-deity
		lues, luis L	plague, pestilence, spreading calamity
.13	quoniam	quoniam L	since now, seeing that, whereas

.13	celebrand	celebrandus L	fit to be frequented, apt to be much visited; about to be solemnized
.14	quoniam	*see 484.13E*	
.15	insulant	insulanus L	islander
.15	hyber	hybris G	wanton violence, pride
		hyper G	over, beyond
.16	avtokinatown	*avtokinêton MG	self-moving thing [automobile]
		*autokinêton G	
.17	vespian	vespa L	wasp
		vespillo L	nocturnal remover of the dead poor
		vesper L	evening
.19	cardonals	cardo L	hinge
.20	Improperial	improperium eccl L	reproach, taunt [of Jesus, by Jews]
.20	Hekkites	hic, haec, hoc L	this, this here; #B
.21	Aud Dub	aud[ens] dub[itanter] L	hesitatingly bold
.22	P.Q.R.S.	S[enatus] P[opulus]q[ue] R[omanus] L	the Roman Senate and People
.23	legatine	legativus L	pertaining to an embassy
.23	episcoping	episkopeô G	to inspect, observe, oversee
.24	circumdeditioned	circumdedi L	to have placed around, to have surrounded
		*circumdeditio L	addiction all around, diligence all around
.25	lapsus langways	lapsus linguae L	a slip of the tongue
.25	langways	Andrew Lang (1884–1912)	translator of Homer into pseudo-archaic English
.28	ruridecanal	*ruridecanalis ML	pertaining to a rural dean
.29	peregrines	peregrinus L	foreigner, stranger; *ML*, pilgrim
.30	Theophrastius	Theophrastos (372–286 b.c.) G	"Divine Speaker": philosopher, disciple of Plato and Aristotle, Aristotle's heir
.30	Spheropneumaticus	*sphairopneumatikos G	of rounded breath

.30	Theophrastius Spheropneumaticus	Theophrastos Sphairopneumat-ikos G	Divine Speaker of Rounded Breath
.32	ochlocracy	ochlokratia G	mob rule
.32	Prestopher	*praestofer L	ready-carrier, superior carrier
		# *P/K Split*: *Chrêstophoros G	bearer of goodness
		*Crestafer ML *Cristafer L	tuft-bearer, crest-bearer, cock's-comb-bearer
.32	Palumbus	palumbes L # *P/K Split*: columbus L	wood-pigeon, ring-dove pigeon, dove
.32	Prestopher Palumbus	# *P/K Split*: (1) Crestopher Calumbus;	Christopher Columbus
		(2) Crestofer Palumbes;	Crested Wood-pigeon
		(3) *etc.*	*etc.*
.32	Porvus	# *P/K Split*: corvus L	crow
.32	Parrio	# *P/K Split*	carrio[n]
.32	Porvus Parrio	# *P/D Split*: corvus carrio fake-L	carrion crow
.33	Terry	terreo L terreus L	to frighten of earth, earthen
.33	per	per L	whereby; through; during, for
.33	Chelly	chelys G	tortoise
.33	lepossette	lepus L	hare
.34	Exquovis	ex quovis L	from whatever you like
.34	sequencias	sequentia L	that which follows; context
.34	fakesimilar	fac simile L	make a likeness
.35	Pappagallus	papa L pappas G	father; bishop; tutor
		gallus L	cock
		Gallus L	1. a Gaul; 2. eunuch priest of Cybele; 3. poet, friend of Vergil's
		Papa Gallus L	Daddy from Gaul (J. Caesar?)
.35	Pumpusmugnus	Cn. Pompeius Magnus L	Roman soldier and politician

.36	Anglicey	Anglice ML	in English
.36	*Eggs squawfish lean yoe nun feed marecurious*	Ex quovis ligno non fit Mercurius L	A Mercury is not made out of just any piece of wood (*proverb*); #B
485.01	laud	laus L	praise
.01	nilobstant	nihil obstat L	nothing stands in the way
.02	tripenniferry	tripennifer L	three-feather-bearing
.02	cresta	crista L	crest, plume
.02	tripenniferry cresta	tripennifera crista L	three-feather-bearing crest (*crest of Prince of Wales*)
.03	caudal	cauda L	tail
.03	mottams	moto L	to move about
		tam L	so, so much, as
.05	Egoname	nam ego L	for surely I . . .
		egônê G	I, for my part
.05	Yod	iota G	letter I
.09	luckat	luceat L	may it shine
.10	sour! Ichthyan	ichthyosauros G	fish-lizard; ichthysaur
.10	Ichthyan	ichthya G	fishery
		ichthyaô G	to fish
		ichthys G	a fish
		I[êsous] CH[ristos] TH[eou] [h]Y[ios] S[ôtêr]	Jesus Christ God's Son Savior
.10	plebsed	plebs L	the common people
.11	consinuantes	*consinuans L	sharing the same bay; sharing a purse
.16	Cum	cum L	with, while
.17	thrupenny croucher	tripennata crista L	three-feathered crest
.19	*Spira in Me Domino*	spira in me Domino L	breathe into me by the Lord
		spero in te Domine L	I hope in thee, O Lord
.20	bonafide	bona fide L	in good faith; #B
.22	dullaphone	phônê G	sound, voice
.24	trifoaled	trifolium L	three-leaved clover; shamrock
.25	hored	hora OL	lady
		hôra G hora L	hour
		horum (*Gen. pl. masc.*) L	of these

.26	harum	harum (*Gen. pl. fem.*) L	of these
.26	lubberintly	lubricus L	slippery
.28	Ho ha hi he hung	hic, haec, hoc (*sing.*), hi, hae, haec (*pl.*) L	this, this here; these, these here #*B*
.30	ludiments	ludimentum L	plaything, toy
.34	boohoomeo	humeo L	to be moist, to be damp
.35	Confucium	confugium L	place of refuge, shelter, asylum
.36	Thot's	Thot	Egyptian god identified with Hermês
486.01	lambdad's	lambda G	letter L
.03	*Quadrigue*	quadriga L	four-horse chariot
		quadrigae L	set of four, yoke of four horses; free *or* rapid course
.05	*Tandem*	tandem L	at length, at last
.08	understudium	studium L	assiduity, zeal, endeavor
.09	verbed	verba L	words
.11	a chink in his conscience	*trans.* *psychosinolog-ia G	spiritual study of the Chinese; *see 486.13*
.13	Minucius	minutius L	very small
		Minucius L	"Very Small": name of a Roman gens
		Minucius Felix (*fl. c.* a.d. 200)	Christian apologist
.13	psychosinology	*psychosinolog-ia G	spiritual study of China *or* the Chinese, study of the Chinese soul
.14	Tuttu	tuto L	to watch, guard, defend
		tutum L	a shelter; safety, security
.17	pliestrycook	pleistos G	most, greatest
.21	serpe	serpens L	creeper, crawler; snake
		herpês G (#*G-to-L*)	1. the shingles; 2. snake
.24	isisglass	Isis	Egyptian deity; #*A*
.32	Bellax ... bellax	bellax L	warlike, martial
.32	triptych	triptychos G	consisting of three layers
.35	oneir	oneiros G	dream
.35	oneir urge	*oneirourgos G	dream-maker

.35	iterimpellant	*iterimpellens L	setting in motion on a journey
.36	*qua*	qua L	as far as, in so far as
487.01	iberborealis	hyperboreos G	"above-northern": pertaining to a people supposed to live in the extreme north
		*Ibêriboreos G	pertaining to northern Spain
.02	bar accidens	per accidens L	accidentally
.02	accidens	accidens L	the non-essential quality of any thing
.11	apert	apertus L	open, free
		aperte L	openly, clearly, plainly
.12	nexword	nex L	murder
.15	ericulous	*ericilus L	little hedgehog
.18	bimiselves	bimi *(pl.)* L	of two years, for two years
.22	Roma	Roma L	Rome
.23	Amor	Amor L	Love
.22	Roma ... Amor	Rome, Venus L	Venus, ancestress of the *Julii*, became special deity of Imperial Rome. Temples of Venus and Rome (AMOR/ROMA) were built back-to-back as mirror images
.33	*simpliciter arduus*	simpliciter arduus [Dog-] L	simply high, simply elevated, simply arduous
.33	ars	ars L	art
.36	Synodius	*Synodius L	belonging to a *synodos*
		synodos G	meeting, assembly, get-together
		[cf. Ekklêsiastês G	member of a congregation]
		Synesius (a.d. 375–413)	bishop of Ptolemais; author
488.03	simplicissime	simplicissime L	most simply
.04	Nola	Nola L	very ancient Ausonian city in Campania (*home of G. Bruno*)
.07	Nola	*see 488.04 F*	

.08	egobruno	ego L egô G	I
.08	seses	sese (*Acc., Abl.*) L	himself, herself, itself; from, with, by himself, herself
.09	alionola	alio L	elsewhither, to another place
		Nola L	city; *see 488.04,07,11*
.09	brunoipso	ipso L	from, with *or* by the self *or* the same
.09	*id est*	id est L	that is
.10	alio	alio L	to another place
.11	Nola	*see 488.04F*	
.11	Poor omniboose, singalow singlearum	pro omnibus, saeculo saeculorum L	for everyone, for an age of ages
		per omnia saecula saeculorum L	through all ages of ages
.14	zoohoohoom	zôon G	animal, living thing
.14	Felin	felinus L	pertaining to a cat, catlike
.15	Nolans	Nolanus L	inhabitant of Nola
		nolens L	unwilling
.15	Volans	volans L	flying
		volens L	willing
.16	alibi	alibi L	someplace else, elsewhere
.20	ostralian	ostra (*pl.*) L	purples, purple garments
		ostrea L	oyster
.20	mults	multus L	much, many
.20	belubdead	lubens L	with pleasure
.21	allaboy	alibi L	elsewhere
.21	Negoist	nego L	to deny, refuse
.22	expulled	pullus L	1. young animal; 2. pure; 3. dark-colored
.24	Cenograph	kenographos G	an empty writing
		kainographos G	a new writing
.26	per	per L	through, during, by
.26	Neuropaths	neuron G	sinew, nerve
		neuropathos G	sinew-experience, nerve-suffering
.29	Alby	albi- L	white-
.29	Sobrinos	sobrinus L	maternal cousin
.35	opulose	opulus L	maple-tree

.35	and bilgenses	Albigenses ML	those from *Albi* (*town in southern France*): medieval heretics
489.03	*V.V.C.*	V.V.C. pseudo-MG	B.B.C.
.04	muxy	muxa G	snot
.06	Oremus poor fraternibus	oremus pro fratribus L	let us pray for [our] brothers
.10	antipathies	antipodes G	with the feet opposite: *legendary people who live at the bottom of the globe*
.10	austrasia	*austrasia L	south Asia
.13	Obiit	obit L	he [she, it] falls, dies
488.16	castor and porridge	Castor and Pollux L	heavenly twins; #*A*
489.17	clarenx	clarens L	brightening
		*clarenx L + G	musical instrument [clarinet?] ?
		modeled on syrinx G	shepherd's pipe
.17	negus	nego L	to deny, refuse
.17	teetotum	totum L	all, the whole
.20	Telewisher	têle- G	at a distance, afar
.27	africot	Africus L	the south-west wind
.27	lupps	lips G	the south-west wind
.29	otiumic	otium L	leisure, freedom, vacation
.31	irismaimed	Iris G L	goddess of the rainbow; the rainbow
490.01	vector	vector L	carrier, bearer
.01–.02	vector victored	victor victus L	the winner defeated
.02	victim vexed	victum vexatum (*Acc.*) L	the loser tormented
.04	ecolites	oiko- G	house-, home-
.08	pronuminally	pro numina L	in place of a god
.10	You reeker	[h]êurêka G	I have found; I have it
.16	mispatriate	misopatris G	a hater of his country
.17	rereally	res L #*Reduplication*	thing, affair
.25	Jenny	geni- L	birth-
.26	Rediviva	rediviva (*fem.*) L	that lives again
.28	contraman	contra L	over against, opposite
		*contramen L	a means of opposing

.35	bosbully	bos L	ox, bull, cow
491.13	tutu	tutus L	safe, secure, out of danger
.14	turturs	turtur L	turtle[dove]
.28	scaliger	scaliger L	ladder-carrier
		Joseph Justus Scaliger (1540–1609)	one of the greatest classical scholars of all time; *son of J. C. Scaliger*
		Julius Caesar Scaliger (1484–1558)	classical scholar, *father of J. J. Scaliger*
.30	Phylliscitations	Phyllis G	girl who was changed into an almond-tree
		phyllis G	foliage; heap of leaves; salad
		phyllis L	almond-tree
492.04	allaughed	alpha G	letter A
.04	baited	bêta G	letter B
.04	gammat	gamma G	letter G
		gamma ut ML	the third *ut*: lowest note on scale
.05	Loonacied	dies Lunae L	Moon's day, Monday
.05	Marterdyed	dies Martis L	Mars' day, Tuesday
.05	Madwakemiherculossed	dies Mercurii L	Mercury's day, Wednesday
		mehercle L	by Hercules!
		Colossus L	statue at Rhodes
		Kolossos G	
.05	Judascessed	dies Jovis L	Juppiter's day, Thursday
.06	Pairaskivvymenassed	Paraskeuê G Paraskivi MG	day before the sabbath of Passover; Good Friday
.06	Luredogged	luridus L	pale yellow, wan, ghastly
		luridatus L	besmeared, defiled
.07	faulscrescendied	crescendum L	fit to be increased
.08	Dias domnas	dies Domini L	the Lord's day, Sunday
.09	diva	diva L	goddess
.09	deltic	*deltikos G	pertaining to the letter D *or* to a rivermouth *or* to the female pudenda
.12	ara	ara L	altar

		ara G	*interrogative particle*
.13	Capilla	capilla (*pl.*) L	hairs
.13	Rubrilla	rubra (*fem.*) L	red, ruddy
.13	Melcamomilla	mel L	honey
		chamaimêlon G	"earth-apple": camomile
		*melichamaimêl-on G	honey-earth-apple
.14	saxy	saxum L	a stone
.15	luters	lutum L	mud
.19	parapotacarry's	*parathêkê G	place where things are
		*paratheca L	laid alongside
		*parathecarius L	clerk in a place where things are laid alongside
		modeled on	
		apothecarius L	warehouseman
		from	
		apotheca L *for* apothêkê G	place where things are laid away, storehouse, warehouse
.20	sedown	sedo L	to settle, lull, quiet
		sedeo L	to sit
.28	mepetition	me- L	*demonstrative particle*
		mephitis L	noxious exhalation from the ground
.32	sexular	sex L	six
		sexus L	sex
.33	volvular	volvula L	little womb
493.03	vallad	*MG pron.*	ballad
.05	nil ensemble	nil insimul L	nothing at the same time
.06	hemifaces	hêmi- G	half-
.08	so light's	solis (*Gen.*) L	sun's, of the sun
.10	propendiculous	propendulus L	hanging down in front
		*propendiculus L	a noose in front
		culus L	arse
.14	Lithia	lithia G	precious stones, jewelry
.18	Fantasy! funtasy on fantasy, amnaes fintasies	Vanitas, vanitas vanitatum, omnis vanitas L	Emptiness, emptiness of emptinesses, all empty ["Vanity, vanity of vanities, all is vanity"—*Ecclesiastes*]
.18	amnaes	amnis L	river

		amnêsia G	forgetfulness
.19	nihil	nihil L	nothing
.23	Ephialtes	ephialtês G	nightmare
		Ephialtês G	the demon of nightmare
		Ephialtês G	giant, brother of Otus (*see 493.24*), stormed heaven, slain by Apollo
		Ephialtês G (*d.* 461 b.c.)	Athenian statesman, murdered
		Ephialtês G (*d.* 468 b.c.)	traitor who helped Xerxes outflank Leonidas at Thermopylae
.24	simplex mendaciis	simplex mendaciis L	simple in [his] lies
.24	Outis	Outis G	Nobody: name Odysseus gave himself
		ôtos G	horned owl; booby, fool
		Ôtos G Otus L	giant, brother of Ephialtes (*see 493.23*), stormed heaven, slain by Apollo
.26	Vide! Vide!	vide L	see!
.28	Irise	Iris G L	goddess of the rainbow; the rainbow
		Isis	Egyptian goddess; #*A*
.28	Osirises	Osiris	Egyptian god; #*A*
.31	Nu-Men	numen L	divine will, divine rule; a god
.35	dearast	erastês G	lover
494.01	strawnummical	nummus L	piece of money, coin
.02	chrome	chrôma G	skin; complexion; color
.06	Orca	orca L	kind of whale; tun; dice-box
		Orcus L	Pluto; abode of the dead; the dead
.06	Bellona	Bellona L	goddess of war
		balaena L	whale
.06	etnat	Aetna L Aitnê G	"Burning": Sicilian volcano, Etna
.06	athos	Athôs G	high mountain in Macedonia
.07	vulcanology	*vulcanologia L + G	the study of Vulcan (*his forge was inside Aetna*); study of volcanoes

.09	Ophiuchus	Ophiouchos G	Serpent-holder: *a constellation*
.09	muliercula	muliercula L	little woman (*constellation* Virgo?)
.10	Satarn's	Saturnus L	Roman god; the planet Saturn
.10	pisciolinnies	pisciculi (*pl.*) L	little fishes (*constellation* Pisces?)
.10	Nova	nova (*fem.*) L	new
.11	Ardonis	Adônis G	beautiful youth loved by Aphrodite
		ardor L	burning heat, ardent desire
.11	Prisca	prisca (*fem.*) L	ancient, of old, antique
.11	Parthenopea	Parthenopê G	"Maiden-face": Siren, drowned herself when Odysseus escaped; Naples (*after the Siren*)
.12	Ers	Erôs G	god of sexual love
		Arês G	god of war = L Mars; #A
.12	Mores	mores (*pl.*) L	customs, habits
		Mars L	god of war = G Arês; #A
.12	Merkery	Mercurius L	messenger of the gods; #A
.12	surgents	surgens L	rising
.13	Arctura	*arctura L	bear-wardress, female
		*arktourê G	bear-guard
		Arcturus L	Bear-guard: a bright
		Arktouros G	star
		Arctos	*in some lists*, apocryphal star from whence Adam's name [Anatole, Dusis, Arctos, Mesembria]
.13	Anatolia	*Anatolia G	the Orient; Rising-up-land; the East
		Anatole, Anatoile	*in some lists*, apocryphal star from whence Adam's name [Anatole, Dusis, Arcis, Mesimbria]
.13	Hesper	Hesperos G	the evening star; the
		Hesperus L	west

.13	Mesembria	Mesêmbria G	city on Black Sea, mod. Neseber, Bulgaria
		mesêmbria G	midday; the south
		Mesembria, Messembrion	some form of this name occurs on all lists of apocryphal stars from which Adam named, *e.g.* Arthox, Dux, Arotholem, Minsymbria
.17	strombolo	Strongyle L*for* Strongylê G	"Round": volcanic island between Sicily and Italy
.19	obesendean	obesus L	"eaten away": 1. lean, meager; 2. fat, plump
.21–.22	Obeisance so their sitinins is the follicity of this Orp	Obedientia civium urbis felicitas L	Dublin's motto; #B
.22	follicity	follico L	to expand and contract like a bellows
.22	Orp	urbs L	city
.23	Guygas	Gygês, Gugês	king of Lydia
		gigas G	giant
.26	heva heva	Heva L	Eve (*first woman*)
.27	emanence	emanens L	1. overstaying a furlough; 2. flowing out, spreading
.33	Synamite	*synamis G *modeled on*	flowing together
		dynamis G *as if* power, might *from*	
		dy- G +	two-
		nama G	stream, spring, running water
495.05	Sylphling	sylphes Mod L *from* sylvestris	"forest nymph": *coinage for* soulless
		nympha LL	being inhabiting the air
.06	anyposs	posse (*infinitive*) L	to be able
.11	Withworkers	*trans.* synergoi G	fellow workers, co-workers
.16	poly	poly- G	much-, many-
.23	pennis	penna L	feather, wing; pen
.30	magistrades	magis L	more completely, more
		magistra L	mistress
.33	Amn.	amnis L	river

.33	Anm.	anima L	breath, vital principle
.33	Amm.	ammos G	sand
.33	Ann.	annus L	year
.34	Frui	fruor L	to enjoy
.34–.35	*artis litterarumque patrona*	artis litterarumque patrona L	patroness of art and letters
.36	silvanes	Silvanus L	deity of woods
.36	salvines	salvus L	saved, preserved, unhurt, sound
496.06	conspued	conspuo L consputus (*pp.*) L	to spit upon spat-upon
.08	Archimandrite	archimandritês G	abbot
.08	minx	minxi L	I have pissed
.10	ecunemical	cuneus L oikoumenikos G	wedge open to the whole world
.10	conciliabulum	conciliabulum L	place of assembly, public place; marketplace, exchange
.13	*Auxilium Meum Solo A Domino*	auxilium meum solo a Domino L	my help [is] from the Lord alone
.13	Amsad	a[uxilium] m[eum] s[olo] a d[omino] L	my help [is] from the lord alone
.20	Ma's da	m[eum] a s[olo] d[omino] a[uxilium] L	my help [is] from the only lord [*poetic syntax*]
.20	Da's ma	D[omino] a s[olo] m[eum] a[uxilium] L	from the Lord only [is] my help
.21	Madas	m[eum] a d[omino] a[uxilium] s[olo] L	from the Lord alone [is] my help [*poetic syntax*]
.21	Sadam	s[olo] a d[omino] a[uxilium] m[eum] L	from the Lord alone [is] my help
.22	*Pater patruum cum filiabus familiarum*	pater patruum [OL] cum filiabus familiarum L	the father of the uncles with the daughters of the families

		pater patrum cum filiabus familiarum L	the father of the fathers with the daughters of the families
.23	ariring	#*Rhotacism*	arising
.24	subjunct	subjunctus (*pp.*) L	annexed; subjugated; substituted
.24	traumaturgid	trauma G turgeo L thaumatourgos G	a wound to swell, to be swollen wonder-worker
.30	Christy Columb	Christi columbus L	the dove of Christ
.34	Rotacist	rota L #*Rhotacism*	wheel *alteration of* -s- *to* -r-
.36	*Quis est qui non novit quinnigan*	Quis est qui non novit *Quinnigan L	Who is he who does not know Quinnigan?
.36	*quinnigan*	#*P/K Split*; #*Labials*	Finnegan
.36	*Qui quae quot*	qui quae quod L	who? which? (*masc., fem., neut.*)
.36	*quot*	quot L	how many, as many as; each, every
497.02	exagmination	ex agmin L	out of the host, out of the multitude [*Joyce's etymology: see Ellmann, p. 626*]
		*exagminatio OL	a swarming, crowding
.02	factification	*factificatio L	making of a thing made, making of an achievement
.02	incamination	*incaminatio L	an enforging
.04	Arra	arra L ara G	earnest-money, security-money, pledge *interrogative particle*
.04	irrara	ira L irrasus L	wrath, anger 1. shaved, scraped; 2. unshaven
.04	hirrara	hir L (*from* cheir G). hira L hirrio L	palm of the hand the empty gut, jejunum to snarl
.05	*Ad Regias Agni Dapes*	ad regias Agni dapes L	to/at the royal feast of the Lamb

.06	panhibernskers	*panhiberniani G + L	all-Irelanders
.07	messicals	messis L	harvest
.08	leggats	legatus L	ambassador
.08	prelaps	praelapsus (pp.) L	bypast, hastened-by
		prae lapsu L	before the fall
		praelatus (pp.) L	carried before, placed before, anticipated
		praelatus ML	ruler, prelate
.09	undecimmed	undecim L	eleven
.09	centries	centum L	hundred
.09	undecimmed centries	undecim et centum L	one hundred and eleven
.10	extraomnes	extra omnes L	outside of all, apart from all
.10	allcunct	cunctus L	all in a body, all together, the whole
		cuncto, cunctor L	to delay
.12	Affrian	affrico L	to rub on, to rub against
		affrio L	to crumble to pieces
		Afri L	Africans
.12	Affrian Way	Via Appia L	the Appian Way: road to Brundisium
.12	Europa	Europa L	girl carried off by Zeus;
		Eurôpê G	the continent of Europe
.15	oppidumic	oppidum L	town
.16	Maximagnetic	maximus L	greatest
		magnus L	great
.18	Luccanicans	Lucanici (pl.) L	people from Lucania, southern Italy
		Lucanica L	kind of sausage (from Lucania)
		Luca L	city in Etruria, scene of conference between Caesar and Pompey (56 b.c.); mod. Lucca
.23	*Uisgye ad Inferos*	usque ad inferos L	all the way to those below, to the dead
.23–.24	*Usque ad Ebbraios*	usque ad ebrios L	as far as the drunkards
		usque ad Hebraeos L	even unto the Hebrews

.26	Hosty's	hostis L	stranger, foreigner, enemy
.35	protemptible	*protemptabilis L	capable of being tried, testable
		*protemptibilis L	admirable
		by false opposition [*pro:* *con*] *to*	
		contemptibilis L	despicable, contemptible
		pro temp[ore] L	for the time
.35	tintanambulating	tintinnabulatus L	wearing a bell
		tintinnabula (*pl.*) L	bells
		ambulatus L	walking
498.03	Leodegarius	Leodegarius LL	French saint (St. Leger)
.04	Amaxodias	[h]amaxa G	wagon
		hodeia G	traveling
		*amaxodeias G	wagon-traveler
.04	Isteroprotos	hysteroprôtos G	back-to-front
		Ister L	the Danube
.06	*Horsibus*	horsum L	hither, this way
		-ibus L	Dat., Abl. pl. suffix
.10	F.P.	F[lamen] P[erpetuus] L	permanent priest
.10	Agiapommenites	agapômenos G	beloved, loved one
		[h]agia (*fem.*) G	holy, sacred
.10	A.P.	A P[opulo] L	from the People
		A[ediliciae] P[otestatis]	of the power vested in the aediles
.10	Antepummelitee	ante L	before, prior
		pumilio L	a dwarf
.11	P.P.	P[ater] P[atriae] L	Father of his Country
		P[rae]P[ositus] L	Prefect
		P[rimi]P[ilus] L	Chief Centurion
		P[ro] P[arte] L	on behalf of, for the part of
.13	gemmynosed	geminus L	twin
.13	sanctsons	sanctus L	holy
.14	epheud	pheu G	alas! oh!
.15	Adamantaya	adamantinos G	of steel; very hard

		adamas G	unconquerable
.18	mona	Mona L	Isle of Man; Anglesea
.19	pani's annagolorum	panis angelorum L	angels' bread, bread of angels
		Panis Angelicus L	Angelic Bread [*the Sacred Host*]: *hymn*
.23	clayroses	klêros G	allotment
.27	circumassembled	circum L	around
.30	cummulium	cumulus L	heap, pile
.30	erica's	erica L ereikê G	heather
.31	spectrem	spectrum L	appearance, form, image, spectre
.32	candiedights	candidatus L	dressed in white
.35	expositoed	expositus L	set forth, open, free, accessible
499.01	rouseruction	eructo L	to belch, to vomit
.04	morties	mortuis (*Abl. pl.*) L	by, with, from those who are dead
.05	calisenic	kalli- G	beautiful-
		senis L	old
.05	neniatwantyng	nenia L	1. funeral-song, dirge; 2. magical song, incantation; 3. popular song, lullaby
.05	Mulo	mulio L	mule-driver
.05	Mulo Mulelo	mulier L	woman
.05	Homo	homo L	person, man
.06	Humilo	humilis L	low, humble, obscure, base
		humilio LL	to abase
.09	Thaunaton	thanatos G	death
		thaunon G	wild animal
.09	Udamnor	damnor L	I am damaged, I am doomed, condemned
.09	Eulumu	eu G	good, well, fine
		eu lelumai G	I was well released
.11	Hamovs! Hemoves	ovum, *pl.* ova L	egg
		oves (*pl.*) L	sheep
.11	Mamor	Mamers Osc.	Mars
		mors L	death
.11–.12	Rockquiem eternuel give donal aye in dolmeny	requiem aeternam dona eis, Domine L	grant them eternal rest, O Lord
.12	Bad luck's perpepperpot loosen his eyis	et lux perpetua luceat eis L	and may perpetual light shine upon them

.12	Psich	psychê G	soul, spirit, consciousness
		sic L	thus
.16	adipose	adiposus LL	fat, lardy
.16	rex	rex L	king
.16	adipose rex	Oedipus Rex L *for* Oidipous Tyrannos G	Swollen-foot the Ruler: tragic king of Thebes
.30	*Tris tris*	tris L	three
		tris G	thrice, three times
.30	*Tris tris a ni ma mea*	tristis anima mea L	my soul [is] sad
.31–.32	*Usque! Usque! Usque!*	usque L	as far as, all the way to, even unto
.30–	*Tris tris a*	Anima mea	"My soul *is* sorrowful
.32	*ni ma mea … Usque*	tristis usque [ad mortem] (*Matt. 26:38*)	even unto [death]"—*Jesus in Gethsemane.*
.32	*Lignum in …*	lignum in … L	[a piece of] wood in …
500.13	Send us	sanctus L	holy
.15	chareman	charis G	grace, favor
		Chaeremon L Chairemôn G	1. tragic poet of the mid 4th C b.c.; 2. a stoic, teacher of Nero
.19	Aure	aureus L	golden
		aude L	hear! listen!
501.13	Sybil	Sibylla G L	female soothsayer, prophetess
.14	Sybil	*see 501.13* G	
.26	Bonafieries	Bonifacius L	"Handsome-Face"; apostle to the Germans; #*A*
		bona fides L bonum fieri (*infinitive*)	good faith; #*B* to become good
.31	flosting	flos L	flower, blossom
502.06	ostscent	occidens L	setting; west
.07	rose	ros L	dew
.10	Lieto galumphantes	[Adeste fideles] laete triumphantes L	[Come all ye faithful] joyfully triumphing
.11	Pacific	pacificus L	peace-making
.12	Muna	Luna L Mênê G	Moon
.15	Quando	quando L	when?

.15	Quonda	quondam L	at one time, formerly, once
.15	Go datey	gaudete L	rejoice!
.16	Latearly! Latearly! Latearly! Latearly!	Laetare L	Rejoice!
		laete L	joyfully
.18	hice	hice OL	this here
.18	calid	calidus L	hot, warm
.19	bruma	bruma L	midwinter
.19–.20	airsighs and hellstohnes and flammballs and vodashouts	air, stones, flames, water:	air, earth, fire, water: *four elements of ancient physics*
.20	flammballs	flamma L	blazing fire, blaze
.23	ahrtides	arti G	exactly; just now, just
.26	formous	formosus L	finely formed, handsome, lovely
.27	fumous	fumus L	smoke, steam
.30	delugium	diluvium L	inundation, flood, deluge
.30	stramens	stramen L	straw, litter
.30	delugium stramens	delirium tremens L	trembling madness
.33	phone	phônê G	sound, voice
.35	flockfuyant	flocces L	dregs
		floccus L	small tuft, flock, fleck; anything insignificant
		fugans L	fleeing
.36	Paronama	paronomasia G	play upon words; punning
		paronomazô G	to call things by a slightly altered name
503.04	stilller	stellaris L	starry
.05	oleotorium	*oleotorium L *from*	place for storing oil
		oleum L	olive-oil, oil
		*oleorium L *from*	giving off of smell; place for giving off smells in
		oleo L *modeled on*	to give off a smell
		auditorium L *from*	a hearing; place for holding hearings
		audio L	to hear
.29	Trickspissers	trixos (*Ionic*) G	threefold

.34–.35	*Thesaurus Plantarum*	thesaurus plantarum L	a storehouse of slips *or* cuttings (*of plants*); a storehouse of soles (*of the feet*)
		Thesaurus Plantarum ML	A Treasury of Plants
504.02	plantagenets	planta genesta L	the broom-plant; *emblem, thence surname of English dynasty 1154–1399*
.07	Cimmerian	Cimmerii L Kimmerioi G	1. fabulous people living in perpetual darkness; 2. ancient people of mod. Crimea
.10	stereo	stereos G	firm, solid
.11	tunc	tunc L	then
.11	tunc committed	nunc dimittis L	Now thou dost dismiss [thy Servant] (*Rheims-Vulgate Luke 2:29*); Now lettest thou [thy servant] depart (*AV Luke 2:29*)
.13	Solve	salve L	be well! hail!
.13	Solve it	solvit L	he [she, it] loosens, sets free
.16	Arber	arbor L	tree
.16	avis	avis L	bird
.16	valley	vale L	farewell!
.13–.16	Solve ... avis ... valley	Salve, Ave, Vale L	Be well; Hail; Farewell; *separate titles of volumes of George Moore's memoirs*, Hail and Farewell
.17	purpurando	purpurando L	by purpling, by making purple
.19	Tonans	Tonans L	Thunderer: *epithet of* Jupiter
.19	Tomazeus	Zeus G	"Brightness"; chief god of the Greeks, identified with Jupiter; #*A*
.19	*O dite*	O dite L audite L	O enrich! hear ye!
.20	Corcor Andy	#*P/K Split:* purpurandi L	those to be turned purple [those to be made cardinals?]

.20	*Udi*	ude L	make wet!
		audi L	hear!
.20	*Udite*	udete L	wet ye!
		audite L	hear ye!
.20	Ominence	ominosus L	full of foreboding
		omnis L	all
.24	Orania	Ouraniê G	"Heavenly": Muse of
		Urania L	Astronomy
.30	anatolies	anatolios G	rising, orient, the East
		ana G	upwards
.31	catastripes	katastrephô G	to overthrow
		katastraptô G	to hurl down lightning
		kata G	down, downwards
505.04	triliteral	triliteralis L	of three letters
.05	plantitude	*plantitudo L	plantness
		planitudo L	evenness, levelness
.07	snakedst-tu-naughsy	*allusion to* Odysseus and Nausicaa	Nausicaa encountered the naked Odysseus when she came to do her laundry by the water's edge
.07	–tu–	tu L	thou, you (*sing.*)
.07	naughsy	nausia, nautia G	seasickness
.08	sathinous	satin L	enough?
		sathê G	penis
		nous G	mind, intelligence
.12	germination	germinatio L	a budding, sprouting
		*germanitio L	being *or* becoming a brother
.12	gemination	geminatio L	a doubling
		geminus L	twin
.13	encircle him circuly	in saeculum saeculi L	in an age of an age; forever
.13	Evovae	evoe L euoi G	shout of joy at Dionysiac festivals
		vae! L	woe!
.14	exaltated	exaltatus (*pp.*) L	raised up, elevated
.14	eximious	eximius L	excepted, exempt; select, choice
.14	excelsiorising	excelsior L	higher, more lofty
.17	aviar	aviarius L	pertaining to birds
.24	Melamanessy	melam- G	black-, dark-
		melas G	black, dark
.24	mens	mens L	mind, intelligence
.32	looseaffair	lucifer L	light-bringing: the morning star

.33	fussforus	phôsphoros G	bringing light
506.03	conconundrums	con- L	with-
		quo nunc L	whither now? [*basis of dog-L "conundrum"*]
.08	bellance	bella (*pl.*) L	wars
		bella (*fem.*) L	pretty
		bellum quod res	*war*, because it would
		bella non sit L	not be *pretty* # *B*
.09	Oh Finlay's cold-palled	O felix culpa L	O happy sin; # *B*
.10	Ahday's	Haidês, Hadês G	god of the nether world; the nether world; the grave; death
		ades L	you (*sing.*) are present
.16	treefellers	trifolium L	three-leaved grass; shamrock
.18	truefalluses	trifolium L	three-leaved grass; shamrock
		phallus L *for* phallos G	image of a penis carried at Dionysiac festivals
.18	Bapsbaps	baptizô G	to plunge, dip
.26	socried	socer L	father-in-law
		socra, socrus L	mother-in-law
.28	pagany	paganus L	villager, rustic, countryman
.31	*Inter nubila numbum*	inter nubila nimbus L	among clouds a rainstorm; among clouds a splendor
.31	*numbum*	num L	not? whether not? (*expecting "No"*)
507.11	font	fons L	spring, well, fountain
.11	tubbernuckles	tabernacula (*pl.*) L	tents
.30	memoirias	memoria L	memory, recollection
.31	pater	pater L patêr G	father
.33	*qua*	qua L	in so far as
.33	arc	arcus L	bow, rainbow
508.06	Pax	pax L	peace
.06	Quantum	quantum L	as much as
.09	evoe	evoe L euoi G	shout of joy at Dionysiac festivals
.11	culious	# *L/R Interchange* culus L	curious arse
.12	*Hodie*	hodie L	today

.12	*casus*	casus L	a falling, fall, event; case (*Gram.*)
.12	*esobhrakonton*	esô G	inward
		bracae L	trousers
		brachiôn G	arm, forearm
.19	questuants	questus L	complaint, a complaining
		*questans L	complaining
.21	semidemihemispheres	semi- L	half-
		dêmi- G	people-
		hêmi- G	half-
		sphaira G	ball
		*semidêmihêmis- phairai L + G	half-people-half-balls
.22	subligate	subligatus (*pp.*) L	bound below, tied on below, tied on
.23	*mutatis mutandis*	mutatis mutandis L	things that require change [being] changed
.27	mute antes	mutandis L	things requiring to be changed
.29	sulks alusty	Gaius Sallustius Crispus (86–34 b.c.)	*Sallust*: Roman historian, of licentious private life
509.20	cocks in Gaul	galli (*pl.*) L	cocks
		Galli (*pl.*) L	1. Gauls; 2. castrated priests of Cybele
.22	haliodraping	hêliotropion G	sundial; heliotrope
.24	Liburnum	Liburnus L	god of lustful enjoyment
.30	claud	claudo L	to limp
.33	volimetangere	*voli me tangere L *based on* noli me tangere L	wish to touch me; touch me do not [wish to] touch me: *Christ to Mary Magdalen* (*John* 20:17)
.34	pantoloogions	pantologos G *pantologion G	ready to say anything place containing all words [dictionary?]
.35	perpersonal	perperus L perperos G	faulty, defective, wrong
.35	puetry	puer L pueritia L	boy, child childhood, youth
510.30	mastrodantic	*mastodontos G	"breast-toothed": mastodon

		mastros G	searcher: financial officer at Athens
.04	troppers	tropos G	turn, direction
.05	stultitiam	stultitiam (*Acc.*) L	folly, foolishness
.06	in veino	in vino L	in wine; *i.e.*, while drunk
.06	ineptias	ineptias (*Acc. pl.*) L	sillinesses, absurdities
.06	veritues	veritas L	truth, reality
		veritus (*pp.*) L	revered, feared
.05–.06	let stultitiam done in veino condone ineptias made of veritues	L?	*proverb?*
.09	Puppaps	puppa L	girl, damsel; doll
.13	Scenography	skênographia G	scene-painting; illusion
.25	Insul	insula L	island; apartment-house
.31	louties	laudes L	praises
.31	genderymen	genimen L	progeny
.33	Whiskway and mortem	[Anima mea tristis] usque ad mortem L	[My soul is sorrowful] even unto death, *Christ in Gethsemane*
.33	puseyporcious	*pusiporcus L	little pig
.34	invitem	*invitem L	unwillingly
		invicem L	alternately
.35	eleft	eleftheros MG	free
		eleutheros G	
511.04	thatseme's	sêma G	sign, mark, token; grave, tomb
		semen L	seed
.11	sesuos	se L	himself, herself, themselves
		suos L	his, her[s], its, their[s]
.13	cygncygn	cygnus L	swan
.14	cacchinic	cachinno L	to laugh aloud
.16	epexegesis	epexêgêsis G	detailed account, explanation
.17	pinnigay	pinniger L	feather-bearing, feathered, winged
.17	pretonsions	*praetonsio L	shaving in advance
.18	a pigs of cheesus	epexêgêsis G	detailed account, explanation
.22	letties	laete L	joyfully
.22	hereditate	hereditate L	by inheritance

.28	stellar	stellaris L	starry
.31	anulas	anulus L	ring
.31	crocelips	krokê G	woof; threads passed between the threads of the warp; thread
		krokos G	saffron
		lips G	the south-west wind
.33	mort	mortuus L	dead; dead person
.35	jungular	jungo L	to join together, yoke, fasten
512.02	serical	serica L	silken garments, silks
		Sericus L	Chinese
.04	allmanox	nox L	night
		alma nox L	nurturing night
.05	Megalomagellan	megalo- G	great-
.07	Crestofer	cristafer, crestafer L	crest-bearing
.07	zodisfaction	zôdion G	small figure; sign of the Zodiac
		*zôdifactio G + L	a making of little figures
.08	He came, he kished, he conquered	*part trans.* Veni, vidi, vici L	I came, I saw, I conquered; #B
.08	Vulturuvarnar	vultur, vulturus L	vulture
.10	Annabella, Lovabella, Pullabella	bella (*fem.*) L bella (*pl.*) L	pretty wars; #B
.10	Pullabella	pulla bella L *pulla bella L	gloomy wars pretty filly, pretty chick
.11	Sabina's	Sabina L	Sabine woman
.16	circumconversioning	circumconversio L	a turning all around, a revolving
.16	antelithual	ante L lithos G	before, prior to a stone
.16	paganelles	*paganillae (*pl.*) L	little country-girls
.17	energuman	energêma G	action, activity, operation
.17	caecodedition	caecus L deditio L	blind a giving up, yielding, surrender
		*caecodeditio L	a blind surrender
.17	absquelitteris	absque litteris L	without letters, contrary to letters, except letters

.21	Nautaey, nautaey	nautae (*pl.*) L	sailors, seafarers
		nautia, nausia G	seasickness
.22	arbatos	arbutus L	wild strawberry-tree
		arbor L	tree
		orbatus L	bereaved
.22	Malkos	Malchos	Carthaginian politician
		malkios G	freezing, benumbing
.27	*Primus auriforasti me*	primus	you, first, earpierced
		*auriforasti me L	me; *i.e.*, you were the first to earpierce me
.35	solarly	solaris L	pertaining to the sun
.36	canicular	canicula L	small dog; bitch
		Canicula L	*Canis Minor*; the lesser dog-star
.36	*Nascitur ordo seculi numfit*	nascitur ordo saeculi novi L	the order of the new age is born
.36	*numfit*	num fit L	it's not going to happen?
513.01	Siriusly	Sirius L Seirios G	the dog-star
.01	selenely	selênê G	moon
.01–.02	*Securius indicat umbris tellurem*	securius indicat umbris tellurem L	more securely he points out the earth to the shadows *or* by means of the shadows
		securus iudicat orbis terrarum L	untroubled, the earth judges; #*B*
.05	Amnis Dominae	amnis Dominae L	the Lady's river
		annus Domini L	the year of the Lord
.05	Marcus	Marcus L	"Hammer": Roman praenomen
.08	*Ex ugola lenonem*	ex Jugula lenonem L	out of Orion's belt a pimp
		ex ungula leonis L	out of the lion's claw
.09	Delphin's	delphin L	dolphin
		[ad usum] Delphini[s] L	[for the use] of the Dauphin: *imprint of the Delphin editions of classical texts*
.11	choreopiscopally	choreios G	pertaining to a chorus *or* choral dance
		episkopikos G	pertaining to inspection
		*choreiôpiskopikos G	pertaining to inspection of the dance *or* chorus

.16	Corumbas	#L/R Interchange	Columbas
		columba L	dove
.17	semi	semi- L	half-
.17	pantaglionic	panta- G	all-
		glion (Hesychius) G	strong
		*pantaglionikos G	all-powerful
.20	Prisky	priscus L	old, ancient, antique, olden, of yore
.20	Poppagenua	[Poppa]genua L	[Poppa]knees
.20	priamite	Priamos G	king of Troy at its fall
		*priamitês G	follower of Priam?
.21	*Oropos*	Ôrôpos G	town in Boeotia bordering on Attica
.21	*Oropos Roxy*	Oedipus Rex L *for* Oidipous Tyrannos G	Swollen-foot the Ruler: tragic king of Thebes
.22	*Pantharhea*	*pantarhea G	all-lightly, all-easily
		pantarhoia G	all-flux
.22	trippudiating	tripudio L	to leap, stamp, dance *as religious exercise*
.24	Bonum's	bonum L	a good, a blessing
.26	Trists	tristis L	sad
.26	trinies	trini L	three each
.29	quobus	quibus (*Dat.*), *Abl. pl.*) L	to, for *or* by, with, from whom
.30	*pace*	pace L	by the leave of
.35	twelvepodestalled	podes (*pl.*) G *for* pedes L	feet
514.04	In sum	insum L	I am in, I belong to
.04	some hum	summum L	1. the top, surface, highest point; 2. at the utmost, for the last time
.04	marrage	marra L	hoe
.11	Heavystost's	Hephaistos G	god of fire; identified with Vulcan; #A
.11	catacalamitumbling	kata G	down, downward
		calamus L	reed; pen
		kalamos G	
		calamitas L	loss, injury, harm
.11	Heavystost's envil catacalamitumbling	*allusion to* the fall of Hephaistos from heaven	he was thrown down by Zeus (*Iliad* I) or Hera (*Iliad* 18) and landed on Lemnos in the Aegean

.12	Vulcuum	Vulcanus L	god of fire; identified with Hephaistos; #A
		vacuum L	empty space, void
.14	Noe et Ecclesiastes, nonne?	Noe et Ecclesiastes, nonne L	Noah and Ecclesiastes, isn't it?
.14	Ecclesiastes	Ekklêsiastês G	member of a congregation
.17	acquinntence	quinque L	five
.20	*etcaetera etcaeterorum*	et caetera et caeterorum L	and the others and the others'; and the rest and the rest's
		in saecula saeculorum L	in ages of ages; forever
.22	Hora	Hora L	"Lady": goddess, wife of Romulus
		hora L	an hour, time
.22	pro	pro L	for
.22	Nubis	nubis L	a cloud
.22	Hora pro Nubis	ora pro nobis L	pray for us
.23	Deimetuus	*Deimetuus L	fearer of God
.23	D'amn	amnis L	river
.25	Auspice	auspicium L	divination by bird-flights
.34	ars	ars L	art
515.01	culping	culpa L	fault, sin
.03	Clam	clam L	secretly, privately
.04	periwhelker	peri G	around, about
.08	Sangnifying	*sanguinificatio L	a blood-making
.09	*Fortitudo eius rhodammum tenuit*	fortitudo ejus Rhodanum tenuit L	his bravery has held the Rhone
		Fortitudo Ejus Rhodum Tenuit L	his strength has held Rhodes; #B
.11	euphonise	*euphônizô G	to make to have a good voice
.11	an isochronism	*anisochronism-os G	unequal periodicity, non-simultaneity
.11	isochronism	*isochronismos G	equal periodicity; contemporaneousness
.14	*ultra vires*	ultra vires L	beyond the powers, outside the authority
.16	blepharospasmockical	blepharon G	eyelid

		spasmôdês G	convulsive
		*blepharospasm-	eyelid-cramps
		ôdês G	
.24	homer's	Homêros G	epic poet
.25	massacreedoed	credo L	I believe
.36	Bones Minor	bonum minus L	a lesser good
.36	chairful	chairô G	to rejoice
516.12	fex	fex, faex L	grounds, sediment, lees
		-fex L	-maker
.12	Miles	miles L	soldier
.15	pyre	pyr G	fire
.20	coaccoackey	koax koax G	croaking of frogs
.24	faketotem	factotum ML	do-all: handyman, man of all work
.24	plantagonist	planta genista ML	broom-sprig: emblem, thence surname of English dynasty
		*plantagônistês L + G	sole-of-the-foot contender, off-shoot contender [Jacob?]
.28	pupparing	puppa L	girl, damsel; doll
.29	compuss memphis	compos mentis L	in control of the mind
.29	memphis	Memphis	city in ancient Egypt
.31	sarsencruxer	crux L	cross, gallows
.32–.33	annusual curse	annuus cursus L	the course of the year, yearly course
.35	celicolar	caelicola L	inhabitant of heaven
.35	finister	finis L	limit, boundary, end
517.02	auradrama	aura L	breeze
.05	angerus	#L/R interchange	angelus
		angelus L	messenger; angel
		angelos G	
.06	medicis	medicus L	physician
.21	Asbestos	asbestos G	unquenchable, inextinguishable, ceaseless; unslaked lime
.26	querqcut	quercus L	oak-tree
.32	rosing	ros L	dew
.35	triduum	triduum L	space of three days, three days
.36	chronos	chronos G	time
518.02	Marses	Mars L	god of war; #A
		Marsi L	people of Latium hostile to Rome

.02	ambiviolent	ambi- L	around-, round about
.04	diabolically	diabolikôs G	slanderously
		diaballomai G	to be at variance with
.05	*pro*	pro L	for
.05	*con*	con[tra] L	against
.07	Milesian	Milesiae [fabulae] L	Milesian tales: dirty stories
.07	Milesian winds	etesiae L etêsiai G	Etesian winds: the trade winds
.15	alias	alias L	otherwise
.19	berebelling	rebello L	to wage war again, to renew war
.21	mere	merum L	pure, unmixed wine
.21	woiney	[w]oinos G # *Digamma*	wine
.22	Scutticules	*scuticula L	little lash, little whip
		Scoticuli (*pl.*) L	little Scots [from Scotia Minor?]
.22	caractacurs	Cara[c]tacus L	British leader against Romans
		Caracalla [?] Celt. *nickname of* Marcus Aurelius Antoninus (176–217)	"Hood": emperor 211–217; murdered his brother and co-emperor; was assassinated
.23	Danos	Danos (*Acc. pl.*) L	the Danes
		Danaos (*Acc. pl.*) G L	the Greëks
.24–.25	Limba romena in Bucclis tucsada	lingua Romana in bucca Tuscana L	"a Roman tongue in an Etruscan [L]/ a Tuscan [ML] mouth": *Dante's formula for literary Italian* (lingua Romana in bocca Toscana [It.]): *Roman grammar, Florentine pronunciation*
.25	Farcing gutterish	Vercingetorix Celt.	"Overwarriorking": Gaulish leader against Caesar
.27	in Feeney's	in fine L	in the end, as far as
.27	Feeney's	finis L	limit, boundary, end
.28	barbarihams	barbari L barbaroi G	foreigners neither Roman nor Greek

.31	In voina viritas	in vino veritas L	in wine [there is] truth
		in [*voina*] virilitas L	in *voina* ["war" *Russ.*][there is] manliness
.31	Ab chaos lex	ab chao lex L	from chaos [comes] legislation
.33	bella	bella (*pl.*) L	wars
		bella (*fem.*) L	pretty, nice
.33	pia	pia (*fem.*) L	dutiful, pious
.33	pura	pura (*fem.*) L	clean, pure
.33	O bella! O pia! O pura!	O bella! O pia! O pura! eccl. L	O fair! O dutiful! O pure! *quasi* hymn to e.g. BVM
		O bella pia pura L	O pious and pure wars!
		bella pia et pura L	pious and pure wars: Vico's idea; #B
.34	Balbus	Balbus L	"Stuttering": Roman cognomen
.36	christmians	chrisma G	anointing, unction; spiritual grace
		Isthmia G	games at Isthmus of Corinth
519.01	neuropeans	neuro- G	sinew-, nerve-
.02	vigil	vigil L	awake, alert, on the watch
.03–.04	concoon and proprey	communis et propria L	public and private
.07	fortey and more fortey	forte L	by chance
		*forte L *for* fortiter L	bravely, strongly (*common schoolboy error*)
.08	Lludillongi	ludi longi L	long games
.15	fere	fere L	nearly, almost; quite, entirely
.19	thathens	Athênai G	Athens
.19	tharctic	arktikos G	near the Bear (*constellation*): far northern
.33	Aunt Tarty	antarktikos G antartês G	opposite to far northern tyrant, rebel against a king
.33	Villa	villa L	farmhouse, country estate
520.15	albs	albus L	white

.21	Foueh	fui L	I was, I have been
		pheu G	alas! oh!
.24	octo	octo L	eight
.27	ar	ar G	*interrogative particle*
.28	fyats	fiat L	let there be
.33	holyhagionous	hagios G	holy
		nous G	mind, intelligence
.34	rubricated	rubricatus (*pp.*)	colored red
		L	
.36	labrose	labrosus L	with large lips
521.04	potators	potator L	drinker, toper
.06	Lucan	M. Annaeus	poet; #*A*
		Lucanus L	
.10–.11	*Pro tanto quid*	pro tanto quid	for so much what shall
	retribuamus?	retribuamus L	we repay?
.11	scotty pictail	Scotia Picta L	Painted Scotland,
			Pictish Scotland
.22	tristy	tristis L	sad
.32	Emania	Emania ML	Eamhain [Macha];
			ancient capital of Ulster
			[*see* Gaelic Lexicon]
		emaneo L	to overstay a furlough
		emano L	to flow out
522.07	melanodactylism	melas G	black, dark
		daktylos G	finger
		*melanodaktylis-	blackfingerism,
		mos G	blackfingering
.17	sylvan	silva L	wood, woodland
.19	silver	*see 522.17 E*	
.30	catheis	katheis G	one by one, one after
			another
		kathiêmi G	to let down, to drop
.31	expert	expertus (*pp.*) L	known by experience
.31	steatopygic	*steatopygikos	having a fat rump
		G	
.32	psychoanolised	*psychoanalysis	loosening-up of the
		G	spirit
		ano L	to, for *or* by means of
			the anus
		nolis L	may you/you may be
			unwilling
.33	nursis	nurus L	daughter-in-law
.33	symaphy	synapheia,	connection, union
		synaphê G	
523.11	mufto	*mufto (Abl.)*	by a civilian *clothe
		fake-L	

		from*muftus, *pl.*	civilian *clothe, *pl.*
		*mufti fake-L	civilian clothes, mufti
.17	vites	vites L	vines, grapevines
.19–.20	The Mod needs a rebus	est modus in rebus L—Horat. *Sat.* I .i.106	there is a moderation in things—Horace, *Satires* I .i.106
.21	Pro	pro L	for
.26	Doddercan Easehouse	Dôdeka Nêsoi G	Twelve Islands: Dodecanese
.27	hosty	hostis L; Hostius Quadra	stranger, foreigner, enemy; #*A*
.33	fict	fictum L	deception, falsehood
.34	epscene	epikoinos G	common to many, promiscuous; of common gender
		obscene L	impurely, indecently, lewdly
524.12	bisectualism	*bisectilis L	divided in two
.15	*Quis ut Deus*	quis ut Deus L	who like God, who like unto God
.20	cunifarm	cuni- L	shit-, dung-
		*cuneiformus L	wedge-shaped
		*cunniformus L	cunt-shaped
.20	supernatently	*supernatans *for* supernans L	swimming above
		nates L	buttocks
.30	Zeus	Zeus G	"Brightness": chief G god; #*A*
.30	olfac	olfactus L	smell
		alpha G	letter A
.31	supperfishies	superficies L	the upper side, top, surface
.31	lamme	lambda G	letter L
.31	scaligerance	*scaligerans L Joseph Justus Scaliger, Julius Caesar Scaliger	being a ladder-carrier classical scholars
.31	pesk	peskos G	skin, rind, hide
		piscis L	fish
		pi G	letter P
.32	flossity	flos L	blossom, flower
		[non] flocci [facio] L	I don't care a straw [*idiom*]
.32	pectoralium	pectoralis L	pertaining to the breast *or* chest

.33	apodictic	apodeiktikos G	affording proof, demonstrative; explained; exact, scientific
.33	briam	bria L	wine-vessel
		Priamos G	king of Troy at its fall
.36	bisectualism	see 524.12 E	
525.02	crux	crux L	cross, gallows
.02	tillicately	tilia L	linden, lime-tree
		tiliaceus L	of linden-wood
.04	testificates	testificatio L	bearing witness, giving testimony
		testis L	1. witness; 2. testicle
		*testificatio L	making a testicle
.04	sugjugation	sub- L	under-
		becomes sug- *before* g-, *as in* sub+gero=	
		suggero L; *since*	to suggest, etc.
		g- *Eng* = j-*Eng*, sub+jugatio *is made*	a bringing under the yoke
		*sugjugatio fake-L	
.05	cungunitals	cunnus L	cunt
		gunê G	woman
.06	coprulation	kopros G	excrement
.07	Pelagiarist	Pelagius L *for*	*Morgan*, "Sea-born":
		Pelagios G	denied original sin; *see* 182.03
.08	absexed	ab L	away from
		*absectus (*pp.*) L	cut away
.08	mackerglosia	makar G	blessed, happy
		*makaraglôssia G	state of having a blessed tongue
		*makroglôssia G	state of having a big tongue
.08	mickroocyphyllicks	mikros G	small
		ôkys G	swift
		kephalos G	head
		phyllikos G	of a leaf, leaf-like
		*mikrokephalik-os G	having a small head
		*mikrookyphylli-kos G	having small, swift leaves

.10	eggoarchicism	*egôarchikismos G	doctrine of putting the self first
.12	*esox*	esox L	fish of the Rhine: kind of pike
		isox G	a fish, *possibly* salmon
.12	*lucius*	lucius L	the pike
.12	*salmo*	salmo L	salmon
.12	*ferax*	ferax L	fertile, prolific
		ferox L	wild, fierce
.14	Lalia	lalia (*fem.*) G	talkative, babbling
.14	Lelia	Laelia L	Crassus' mother-in-law; *see 340.22*
.14	Lilia	lilia (*pl.*) L	lilies
.14	Lulia	luela L	expiation, punishment
.15	Gubbernathor	gubernator L	steersman, pilot; director, ruler
.16	ova	ova (*pl.*) L	eggs
.17	monach	monachos G	unique, solitary; a monk
.19	Hosty	hostis L	stranger, foreigner, enemy
		Hostius L	epic poet, 2d C b.c.
		Hostius Quadra L	voyeur and lecher; # *A*
.20	*Magnam Carpam*	magnam *carp*-am (*Acc.*) L	the great *carp* [Eng. word]
		Magna Charta L	The Great Letter: *Magna Carta*
		magnam *carptam (*fem. Acc.*) L	the great plucked, gathered, enjoyed
.20	*Carpam*	karpos G	1. fruit; 2. wrist
.31	cumule	cumulus L	heap, pile
.32	Manu	manu (*Abl.*) L	by hand
.33	Romunculus	homunculus L	little weak man, manikin
		*Romunculus L	little weak Romulus
		Romulus Augustulus L	last emperor (475–476) of Rome
		ranunculus L	little frog, tadpole
.34	Remus	Remus L	brother of Romulus; # *A*
526.11	anglers or angelers	non sunt Angli sed angeli L	they are not Angles but angels—*Pope Gregory I upon seeing Anglo-Saxon slaves on sale in Rome*

.12	*tertium quid*	tertium quid L	a third something
.18	patmost	Patmos G	island in Aegean used by Romans for banishment; *John the Divine wrote Revelation there*
.18	unpackyoulloups	apokalypsis G	uncovering, discovery, revelation; G title of John's Revelation
.23	glans	glans L	acorn; glans penis (top of the penis)
.23	Stilla	stilla L	drop
		stella L	star
.25	superflowvius	superfluus L	running over, overflowing
.30	Tarpeyan	Mons Tarpeius L	Tarpeian Rock
.30	Vesta	Vesta L	goddess of flocks and herds
.30	Tully	Tullius L	name of a Roman gens
		M. Tullius Cicero L	orator
		Servius Tullius L	sixth king of Rome
.32	salices	salices (*pl.*) L	willows, willow-trees
.33	playactrix	actrix L	woman who does *or* performs something
.34	add shielsome	ad sum L	I am present
.34	Nircississies	Narcissus L	youth who loved himself
.35	Secilas	salices (*backwards*) L	willows, willow-trees
		saecula L	ages, centuries
		Caecilia L	patroness of music
527.01	Gotellus	tellus L	earth, dry land; the planet Earth
.05	viry	vir L	man, male person
.12	Eulogia	eulogia G	fine language; plausibility; praise; blessing
.16–.17	vickyvicky veritiny	veni vidi vici L	I came, I saw, I conquered; #*B*
.22	conavent	conamen L	effort, struggle
.23	ethernal	aether L aithêr G	air, pure air; the fifth element

		aeternalis L	enduring forever
.26	D.V.	D[eo] V[olente] L	God willing
.26	colombinas	columba L	dove, pigeon
.31	labs	labia (*pl.*) L	lips
.33	picious	piceus L	of pitch; pitch-black
.34	futuous	futuo L	to fuck
		fututus (*pp.*) L	fucked
528.01	novene	novenus L	nine each
		novennis L	nine-year-old
.03	Clothea	Clotho L	"Spinster, Weaver":
		Klôthô G	one of the three Moirai, the Fates
		thea G	goddess
.06	Audiens	audiens L	hearer, auditor; pupil
.08	Blesius	blaesus L	lisping, stammering
		blaisos G	
.08–.09	Kyrielle elation! Crystal elation! Kyrielle elation!	Kyriê eleêsôn, Christê eleêsôn, Kyriê eleêsôn G	Lord have mercy, Christ have mercy, Lord have mercy
.09–.10	Sing to us, sing to us, sing to us	sanctus sanctus sanctus L	holy holy holy
.11	hister	# *G-to-L*	sister
		hister Etr	stage-player, actor
		Hister L	lower Danube
.14	Eusapia	eusebeia G	reverence, piety
		*eusophia G	good-wisdom
		*eusapia G + L	
.23	liryc and themodius	Cyril and Methodius	apostles to the Slavs
.23	iris	Iris G L	goddess of the rainbow; the rainbow
.23	vals	valles L	valley
.24	euphemiasly	euphêmia G	use of words of good omen; abstinence from inauspicious language; religious silence; praise, worship, honor, good repute
.24	ambidual	ambidualis L	around about two
.26	tether, a loguy O	[hoi] tettara logioi G	the four narrators (evangelists?)
		tetralogia G	group of four (plays, dialogues, etc.) tetralogy

529.04	pro mile	Pro Milone L	"On Behalf of Milo": defence speech delivered by Cicero 52 b.c.
.07	uniformication	formica L	ant
.16	ex	ex L	out of
.25	V.D.	V[icarius] D[ei] L	Vicar of God
.34	Ptolomei	Ptolemaios G	"Warlike": Macedonian dynasty of Egypt; # A
530.05	*certiorari*	certiorari LL	"to be made certain": legal writ requesting the record of a case
.10	surdumutual	surdus L	deaf
		mutus L	dumb
		*mutualis ML	mutual
.10	litterydistributor	litterae L	a letter
.11	chayr	cheir G	hand
		chaire G	hail!
.16	paroply	paroplizô G	to disarm
		*paroplia G	state of being disarmed
		modeled on	
		panoplia G	full suit of arms and armor
.16	Heliopolitan	Hêliopolitês G	citizen of Heliopolis
		Heliopolitanus L	
		Hêliopolis G	Sun-City: city in Lower Egypt; *also* city in Syria
.18	auxiliar	auxiliarius L	allied soldier, ally
.18	arianautic	Aria G L	Persian province
		nautikos G	seafaring, naval
.21	magnon	magnus L	big, great
		non L	not
.24	*orchid*	orchis G	testicle
.25	orchid	*see 530.24 I*	
.33	Mandame	mandare (*infinitive*) L	to commit to one's charge, to commission
		mandamus L	"we command": writ from a higher to a lower court
.33	succuba	succuba L	1. one who lies under: lecher, strumpet; 2. supplanter, rival

		succubus ML	female demon who has sexual intercourse with sleeping men
.36	farternoiser	pater noster L	our father
531.01	gibbous	gibbus L	hump
.03	Pave Pannem	#P/K Split:	
		Cave Canem L	Beware the Dog
.03	Pannem	panem (Acc.) L	bread
		pannum L	cloth, garment, rag
.05	dilltoyds	*deltoeidês G, recte	in the shape of the letter *delta*,
		deltôtos G	triangular
.11	noas	Noa L	Noah
		noas (Acc. pl.) G	minds, wits
		Naso L	"Large-nosed": Roman family name; *esp.* P. Ovidius Naso; #A
.15	Katty	kathairô G	to cleanse
.19	gause	gaude L	rejoice!
		gausapa L	a shaggy woolen cloth
.19	meter	mêtêr G	mother
.21	pantamine	panta- G	all-
		pantomimos G	imitating all, acting[-out] everything
.24	quamquam	quamquam L	though, although, albeit
.24	potapot	potapos, podapos G	whence? of what sort?
		#P/K Split:	
		quotquot L	how many soever
.25	panapan	pan, pana- G	all, all-
.25	kickakickkack	brekekekex G	croaking of Aristophanes' *Frogs*
.29	sylph	sylphes Mod L for	soulless being inhabiting the air
		silvestris nympha L	wood-nymph
.30	tritons	Tritôn G L	sea-god, son of Neptune
.33	primapatriock	primipatriarches L [+G]	first patriarch, first father
.33	archsee	arch[i]- G	chief
.34	Trancenania	trans L	across
		cena L	dinner
		kenangia G	hunger

532.01	eirenarch's	eirênarchês, eirênarchos G	"peace-ruler": a police magistrate (justice of the peace)
.01	custos	custos L	guard, keeper, protector, attendant
.01	eirenarch's custos	*trans.* Gárda Síochána Gael.	"Guard of the Peace": Irish national policeman
.01	meg of megs	megas G	big
.06	Eternist cittas	Civitas aeterna L	the eternal City: Rome
.09	MacAuscullpth	ausculto L	to hear, to listen
.09	pontofacts massimust	pontifex maximus L	"greatest bridgemaker": chief Roman high-priest
.11	Augustanus	Augustanus L	pertaining to Augustus; imperial; Roman knight appointed by Nero
.12	Ergastulus	ergastulus LL	foreman in a workhouse
.15	fict	fictum L	deception
.18	verawife	verax L	true
.31	Floss Mundai	flos mundi LL	the flower of the world
.31	Mundai	Munda L	Caesar's last battle; #A
533.02	heliotrope	hêliotropos G	sundial
.17	Mellos	mellosus L melos G	honey-like tune, air, song
.17	euphonium	euphônia G	goodness of voice; excellence of tone
.21	Johannes	Johannes L	John
.24	Katakasm	katachêsis G katakassa, kasalbas G	flouting, mockery strumpet
.28	parruchially	paroikos G	dwelling near, neighboring
.30	phoney	phônê G	noise, sound, voice, speech
.31	clairaudience	clara audientia L	clear hearing
.33	Hiemlancollin	hiems L collis L	winter hill
534.02	Abbreciades	ab L	away from
.11	contango	*contango L	to bring into contact, to touch; to contaminate
.12	Pynix	Punicus, Poenicus L	Punic, Carthaginian

		Phoenix L	fabulous bird; *see*
		Phoinix G	*265.08*
		Pnyx G	low hill at Athens, meeting-place of the Assembly
.16	caveat	caveat L	let him beware
.20	cunvesser	cunio L	to shit
		cunnus L	cunt
.21	Noceletters	noceo L	to harm, injure
.26	caca	caco L	to go to stool
.34	Eristocras	eristês G	wrangler, arguer
		eristos G	that may be contested, contestable
		cras L	tomorrow
535.03	immitiate	immitis L	harsh, stern
.03	chry	chreia G	need
		chrysos G	gold
.03	urs	ursus L	he-bear
.04	Sexencentaurnary	sex L	six
		centaurus L	wild people of Thessaly who fought on horseback; mythological creatures part-horse, part-man
		kentauros G	
.06	Majuscules	majusculus L	somewhat larger; somewhat great
.07	Magnus	Magnus L	the Great
.07	Maggerstic	magister L	master, leader, head
.08	Nova Tara	Nova *Tara L	New Tara
.09–.10	oar . . . fanned	*allusion to* Odysseus	required to go inland so far his oar would be mistaken for a threshing-fan
.12	ecclesency	ekklêsis G	appeal, challenge
.18	hystry	hystera G	womb
		hysterêsis G	shortcoming, deficiency
.20	porcupig's	porcus L	pig
.25	fish for Christ's	ichthys G	fish
		I[êsous] CH[ristos] TH[eou] [h]Y[ios] S[ôtêr] G	Jesus Christ God's Son Savior
.29	profundust	profundus L	deep, vast, profound
.33	freeandies	friandis L	by means of things to be crumbled into small pieces

.33	celeberrimates	celeberrimus L	most frequented, most honored, most celebrated
536.01	Sebastion	Sebasteion G	temple of *Sebastos* (*Augustus*)
.05	psychous	psychos G	cold
		ous G	ear
		psychê G	life, soul
.08	Felix	felix L	happy, lucky, blessed
.08–.09	Felix Culapert	felix culpa L	happy sin; #*B*
.09	Culapert	culus apertus L	open arse
.11	eleathury ...	eleatros G	steward, seneschal
	eleathury	eleaô G	to have pity, to show mercy
		thus, thuris L	incense
		eleutheria G	freedom
.13	achershous	Acherôn G	"Stream of woe": river of the netherworld
.16	puertos mugnum	porta magna L	great gate
		portus magnus L	great port
.18	vestas	Vesta L	goddess of flocks and the hearth.
.19	nephos	nephos G	cloud, mass of clouds
		nepos L	grandson
.19	neberls	nebula L	mist, vapor, fog, smoke
.31	Skivinis	skeuê G skivi MG	apparel, equipment, attire, fashion
.33	jurats	jurat L	he swears
.36	leuther	eleutheria G	freedom
537.05	miscisprinks	misceo L	to mix, mingle
.06	umbracing	umbra L	shade, shadow
.10	*viktrae*	victoriae (*Dat.*) L	to victory
.17	*in toto*	in toto L	in all, as a whole
.18	confoederated	confoederatus (*pp.*) L	united by a league
.18	prebellic	*praebellicus L	pertaining to before the war
.21	locum	locum (*Acc.*) L	place, spot
.23	byusucapiture	usucapione (*Abl.*) L	by usucaption, by acquiring ownership through long use
.26	Deuterogamy	*deuterogamia G	second marriage

.36	erithmatic	eritheumai G	to work for hire; to canvass for office; to compete with; to indulge in petty intrigue
538.01	Juno Moneta	Juno Moneta L	Juno the Reminder, in whose temple at Rome money was coined
.03	Salvatorious	*Salvatorius L	pertaining to the Savior
.05	angars	angarius L	messenger, courier
		angaria L	service, service to a lord
.07	ochtroyed	ochos G	carriage, chariot
.08	melkkaart	Melkart	a Carthaginian god
.10	honnibel	Hannibal	Carthaginian general
.11	orgias	orgia G	secret rites, secret worship; sacrifices, mysteries
.12	cartage	Carthago L *for* Kart-Hadasht Punic	New-Town: Phoenician city in North Africa, Rome's chief rival until its destruction 146 b.c.
.12	improperable	*improperabilis L	1. hastenable; 2. delayable; 3. reproachable
.13	Crusos	chrusos G	gold
.14	panis	panis L	loaf, bread
.15	testey	testis L	1. witness; 2. testicle
.16	ecus	acus L	needle, pin
.18	surdity	surditas L	deafness
.23	hespermun	hesperos G hesperus L	evening; the evening star
		sperma G	seed, semen, sperm
.26	Ous	ous G	ear
.29	Deucollion	Deucalion L Deukaliôn G	the classical Noah; #A
.30	Deucollion	*see 538.29 D*	
.33	ekeascent	ekêa G	I was burning
.33	Deucollion	*see 538.29 D*	
.36	Pelagios	Pelagios	"Of the Sea": Irish heretic
539.03	erectheion	Erechtheion G	Temple of *Erechtheus* ["Breaker," fabulous king] at Athens
.11	perplagued	*perplagatus L	1. thoroughly struck, thoroughly whipped; 2. thoroughly netted, thoroughly tangled

.23	soccage	soccus L	slipper, sock
.25	Serbonian bog	*trans.* Serbônis limnê G	lake *or* bog in Egypt *supposed to have swallowed up whole armies*
.26	talus	talus L	ankle, heel; die, knucklebone
.28	that year which I have called myriabellous	*part trans.* Annus Mirabilis L	The Year of Wonders (1665–1666): poem by Dryden
.29	myriabellous	myrias G bellum, *pl.* bella L	ten thousand war
.33	tenenure	tenens L uro L	holding to burn
.36	oppedemics	oppidum L dêmos G	town district, country, land
540.01	compolitely	com- L politikôs G	with- civilly, courteously
.06	delited	delitus (*pp.*) L	1. obliterated; 2. besmeared
.07	Ptolemy	Claudius Ptolemaeus	geographer who first put Dublin on the map; #*A*
.07	Libnia	Eblana G	Dublin
.07	Labia	labia (*pl.*) L	lips
.13	Pro	pro L	for
.13	clam	clam L	secretly, in private
.14	Ubipop	ubi L	where
.14	ibipep	ibi L	there
.17	Estoesto!	esto; esto L	thou shalt be!; he shall be!
.17	Estote	estote L	you (*pl.*) shall be!
.17	sunto!	sunto L	they shall be!
.17	Estoesto! Estote sunto!	esto, esto, estote, sunto L	*full paradigm of Future Imperative of* sum, "*I am*"
.18	capt	caput L	head
.18	in altitude	in altitudine L	on high
.23	quaysirs	Caesar L	Roman name become a title; #*A*
.25–.26	Obeyance from the townsmen spills felixity by the toun	Obedientia civium urbis felicitas L	Dublin's motto; #*B*
.33	esculapuloids	Asklêpidês G	"son of *Asklêpios* (*physician in* Iliad; *god of healing*)": physician

		Asklêpiadeios G	physician of the school of *Asklêpios*
.34	waldy bonums	valde bonum L	exceedingly good
.36	skivs	skeuês G skivis MG	apparel, equipment
541.01	seven ills	*allusion to* Rome	*see below* 541.02-.04
.02	inkeptive	inceptus L	1. (*pp.*) begun; 2. beginning
.02-.04	Braid Blackfordrock, the Calton, the Liberton, Craig and Lockhart's, A. Costofino, R. Thursett	Aventinus, Caelius, Capitolium, Esquiliae, Palatium, Quirinalis, Viminalis L	seven hills of Rome (*except for the number, the correspondences, if real, elude us*)
.09	murage	*muratia L	condition of being surrounded *or* defended by walls
.11	percussors	percussor L	one who hits, a murderer
.16	Luc	lux, lucis L	light
.16	Leonden	leôn G	lion
.24	plumbate	plumbatus L	leaden, made of lead
.25	acorpolous	akropolis G	upper city, citadel, castle
.27	unoculated	*inoculatus L unoculus L	eyeless, unseeing one-eyed [*cf.* Cyclops]
.28	ad liptum	ad libitum L	at pleasure, as one wills
.32	belluas	belua L	monster, huge wild beast
.32	tendulcis	dulcis L	sweet
.36	tuberclerosies	tuberculum L tuber L klêros G	little swelling *or* bump 1. kind of mushroom; 2. kind of apple-tree allotment
542.02	pletoras	pletura L	fulness; excess of blood
.08	kommeandine	commeandi (*Gen.*) L	of coming and going
.09	fontaneously	fontanus L	pertaining to a spring *or* well
.12	obtemperate	obtemperate L	attend! obey! (*pl.*)
.14	tot the ites	toties L totietas LL	so often, so many times entirely
.16	Janus's	Janus L	god of beginnings

.16	syndic	syndikos G	lawyer, advocate
.17	podestril	*podestris G+L for pedester, pedestris L	on foot; prosaic
.18	Forum	forum L	public place, marketplace
.18	demosthrenated	dêmos G	country, province
		thrêneô G	to lament, bewail
.18	pupuls	pupulus L	little boy
.19	Sapphrageta	Sapphô G	Lesbian poetess
		suffragatio L	voting for someone
		Geta, Lucius Septimius L	brother and co-emperor with Caracalla, by whom he was killed
		Geta, Hosidius L	poetaster
.20	Consciencia	conscientia L	joint knowledge, knowledge along with others, privity
.21	auntiparthenopes	Parthenôpeia G	"Maidenly aspect": 1. a Siren; 2. Naples
		*antiparthenôp-ês G	one opposed to maidenly aspect; one hostile to Naples
.23	rogated	rogo L	to ask, question
		rogatus L	request, entreaty
.28	rotundaties	rotunditas L	roundness
.29	raped lutetias	allusion to rape of Lucretia L	immediate cause of expulsion of the Roman kings; see 277.F2
.29	lutetias	Lutetia L	city in Gaul; mod. Paris
.29–.30	bax of biscums	pax vobiscum L	peace [be] with you
.33	farinadays	farina L	flour
.35	amnibushes	amnis L	river
543.01	megalopolitan	megalopolitês G	citizen of a large city
.06	reciping	recipiens L	taking back, getting back, getting back, bringing back; regaining
.06	omominous	omômi G	Persian plant used in offerings to Ahriman; identified with môly
		nous G	mind, intelligence
.10	bi	bi- L	two-
.10	palastered	palaistra G	wrestling-school,
		palaestra L	gymnasium; rhetorical exercise; school

.16	Ostmanorum	Ostmanorum (*Gen. pl.*) L	of the Ostmans (Turks'); of the Ostmen (Vikings')
.17	*recte*	recte L	1. in a straight line; 2. correctly
.19	Saltus	saltus L	1. leap, spring, bound; 2. forest-pasture, woodland; mountain-valley; female pudenda
.30	quasi	quasi L	as if, just as, as it were
544.24	Leo	Leo L	Lion: name of 13 popes; Leo XII (1823–1829), Leo XIII (1878–1903)
545.10	amblyopia	amblyôpia G	dim-sightedness
.12	orable	*orabilis L	arguable, prayable
.12	amission	amissio L	loss
.23	Enwreak us wrecks	[H]enricus Rex L	King Henry
.24	milles on milles	mille L	thousand
.25	mancipelles	mancipium L	formal possession
.28–.29	parciful of my subject ... I debelledem superb	parcere subiectis, et debellare superbos—*Aen.* VI 853 L	to be sparing of inferiors, and to vanquish the arrogant: *Rome's imperial mission, Vergil*, Aeneid *VI . 853*
.33	revolucanized	volucer L	flying, winged
		M. Annaeus Lucanus L	Roman poet; #*A*
546.01	obstain	*obstineo L *modeled on* abstineo L	to hold for, to keep in front of / to keep away, to hold off
.02	lento	lento L	I make flexible, I bend
.02	*Quo warranto*	quo warranto ML	by what warrant (*Law*)
.04	nomen	nomen L	1. name; 2. middle of three names borne by freeborn Romans
		Nemo L	Nobody: name Ulixes gave himself; #*A*
.05	genteelician	gentilicius L	pertaining to a particular clan *or* gens

.04–.05	nomen . . . genteelician	nomen gentilicum L	middle of three names born by a freeborn Roman, signifying his gens
.07	coleopter	koleopteros G	"sheath-winged": beetle
.07	pondant	ponderans L	weighty, heavy
.08	sinister	sinister L	on the left
.10	embusked	emboskomai G	to feed on
.10	sinople	*Sinopolis L+G	Bay-city
		Sinôpê G	1. G colony on the Black Sea, *mod.* Sinop; 2. name of a courtesan
.10	*Hery*	heri L	yesterday
.10	*Crass*	cras L	tomorrow
.11	*Evohodie*	evoe L	shout of joy at Bacchic festivals
		hodie L	today
.13	holocryptogam	*holokryptogamos G	completely secret marriage
.16	pritticoaxes	praecox L	ripe before time, premature
.17	trine	trini L	three each, three
.19	virtus	virtus L	manliness, strength, vigor, virtue
.22	reclam	reclamo L	to cry out against, contradict loudly
		clam L	secretly, in private
.23	hek	hic, haec L	this, this here (*masc.*, *fem.*)
.25	numb?	num L	*interrogative particle anticipating negative reply*
.26	numb	*see 546.25 D*	
.29	Televox	têle- G	afar, at a distance
		vox L	voice
.30	Fulvia	Fulvial	"Blonde": *name of, e.g., wife successively of P. Clodius, C. Curio and Mark Antony*
.35	Fluvia	fluvia L	river
547.05	Fulvia Fluvia	fulvia fluvia L	blonde river
.08	undines	undina Mod L	wave-spirit
		unda L	wave, billow
.16	flumingworthily	flumen L	flood, stream, river

.22	taillas	talis L	such, of such a kind, such like
.22	quailless	qualis L	of what sort, what kind of, the like of which
.23	Highjakes	Ajax L Aias G	G. hero at Troy
.22–.23	taillas Cowhowling quailless Highjakes	talis [Cúchulainn] qualis Ajax L	Cúchulainn [is] of the same sort as Ajax
.23	tridont	triodous, triodontos G	with three teeth, three-pronged
.24	polyfizzyboisterous	polyphloisbos G	loud-roaring: *Homeric epithet of the seas.*
.25	os	os L	1. mouth; 2. bone
.26	stamoror	sta- *root of* sto L	to stand
		moror L	to delay, tarry, stay
.29	Heydays	Haidês, Hadês G	god of the lower world; the nether world; place of departed spirits; the grave, death
.30	blissforhers	Bosphoros G	"Heifer's Ford": strait at Istanbul; #*A*
.32	Galata! Galata!	Galata L	a Galatian: Celt of Asia Minor
		Galateia G	"Milk-white": a sea-nymph
		Thalatta! Thalatta!	Sea! Sea!:*cry of Xenophon's men*; #*B*
.33	iern	Ierne L	Ireland
.34	iday	hodie L	today
548.01	hoks	hoc (*neut.*) L	this, this thing here
.01	zivios	vios MG bios G	life
.01	vives	vives L	you (*sing.*) will live
.02	Impress	Imperatrix L	Empress
.02	pairanymphs	paranymphos G	best man; bridesmaid
.06	Appia	Appia [Via] L	the Appian Way; road south from Rome
		Appia [aqua] L	aquaduct built by Appius Claudius Caecus; terminated at temple of Venus
.06	Lippia	lippa (*fem.*) L	bleary-eyed
.06	Pluviabilla	pluvia L	rain; rainwater
		*pluviabilis L	able to rain, prone to rain

.10	pisoved	ovum L	egg
.16	constantonoble's	Konstantinou polis G	Constantine's city: *Byzantium after* a.d. *330*
.17	vermincelly	vermiculi (*pl.*) L	little worms; grubs, maggots
.21	*passim*	passim L	here and there, now and then, at random
.27	loomends	lumen L	light
.28	*Pyrrha*	Pyrrha G	"Red": Deucalion's wife; #*A*
.28	*Pyrrhine*	pyrrias G	redhead
		pyrinos G	1. fiery; 2. wheaten, of wheat
.30	tortuours	tortuosus L	crooked, winding
		turtur L	turtledove
.35	oloss	olor L	swan
549.01	Cunnig's	cunnus L	cunt
.03	quintacasas	quinta casa L	the fifth cottage
.07	pacis	pacis (*Gen.*) L	of peace
.09	septuor	septem L	seven
		quattuor L	four
.13	lunas	luna L	the moon
.14	*coloumba mea, frimosa mea*	columba mea, formosa mea L	my dove, my beautiful one (*Vulgate, Canticum Canticorum 2:10*)
.15	strate	strata L	paved road, street
.16	Liviania's	Livia L	Liffey; etc. #*A*
.16	volted	volutus (*pp.*) L	turned about, rolled around
.17	anodes	anodos G	way up
.17	cathodes	kathodos G	way down
.17	anodes to cathodes	hodos anô katô mia kai hôutos G	The way up and down is one and the same: *Heraclitus, Fragment 60*
.25	seizer	Caesar L	family name become a title; #*A*
.27	I took my plowshure sadly	*part trans.* In tristitia hilaris hilaritate tristis L	In sadness cheerful, in gaiety sad *Giordano Bruno's motto; see 021.12*
.31	potatums	potatum (*Acc.*) L	a drink, draught
550.01	bissed	bis L	twice

.01	trissed	tris L	three
		tristis L	sad
.02	*processus prophetarum*	processus prophetarum L	the progression of the prophets
.03	plauded	plaudo L	to clap
.04	buum	boum (*Gen. pl.*) L	bulls', cows', of bulls, of cows
.06	collegtium	collegium L	colleagueship, partnership, partnership; corporation, fraternity
		collectio L	a collecting together
.15–.16	shallots out of Ascalon	[caepa] Ascalonia L	onion of Ascalon: scallion, shallot, leek
.18	powlver	pulver L	dust, powder
.18	Uliv's	oliva L [*uliva]	olive [*Joyce harbored a persistent delusion that L for "olive" is* *uliva—see Portrait 105 (118)]*
.18	Uliv's oils	olivum L [*ulivum]	oil
.18	cuticure	*cuticura L	skin-care
.20	tussy	tussis L	cough
.21	mopsa's	Mopsos G	legendary diviner [*or two*]: prophet
		Mopsopia G	old name for Attica
.25	librariums	librarium L	bookcase
551.01	palast	palaistra G palaestra L	wrestling-school, gymnasium; rhetorical exercise; school
.07	pantocreator	panto- G ho Pantokratôr G	all- the Almighty
.12	prevened	praevenio L	to come before, precede
.13	*pelves ad hombres sumus*	pelves ad homines sumus L	we are basins to men
.20	latification	*latificatio L	a making wide, a broadening
.24	*Urbs in Rure*	urbs in rure L	a city in the countryside
		rus in urbe L	a bit of country in the city

.30	stellas	stella L	star
.31	hieros	hieros G	divine; holy, hallowed, blessed
.31	gregos	grego L	to collect into a flock *or* herd
		grex L	flock, herd
.31	democriticos	*dêmokritikos G	able to discern the people, critical of the people
.31	tricastellated	tris L	three
		castella (*pl.*) L	castles, forts
		stella L	star
.32	Hibernska	Hibernia L	Ireland
.34	Vicus Veneris	vicus Veneris L	Venus's street, Venus's village
.35	kolossa kolossa	kolossos G	giant statue; esp. as at Rhodes
		Thalatta!	Sea! Sea! *cry of*
		Thalatta! G	*Xenophon's men*; # B
.35	Oi polled	hoi polloi G	the many; the majority
552.01	Sarum	Sarum ML	Salisbury (England)
.01	staties	statio L	a standing still; that which is established; post, station
		toties L	as often, so many times
.03	sept	septem L	seven
.03	sept up	septuplum L	group of seven
.03	pro	pro L	for
.03	con	con[tra] L	against
.07	Hagiasofia	Hagia Sophia G	Holy Wisdom: *cathedral in Byzantium*
.07	Astralia	*Astralia L	Starland
.07	absedes	absida L	arch, vault; choir *or* apse [*church*]
		*absedes L	seats away, distant seats
.08	aeone	aiôn G aeon L	age, eternity
.08	aeones	*see 552.08 B*	
.14	tect	tectum L	roof
.14	gentes	gens, *pl.* gentes L	race, clan: several families united by a common name
.15	oathiose	otiosus L	at ease, at leisure
.19	Blabus	Balbus L	"Stuttering": Roman cognomen

.24	duominous	duo L	two
		dominus L	lord, master
		*duominus L	less two?
		modeled on	
		*terminus L	less three times?
		terminus L	boundary, limit, end
522.25	oragel	ora L	border, brim, edge
		oraculum L	divine announcement
552.25	lauds	laus L	praise
.31	Hoke	hoc (*neut.*) L	this one here
	Hoke	*see 552.31 A*	
.36	chalix	calix L	goblet, cup
		kalyx G	seed-pod; cup of a flower
553.01	vergin	P. Vergilius Maro L	Roman poet
.02	ana	ana G	up, upwards
.02	alphabeater cameltemper	alpha, bêta, gamma, delta G	letters A,B,G,D (*1st four of G alphabet*)
.04	Livvy	Titus Livius L	Roman historian; #*A*
.05	Cammomile	chamomilla L chamaimêlon G	earth-apple: a plant
.09	my carpet gardens of Guerdon City	*allusion to* hanging gardens of Babylon	part of one of the seven wonders of the world
.10	chopes pyramidous	*allusion to* the pyramids of Egypt	one of the seven wonders of the world
.10	pyramidous	pyramis, pyramidos G	pyramid
		pyramous G	cake used as a prize; a prize
.10	mousselimes	Mausoleum L Mausôleion G	tomb of King Mausolus of Caria; one of the seven wonders of the world
.10	beaconphires	*allusion to* Pharos	island with lighthouse off Alexandria; one of the seven wonders of the world
.10	colossets	*allusion to* Colossus L Kolossos G	giant statue-lighthouse at Rhodes; one of the seven wonders of the world
.11	pensilled	pensilis L	hanging downward

.11	turrises	turris L	tower
.11	pensilled turrises	*allusion to* hanging gardens and the walls of Babylon	one of the seven wonders of the world
.11	summiramies	Semiramis	semi-historical queen of Assyria, in G legend builder of Babylon
.12	statuesques	*allusion to* statue of Zeus at Olympia	one of the seven wonders of the world
.12	templeogues	*allusion to* temple of Artemis at Ephesus	one of the seven wonders of the world
.12	Pardonnel	Parthenôn G	celebrated temple of Athena at Athens; a wonder of the classical world
.14	Guglielmus	Guglielmus ML	William
.14	Caulis	caulis L	cabbage-stalk, cabbage; penis
.15	ediculous	aedicula L	small dwelling; chapel
.15	Passivucant	passivus L	1. spread-about, general, common 2. capable of feeling *or* suffering
		vocans L	calling, summoning, evoking
.15	glorietta's inexellsiored	gloria in excelsis [Deo] L	glory [to God] in the highest
.16	comple anniums	*complennium L *backformed from*	filled-out year
		e.g. compleaños Span.	birthday
.16	calendarias	Kalendarium, *pl.* Kalendaria L	account-book, debt-book; interest-book of a moneylender
		Kalendarius L	pertaining to the Kalends
.16	gregoromaios	Gregorius L	"Shepherdly": name of 16 popes; Gregory XIII reformed the calendar in 1582

		[mensis] Maius L	the month of *Maja* (*mother of Mercury*):May
.17	gypsyjuliennes	C. Julius Caesar L	Roman dictator; reformed the calendar
		Julianus L	pertaining to *Julius*
		[mensis] Julius L	the month of *Julius*: July
.18	lisbing	Lesbia G L	woman of Lesbos; passionate woman; Catullus's name for his mistress
.20	villas	villa L	farmhouse, country estate
.21	animos	animus L	breath, life, rational soul
.21	pons	pons L	bridge
.22	aguaducks	aquaeductus L	conveyance of water, conduit
.25	phoenix	phoenix L phoinix G	fabulous bird of Arabia
.26	plurabelle	pleura G	rib
		pluralis L	pertaining to many
		plorabilis L	lamentable, deplorable
.29	eblanite	*Eblanitês G	Dubliner
.30	circulums	circulum (*Acc.*) L	circle
.33	cundoctor	cunnus L	cunt
.35	claudesdales	claudus L	lame
.36	Hispain's	Hispania L	Spain
554.01	bronchos	bronchos G	trachea, windpipe; throat
.03	sedated	sedeo L	to sit
.08	lalaughed	lalageô G	to babble
555.01	mult	multum L	much
.08	sycomores	sykomoros G	sycamore-fig
		*psychomôros G	soul-foolish
.09	majorchy	major L	greater, bigger, elder
		-archia G	-rule
.09	minorchy	minor L	lesser, smaller, younger
		-archia G	-rule
.10	tetranoxst	tetra- G	four-
		nox L	night
.11	pallyollogass	palaiologos G	one who discusses old times

		Palaiologoi G	last Byzantine dynasty
.18	auspices	auspicia (*pl.*) L	divination by observing flight of birds
.19	onage	onager L	wild ass
.23	lemoncholy	xanthê cholê G	yellow bile
		melainecholê G	black bile
.24	rhubarbarorum	rhus barbarorum L	sumac of the barbarians: rhubarb
556.18	daphnedews	daphnê G	laurel-tree, bay-tree
.24	seequeerscenes	sequestro L	to give up for safekeeping, to surrender
.32	Kothereen	katharion G	purgative medicine
		katharos G	clean, cleanly
557.02	apolkaloops	apokalypsos G	uncovering, disclosure, revelation; Revelation
.03	stirkiss	stercus L	dung
.06	hapspurus	Bosphoros G	"Heifer's Ford": strait at Istanbul # *A*
		Hesperus L	the evening star
		Hesperos G	evening, evening star, west
		purus L	clean, unstained, pure
.10	fingerhals	hals G	salt; the sea
.15	juremembers	jure L	by law
.16	reverendum	reverendum (*neut. or Acc.*) L	inspiring awe, venerable, reverend
.17	fornicolopulation	fornix L	arch, vault; brothel
		colaphus L	a punch, blow (with the fist)
		colo L	cultivate, till, take care of
.17	albowcrural	*albocruralis L	white-legged
.20	conjugation	conjugatio L	combination, mingling, mixture
.21	carnation	carnatio L	fleshiness, corpulence
.22	deretane	rete L	net
.33	festination	festinatio L	haste, hurry
.34	complore	comploro L	to bewail together loudly
.35	obsecration	obsecratio L	a beseeching, imploring, plea
558.12	extinuation	*extinuatio L *modeled on*	disconnection, holding out of

			continuatio L	connection, unbroken series, holding together
	.14	Sully	Sulla	Roman soldier-politician; # A
	.18	Nolans Volans	nolens volens L	unwilling [or] willing, willy-nilly
	.18	Volans	volans L	flying
	.27	Albatrus	albatus L	clothed in white
	.28	Victa	victa (fem.) L	defeated, overcome, vanquished
559.13		Limes	limes L	cross-path; boundary between fields; limit, street, boundary
	.24	homoplatts	*homoplatê G	companion-widths
	.24	ghazometron	metron G	measure; measurer
	.24	pondus	pondus L	weight; heaviness; importance
	.35	Mesopotomac	Mesopotamia G	"Between Rivers": land between Tigris and Euphrates
560.01		Promiscuous Omebound	Promêtheus Lyomenos G	Prometheus Unbound: play by Aeschylus
	.03	Circus	circus L	circular line, circle
	.14	Limen	limen L	threshold
	.16	ephort	ephoros G	overseer, guardian, ruler
	.17	hominous	hominis (Gen.) L	a person's, of a person
	.28	pateramater	pater L	father
			mater L	mother
561.05		noe	Noe L	Noah
	.09	Cunina	Cunina L	goddess who protects children in the cradle
	.09	Statulina	*Statulina, Statina L	deity who presided over the standing of children
	.09	Edulia	Edulia L	goddess who presides over children's food
	.10	pessname	pessum L	to the ground, down
	.11	passim	passim L	here and there, all over, at random
	.19	Loreas	lorea L	wine of the second press, after-wine
	.19	lillias	lilia (pl.) L	lilies
	.19	flocaflake	[non] flocci facio L	to regard as worthless, to care not a speck for

.19	arrosas	arrosas (*pp. fem.* *Acc. pl*) L	nibbled at, gnawed at
.20	heliotrope	hêliotropos G	sundial
.21	amaranth	amarantos G	unfading
		amaranthis G	a kind of plant
.22	Charis	Charis G	a Grace, one of the Graces
.22	Charissima	carissima (*fem.*) L	dearest
.24	Enameron	*enameron ML *for* henahêmeron G *modeled on* decameron ML *for* dekahêmeron G	a thing of one day / a thing of ten days
.28	dormition	dormitio L	a sleeping
562.03	barytinette	bary- G	heavy-
.06	Dulce	dulce L	sweetly
.06	delicatissima	delicatissima (*fem.*)L	most alluring
.09	chrysming	chrisma G	anointing, unction; grace
		chrysos G	gold
.15	plikaplak	plico L	to fold up, to wind together
		placo L	to reconcile, to assuage
.16	amnessly	amnis, *pl.* amnes L	river
.17	twobis	bis L	twice
.21	tattached	tat L	what!
.26	semiope	semi- L	half-
		ôps G	eye, face
.31	Amorica	amor L	love
		Armorica L	north Gaul: Brittany; #A
.32	nonsolance	non solans L	1. not comforting, not consoling; 2. not making lonely, not desolating
.33	audorable	audeo L	to dare
		audio L	to hear
		*orabilis L	mouthable, speakable
.33	eunique	eunê G	bed, bedding
		eunikêtos G	easily overcome

.36	venials	venia L	pardon, permission
563.14	bannars	ars L	art
.17	anemone's	anemône G	wind-flower: poppy
.18	Donatus	Donatus L	"Gift": Roman name
		Aelius Donatus L	Roman grammarian
.25	costarred	costa L	rib
.34	Vellicate	vellicatio L	a plucking, twitching; taunting
		vellico L	to pluck, twitch, pinch, nip
.34	nyche	nycheia G	nightly watch
564.01	Jemini	gemini L	twins
.04	meseedo	mesê G	a musical tone: top note of the lower tetrachord in the octave
		sedo L	to allay, settle, calm
		Mi[ra] (*pl.*) L	Wonders: *third upward note in sol-fa*
		S[ancte] I[ohannes] L	O Saint John: *fifth upward note in sol-fa*
		Do L *for*	I give
		Ut L	That: *base note in sol-fa*
.05	Helius	Hêlios G	Sun: the sun-god
.05	Croesus	Croesus L Kroisos G	famous wealthy king of Lydia
.05–.06	white and gold elephant in our zoo-park	*allusion to* chryselephant-ine statue of Zeus	(*at Olympia*): one of the seven wonders of the world
		chryselephantin-es G	of ivory and gold
.21	pappasses	pappas G	father (*child's word*)
		pappas L	tutor, governor
.25	sylvious	Silvius L	name of several kings of Alba Longa
.31	Hystorical	hysterikos G	suffering in the womb; hysterical
.33	Lucan's	M. Annaeus Lucanus	Roman poet; #*A*
.35	fundus	fundus L	bottom; piece of land
565.03	duol	duo L	two
.03	wankyrious	ankyra G	anchor, hook

		[w]anax G; # *Digamma*	lord, master
		kyrios G	lord, master
.04	pentapolitan	pentapolitês G	citizen of five cities; citizen of the Pentapolis (*district on Dead Sea*)
.05	Ulvos! Ulvos!	ulva L	sedge, marsh-grass
		ulmus L	elm-tree
.19	phanthares	*phantharsos [?] G	bright courage
.25	*ne dormis?*	ne dormis L	are you (*sing.*) not sleeping?
.26	*Malbone*	male L	badly
		bene L	well
.26	*dormas*	dormias L	you (*sing.*) might sleep
.35	pickts	Picti L	"Painted People": a people of north Britain, the Picts
.35	saxums	saxum L	stone, rock
		Saxones L	the Saxons, a German people
566.09	penisills	penicillus L	little tail, little penis; painter's brush, pencil
.10	boufeither	bous G	bull, ox, cow
.11	Katya	Kathairô G	to cleanse
.12	duedesmally	duodecimus L	twelfth
.13	arums	arum L	a kind of plant
.15	magnum chartarums	magnum chartarium L	the great archive
		magna charta L	the great letter, the great writing: Magna Charta
.16	harrums	harum (*Gen. pl. fem.*) L	of these, of these women, these women's
.21	duffgerent	gerens L	bearing, carrying, wearing; acting, behaving
562.24	duffgerent	*see 566.21 H*	
566.24	futherer	futuo L	to fuck
.32	non	non L	not
567.11	Courtmilits'	militis (*Gen.*) L	soldier's, of a soldier
		cohors militum L	a cohort of soldiers, division of troops
.25	faxes	fax L	torch, firebrand; incitement

.30	Zosimus	Zôsimos	"Viable": 1. G historian, 5th C a.d.; 2. Pope who condemned Pelagios
.31	Plentifolks Mixymost	Pontifex Maximus L	"Greatest Bridgemaker": chief Roman high-priest
.35	Sibernian	*Sibernia pseudo-L *for* *Hibernia pseudo-G; # *G-to-L*	Ireland
.35	Pelouta	pêlos G	clay, earth
.36	lawncastrum	castrum L	fort
568.02	ruber	ruber L	red
.02	fullvide	fulvus L	yellow
		vide L	see!
.02	veridust	viridis L	green
.03	crerdulous	caerulus L	blue
.05	plurity	pluri- L	many-
		ploratus L	lamentation, wailing
		pleura G	rib
.08	Britus	Brutus	fictitious eponymous founder of Britain
		M. Junius Brutus L	assassin of Caesar; # *A*
.08	Gothius	Gothus L	a Goth, member of great north-German tribe
		C. Cassius Longinus L	assassin of Caesar
.09	mark one autonement	Marcus Antonius L	triumvir, defeated Brutus and Cassius
.09	autonement	auto- G	self-
.09	si	si L	if
.10	Cloudia	Clodia L	notorious sister of P. Clodius Pulcher; Catullus's Lesbia
		[Aqua] Claudia L	aquaduct to Rome completed by emperor Claudius
.10	Aiduolcis	aei G	ever, always
		aio L	to say yes
		duo L	two
		dulcis L	sweet

		cis L	on this side
.15	sayeme	sêma G	sign, mark, token; gravestone; symbol; constellation
.20	necknoose	necnon L	and also, and yet, in fact
.20	aureal	aureolus L	golden
.24	pompey	Cn. Pompeius Magnus L	Pompey the Great, triumvir
.25	Pompkey	Cn. Pompeius Magnus L	Pompey the Great, triumvir
.29	Sole	Sol L	the Sun
.32	alfi byrni gamman dealter etcera zezera eacla treacla youghta kaptor lomdom noo	alpha bêta gamma delta epsilon zêta êta thêta iota kappa lamda mu nu G	letters A, B, G, D, E, Z, Ê, TH, I, K, L, M, N
.32	etcera	et cetera L	and the rest, and the others
.35	edify	aedifico L	to erect a building, to build
.35	Rex	rex L	king
.36	canule	cannula L	little reed; flute; windpipe
569.05	Presbutt	presbuteros G presbus G	elder old man
.09	audialterand	*alteraudiens L	listening to another, hearing the other
.10	Stillamaries	stella maris L	star of the sea
.11	Audeons	audens L audiens L	daring, bold, intrepid hearer, auditor; catechumen
.14	Agithetta	Agathê G agitata (pp. fem.) L	"Good": fem. name driven, impelled, shaken
.14	Tranquilla	tranquilla (fem.) L	quiet, calm, still
.14	demure	*demuro L	to unwall
.14	umclaused	clausus (pp.) L	closed, shut, enclosed
.16	virgilances	P. Vergilius Maro L	Roman epic poet
.16	Beata	beata (fem.) L	blessed
.16	Basilica	basilica L	public building; cathedral
.16	pontification	*pontificatio L	bridge-building; being a high-priest

.18	supprecate	*supprecor L	to ask humbly, to beg, pray humbly
.21	*Benedictus benedicat*	benedictus benedicat L	may the blessed one bless (*form of Grace used in Trinity College, Dublin*)
.22	frust	frustum L	piece, morsel
.29	Ithalians	ithys G	straight
.29	Moll Pamelas	molpêtis, molpatis G	she who sings and dances
		Melpomenê G	"Songstress": Muse of tragedy and lyric
.31	Veruno	veru L	roasting-spit; dart; railing
.33	rhoda's	rhoda (*pl.*) G	roses
		Rhoda G	ceremony at which graves were decked with roses
570.03	Dalchi	dulcis L	sweet
.03	Dolando	dolando L	1. by chipping with an axe; by cudgeling soundly; 2. by one to be cudgeled soundly
.05	viceuvious	Vesuvius L	"Quenched[?]": famous volcano in Campania, dormant before a.d. 79
		uva L	grape
		uvidus L	moist, damp
.06	pyrolyphics	pyro- G	fire-
		*pyroglyphikos G	pertaining to fire-carving
.07	Mamnesty	amnes (*pl.*) L	rivers
.17	herculeneous	Herculaneus L	pertaining to Herculaneum (*town buried along with Pompeii by Vesuvius, a.d. 79*)
		hircus L	he-goat
.19	aproham	aper L	wild boar
.20	Pournterfamilias	paterfamilias L	father of an extended family, patriarch
.32	Sylvanus Sanctus	Silvanus Sanctus L	Holy Silvanus (*god of woods*)
.33	retrorsehim	retrorsum L	backwards, back, behind

.36	sui	sui L	of himself, herself, itself, themselves; himself, herself, etc.
571.10	ferm	ferme L	nearly, almost, for the most part
.14	triste	triste L	1. a sad thing; 2. sadly, sorrowfully
.22	limmenings	limen L	threshold
.22	lemantitions	Lemanus L	Lake Geneva
.31	Qui	qui L	who? which?
.36	saltklesters	kleistos, klêstos G	that can be shut
572.16	eskmeno	eskemmenôs G	deliberately
.19	procurator	procurator L	manager, overseer, superintendent, deputy, collector of taxes
.19	Interrogarius	interrogatorius L	consisting of questions
		*interrogarius L	questioning
.19	Mealterum	me alterum L	another me
.21	Honuphrius	*Onopherios G	he who carries an ass
		Honuferius L	load-carrying
.23	Felicia	*Felicia L	she who is fertile
.24	Eugenius	Eugenius L for Eugenios G	well-born; noble, generous; *name of 4 popes.*
.24	Jeremias	Jeremias eccl. L	Jeremiah (*Hebrew prophet*)
.25	philadelphians	philadelphoi (*pl.*) G	those who love their brother[s] *and/or* sister[s]
.25	Honuphrius	*see 572.21 A*	
.25	Felicia	*see 572.23 G*	
.25	Eugenius	*see 572.24 I*	
.26	Jeremias	*see 572.24 K*	
.27	Honuphrius	*see 572.21 A*	
.27	Fortissa	*Fortissa L	she who is strong
.28	Honuphrius	*see 572.21 A*	
.29	Mauritius	Mauritius L	Moor, Mauritanian, Moroccan
.30	Magravius	*Magnigravius L	he who is very heavy
.32	Fortissa	*see 572.27 K*	
.32	Mauritius	*see 572.29 H*	
.33	Gillia	*Gillia L	she who has to do with a *gillo* [wine-cooler]

.33	Magravius	*see 572.30 B*	
.34	Honuphrius	*see 572.21 A*	
.35	Jeremias	*see 572.24 K*	
.35	Gillia	*see 572.33 B*	
.36	*ex equo*	ex equo L	out of a horse
		ex aequo L ex equo LL	out of fairness
.36	Poppea	Poppaea L	Nero's mistress and 2nd wife
.36	Arancita	aranea L	spider
.36	Clara	clara (*fem.*) L	clear, bright, shining
573.01	Marinuzza	marinus L	pertaining to the sea
.01	Iodina	ion eidos G	like a violet
.02	Honuphrius	*see 572.21 A*	
.02	Magravius	*see 572.30 B*	
.04	Michael ... Cerularius	Michael Cerularius (*d.* 1058)	patriarch of Constantinople under whom final breach was made between G and L Churches despite mediation of Constantine Monomachos (*see 017.01* D]
		name may be *Keroularios G or* *Kairoularious G from* *Caerularius L	*something having to do with goats* having to do with the blue sea
.05	Eugenius	*see 572.24 I*	
.05	Magravius	*see 572.30 B*	
.06	Sulla	L. Cornelius Sulla Felix	Roman dictator; # A
.07	Sullivani	Sullani L *Sullivani L	partisans of Sulla Sullivans
.07	Felicia	*see 572.23 G*	
.08	Gregorius	Gregorius L	"Shepherdly": name of 16 popes
.08	Leo	Leo L	"Lion": name of 13 popes
.08	Vitellius	Vitellius L	"Veal" *or* "Eggyolk": emperor A.D. 69; # C
.08	Macdugalius	*Macdugalius L	pertaining to Macdugal
.09	Honuphrius	*see 572.21 A*	

.11	Eugenius	*see 572.24 I*	
.12	Honuphrius	*see 572.21 A*	
.13	Sulla	*see 573.06 B*	
.13	Sullivani	*see 573.07 C*	
.15	Felicia	*see 572.23 G*	
.15	Magravius	*see 572.30 B*	
.16	Gillia	*see 572.33 B*	
.17	Eugenius	*see 572.24 I*	
.18	Jeremias	*see 572.35 G*	
.19	Honuphrius	*see 572.21 A*	
.20	*turpiter*	turpiter L	in an ugly manner, shamefully
.21	*ex cathedris*	ex cathedris L	out of seats, out of chairs
		ex cathedra L	out of the chair [*of authority*]
.21	Gerontes	gerontes (*pl.*) G	old men; senators
.21	Cambronses	*Cambronses (*pl.*) Mod. L	of Cambronne (*le mot de Cambronne =* "*merde*")
.21	Gerontes Cambronses	Giraldus Cambrensis L	Gerald of Wales, chronicler; *see 151.32 A*
.23	subdolence	subdolens L	somewhat painful
		*subdolentia L	moderate pain
		subdolositas L	craft, cunning
.23	comminates	comminatio L	a threatening, menace
		comminor L	to threaten
.24	Guglielmus	Guglielmus ML	William
.25	affrication	affricatio L	a rubbing against
.27	Fortissa	*see 572.27 K*	
.28	Gregorius	*see 573.08 A*	
.28	Leo	*see 573.08 B*	
.28	Viteilius [misprint?]	*see 573.08 C*	
.28	Magdugalius	*Magdugalius L	pertaining to Magdugal
.29	Honuphrius	*see 572.21 A*	
.30	*turpissimas*	turpissimus (masc.), turpissima (fem.) L	most foul, most filthy, most shameful
.30	Canicula	Canicula L	"Little Bitch": the lesser dogstar, *Canis Minor*
.31	Mauritius	*see 572.29 H*	
.31	Sulla	*see 573.06 B*	
.31	abnegand	abnegans L	being unwilling, refusing

574.05	Tangos	tango L	I touch
.12	Jucundus	jucundus L	pleasant, agreeable, delightful
.12	Fecundus	fecundus L	fruitful, fertile, abundant
.12	Xero	xêros G	dry
.12	Pecundus	pecus L	cattle
		pecuniosus L	rich, moneyed, wealthy
.20	Tangos	*see 574.05 H*	
.28	Pango	pango L	I fasten; I drive in, I sink in
.35	*mandamus*	mandamus L	we command (*legal term*)
575.05	absolete	*absoletus L	grown away, worn away
.09	*in re*	in re L	in the matter
.13	corruberation	*corruberatio L	a reddening-together
.19	tetigists	tetigi L	I have touched (*perfect tense of* tango)
.23	*in camera*	in camera L	in the chamber: secretly, privately
.24	*annias*	alias L	otherwise
.29	Pepigi	pepigi L	I have driven in (*perfect tense of* pango)
.36–.01	*occupante extremum scabie*	occupante extremum scabie L	an itching having seized the end
576.02	tact	tactus L	1. touched (*pp. of* tango); 2. a touch
.04	mancipium	mancipium L	a taking by hand, formal acceptance, taking possession
.06	Una	una L	in one and the same place
		una (*fem.*) L	one
.06	Bellina	Bellona L	goddess of war
		belluina (*fem.*) L	brutal, bestial
.06	Pepigi's	pepigi L	I have driven in (*perfect tense of* pango)
.06	pact	pactus (*pp.*) L	fixed, driven in (*pp. of* pango)
.07	rhino	rhino- G	nose-
		rhinos G	skin, hide
.08	pango	pango L	I fasten, I fix, I drive in, I determine

.08	Pepigi	pepigi L	I have fixed, I have driven in (*perfect tense of* pango)
.20	perambulaups	perambulo L	to ramble through
.28	cunnyngnest	cunnus L	cunt
.28	Phenicia	Phoenicia L	a country of the Levant
.33	alteregoases	alter ego L	another I, the other I
.34	ligious	*ligius L	pertaining to tying *or* binding
		ligo L	to tie, to bind
577.01	mandragon mor	mandragoras G L	a plant; mandrake
.01	Morionmale	morion L	deadly nightshade
		môrios G	male-mandrake: a species of mandrake
.01	Thrydacianmad	thrydakias G	female-mandrake: a species of mandrake
		thrydakinê G	lettuce
		Dacia L	Roman province, country of the Dacii; *roughly mod.* Romania
.02	basilisk	basiliskos G	princeling, kinglet; cobra
		basiliscus L	a kind of lizard
.11	lymph	lympha L	clear water
.11	boniface	bona facies L	nice face
		Bonifacius L	English saint; #*A*
.15	abunda	abunda (*fem.*) LL	copious
		abundans L	overflowing
.15	Regies	Regis (*Gen.*) L	King's, of the King
.23	via mala	via mala L	the evil way
.23	hyber	hybris G	wanton violence, pride, arrogance
		hyper G	over, above
.23	heckhisway	hic, haec (*masc., fem.*) L	this, this here
		his L	to *or* by these
.23	per	per L	through, by, during
.27	pinguind	pinguis L	fat
.28	arthruseat	arthron G	limb
.31–.32	curious	kurios G	lord, master [*MG*: Mister]
.32	deman ... dayman	daimôn G	spirit, deity; demon
.32	plagiast	plagiasmos G	obliquity; deceit

.34	karkery	carcer L	prison
		karkaros G	
578.04	chrismy	chrisma G	anointing, unction; grace
.06	pharrer	pharos G	plough
		Pharos G	island with famous lighthouse; #A
.10	Misthra	Mithras	Persian sungod whose worship in the Roman empire rivaled early Christianity
.17	trixiestrail	trixago L	a kind of plant
		trixos (Ionic) G	threefold
.18	lucre	lucrum L	gain, profit
.22	steptojazyma's	septuagesimus L	the seventieth
.22	culunder	culus L	arse
579.08	Cave and can em	cave canem L	beware the dog
.09	wrecks	rex L	king
.09–.10	quick queck quack	qui, quae, quod L	who? which? what? (masc., fem., neut.)
		echo of hic, haec, hoc L	this, this here (masc., fem., neut.) #B
.10	radiose	radiosus L	radiant, emitting many beams
.10	Renove	renovo L	to renew, restore
.10	bible	biblion G	book
.15	plethoron	*plêthôron (pseudo-sing.) of *plêthôra (pseudo-pl.) plêthôra [sing.] G	fullness, satiety
		plêtrion G	a little rudder
.20	dives	dives L	rich
.20	freund	Wilhelm Freund (1806–1894)	German lexicographer; his Worterbuch der lateinischen Sprache underlies all subsequent L dictionaries in Eng.
.31	extramurals	extramuralis L	pertaining to outside the [city] walls
580.12	Multaferry	multifarie L	in many ways, variously
		multifer L	bearing much, fruitful
.17	Pervinca	pervinca L	periwinkle (flower)

.18	Soloscar	solus L	alone
		Sol L	the Sun
.25	hydrocomic	*hydrokômikos G	a *watercomedian
.25	limfy	lympha L	clear water
.36	Hosty	hostis L	stranger, foreigner, enemy
		Hostius L	epic poet, 2d C b.c.
		Hostius Quadra L	Roman voyeur, murdered; #A
581.01	peniloose	peniculus L	brush, sponge
.03	vective	*vectivus, vectus (pp.) L	borne, carried, conveyed
.13	consollation	sollers L	skilful, clever
		sollicito L	to annoy, disturb
.13	sursumcordial	sursum corda L	hearts upward; lift up [your] hearts
.17–.18	mens conscia recti	mens [sibi] conscia recti—Vergil. Aen. I .604 L	a mind [self-] aware of what is correct—Vergil, Aeneid I, 604
.18	omniwomen	omnis L	all
.20	illian	illa L	she
		Ilias G L	"The Trojan Woman": Helen
.22	awlus plawshus	Aulus Plautius	commander of Claudius' conquest of Britain, a.d. 43
.22–.23	happyass cloudious	Appius Claudius	Roman decemvir; #A
.23	cloudious	Tiberius Claudius Drusus Nero Germanicus (10 b.c.–a.d. 54)	Claudius I, 4th Roman emperor, feigned imbecility to avert murder by Caligula; scholar; murdered by his wife Agrippina, Nero's mother
.24	monomyth	monomythos G	a single word, sole speech
.27	hebdromadary	hebdomadikos G	weekly
		dromadarios G	"running": a kind of camel
.32	alter	alter L	other, the other, another [of two]
.33	anander	anandros G	unmanly, cowardly

582.07	clooshed	kluô G	to hear
.15	semperidentity	semper idem L	forever the same
		sempiternitas L	perpetuity, eternal duration
.17	surprends	*superprendo L	to lay hold of above, to over-catch
.20	megaron	megaron G	large room, hall; bedchamber
.36	villa's	villa L	farmhouse, country house
583.02	arx	arx L	citadel, castle
.03	dinties	dentes L	teeth
.10	io, io	Iô G L	girl loved by Zeus; changed to a cow
		iô, iô G L	oh, oh!; ho, ho!; hurray!
.11	ganymede	Ganymêdês G	beautiful youth carried to heaven to be Zeus's darling
.12	Bossford	*part trans.*	"Heifer's Ford" (named
		Bosphoros G	for Io); strait at Istanbul; #*A*
.13	phospherine	phôsphorion G	figure of *hê Phôsphoros* on a ring
		hê Phôsphoros G	"the Light-bringer": Artemis
.14	setalite	saeta L seta LL	bristle
.15	Photoflashing	phôto- G	light-
.16	Urania	Urania L	"Heavenly": Muse of
		Ouraniê G	astronomy
.17	titaning	Titan G L	1. elder brother of Kronos; ancestor of the Titans (giants); 2. the Sun
.17	rhean	rhea G	easily, lightly
		Rhea G	mother of Zeus
		Rhea Silvia L	mother of Romulus and Remus
.18	rhodagrey	rhoda (*pl.*) G	roses
.19	Satyrdaysboost	Satyros G	wood-god resembling
		Satyrus L	an ape; lewd, goatish person
.19	Phoebe's	Phoebe L	the moon-goddess; the
		Phoibê G	moon
.22	nivia	nivea (*fem.*) L	snowy

.33	loomph	lympha, lumpha L	clear water
584.04	linguish	lingua L	tongue; language
.05	hek	haec (fem.) L	this, this here
.05	hok	hoc (neut.) L	this one here
.05	hucky	huc L	to this place, hither
		hucine L	to this? so far?
.21	kikkery	kiki G	castor oil
		kikinos G	ringlet
		kikiourgos G	castor-oil worker
.28	Armigerend	armiger L	bearing weapons, armed, warlike
.31	Tellaman	Telamôn G	"Supporter": Argonaut, father of Ajax
		telamôn G	"bearer": (Architecture) male figure supporting an entablature
.33	contractations	contractatio L	touch; stealing, theft
.34	choree	choreios G	pertaining to the chorus (metrics), i.e, trochee, tribrach
.35	gratias	gratias (Acc. pl.) L	favors, regards, thanks
585.01	eon's	aiôn G	lifetime, age
.02	Neptune's	Neptunus L	god of the sea
.02	Centinel	centi- L	hundred-
.02	Tritonville	Tritôn G L	son of Poseidon [Neptune]
.03	choree	choreios G	choric meter; see 584.34
.04	choree	see 585.03 I	
.11	Malthus	Malchos	Carthaginian politician
.11	paratonnerwetter	para G	beside, along
		paratonos G	stretched beside; ill-sounding; ill-strung
.17	condeal	con- L	with-, together-
.18	verbumsaps	verbum sapienti L	a word to the wise
.22	annastomoses	anastomôsis G	outlet, opening; opening up, keeping open
.24	Totumvir	*totusvir L	an all-man, all-male
.27	abjourned	*abdiurno LL	to put off from a day
		modeled on	
		*addiurno LL	to put off until a day set, to adjourn

.32	Aunty Dilluvia	antediluvium LL	before the flood
.34	misturbing	*misturbo L	to mix by violence
586.05	*non*	non L	not
.05	*coram*	coram L	in the presence of, before the eyes of, in the face of; personally
.05	*ex*	ex L	out of
.24	multaplussed	multo plus L	by much more
.25	ell a fee and do little ones	LVII L	57
.27	parasangs	parasangês G	1. measure of distance, slightly less than 3.5 miles; 2. a messenger
.29	tanquam	tanquam L	as much as, so as, as if
.31	windopes	ôps G	eye
587.03	cert	certo, certe L	certainly, surely
.04	auxy	auxilium L	help, aid
.08	Theoatre	Theos G	God
.15	Lawd	laus L	praise
.22	vivaviz	viva (*fem.*) L	alive
		viz. *abbrev. for* videlicet L	it is easy to see, clearly, plainly
588.06	Jamessime	*Jamessime (*adv.*) fake-L	most *Jamesily
		*jamissime [*from* jam] dog-L	most precisely now, very much just now
.12	*oloroso*	olor L	1. a smell; 2. swan
.20	fulmenbomb	fulmen L	lightning that strikes, thunderbolt
.29	Arrah	ara G	*interrogative particle implying anxiety or impatience*
.29	Triss	tris L	three
		trissos G	threefold
.32	magill o'dendron	*megalodendron G	a big tree
		megalodendros G	full of large trees
589.06	urbanorb	Urbi et Orbi L	to the City and the World (*papal blessing* or *announcement*)
.07	mayom and tuam	meum et tuum L	mine and thine

.28–.29	were spared a just two of a feather in wading room only	*allusion to* Deucalion and Pyrrha	classical Noah and wife; #*A*
.35	ultimatehim	ultimatum (*neut. pp.*) L	come to an end, ended
.36	explosium	*explosium fake-L *for* *explosion fake-G	#*G-to-L*
590.02	heptark	heptarchos G	magistracy of one-seventh (*of a country, etc.*)
		arca L	chest, box
.03	bankrump	rumpo (*pp.* ruptus) L	to break
.05	Phoenis	Phoenix L Phoinix G	fabulous bird of Arabia
		finis L	boundary, limit, border, end
.10	tryomphal	triumphalis L	pertaining to a *triumphos*
		omphalos G	navel
.11	plemyums	plenum L	space occupied by matter; stout, bulky
		#*L/R Interchange*: praemium L	profit derived from booty; booty; profit, reward
.15	integer integerrimost	integer integerrimus L	perfect most perfect, untouched most untouched
.15	formast	formaster L	one who beautifies himself; a dandy
.17	concloud	*conclaudo L	to shut up closely, to confine
.17	Nephilim	nephelê G	cloud, mass of clouds
.20	mand	mando L	to chew
		mandatum L	command, commission
593.01	Sandhyas! Sandhyas! Sandhyas!	sanctus sanctus sanctus L	holy holy holy
		dies L	day
		deus, divus L dios G *from* *dyavi	god, sky, day
.02	Surrection	surrectio L	a raising up, erection
.03–.04	O rally, O rally, O rally ... O rally	orate L	pray ye!

.04	Phlenxty	phlexis G	burning
.11	orther	orthros G	dawn
		arthron G	joint
.13	Securest	securus L	free from care
		secures (*pl.*) L	axes
.13	jubilends	jubilans L	rejoicing, jubilant
.13	albas	albus (*masc.*)	white
		alba (*fem.*) L	
.13	Temoram	timorem (*Acc.*) L	fear
		te L	thee
		mora L	delay
.13	Securest jubilends albas Temoram	securus judicat orbis terrarum L	untroubled, the world judges; #*B*
.15	humuluation	humus L	earth, the ground, soil
		humo L	to cover with earth, to bury
.17	pewtewr publikumst	puteus publicus L	a public well *or* cistern
		pudor publicus L	a public shame
.17	pratician pratyusers	pratum L	meadow
.21	domnatory	dominator L	ruler, lord
		domator L	a tamer, subduer, conqueror
		domatorium L modeled on	room for taming in
		dormitorium L	sleeping-room
.24	Ntamplin	*MG spelling for* *Dablin	Dublin?
.24	tohp	phôt- G	light-
594.02	agnitest	agnitus (*pp.*) L	recognized, acknowledged
.02	Arcthuris	Arktouros G	"Bear-Guard": the star;
		Arcturus L	the time of its rising (*mid-September*)
		arcus L	bow, arch, rainbow
		thuris (*Gen.*) L	of incense
.02	Verb umprincipiant	verbum principians L	beginning to speak the word
		In principio erat Verbum L	In the beginning was the Word (*John 1:1*)
.04	salve!	salve L	hail! be well!
.07	iteritinerant	*iteritinerans L	a journey-traveler; journey-traveling; traveling again

.08	semitary	semita L	path, lane
.08	Somnionia	somnium L	a dream
.08	Heliotropolis	Hêlios G	Sun: the sun-god
		hêliotropion G	sundial
		polis G	city
		*Hêliotropopolis G	Sundial-city
.14–.15	Qui stabat ... qui stabat	qui stabat L	who was standing?
.14	Meins	minus L	less
		minae (pl.) L	threats
.14	quantum	quantum L	as much as, so much as
.15	Peins	penis L	tail; penis
		Poenus L	a Carthaginian
		poena L poinê G	compensation, punishment
.14–.15	Qui stabat Meins quantum qui stabat Peins	qui stabat [minus?] quantum qui stabat [peius?] dog-L	who was standing [less?] as much as who was standing [worse?]
.17	pasch	pascha G L	Passover, Easter [Hebrew pesach]
.19	Atriathroughwards	atria (pl.) L	entrance-halls of Roman houses
.22	macroliths	*makrolithos G	a long-stone
.23	Helusbelus	helus OL	kitchen vegetables, cabbage
		Belus L Bêlos G	legendary Asian king, builder of Babylon
		bêlos G	threshold
.23	peneplain	paene L	almost, nearly
.24	erge	ergon G	work
.25	floran	Flora L	goddess of flowers
		florens L	blossoming, flowering; glittering
.25	isthmians	isthmion G	pertaining to the neck or throat; necklace
		isthmiastês G	spectator at the Isthmian Games; *dweller on an isthmus
.27	Cur	cur L	why, wherefore
.28	byelegs	lex L	law, legislation
.28	humuristic	humus L	earth, soil
		humo L	to bury

.29	cur	cur L	why, wherefore
.29	noxe	nox L	night
		noxa L	hurt, harm, injury
.30	Gallus	Gallus L	1. a Gaul; 2. castrated priest of Cybele
		gallus L	cock
.33	invasable	invado, *pp.* invasus L	to go, to come, to enter, to attack
595.07	Geoglyphy's	*geôglyphê G	earth-carving
.14	lungfortos	fortis L	strong
.18	Bruton	Brut, Brutus L	fictitious eponymous founder of Britain; # *A*
.20	perporteroguing	perporto L	to transport (*something to someplace*)
		rogo L	to ask, to question
.22	apad	apud L	with, at, by, near
.22	muniment	munimentum L	defence, fortification, intrenchment
.23	etceterogenious	et cetera L	and the rest, and the others
		heterogenês G	of different kinds
.26	topaia	topoi (*pl.*) G	places
		topia L	ornamental gardening
596.01	thetheatron	to theatron G	the theater
		thea G	goddess
.01	lemoronage	môros G	foolish
		onager L	wild ass
.06	chrest	chrêstos G	useful, serviceable, good
.06–.07	*victis poenis hesternis*	victis poenis hesternis L	yesterday's punishments having been overcome
		victis Poenis hesternis L	yesterday's Carthaginians having been conquered
		victus poenis hesternis L	conquered by punishments of a former day
.07	fostfath	phôs G	light
		phathi G	say!
		fostis L (= hostis)	stranger, foreigner, enemy
.07	solas	sola (*fem.*) L	alone
		solatus L	sun-struck, sun-burnt
.09	consecrandable	consecrandus L	[one] to be made sacred

.10	pesternost	pater noster L	our father
.14	angalach	angelus L	messenger, angel
		gala G	milk
.14	gnomeosulphidosalam-ermauderman	gnômê G	means of knowing, mark, token
		sulfoeidês L + G	looking like brimstone
		dos L	dowry
.15	fert	fert L	[he] carries
.15	fert in fort	fortitudo ejus	his strength has held
		Rhodum tenuit L	Rhodes; #B
.18	pamphilius	Pamphilos G	"Beloved of All": name of several distinguished persons
		Pamphylia G L	"Of mingled tribes": country on the coast of Asia Minor
.18	vintivat	vindicat L	[he] lays legal claim to
		vinea L	vineyard
.19	niviceny	nivis (Gen.) L	of snow
		cena L	dinner
.23	gygantogyres	gigantoguroi (pl.) G	giant circles
		Gygês	king of Lydia
.24	parasama	parasama (pl.; Doric),	marginal marks or notes; insigniae,
		parasêma G	emblems
.26	temperasoleon	temperans L	sober, moderate
		tempora (pl.) L	the times, the circumstances
		soleo L	to be accustomed
		leôn G	lion
.28	inspectorum	inspectorum (Gen. pl.) L	of observers; [LL] of inspectors, of examiners
.29	fabulafigured	fabula L	narrative, account, story; fable
		figuratus L	formed, fashioned
		fabulafiguratus L	fashioned by story
.34	antar	antar Etr.	eagle
		antar G	warp (in weaving)
597.01	Soe	Sol[ve] L	Absolve, Dissolve: fifth upward note in sol-fa
.01	La	La[bii] L	of the Lip: sixth upward note in sol-fa

.01	Soe? La	Sol L	the Sun
.14	sponthesite	sponte (*Abl.*) L	voluntarily
.16	breakfedes	foedus L fedus LL	league, treaty
		fides L	faith
		fedus Sab.	young goat
.17	parricombating	parri- OL	father-
.21	systomy	systolê G	contraction
		systomos G	with a narrow mouth; mouth-to-mouth
.21	dystomy	dystomia G	"hard-mouthedness": difficulty in pronouncing
		diastolê G	dilatation, drawing apart
.24	anilancinant	*anila L	little old woman
		lancinans L	tearing to pieces; squandering
.31	excelsius	excelsius L	higher, more highly
.32	Anemone	anemônê G	wind-flower: poppy
		anemos G	wind
.32	activescent	active L	actively
		activus L	practical
.32	torporature	torpor L	numbness
598.02	dromo	dromos G	course, race, running
		dromoô G	to hasten
.05	Nuctumbulumbumus	noctu L	at night, in the night
		noctu ambulabamus L	we were walking in the night
		noctuabundus L	having traveled all night
.06	Nil	nil L	nothing
.06	neantas	nea (*fem.*) G	new
		neanthês G	new-blown
.09	Diu	diu L	1. by day; 2. a long time, long
.10	Dormidy	dormite L	sleep ye!
.14	Adya	ad L	to, at
		dies, deus, dyavi, *etc.*	day; *see 593.01*
.17	supernoctural	*supernocturnus L	above *or* beyond the night
.18	Panpan	pan G	all
.23	accoustomology	akoustos G	heard, audible; that should be heard

		*akoustologia G	the skill *or* science of what is audible
.25	adyatants	adjutans L	helping, assisting
		agitans L	driving, impelling
		adya	*see 598.14*
.28	urb it orbs	Urbi et Orbi L	to the City and the World: *papal blessing or announcement*
.32	diurn	diurnus L	pertaining to the day; [LL] day
.34	hugibus	*hugibus (*Dat.*, *Abl. pl.*) fake*-L *modeled on*	to, for *or* by, with [*those who are*] huge[?]
		jugibus L	to, for *or* by, with [*those who are*] joined together
.34	hugibum	*hugium (*Gen. pl.*) fake*-L *modeled on*	of [*those who are*] huge[?]
		jugium L	of [*those who are*] joined together
599.01	cognance	cognatii (*pl.*) L	kinsmen
.01	orts	ortus L	rising, origin
.03	Time-o'-Thay	Timotheus G	"Honoring God": companion of Paul
.06	liofant	lio L	to plaster over, make smooth
		leios G	smooth
		fans L	speaking, saying
		*liofans L	speaking smoothly
.06	thurst	thus, thuris L	incense
.08	padapodopudupedding	pous, podos G	foot
		pes, pedis L	foot
.12	fulminance	fulmen L	lightning that strikes, thunderbolt
		fulminans L	hurling lightning
.17	equonomic	equo (*Dat.*, *Abl.*) L	to, for *or* by, with a horse
		equus L	horse
		aequus L	level, even
		oikonomikos G	skilled in household management
		*equonomicus L + G	skilled in horse management
.18	ecolube	oikos G	house
		lubricus L	slippery

.18	equalobe	equa L	mare
.18	equilab	equi (*Gen.*) L	horse's, of a horse
		aequi- L	equal-
.18	equilibbrium	*equilibrium L	a horse's balance
		aequilibrium L	level position, equilibrium; perfect equality
.18	Nomomorphemy	*nomomorphop- hêmê G	utterance in the form of law
.20	tache	tacha G	presently; perhaps
.20	Aecquotincts	aequitinctus L	equally dyed
		ecquo L	anywhere?
.23	Tamotimo	tamon (*Thessalian*) G	today
		timaô G	to honor
		timeo L	to fear
.25	Cumulonubulocirrhoni- mbant	cumulus L	heap, pile
		nubes L	cloud
		nubilum L	cloudy sky
		nebula L	mist, fog, smoke
		cirrus L	lock, curl
		nimbus L	rainstorm, thundercloud
		*cumulonubilo- cirronimbans	heaped-cloudy-curly- thunderclouding
600.05	Polycarp	poly- G	much-, many
		Polykarpos G	"Fruitful": Church father
.05	Innalavia	lavo L	to wash
.06	Deltas	delta G	letter D; female pudenda, rivermouth
.06	Piscium	piscium (*Gen. pl.*) L	of fishes, fishes'
.06	Sagittariastrion	Sagittarius L	The Archer: constellation
		astrion G	little star: an ornament
		Sagitarii L	the Archer's asterisk
		astrion G	
.07	alve	ave L	hail!
		alveus L	hollow, cavity; hull of a ship; bathtub, riverbed
.07	vale	vale L	farewell!
.09	apparentations	parentatio L	funeral obsequies for a parent
.11	Alieni	alieni (*pl.*) L	others; foreigners

.13	Linfian	lympha L	clear, running water
.17	preterpost	praeter L	past, beyond
		post L	behind, after
.22	Vitalba	vita L	life
		alba (*fem.*) L	white
		vita alba L	a white life
.24	anscessers	cessator L	loiterer, idler
.29	*Homos*	homos G	one and the same, common, joint
		homo L	man, person
.29	*Circas*	circa L	around, in the neighborhood
		circus L	circle, race-course
.29	*Elochlannensis*	e L	out of
		Lochlannensis L	pertaining to *Lochlann* (*Gaelic:* "Scandinavia"): Scandinavian
.29	*Homos Circas Elochlannensis*	homos homo circa e Lochlannensis dog-G-L-Gael.	the same person in the neighborhood out of Scandinavia
.33	arrah	ara G	*particle implying impatience*
.34	ferial	feria L	holiday
.35	celibrate	celebro L	to frequent, to go in great numbers
		caelibatus L	unmarried life, celibacy
.35	pirigrim	peregrinus L	foreigner; ML, pilgrim
		pyr G	fire
601.04–.05	lake lemanted	Lacus Lemanus L	Lake Geneva
.05	Is is	Isis	Egyptian goddess; #A
.05	atlanst	Atlas	giant changed into a mountain who holds up the sky
		atlantis L	pertaining to Atlas
.05–.06	urban and orbal	Urbi et Orbi L	to the City and the World: *papal utterance*
.14	novanas	nova (*fem.*) L	new
		novena (*fem.*) L	nine each
.14	ayand	aiens L	saying yes; assenting; asserting
.14	decadendecads	dekas, dekados G	group of ten
		[h]endeka G	eleven

		[h]endekas, [h]endekados	group of eleven
		*deka[h]endeka G	ten-eleven [*intended for* 111?]
		cadens L	falling
.16	*Sicut campanulae petalliferentes*	sicut	1. just like
		campanulae	metal-plate-bearing
		petaliferentes	little bells; 2. just like
		(1) LL; (2) Mod L	petal-bearing little bells
.16	coroll	corolla L	garland
.21	Phibia's	Phibi G	name for the Egyptian ibis
.23	Rhodamena's	*Rhodamênê G	Rosy-moon
.24	Una	una (*fem.*) L	one
		una (*adv.*) L	in one and the same place
.24	Vestity's	vestitus L	clothing, apparel, dress
.25	Bellavistura's	bella (*pl.*) L	wars
		bella (*fem.*) L	pretty; #*B*
.27	Glacianivia's	glacies; glacia- L	ice; ice-
		nivea (*fem.*) L	snowy
		*glacianivea (*fem.*) L	ice-snowy
.30	Euh!	eu G	well; good, fine
		heu L	alas! ah!
.32	Kathlins	kathairô G	to cleanse
.33	Soros	soror L	sister
.33	ma brone	mavros MG	dark, blind
		mauros G	
.33	exterra	ex terra L	out of land, from land
		extra L	outside
.33	acquarate	aqua L	water
		aquate L (*adv.*)	by the use of water, with water
.33	interirigate	interirrigo L	to conduct water among
.34	arkypelicans	arcus L	bow, arch; rainbow
		*archipelagos G	chief-sea: the Aegean
.34	austrologer	*austrologos L + G	expert on the south
.36	Milenesia	mille L	thousand
		nêsoi (*pl.*) G	islands
		mille L nêsoi G	a thousand islands

		*Millenêsia L + G	Land of a thousand islands
602.12	Roga	roga L	ask!
		roga (pl.) L	funeral piles, graves
.13	Roga	see 602.12 D	
.14	adestance	adeste L	draw near! be at hand! be present!
.17	independant	*independans recte independerans L	not weighing down
.20	collispendent	*collispendens L	hill-hanging
.22	Saturnights	Saturnus L	old Italian deity
.22	exhabiting	*exhabitans L	1. usually having-out; 2. living outside (a place)
.27	Patathicus	patheticus L for pathêtikos G	full of pathos, affecting
		patageô G	to clatter, clash
.35	noxer	nox L	night
		noxa L	harm, injury
603.05–.06	Tay, tibby, tanny, tummy, tasty, tosty, tay	tu (Nom.), tui (Gen.), tibi (Dat.), te (Acc.), te (Abl.) L	thou; of thee; to thee; thee; from, with, by thee
		tuus, tua, tuum L	thy, thine (masc., fem., neut.)
.14	alter	alter L	other, the other
.15	hydes of march	Idus Martiae L	March 15: date of Caesar's assassination (44 b.c.)
.28	Hyacinnsies	Hyakinthos G Hyacinthus L	beautiful youth turned to a flower
		cincinnus L	curl of hair
.28	heliotrollops	hêlios G	sun
		hêliotropos G	sundial; heliotrope
.29	iction	ictus L	blow, stroke, stab, sting
.30	summum	summum L	top, surface; highest place; at the utmost; for the last time
.31	quound	quo L	where; because; why
.32	sunt	sunt L	they are
.34	fostard	phôs G	light
.34	Tyro	Tyrô G	woman seduced by Poseidon

		tiro L	army recruit; beginner
		Tiro L	Cicero's secretary
.34	tora	torus L	couch, cushion
.35	novened	novenus L	nine each
.35	iconostase	eikonostasion G	shrine
.36	Phosphoron	Phôsphoron (*Acc.*) G	"Torch-bearing": *epithet of* Artemis
604.02	Roga's	roga L	ask!
		roga (*pl.*) L	funeral piles, graves
.05	fructed	fructus (*pp.*) L	enjoyed
.07	Malthus	Malchos	Carthaginian politician
.08	loiter on	eleutheron (*neut.*) G	free
.08	primilibatory	*primilibatorius L	pertaining to the one who makes the first libation (*drink-offering*)
.09	solicates	solicatio L	a sunning, sunbath
.12	Sideral	sidêrios G	made of iron
		sidereus L	starry
.14	vialact	via lactea L	the milky way
.15	gallaxion	ho galaxias G	the milky way
.15	rotatorattlers	rota L	wheel
		rotator L	a whirler round
.18	Rogua	rogus *or* rogum L	funeral-pile, grave
		roga L	ask!
.19	Taceate	tacete L	be ye silent!
		taceat L	let him be silent
.19	*Hagiographice*	hagiographê G	holy-writing
		Hagiographa G	"Holy Writings": last division of Old Testament, after Law and Prophets
.19	*Hagiographice canat Ecclesia*	hagiographice canat Ecclesia ML *or* Mod L	the Church sings hagiographically
.19	*Ecclesia*	ekklêsia G	duly summoned assembly; congregation; the Church
.22	protonotorious	protonotarius ML	chief clerk; *in the Vatican*: a recorder of pontifical events
		prôtos G	first
		notarius L	stenographer, shorthand-writer

.23	mitrogenerand	*mitragenerand-us L	(one) to be created a miter; one suitable to be a bishop
		*mitragenerans L	producing a miter
		*mitragerens L	miter-bearing
.25	Meganesia	*Meganêsia G	land of big islands
.25	Habitant	habitant L	they frequently have; they dwell
		habitans L	dwelling, abiding
605.04	encyclical	enkyklios G	circular, round
.07	praviloge	*pravilogeion L + G	depraved pulpit
		*pravilogos L + G	ugly talk, depraved idea, crooked thought
.08	postcreated	post L	after, behind
.08	*altare cum balneo*	altare cum balneo LL	altar together with bath
.09	invented	invenio, *pp.* inventus L	to find, to come upon
.14	triune	triunus eccl. L	three-one
.14	trishagion	trishagion G	thrice holy, holy trinity
.14	conducible	conducibilis L	advantageous, expedient
.15	super	super L	above, on top of
.15	hibernian	Hibernianus L	Irish
.17	ventrifugal	*ventrifugalis L	pertaining to fleeing from the belly, belly-fleeing
.21	*propter*	propter L	near, hard by, beside, besides
.22	extremely	extremum L	for the last time
.25	arenary	[h]arenaria L	sand-pit
.29	ubidience	ubi L	where, in what place
.30	gregorian	Gregorianus Mod L	pertaining to Pope Gregory I (*plain chant*) *or* Gregory XIII (*calendar*)
.30	ambrosian	Ambrosianus ML	pertaining to St. Ambrose (*chant*)
.32	*unacumque*	una cumque L	one, however; one, howsoever
		*unacumque L	and with one
.33	lector	lector L	reader
.34	effused	effundo, *pp.* effusus L	to pour out

606.03	translated	translatus (*pp.*) L	carried across
.05	Hydrophilos	hydrophilos G	water-lover
.05	*cappa magna*	cappa magna LL	great cloak
.07	*doctor insularis*	doctor insularis L	insular teacher, instructor belonging to an island
.09	*extempore*	ex tempore L	out of a [set] time; offhand
.11	affusion	*affusio L	a pouring upon
.13	Nuotabene	nota bene L	note well!
.23	*O ferax cupla*	O ferax cupla L	1. O fertile tub; O fruitful burial-vault; 2. O fruitful bond *or* connection; 3. O fertile *cúpla* (Gaelic: "couple")
		O felix culpa L	O happy sin; #B
.24	ablations	ablationes (*pl.*) L	takings-away
.26	anticidingly	*anticido L	to cut in front
.27	stigmataphoron	stigmatophoron (*neut.*) G	a thing bearing tattoo-marks
607.01	Missas	Missa (*fem. pp*) L	"Sent": the Mass
.02	veriters verity	veritas veritatis L	truth of truth
.02	maximollient	*maximolliens L	most softening
.03	ludubility	*ludibilitas L	playfulness
		Laudibiliter L	"Laudably": Pope Adrian's bull; #A
.03	Facst	fax L	torch, firebrand
.06	socerdatal	socer L sacerdotalis L	father-in-law priestly
.07	horolodgeries	horologiaris L	pertaining to a clock; provided with a clock
.09	Messagepostumia	Mesopotamia G Postumia L	Between the Rivers "Last": name of a Roman gens
.11	anniverse	*anniverse, anniversarie L	annually
.11	nam	nam L	for, for instance, certainly, on the other hand

.12	nam	*see 607.11 K*	
.20	Sveasmeas	meas (*Acc. pl. fem.*) L	my, mine
.21	sublumbunate	sub lumbo L	under the loin
		*subluminatus L	faintly illumined
.21	A polog	apologia G	speech in defense
.22	Excutes	ex cute L	out of the skin
.28	Solsking	Sol L	the Sun
.30	whereupont	pons, pontis L	bridge
.35	mensy	mensis L	month
.35	upponnus	pondus L	weight
608.04	essenesse	esse (*infinitive*) L	to be
		*nesse *for* non esse L	not to be
.07	Arth	arthron G	joint
.10	Sphygmomanometer	sphygmomanom-etron G	pulse-infrequent-measur-er
.17	salaciters	*salaciter L	lustfully, lecherously, salaciously
.23	pubably	pubens L	at the age of puberty
.29	*Sorte*	sorte L	by lot, by chance
.32	Phoenican	Phoenicus L	Phoenician, Carthaginian
.36	diar, ah diar	diarium L	daily allowance; diary
609.01	sinegear	sine L	without
.02	absolent	absolens L	away from the custom, far from usual
.02	populose	populus L	the people
		populos (*Acc. pl.*) L	peoples
.03	magnumoore	magnum (*neut.*) L	big, great
		môros G	foolish
.12	Amaryllis	Amaryllis G	"Twinkling[?]": shepherdess in Vergil's *Eclogues*
.14	milletestudinous	mille L	thousand
		testudineus L	belonging to a tortoise
.17	Hockeyvilla	hoc (*neut.*) L	this thing here
		villa L	farmhouse, country place
.18	Fockeyville	foci (*Gen.*) L	of the hearth
		foci (*pl.*) L	hearths, fireplaces
		villa L	farmhouse, country place

.22	houram	horam (*Acc.*) L	hour
.24	*Muta*	Muta L	"Dumb": a goddess
.24	Quodestnunc fumusiste volvhuns ex Domoyno?	Quod est nunc fumus iste volvens ex Domino? L	What now is that smoke rolling out of the Lord?
.24	Domoyno	dôma oinou G	house of wine
.25	*Juva*	*juva L	help, aid
.26	*Muta*	see 609.24 A	
.28	*Juva*	see 609.25 A	
.28	Dies is Dorminus master and commandant illy tonobrass	Deus est Dominus noster et commandat ille tenebras LL	God is our Lord and he commands the darkness
		Dies est Dominus noster et ... LL	Our Lord is the Day and ...
		Dies est dormitio nostra et ... LL	Day is our sleeping and ...
.28	commandant	commandant LL	they chew
.30	*Muta*	see 609.24 A	
.30	Diminussed	*diminutus L	broken into small pieces
.30	aster	astêr G	star
.30	Diminussed aster	diminutus aster LL	a star broken into bits
		Dominus noster L	our Lord
.32	*Juva*	see 609.25 A	
.32	Chrystanthemlander	chrysanthemon G	golden–flower: garden ranunculus
.35	*Muta*	see 609.24 A	
610.01	*Juva*	see 609.25 A	
.01	fundementially	fundamentum L dementia L	foundation, basis insanity
.01	theosophagusted	*theoisophagos G	god–gullet
		theosophia G theophagos G	god–wisdom god–eater
.03	*Muta*	see 609.24 A	
.03	Petrificationibus	*petrifactionibus (*Dat., Abl. pl.*) L	to, for *or* by, with, from stonemaking

.04	rearrexes	*reerigo L	to re-erect
		rex L	king
.04	memorialorum	memorialium	of memoirs
		(*Gen. pl.*) L	
.05	*Juva*	*see 609.25 A*	
.06	*Muta*	*see 609.24 A*	
.06	Ulloverum	ullum verum L	1. any truth; 2. any duty
		ullo verum L	to, for *or* by, with, from anybody, certainly
.06	Fulgitudo ejus Rhedonum teneat	fulgitudo ejus Rhedonum teneat L	his brightness holds of the *Rhedones* (*people of north Gaul*)
		fortitudo ejus Rhodum tenuit L	his strength has held Rhodes; #*B*
.07	*Juva*	*see 609.25 A*	
.07–.08	ubidientia of the savium is our ervics fenicitas	obedientia civium urbis felicitas L	Dublin's motto; #*B*
.07	ubidientia	ubi L	where
		deinde L	thereafter, then
.08	savium	suavium L	kiss
.08	fenicitas	*Phoenicitas L	Phoenixness; Phoenicianness, Carthaginianness
.09	*Muta*	*see 609.24 A*	
.09	soly ... supremest	Sol supremus L	Supreme Sun[–god]
.10	rugular	ruga L	wrinkle
.11	*Juva*	*see 609.25 A*	
.14	*Muta*	*see 609.24 A*	
.14	velleid	vello L	to pluck
		velle L	pluck! shear!
		id L	it, that thing
.14	paridicynical	Paridis (*Gen.*) G L	Paris's, of Paris [Helen's lover]
		kynikos G	dog–like: Cynic
.16	*Juva*	*see 609.25 A*	
.16	Ut vivat volumen sic pereat pouradosus	ut vivat volumen sic pereat paradisus L	1. that the volume may live, so may paradise perish; 2. that the revolution may live, thus let paradise perish
.17	*Muta*	*see 609.24 A*	
.18	*Juva*	*see 609.25 A*	

.19	*Muta*	*see 609.24 A*	
.19	Suc	suco L	a sucker
.20	*Juva*	*see 609.25 A*	
.21	*Muta*	*see 609.24 A*	
.21	Ad	ad L	to, at, toward, for
.21	Piabelle	pia (*fem.*) L	pious, dutiful
		bella (*fem.*) L	pretty
.21	et	et L	and
.21	Purabelle	pura (*fem.*) L	clean, chaste, pure
		bella (*fem.*) L	pretty
.21	Ad Piabelle et Purabelle	at pia et pura et bella L	indeed pious and pure and fair
		pia et pura bella L	pious and clean wars: Vico's phrase; # *B*
.22	*Juva*	*see 609.25 A*	
.23	*Muta*	*see 609.24 A*	
.28	*Juva*	*see 609.25 A*	
.30	*Muta*	*see 609.24 A*	
.32	*Juva*	*see 609.25 A*	
.34	Peredos	peredo L	to eat up, to consume
		parodos G	entrance [*of Chorus in drama*]
.35	Velivision	velum L	a sail
		*velivisio L	a sail-seeing; a veil-seeing
		*velivisio L	a wish-seeing, seeing what you wish
.35	Velivision victor	veni vidi vici L	I came I saw I conquered; # *B*
.36	Winny Willy Widger	veni vidi vici L # *Labials*	I came I saw I conquered; # *B*
.36	Heliotrope	hêliotropion G	sundial
611.04	Tunc	tunc L	then
.06	heptachromatic	heptachrômatik- os G	seven-colored
.06	septicoloured	septicoloratus L	seven-colored
.07	Patholic	patho- G # *P/K Split* # *L/R Interchange*	suffering-, -suffering Catholic Pathoric
.10	Patholic	*see 611.07J*	
.10	quoniam	quoniam L	since now, whereas
.11	scilicet	scilicet L	"you may know": it is evident, of course
.13	photoprismic	*phôtoprismos G	gripping light tightly

		*phôtoprismatik-os G	pertaining to sawdust of light; light-prismatic
.13	velamina	velamina (*pl.*) L	coverings, robes, garments, veils
.13	panepiphanal	*panepiphanês G	all-visible, completely manifest, totally famous
.14	spectacurum	spectaculum L #*L/R Interchange*	show, sight, spectacle
.14	zoantholitic	zôon G	animal
		anthos G	flower
		lithos G	stone
		zôon-anthos-lith-os G	*three stages downward in Great Chain of Being: animal, vegetable, mineral*
.16	photoreflection	phôto- G	light
		reflexio L	bending back
.17	iridals	*iridalis L	pertaining to the rainbow
.17	gradationes	gradationes (*pl.*) L	series of steps, flights of stairs
.18	heupanepi	heu L	alas! oh!
		eu G	well; good, fine
		pan G	all, everything
		epi G	upon
.19	huepanwor	heu L	alas! oh!
		eu G	well; good, fine
		pan G	all, everything
.19	absorbere	absorbere (*infinitive*) L	to swallow down, to devour, to eat up
.19	puraduxed	pura (*fem.*) L	pure, clean
		dux L	leader, chief
.20	Entis-	entis (*Gen.*) L	of a being, being's
.20	-Onton	ontôn (*Gen. pl.*) G	of beings, of reality, of things that actually exist
.21	id est	id est L	that is
.22	panepiwor	pan G	all, everything
		epi G	upon
.22–.23	in ... coloribus	in coloribus L	in colors
.23	sextuple	sex L	six
.23	gloria	gloria L	fame, honor, glory
.24	untisintus	unde L	whence
		intus L	on the inside, within

.24	obs	obs OL	about, in front of, for
.24	epiwo	epi G	upon
.25	stareotypopticus	*stereotypos G	solid impression, firm blow, hard principle
		*stereoptikos G	pertaining to solid eyes, solid vision
		*steatopygikos G	having a fat rump
.25	utpiam	utpiam L	anyway
.25	ontesantes	omnes sancti L	all saints
		onta G	reality, things that actually exist
.29	verbigratiagrading	verbi gratia L	"for a word": for example, for instance
.29	murmurulentous	murmurillo L	to mutter
		lentus L	slow, sluggish
.29	stridulocelerious	stridulus L	creaking, hissing
		celer L	swift, quick, hasty, speedy
.30	comprehendurient	*comprehenduri-ens L	longing to grasp, wishing to seize
.31	claractinism	clarus L	clear, bright
		aktis G	ray, beam
		*claraktinismos L + G	brightrayism
.31	augumentationed	augumentum L	increase, growth, augmentation
.32	caloripeia	kalopoiêsis G	a doing good
		*caloripoiia L + G	a making of heat, a heating
612.01	mutismuser	mutis L	you (sing.) are mumbling
		mutus L	dumb, mute
		musso L	to mutter
		Musa L	Muse
.01	compyhandy	comprehendo L	to grasp, seize, lay hold of
.03	pace	pace L	with [someone's] leave
.03	Exuber	exubero L	to grow luxuriantly, to be abundant
		exuberans L	superfluous
.06	bulopent	boulê G	will, determination
		ôpê G	view; aspect, appearance
		*boulôpê G	desired appearance, wished-for view

.08	nos	nos L	we
.11	undesendas	unde L	whence
		unda L	wave, billow
.11	contusiones	contusiones (*pl.*) L	crushings, breakings, batterings, bruisings; bruises
.12	Sublissimime	sublimissime L	most loftily
.14	seecut	sicut L	so as, just as, as
.16	Punc	punctus L	prick, sting, puncture; a point
		punctim L	with the point
.19	aposterioprismically	a posteriori L	from the following, from what follows
		prismatikos G	pertaining to sawdust, pertaining to a prism
.19	apatstrophied	apostrophos G	a turning away
		atrophia G	want of food; atrophy
.19	periparolysed	*periparalysis G	secret undoing all around; allaround paralysis
.20	Irismans	Iris G L	goddess of the rainbow; the rainbow
.22	neutrolysis	neutro L	to neither one side nor the other, neither way
		*neurolysis G	loosening of the sinews
.23	viriditude	viriditas L	greenness
.23	eruberuption	erubesco L	to redden
		*eruberuptio L	a red breaking-out
.24	tappropinquish	appropinquo L	to approach
.24	gnosegates	gnôsis G	inquiry, investigation, knowledge
.27	Balenoarch	*balaenarchos L + G	whale-chief
.28	Balenoarch	*see 612.27 A*	
.29	sympol	sympolloi G	many together
613.01	heliots	hêlios G	sun
		Heilôtês G	Spartan serfs
.03	Adie	a die L	from the day
		ad die L	to the day
		hodie L	today
.03–.04	Per ye comdoom doominoom noonstroom. Yeasome priestomes. Fullyhum toowhoom	per jucundum Dominum nostrum Jesum Christum Filium tuum L	through our dear Lord Jesus Christ thy Son

.09	Taborneccles	tabernaculum L	tent
		ekklêsis G	appeal
.09	scenopegia	skênopêgia G	setting-up of tents; Feast of Tabernacles
.11	eggons	ego L egô, egôn G	I, myself
.12	pancosmos	*pankosmos G	all-order, whole-universe
.14	*Fuitfiat*	fuit L	there was
		fiat L	let there be
.15	laud	laus L	praise
.15	orielising	orior L	to rise (*the sun*)
.15	benedictively	benedictio eccl. L	praising, blessing
.17	spathe	spathê G	broad blade; leaf-like enclosing part of a flower
.17	calyptrous	kalyptra G	veil, cover; seed-capsule
.17	glume	gluma L	corn-husk, hull
.17	involucrumines	involucrum L	wrapper, case, envelope
.17	perinanthean	periantheô G	to bloom
		perianthês G	with flowers all around
		perinaietês G	neighbor
.18	Amenta	amenta (*pl.*) L	straps, thongs, shoe-strings
		amentia L	madness, insanity
.18	fungoalgaceous	fungus L	mushroom
		alga L	seaweed
.18	muscafilicial	musca L	fly
		filix L	fern
.18	graminopalmular	*graminopalmes L	grass-shoot
		palma L	palm-tree, palm (*of the hand*)
.18	planteon	planta L	1. sprout, shoot, twig, cutting; plant; 2. sole (*of the foot*)
		*planteon LL	place of plants
.19	livivorous	*vivivorus L	feeding on life, eating what is alive
.19	luxuriotiating	luxurio L	to be rank, to abound to excess
		otior L	to be at leisure
.22	theas	thea G	goddess
.25	runcure	runco L	to weed, to weed out

.25	amullium	*amulium LL *for* amulion G	cake
.26	chlorid	chlôris, chlôridis G	greenfinch; a kind of grape
.27	chalce	chalkê G	bronze statue
		chalkê *or* kalchê G	a purple flower; purple
.28	folgor	fulgur L	lightning-flash
.28	optimominous	*optimominosus L	full of the best omens
.35	Monogynes	*monogynês G	(*one with*) one woman, a one-womaner, a one-woman man
.36	Diander	*diandros G	two-man
		Diana L	goddess, of the hunt, moon
614.01	Mopsus	Mopsus L Mopsos G	name of several soothsayers; also a shepherd in Vergil's *Eclogues*
.01	Gracchus	Gracchus L	name of a family of prominent Roman statesmen
.02	horodities	Hêrodotos G	G historian
.02	incessantlament	antlos G	bilge-water
.02	Annone	Annona L	goddess of the yearly produce; the yearly produce; dearness; prices
.11	surviva	viva (*fem.*) L	alive
.11	iorn	Ierne L	Ireland
.13	Noxt	nox L	night
.16	prives	prives L	you (*sing.*) may bereave, deprive, rob
.25	Eblania's	Eblana G *Eblania G L	Dublin Dublin-land
.25	delty	deltoeidês G	shaped like the letter *delta*, triangular
.25	Deva	Deva L	river in north Britain; *mod.* Dee *in Scotland*
.27	vicociclometer	*vicokyklometron L + G	street-circle-measurer, village-circle-measurer
.27	tetradomational	tetra G dôma G domator L	four house tamer, (animal-)breaker

.28	gazebocroticon	*gazebo fake- L	I shall gaze
		krotêtikos G	plausible
		kritikos G	able to discern
		kritikon (*neut.*) G	something picked out, choice
		*gazebo kritikon	a choice gazebo
.28	Mamma	mamma G L	female breast
.30	autokinatonetically	*autokinêtonik- os G	pertaining to a self-moving thing
.33	dialytically	dialytikos G	able to sever; relaxing; embodying a compromise
615.01	type	typos G	blow, impression, mark
.01	tope	topos G	place
.01	litter	littera L	letter
.02	Plooney	Plinius L	Roman gens, numbering two famous authors; *see 255.18, 281.04*
.02	Columcellas	Columella L	Roman agricultural writer; #*A*
.04	ghoulish	Gallia L	land of the Gauls, *including mod.* France, north Italy, Belgium, Netherlands
.04	illyrical	Illyria	ancient country, *covering mod.* Jugoslavia *and* Albania
.04	innumantic	Numantia L	city in Hispania Tarraconnensis (*north Spain*)
.05	anastomosically	anastomôtikos G	suitable for opening
.05	preteridentified	*praeteridentific- atus ML	previously identified
.05	paraidiotically	*paraidiôtikos G	alongside the private, almost privately
.06	adomic	*adômikos G	houseless
.08	Cockalooralooraloome- nos	*[Cockalooraloo- ral]oumenos G	[Cockalooralooral]ing
.23	besidus	sidus L	constellation, group of stars
.24	pulltomine	pulto L	to beat
.25	paladays	palai G	long ago
616.05	Hibernia	Hibernia L	Ireland

.06	carpus	corpus L	body
		carpo L	to pluck, gather; enjoy, consume; divide, distinguish
		karpos G	1. fruits of the earth, corn; seed 2. wrist
.10	delitious	delitisco L	to lie hidden
.12	chloras	chlôra (*fem.*) G	pale green
.16	exgust	*exgusto L	to taste out of, to eat a little of
.20	coerogenal	*coerogo L	to expend together, to pay out together
		*erôgenos G	love-engendering
		*coerogenos Mod L	engendering love together
.24	metropolonians	mêtêr, mêtro- G	mother, mother-
		Polonia ML	Poland
.25	Cumsensation	cum L	with
.30	manunknown	manu L	by hand
.35	Pondups	pondus L	weight
617.01	Levia	*Levia L	[she who is] light *or* trifling
.06	Danis	Danis (*Dat.*, *Abl.*, *pl.*) L	to, for *or* by, with, from the Danes
.12	Force in giddersh	Vercingetorix	Gallic leader; *see* 281.F1
.12	Tomothy	Timotheus G	companion of Paul; *see* 258.35
.14	characticuls	Cara[c]tacus	British king
.25	moracles	mora L	delay
		moracillum L	anything small and hard
		*moracula L	a little delay
.30	erronymously	*erronymos L + G	with wrong name, misnamed
618.01	O, felicious coolpose	O felix culpa L	O happy sin; #B
.02	virgils	P. Vergilius Maro	Roman epic poet; *see* 270.25
.02	Armsworks	Arma virumque L	"Arms and the man": *first words of Vergil's* Aeneid
.08	Sully	Sulla	Roman soldier-politician; #A
.14	scissions	scissio LL	a cleaving, dividing
.14–.15	Marie Reparatrices	Maria Reparatrix L	Mary the Restoress

.22	cubarola	Cuba L	goddess who protects the lying-down of children
.23	beaux	bos L	bull, ox, cow
.23	alce	alces L alkê G	elk
.24	Item	item L	just so, likewise, also
.25	bitem	bis L	twice
.29	Sully	see 618.08 J	
.30	herearther	arthron G	joint
.31	Laraseny	Lara	talkative nymph whose tongue was cut out by Jupiter; renamed *Muta* (*see 609.24 etc.*); identified with *Tacita* (*see 213.30*)
619.02	urogynal	uro L	to burn
		gynê G	woman
		*erôgenês G	generating love
.02	that ... pan	to pan G	the All: the world, the universe
.07	amphybed	amphi G	on both sides
.16	Alma	alma (*fem.*) L	nourishing, cherishing, kind
.16	Luvia	*luvia (*fem.*) L	pertaining to washing
.16	Pollabella	Polla = Paula L	"Little": *fem. pers. name*
		bella (*fem.*) L	pretty
		bella (*neut. pl.*) L	wars
		Polla bella	pretty Paula, pretty Polly
		paula bella L	little wars
.19	deckhuman	decumanus L	1. tithe-gatherer; 2. east-to-west boundary line
		Decuma L	one of the Three Fates
.27	cape	caput L	head
.27	pede	pes, *pl.* pedes L	foot
.29	Norvena's	novena (*fem.*) L	nine each
.30	silve	silve ML silvae (pl.) L	woods
.30	exsogerraider	exô G	out of, outside
620.01	umbr	umbra L	shade, shadow
.03	nill	nil L	nothing
.05	Proudpurse Alby	Perfidiosus Albion L	Treacherous Britain

.06	Eireen	eirêne G	peace
.08	Lucan	M. Annaeus Lucanus	Roman poet; #A
.09	Iren	Ierne L Iernê G	Ireland
		eirênê G	peace
.18	crony aunts	Kroniôn G	son of Kronos: Zeus; #A
.21	Minssions	mingo L	to urinate
.30	gricks	Graeci L	Greeks
.31	ledden	[lingua] Latina L	the L language
.32	Is is	Isis	Egyptian goddess; #A
621.01	Phoenix	Phoenix L	fabulous bird of Arabia; see 265.08
.03	lausafire	laus L	praise
		lucifer L	light-bearer: the morning star
.08	Arctur	Arktouros G	Bear-Guard: star; the
		Arcturus L	time of its rising (mid-September)
.14	Oaxmealturn	me alterum (Acc.) L	another me
.18	nolly	noli L	do not wish to, do not
.20	arthou	Artus L	original of King Arthur; see 252.20
		arktos G	bear
.22	languo	langueo L	to be faint, weary
		languor L	faintness, feebleness
		lingua L	tongue, language
.26	infams	infamis L	of ill repute, notorious
		infans L	speechless; infant
.35	Pax	pax L	peace
622.03	elicted	*elictus L	tied out; unbandaged
.03	elicitous	elicitus (pp.) L	drawn out, enticed forth
.09	antilopes	*antilôps G	counter-mantle
.11	possumbotts	possum L	I can
.21	nos	nos L	we
.23	Olobobo	ololuzô G	to cry aloud
		boaô G	to cry aloud, to shout
.36	Platonic	Platônikos G	follower of Plato
623.21	Flura's	fluor L	a flow
		Flora L	goddess of flowers

.25	quolm	quo L	where; because, wherefore
.28	Lonu nula	Luna L	the Moon
.34	crux	crux L	cross, gallows
624.09	bubel	bubile L	stall for oxen
		bubleum L	kind of wine
		bubo L	owl
		boubalos G	antelope
		boubôn G	swollen gland
.10	Jove	Jovis-Pater L	Brightness-Father: Jupiter; #A
.15	limpidy	limpide L	clearly
		Lampetiê G	"Shiner": daughter of the sun-god, changed into a tree
		lampades (pl.) G	torches, lamps, lights
.25	Yhesters	hesternus L	of yesterday, yesterday's
.26	nasturtls	nasturtium L	nose-twister: a kind of cress
.26	Medeurscodeignus	medeus, medius L	by god!
		dignus L	worthy, deserving
		medeus condignus L	by the most worthy god!
.28	cumhulments	cumulus L	heap, pile
625.03	Pharaops	Pharos G	island with lighthouse near Alexandria; #A
		ôps G	eye, face
		*pharôps G	lighthouse-eye; plow-face; etc.
.04	Aeships	aes L	crude metal; copper; bronze
.07	*Quid superabit*	quid superabit L	what shall surpass?
		quis superabit L	who shall overcome?
		quis/quid separabit L	who/what shall separate?
.07	villities	vilitas L	cheapness
.07	valleties	valetudo L	health, state of health
.07	villities valleties	vanitas	emptiness of
		vanitatum L	emptinesses, vanity of vanities
.20	agres	ager L	territory, soil, cultivated land; field

.21	Steadyon	stadion G	1. measure of distance, approx. 606 feet; 2. place for footraces
.22	Cooloosus	Colossus L	giant statue, *esp. at*
		Kolossos G	*Rhodes*
		Colosseum L	"The Huge Place": Vespasian's amphitheater (still) at Rome
.26	Eblanamagna	Eblana G	Great Dublin
		Magna L	
626.05	Apophanypes	apophainô G	to show forth, display
		apokalypsis G	uncovering, revelation
		epiphaneia G	appearance, coming into view
		*apophaneia G	disappearance, going away from view
.14	duohs	duo L	two
.19	non	non L	not
.27	Vulking	Vulcanus L	god of fire; #A
.27–.28	Vulking Corsergoth	Vercingetorix	Gallic chieftain; *see* 281.F1
.31	delth to	delta G	letter D; rivermouth; female pudenda
.34	Illas	Ilias G L	"The Trojan Woman": Helen
		illa L	she
627.28	pulchrabelled	pulchra (*fem.*) L	beautiful
		bella (*fem.*) L	pretty
.28	Amazia	*amazeia,	breastlessness, lack of a
		*amazia G	breast (*ancient etymology for* Amazon)
.30	Niluna	nil L	nothing
		luna L	the moon
.32	Auravoles	aura L	air, breeze
		volens L	willing, voluntary
		voles L	you (*sing.*) may fly
628.05	therrble prongs	*trans.* tridens L	three-pronged, treble-pronged: trident: *attribute of Neptune* [*Tridentifer, Tridentiger*]
.06	moremens	mora L	delay
.06	Avelaval	ave L	hail!
		lavo L	to wash

		vale L	farewell!
.14	mememormee	memini L	to remember
		memoro L	to remind, to bring to remembrance

Glossary for Joyce's Other Works

The Latin and Greek Words, Phrases and Allusions in the Poems (*Chamber Music, The Holy Office, Gas from a Burner, Pomes Penyeach, Ecce Puer*), *Dubliners, Stephen Hero, A Portrait of the Artist as a Young Man, Exiles,* and *Ulysses*

Because of the relative sparsity of classical instances in the poems, and because the poems themselves are widely reprinted, the citations for the poems are limited to line number only, within each poem, and without reference to any edition. The single citation for *Exiles* is identified by its position in the play. Likewise citations for *Dubliners* are to page only, not to line number, although we specify three representative editions. In general, *Stephen Hero, A Portrait of the Artist,* and *Ulysses* are dealt with on the pattern of *Finnegans Wake.* Since citations for *Stephen Hero* serve equally to all editions to the extent the editions share the same text, we have been able to follow the *Finnegans Wake* model exactly for that work, citing only the edition of 1963, by page and line, without complication. *A Portrait* and *Ulysses* have also been cited by page and line for the base texts, but by page number only for the additional representative editions cited.

The entries for *Dubliners* are listed successively after the title of each story; chapter divisions are indicated for *Stephen Hero, A Portrait,* and *Ulysses.* Variant readings among the editions are either ignored or tacitly conformed.

The following are the relevant editions used:

Dubliners: Text, Criticism, and Notes, ed. Robert Scholes and A. Walton Litz. The Viking Critical Library (1969). *Base text.*

Dubliners. Modern Library (1926, 1954). Cited as M.

Dubliners. In *The Portable James Joyce,* ed. Harry Levin. The Viking Press (1949). Cited as P.

Stephen Hero. New Directions, ed. Spencer, Slocum, and Cahoon (1963).

A Portrait of the Artist as a Young Man. Viking: Compass Books (1956). *Base text.*

A Portrait of the Artist as a Young Man. Modern Library (1928). Cited as M.

Ulysses. Vintage Books, Random House, "new ed., corrected and reset" (1961). *Base text.* [N.B. This edition is textually identical with the Modern Library edition of 1961 cited in *A Gaelic Lexicon* as M.]
Ulysses. Modern Library (1934). Cited as M.
Ulysses. Shakespeare & Co., Paris (1922–1930). Cited as P.

Chamber Music
XII

line 3	plenilune	plenilunium L	the full moon
XIII			
line 4	Epithalamium	epithalamium L *for* epithalamion G	"at the bridal-chamber": a weddingsong
XXV			
line 4	Oread	oreias, oreiados G	mountain-nymph
XXVII			
line 1	Mithridates	Mithridates VI (Eupator Dionysos)	"gift of Mithras": king of Pontus (120–63 B.C.); fought 3 wars against Rome; driven to suicide by defeat, he found his prophylactic diet had made him immune to poison

The Holy Office

lines 2,55	Katharsis	katharsis G	cleansing, purification

Gas from a Burner

line 98	*Memento homo*	memento, homo [quia tu pulvis es] L	remember, man [that thou art dust]: *Ash Wednesday prayer*

Pomes Penyeach
"Simples"

line 9	a waxen ear	*allusion to* Odysseus	*Odysseus stopped the ears of his crewmen with wax so they would not hear the fatally alluring song of the Sirens*

Ecce Puer

title	Ecce Puer	ecce puer L	behold the boy!

Dubliners
"The Sisters"

p. 12, M10, P22	*R.I.P*	R[equiescat] I[n] P[ace] L	May he rest in peace

p. 13, M12, P23	to pronounce Latin properly	*an enigma*	*at least three systems* *might have been taught* *as "proper"*
"A Little Cloud"			
p. 72, M87, P82	Atalantas	Atalanta L Atalantê G	swift-footed maiden
p. 74, M91, P85	Lithia	lithia G	marble; jewelry
"Counterparts"			
p. 93, M115, P105	the eclogues	ecloga L eklogê G	"selection": excerpt of fine passages; a short poem
		Eclogae L	"Eclogues": *grammarians' name for* *Vergil's* Bucolica, *pastoral poems*
"A Painful Case"			
p. 109, M135, P120	Rotunda	rotunda (*fem.*) L	circular, round
p. 113, M141, P124	*Secreto*	secreto L	in private, without witnesses
p. 114, M143, P126	Leoville	leo L	lion
"Ivy Day in the Committee Room"			
p. 120, M151, P132	imminent	imminens L	hanging down over, overhanging
p. 122, M153, P133	Edward Rex	[Edward] Rex L	King [Edward]
p. 122, M153, P133	spondulics	spondulos G	vertebra, backbone; voting pebble
"Grace"			
p. 159, M201, P172	thorax	thôrax G	coat of mail; the chest
p. 159, M202, P173	*bona-fide*	bona fide L	in good faith; #*B*
p. 167, M212, P181	Leo	Leo L	"Lion": name of 13 popes
		Leo XIII	pope 1878–1903
p. 167, M213, P182	*Lux upon Lux*	lux L	light
p. 167, M213, P182	*Lux in Tenebris*	lux in tenebris L	a light in the darkness
		Lumen in Coelo L	a light in the heaven: *formula corresponding* *to Leo XIII in the* *pseudo-medieval* *prophecy of St. Malachy*

p. 167, M213, P182	*Tenebrae*	tenebrae L	darkness (a Good Friday service)
p. 167, M213, P182	Pius	Pius L	"Dutiful": name of 12 popes
		Pius IX	pope 1846–1878
p. 167, M213, P182	*Crux upon Crux*	crux L	cross, gallows
		Crux de Cruce L	a cross from the cross: *formula corresponding to Pius IX in the prophecy of Malachy*
p. 169, M214, P183	one of Pope Leo's poems was on the invention of the photograph—in Latin	"Ars Photographica (An[no] MDCCCLXVII)": Expressa solis spiculo / Nitens imago, quam bene / Frontis decus, vim luminum / Refers, et oris gratiam. / O mira virtus ingeni / Novumque monstrum! Imaginem / Naturae Apelles aemulus / Non pulchriorem pingeret. L	"The Photographic Art (In the Year 1867)": Shining image produced by the sun's beam, how well you give back the brow's dignity, the force of life, the features' grace. O admirable excellence of mind, and a new marvel! Apelles, Nature's rival, could not paint a lovelier picture.
pp. 168, 169, M214, 214–15, P183	*ex cathedra*	ex cathedra L	from the seat [of authority]
p. 169, 170, M216, P185	*Credo*	credo L	I believe
p. 172, M220, P187 "The Dead"	quincunx	quincunx L	five-twelfths; the form of five spots on dice

| p. 204, M262, 263, P222 | the Three Graces | hai Charites G | three (*or more*) attendants on Aphroditê; *Hesiod names* Aglaia *("Splendor"),* Euphrosynê *("Mirth") and* Thaliê *("Abundance"), daughters of Zeus and Eurynomê* |
| p. 204, M263, P222 | the part that Paris played | *allusion to* Paris-Alexander of Troy | *selected to judge the beauty of Hêra, Athênê and Aphroditê, he accepted Aphroditê's bribe of Helen and so occasioned the Trojan War* |

Stephen Hero
Chapter XV

| 028.06 & sqq. | Daedalus | Daedalus L *for* Daidalos G | "Cunning Worker," "Artist": *legendary craftsman and inventor;* #A |
| 030.26,29 | Eucharist | eucharistia G | thankfulness, gratitude; thanksgiving |

Chapter XVI

033.02	*Poeta nascitur non fit*	poeta nascitur, non fit L	a poet is born, not made
033.03–04	*Poema fit, non nascitur*	poema fit, non nascitur L	a poem is made, not born
033.14	pleisiosauros	*plêsiosauros G	near-lizard (*mod. coinage*)
041.23	*Index*	Index Expurgatorius Mod L	"List for Purifying": *former list of books required by Catholic Church to be expurgated before read by the faithful*
		or Index Librorum Prohibitorum L	"List of Forbidden Books": *list of books forbidden to be read by the faithful*

Chapter XVII

| 052.11 | *paterfamilias* | paterfamilias OL | patriarch of an extended family |

Chapter XIX

077.05	patria	patria L	fatherland
080.01	*Noli Tangere*	noli tangere L	do not [wish to] touch
		Noli me tangere L	"Touch me not": Christ to Mary Magdalen after the Resurrection (*John 20:17*)
089.31	Attica	Attica L Attikê G	G province of which Athens is capital
092.35	*Apologia*	apologia G	defense-speech
095.19	*Pulcra sunt quae visa placent*	pulchra sunt quae visa placent L	those things are beautiful which, when seen, please
		Pulchra enim dicuntur ea quae visa placent L—*Summa Theologica* I.q.5, art. 4	For those things are said to be beautiful that please when seen: *what St. Thomas actually wrote*
096.08	*Ad pulcritudinem tria requiruntur*	ad pulchritudinem tria requiruntur L	for beauty three things are required
096.10	*Integritas, consonantia, claritas*	integritas, consonantia, claritas L	completeness, agreement, clearness
097.01 & sqq.	Eschylus	Aeschylus L Aischylos G	eminent Athenian dramatist
097.11	Menander	Menandros G	Athenian writer of "New" Comedy

Chapter XX

103.29	*ex cathedra*	ex cathedra L	from the chair [of authority]
103.33	*advocatus diaboli*	advocatus diaboli eccl. L	the devil's attorney, the devil's advocate
106.07	*Atque ad duas horas in Wicklowio venit*	Atque ad duas horas in Wicklowio venit dog-L	And then it comes into Wicklow at two o'clock
106.08	*Damnum longum tempus prendit*	Damnum longum tempus prendit dog-L	It takes a damn long time
106.10	*Quando*	Quando L	When? At what time?
106.10	*quo in*	quo in L	in what, in which

106.12	*Quo in batello?*	Quo in battello dog-L	In what boat?
106.12	in *"Regina Maris"*	in Regina Maris dog-L	in the "Queen of the Sea" [*i.e., the "Seaqueen"*]
106.18	*Ecce orator qui in malo humore est*	Ecce orator qui in malo humore est dog-L	Behold the rhetorician who is in a bad humor
106.19	*Non sum*	Non sum L	I am not
106.20	*Credo ut estis*	Credo ut estis dog-L	I believe you are
106.21	*Minime*	Minime [dog-]L	[not] the least: no
106.22–23	*Credo ut vos sanguinarius mendax estis quia facies vestra mostrat ut vos in malo humore estis*	Credo ut vos sanguinarius mendax estis quia facies vestra monstrat ut vos in malo humore estis dog-L	I think you are a bloody liar because your face shows that you are in a bad humor
107.21	*Habesne bibitum?*	Habesne bibitum dog-L	Have you drunk? Are you drunk?
108.05	*Bellam boccam habet*	Bellam buccam habet dog-L	He has a nice cheek
108.08	*Patrioticus est*	Patrioticus est dog-L	He is patriotic
109.11	*Feuc an eis super stradam . . . in Liverpoolio*	[Feuch an *Gaelic*][eis *German*] super [strada *Ital.*] stratam . . . in Liverpoolio dog-L *etc.*	[See the][ice] on the street . . . in Liverpool
113.21	*Pax*	pax L	peace
113.29, 114.02	*Viginti-uno denarios*	viginti-uno denarios dog-L	twenty-one pence
114.03	*Sicut bucketus est*	Sicut bucketus est dog-L	It is just like a bucket
115.08	*Nos ad manum ballum jocabimus*	Nos ad manum ballum jocabimus dog-L	We are going to play at handball
116.10	Tenebrae	tenebrae L	darkness (*Good Friday service*)

116.23–25	*Dixit enim Dominus: in tribulatione sua consurgent ad me; venite et revertamur ad Dominum*	Dixit enim Dominus: in tribulatione sua consurgent ad me; venite et revertamur ad Dominum L	For the Lord has said: in their tribulation they rise up to me; come and let us turn back to the Lord
116.31	*advocatus diaboli*	advocatus diaboli eccl. L	the devil's attorney, devil's advocate
116.n	*Haec dicit Dominus*	Haec dicit Dominus L	This saith the Lord
118.22	Tenebrae	Tenebrae L	Darkness: *Good Friday service*
119.13	*Consummatum est*	Consummatum est L	It is completed, it is finished (*one of Christ's "Seven Last Words"*)
Chapter XXI			
136.33	*oracle*	oraculum eccl. L	the mercy-seat
		oraculum dog-L	little mouth?
136.34	*oracular*	oracularius L	prophetic; pertaining to oracles
141.21	hypostatic	hypostatikos G	substantial, real
Chapter XXII			
147.28–29	anabolism	*anabolismos G	building-up, bubbling up; prelude
Chapter XXIII			
171.26	Aula Maxima	Aula Maxima ML	Biggest Hall
179.34–35	*bonum simpliciter*	bonum simpliciter L	a good, simply; simply a good
180.01–02	*bonum arduum*	bonum arduum L	a difficult good
180.03	*bonum . . . simpliciter*	bonum simpliciter L	a good, pure and simple
Chapter XXIV			
182.33	Toga Girilis	toga virilis L	toga of manhood: the civil dress of a Roman citizen; *see* Finnegans Wake *112.30*
185.01	Sitio	Sitio L	I thirst (*one of Christ's "Seven Last Words"*)
192.06	*Scortum*	scortum L	prostitute, harlot
192.06	*moechus*	moechus L *for* moichos G	adulterer, paramour (*a masculine, not a neuter noun*)

192.35–193.03	*Question*—What great truth do we learn from the *Libation-Pourers* of Eschylus? *Answer*—We learn from the *Libation-Pourers* of Eschylus that in ancient Greece brothers and sisters took the same size in boots	*allusion to crucial episode in Choêphoroi* of Aeschylus	*Elektra recognizes that the messenger bringing news of her brother Orestes' death in exile is really Orestes himself by means of the identity of his and her footprints*
193.21	Alma Mater	alma mater L	nourishing mother
194.08	Callista	Kallistê G	"Most Beautiful": martyr-saint heroine of Newman's novel *Callista; locusts are in Ch. XV*

Chapter XXV

211.17	epiphany	epiphaneia G	appearance, coming into light, coming into view
213.07	*Claritas*	claritas L	clearness, brightness
213.07	*quidditas*	quidditas ML	whatness

Chapter XXVI

| 223.17 | *Druncus* es | druncus es dog-L | you are drunk |

Additional Manuscript Pages

| 250.11 | scaphoid | skaphoeidês G | like a bowl, bowl-shaped, hollow |

A Portrait of the Artist as a Young Man

| half-title, M1 | *Et ignotas animum dimittit in artes.*—Ovid, *Metamorphoses,* VIII , 188 | [Daedalus interea Creten longumque perosus / Exsilium tactusque soli natalis amore / Clausus erat pelago. "Terras licet" inquit "et undas / Obstruat; at | [Daedalus, meanwhile, hating his long Cretan exile and stirred by love of his native land, was cut off by the sea. "Let him," he said, "make the lands and the waves impassable; yet the sky is still open: we shall go that way. Minos may control everything, but he does |

		coelum certe patet: ibimus illac. / Omnia possideat, non possidet aëra Minos." / Dixit] et ignotas animum dimittit in artes, / [Naturamque novat.] L	not control the air." He spoke,] and sent forth his mind into unknown arts, [and altered Nature.]—Ovid, *Metamorphoses*, VIII, 183-189
Chapter I			
008.33, M3 & sqq.	Dedalus	Dedalus ML *for* Daedalus L *for* Daidalos G	"Artist": fabulous artificer; #A
043.18, M45	*Balbus*	Balbus L	"Stuttering": Roman cognomen
043.18, M45	*Balbus was building a wall*	*trans.* Balbus murum aedificabat L	*sentence from L primer; see* Finnegans Wake *004.30*
043.23, M45	*Julius Caesar*	C. Julius Caesar	Roman soldier and dictator; #A
043.23, M45	*The Calico Belly*	de Gallico Bello L	*Concerning the Gallic War.* Caesar's commentary on his conquest of Gaul
044.01, M46	*ferulae*	ferulae (*pl.*) L	whips, rods
047.19, M50	*mare*	mare L	the sea
047.20, M50	the ablative singular	mari (*Abl.*) L	by sea
047.21, M50	the plural	maria (Nom.) marum (Gen.) maribus (Dat.) maria (Acc.) maribus (Abl.) L	seas; of seas; to *or* for seas; seas; by, with, from seas

053.10, 26–27, 054.09–10, M57,58	The senate and the Roman people	*trans.* Senatus Populusque Romanus L	*formulaic phrase indicating source of Roman authority; abbreviated* S.P.Q.R.
054.12,13,15, M58	Peter Parley	penname of Samuel G. Goodrich (1793–1860)	American publisher, popularized myths for children; *see* Finnegans Wake *288.F6*
55.35–56.01, M60	*Ad Majorem Dei Gloriam*	ad majorem Dei gloriam L	for the greater glory of God; *#B*
Chapter II			
070.12, M77	A.M.D.G.	A[d] M[ajorem] D[ei] G[loriam] L	for the greater glory of God; *#B*
071.04, M78	L.D.S.	L[aus] D[eo] S[emper] L	praise to God forever; *#B*
078.09, M86	*Confiteor*	confiteor L	I confess (*prayer of confession*)
082.17, M91	*Confiteor*	confiteor L	I confess
094.07, M105	Dilectus	Dilectus L	The Favorite
094.08–09, M105	*Tempora mutantur nos et mutamur in illis*	Tempora mutantur nos et mutamur in illis L *well-known, source unknown, perhaps Lothair I* (c. 840): Omnia mutantur nos et mutamur inillis L	Times are changed and we are changed in them; *preferable version, scans as perfect hexameter* (*naturally short* et *made long "by position"*): Tĕmpŏrǎ|mūtānt|ūr| |nōs|ēt mŭt|āmŭr ĭn|ĭllīs All things are changed and we are changed in them (*Lothair*)
094.09, M105	*Tempora mutantur et nos mutamur in illis*	Tempora mutantur et nos mutamur in illis L	Times are changed and we are changed in them; *meaning identical with first version but hexameter spoiled by short* et *in this position*

Chapter III

105.03–04, M118	*Quasi cedrus exaltata sum in Libanon et quasi cupressus in Monte Sion.*	Quasi cedrus exaltata sum in Libano et quasi cypressus in monte Sion. L —*Ecclesiasticus 24:17, Vulgate*	I am like a cedar exalted on Lebanon and like a cypress on Mount Zion. "I was exalted like a cedar in Libanus, and as a cypress tree on mount Sion." (*Douay*); "I was exalted like a cedar in Libanus, and as a cypress tree on the mountains of Hermon." (*Rev. AV*)
105.04–05, M118	*Quasi palma exaltata sum in Gades et quasi plantatio rosae in Jericho.*	Quasi palma exaltata sum in Cades et quasi plantatio rosae in Jericho. L *Ecclesiasticus 24:18, Vulgate*	I am as a palm-tree exalted in Cades and like the transplanting of a rose in Jericho. "I was exalted like a palm tree in Cades, and as a rose plant in Jericho:" (*Douay*); "I was exalted like a palm tree on the sea shore, and as rose plants in Jericho," (*Rev. AV*)
105.04, M118	*Gades*	Gades L	city in Hispania; *mod.* Cadiz
105.05–06, M118	*Quasi uliva speciosa in campis et quasi platanus exaltata sum juxta aquam in plateis.*	Quasi oliva speciosa in campis et quasi platanus exaltata sum juxta aquam in plateis L —*Ecclesiasticus 24:19, Vulgate*	Like a splendid olive in the fields and like a plane-tree beside the water in the open spaces I am exalted. "As a fair olive tree in the plains, and as a plane tree by the water in the streets, was I exalted." (*Douay*); "and as a fair olive tree in the plain; and I was exalted as a plane tree." (*Rev. AV*)
105.05, M118	*uliva*	oliva L	olive, olive-tree; *Joyce maintained this aberrant spelling into* Finnegans Wake; *see* Finnegans Wake 550.18

105.06–08,
M118

*Sicut
cinnamomum et
balsamum
aromatizans
odorem dedi et
quasi myrrha
electa dedi
suavitatem odoris*

Sicut
cinnamomum et
balsamum
aromatizans
odorem dedi et
quasi myrrha
electa dedi
suavitatem
odoris L
—*Ecclesiasticus
24:20, Vulgate*

Just like cinnamon and
aromatic balsam I have
given off an odor and
like choice myrrh I
have yielded a sweet
smell. "I gave a sweet
smell like cinnamon,
and aromatical balm: I
yielded a sweet odour
like the best myrrh:"
(*Douay*); "As cinnamon
and aspalathus I have
given a scent of
perfumes; and as choice
myrrh, I spread abroad
a pleasant odour;"
(*Rev. AV*)

108.11–12;
M122

*ad majorem Dei
gloriam*

ad majorem Dei
gloriam L

for the greater glory of
God; #*B*

117.28, M134

non serviam

non serviam L

I shall not serve, I shall
not be a servant

128.22, M147

poena damni

poena damni L

the punishment of loss

143.31, M165

Confiteor

Confiteor eccl.
L

I confess

146.22,30
M169

*Corpus Domini
nostri*

Corpus Domini
nostri L

The Body of our Lord

146.26, M169

In vitam eternam

in vitam
aeternam L

for eternal life

Chapter IV

152.19–20,
M176

*Inter ubera mea
commorabitur*

Inter ubera mea
commorabitur
L—*Canticum
Canticorum I
.12, Vulgate*

He shall linger between
my breasts—Song of
Songs 1:12, "he shall
abide between my
breasts" (*Douay*); "he
shall lie all night
betwixt my breasts"
(*AV, Song of Solomon,
1:13*)

159.03, M184

Ite, missa est

Ite, missa est L

Go, it is a dismissal [*or,*
Go, it (*sacrificio,* the
sacrifice) is sent (*i.e.,*
offered)]: *final words of
the ordinary of the
Mass. (Missa in this
sentence is the etymon
of "Mass."*)

159.17, M185	Simon Magus	magus L magos G	sage, learned man, magician
167.35, M195	Stephanos	stephanos G	1. that which surrounds, *e.g.*, a town wall; 2. crown, wreath
167.36, M195	The Dedalus	Dedalus ML *for* Daedalus L *for* ho Daidalos G	the Artist
168.04, M195	Bous Stephanoumenos	bous stephanoumenos G	a garlanded ox; wreathing an ox [*for being sacrificed*]
168.04–05, M195	Bous Stephaneforos	bous stephanêphoros G	an ox wearing a wreath
168.28, M196	Stephanos	stephanos G	circlet; crown, wreath
168.28, M196	Dedalos	dedalos pseudo-G *for* daidalos G	artist, craftsman
168.29, M196	Bous Stephanoumenos	bous stephanoumenos G	a wreathed ox; crowning an ox
168.29–30, M196	Bous Stephaneforos	bous stephanêphoros G	an ox wearing a wreath
169.01–02, M196	the fabulous artificer	Daidalos G	"Artist": legendary designer of the labyrinth; escaped from Crete by making wings; #*A*
169.25,33, M197	Stephaneforos	stephanêphoros G	wearing a crown, wreath, *or* garland
Chapter V			
176.35–36, M206	Aristotle's poetics	Poetica L *for* hê Poiêtikê G	*The Poetics*: an extensive fragment chiefly on tragedy as Aristotle knew it
176.35–36, M206	Aristotle's . . . psychology	*probably* De Anima L peri Psychês G	*Concerning the Soul*; several other works deal with psychology
176.35–177.01 M205	*Synopsis Philosophiae Scholasticae ad mentem divi Thomae*	Synopsis Philosophiae Scholasticae ad mentem divi Thomae ML	A Summary of Scholastic Philosophy according to the thought of St. Thomas
179.15, M208	*ebur*	ebur L	ivory

179.16, M208	*India mittit ebur*	India mittir ebur L	India sends [*i.e.*, exports] ivory
179.23, M208	*Contrahit orator, variant in carmine vates*	Contrahit orator, variant in carmine vates L	The orator assembles, the poets diversify in songs
179.25, M208	*in tanto discrimine*	in tanto discrimine L	in so great an emergency (*a Caesarian phrase*)
179.27, M208	*implere ollam denariorum*	implere ollam denariorum L	to fill a pot with *denarii* (*Roman silver coins*)
179.29, M209	Horace	Q. Horatius Flaccus	Roman poet
186.01–02, M216	*Pulcra sunt quae visa placent*	Pulchra sunt quae visa placent L Pulchra enim dicuntur ea quae visa placent—*Summa Theologica* I q.5 art. 4	Beautiful things are those which please when seen For those things are called beautiful which please when seen—*what St. Thomas wrote*
186.07, M216	*Bonum est in quod tendit appetitus*	Bonum est in quod tendit appetitus L	The good is that to which the appetites incline, The good is that to which desire extends
186.27–29	*Similiter atque senis baculus* ... like a staff in an old man's hand	*part trans.* similiter atque senis baculus ... qui eum manu tenet—Ignat. *Summarium Constitutionum*, p. 397	even just like the stick of an old man ... who holds it in his hand: Ignatius Loyola, *A Summary of the Constitution* [of the Society of Jesus]
187.19, M218 & sqq.	Epictetus	Epictetus	Stoic philosopher
190.19, M222	*Per aspera ad astra*	per aspera ad astra L	through hardships to the stars
194.26, M227	*Ego habeo*	ego habeo dog-L	I have
194.28, M227	*Quod*	Quod [dog-]L	What?
194.32, M227	*Per pax universalis*	Per [Pro?] pax universalis dog-L	For universal peace

195.05, M227	*Credo ut vos sanguinarius mendax estis*	Credo ut vos sanguinarius mendax estis dog-L	I think that you are a bloody liar
195.05–06, M227	*quia facies vostra monstrat ut vos in damno malo humore estis*	quia facies vestra monstrat ut vos in damno malo humore estis dog-L	because your face shows that you are in a damn bad humor
195.18, M228	*Quis est in malo humore, . . . ego aut vos?*	Quis est in malo humore, ego aut vos? dog-L	Who is in a bad humor, I or you?
198.03, M231	*Pax super totum sanguinarium globum*	Pax super totum sanguinarium globum dog-L	Peace over the whole bloody globe
198.31, M232	*Nos ad manum ballum jocabimus*	Nos ad manum ballum jocabimus dog-L	We are going to play at handball
200.28, M234	*super spottum*	super spottum dog-L	on the spot
204.26, M239	Aristotle has not defined pity and terror	*not quite true*	*Aristotle does not define pity and terror in the* Poetics, Stephen's *source, but he defines and discusses both emotions at length in the* Rhetoric
204.32–34, M239	Pity is the feeling which arrests the mind in the presence of whatsoever is grave and constant in human sufferings and unites it with the human sufferer	*cf.* estô dê eleos lypê tis epi phainomenô kakô phthartikô ê lypêrô tou anaxiou tynchanein, ho kan autos prosdokêseien an pathein ê tôn autou tina, kai touto hotan plêsion phainêtai G *Rhêtorikê* B 8	pity [*eleos*] is a sort of pain at an evident evil of a destructive or painful kind in the case of someone who does not deserve it, the evil being one to which we may naturally expect ourselves or someone belonging to us to be subject, and this when it appears to be at hand *Rhetoric* II.viii

204.34–37, M239	Terror is the feeling which arrests the mind in the presence of whatsoever is grave and constant in human sufferings and unites it with the secret cause	*cf.* estô dê ho phobos lypê tis ê tarachê ek phantasias mellontos kakou phthartikou ê lypêrou G—*Rhêtorikê* B 5	terror [*phobos*] is a sort of pain or disturbance from an anticipated appearance of a destructive or painful evil *Rhetoric* II,v
205.24, M240	Venus	Venus L	Roman goddess of sexual love; #*A*
205.24, M240	Praxiteles	Praxitelês G (4th C b.c.)	"Acting afar": celebrated G sculptor
207.32, M243	*Pulcra sunt quae visa placent*	pulchra sunt quae visa placent L	those things are beautiful which please when seen
207.33, M243	*visa*	visa (*pp., neut. pl.*) L	seen, things seen
210.07, M246	*Pange lingua gloriosi*	Pange lingua gloriosi L [*not by Aquinas but by Fortunatus*]	Discourse, O tongue, of the glorious . . .
210.10–11, M246	Venantius Fortunatus	Honorius Clementianus Venantius Fortunatus	Christian hymnwriter (7th C)
210.10, M246	*Vexilla Regis*	vexilla regis L	the king's banners
210.14–15, M246	*Impleta sunt quae concinit / David fideli carmine /*	Impleta sunt quae concinit David fideli carmine L	Fulfilled are those things which David sang in his truthful song
210.16–17, M246	*Dicendo nationibus / Regnavit a ligno Deus*	Dicendo nationibus regnavit a ligno Deus L	Telling the nations God has reigned from the tree
212.01–02, M248	*ad pulcritudinem tria requiruntur, integritas, consonantia, claritas*	ad pulchritudinem tria requiruntur, integritas, consonantia, claritas L	for beauty three things are needed, completeness, agreement, clearness
212.22, M249	*integritas*	integritas L	undiminished *or* unimpaired condition, completeness, soundness, the whole; purity, correctness

212.32, M249	*consonantia*	consonantia L	agreement, harmony, consonance
212.34, M249	*claritas*	claritas L	clearness, brightness, splendor, distinctness
213.05, M249	*claritas*	claritas L	clearness
213.15, M250	*quidditas*	quidditas ML	whatness
216.20–21, M254	*Ego credo ut vita pauperum est simpliciter atrox, simpliciter sanguinarius atrox, in Liverpoolio*	Ego credo ut vita pauperum est simpliciter atrox, simpliciter sanguinarius atrox, in Liverpoolio dog-L	I believe that the life of the poor is simply atrocious, simply bloody atrocious, in Liverpool
224–226, M263–265	[watching the birds, seeking to interpret their flight and predict his future]	*Stephen is practicing* auspicium L	divination by observing the flight of birds [*see* Ulysses *217.31 etc.*]
230.08, M270	Giraldus Cambrensis	Giraldus Cambrensis L	Gerald of Wales; medieval historian
230.14, M270	*Pernobilis et pervetusta familia*	pernobilis et pervetusta familia ML	a very noble and very ancient family
230.24, M271	*paulo post futurum*	paulo post futurum L	a little after the future
233.36, M275	Cornelius a Lapide	Cornelius a Lapide L (1567–1637)	"Cornelius from the Stone": L name of Cornelis van den Steen, Jesuit Biblical exegete
235.14–15, M275	*ipso facto*	ipso facto L	by the very same fact
236.21,25,36, 237.07,11, M278,279	limbo	limbo (*Abl.*) L	"at the edge": region bordering on hell
244.13, M288	*Mulier cantat*	mulier cantat L	a woman is singing
244.24, M288	*Et tu cum Jesu Galilaeo eras*	Et tu cum Jesu Galilaeo eras L—*Matt. 26:69,* *Vulgate*	Thou also wast with Jesus the Galilean (*Rheims*), Thou also wast with Jesus of Galilee (*AV*)
244.27, M288	proparoxyton	proparoxytonos G	with the acute accent on the antepenult
248.14, M293	Item	item L	just so, likewise, also

Exiles
Act II

[*about*	Neither an angel	*allusion to* Non	They are not Angles
one-quarter	nor an	sunt Angli sed	but angels: *Pope*
through the	Anglo-Saxon	angeli L	*Gregory's comment on*
act, Robert			*English slaves at Rome*
conversing			
with Richard,			
speaks of			
Richard's son]			

Ulysses

title	Ulysses	Ulysses ML	"Hated": king of
		from Ulixes L	Ithaka, hero of Homer's
		+ Odysseus G	*Odyssey*

"Telemachus" (Martello Tower)

title	Telemachus	Telemachus L	"Fighting from afar":
		for Telêmachos G	son of Odysseus
003.05, M5, P3	*Introibo ad altare Dei*	Introibo ad altare Dei L	I will go in to God's altar: *first words of the Mass*
003.28, M5, P3	Chrysostomos	chrysostomos G	of golden mouth, golden-mouthed: *conventional epithet of orators*
003.40, M5, P4	Dedalus	Dedalus ML *for* Daedalus L *for* Daidalos G	Artist, Craftsman; *name of fabulous artificer;* #A
005.07, M7, P5	*Epi oinopa ponton*	epi oinopa ponton G	upon the wine-colored sea: *Homeric phrase*
005.08, M7, P5	*Thalatta! Thalatta*	Thalatta! Thalatta! G	Sea! Sea! —*cry of Xenophon's men;* #B
007.08, M9, P7	oxy	oxys G	sharp
007.26, M9, P7	Ades	Aidês G Hades L	god of the netherworld
007.33, M9, P7	omphalos	omphalos G	navel; stone marking the middle of the earth (*at Delphi*)
010.23–24, M12, P10	*Liliata rutiliantium te confessorum turma circumdet:*	Liliata rutilantium te confessorum turma circumdet: L	May a lilied crowd of glowing confessors surround thee:
010.24, M12, P10	*iubilantium te virginum chorus excipiat*	jubilantium te virginum chorus excipiat L	May a chorus of rejoicing virgins follow after thee

012.27, M14, P12	*In nomine Patris et Filii et Spiritus Sancti*	In nomine Patris et Filii et Spiritus Sancti L	In the name of the Father and of the Son and of the Holy Spirit
017.37, M19, P17	*omphalos*	omphalos G	navel; stone at Delphi
020.42–021.01 M22, P20	*et unam sanctam catholicam et apostolicam ecclesiam*	et unam sanctam catholicam et apostolicam ecclesiam eccl. L	and one holy catholic and apostolic church
021.03, M22, P20	Marcellus	Marcellus L	"Little *Marcus* ['Hammer']": name of 2 popes, one martyred 310, other d. 1555
021.07, M22, P20	Photius	Phôtios G (820–891)	"Belonging to Light": leader of the Eastern Church in schism with the Western Church
021.08, M22, P21	Arius	Areios G (260–336)	"Belonging to *Ares*": denied the equality of the Trinity; condemned by the Council of Nicea; poisoned
021.09–10, M22, P21	Valentine	Valentinus L (2d C)	"Strong": founder of a sect against which Tertullian wrote a book
021.12, M22, P21	Sabellius	Sabellius (3rd C)	elder of the Christian Church at Rome, founded heretical sect in Egypt
023.16, P23	*Liliata rutiliantium*	liliata rutiliantium L	lilied ... of glowing
023.17, M24, P23	*Turma circumdet*	turma circumdet L	May a crowd ... surround
023.18, M24, P23	*Iubilantium te virginum*	jubilantium te virginum L	of rejoicing virgins ... thee
"Nestor" (Mr. Deasy's School) title	Nestor	Nestôr G	king of Pylos; most aged of the Homeric heroes; called "horse-tamer"
024.02, M25, P24	Tarentum	Tarentum L	city in southern Italy, *mod.* Taranto

024.13, M25, P24	Asculum	Asculum L	city in eastern Italy, *mod.* Ascoli; *site of Pyrrhus's second "Pyrrhic victory" over the Romans, 279 b.c.*
024.23,24,27,3-3 M25, P24	Pyrrhus	Pyrrhos G (319–272 b.c.)	"Red": king of Epirus, unsuccessful antagonist of Rome 280–275 b.c.
025.14, M26, P25	Pyrrhus … fallen by a beldam's hand in Argos	*allusion to death of Pyrrhus*	Pyrrhus was killed by a rooftile thrown during street-rioting in Argos; who threw it is unknown
025.15, M26, P25	Julius Caesar knifed to death	*allusion to assassination of Caesar*	Caesar was stabbed to death at the Capitol by a large number of senators, March 15, 44 b.c.
025.36, M26, P26	Aristotle's	Aristotelês G	materialist philosopher; #*A*
028.25, M29, P28	*Amor matris:* subjective and objective genitive	amor matris L	(*subjective*) a mother's love
		amor matris L	(*objective*) love of a mother, love for a mother
031.32, M32, P31	*per vias rectas*	per vias rectas L	through straight ways
033.06, M34, P33	pluterperfect	plusquam perfectus L	more than finished
033.07, M34, P33	Cassandra	Kassandra G	daughter of King Priam of Troy, she had the gift of accurate prophecy with the curse her predictions would never be believed
034.41, M35, P34	Helen	Helenê G	daughter of Zeus and Leda, her abduction by Paris occasioned the Trojan War
034.41, M35, P34	Menelaus	Menelaos G	"Abiding-men": younger brother of Agamemnôn, king of Mycenae; abduction of his wife, Helen, occasioned the Trojan War

034.41–42, M35, P34	ten years the Greeks made war on Troy	allusion to Trojan War	the siege of Troy lasted ten years

"Proteus" (Sandymount Strand)

title	Proteus	Prôteus G	"Very First," "Primal": sea-god who often changed his form
037.05,08,09, M38, P37	diaphane	diaphanês G	translucent, transparent; distinct
037.08, M38, P37	*maestro di color che sanno*	*allusion to* Aristotle	"master of those who know": Dante's epithet for Aristotle; #*A*
037.09,29, M38, P37	adiaphane	adiaphanês G	opaque
037.21, M38, P37	*Demiurgos*	dêmiourgos G	one who works for the people, skilled workman, handicraftsman; maker, creator, producer
038.03, M39, P38	omphalos	omphalos G	navel
038.04, M39, P38	alpha	alpha G	letter A
038.06, M39, P38	Kadmon	Kadmos G	legendary founder of Thebes; sowed dragon's teeth to grow warriors
038.06, m39, P38	Heva	Heva L	Eve, *first woman*
038.14, M39, P38	*lex eterna*	lex aeterna L	an eternal legislation
038.16, M39, P38	Arius	Areios G	denied the Trinity; *see 021.08*
038.17–18, M39, P38	contransmagnific- andjewbangtantia- lity	con- L	with-
		contra L	against
		trans L	across
		magnificans L	making much of, esteeming highly; glorifying, worshipping
		magnificandus L	(one) worthy to be worshipped
038.21, M39, P38	omophorion	ômophorion G	short cloak
039.08–09, M40, P39	*Duces Tecum*	duces tecum L	you (*sing.*) shall bring forward with you

039.09–10, M40, P39	*Requiescat*	requiescat L	may [he] rest
039.16, M40, P38	lithia	lithia G	fine marbles; jewelry
039.37, M40, P40	Joachim Abbas	Joachim Abbas (1145–1202)	Joachim the Abbot: Joachim of Floris, Italian mystic
039.42, M40, P40	Abbas	abbas eccl. L	abbot
040.01–02, M41, P40	*Descende, calve, ut ne nimium decalveris*	descende, calve, ut ne nimium decalveris L *altered from*	get down, baldhead, lest you be excessively baldened
		Ascende, calve, ut ne amplius decalveris, [qui non vereris decalvere sponsam, ut comam ursae nutrias] Joach. *Vaticinia*	Go up, baldhead, lest you be more fully baldened, you who will not scruple to balden the spouse, that you may nourish the she-bear's locks—*one of Joachim's prophecies*
040.03, M41, P40	*descende*	descende L	get down, come down!
040.14, M41, P40	hypostasis	hypostasis G	substance; existence; reality
042.08, M43, P42	Columbanus	Columbanus L (543–615)	"Belonging to *Columba* ['Dove']": Irish monastic missionary to Gaul
042.08, M43, P42	Scotus	Johannes Duns Scotus (1265–1308)	John Dunne the Scot, "The Subtle Doctor": critic of Aquinas; highly orthodox
		Johannes Scotus Erigena (813–880)	John the Irish-born Scot; regarded as a heretic; #*A*
042.10, M43, P42	Euge! Euge!	euge G L	well done! good! bravo!
045.22–23, M46, P45	*Terribilia meditans*	terribilia meditans L	contemplating terrible things
047.38, M48, P47	*oinopa ponton*	[epi] oinopa ponton G	[upon] the wine-colored sea
048.01, M48, P47	*Omnis caro ad te veniet*	omnis caro ad te veniet L	all flesh will come to thee

049.10, M50, P48	*Et vidit Deus*	Et vidit Deus ... L *Vulgate*	And God saw ... (*Genesis 1:4,10,12,18,21,25*)
049.10, M50, P48	*Et erant valde bona*	... et erant valde bona L *Vulgate*	... and they were very good (*Genesis 1:31*)
049.20, M50, P48	tripudium	tripudium L	measured stamping, solemn religious dance
049.41–42, M50, P49	*diebus ac noctibus iniurias patiens ingemiscit*	diebus ac noctibus injurias patiens ingemiscit L	suffering wrongs by days and by nights it sighs
050.25, M51, P49	*Lucifer, dico, qui nescit occasum*	Lucifer, dico, qui nescit occasum L	The light-bringer [morning star] I say, who does not know a setting

"Calypso" (Bloom's Breakfast)

title	Calypso	Kalypsô G	"She that conceals": nymph with whom Odysseus lived, and who bore him a son
059.16, M59, P57	Tiberias	Tiberias	[city of] Tiberius: in Galilee, on Lake Galilee
060.18, M60, P58	eucalyptus	eukalyptos G	well-hidden; *cf. Kalypsô*
064.18, 20, M64, P62	Metempsychosis	metempsychôsis G	transmigation of souls

"Lotus-Eaters" (Toward the Bath)

title	Lotus-Eaters	*trans.* Lôtophagoi G	mythical people on the coast of North Africa
070.41, M70, P69	Azotes	azôtes G	(animals, plants) that do not exist in the same habitat
080.12, M79, P77	Ecce Homo	Ecce homo L *Vulgate*	Behold the man! (*John 19:5*): *Pilate to the mob, showing them Jesus whom he had had flogged*
080.34, M79, P77	*Corpus*	[hoc est enim] corpus [meum] L	[for this is my] body: *priest's words while distributing communion wafers*
081.20, M80, P78	I.N.R.I.	I[esus] N[azarenus] R[ex] I[udaeorum] L	Jesus the Nazarene King of the Jews: *title Pilate had placed over Jesus's cross*

081.20, M80, P78	I.H.S.	IHS[OYS] = Iês[ous] G	JES[US]; (not initials)
082.09, M81, P78	Stabat Mater	stabat Mater L	the Mother was standing
082.15, M81, P79	Quis est homo	Quis est homo L	Who is the man?
082.17, M81, P79	Gloria	gloria L	fame, glory
		Gloria [Patri et Filio et Spiritui Sancto] L	Glory to the Father and to the Son and to the Holy Spirit
084.20, M83, P81	Aq. Dist.	Aq[ua] Dist[illata] L	distilled water (Pharmacy)
084.20, M83, P81	Fol. Laur.	Fol[ia] Laur[ocerasi] L	cherry-laurel leaves
084.20, M83, P81	Aq. Dist. Fol. Laur.	Aq[ua] Dist[illata] Fol[iarum] Laur[ocerasi] L	Distilled Water of Cherry-Laurel Leaves (Pharmacy)
084.20, M83, P81	Te Virid.	Te[rebinthum] Virid[is] L *Te Virid[is] L	green turpentine (Pharmacy) green tea
"Hades" (The Funeral)			
title	Hades	Haidês, Hadês G	"Unseen": god of the underworld; place of departed spirits; the grave, death
088.15, M87, P85	fidus Achates	fidus Achates L	trusty or faithful Achates; faithful companion of Aeneas in the Aeneid
090.20, M89, P87	Athos	Athos G	mountain-headland in eastern Greece
097.22, M96, P94	Mater Misericordiae	Mater Misericordiae L	Mother of Mercy
103.27–28, M102, P99	Dominenamine	probable conflation of in nomine Domini L and Domine non sum dignus L	in the name of the Lord Lord, I am not worthy
103.34, M102, P100	Non intres in judicium cum servo tuo, Domine	Non intres in judicium cum servo tuo, Domine L	Enter not into judgment with thy servant, Lord

104.12, M102, P100	*Et ne nos inducas in tentationem*	et ne nos inducas in tentationem L	and lead us not into temptation
104.25, M103, P100	*In paradisum*	in paradisum L	into paradise
107.36, M106, P103	*Habeat corpus*	habeat corpus L	[he] may have the body
	Habeas corpus	habeas corpus L	you may have the body
109.16, M107, P105	*De mortuis nil nisi prius*	de mortuis nil nisi prius L	of the dead nothing unless before
		conflation of de mortuis nil nisi bonum L	of the dead [say] nothing unless [it is] good
		and nisi prius L	unless before: *legal term*
109.27, M108, P105	ides of March	Idibus Martiis L	on the Ides of March: March 15, *day of Caesar's assassination*
109.28, M108, P105	or June	Idibus Juniis L	on the Ides of June: June 13, *three days prior to the day of the book's action*
		[June 16 = a.d. XVI Kal. Julias L	the sixteenth day before the Calends of July; *N.B. Bloomsday is not dated with reference to the Ides*]
111.30, M110, P107	dismal	dies mali L	evil days (*etymon of "dismal"*)
		Dis L	god of the underworld, equated with Hades
111.30, M110, P107	dismal fields	Ditis campi L	the fields of Dis: the netherworld
113.39–40, M112, P109	Apollo	Apollôn G Apollo L	G god of young masculine beauty, of music, archery, prophecy
"Aeolus" (Newspaper Office)			
title	Aeolus	Aeolus L *for* Aiolos G	deity: ruler of the winds

126.01, M125, P121	DORIC	hê Dôrikos G	the Doric dialect of G, *spoken at Sparta and in general over the southwestern G settlements, including Sicily; in literature it was conventional for Choric Odes and Pastoral; its most obvious characteristics are* a *for* ê, *and retention of* # *Digamma*
127.12, M126, P122	cretic	krêtikos G	"Cretan": metrical foot of a long, a short and a long syllable
127.13, M126, P123	EOLIAN	Aeolianus ML *for* Aeolius L *for* Aiolios *or* Aiolikos G	1. pertaining to Aiolos, god of the winds; 2. the Aeolian dialect of G, *spoken on Lesbos and the nearby mainland of Asia Minor, used in literature for Sapphic Odes*
129.07, M127, P124	*anno Domini*	anno Domini L	in the year of the Lord
		anni Domini L	years of the Lord
130.35, M129, P126	*Imperium romanum*	imperium romanum L	Roman sovereignty, Roman sway, Roman empire
131.12, M130, P126	Cloacae	cloacae (*pl.*) L	sewers
131.17, M130, P126	toga	toga L	ordinary civil dress of a Roman citizen
133.15, M132, P128	*Dominus*	dominus L	lord, master
133.18, M132, P128	KYRIE ELEISON	Kyrie eleêson G	O Lord be merciful
133.21, M132, P128	*Kyrios*	kyrios G	lord, master
133.22, M132, P128	*Kyrie*	kyrie G	O lord (*Voc.*)
133.24, M132, P128	*Kyrie eleison*	Kyrie eleêson G	O Lord be merciful
133.27, M132, P128	*imperium*	imperium L	order, command; the right to command; sway, rule, government, empire

133.28, M132, P129	Aegospotami	Aegospotami L *for* Aigos Potamoi G	"Goat Rivers": river and town in Thrace where Spartans defeated Athenian fleet to decide the Peloponnesian War (405 b.c.) [*a century before Pyrrhus and in no way involving Rome*]
133.29, M132, P129	Pyrrhus	Pyrrhos G	"Red": king of Epirus who invaded Italy but failed to conquer Rome
133.34–134.01 M132, P129	a brick received in the latter half of the *matinée.* Poor, poor, poor Pyrrhus!	*allusion to* the death of Pyrrhus	Pyrrhus was killed by a rooftile thrown during street-rioting in Argos (272 b.c.)
134.10, M132, P129	Sallust	Gaius Sallustius Crispus	Roman historian
135.01, M133, P130	OMNIUM	omnium (*Gen. pl.*) L	of all
135.01, M133, P130	OMNIUM GATHERUM	omnium gatherum fake-L	a gathering of all
139.01, M137, P133	*qua*	qua L	to what degree *or* extent
139.30, M138, P134	ITALIA, MAGISTRA ARTIUM	Italia, magistra artium L	Italy, mistress of the arts
139.33, M138, P134	*lex talionis*	lex talionis L	a law of retaliation in kind (*an eye for an eye*)
140.25, M138, P135	Muchibus thankibus	muchibus thankibus (*Abl. pl.*) dog-L	with many thanks
144.25, M142, P138	*Fuit Ilium*	fuit Ilium L	Troy has been
147.16, M145, P141	*Nulla bona*	nulla bona (*neut. pl.*) L	no good things, nothing good
148.14, M146, P142	AEROLITHS	*aerolithoi G	air-stones
148.30, M147, P142	Antisthenes	Antisthenês G (455–360 b.c.)	follower of Socrates, teacher of Diogenes, founder of the Cynic philosophical sect
148.31, M147, P142	Gorgias	Gorgias G (483–376 b.c.)	sophist and rhetor who taught that truth cannot be attained

149.02–04, M147, P142	a book in which he took away the palm of beauty from Argive Helen and handed it to poor Penelope	*only fragments of Antisthenes' writings survive*	Antisthenes taught that happiness is based on virtue, most pleasures do not contribute to happiness; only pleasure derived from exertion is lasting. He preferred (like Joyce) Odysseus to Ajax, because wisdom is superior to bodily strength
149.03, M147, P142	Argive	Argivus L Argeios G	belonging to *Argos* (*sacred city in the Peloponnesus*); *poetic*: Greek
149.04, M147, P142	Helen	Helenê G	woman who occasioned the Trojan War
149.04, M147, P142	Penelope	Pênelôpeia G	"Weaver": faithful wife of Odysseus
149.24, M147, P143	*deus nobis haec otia fecit*	deus nobis haec otia fecit L Verg. *Ec.* I.6	a god has made these pastimes for us—Vergil's first *Eclogue*, line 6

"Lestrygonians" (Lunch)

title	Lestrygonians	Laestrygones L Laistrygones G	ancient people of southern Italy fabled to have been cannibals
176.26, M174, P168	Venus	Venus L	Roman goddess of sexual love; #*A*
176.26, M174, P168	Juno	Juno L	chief Roman goddess
176.30, M174, P168	Pygmalion	Pygmaliôn G	legendary king of Cyprus, made an ivory statue of a woman and fell in love with it; Aphrodite brought it to life
176.30, M174, P168	Galatea	Galateia G	"Milk-white": seanymph pursued by Polyphemus the Cyclops

"Scylla and Charybdis" (National Library)

title	Scylla	Skylla G	sea monster on strait between Italy and Sicily, opposite Charybdis

		cf. skylax G	puppy
title	Charybdis	Charybdis G	whirlpool on the coast of Sicily, opposite Scylla
185.01, M183, P177	ave	ave L	hail!
185.24, M183, P177	Aristotle was once Plato's schoolboy	approximately true	Aristotle was a member of Plato's Academy for 20 years (age 17 to 37—367–347 b.c.), first as a pupil, ultimately as a research associate until Plato's death
185.30, M183, P178	Hiesos	*hiesos pseudo-G *hiêsos pseudo-G	thrower shooter
185.30, M183, P178	Hiesos Kristos	mystic garble of Iêsous Christos	Jesus Christ
185.31, M183, P178	the Logos	[en archê ên] ho Logos G	[in the beginning was] the Word (John 1:1)
185.33, M183, P178	Arval	arvalis L	pertaining to a cultivated field
		Fratres Arvales L	Arval Brothers: college of 12 priests concerned with fruits of the field
185.38, M183, P178	sophia	sophia G	wisdom (a Gnostic entity, involved in fall from perfection)
187.05, M185, P179	Homer's	Homêros G	celebrated epic poet
187.05, M185, P179	Phaeacians	Phaeaces L Phaiakes G	fabled luxurious inhabitants of the isle of Scheria; the climate is mild, the people are seafaring, fond of pleasure, unwarlike, kindly and hospitable
188.10, M186, P180	from limbo patrum	ex limbo patrum eccl. L	from the border-region of the [Church] fathers
190.15, M188, P182	Liliata rutilantium	liliata rutilantium L	lilied ... of shining
190.28, M188, P182	Socrates	Sôkratês G	noted philosopher
190.28, M188, P182	Xanthippe	Xanthippê G	"Tawny Mare": wife of Socrates' middle age, notorious in legend as a shrew

190.31, M188, P183	Myrto	Myrton G	"Myrtle-berry": Diogenes Laertius, *Vita Socratis* 26, reports Myrto as a wife either earlier or later than Xanthippe; the name was also slang for the female pudenda
190.31, M188, P183	*absit nomen!*	absit omen L	may the omen be away! may there be no omen in it!
		absit nomen L	may the name be away (*pun on above*)
190.31, M188, P183	Socratididion's	Sôkratidion G	"Dear Little Socrates"—*in Aristophanes'* Clouds
190.31-32, M188, P183	Epipsychidion	*epipsychidion G	1. cooler, chiller, refrigerator; 2. upon-a-little-soul
190.33, M188, P183	archons	archôn G	ruler, commander, chief, king, magistrate; chief magistrate at Athens
191.04, M188, P183	*Venus*	Venus L	Roman goddess of sexual love; #*A*
191.05, M188, P183	*Adonis*	Adônis G	beautiful chaste youth beloved by Aphrodite (Venus); killed by a boar
191.07, M188, P183	*Antony*	Marcus Antonius L	Roman triumvir
191.08, M188, P183	*Cleopatra*	Kleopatra G	notorious queen of Egypt; #*A*
191.16, M189, P183	Adonis	Adônis G	youth beloved by Aphrodite
191.26, M189, P183	Paris	Paris G	abductor of Helen
191.31, M189, P184	*Isis*	Isis	Egyptian goddess; #*A*
191.39, M189, P184	logos	logos G	word, discourse, idea, plan, speech
193.32–33, M191, P186	Caesar ... had he believed the soothsayer	*allusion to Caesar's assassination*	*Caesar was warned by a soothsayer shortly before his assassination to "Beware the Ides of March"; he took inadequate precautions*

193.35–36, M191, P186	what name Achilles bore when he lived among women	*allusion to* Achilles' attempt to avoid the Trojan War	*according to post-Homeric poets, Achilles' parents, knowing he was fated to die at Troy, hid him at Skyros, dressed as a girl*
193.35, M191, P186	Achilles	Achilleus G	barbarian hero of the Iliad
195.16, 32, M193, P187	Marina	marina (*fem.*) L	pertaining to the sea
195.32, M193, P187	Miranda	miranda (*fem.*) L	she who is worthy of being marvelled at, she who is to be wondered at
195.33, M193, P187	Perdita	perdita (*fem. pp.*) L	lost, she who is lost
197.28, M195, P189	Photius	Phôtios G	leader of the Eastern Church in schism with the West; *see 021.07*
197.28, M195, P189	pseudomalachi	pseudo[Malachi] G	false [Malachi]: the unknown 16th C forger of the *Prophecy* of the 12th C St. Malachy
197.34, M195, P189	*Glo-o-ri-a in ex-cel-sis De-o*	Gloria in excelsis Deo L	Glory to God in the highest
199.07, M196, P191	Jove	Jovis-Pater L	"Brightness-Father": Jupiter, chief Roman god
201.04–05, M198, P192	foamborn Aphrodite	Aphroditê G	"Foam-born": goddess of love and beauty
201.11, M198, P192	Venus Kallipyge	Venus L *for* Aphroditê Kallipygos G	Aphrodite with Beautiful Buttocks: *epithet of Aphrodite*
201.16, M198, P193	Penelope	Pênelopeia G	"Weaver": faithful wife of Odysseus
201.17, M198, P193	Antisthenes	Antisthenês G	founder of the Cynic sect; *see 148.30*
201.17–20, M198, P193	Antisthenes ... took the palm of beauty from ... Helen ... to poor Penelope	*only fragments of Antisthenes' writings survive*	see 149.02-04
201.17, M198, P193	Gorgias	Gorgias G	sophist and rhetor; *see 148.31*

201.18, M198, P193	Kyrios Menelaus'	Kyrios Menelaos G	Lord Menelaus: husband of Helen; see 034.41
201.19, M198, P193	Argive	Argivus L Argeios G	belonging to Argos; Greek; see 149.03
201.19, M198, P193	Helen	Helenê G	wife of Menelaus, occasion of Trojan War
201.19–20, M199, P193	the wooden mare of Troy in whom a score of heroes slept	*allusion to* the Trojan Horse	*the Greeks ostensibly abandoned the siege of Troy, leaving behind as an offering a large wooden horse; the Trojans took the horse inside the walls as a trophy; at night the Greek fleet returned, and a party hidden in the horse [Vergil names them, nine in all] opened the gates. The implied aspersion on Helen is not justified by her legend; she is not promiscuous*
201.20, M199, P193	Penelope	Pênelôpeia G	"Weaver": Odysseus's wife
201.30, M199, P193	scortatory	*scortatorius L	pertaining to whores
		scortum, *pl.* scorta L	whore, harlot, prostitute
204.01, M201, P195	*separatio a mensa et a thalamo*	separatio a mensa et a thalamo L	separation from table and from marriage-bed (*type of Roman Catholic quasi-divorce*)
204.05–10, M201, P195	Antiquity mentions . . . his villa	*allusions to* Aristotle	*the information in this paragraph is all contained in the brief "Life" of Aristotle by Diogenes Laertius*
205.05, M201, P195	Stagyrite	Stageiritês G	"man from Stageira" (*Aristotle's birthplace*): Aristotle

204.09, M201, P195	Herpyllis	Herpyllis G	"Grasshopper": widower Aristotle's domestic mistress; bore him a son, Nicomachus [*Aristotle's will is reproduced in Diogenes Laertius*]
204.22, M202, P196	Catamite	Catamitus L *corruption* of Ganymêdes G	1. beautiful youth borne to heaven to be Zeus's cupbearer; 2. submissive homosexual male
205.13, M202, P196	*Mingo, minxi, mictum, mingere*	mingo, minxi, mictum, mingere L	I piss, I have pissed, pissed, to piss (*principal parts of the verb*)
		misceo, miscui, mixtum, miscere L	I mix, I have mixed, mixed, to mix
205.16, M202, P197	*Sufflaminandus sum*	sufflaminandus sum L	I must be stopped [*allusion to Ben Jonson's quotation of Seneca in criticism of Shakespeare (in* Timber): "*it was necessary he should be stop'd*: Sufflaminandus erat; *as Augustus said of* Haterius."]
205.21–22, M203, P197	*Amplius. In societate humana hoc est maxime necessarium ut sit amicitia inter multos*	Amplius. In societate humana hoc est maxime necessarium ut sit amicitia inter multos L	More. In human society this is most necessary in order that there may be friendship among the many
205.24, M203, P197	*Ora pro nobis*	Ora pro nobis L	Pray for us
206.12, M203, P197	*Requiescat*	requiescat L	may [she] rest
206.29, M204, P198	*inquit Eglintonus*	inquit Eglintonus L	said Eglinton
206.29–30, M204, P198	*Chronolologos*	*Chronologos G	time-recorder
207.27, M205, P199	*Amor matris,* subjective and objective genitive	amor matris L	(*subjective*) a mother's love, love felt by a mother

			(*objective*) love of a mother, love felt for a mother
207.33, M205, P199	*Amplius*	amplius L	more, further, besides
207.33, M205, P199	*Adhuc*	adhuc L	hitherto, thus far
207.33, M205, P199	*Iterum*	iterum L	again, once more
207.33, M205, P199	*Postea*	postea L	after this, hereafter, afterwards
207.40, M205, P199	queens with prize bulls	*allusion to* Pasiphaë	queen of Minos of Crete, she fell in love with his prize bull, had Daidalos build her a cow-disguise, and mothered the Minotaur by the bull
208.07, M205, P199	Sabellius	Sabellius L	"Sabine": 3rd C elder of the church at Rome, founded a heretical sect in Egypt; *see 021.12*
208.25, M206, P199	Pallas Athena	Pallas Athênê G	Athena the Virgin *or* Athena the Brandisher: *epithet of Athena*
208.30, M206, P200	Volumnia	Volumnia L	"Well-Wisher": wife of Coriolanus
208.30, M206, P200	*Coriolanus*	Caius Marcius Coriolanus	Roman general; disgruntled, led an enemy attack on Rome but was dissuaded by his mother
208.33, M206, P200	Cleopatra	Kleopatra G	notorious queen of Egypt; #*A*
208.34, M206, P200	Venus	Venus L	Roman goddess of sexual love; #*A*
210.04, M207, M201	honorificabilitudi-nitatibus	*honorificabilitu-dinibus (Dat., Abl. pl.)* L	to, for *or* by, with, from honorablenesses
210.08, M207, P201	Venus	Venus L	Roman goddess of sexual love; #*A*
210.09, M207, P201	delta	delta G	letter D
210.09, M207, P201	Cassiopeia	Cassiopea L Kassiopeia G	mother of Andromeda; *now* a constellation

210.19, M207, P201	*Autontimerumen- os*	Heautontimoru- menos G-L *for* Heauton Timôroumenos G	*Self-Tormentor*: L play by Terence adapted from G of Menander
210.19, M207, P201	*Bous Stephanoumenos*	bous stephanoumenos G	a garlanded ox; garlanding an ox
210.08, M208, P202	*Stephanos*	stephanos G	crown, wreath, chaplet, garland
210.37, M208, P202	Icarus	Icarus L Ikaros G	son of Daidalos; *on their flight from Crete he flew too near the sun,* melted the wax in his wings, *fell into the Aegean and drowned*
210.37, M208, P202	*Pater, ait*	Pater, ait L	"Father," he says [*in Ovid Daedalus several times calls to Icarus, but Icarus never to his father*]
211.12, M208, P202	rectly ... rectly rectly ... rectly	recte L	correctly
212.11, M209, P203	protasis	protasis G	putting forward, that which is put forward; proposition; first part of a classical drama
212.11, M209, P203	epitasis	epitasis G	stretching, tightening; second part of a classical drama
212.11, M209, P203	catastasis	katastasis G	settlement, establishment, presentation
212.11–12, M209, P203	catastrophe	katastrophê G	end, conclusion; denouement of a classical drama
213.28, M211, P204	*Eureka! ... Eureka!*	heurêka G	I have found, I have it (*Archimedes' exclamation*)
213.36, M211, P205	Johannes	Johannes LL	John
214.05, M211, P205	Eclecticon	*eklektikon G	something deserving moral choice
214.16–17, M211, P205	*Egomen*	egômen G	I, for one

214.29, M212, P205	*Summa contra Gentiles*	Summa contra Gentiles L	*The Principal Material against the Heathens*: work by Thomas Aquinas on natural religion
215.26, M212, P206	Mincius	Mincius L	river of Cisalpine Gaul, *mod*. Mincio; *runs by Mantua, Vergil's home*
215.42, P213, P207	Phedo	Phaedo L Phaidôn G	disciple of Socrates after whom Plato named his dialogue on the immortality of the soul and the last hours of Socrates
216.28, M213, P207	Homer	Homêros G	epic poet
217.31, M214, P209	Here I watched the birds for augury	auspicium L	divination by observing flight of birds
217.31, M214, P209	augury	auguria L	divination

"Wandering Rocks" (Streets of Dublin)

title	Wandering Rocks	*trans.* Planktai Petrai G	rocks near Scylla and Charybdis mentioned in the *Odyssey*; later identified with the Symplêgades encountered by the Argonauts [*name may really mean* "clashing" *rather than* "wandering" *rocks*]
219.04–05, M216, P210	*Vere dignum et justum est*	Vere dignum et justum est [pro mortuis orare] L	It is truly fit and just [to pray for the dead]
220.39, M217, P212	D.V.	D[eo] V[olente] L	God willing
223.09, M220, P214	D.V.	D[eo] V[olente] L	God willing
223.31, M220, P214	*eiaculatio seminis inter vas naturale mulieris*	ejaculatio seminis inter vas naturale mulieris L	the ejaculation of semen within the natural vessel of the woman

224.17, M221, P215	Nones	nona L	the ninth hour of the day, the third hour before sunset; *eccl. L:* the service for the hour, *usually now* before 3:00 p.m.
224.19, M221, P215	*Pater*	Pater [noster] L	[Our] Father
224.19, M221, P215	*Ave*	Ave [Maria] L	Hail [Mary]
224.20, M221, P215	*Deus in adiutorium*	Deus, in adjutorium [meum intende] L (*Ps. 70:1, Vulgate*)	God, [turn] to [my] help: "O God, come to my assistance" (*Douay, Ps. 69:1*); "Make haste, O God, to deliver me" (*AV, Ps. 70:1*)
224.22, M221, P215	*Res*	[res L	thing, affair]
		Res L	the Hebrew letter *Resh* (= R)
224.22, M221, P215	*Beati immaculati*	Beati immaculati L (*Ps. 119:1, Vulgate*)	Blessed [are] the undefiled (*Douay, Ps. 118:1; AV, Ps. 119:1*)
224.22–24, M221, P215	*Principium verborum tuorum veritas: in eternum omnia iudicia iustitiae tuae*	Principium verborum tuorum, veritas: in aeternum omnia judicia justititiae tuae L (*Ps. 119 [Res]:160, Vulgate*)	"The beginning of thy words [is] truth: all the judgments of thy justice *are* for ever" (*Douay Ps. 118 [Res]:160*); "Thy word *is* true *from* the beginning: and every one of thy righteous judgments *endureth* for ever" [*AV, Ps. 119 [Resh]:160*)
224.31, M221, P215	*Sin*	Sin L	the Hebrew letter *Sin, Shin* (=S, SH)
224.31–32, M221, P215	*Principes persecuti sunt me gratis: et a verbis tuis formidavit cor meum*	Principes persecuti sunt me gratis: et a verbis tuis formidavit cor meum L (*Ps. 119 [Sin]:161, Vulgate*)	"Princes have persecuted me without cause: and my heart hath been in awe of thy words" (*Douay Ps. 118 [Sin]:161*); "Princes have persecuted me without a cause: but my heart standeth in awe of thy word" (*AV, Ps. 119 [Schin]:161*)

232.10, M228, P223	Nisi Prius	nisi prius L	unless before: *legal term*
233.14, M229, P224	Marcus	Marcus L	"Hammer": Roman praenomen
233.14, M229, P224	Tertius	Tertius L	Third, the Third
235.01, M231, P225	Hercules	Hercules L Heraklês G	demi-god
235.19, M232, P226	Aristotle's *Masterpiece*	*nothing to do with Aristotle*	a post-medieval anatomical work falsely attributed to Aristotle; *of prurient appeal for its detail*
236.33, M233, P227	exparte	ex parte L	from the side, in the interest of one side only
236.34, M233, P227	Mona	Mona L	Anglesea; Isle of Man
242.04, M238, P232	Antisthenes	Antisthenês G	student of Socrates; founder of Cynic sect
242.25, M239, P232	proposed	*trans.* proposuit L	set before, displayed
242.31–32, M239, P232	*Stephano Dedalo, alumno optimo, palmam ferenti*	Stephano Dedalo, alumno optimo, palmam ferenti L	for Stephen Dedalus, the best pupil, carrying off the palm
242.41, M239, P233	*femininum*	femininum (*masc. Acc.* or *neut. Nom./Acc.*) L	feminine, pertaining to women
242.41, M239, P233	*Amor*	amor L	love
242.41, M239, P233	*me solo*	me solo (*Abl.*) L	by me alone
242.41, M239, P233	*Sanktus*	sanctus L	holy
243.03, M239, P233	Joachim's	Joachim Abbas	medieval Italian mystic; *see 039.37*
243.03–04, M239, P233	Down, baldynoddle, or we'll wool your wool	*trans.* descende, calve, ut ne nimium decalveris L	get down, baldhead, lest you be excessively baldened; *see 040.01-02*
243.13, M239, P233	*femininum*	femininum (*masc. Acc.* or *neut. Nom./Acc.*) L	feminine

247.13, M243, P237	the conscript fathers	*trans.* patres conscripti L	the enrolled fathers: the Senate
247.22, M243, P237	*locum tenens*	locum tenens L	holding the place
250.12, M246, P240	*Coactus volui*	coactus volui L	constrained, I have desired
254.32, M251, P244	Mirus	mirus L	wonderful, marvelous

"Sirens" (Ormond Hotel)

title	Sirens	Seirênes G	birds with faces of virgins who enticed seamen ashore with sweet singing, then killed them
		cf. seireô G	to drain dry
257.04, M253, P246	Naminedamine	[in] nomine Domini L	in the name of the Lord
258.17, M254, P247	lithia	lithia G	fine marble; jewelry
264.22, M260, P253	duodene	duodeni L	twelve each, twelve
277.27, M273, P266	*Corpus*	corpus L	body
277.27–28, M273, P266	*paradisum*	[in] paradisum L	into paradise
282.22, M278, P270	*quis est homo*	quis est homo L	who is the man?
284.41, M278, P271	Doric	hê Dôrikos G	the Spartan dialect of G; *see 126.01*
284.03, M279, P272	*in nomine Domini*	in nomine Domini L	in the name of the Lord
284.05, M279, P272	*mea culpa*	mea culpa L	by my fault
284.07, M279, P272	corpus	corpus L	body
284.08, M279, P272	*corpusnomine*	*conflation of* corpus Domini nostri L *and* in nomine Domini L	the body of our Lord in the name of the Lord
286.40, M282, P274	Dolor	dolor L	pain, grief
289.39, M285, P277	*nominedomine*	in nomine Domini L	in the name of the Lord

"Cyclops" (Barney Kiernan's Pub)

title	Cyclops	Kyklôps G	"Round-eye": one-eyed cannibal giant encountered by Odysseus
292.42, M287, P281	videlicet	videlicet L	one may see; plainly, obviously, evidently, manifestly
294.13, M289, P282	Eblana [misprint all eds.]	Eblana G	Dublin
296.14, M291, P284	Ulex Europeus	ulex Europeus L	European ulex (shrub resembling rosemary)
297.06–07, M292, P285	Cleopatra	Kleopatra G	notorious queen of Egypt; #A
297.07, M292, P285	Julius Caesar	Gaius Julius Caesar L	Roman dictator; #A
297.07, M292, P285	Paracelsus	Paracelsus [for Parakeleusis G ?]	["Exhorting"?]: name coined for himself by Theophrastus Bombastus von Hohenheim (1493–1541), physician, chemist, alchemist, mystic
297.12, M292, P285	Nemo	Nemo L	nobody
		[trans. Outis G	Nobody: name Odysseus called himself to the Cyclops; #A]
297.17, M292, P285	Herodotus	Hêrodotos G	early G historian
299.33, M294, P287	the sons of deathless Leda	Kastôr G Castor L and Polydeukês G Pollux L	the heavenly Twins; #A
299.33, M294, P287	Leda	Lêda G	young woman approached by Zeus as a swan, by whom she bore the Twins, Helen, and Clytemnestra
304.17, M299, P291	Erebus	Erebus L Erebos G	god of darkness; the nether world
305.03, M299, P292	corpora cavernosa	corpora cavernosa L	the bodies full of hollows
305.08–09, M299, P292	in articulo mortis per diminutionem capitis	in articulo mortis per *deminutionem capitis L	at the point of death through lessening of the head

305.08–09, M299, P292	*per diminutionem capitis*	per deminutionem capitis L (*Roman law*)	through forfeiture of civil rights
307.26, M302, P294	Athanatos	athanatos G	deathless, immortal
307.27, M302, P294	Lokum	locum (*Acc.*) L	place, spot
307.28, M302, P294	Paternoster	Pater noster L	Our Father
308.21, P295	*Gladiolus Cruentus*	gladiolus cruentus L	bloodstained small-sword
308.29, M303, P295	*polla kronia*	polla *chronia G	many *longtimes
		polla kronia MG	many ages; long life
309.28, M304, P296	*nec*	nec L	not, and not, also not
309.28–29, M304, P296	*nec ... plus ultra*	nec plus ultra L	and no farther; unsurpassed
309.29, M304, P296	*non plus ultra*	non plus ultra L	no farther; unsurpassed
310.23, M305, P297	Albion's	Albion	ancient name for Britain
311.30, M306, P298	*pro bono publico*	pro bono publico L	for the public good
311.37, M306, P298	cynanthropy	*kynanthrôpia G	man-dogness, dog-manness
314.15, M308, P301	Manuo	manuor [?] L	to steal
315.01, M309, P301	Hairy Iopas	*trans.* crinitus Iopas L (Vergil. *Aen.* I.740)	long-haired [*or* hairy] Iopas: minstrel at Dido's court
319.06, M313, P305	Eblanite	*Eblanitês G	Dubliner
319.37, M314, P306	Calpe's	Kalpê G	"Urn," "Bowl": the rock of Gibraltar
320.40, M315, P307	*compos mentis*	compos mentis L	in control of the mind
320.41, M315, P307	*Compos*	compos L	having mastery *or* control
322.34–35, M317, P309	the month of the oxeyed goddess	Junius L	June: month of Juno
		Juno L	chief Roman goddess, identified with Hêra

		boôpis G	ox-eyed: *epithet of Hêra*
323.01, M317, P309	*in re*	in re L	in the matter
324.06, M318, P310	*nisi*	nisi L	unless
326.15, M320, P312	Juvenal	D. Junius Juvenalis (a.d. 55–140)	Roman satirical poet
326.22, M320, P312	the pillars of Hercules	*trans.* Herculis Columnae L	the promontories flanking the Strait of Gibraltar
326.24, M320, P312	Tacitus	Cornelius Tacitus	Roman historian
326.24, M320, P312	Ptolemy	Claudius Ptolemaeus	Alexandrian geographer, first to put Dublin on a map; #*A*
326.25, M320, P312	Giraldus Cambrensis	Giraldus Cambrensis L	Gerald of Wales, medieval chronicler; *see* Finnegan's Wake *151.32*
326.29, M320, P312	Anglia	Anglia ML	England
327.15, M321, P313	Regis	regis (*Gen.*) L	king's, of the king
327.17, M321, P313	Glands [*error?*]	glans L	acorn
327.31–32, M321, P313	*in Horto*	in horto L	in the garden
330.23, M324, P316	Albion	Albion	ancient name for Britain
330.39, M325, P316	pax	pax L	peace
337.31, M331, P323	Junius	Junius L	"belonging to Juno": *in context, pseudonym of unknown writer of antigovernment pamphlets in England (1768–1772); adopted from*
		Lucius Junius Brutus L	founder of the Roman republic, #*A*
338.39, M332, P324	crucifer	crucifer eccl. L	cross-bearer, carrier of the cross in processions
338.40, M332, P324	thurifers	thurifer eccl. L	incense-bearer

338.40, M332, P324	ostiarii	ostiarii (*pl.*) eccl. L	doorkeepers
339.03, M332, P324	Premonstratesi-ans	praemonstratio L	a showing beforehand
		Praemonstratesi-ani L	order of Augustinian canons founded 1120 by St. Norbert
339.04, M332, P324	Servi	Servi L, *members of*	Servants
		Ordo Servorum L	The Order of Servants: monastic order founded in Florence by 7 rich city councilmen (1240)
339.08, M333, P324	minimes	minime L	least of all, least, very little
339.13–14, M333, P324	Isidor Arator	Isidorus Arator (*d.* 1170)	Isidor the Farmer, native and patron saint of Madrid
339.14, M333, P324	Phocas	Phôkas G	"Seal": G *Christian name*
339.14, M333, P324	Sinope	Sinôpê G	town on south shore of Black Sea
339.14, M333, P324	Phocas of Sinope	Phôkas [*of*] Sinôpê	Bishop of Sinope martyred under Trajan, a.d. 117
339.15, M333, P324	Julian Hospitator	Julianus Hospitator L	Julian the Hospitaller: legendary saint. *In penance for killing his parents kept a hospice for the poor and travelers by a river; patron of boatmen, innkeepers, travelers.*
339.15, M333, P324	Felix de Cantalice	Felix Cantalicensis L (1513–1587)	"Happy" from Cantalice [*village in Apulia*]; Capuchin laybrother nicknamed *Deo Gratias*, noted for happy disposition; *canonized 1724*

339.15–16, M333, P324	Simon Stylites	Simeon Stylitês (I) G (390–459) Simeon Stylitês (II) G (521–597)	Simeon Dwelling-on-a-pillar: *name of two saints*: (I) the 1st pillar ascetic, became anchorite near Antioch aged 16, began constructing a pillar on top of which he lived as it grew higher; (II) imitator of (I), lived 69 years atop pillars, his last 45 years on one pillar, never descending
339.16, M333, P324	Stephen	Stephanos G	"Crown": G Christian name
339.16, M333, P324	Protomartyr	prôtomartyros G	first witness
339.16, M333, P324	Stephen Protomartyr	Stephanos Prôtomartyros G	Stephen the First Witness: young man stoned to death in the presence of Saul/Paul; canonized as 1st Christian martyr
339.17, M333, P324	Theodotus	Theodôtos G	"God-given": name of several saints; *perhaps Theodotus of Ancyra, martyr, patron of innkeepers*
339.21, M333, P324	Caniculus	caniculus L	little dog, puppy [*St. Garryowen?*]
339.21, M333, P324	Anonymous	anônymos G	nameless
339.22, M333, P324	Eponymous	epônymos G	significantly named, surnamed
339.22, M333, P324	Pseudonymous	pseudônymos G	falsely named, given a false name
339.22, M333, P324	Paronymous	parônymos G	derivatively named, punningly named
339.23, M333, P324	Synonymous	synônymos G	1. having the same name; 2. having a different name with the same sense
339.25, M333, P324	Columba	Columba L (521–597)	"Dove": *Colmcille*, Irish missioner to North Britain

339.36, M333, P324	Frigidian	*Frigidianus L	"belonging to *Frigidus* ['cold']"
		Frigidandus [?] (*d.* 740)	Irish saint; monk and abbot of Kerkelodor near Antwerp
339.27, M333, P324	Columbanus	Columbanus L (543–615)	"belonging to *Columba* ['Dove']": Irish monastic missionary to Gaul
339.32, M333, P325	Gervasius	Gervasius L (*fl.* 1188)	English monk and chronicler
339.32, M333, P325	Servasius	Servatus [?] L (*d.* 384)	saint, archbishop of Tangres in Netherlands (Fr. *Servais*)
339.32, M333, P325	Bonifacius	Bonifacius L	"Handsome": English apostle to the Germans, #*A*
339.35, M333, P325	Pacificus	pacificus L	peaceful
339.35, M333, P325	Bellicosus	bellicosus L	warlike
339.38, M333, P325	Calpensis	Calpensis (*Gen.*) L	of *Calpe* (Gibraltar)
339.40, M333, P325	Scholastica	Scholastica (*fem.*) L (*d.* 550)	"belonging to a school": saint, sister of St. Benedict
339.41, M333, P325	nimbi	nimbi (*pl.*) L	cloud-shaped splendors
339.41, M333, P325	gloriae	gloriae (*pl.*) L	glories
340.09, M334, P325	introit	introit L	he goes in
		introitus L	entrance: the first part of the Mass
340.09–10, M334, P325	in *Epiphania Domini*	in Epiphania Domini L	on the feast of the Epiphany of the Lord
340.10, M334, P325	*Surge, illuminare*	surge, illuminare L	rise, be enlightened!
340.11, M334, P325	*Omnes*	omnes L	all
340.11, M334, P325	*de Saba venient*	de Saba venient L	from Saba they will come
340.31, M334, P325	*Adiutorium nostrum in nomine Domini*	adjutorium nostrum in nomine Domini L	our help [is] in the name of the Lord

340.32, M334, P325	*Qui fecit coelum et terram*	Qui fecit coelum et terram L	Who made heaven and earth
340.33, M334, P325	*Dominus vobiscum*	Dominus vobiscum L	The Lord [be] with you
340.34, M334, P325	*Et cum spiritu tuo*	Et cum spiritu tuo L	And with thy spirit
340.37, M334, P326	*Deus, cuius verbo sanctificantur omnia,*	Deus, cujus verbo sanctificantur omnia L	God, by whose word all things are made holy,
340.37–38, M334, P326	*benedictionem tuam effunde super creaturas istas:*	benedictionem tuam effunde super creaturas istas L	pour forth thy blessing over these creatures:
340.38–40, M334, P326	*et praesta ut quisquis eis secundum legem et voluntatem Tuam cum gratiarum actione usus fuerit*	et praesta ut quisquis eis secundum legem et voluntatem Tuam cum gratiarum actione usus fuerit L	and grant that whosoever may use them according to Thy law and will with thanksgiving
340.40, M334, P326	*per invocationem sanctissimi nominis Tui*	per invocationem sanctissimi nominis Tui L	through invocation of Thy most holy name
340.40–41, M334, P326	*corporis sanitatem et animae tutelam Te auctore percipiat*	corporis sanitatem et animae tutelam Te auctore percipiat L	may receive health of body and protection of the soul, Thou being the creator, [*or*, from Thee, the creator]
340.41–42, M334, P326	*per Christum Dominum nostrum*	per Christum Dominum nostrum L	through Christ our Lord
343.21, M337, P328	mastodontic	*mastodontikos G	breast-toothed, having teeth on the breast
344.34–35, M338, P329	*missa pro defunctis*	Missa pro defunctis eccl. L	Mass for the deceased
345.03, M338, P329	Hercules	Hercules L Heraklês G	hero and demigod
345.03, M338, P329	Hannibal	Hannibal	Carthaginian general against Rome
345.03–04, M338, P329	Habeas Corpus	habeas corpus L	you may have the body (*legal term*)

345.04, M338, P329	P.C.	P[ater] C[onscriptus] L	Enrolled Father: Senator
"Nausicaa" (Sandymount Strand)			
title	Nausicaa	Nausikaa G	(from *naus*, "ship"): daughter of king Alcinous of the Phaeacians, met and succoured the shipwrecked Odysseus near the shore, where she had come to do her laundry
358.22, M352, P342	*Ora pro nobis*	ora pro nobis L	pray for us
360.06, M353, P344	*Tantum ergo*	tantum ergo L	how great, therefore
360.07–08, M353, P344	*Tantumer gosa cramen tum*	Tantum ergo sacramentum L	How great a sacrament, therefore: *beginning of a hymn used at Benediction of the Most Blessed Sacrament*
361.27, M355, P345	*Tantum ergo*	Tantum ergo L	How great ... therefore
362.10, M356, P346	*Panem de coelo praestitisti eis*	Panem de coelo praestitisti eis L	Thou hast shown them bread from heaven: *line from the service of* Benediction
365.08, M358, P348	*Laudate Dominum omnes gentes*	Laudate Dominum, omnes gentes L (*Ps. 117:1, Vulgate*)	"O praise the Lord, all ye nations" (*Douay, Ps. 116:1; AV, Ps. 117:1*)
370.22, M364, P353	*Lacaus esant taratara*	not real L	*garbled syllables from* Tantum Ergo *hymn*
377.30–33, M371, P360	Metempsychosis	metempsychôsis G	transmigration of souls
378.13–14, M371, P360	that wise man what's his name with the burning glass	*allusion to* Archimêdês G	Syracusan mathematician:set fire to besieging Roman ships with burning-glasses
378.17, M371, P360	Archimedes	Archimêdês G	Syracusan mathematician
378.17, M371, P360	I have it!	*trans.* heurêka G	Archimedes' exclamation when he discovered the way to determine specific gravity

379.05, M372, P361	cockalorum	cockalorum dog-L	cocks', of cocks
379.06, M372, P361	Mirus	mirus L	wonderful, marvelous

"Oxen of the Sun" (Holles Street Hospital)

383.01–02, M377, P366	EAMUS ... Eamus	eamus L	let us go, let us be going
383.20–21, M377, P366	omnipollent	omnipollens L	all-powerful, almighty
383.24, M377, P366	lutulent	lutulentus L	muddy
383.30–31, M377, P366	inverecund	inverecundus L	shameless, immodest
384.39, M378, P368	sejunct	sejunctus L	separate, divers
385.41, M379, P368	Mona	Mona L	1. Anglesea; 2. Isle of Man
386.28, M380, P369	misericord	misericordia L	pity, mercy
386.33, M380, P369	as much as he might suffice	*trans.* quantum sufficiat L	as much as may suffice (*Pharmacology*)
388.22, M382, P371	Alba Longa	Alba Longa L	"Long White": the mother-city of Rome (*here* Alba, *Gaelic,* "*Scotland*"; *see* Gaelic Lexicon)
388.40, M382, P371	Eblana	Eblana G	Dublin
389.32, M383, P372	Alba Longa	Alba Longa L	"Long White"; *see 388.22*
390.04, M383, P372	Virgilius	*probably* Polydorus Virgilius (1470–1555)	Polydore Vergil, Italo-English historian, author of, *inter alia, De Prodigiis* (1526), a treatise on natural wonders
390.06, M383, P372	*effectu secuto*	effectu secuto (*Abl.*) L	by following effect, by effect of following
391.23–24, M385, P373	*Omnis caro ad te veniet*	omnis caro ad te veniet L	all flesh will come to thee
391.27–28, M385, P374	*omnipotentiam deiparae supplicem*	omnipotentiam deiparae supplicem L	an all-powerful beseeching of her who gave birth to God
391.36, M385, P374	Piscator	Piscator L	The Fisherman: *surname of St. Peter from his trade; title of the popes*

393.01, M386, P375	kyries	Kyrie G	O Lord
393.01–02, M386, P375	*Ut novetur sexus omnis corporis novetur*	ut novetur sexus omnis corporis mysterium L	that the mystery of the sex of all bodies may be known [*or*, may be renewed]
393.09, M386, P375	paranymphs	paranymphos G	bridal attendant: best man, bridesmaid
393.20, M387, P375	regius	regius L	royal
393.24, M387, P375	*Orate, fratres, pro memetipso*	orate, fratres, pro memetipso L	pray, brothers, for my very own self
393.30, M387, P375	the slave of servants	*distorted trans.* servus servorum [Christi] L	slave of the slaves, servant of the servants [of Christ]: *papal title*
393.31, M387, P375	Milesian	Milesianus ML	follower of Milesius, legendary settler of Ireland (*see* Gaelic Lexicon)
		Milesia [fabula] L	a Milesian tale: a dirty story
394.03, M387, P376	foraneous	*foranius for forasticus L	out of doors, exterior
394.03, M387, P376	Assuefaction	*assuefactio L	an accustoming, habituation, inuring
394.03, M387, P376	minorates	minoro L	to lessen, diminish
394.03, M387, P376	atrocities	atrocitas L	fierceness, harshness
394.03, M387, P376	Assuefaction minorates atrocities	*Assuefactio minorat atrocitatem L	Getting used to it diminishes hardship (*or words to that effect*)
394.04, M387, P376	Tully	Marcus Tullius Cicero L	Roman philosopher-statesman
394.05, M387, P376	adiaphane	*adiaphaneia G	opacity
394.07, M387, P376	*ubi*	ubi L	where
394.08, M387, P376	*quomodo*	quomodo L	how, by what means
395.25 & sqq., M389, P377	Phenomenon	phainomenon (*neut. pp.*) G	appeared, a thing that has appeared
401.05, M394, P383	*Bos Bovum*	bos bovum L	bull of bulls, ox of oxen

402.04–05, M395, P383	Quidnunc	quid nunc L	what now
402.31, M396, P384	Omphalos	omphalos G	1. navel; 2. stone at Delphi thought to be the world's navel
403.16, M396, P384	Talis ac tanta depravatio hujus seculi, O quirites,	Talis ac tanta depravatio hujus saeculi, O Quirites L	Of such kind and so great is the depravity of this age, O Roman citizens,
403.16–17, M396, P384	ut matres familiarum nostrae lascivas	ut matres familiarum nostrae lascivas L	that our wanton mothers of families
403.17–19, M396, P384	cujuslibet semiviri libici titillationes testibus ponderosis atque excelsis erectionibus centurionum Romanorum magnopere anteponunt	cujuslibet semiviri [Libici? Libyci? libidini? librici?] titillationes testibus ponderosis atque excelsis erectionibus centurionum Romanorum magnopere anteponunt L	much prefer the titillations of any [North Italian? African? licentious? lewd?] pansy to the weighty testicles and lofty erections of Roman centurions [the style is the style of Cicero but the words are the words of Mulligan]
406.13, M399, P387	Mater	Mater [Misericordiae] L	Mother [of Mercy]
408.22–23, M401, P389	Ephesian matron	allusion to the widow of Ephesus	Milesian tale (recounted by Petronius) of a widow who exchanged her husband's corpse for a criminal lover
410.04, M403, P390	quondam	quondam L	at a certain time, once, formerly
410.31, M403, P391	acardiac	akardios G	lacking a heart
410.32, M403, P391	foetus in foetu	foetus in foetu Mod. L	foetus in a foetus
410.32, M403, P391	aprosopia	*aprosôpia G	facelessness, lack of features
410.32, M403, P391	agnatia	*agnatia L	the condition of being connected by birth, blood-relatedness

		agnathia G	jawlessness [*probably the word intended*]
411.04, M404, P391	catamenic	*katamênikos G	monthly
		katamênia G	menses
411.18, M404, P391	*primafacie*	prima facie L	on first appearance
411.29, M404, P392	Minotaur	Minotaurus L Minotauros G	[Minos + *tauros*, "bull"]: monster with bull's head and man's body shut up by Minos in the labyrinth at Crete
411.29, M404, P302	the elegant Latin poet	*allusion to* Publius Ovidius Naso	amatory poet; #*A*
411.30, M404, P392	Metamorphoses	Metamorphoses L *from* G	"Transformations": poem by Ovid in 15 books; *Book VIII deals with the genesis of the Minotaur through coupling of Queen Pasiphaë with a bull (and with the complex involvement of Daedalus in Cretan affairs)*
411.41, M405, P392	Coadjutor	coadjutor L	assistant, helper
412.29, M405, P393	*Lex talionis*	lex talionis L	a law of equal retribution
413.36, M406, P394	*fiat!*	fiat L	let there be!
414.13, M407, P394	upupa	upupa L	hoopoe (*bird*)
414.19–20, M407, P394	*Lacus Mortis*	Lacus Mortis L	Lake of the Dead [the Dead Sea?]
414.29, M407, P394	Virgo	Virgo L	The Maiden; *epithet* of several goddesses; a constellation
414.29, M407, P394	metempsychosis	metempsychôsis G	transmigration of souls
414.33, M407, P395	Pleiades	Pleiades G	the seven daughters of Atlas and Pleione; a constellation

414.33–34, M407, P395	antelucan	antelucanus L	before light, before day
414.40, M407, P395	Alpha	alpha G	letter A
414.41, M407, P395	Taurus	Taurus L	The Bull: a constellation
415.02, M407–408, P395	Glaucon	Glaukos G	"Gleaming," "Grey": personal name
415.02, M408, P395	Alcibiades	Alkibiadês G	"Vigorous": Athenian general and playboy
415.02, M408, P395	Pisistratus	Pisistratus L *for* Peisistratos G (600–527 b.c.)	"Army-persuader": benevolent tyrant of Athens
415.05, M408, P395	Lethe	Lêthê G	"Forgetfulness": river in the underworld; [*it was* Styx *that the dead crossed*]
415.06, M408, P395	Bous Stephanoumenos	bous stephanoumenos G	a garlanded ox; garlanding an ox
415.23,27, M408, P395	Phyllis	Phyllis G	"Leafy": *fem. pers. name*
415.28, M408, P395	Juno	Juno L	chief Roman goddess
415.40, M408, P396	Lalage	Lalagê G	"Prattle": name of a girl mentioned by Horace in three poems
416.04, M409, P396	Periplepomenos	*Periplêpômen-os G	"Full of drinking water" ["*his booth near the bridge*" *is the Cabman's Shelter of the Eumaeus chapter—a temperance canteen*]
416.13, M409, P396	Glycera	Glykera G	"Sweet": *girl mentioned by Horace in three odes.*
416.13, M409, P396	Chloe	Chloê G	"Verdant": *fem. name mentioned by Horace*
416.28,30, M409, P396	Theosophos	*Theosophos G	"God-wise"
416.31, M409, P396	Alpha	alpha G	letter A
418.03, M410, P397	hippodrome	hippodromos G	horse-racecourse

418.10–11, M411, P398	Div. Scep.	Div[initatis] Scep[ticus] ML	Doubter of Divinity
418.20, M411, P398	Empedocles	Empedoklês G (d.c. 430 b.c.)	"Famous for Steadfastness": Sicilian naturalist; allegedly killed himself by leaping into Aetna
418.20, M411, P398	Trinacria	Trinakria G	"Three-pointed": Sicily
418.22–23, 27–28, M411, P398	nemasperms ... nemasperm	nemasperma Mod. L *from* G	thread-seed
418.27, M411, P398	*nisus formativus*	nisus formativus ML	formative effort
418.29, M411, P398	*succubitus felix*	succubitus felix L	a lucky lying-underneath
418.33, M411, P398	Hyg. et Eug. Doc.	Hyg[eae] et Eug[enicae] Doc[tor] *or*	Doctor of Health and Eugenics
		Hyg[ieinae] et Eug[enicae] Doc[tor] Mod. L	Doctor of Hygiene and Eugenics
418.42, M411, P398	Kalipedia	*Kallipaidia G	Education in beauty
419.03, M411, P398	Venus	Venus L	goddess of sexual love; # *A*
419.04, M411, P398	Apollo	Apollôn G	god of masculine beauty, the sun, prophecy, etc.
419.07, M412, P398	Disc. Bacc.	Disc[iplinae] Bacc[alaureus] Mod. L *or*	Bachelor of Discipline
		Disc[ipulus] Bacc[hi] L	Disciple of Bacchus
419.21, M412, P399	Bacc. Arith.	Bacc[alaureus] Arith[metici] Mod. L	Bachelor of Arithmetic
419.42, M412, P399	Div. Scep.	Div[initatis] Scep[ticus] Mod. L	Doubter of Divinity
421.19, M414, P401	Cronion	Kroniôn G	son of Kronos: Zeus; *error for* Kronos, *taken for* Chronos, "Time"
423.22, M416, P402	*coelum*	coelum, caelum L	the sky, heaven

423.23, M416, P402	cessile	*cessilis L	yielding
424.12, M416, P403	rutilant	rutilans L	glowing redly, shining
424.17–18, M417, P403	*Per deam Partulam et Pertundam nunc est bibendum*	Per deam Partulam et Pertundam nunc est bibendum L	By the goddess Partula and Pertunda now we must drink!
424.17, M417, P403	*Partulam*	Acc. of Partula L	goddess who presides over childbirth
424.17, M417, P402	*Pertundam*	Acc. of Pertunda L	goddess who presides over loss of virginity
424.20, M417, P403	Bonafides	bona fides L	good faith; # *B*
424.25–26, M417, P403	*Benedicat vos omnipotens Deus, Pater et Filius*	Benedicat vos omnipotens Deus, Pater et Filius L	May the almighty God, the Father and the Son, bless you
424.30–31, M417, P404	Thence they advanced five parasangs	*typical sentence from Xenophon's* Anabasis: parasangês G	Persian measure of distance, about 3.5 miles
424.39, M417, P404	*Silentium*	silentium L	silence
425.13, M417, P404	Avuncular's	avunculus L	uncle
425.14, M418, P404	pectoral trauma	trauma pectorale (*Medic.*) LL	chest wound
425.16, M418, P404	Mater	Mater [Misericordiae] L	Mother [of Mercy]
425.26, M418, P404	hoi polloi	hoi polloi G	the many
425.31–32, M418, P404	orchidised	orchis, orchidis G	testicle
425.32, M418, P404	polycimical	poly- G	much-, many-
		cimex L *polycimicalis G + L	bug much-bugged, full of bugs
425.40, M418, P405	Venus Pandemos	Venus *for* Aphroditê Pandêmos G	Aphrodite of the Whole People, Vulgar Aphrodite: *title of* Aphrodite

426.03, M418, P405	*Ex*	ex L	out of
426.06, M418, P405	*ad lib.*	ad lib[itum] L	at pleasure
426.19, M419, P405	Gemini	Gemini L	The Twins: Castor and Pollux; #*A*
427.02–03, M419, P406	*Nos omnes biberimus viridum toxicum diabolus capiat posteriora nostra*	Nos omnes biberimus viridum toxicum diabolus capiat posteriora nostra dog-L	We shall all have drunk green poison let the devil take our hindmosts [backsides]
427.12, M419, P406	Item	item L	just so, also
427.26, M420, P406	Nix	nix L	snow
427.41,42, M420, P407	Mona	Mona L	1. Anglesea; 2. Isle of Man
427.42, M420, P407	Ook	ouk G	no, not
428.07–08, M420, P407	*Laetabuntur in cubilibus suis*	Laetabuntur in cubilibus suis L	They shall be gladdened in their beds
428.11, M420, P407	*Ut implerentur scripturae*	Ut implerentur scripturae eccl.L	That the scriptures may be fulfilled

"Circe" (Nighttown)

title	Circe	Kirkê G	"Hawk?": daughter of the Sun who changes men to beasts
431.11, M424, P410	introit	introit L	he goes in
		introitus L	entrance: the first part of the Mass
431.15, M424, P410	*Vidi aquam egredientem de templo a latere dextro*	Vidi aquam egredientem de templo a latere dextro L	I saw water coming out of the temple from the right side
431.22, M424, P410	*Altius aliquantulum*	altius aliquantulum L	somewhat higher
431.23, M424, P410	*Et omnes ad quos pervenit aqua ista*	Et omnes ad quos pervenit aqua ista L	And that water reached unto all men
432.10, M425, P411	*Triumphaliter*	triumphaliter L	triumphantly
432.10, M425, P411	*Salvi facti i sunt*	Salvi facti i sunt LL	They are made sound

432.22, M424, P411	Pornosophical	*pornosophos G	one learned about prostitutes *or* fornication
432.33, M425, P411	philotheology	*philotheologia G	love of the study of God
432.25, M425, P411	Socrates	Sôkratês G	celebrated philosopher
432.26, M425, P411	stagyrite	Stageiritês G	man from Stageira: Aristotle
433.09, M426, P412	*ad deam qui laetificat juventutem meam*	ad deam qui laetificat juventutem meam	to the goddess who gladdens my youth
		irreverent parody of ad Deum qui laetificat juventutem meam L	to God who gladdens my youth: *first response of the Introit of the Mass*
434.27, M427, P413	*Aurora borealis*	aurora borealis L	"the northern dawn": northern lights
438.29, M431, P417	*Agnus Dei*	Agnus Dei L	Lamb of God
440.02, M432, P418	Feminimum [*error?*]	femininum (*masc. Acc.* or *neut. Nom.* / *Acc.*) L	feminine, pertaining to a woman
449.23, M442, P427	Marcus	Marcus L	"Hammer": Roman praenomen
449.23, M442, P427	Tertius	Tertius L	Third, the Third: Roman praenomen
453.20, M445, P430	Bloom. Of Bloom. For Bloom. Bloom.	*Bloomos (*Nom.*). *Bloomou (*Gen.*). *Bloomôi (*Dat.*) *Bloomon (*Acc.*)	*cases of the G noun*
454.25–26, M446, P431	*Leo ferox*	leo ferox L	the wild lion [*Zoological name:* Felis Leo, "*Cat Lion*" or "*Lion Cat*"]
455.22, M447, P432	alibi	alibi L	elsewhere
456.07, M448, P432	THE DARK MERCURY	Mercurius *for* Hermês Psychopompos G	Mercury, Soul-Conductor: led the shades of the dead to the netherworld

459.22, M451, P435	*corpus delicti*	corpus delicti L	the body of the crime: the material evidence of the crime (*Law*)
463.15, M455, P439	*Prima facie*	prima facie (*Abl.*) L	on first appearance
464.02, M455, P439	Hades	Hadês, Haidês G	"Unseen": god of the underworld; place of departed spirits; death, the grave
473.10, M464, P447	metempsychosis	metempsychôsis G	transmigration of souls
473.27–28, M465, P448	Namine. Jacobs Vobiscuits	*conflation of* in nomine Domini L *and* Dominus vobiscum L	in the name of the Lord the Lord [be] with you
475.10, M466, P449 & sqq.	*Zoe*	zôê G	living, livelihood, life
478.23, M469, P452	*Cui bono?*	cui bono L	for whose good?
478.28, M469, P452	*aurora borealis*	aurora borealis L	"the northern dawn": northern lights
479.07, M470, P452	*locum tenens*	locum tenens L	holding the place
482.21–22, M473, P456	*Gaudium magnum annuntio vobis*	Gaudium magnum annuntio vobis L *for* evangelizo vobis gaudium magnum—*Luc.* 2:10, *Vulgate*	I proclaim to you great joy "I bring you good tidings of great joy" (*Rheims, Luke 2:10; AV, Luke 2:10*)
482.22, M473, P456	*Habemus carneficem*	Habemus carnificem L	We have an executioner
482.28, M473, P456	*Mirus*	mirus L	wonderful, marvelous
483.09–10, M473, P456	Copula Felix	copula felix L	the happy bond, the blessed tie (*matrimony; friendship*)
		felix culpa L	happy sin; #*B*
483.12,14, M473–474, P456	Selene ... *Selene*	Selênê G	Moon: goddess of the moon

484.08, M474, P457	*Bonafide*	bona fide L	in good faith; #*B*
484.23, M475, P458	Nova Hibernia	Nova Hibernia L	New Ireland
485.07, M475, P458	*Morituri te salutant*	morituri te salutant L	they, about to die, salute thee
		for morituri te salutamus L	we, about to die, salute thee: *gladiators' salutation to the emperor*
485.34, M476, P459	*Vade Mecum*	vade mecum L	"go with me": handbook
488.13, M478, P461	Tinct. mix. [*error for* nux *all eds.*] vom.	Tinct[ura] nux [*recte* nucis] vom[icae] *pharmaceutical pidgin-*L	Tincture of *nux vomica*
		nux vomica Mod L	the foul nut (*perhaps intended as* nux vomifica, "*emetic nut*"): *a heart stimulant made from the poisonous nut of an Asian tree*
488.14, M478, P461	Extr. taraxel. lig.	Extr[actum] tarax[asterolae] lig[ni]	Extract of the wood of gentian
		or Extr[actum] tarax[aci] lig[ni] *pharmaceutical* L	Extract of the wood of dandelion root
488.15, M478, P461	Aq. dis. ter in die	Aq[ua] dis[tillata] ter in die L	Distilled water three times a day
489.06, M479, P462	pater	pater L	father
490.15, M480, P463	*Venus Callipyge*	Venus *for* Aphroditê Kallipygos G	Aphrodite of the Beautiful Buttocks: *Epithet of* Aphrodite
490.16, M480, P463	*Venus Pandemos*	Venus *for* Aphroditê Pandêmos G	Aphrodite of the Whole People: *epithet of Aphrodite*
490.16, M480, P463	*Venus Metempsychosis*	Venus *for* Aphroditê Metempsychôse-ôs G	Aphrodite of Transmigration of Souls: *not an epithet of Aphrodite*

490.18, M480, P463	*Amor*	amor L	love
491.17, 492.01, M481, 482, P464	Sibyl	Sibylla G L	female soothsayer
493.17, M483, P465	*virgo intacta*	virgo intacta L	an untouched maiden
493.20, M483, P465	Hypsospadia	*hypsospadia G *for* hypospadias G	sublime impotence one having orifice of the urethra too low (*congenital malformation of the penis*)
493.27, M483, P466	*fetor judaicus*	fetor judaicus L	Jewish stench
494.31, M484, P467	*Chrysostomos*	chrysostomos G	golden-mouthed
494.32, M484, P467	*Panargyros*	panargyros G	all-silver
495.24, M485, P468	*Leopoldi autem generatio*	Leopoldi autem generatio L: *"Chi-rho" page of Book of Kells reads* Christi autem generatio, *corresp. to Matthew 1:18*	But now the begetting of Leopold But now the begetting of Christ "Now the birth of Jesus Christ [was on this wise . . .]"
495.33, 496.01, M485, P468	Magnus	Magnus L	the Great
496.07–08, M486, P468	*et vocabitur nomen eius Emmanuel*	et vocabitur nomen ejus Emmanuel L	and his name shall be called Emmanuel
496.19, M486, P468	*frons* [error *front* in all eds.]	frons L	forehead, brow
496.19, M486, P468	*nates*	nates L	buttocks
497.16, M487, P469	*bonafide*	bona fide L	in good faith; #*B*
498.16, M488, P470	*I.H.S.*	IHS[OYS] = Iês[ous] G	JES[US]
498.17, M488, P470	*phoenix*	phoenix L	fabulous bird of Arabia; *see* Finnegan's Wake 265.08

504.01, M493, P475	Demeter	Dêmêtêr G	"Dê [meaning unknown] Mother": G corn goddess
504.01–02, M493, P475	Caela enarrant gloriam Domini	Caela enarrant gloriam Domini L for Coeli enarrant gloriam Dei (Ps. 19:1, Vulgate)	The heavens relate the glory of the Lord, for "The heavens shew forth the glory of God" (Douay Ps. 18:1), "The heavens declare the glory of God" (AV, Ps. 19:1)
504.04, M493, P475	Circe's	Circe L Kirkê G	goddess who turned men to beasts
504.05, M493, P475	Ceres'	Ceres L	Roman goddess of agriculture, esp. of grain
510.15–16, M499, P481	Hermes Trismegistos	Hermês Trismegistos G	clumsy trans. of Egyptian "Thoth the very great": reputed author of mystical works
511.21–22, M500, P482	basilicogrammate	basilikos grammateus G	royal scribe: official in Egyptian provinces
512.31, M502, P483	Rualdus	Rualdus ML	masc. name: Raoul
512.31, M502, P483	Colombus	columbus L	dove, pigeon (c'est le pigeon)
512.31, M502, P483	Rualdus Colombus	Rualdus + Columbus ML	Raoul the discoverer (Sweets of Sin)?
514.28–29, 514.11, M502, 503, P484	Lycopodium . . . lycopodium	lycopodium ML from G	"wolf-foot": club moss
514.01–02, M502–503, P484	Argumentum ad feminam	argumentum ad feminam L parody of argumentum ad hominem L	demonstration to the woman demonstration, proof or argument directed at the person (loosely trans. as "at the man")
514.04, M503, P484	Diplodocus	diplodocus Mod L for diplodokos G	double-beam, double-bar; name of a dinosaur
514.04, M503, P484	Ichthyosaurus	ichthyosauros G	fish-lizard; name of a dinosaur
514.23, M503, P484	Mnemo	mnêmô G	remembrance, memory

Reference	Term	Source	Meaning
514.28, M503, P484	pulsatilla	pulsatilis L	throbbing
516.22, M505, P486	Elephantuliasis	*elephantuliasis L *modeled on*	[imaginary] disease which causes resemblance to a little elephant
		elephantiasis G L	form of leprosy; disease that causes the skin to resemble elephant hide
519.01, M507, P488	*Zoe mou sas agapo*	Zôê mou sas agapô MG	My life I love thee
519.29, M508, P489	pudor	pudor L	shame
520.01, M508, P489	*Coactus volui*	coactus volui L	constrained, I have desired
520.07, M508, P489	glorias	Gloria [Patri *etc.*] L	Glory [be to the Father, *etc.*]
520.22, M509, P490	Iacchias	Iakchiastês G	worshipper of *Iakchos* (*mystic name of Dionysos*)
521.21–22, M510, P491	genitories	genitoris (*Gen.*) L	creator's, father's
521.25, M510, P491	Hik! Hek! Hak! Hok!	hic, haec, hoc L	this, this here (*masc., fem., neut.*)
521.23, M510, P491	Huk!	huc L	to this place, hither
523.09, M511, P492	*Exeunt*	exeunt L	[they] go out, [they] leave
523.13, M512, P492	Antisthenes	Antisthenês G	pupil of Socrates, founder of Cynic philosophical sect
523.13, M512, P492	the dog sage	*allusion to* Diogenês ho Kynikos G	Diogenes "the dog-like" (*trans. as* Cynic), from his personal habits
523.13, M512, P492	Arius	Areios G	denied equality of the Trinity; *see 021.08*
523.14, M512, P492	Heresiarchus	Heresiarchus L ho Hairesiarchês G	the Sect-Leader
526.25, M515, P495	Mnemo	mnêmô G	remembrance, memory
526.26, M515, P495	lupus	lupus L	wolf
527.01, M515, P495 & sqq.	*Bella*	bella (*fem.*) L	pretty

		bella (*neut. pl.*) L	wars
530.16, M518, P499 & sqq.	BELLO	bello (*Abl.*) L	by means of war
536.34, M525, P504	*Vice Versa*	vice versa L	turned around reciprocally
544.05, M531, P511	procurator	procurator L	manager, overseer, deputy, imperial tax collector
544.22, M532, P511	*pneuma*	pneuma G	blast, wind, air, breath; divine inspiration
545.14, M533, P512	Aurora	Aurora L	Dawn
545.28, M533, P512	exuber	exubero L	to overflow, to abound in
548.15–16, 17, 22, M535, P514–515	Halcyon days . . . *Halcyon days* . . . HALCYON DAYS	alkyonides hêmerai G	winter days when the halcyon nests on the calm sea
		[h]alkyôn G	"Sea-conceived" (*false etymology*): mythical bird that nests on the sea; kingfisher
549.03, M536, P515	*hamadryads*	hamadryades G	"together-with-trees": spirits whose lives were bound up with those of trees to which they were attached
549.16, M536, P515	fauns	fauni (*pl.*) L	sylvan deities identified with G satyrs
551.16, M538, P517	Peccavi	peccavi eccl. L	I have sinned
553.19, M540, P519	Nekum!	neco L	to kill, to slay
556.26–27, M543, P522	*brevi manu*	brevi manu L	with brief hand
559.10, M545, P524	Proparoxyton	proparoxytonos G	having an acute accent on the antepenult
560.16–17, M546, P525	*Dona nobis pacem*	Dona nobis pacem L	Give us peace
561.04, M547, P526	Mars	Mars L	god of war; #*A*
566.19, M552, P530	poppysmic	poppysma, poppysmos G, L	smacking *or* clucking with the tongue

567.25, M553, P531	Thursdaymomun Thursday momum	mômon (*Acc.*) G	blame, reproach
569.08, M554, P533	*Et exaltabuntur cornua iusti*	Et exaltabuntur cornua justi L	And the horns of the just shall be raised up
569.09, M554, P533	Pasiphae	Pasiphaë L Pasiphaê G	"All-Shining": Circe's sister, wife of Minos, mother, by Minos's bull, of the Minotaur
569.09–10, M554, P533	my grandoldgrossfather made the first confession box	*allusion to* Daedalus L Daidalos G	made a hollow cow in which Pasiphaë enjoyed congress with the bull
572.03, M557, P535	*Pater*	pater L	father
573.30, M559, P537	*Per vias rectas*	per vias rectas L	through straight ways
574.21, M559, P537	augur's	augur L	soothsayer, diviner
574.22, M559, P537	*tripudium*	tripudium L	solemn religious stamping dance
580.02, M564, P542	*Liliata rutilantium te confessorum*	Liliata rutilantium te confessorum L	Lilied ... of glowing confessors ... thee
580.03, M564, P542	*Iubilantium te virginum*	Jubilantium te virginum L	of rejoicing virgins ... thee
580.15, M565, P543	Lemur	lemur L	ghost, spectre of a dead person
580.21, M565, P543	*Epi oinopa ponton*	epi oinopa ponton G	upon the wine-colored sea
582.14, M567, P545	*Non serviam*	non serviam L	I shall not serve
587.30, M572, P550	Sisyphus	Sisyphos G	robber, condemned in underworld to roll a stone uphill forever
589.26, M574, P552	philirenists	phileirênistês G	peace-lover
598.33–34, M583, P560	*It rains dragon's teeth. Armed heroes spring up from furrows*	*allusion to* Kadmos G Cadmus L	prior to founding Thebes he sowed dragon's teeth from which sprang armed men. Their survivors founded the First Families of Thebes.

599.21, M583, P560	Introibo ad altare diaboli	Introibo ad altare diaboli L parody of Introibo ad altare Dei L	I will go in to the devil's altar I will go in to God's altar: beginning of the Introit of the Mass
599.23, M583, P560	To the devil which hath made glad my young days	(pseudo-Anglic- an) trans. Ad diabolum qui laetificat juventutem meam L parody of Ad Deum qui laetificat juventutem meam L	To the devil who gladdens my youth To God who gladdens my youth: first response of the Introit
599.26, M583, P561	Corpus Meum	corpus meum L	my body
600.26, M585, P562	Exit Judas	exit Judas L	Judas goes out
600.26, M585, P562	Et laqueo se suspendit	et laqueo se suspendit L	and hangs himself with a noose
600.26, M585, P562	Exit Judas. Et laqueo se suspendit	for et abiens laqueo se suspendit (Matt. 27:5, Vulgate)	"and went and hanged himself with an halter" (Rheims, Matt. 27:5), "and went and hanged himself" (AV, Matt. 27:5)

"Eumaeus" (Cabmen's Shelter)

title	Eumaeus	Eumaios G	"Well-born": faithful swineherd of Odysseus who helped him regain control of Ithaca
614.06, M598, P574	Jupiter Pluvius	Juppiter Pluvius L	Jupiter the Rain-Dispenser; # A
614.22–23, M598, P574	fidus Achates	fidus Achates L	faithful or trusty Achates: friend and companion of Aeneas in the Aeneid
614.32, M598, P574	re	[in] re L	[in] the matter
616.03, M600, P576	quondam	quondam L	one time, formerly, once
617.35, M601, P577	haud ignarus malorum miseris succurrere disco, etcetera	haud ignarus malorum miseris succurrere disco, et cetera L	by no means unacquainted with evils, I know how to aid the wretched, and the rest

		misquotation of Non ignara mali, miseris succurrere disco—Verg. *Aen.* I .630	Not unacquainted with ill, I know how to aid the wretched, *Aeneid* I .630
619.09, M603, P579	*rara avis*	rara avis L	an extraordinary bird (Horace, of the peacock, *Sat.* II .2,26)
619.24, M603, P579	Eblana	Eblana G	Dublin
621.43, M606, P581	*homo*	homo L	human being, man, person
622.08, M606, P581	*hoi polloi*	hoi polloi G	the many
622.41, M607, P582	Cicero	Cicero L	"Chick-pea": Roman cognomen in the gens Tullia
		Marcus Tullius Cicero L	Roman orator and statesman
624.41, M609, P584	*post mortem*	post mortem L	after death
626.27, M610, M586	*bona fides*	bona fides L	good faith
626.29, M610, M586	*via*	via (*Abl.*) L	by way [of]
629.15, M613, P588	*alias*	alias L	otherwise
630.20, M614, P589	nil	nil L	nothing
630.22, M614, P589	*minutiae*	minutiae (*pl.*) L	smallnesses, trifles
633.16, M617, P592	*instanter*	instanter L	vehemently, earnestly
633.20, M617, P592	*paterfamilias*	paterfamilias OL	father of an extended family, patriarch
633.39–40, M618, P593	*corruptio per se*	corruptio per se L	a corrupting through itself
633.40, M618, P593	*corruptio per accidens*	corruptio per accidens L	a corrupting through chance, a spoiling through an extraneous circumstance
634.23, M618, P593	*in toto*	in toto L	in all
635.21, M619, P594	*sine qua non*	sine qua non L	without which, not

636.18, M620, P595	*Hesperus*	hesperus L	the evening star; the west
636.18, M620, P595	etcetera	et cetera L	and the rest
636.34, M620, P595	*alias*	alias L	otherwise
638.14,16, M622, P597	*Mona ... Mona's*	Mona L	1. Anglesea; 2. Isle of Man
639.11, M623, P598	Morpheus	Morpheus G	"Shaper": god of dreams
640.03, M624, P598	*cum*	cum L	with, along with, as well as, while
640.35,37, M625, P599	Achilles heel ...	Achilleus G Achilles L	G hero in the Trojan War, hero of the *Iliad*, could be mortally wounded only in his heel
643.11, M627, P601	*Ex quibus*	ex quibus L	from which [things]
643.12, M627, P601	*Christus*	Christus L *for* Christos G	"Anointed": Christ
643.13, M627, P601	*secundum carnem*	secundum carnem L	according to the flesh
644.17, M628, P602	*pro rata*	pro rata [parte] L	according to the calculated [share]
644.23, M628, P603	*Ubi patria*	ubi patria L	where the fatherland [is]
644.24, M628, P603	*Alma mater*	alma mater L	nourishing mother
644.24, M628, P603	*vita bene*	vita L	life
		bene L	well
644.23–24, M628, P603	*Ubi patria ... vita bene*	*garble of* Ubi bene, ibi patria L (Cicero, *Tusc. Disp.* V ,108)	Where [it is] well, in that place [is my] country—*Cicero*
644.36, M629, P603	pro. tem.	pro tem[pore] L	for the time
644.40, M629, P603	kudos	kudos G	1. glory, renown; 2. reproach, abuse
647.24, M631, P605	R.I.P.	R[equiescat] I[n] P[ace] L	May he rest in peace
650.12, M634, P608	*Bella*	bella (*fem.*) L	pretty
		bella (*neut. pl.*) L	wars; #B

653.36, M637, P611	*sic*	sic L	thus
654.14,15, M638, P612	*nisi*	nisi L	unless
655.06, M639, P612	kudos	kudos G	1. honor; 2. reproach
656.09, M640, P613	*conditio sine qua non*	conditio sine qua non L	a stipulation without which, not
656.38, M641, P614	*quasi*	quasi L	as if, as it were
657.20, M641, P615	pros	pro L	for
657.20, M641, P615	cons	con[tra] L	against
658.18, M642, P615	*passim*	passim L	here and there, at random, in every direction
658.23, M642, P616	tender Achilles	tendo Achillis ML tenôn Achilleôs G	Achilles' tendon: muscular connection in the heel *which was Achilles' mortal spot*
660.26, M644, P618	tender Achilles	tendo Achillis *etc.*	*as above*
641.10, M645, P618	*Gloria*	Gloria [Patri, *etc.*] L	Glory [be to the Father, *etc.*]
661.16, M645, P618	*Stabat Mater*	stabat mater L	the mother was standing
661.39–40, M646, P619	*anno ludendo hausi, Doulandus*	annos [sic] ludendo hausi L *anagram of* [Iohannes] Doulandus L	I have consumed years in playing John Dowland
662.01, M646, P619	*dux*	dux L; ML	leader, chief; duke
662.02, M646, P619	*comes*	comes L; ML	companion; earl, count
662.43, M647, P620	*in medias res*	in medias res L	in the middle of the plot: *place to begin narrating an epic*
663.20, M647, P620	*extempore*	ex tempore L	out of the time, outside the [set] time: offhand, without preparation
664.21, M648, P621	*genus omne*	genus omne L [hoc] genus omnes L	all the kind, the whole tribe all that sort

664.30, M648, P621	iota	iota G	letter I
"Ithaca" (Bloom's House)			
title	Ithaca	Ithakê G	the kingdom of Odysseus; *perhaps the island of that name* (*mod. Thiaki*) [does not fit the description], *or perhaps the island Leukas* [fits the description]
666.13, M650, P623	duumvirate	duumviratus L	two men jointly holding office
666.17, M650, P623	paraheliotropic	*parahêliotropos G	turning with the sun
666.26, M650, P623	cisatlantic	cis L	on this side
667.14, M651, P624	paraheliotropic	*parahêliotropos G	turning with the sun
668.34, M652, P626	bissextile	bisextilis L	"having a double sixth": having an intercalary day (VI Kal. Mart. = Feb. 24, was doubled in Roman leap year)
669.02, M653, P626	MXMIV [*error in all eds.*]	*MXMIV = MCMXCIV L *should be* MCMIV L	1994

1904 |
671.40, M655, P628	multisecular	multisaecularis L	of many centuries
671.41, M655, P628	luteofulvous	luteofulvus L	1. yellow-tawny; 2. muddy-yellow
672.15, M656, P629	rhabdomantic	rhabdomantikos G	pertaining to divination by a rod *or* wand
672.33–34, M656, P629	anacoustic	anakoustos G	unhearing, deaf
672.34, M656, P629	photophobe	*phôtophobos G	fearer of light; light-fearing
673.35, M657, P630	foliated	foliatus L	leaved, having leaves
673.36, M657, P630	decidua	decidua L	things that have fallen down
674.29, M658, P631	humected	humectatus (*pp.*) L	moistened

679.01, M663, P635	posticipated	posticipatus (*pp.*) L	received afterwards
681.02, M665, P637	*vice versa*	vice versa L	turned around reciprocally
685.35, M669, P642	videlicet	videlicet L	it is easy to see, plainly, of course, manifestly
686.31, M670, P643	metempsychosis	metempsychôsis G	transmigration of souls
686.32, M670, P643	*alias*	alias L	otherwise
		Ananias G	*Hananiah* (Heb.): "God is merciful": *was struck dead for lying under oath* (Acts 5:1-10)
687.27, M671, P644	Aristotle	Aristotelês G	well–known philosopher; #*A*
687.31, M672, P644	anapocryphal	anapokryphos G	unhidden, not concealed
689.16, M673, P645	virgular	*virgularis L	striped
689.17, M673, P645	quinquecostate	*quinquecostat-us L	having five ribs, five-ribbed
689.29, M674, P646	hypostasis	hypostasis G	substance, reality
689.30, M674, P646	Johannes Damascenus	Johannes Damascenus L (a.d. 676–754)	[St.] John of Damascus; theologian, hymnwriter; wrote *Barlaam and Joasaph*, a disguised life of Buddha
689.30, M674, P646	Lentulus Romanus	Lentulus Romanus *probably* Publius Lentulus	"Somewhat-slow, the Roman" fictitious governor of Jerusalem, supposedly sent the Roman Senate a description of Jesus; his letter (a pious forgery) was found in the 15th C.
689.31, M674, P646	Epiphanius	Epiphanius LL	"belonging to the Epiphany": *name of several saints*
689.31, M674, P646	Monachus	monachus LL	monk

689.31, M674, P646	Epiphanius Monachus	Epiphanius Monachus LL (310–403)	Epiphanius the Monk: saint, preacher against Arianism
689.31, M674, P646	leucodermic	leukodermatos G	white-skinned
689.31, M674, P646	sesquipedalian	sesquipedalis L	a foot and a half long; having one and a half feet
689.32, M674, P646	winedark	*trans.* oinops G	winecolored
694.03,07,10,1-4, M678, P651	cf.	c[on]f[er] L	compare!
694.07, M678, P651	locus	locus L	place, spot
694.27–28, M679, P651	*videlicet*	videlicet L	it is easy to see, manifestly
695.01, M679, P652	diambulist	*diambulator L	one who walks by day
695.02, M679, P652	noctambulist	noctambulator L	one who walks by night
696.07, M680, P653	peripatetic	peripatetikos G	strolling about; belonging to Aristoteles' philosophical school
696.25, M681, P653	imprevidibility	*impraevidibili-tas L	unforeseeableness
698.05, M682, P655	*secreto*	secreto (*Abl.*) L	in private
698.07, M682, P655	*modus peregrinus*	modus peregrinus L modo peregrini ML	a foreign manner in the manner of a pilgrim
698.07–08, M682, P655	*In exitu Israël de Egypto:*	In exitu Israël de Egypto L *Ps. 114:1, Vulg.*	When Israel went out of Egypt (*Douay, Ps. 113:1; AV. Ps. 114:1*)
698.08, M682, P655	*domus Jacob de populo barbaro*	domus Jacob de populo barbaro, *Ps. 114:1, Vulg.*	the house of Jacob from a barbarous people (*Douay Ps. 113:1*); the house of Jacob from a people of strange language (*AV Ps. 114:1*)
698.26, M683, P655	Sirius	Sirius L Seirios G	the dog star
698.26, M683, P655	alpha	alpha G	letter A

698.26–27, M683, P655	Canis Major	Canis Major L	The Greater Dog: constellation *of which Sirius is the brightest star*
698.28, M683, P655	Arcturus	Arcturus L Arktouros G	"Bear-Guard": a star
698.29, M683, P655	Orion	Ôriôn G	fabulous hunter changed to a constellation
698.29, M683, P655	theta	thêta G	letter TH
698.29, M683, P655	nebula	nebula L	mist, smoke, fog
698.31, M683, P655	Nova	nova (*fem.*) L	new
698.32, M683, P655	Hercules	Hercules L Heraklês G	hero and demigod
700.32, M685, P657	astroscopist	astroskopistês G	star-watcher
700.40, M685, P657	delta	delta G	letter D
700.41, M685, P657	Cassiopeia	Cassiopia L Kassiopeia G	mother of Andromeda; a constellation
701.02–03, M685, P657	Corona Septentrionalis	corona septentrionalis L	the northern crown: Ariadne's crown; a constellation
701.06, M685, P657	Andromeda	Andromeda L Andromêdê G	maiden rescued by Perseus, *now* a constellation
701.07, M685, P657	Auriga	auriga L	charioteer: the waggoner, a constellation
701.19, M686, P658	Utopia	*Outopia G	Nowhere-land
703.03, M687, P659	irruent	irruens L	rushing in
703.14, M687, P659	pelosity	pêlos G	mud
		*pelositas G + L	muddiness
703.20, M688, P660	hyperduly	hyperdoulia eccl. G	superservility: the special class of veneration accorded to the Blessed Virgin
703.20, M688, P660	latria	latreia G	service, worship

703.26, M688, P660	Berenice	Berenikê (*Macedonian*) G	"Victoria," "Bearing Victory": daughter of Ptolemy Philadelphus, wife of Ptolemy Euergetes; her hair is a constellation
703.27, M688, P660	Leo	Leo L	The Lion: constellation
703.30, M688, P660	arruginated	*arruginatus (*pp.*) L	wrinkled, corrugated
704.10, M688, P660	*Liliata rutilantium*	Liliata rutilantium L	Lilied ... of glowing
704.10, M688, P660	*Turma circumdet*	Turma circumdet L	May a crowd ... surround
704.11, M688, P660	*Iubilantium te virginum*	Jubilantium te virginum L	... of rejoicing virgins ... thee
704.11, M688, P660	*Chorus excipiat*	Chorus excipiat L	A chorus ... follows ...
705.02–03, M689, P661	Mater Misericordiae	Mater Misericordiae L	Mother of Mercy
705.12, M689, P661	paraphenomena	*paraphainôm-ena G	things disclosed
706.29, M691, P663	*ad libitum*	ad libitum L	to one's liking, as one wishes
706.29, M691, P663	*forte*	forte L	by chance, accidentally
707.20, M692, P663	homothetic	*homothetikos G	placed the same
708.01,03, M692, P664	ipsorelative	ipso L	to, for *or* by, with, from the same *or* the self
708.01,06, M692, P664	aliorelative	alio L	to, for *or* by, with, from another ("same/other"—*Platonic categories*)
708.35, M693, P665	Viator	viator L	wayfarer, traveler
709.23, M694, P660	MDCCXI	MDCCXI L	1711
709.36, M694, P666	incuneated	*incuneatus (*pp.*) L	wedged-in
710.15, M695, P667	Narcissus	Narcissus	beautiful youth who loved his own reflection; changed into a flower

712.23, M697, P669	*Rus in Urbe*	rus in urbe L	[bit of] country in the city
715.32, M700, P672	*Semper paratus*	semper paratus L	always prepared
715.33, M700, P672	P.C.	P[ater] C[onscriptus]? L	Enrolled Father: Senator (*here*, City Councilman)
715.34, M700, P672	*honoris causa*	honoris causa L	by reason of honor
721.14–15, M706, P677	boustrophedontic	boustrophêdonti-kos G	in the manner of an ox turning: written with alternate lines left-to-right and right-to-left
722.02, M706, P678	thaumaturgic	thaumaturgos G	wonder-working
724.13, M709, P680	hebdomadary	hebdomadikos G	weekly
724.16, M709, P680	tetragrammaton	tetragrammaton G	word of four letters; *the sacred Hebrew name* YHWH
725.21, M710, P681	helotic	heilôtikos G	pertaining to Spartan serfs
726.02, M710, P682	latration	*latratio L	barking
727.03, M711, P683	Parthenon	Parthenôn G	"Temple of the Virgin": famous temple of Athena at Athens
727.12, M712, P683	septentrional	septentrionalis L	northern
727.13, M712, P683	beta	bêta G	letter B
727.13,16, M712, P683	alpha	alpha G	letter A
727.14,16–17, M712, P683	Ursa Major	Ursa Major L	The Greater Bear; a constellation
727.14, M712, P683	omega	ô mega, ômega G	letter *Ô*, *great O*
727.16, M712, P683	delta	delta G	letter D
727.31,34, M712, P683	Noman	*trans.* Outis G	Nobody: name Odysseus gave himself to the Cyclops; #*A*
727.34, M712, P683	nymph immortal ... the bride of Noman	*allusion to* Kalypsô	"She that conceals": Odysseus spent seven years with her, during which she bore him a son

728.06, M712, P684	delta	delta G	letter D
728.06, M712, P684	Cassiopeia	Cassiopia L Kassiopeia G	mother of Andromeda; a constellation
728.07–08, M712, P684	return an estranged avenger, a wreaker of justice on malefactors	*allusion to* return of Odysseus to Ithaca	unrecognized he returned to his home and slew the suitors who had occupied his house, and the maids who had abetted them
728.23, M713, P684	Narcissus	Narcissus	beautiful youth who loved his own reflection; changed into a flower
731.07, M715, P687	radii	radii (*pl.*) L	rays, beams, spokes
731.34, M716, P687	Argus	Argos G	"Bright": giant with 100 eyes
735.21, M720, P691	peccaminous	peccamen LL	fault, sin
		*peccaminosus LL	sinful
735.24, M720, P691	postcenal	*postcenalis L	after-dinner
736.09,14–15, M720, P691	ejaculation of semen within the natural female organ	*trans.* ejaculatio seminis inter vas naturale mulieris L	see 223.31
737.08, M721, P692	Gea-Tellus	Gaia G	Earth (*goddess*)
		Tellus L	Earth (*goddess*)
"Penelope" (Molly) *title*	Penelope	Pênelopeia G	"Weaver": Odysseus' faithful wife
739.05, M724, P695	Myriorama	*myriôrama G	sight of ten thousand things
745.33, M730, P701	*Ave Maria*	Ave Maria L	Hail Mary
748.33, M733, P704	*Stabat Mater*	stabat mater L	the mother was standing
759.20, M744, P713	vatican	*Mollyism for* viaticum L viaticum eccl. L	provisions for a journey the last sacrament
761.26, M746, P715	Calypso	Calypso L Kalypsô G	"She who conceals": nymph with whom Odysseus stayed seven years

761.40, M746, P716	Europa	Europa L Eurôpê G	girl carried off by Zeus in form of a bull; the continent named for her
775.26, M760, P728	Europa	Europa L Eurôpê G	*as at 761.26*
776.28, M761, P729	hypocrites	hypokritês G	actor (*Molly's spicy reading must have shown her a Comic actor with conventional exaggerated phallic erection*)
776.28–29, M761, P729	Julius Caesar	C. Julius Caesar L	famous dictator; #A [*no doubt all antiquity was "the time of Julius Caesar"*]
776.43, M762, P729	etcetera	et cetera L	and the others, and the rest

APPENDIX A

A List of Classical Names Requiring Further Annotation

Amnis Livia See *Livia*.

Amor Roman love god, son of Venus; also Venus herself. See *Venus*.

Aphroditê G goddess of love, identified with Venus. See *Venus*.

Arês G god of war, identified with Mars. See *Mars*.

Aristotle Aristotelês ("Best-Complete") (384-322 b.c.), Athenian scientist and philosopher, born at Stagiros (later called Stagira), son of a physician and surgeon. From his birthplace he is sometimes called the Stagirite (often misspelled Stagyrite). At the age of 17 he entered Plato's school, where he stayed about 20 years, as a student and then as a researcher. After Plato's death he left, and thereafter taught and studied at various places, including a spell at Pella in Macedonia as tutor to the young prince who became Alexander the Great. Later he founded his own school, research center, and museum at Athens, near a grove dedicated to Apollo Lyceius, from which the school was known as the Lyceum. The buildings included a covered court (*peripatos*), from which the school was also named; "peripatetic" has become a generic term for Aristotelian philosophy and method.

Aristotle was married twice, first to a woman named Pythias, and after her death to Herpyllis, who bore his son, Nicomachus. It is possible he did not in fact marry Herpyllis, but unquestionably he lived with her. His will is preserved, in which he makes thoughtful disposition of his property, providing for the welfare of his family and slaves, with expressions of affection and gratitude. This personal side of Aristotle is alluded to most frequently in *Ulysses*.

Aristotle was an extremely prolific researcher and writer, whose extant corpus, despite considerable losses, remains formidable. Perhaps because he was more interested in biology than in mathematics, his thought moved far from its Platonic origins, and he rejected the Platonic notion of the separate existence of "Ideas." His distrust, if it may be so called, of mathematics was the greatest weakness in his system, and had a retarding effect on science throughout the millenium or so in which his theories dominated scientific thought. But that he should have been so dominant is thoroughly understandable, for he was a tireless researcher, interested in every aspect of knowledge. His mind has been characterized as one of inspired common sense governed by tidiness and love of order. Both these qualities are responsible for Aristotle's major contribution to subsequent philosophy and science: (1) the classification of the sciences—e.g., the separation, for purposes of study and research, of ethics from mathematics, or physics from theology; (2) the development of a clear terminology for philosophy—*universal* and *particular*, *premise* and *conclusion*, *potentiality* and *actuality*— these are all terms that Aristotle first defined, named, and introduced into philosophic discourse.

St. Thomas Aquinas in his methodology was much influenced by Aristotle, and such philosophical instruction as Joyce received in his Jesuit education would have been Aristotelian-Thomistic in color. Although the melting morass of *Finnegans Wake* is anything but Aristotelian, Joyce seems to have remained emotionally loyal to "the master of those who know," in Dante's famous phrase. One suspects he felt his own work, certainly through *Ulysses*, to be commonsensical in an Aristotelian way, dealing with the present world of daily fact, by contrast with the "Platonic" work of the only other Irish writer of his own stature, W. B. Yeats.

Armenia This ancient kingdom, mentioned frequently by classical writers, may be alluded to a number of times in *Finnegans Wake* (e.g., 339.29), but if the references are actual, Joyce's intent is not entirely clear to us. A few salient facts concerning Armenia are here offered in the hope the reader may find some enlightenment in them.

Armenia was a mountainous country of Asia, occupying the plateau east of the Euphrates river. Strabo describes it as bounded by Media Atropatene, Iberia, Albania, Colchis, the Euphrates, Cappadocia, and Commagene. "Albania" is not, of course, the modern country of that name on the Adriatic; "Iberia," likewise, is not the peninsula occupied by modern Spain and Portugal, but approximately the territory of the Soviet Republic of Georgia. In medieval manuscripts dealing with Ireland, however, "Iberia" sometimes represents Ireland, and Isidore of Seville derives the name "Hibernia" from "Iberia." Similarly, "Albania" frequently designates Scotland (from Gaelic *Alba*, "Britain" or

"Scotland"). Moreover, in medieval Irish manuscripts the word "Armenia" itself often stands, by scribal confusion, for Armorica. This onomastic confusion, if Joyce was sensible of it, would certainly have attracted Armenia into *Finnegans Wake* (See *Armorica; Hibernia*).

Ancient Armenia had been a part of the Persian Empire, but was annexed to the Roman Empire. For centuries it was the subject of a tug-of-war between the Roman and the Parthian Empires. A local dynasty long managed to maintain a balance between the claims of the two empires. Armenia was the first country in the world to become officially Christian. Christianity became identified with nationalism, and Armenia has remained an embattled Christian enclave in a largely Moslem part of the world. Some analogy may be felt between the Armenian identification of Christianity and nationalism and the Irish identification of Catholicism and nationalism.

Armorica Armorica, mentioned on the first page of *Finnegan's Wake* and fairly frequently thereafter, is the classical name for that part of Gaul represented in modern France by Brittany and part of Normandy. The name is properly plural, *Armoricae*, G *Armorikai*, and means "those [tribes *or* provinces] at the sea." The name is Celtic (Gaulish), compounded of *ar*, "at, on" and *mor*, "sea." This compound would be very similar in OL, Celtic *ar+mor* becoming OL *ar+mare* (L *at+mare* or *ad+mare*).

In medieval writing the name Armorica was revived as a pseudo-L name for Britanny, because of a historical misunderstanding. When the Romans conquered Gaul, all the Gauls, including those "at the sea," spoke a Celtic language—Gaulish. In time *all* the inhabitants of Gaul came to speak a version of L, Gallo-Romanic, the ancestor of French. The inhabitants of southern Britain spoke a language—British —related to Gaulish, and presumably, unlike the Gauls, continued to speak it after their conquest by the Romans. When the Roman occupation of Britain ended, the island was invaded by Angles, Saxons, and Jutes from Denmark or thereabouts, and thousands of British-speaking refugees fled to northwestern France, bringing their Celtic language to a country that had lost its own Celtic language. The area of France these Britons settled in is called after them— Brittany or Bretagne— and they themselves are now called Bretons, and their language Breton. The scribes of medieval manuscripts were not the last to imagine incorrectly that the Celtic-speaking Bretons were the remnants of the Celtic-speaking Gauls-at-the-sea, the Armoricans, instead of late intruders into roughly the same territory as ancient Armoricae, and so, as stated above, *Armorica* came to be the accepted L name for Brittany.

In *Finnegans Wake* Armorica comes to be mantioned primarily because Tristan, of the Tristan and Isolde legend, is usually represented to have been Breton, or at least to have ended his life in Brittany. The story of Tristan, Isolda, and Mark is of Celtic, or rather specifically Irish, origin, being derived from the Irish saga of the "Pursuit of Diarmaid and Grainne" (*Toruigheacht Dhiarmada agus Ghráinne*—see *Gaelic Lexicon*), which derives from the older tragedy of Derdriu (Deirdre) (see Gertrude Schoepperle, *Tristan and Isolt*, London, 1914). In Irish sagas Armorica is mentioned frequently, sometimes apparently standing for France as a whole. In later manuscripts, when the name "Armorica" had become unfamiliar to the scribes, they frequently substituted the exotic name "Armenia"—thus we have Irish heroes engaged in improbable journeys to remote Armenia instead of to nearby Brittany. We do not know if Joyce was aware of this fact (but see *Armenia*).

Arthox, Dux Although the Arthur-Dux combinations so frequent in *Finnegans Wake* probably refer primarily to Arthur Wellesley (Duke of Wellington and the victor of Waterloo) mixed very largely with Artorius or Artus Dux, (earlier representations of King Arthur) another bizarre set of names seems also to be involved. The apocryphal supplement to Genesis called *The Book of the Secrets of Enoch* established a medieval tradition that Adam was named for four stars in the four directions of the universe. The early Irish *Lebor Gabála* ("Book of Invasions") gives this version:

When Man was made and as he had no name, God said to four angels to go in search of a name for him. Michael went to the east, and saw a star, *Anatole* its name, and he brought with him the first letter of that name. Raphael went southward, and saw a star there, *Dusis* its name, and he brought its first letter. Gabriel went northward, and saw the star *Arctos*, and brought with him the first letter of the name. Uriel went westward, and saw a star in the sunset called *Mesembria*, and brought with him the first letter. God said: Uriel, read these letters. Uriel said:

Adam. And God said: So be it. (Macalister's trans.)

In the Irish text the stars are actually named Anatoile, Dissis, Arethos, and Mesimbria. In *The Dialogue of Salomon and Saturnus* the stars are: Arthox, Dux, Arotholem, Minsymbrie; in a British Museum manuscript they are Anathole, Disis, Arctos, Mesembrios. The *Master of Oxford's Catechism* has Artax, Dux, Arostolym, and Momfumbres, and an old English *Lyff of Adam and Eue* lists Anatalim, Dysus, Arcis, Messembrion. We believe most of these stars are to be found in *Finnegans Wake*, and list them where we suspect their presence.

Bonifacius Bonifacius, *anglicé* Boniface, is the name of nine popes, but the Boniface Joyce has in mind is almost certainly St. Boniface (675–754), "the Apostle of Germany." The name *Bonifacius*, although perhaps construed as meaning "Doing-good," is more likely a nominal derived from *bonifacies*, "having a handsome face," and occurrences of the name in *Finnegans Wake* more than once lean toward that interpretation (315.09, *Burniface*; 577.11 *boniface and bonny features*). St. Boniface was born (*né* Winfrid) in England, and early became a Benedictine monk in Exeter. In 718 he set out with a commission from Pope Gregory II to preach the gospel to all the tribes of Germany. He was immensely successful, baptizing thousands and founding numerous bishoprics; in 732 he became archbishop and primate of Germany. In 754, at the age of 79, he resigned the archbishopric and set out to convert the Frisians, who almost immediately killed him.

Since the life-work of Boniface has been described not as bringing the heathen to the light of Christ, but as undoing the work of previous Irish missionaries, "bringing everything into accordance with Roman Catholic order and suppressing the irregularities of Irish or Columban Christianity," in *Finnegan's Wake* he must feature as an avatar of Shaun, whose face is also bonny, and whose mission is to rectify the creations of his Shemese brother.

Bosphorus The Bosphorus (G Bosphoros) as a geographical feature requires no annotation here. It received its G name, "Heifer's Ford," from the legend that Io, in the form of a heifer, crossed here from Europe into Asia, on her way to Egypt. Io, according to the legend, was a priestess beloved of Zeus, who turned her into a heifer to hide her from the jealousy of Hera. Hera, however, drove her away by means of a gadfly, until she settled in Egypt. In classical times Io was identified with the Egyptian Isis. See *Isis*.

Brittany See *Armorica*.

Brut, Brutus "Brut" is the anglicized form of "Brutus," the factitious name of an imaginary person. Medieval English writers, like those of other emerging northern countries, notably France, seeking to endow their own national patrimony with an effulgence comparable to that shed on Rome and Italy by Vergil's Aeneas, invented Brutus as the eponymous first father of Britain. Like Aeneas, Brutus was supposed a fugitive from the downfall of Troy, driven by the gods into far wandering until he reestablished Trojan *lares et penates* in the distant foggy island. "Britain" or "Britannia," according to this fiction, was originally, therefore, "Brutannia." Needless to say, there is neither truth nor antiquity to this legend, created out of the whole cloth of the *Aeneid*, with a little help from the spurious Dares and Dictys. Nevertheless, the Brutus thesis was taken seriously in medieval English literature—for instance in *Sir Gawaine and the Grene Knight*—and was the subject of separate works, most notably the Middle English *Brut* written by a man named Layamon or Lawman (*Finnegans Wake* 359.17). Presumably the substance of this Brutus was to some extent enhanced by the glories of the historic Roman family of the Junii Bruti, most particularly the renown of *Lucius Junius Brutus* (q.v.), founder of the Roman republic.

The etymology of Britain or Britannia is more prosaic. L derived the name from G. Pytheas, the first Greek to record a visit to the British Isles, called them *Pretannikai nêsoi*— the islands of the *Pretanoi*. *Pretanoi*, later *Bretanoi* (whence G *Brettania*, L *Brittania*, *Britannia*) is clearly recognizable as the G form of the Celtic name for the Picts. The medieval *soi-disant* descendants of Brutus would have been horrified to know the name of their island really signifies Pictland.

Brutus, Lucius Junius Sixth century b.c.; the semi-historical founder of the Roman Republic, leader of the popular movement that overthrew the monarchy. A byword for republican rectitude, his legend partly inspired his descendant, Marcus Junius Brutus, to take part in the assassination of Julius Caesar. The allegation that Caesar intended to restore the monarchy was invoked by the conspirators, and Marcus was led to believe he was emulating his ancestor in upholding republican values. In the 18th-century resurgence of republican enthusiasm both Junii were restored to a regard neither had held since the Roman Empire.

Brutus, Marcus Junius Tyrannicide—i.e., assassin of Julius Caesar. One of the leaders of the conspiracy against Caesar, his name is linked to that of Cassius to a considerable extent because of Shakespeare's *Julius Caesar.* In 42 b.c. he and Cassius encountered the forces of Antony and Octavian at Philippi, and they were defeated. Thereafter Brutus committed suicide. In *Finnegans Wake* Brutus and Cassius are linked under the names of "Burrus" and "Caseus," apparently intended to mean "Butter" and "Cheese." "Burrus," however, is not real L (or G) for "butter." The real L word is *butyrum,* and Joyce presumably derived "Burrus" from French *beurre.* Two moderately prominent persons named Burrus are, however, known to classical literature.

Burrus "Burrus" is an old L word meaning "Red." It is equivalent to G *pyrros* and, according to Cicero, is an old L form of the G name *Pyrrhos.* Several persons named Pyrrhus are known to classical letters, two of special importance: (1) a son of Achilles who is also known as Neoptolemus. He served at the siege of Troy, was one of the picked party inside the wooden horse, and survived the war. According to the *Aeneid,* it was he who killed Priam. (2) Pyrrhus (319-272 b.c.), king of Epirus. He fought and beat the Romans several times, but never decisively; a technically successful campaign against the Romans reduced his expeditionary force to one-third its original strength. His victories are the original "Pyrrhic victories." He was killed in an obscure fashion during a street-riot in Argos, having been hit by a brick or roof-tile.

Burrus, Sextus Afranius Sextus Afranius Burrus is the only person of antiquity actually named Burrus to have attained recorded distinction. He was a responsible household official to Livia (wife of Augustus), to Tiberius, and to Claudius. He was tutor of the young Nero and, together with Seneca, was Nero's closest advisor during the early part of the reign. The first six to eight years of Nero's reign (a.d. 54 to 60 or 62) are the "good" years. Nero became restive about 59, and in 62, with the retirement of Seneca and the death of Burrus, the fatally extravagant part of the reign began.

Byzantium See *Constantinople.*

Caesar The name *Caesar,* etymologized as meaning either "hairy" or "of a bluish color," was a cognomen, or family name, in the gens *Julia.* The most illustrious bearer of the name was, of course, Gaius Julius Caesar. Because the ruler conventionally recognized as the first Roman emperor, C. Octavius [Caesar Augustus], was the adopted heir of his uncle C. Julius, and thus bore the name Caesar, and because the first dynasty of emperors were members of the same family, bearing the name through birth or adoption, the name Caesar, linked with the honorific "Augustus," came to be regarded as a title of rank rather than a personal name. Until the time of the Emperor Hadrian, the emperors all bore the name Caesar with the title Augustus, the two words in combination—Caesar Augustus— having the force of a title. Under Hadrian a distinction was made: "Augustus" designated the ruling emperor, and "Caesar," finally become nothing but a title, designated the heir to the throne appointed by the emperor. The G transliteration of the name—Kaisar—was a title almost from the start, and is the etymon of such later European titles as Kaiser and Czar (*or* Tsar).

C. Julius Caesar was born c. 102 b.c. and was assassinated on March 15, 44 b.c. by a group of conspirators headed by Brutus and Cassius. His career began as a political adventurer and demagogue, alternating with military exploits on a major scale. He brought Gaul under Roman control in a long campaign of which he himself is the eulogistic chronicler. In January 49 he commenced a civil war against his former patron, Pompey; despite Caesar's successes and Pompey's death, the war continued until March 45. In addition to Caesar's assassination on the Ides of March (March 15), Joyce seems interested in the following aspects of his career: (a) he crossed the Rubicon, a stream in northern Italy, against the command of the Senate, to commence his civil war against Pompey; (b) his major opponent in that war was Pompey (Cn. Pompeius Magnus); (c) his last battle was at Munda (see *Munda*); (d) his chief assassins were Brutus (see *Brutus, Marcus Junius*) and Cassius; (e) Caesar's posthumous vindication was taken up by Marcus Antonius; (f) among Caesar's writings is his Commentary on his conquest of Gaul, *de Bello Gallico;* (g) his most formidable Gallic opponent was Vercingetorix (see *Vercingetorix*); and (i) for a time he was the lover of *Cleopatra* (q.v.), having placed her on the throne of the Ptolemies (her own family) whom he had defeated in the wars.

Castor, Kastor See *Gemini.*

Claudius, Appius Although Appius Claudius (fl. 451 b.c.) is not a major character in Joyce's work, he is mentioned unequivocally in *Finnegan's Wake* and his presence is latent in several places. Although his story is well known it is perhaps useful to rehearse it, even if only because Adaline Glasheen has misidentified him (*Second Census*). Claudius was the popular leader of the *decemviri*—the board of ten— who ruled Rome following the overthrow of the monarchy. But according to legend, he seized, by a legal ruse, the person of Verginia, daughter of a soldier named Verginius. Verginius brought suit to regain his daughter, but through corruption and venality the court ruled for Claudius. Verginius thereupon, with his daughter's consent, cut off Verginia's head to preserve her honor. The episode so inflamed the populace that a rebellion overthrew the *decemviri* and destroyed Appius Claudius, establishing in the process a more democratic republic. This fabulous episode is similar to, and perhaps based on, the famous rape of Lucretia that led to the expulsion of the kings. In *Finnegans Wake* the *decemviri* and the rape of Lucretia are somewhat more evident than Appius Claudius, but it is doubtless this, the most famous, or infamous, Appius Claudius that Joyce had in mind, rather than his obscure descendant, Cicero's correspondent.

Cleopatra Cleopatra ("Fatherly Renown") was the name of seven Ptolemaic or Macedonian queens of Egypt, but Cleopatra VII , mistress successively of Julius Caesar and Mark Antony, is the person the name most usually denotes, both in common reference and in *Finnegans Wake.* She was the first of the Ptolemaic dynasty to speak the Egyptian language of her subjects, and she identified herself publicly with the goddess Isis (see *Isis*), daughter of Re, the sun-god. Through this identification she becomes, in *Finnegans Wake,* identified with Isis and HCE's daughter Issy, as the eternally seductive yet narcissistic feminine. Cleopatra was 22, in exile from her throne, when Caesar reached Egypt. She became his mistress in order to regain her throne, and followed him back to Rome to gain greater independence for Egypt. Upon Caesar's assassination in 44 b.c. she returned to Egypt, until in 41 b.c. she took up with Antony in hope of obtaining from him what Caesar's death had frustrated. In 37 Antony married her, and thereafter Antony, based in Egypt, struggled against Octavian for control of the Roman world. Defeat of Antony's fleet at Actium in 31 decided the contest, and in 30 Octavian captured Alexandria, the Egyptian capital. Antony killed himself before the city's fall, but Cleopatra fell alive into Octavian's control. He encouraged her suicide; she chose the "asp" (cobra) because it was sacred to her divine father, the sun. This ensured her return to her father, Re. Her effect on the Roman imagination (as well as on later literature in Europe) was profound; Vergil's Dido reflects the ambivalence she aroused.

In *Finnegans Wake* Cleopatra at times is also a fusion of Clio (G Kleiô), the Muse of History, and St. Patrick.

Columella, Lucius Junius Moderatus Columella was a writer on agriculture of the first century a.d. Two of his works survive, *De Re Rustica* (a.d. 60) and *De Arboribus*. *De Re Rustica* is in twelve books, one (No. 10) in Vergilian verse. Columella is mentioned six times in *Finnegans Wake*, *De Re Rustica* at least once (430.06: "the rarerust"). What his attraction for Joyce was is not clear: his name, Columella, is rather like that of a number of Irish saints (he was Spanish); he wrote on the evils of absentee landlordism; he imitated Vergil in verse; he wrote excellent Silver-Age prose.

Cupido See *Venus*.

Cypria, Kypria See *Venus*.

Daedalus "Daedalus" is the L form of G *Daidalos*, a name that means "artist, craftsman." The Greeks called all archaic and impressive art, native or foreign, *daidala*, and in classical antiquity several works of art were exhibited as the handiwork of the mythical Daedalus. Daedalus, according to the legend, was born at Athens, son of Eupalamos ("Skillhand"); in Crete he made the brazen cow to gratify Pasiphaë's lust for the bull, and subsequently the labyrinth in which the consequent Minotaur was imprisoned. King Minos imprisoned Daedalus, but Daedalus constructed two pairs of wings for himself and his son Icarus and flew safely to Sicily. Icarus flew too near the sun, melted his wings, and fell to death in the Aegean. Thereafter Daedalus continued a long and creative career, involving the suffocation of the pursuing King Minos in a steam-bath of Daedalus's creation, the invention of carpentry, building the pyramids and numerous famous temples.

Joyce knew Daedalus apparently primarily from the narration of the legend by Ovid in the *Metamorphoses* (whence the epigraph of *Portrait of the Artist*), and chose his name originally as his own pen-name (Stephen Daedalus), under which he first published some of the short stories later collected in *Dubliners*. At the same time he also used the name for the hero of his autobiographical novel, *Stephen Hero*. Later, modernized to "Dedalus," the name became the surname of the hero of *A Portrait of the Artist* (a "quibbling" title, since "Artist" = *Daidalos*), and of the youthful Joyce-figure in *Ulysses*. Originally Joyce no doubt chose the name because of his self-identification with the great artificer imprisoned on an island (Crete; Ireland) from which he looked to his art for a means of escape. But at the end of *A Portrait* Stephen invokes Daedalus as his *father* ("Old father, old artificer"), thus unconsciously identifying himself with the unfortunate Icarus. In *Ulysses* this new ironic identification becomes explicit: "Fabulous artificer, the hawklike man. You flew. Whereto? Newhaven-Dieppe, steerage passenger. Paris and back. Lapwing. Icarus." (*Ulysses* 210.37, etc.)

The references to Daedalus in *Finnegans Wake* are rare or tenuous. In her *Second Census* (p. 60), Adaline Glasheen could not "help feeling there are more Daedalus references than [she had] found in *Finnegans Wake*." Her *Third Census* identifies some more, but the tenuousness we mention may be illustrated by "his own surname (yes, yes, less!)" (108.21) where Mrs. Glasheen sees "Daedalus" while to us "Ulysses" seems equally plausible. We have glossed neither. The word "dedal" (179.17) we have of course glossed, but fail to perceive it as inescapably alluding to Daedalus. Mrs. Glasheen also cites "Deaddleconch" (390.17); we are insufficiently persuaded. The most dedalian reference to Daedalus, however, is the "pseudojocax axplanation" (063.30-31).

Dedalus See *Daedalus*.

Deucalion and Pyrrha Deucalion (G Deukaliôn) and his wife Pyrrha are the G equivalents of Noah and his wife and also, to some extent, of Adam and Eve (and therefore are types of HCE and ALP). He was the son of Prometheus, she of Prometheus's brother Epimetheus. Zeus flooded the earth in wrath at sin; Deucalion built an ark (*larnax*) and floated until the waters subsided. After the flood they were advised by a friendly god or goddess to throw their mother's stones over their shoulders. Deucalion threw stones (mother Earth's bones) over his shoulder, and they became men; Pyrrha threw over her shoulder stones that became women. Thus they are the progenitors of the present human race. The myth (like that of Daedalus) is best known in the version presented by Ovid in the *Metamorphoses*, which was probably Joyce's first acquaintance with it.

Dioscuri, Dioskouroi See *Gemini*

Eblana Eblana is the name of a town or settlement that appears on the east coast of Ireland on the map of Europe in the *Geography* (*Geôgraphikê hyphêgêsis*) of Claudius Ptolemaeus (see *Ptolemy*) that appeared about a.d. 150. This map, the earliest drawn on more or less scientific principles on which Ireland appears, remained a standard of world geography until early modern times. Eblana, from its position on the far-from-accurate map, and from somewhat dubious etymological guessing, has been identified with Dublin. Our glosses, identifying Eblana as G for Dublin, or as the earliest external recognition of the existence of Dublin, reflect a common Irish or Dublin belief that was evidently shared by Joyce. "Eblana" occurs frequently in the names of Dublin commercial and cultural enterprises. It must be noted, however, that Professor Thomas F. O'Rahilly (*Early Irish History and Mythology*) argues that Eblana must have been situated near the village of Dunleer in County Louth, close to 40 miles north of Dublin. Yet again, it may be suggested that O'Rahilly was even more of a crank than Joyce was.

Erigena, Johannes Scotus Johannes Scotus Erigena (813-880) was a precursor of Joyce—an emigrant Irishman who set the Continent on its ear. His name "Scotus" means that he was "a Scot," namely, an Irishman. "Scotia" was a very early medieval L name for Ireland; the portion of North Britain occupied by a Gaelic offshoot of the Irish was called "Scotia Minor," although that region alone in modern times has retained the name Scot-land. "Erigena" as likely as not means or intends "born in *Eriu* (modern *Eire*)—i.e., Ireland". He was head of the court school of Charles the Bald, king of France, and taught that evil has no real existence, and consequently hell and damnation are subjective states. His doctrines were condemned by the Papal church as an invention of the devil. He became Abbot of Malmesbury in England, where his students stabbed him to death with their pens. Joyce obviously saw him as a Shem-figure, and a type of himself, particularly in contrast with Johannes Duns Scotus (1265-1308), a genuine Scot from Roxburghshire, one of the most eminent of the orthodox schoolmen, a perfect avatar of Shaun.

Erôs See *Venus.*

Gemini Gemini L, "The Twins," is a constellation identified with the *Dioscuri* (G *Dioskouroi,* "Zeus's Lads"), Castor (G Kastôr) and Pollux (G Polydeukês). They are the brothers of Helen, sons of Leda and of Zeus (as the swan); or sons of Tyndareus; or Polydeuces is the son of Zeus, his twin Castor of Tyndareus. The *Iliad* regards them as dead, but the *Odyssey* as alive but held within the earth. Horace says they were hatched out of one egg, like Helen. Versions of their legend have them (a) alternately dead (in Hades) and in Olympus, taking turns, (b) both in Hades and both in Olympus, together, for alternate spells of time. The basic idea is that the Twins share equally the immortality of one only. They are particularly noted as saviors of those in peril on the sea, although on a number of occasions they were believed to have intervened decisively in human warfare. Although they are frequently depicted as fighters, they never, unlike Shem and Shaun, oppose one another; on the contrary they are models of fraternal love.

Heliopolis Hêliopolis (G "Sun-city") was the name of two cities in the classical world, both religious centers of sun-worship. One was in Lower Egypt, the other, better-known, in what is now Lebanon (modern *Baalbek*). In *Finnegans Wake,* however, "Heliopolis" is neither of these cities, but rather Healy-polis, the city of Tim Healy— i.e., Dublin. Healy (1855-1931) had been one of Parnell's lieutenants, but led the revolt against the Chief over the O'Shea affair (supposedly evoking Joyce's earliest, no longer extant literary effusion, "Et tu, Healy."). With the establishment of the Irish Free State in 1922 Tim Healy became Governor-General, i.e., representative of the Crown.

Hephaestus, Hephaistos See *Vulcan.*

Hermes See *Mercurius.*

Hiberia See *Hibernia.*

Hibernia Hibernia, the classical L name for Ireland, alternated in L with Iverna, Juverna and, from the G, Ierna and Ierne. Ptolemy on his map calls the island Iouernia, and the earliest G references call it Iernê. The form *Hibernia* came about possibly under the influence of *hiberna* (fem.) L, "wintry" (*hiberna insula?*). The word is etymologically completely distinct from *Hibêria*, the G name for Spain (whence, incorrectly, *Iberia* L), but in the late classical and earlier medieval periods the two names were frequently associated. Discrimination was not helped by the fact that Hiberia/ Iberia was also the name of a country in the Caucusus (modern Georgia).

St. Isidore of Seville, alias Isidorus Hispalensis (560-636), among his voluminous writings uttered a book called *Etymologiarum sive Originum* that was immensely influential in forming medieval ideas, not least in Ireland. In that work Isidore derives the name *Hibernia* from *Hiberia*, by which he deduces that the Irish originated in Spain. The Irish were so flattered by this ascription they invented for themselves a Spanish ancestor, Míl Espáine, whose name transparently means no more than "The Spanish Soldier." The Irish have since persuaded themselves that they are *Mílid*, "Milesians" or "Milesii"—descendants of Míl— and have carried on ever since a still unrequited love-affair with Spain ("and Spanish ale shall give you hope, my Dark Rosaleen"). Joyce, too, has accepted the myth of Spanish ancestry. See *Milesiae/ Milesii*; see also *Gaelic Lexicon*, "Colonies, Colonists, Colonizations."

Hostius Quadra Because Hosty in *Finnegans Wake* is hostile to HCE, we may safely assume that *hostis* L, "enemy," has gone into the composition of his name. Since he is the composer of a frequently-cited ballad, he may have received some contribution from Hostius, a Roman epic poet of the second century b.c., whose work survives only in a few fragments. But his character perhaps owes most to that of Hostius Quadra, a licentious old Roman nobleman of the time of Augustus (31 b.c.-a.d.14). This Hostius invented a system of magnifying mirrors (*see* his "mirification," *Finnegans Wake 372.23-24*) so that he could view his sexual escapades from all angles. He was plainly a devoted voyeur, who loved to watch as well as participate in polymorphous couplings. So unsavory a citizen was he that when he was finally murdered by his exasperated slaves, Augustus decided that no reprisal against them was necessary. He is discussed with prurient disapproval by Seneca, *Naturales Quaestiones*, I.16.

Iberia See *Hibernia*.

Iernê See *Hibernia*.

Isis (and *Osiris*) Isis was an Egyptian goddess, wife of Osiris and mother of Horus. From the fourth century b.c. she was established in Greece, and in the course of time her worship spread in the classical world so that evidence of it is to be found in all corners of the Roman Empire. Isis was identified with Demeter, with Aphrodite (Venus), and with the Ptolemaic queens of Egypt, notably Cleopatra (see *Cleopatra*). The association of Isis, mother and wife, with the myth of the death and resurrection of Osiris engendered a deeply emotional religious devotion widespread in the classical world, the equivalent to and precursor of medieval devotion to the Blessed Virgin. Her rôle also makes her a type of ALP for Joyce, and her name is echoed in variants of the name of ALP's daughter, Issy-la-Belle.

Jove. See *Jupiter.*

Juba The L word *juba* means "mane [of a horse, etc.]," and we have so glossed its occurrences in *Finnegans Wake*. But Joyce's references to "juba-" have little clear connection with manes. The allusions are usually bound in with allusions to the biblical Jubal and Tubal Cain, and may therefore include two North African kings, father and son, named Juba. Juba I (*Iobas*), notorious for tyrannical cruelty, fought on the side of the Senate and Pompey in the Civil War against Caesar, and after defeat killed himself (46 b.c.). Juba II, his infant son, was raised in Rome, a close friend of Octavian, who in 25 b.c. made him king of Mauretania. A cultured man, he wrote many books (in G), all of which are lost except for citation and quotation in Plutarch and Pliny. A third Juba of antiquity also lived in Mauretania, the 2nd century a.d. author of a treatise on metrics.

Closer to Joyce's heart and hand than any of these historical Jubas, however, is the character Juba in John Henry Newman's *Callista: A Sketch of the Third Century* (1856)[see *Stephen Hero* 194.08, supra]. Juba is a Shem-figure to the Shaun of his brother Agellius. Both have received Christian instruction and Agellius opts for an at first luke-warm Christianity while Juba holds out for "honest paganism." He is a young man remarkably resembling the attitudinizing Stephen Deda-lus: in a stilted colloquy with a Christian priest that cries out for extended quotation space will not permit, "'I will never fawn or crouch,' said Juba; 'I will be lord and master in my own soul. Every faculty shall be mine; there shall be no divided allegiance.'"

Julius Caesar See *Caesar*

Junius See *Brutus*

Jupiter Jupiter, commonly Iuppiter (*Diou-pater) was the Italian sky-god
and chief municipal god of Rome. The oblique cases of the name are
declined on the stem *Jov-*, e.g., Vocative *Jove*, whence English "Jove."
The oblique declension then is essentially only of the element *Diou*
in the name, dropping the epithet *pater*, "father." *Diou* is etymologically identical with G *Zeus* [-*patêr*]. This sky-god is evidently a primitive Indo-European development, and appears at first to have been a
rather vague *numen*, the source of weather, rain, hail, thunder and
lightning, etc. The Romans on their own seem never to have evolved
a very anthropomorphic concept of Jupiter, but the Etruscan kings of
Rome introduced, from their own pantheon, the cult of Iuppiter Op-
timus Maximus [Jupiter the Best and Greatest] on the Capitoline, who
continued to be regarded as a *king*. Meanwhile the Greeks, in their
separate development of the Indo-European sky-god into the person of
Zeus, produced the highly-anthropomorphic father of the gods and
promiscuous lover of so many myths. With the merging of the cultural
worlds of Greece and Rome, the Romans by the process called *interpretatio Romana* applied the name Jupiter to Zeus, and so began the
process of utterly confusing the two gods. At least nine-tenths of the
surviving myths and anecdotes about "Jupiter" are correctly attributable only to Zeus.

   The Roman Jupiter was the god of lightning, and his *numen* was
incorporated in numerous holy stones, believed to be thunderbolts,
which were used in taking oaths. This function, as god of oaths and
lightning, is perhaps the primary function of Jupiter in the Viconian
scheme of *Finnegans Wake*. Epithets of Jupiter in *Finnegans Wake*
include *Pluvius* (Rain-bringing) and *Stator* (the Sustainer). The myth
of his birth and upbringing on Mount Ida in Crete, by the goat Amal-
theia, alluded to several times in *Finnegans Wake*, pertains properly
only to Zeus, not to the Roman Jupiter. Likewise the story of the
overthrow by Jupiter of his cannibalistic father, Saturn, is merely
interpretatio Romana for the overthrow of Kronos by Zeus—a tale
itself a secondary development from the tale of the overthrow by
Kronos of *his* father Ouranos, which is really a creation-myth. The
story of the war against the Titans also is properly a Zeus rather than
a Jupiter myth.

Joyce, like most products of his latinized educational background, usually follows the *interpretatio Romana*: it is not unexpected, then, to find in *Finnegans Wake* forms of the name Jupiter occurring up to 13 times, as against four clear occurrences of the name Zeus.

Although, as noted above, the name Jupiter is a form of *Diou-pater, meaning either "Sky-father" or "Brightness-father" (there is no necessary distinction between the two), a popular etymologizing of the name derived it from *Jus-pater*, i.e., "Oath-father" or even "Justice-father." We can find no incontrovertible evidence in *Finnegans Wake* that Joyce knew or used this interpretation, but we offer it to the reader for whatever it may be worth.

Laudabiliter *Laudabiliter* is the name (from its first word) of a Bull allegedly uttered by Pope Adrian IV , between 1155 and 1159, by which he granted to King Henry II of England the overlordship of Ireland, to check the wickedness of the Irish and to enforce the collection of Peter's Pence. No authentic copy of *Laudabiliter* is extant, and a large body of scholarship (much of it emanating from Papal apologists seeking to exonerate the Holy See from responsibility for the long Irish nightmare) has sought to prove the Bull a forgery. The exercise is merely academic, however, for the Irish historically never doubted the authenticity of the Bull, and argued merely (as in a petition of 1318 to Pope John XXII) that *Laudabiliter* was granted because of false representations to Adrian IV . More importantly, that Bull, whether genuine or forged, was but one document out of many in the reigns of Adrian IV and Alexander III by which the Papacy pretended the right to grant Ireland as a Papal fief to the Lordship of the English kings. As late as 1555 Pope Paul IV "erected" Ireland into a kingdom, and granted its kingship to Mary I and Philip (theretofore the kings of England had claimed to be "Lords" rather than "Kings" of Ireland). In 1570 the Pope denied the right of the Irish to confer the crown of their own kingdom on Philip II of Spain. Only with the excommunication of Elizabeth I in 1571 did it perhaps strike the Papacy that it had, for the sake of temporal expediency, backed the wrong horse.

L texts of *Laudabiliter* are hard to come by. Arthur Ua Cleirigh, author of the *Catholic Encyclopedia* article on "Adrian IV ," asserts that the text is preserved in the 12th-century *Book of Leinster*, but we have been unable to find it in the five-volume edition by Best, Bergin and O'Brien (Dublin, 1954-1967). The following text is transcribed from *Historiae Catholicae Iberniae Compendium* by Don Philip O'-Sullivan Beare [*a D. Philippo Osulleuano Bearro Iberno*] (Lisbon, 1621), pp. 59-60. Unfortunately, O'Sullivan gives no source for his version.

Adrianus Episcopus servus servorum Dei charissimo in Christo filio illustri Anglorum Regi salutem, & Apostolicam benedictionem.

LAUDABILITER, & fructuose de glorioso nomine propagando in terris, & aeterna faelicitatis praemio cumulando in coelis tua magnificentia cogitat, dum ad dilatandos ecclesiae terminos, ad declarandum indoctis, & rudibus populis Christianae fidei veritatem, & vitiorum plantaria de agro dominico extirpando, sicut Catholicus Princeps, intendis, & ad id convenientius exequendum consilium Apostolicae Sedis exigis, & favorem. In quo facto quanto altiori consilio, & maiore discretione procedis, tanto in eo faeliciorem progressum te praestante Domino confidimus habiturum, eo quod ad bonum exitum semper, & finem soleant attingere, quae [*sic; read* qui] de ardore fidei, & Religionis amore principium acceperunt. Sane Iberniam, & omnes insulas, quibus sol iustitiae Christus illuxit, & quae documenta Christianae fidei ceperunt, ad ius Beati Petri, & sacrosanctae Romanae Ecclesiae (quod tua etiam nobilitas recognoscit) non est dubium, pertinere. Vnde in eis tanto libentius plantationem fidelem, & germen gratum Deo inserimus, quanto id à nobis interno examine distinctius prospicimus exigendum. Significasti siquidem (fili charissime) nobis, te Iberniae insulam ad subdendum illum populum legibus, & vitiorum plantaria inde extirpanda, velle intrare, & de singulis eius domibus annuam unius denarii Beato Petro solvere pensionem. Nos itaque pium, & laudabile desiderium tuum cum favore congruo prosequentes, & petitioni tuae benignum impendentes assensum, gratum, & acceptum habemus, ut pro dilatandis ecclesiae terminis pro vitiorum restringendo decursu, pro corrigendis moribus, pro Christianae Religionis augmento insulam illam ingrediaris: & quod ad honorem Dei, & salutem illius terrae spectaverit, exequaris, & illius terrae populus te honorifice recipiat, & sicut Dominum veneretur, iure nimirum Ecclesiastico illibato, & integro permanente, & salva Beato Petro, & Sacrosanctae Romanae Ecclesiae de singulis domibus annua unius denarii pensione. Si ergo quod concepisti, effectu duxeris complendum, stude gentem illam bonis moribus informare: & agas tam per te, quam per illos, quos adhibes, quos fide, verbo, & vita idoneos esse perspexeris, ut decoretur ibi Ecclesia, plantetur, & crescat Fidei Christianae Religio, & quae ad honorem Dei, & salutem pertinent animarum, per te taliter ordinentur, ut á Deo sempiternae mercedis cumulum consequi merearis, & in terris gloriosum nomen valeas obtinere.

Datum Romae anno salutis 1156.

Adrian, Bishop, slave of the slaves of God, to his dearest son in Christ, the illustrious King of the English, greeting, and Apostolic blessing. PRAISEWORTHILY is Your Excellency concerned with both engendering a glorious name upon earth and with amassing the prize of eternal bliss in heaven, while you exert yourself, as a Catholic Prince should, on expanding the frontiers of the Church, on making plain the truth of Christian faith to untaught and savage peoples, and on rooting out the weeds of vice from the field of the Lord, and you request for the more fitting execution of that purpose the counsel and favor of the Apostolic Seat. In this matter the higher the counsel and the greater the discretion with which you proceed the more fortunate, we trust in the Lord, will be your progress in it, in that they are wont always to arrive at a good conclusion and finish, who [*reading* qui *for* quae] have taken their beginning from the warmth of faith and love of religion. There is no doubt that Ireland, and all islands that Christ, the sun of justice, enlightens, and that have received the lessons of the Christian faith, belong (as even your excellence recognizes) to the jurisdiction of St. Peter and of the most holy Roman Church. Wherefore with all the greater will we engraft in them a faithful transplant and a sprout acceptable to God, to the degree that we from our inward consideration deem to be requisite. Inasmuch as you have indicated to us, dearest son, that you intend to enter upon that island of Ireland to subdue that people to the rule of laws, and to root out the growths of vices from thence, and from each of their houses without exception deliver to St. Peter the yearly payment of a penny; accordingly, accepting with suitable favor your pious, laudable and kind desire, and granting benign assent to your petition, we are pleased to consent to your entering into that island for the expansion of the church's frontiers, for restraint of the career of vices, for the correction of manners, for the increase of the Christian Religion: and whatever shall be in view to the honor of God, and the welfare of that land, you shall carry out, and the people of that land are to receive you with honor, and are to reverence you as Lord, provided always that the law of the Church remain unimpaired and undiminished, and that there be unbroken yearly payment of a penny from each home without exception to St. Peter and to the Most Holy Roman Church. If, therefore, you bring effectively to completion what you have planned, take pains to mould that people with good morals: and see to it that through your own person and those whom you employ, whom you shall see to be suitable in faith, word, and life, the Church there may be ornamented, the Religion of the Christian Faith may be planted and may grow, and that those things that pertain to the honor of God and to the health of souls shall be so ordered by you, that you may merit therefor from God a mound of eternal mercy and on earth you may deserve to obtain a glorious name.

Dated at Rome in the year of salvation 1156.

To modern eyes this astounding document, genuine or forged, seems a damning indictment of the ignorance and cupidity of Pope Adrian. Yet O'Sullivan accepted it as genuine, albeit elicited by false information, and his book appeared both with the blessing of his (Franciscan) Order and with the approval of the Holy Inquisition of Portugal. He offers the ingenious interpretation of Henry's Lordship, that it was not of Ireland, but merely applied to the office of bailiff for collecting Peter's Pence, glossing *sicut Dominum veneretur,* "ut Principem dignum magno honore, non Dominum Iberniae, sed praefectum causa colligem di [sic] tributi ecclestastici [sic]."

Laudabiliter is named frequently in *Finnegans Wake.* It is also "that same bull that was sent to our island by farmer Nicholas" in the "Oxen of the Sun" chapter of *Ulysses* (M399 etc.). His Holiness Adrian IV was—perhaps not surprisingly—an Englishman by birth, *né* Nicholas Breakspear.

Liddell, Henry George Henry George Liddell (1811-1898) deserves mention in a Classical Lexicon because his presence in *Finnegans Wake* has been obscured by the presence of his daughter. Together with Robert Scott he published in 1843 the great *Greek Lexicon* that is the standard G dictionary throughout the English-speaking world. What Liddell & Scott is to G, so is Lewis and Short's *A Latin Dictionary* to L. Without those works this book could not have been compiled.

Both works appear to be conflated at *Finnegans Wake* 269.F4: "Llong and Shortts Primer of Black and White Wenchcraft."

"Wenchcraft" enters Liddell's biography by a fortuitous irony. He was a scholar of Oxford, and his daughter, Alice, became one of the child playmates and models of a neighboring bachelor, fellow-scholar, and amateur photographer named Charles Lutwidge Dodgson. Dodgson under the pen-name of Lewis Carroll wrote *Alice's Adventures in Wonderland*, the heroine of which is based on Liddell's little girl. (The wenchcraft is black and white presumably because of the then state of the photographic art.) Alice has been recognized as a frequent apparition in *Finnegans Wake*; her father is also entitled to his due.

Livia Livia as a latinized form of Liffey is not the concern of this note; that identification is obvious and leads nowhere in particular. But the major historical Livia (58 b.c.-a.d. 29) was a woman of immense influence and importance. The daughter of M. Livius Drusus Claudianus, she married Tiberius Claudius Nero, one of Caesar's military commanders, by whom she bore sons Tiberius and Drusus. In 38 b.c. Nero divorced her so that she could marry Octavian, to whom she was an excellent wife for the remaining 52 years of his life. As consort of Augustus she wielded immense power with tact and intelligence. Under the will of Augustus she had bestowed upon her the title "Julia Augusta." As Augustus had no son, his successor as Emperor was Livia's son by Nero, Tiberius.

Livius, Titus Titus Livius ["Livy"] (59 b.c.-a.d. 17), the eminent Roman historian, seems to have entered *Finnegans Wake* for much the same reason as did his contemporary, Livia—the resemblance of his name to that of the Liffey. (The gens-name Livius, feminine Livia, probably meant "bluish"— a not inapt name for a river.) Livy began work at the age of 30 and continued for 40 years a history of Rome, from its founding, in 142 books. The work at Livy's death had been brought down to 9 b.c., the death of Livia's son Drusus. Only 35 of these books are extant—perhaps the *parva chartula liviana* of *Finnegans Wake* 287.21 is one of the lost books, written on papyrus named for Livia.

The English name "Livy" is appropriated to the historian Titus Livius exclusively. There is another Livius, however, whom Joyce could conceivably have had also in mind. Lucius Livius Andronicus (284-204 b.c.) was a Greek slave who became a L playwright who composed and acted in both the first L comedy and the first L tragedy (240 b.c.). Although he was a prolific writer and translator from G, only fragments of his works remain.

Lucanus, Marcus Annaeus Marcus Annaeus Lucanus ["Lucan"] (a.d. 39-65), the author of *Pharsalia* (correctly *Bellum Civile*), an epic poem in 10 books about the Civil War between Caesar and Pompey, is another person who perhaps owes his prominence in *Finnegans Wake* as much to the associations of his name as to his own life and accomplishments. *Marcus* is the name of the evangelist Mark, and so of one of the Four Old Men, as well as, by extension, of King Mark the cuckold in the Tristan-Isolda story. *Annaeus* looks like a masculine form of Anna, and could be wilfully construed as meaning "belonging to Anna." *Lucanus* suggests the Lord who lived at Lucan, the Dublin suburb that reiterates itself throughout *Finnegans Wake*.

The original Lucan was born at Corduba (Cordova) in Spain, the nephew of the philosopher-dramatist Seneca. For a while he was a favorite of the Emperor Nero, but after Nero had taken a dislike to him he became involved in an unlucky revolutionary conspiracy and was forced to commit suicide. He was a voluminous writer in his brief life, but only the *Pharsalia* has survived at length. His narrative of the contest between Caesar and Pompey, which is a recurrent theme in *Finnegans Wake*, may also have contributed to his own presence here.

Marcus Marcus, meaning "Hammer," is the only name among those of the four evangelists to have (whatever Semitic name it may represent) a genuine classical (L) morphology and existence. The name was a praenomen extremely common among the Romans; Marcus Junius Brutus and Marcus Tullius Cicero are merely among the more prominent men who bore the name.

Mars Mars, whose name also occurs as Mavors, Mamers, Maris, and Marmar, next to Jupiter was the chief Italian god. He was a god of war and the martial arts (the word "martial" derives from his name) and to some extent also of agriculture. The month of March (beginning of both the campaigning and the growing season) was named for him, as was also, in later times, Tuesday (Dies Martis). The Romans celebrated many festivals in his honor, but aside from the story of his marriage to Anna Perenna, goddess of the returning year whose feast was March 15 (which may be entirely an invention of Ovid's), they had no mythology concerning him. By the *interpretatio Romana* Mars was identified with the G war-god Arês, and all the mythology since purveyed as pertaining to Mars is the original property of Arês. Mars/Arês is portrayed in mythology as closely associated with Venus/Aphrodite, either as her husband or (when she is represented as wife of Vulcan/ Hephaistos) as her paramour. In the well-known story from the latter myth (*Odyssey* VIII 266–369) Mars and Venus were caught *in flagrante delictu* in a net constructed by Vulcan. In the former myth he and Venus are the parents of the goddess Harmonia. It is probably his rôle in the marital triangle, in addition perhaps to his Roman marriage to Anna Perenna, that has earned Mars his nine or more references in *Finnegans Wake*.

Mater Misericordiae Mater Misericordiae, "Mother of Mercy," is an epithet or title of the Virgin Mary, and as such requires no comment. Joyce's preoccupation with the name derives, however, not from the context of conventional piety but from the fact that one of the principal hospitals of Dublin—colloquially known as "The Mater"—is named for this aspect of the Virgin. The Mater hospital overshadowed Bloom's house on Eccles Street, and reappears in Joyce's writings more frequently as a Dublin landmark than as a personal object of devotion.

Mercurius Mercurius (Merqurius, Mirqurios, Mircurios) the Roman god of traders, is identified with the G Hermês. The process of identification is not, however, the usual *interpretatio Romana* by which an indigenous Roman god is associated with an indigenous G god. Mercurius appears to be the genuine G Hermês under a L name (derived from *merx* or *mercor*) to denote his function. Everything said here about Mercurius *a fortiori* applies to Hermês. His mythical parentage is Jupiter/Zeus and the goddess Maia; he was born on the fourth of the month and four is his number (probably from his evolutionary origin from a sacred pile of stones marking a crossroads). He is tricky and clever, inventor of the lyre, patron of oratory, poetry, craft and thefts. In human form he is the messenger of the gods, having one serious function: conductor of the souls of the dead to the Underworld (Hermês Psychopompos). His usual representation is as a stone or a log of wood, with a human head at the top and a prominent phallus half-way up. These representations were placed at doors and gates and in gardens, and associate Mercurius with fertility, and so with the goddess Venus/Aphrodite (by Aphrodite Hermês was the father of Hermaphroditus). He came to be the particular patron of literature in general, and of young men in particular. Joyce seems aware of Mercurius/Hermês under most of his aspects.

Milesiae/Milesii These words in their classical aspect refer to the city of Miletus in Asia Minor and its inhabitants. Until the beginning of the 6th century b.c. Miletus was a progressive important city, home of the Milesian philosophers Thales, Anaximander and Anaximenes, famous for its pottery and woolen goods. By Roman times, however, the city after many vicissitudes had gained a reputation for idle dissipation. In L the Milesii were proverbial for luxury and wantonness; *Milesia carmina* simply meant obscene songs, and *sermo Milesius* a dirty story. *Milesiae*, or *Milesiae fabulae*, was the name for a genre of ribald stories. All of this Joyce probably knew, and alluded to in *Finnegans Wake*. But in the Irish early medieval context, *Milesii* did not signify depraved citizens of Miletus, but rather the descendants of Míl Espaine —the Miletians— that is, according to their own manufactured origin-myth, the Irish Gaels. (See *Hibernia*.) Joyce presumably rejoiced at this opportunity to mix up gallous deeds with dirty stories.

Munda Munda, a town in Spain, was the scene of Caesar's last battle, and his hardest. By mid-46 b.c. he had apparently defeated all his foes in the Civil War, Pompey himself had been dead for two years, and Caesar was enabled to celebrate four triumphs. But in 45 Pompey's sons raised forces in Spain, and Caesar was obliged to hurry to Spain, where his final victory at Munda was his closest and hardest fought. Although this was a signal battle in Caesar's career, if we are correct it is alluded to at least four times in *Finnegans Wake*, a fact that seems to call for explanation. Perhaps the explanation is that the battle was fought on March 17, 45 b.c.—that is, on [what would become] St. Patrick's Day!

Naso See *Ovidius Naso*.

Nemo See *Odysseus*.

Odysseus The Joycean reader needs no reminder that our author was deeply interested in the career of the G hero whom he thought of as Ulysses, and who appears in many guises throughout *Finnegans Wake* as well as, of course, in *Ulysses*. The form *Ulysses* is actually an unwarranted corruption of the name. As briefly noted in the glosses,

Ulixes was the usual L rendition of a G dialectical variation of Odysseus; the spelling "Ulysses" is a combination of the L Ul- with the G -ysseus.

Ulixes/Odysseus, king of Ithaca, was famed among the G heroes at Troy for craft and eloquence; husband of Penelope ("the Weaver") and father of Telemachus, his return from the Trojan War was beset with adventures that compose the substance of the *Odyssey*. One incident of his adventures is alluded to up to ten times in *Finnegans Wake*, and therefore requires some comment here.

When the hero encountered the Cyclops, Polyphemus, he prudently withheld his real name, calling himself No-man (G *Outis*, L *Nemo*). Both these anonymous pseudonyms occur innumerably in *Finnegans Wake*. Apart from whatever pleasure Joyce took from contemplating the fact that although his hero (Leopold Bloom or HCE) is a nobody, the famous Greek also declared himself to be a nobody, another interpretation of the episode may have come to his attention. This is the rather strained etymologizing (what more congenial to Joyce?) by which the name Odysseus can be interpreted as containing both *Outis*, "Nobody" (i.e., *Odys-), and *Zeus*, the name of God (i.e., *-seus). According to this, when the hero suppresses the divine in himself, he becomes nobody. Absolute nonsense, of course—but then, what isn't!

Osiris See *Isis*.

Outis See *Odysseus*.

Ovidius Naso, Publius Publius Ovidius Naso ["Ovid"](43 b.c.-a.d. 18), achieved fame, disgrace, and posthumous reputation from his amatory verse, particularly *Ars Amatoria*, in 3 books, in which in a parody of scientific style he presents himself as a Professor of Sexual Love. This appeared when Ovid was about 40, and, together with some mysterious "error"—something he had seen and concealed concerning the family of Augustus—earned him lifelong exile at Tomis on the Black Sea (mod. Constantsa in Romania). The mystery of Ovid's exile has never been solved, and has maintained a focus of attention on his amatory poems. But Ovid's major contribution to the subsequent culture of western Europe is contained less in the *Ars Amatoria* than it is in his *Metamorphoses*, 15 books in hexameter verse, narrating mythical changes of shape, beginning with the change of chaos into cosmos and ending with the change of Julius Caesar into a star. It is a vast storehouse of mythology, and the unacknowledged or unrecognized source of most of the classical mythology in European art and literature through the Middle Ages and the Renaissance down to the present. Shakespeare learned classical mythology from the *Metamorphoses*, as did Chaucer; for centuries it was virtually a Latin primer for school-boys. The Victorian children's books of tales from the classics were mostly reworkings of Ovid, as was a considerable proportion of the mythological content of such works as *Peter Parley's Tales about Ancient Rome*, and *About Ancient and Modern Greece* that young James Joyce studied at Clongowes Wood. Ovid is the virtual creator of that peculiar now-fading hybrid European imaginative world filled with G gods bearing L names, the "classical mythology" that never existed in the real classical world. Sometime during his education Joyce encountered Ovid's *Metamorphoses* directly, and in the 8th book came upon the story of Daedalus. How he responded to it constitutes in itself the justification of this comment.

Paulus Probably everyone knows that St. Paul was originally named Saul, and has learned to associate his name-change somehow with his conversion. The book of Acts, in which Saul-Paul's career is recounted, fails to substantiate the supposition. On the road to Damascus the Lord addressed Saul particularly as "Saul," so an explanation for the name-change, if there is one, must come from elsewhere.

The name "Saul" first occurs in Acts at Ch. 7, v. 58, and occurs thereafter for a total of 17 mentions until Ch. 13, v. 9, which begins "Then Saul (who also *is called* Paul)." From that point onwards the Apostle is never called anything but Paul. The last previous mention of Saul had been two verses earlier (13:7), in which we are told that "the deputy of [Cyprus], Sergius Paulus, a prudent man . . . called for Barnabas and Saul, and desired to hear the word of God." The shift in name from Saul to Paul occurs then in the narrative of Saul/Paul's successful evangelizing of the Roman official Sergius Paulus. It is permissible to assume that Saul adopted the name Paul (L Paulus) as a compliment to, or while under the protection of Sergius Paulus. But why?

The Hebrew name "Saul" (meaning, apparently, "called-for") had been long established, including among its bearers the first king of Israel. But when Saul of Tarsus began his missionary work in the

G-speaking eastern Mediterranean he would have had to preach in G, and would have hellenized his name to Saulos. But unfortunately, the word *saulos* already existed in G and meant "mincing"—i.e., effeminate. It was not an auspicious name for a preacher to the heathen, and no doubt caused many a snigger among the reprobate. One may guess that the amiable Sergius Paulus pointed out to "Saulos" the unfortunate connotations of his name, and it was then the offensive G name was exchanged for the homely L one: *Paulus* in L means "Little." It was as if Mr. Pansy had changed his name to Mr. Small.

Pharos The G neuter noun *pharos* means "a plough." *Pharos* was also the name of an island off the harbor of Alexandria in Egypt (either because of some association with a plough or because derived from some accidentally similar native word) on which was built a famous lighthouse regarded as one of the seven wonders of the world. Because of the lighthouse at Pharos, the name Pharos came to suggest a lighthouse, and ultimately to mean "lighthouse." Joyce's use of the word *pharos* seems to be mostly in the sense of "lighthouse," but since the sense of "plough" is not amiss when Joyce emphasises the phallic aspects of a *pharos*, we have glossed both senses.

Pollux, Polydeuces See *Gemini.*

Ptolemaeus, Ptolemaios Ptolemaios [Ptolemy] (meaning "Warlike" in Macedonian G) was the name of one of Alexander's generals who, after the death of the Conqueror, assumed the kingship of Egypt and founded a dynasty that lasted until Egypt was absorbed into the Roman Empire. All fifteen kings of that dynasty ruled under the name of Ptolemy, most distinguished by a surname. Among the more prominent of these surnames are *Soter*, "Savior," *Philadelphus*, "Brother-loving," *Euergetes*, "Beneficent," *Epiphanes*, "Illustrious," *Philometor*, "Mother-loving," and *Philopator*, "Father-loving." Most of these surnames occur or are alluded to in *Finnegans Wake*, for obvious reasons, but two other factors qualify the Ptolemaic dynasty for appearance in *Finnegans Wake*: (1) Cleopatra was a member of that dynasty (the last to rule independently); and 2) their name is shared with Claudius Ptolemaeus (q.v.).

Ptolemaeus, Claudius Claudius Ptolemaeus of Alexandria was a mathematician and geographer who made mathematical observations of the globe between a.d. 121 and 151. His *Geography* was a treatise in 8 books with an atlas of maps, designed to correct all previous maps of the world. In his mapping of the British Isles Ireland appears as the land of the *Iverni*, and on the east coast of the island, at approximately the position of Dublin, occurs a place called Eblana (see *Eblana*). Eblana being assumed to *be* Dublin, Ptolemy can claim the credit of having been the first to put Dublin on the map. In return, Dublin's artist has given Ptolemy due recognition in *Finnegans Wake*.

Pyrrha See *Deucalion*.

Remus See *Romulus*.

Roma Although the city of Rome according to the legend derived its name from Romulus (see *Romulus*), the city in imperial times if not later was personified in a goddess, Roma. This rather artificial creation probably arose by a peculiar process out of the claim of the family of the Caesars to be descended from Venus (see *Venus*). Once Rome had become the patrimony of the Caesars (real or adopted members of the gens *Iulia*), the Caesars, beginning with the deified Julius, became themselves tutelary gods of Rome. But they were sons of Venus, and the son of Venus was Cupid or Amor. And "Amor" is "Roma" spelled backwards! What might be judged as puerile word-juggling was taken as a serious divine token, and in Rome temples of Venus and Rome (i.e., Amor et Roma) were built back-to-back as mirror images: wordplay in masonry and marble.

Medieval Christians engaged in similar wordplay with Eve and the Virgin. Eve was the woman through whom woe came into the world, Mary the woman through whom came salvation. Thus Mary is often called the Second (redemptive) Eve. Mary was universally hailed in the L prayer, *Ave Maria*, so that "Ave" came to seem virtually part of her name. And "Ave" is "Eva" spelled backwards! Both the Amor/Roma and Ave/Eva nonsense sound like something from *Finnegans Wake*, as indeed they are: *Aveh Tiger Roma* (445.13) is a palindrome of *Amor Regit Heva*.

Romulus The legend of Romulus and Remus is not an ancient Italian myth but a foundation-tale for Rome invented on G models. It is, however, fairly old for a concocted legend. According to it, Rhea Silvia, a Vestal Virgin, was ravished by the god Mars and bore twin sons. The twins were set adrift on the Tiber, found and suckled by a she-wolf, then raised by a shepherd. They founded their own new city of Rome, but

Romulus killed Remus when the latter committed the ill-omened sacrilege of leaping over the city wall. Romulus married a woman called
Hersilia, later deified as Hora (both names are probably forms of *hera*
L, "lady"), reigned as King of Rome until one day he disappeared and
ascended into heaven to become the god Quirinus, one of the three
leading gods of Rome (Jupiter and Mars the others).

The city of Rome is supposed to have derived its name from that of
Romulus, but *Romulus* is etymologically identical to *Romanus* and so
means simply "the Roman." The legendary Romulus, therefore, in
reality draws his name from that of the city, not vice-versa. The name
of Remus is less immediately clear. It was either formed analogously
to Romulus, substituting -e- for -o- on the model of such doublets as
G *Kerkyra*, L *Corcyra*, or backformed from placenames near Rome
such as Remona. In *Finnegans Wake* at times Joyce seems to accept
the derivation of *Roma* from *Romulus* in order to invent the opposite:
had Remus killed Romulus the Italian capital would now presumably
be called Reme (see *Finnegans Wake* 098.32) instead of Rome.

The pertinence of the Romulus-Remus fratricide to the relationship
of Shem and Shaun has been long noted and requires no comment here.

Saulos See *Paulus.*

Scotus Erigena See *Erigena, Johannes Scotus.*

Stagyrite See *Aristotle.*

Sulla, Lucius Cornelius Lucius Cornelius Sulla, nicknamed Felix ("the
Lucky")(137-78 b.c.), was undistinguished except as a soldier until he
was almost 50. He was given command of the Roman forces in the war
against Mithridates, King of Pontus, that broke out in 88 b.c. Political
influence in the Senate transferred the command to Marius, but Sulla
shocked everyone by refusing to vacate his post, instead marching his
troops on Rome. Securing power there, he returned to defeat Mithridates, then came back to Rome and had himself made dictator. He was
thus the first of the series of military dictators who ruled the Roman
republic during the first century b.c., culminating with Julius Caesar
and the Principate of Augustus. He reorganized the administration of
government for greater efficiency and centralization of power, but his
regime was looked back on as a harsh and gloomy time. In *Finnegans
Wake* Sulla seems to be mixed up with Sully the Thug, and he was
somewhat of a thug.

Ulixes See *Odysseus.*

Ulysses See *Odysseus.*

Venus The name *Venus* means in L "charming, attractive." The original Italian goddess was no more than the *numen* of vegetables, i.e., of edible greens and herbs, unrelated to animal procreation. Quite early, however, Venus became identified with the G Aphrodite, and the Venus later venerated at Rome, even under special Roman-developed forms, is really Aphrodite under an alias. At Rome during the Empire, Venus, under the title of *Venus Generatrix*, was especially honored as ancestress of the Caesars (see *Caesar, Roma*). According to the adopted legend (set forth at full in the *Aeneid*), the goddess Venus by the mortal Trojan Anchises became the mother of Aeneas. Aeneas's son Iulus, grandson of Venus, was regarded as eponymous ancestor of the gens Julia—the Julii, of whom C. Julius Caesar became the most prominent member. Since the first dynasty of Roman emperors were members of the Julian clan, at least by adoption, Venus was worshipped as their ancestress and as a special goddess of Rome.

Apart from this special Roman development, Venus is best regarded as G, and most intelligibly discussed under the name Aphrodite. Primarily she is the goddess of generation and fertility, animal and sexual as well as vegetational. She was derived by the Greeks from the east, and is akin to Astarte and Ishtar. The meaning of the name Aphrodite is unknown and probably non-G, but the Greeks derived it from *aphros*, "foam," whence the myth of her birth from the sea-foam at Cyprus. Her epithet "the Cyprian," reflects her origin, and also indicates her Asian background. Later the god Adonis came to Athens from Cyprus, and became incorporated into the myth of Aphrodite and Adonis ("Venus and Adonis," as in Shakespeare), but in the east Adonis was already earlier the consort of Astarte.

In other myths she is associated with Ares (Mars), as wife and as paramour, and by him mother of Harmonia as well as of Eros (Amor, Cupid). As paramour of Ares she was caught with him in a net prepared by her husband Hephaistos (Vulcan). Her association with the god of war and the god who forges weapons is not incompatible with her rôle as goddess of sexual love. She herself was worshipped as a war goddess in Sparta and elsewhere. In cult she is also often associated with Hermes (see *Mercurius*). The myrtle and the dove are both sacred to Aphrodite/Venus. Two very common titles given to her are *Ourania* ("Heavenly") and *Pandêmos* ("Of all the people"). The conversion of these titles into the opposing concepts of Heavenly and Profane Venus is a Platonic development (*Symposium*).

Aphrodite/Venus functions as combined war and love goddess in the part she played in bringing about the Trojan War. As a reward to Paris for adjudging her most beautiful of goddesses she brought him Helen, wife of Menelaus. Throughout the Trojan War she sides with the Trojans.

Joyce seems to have been well acquainted with the extensive mythology of Aphrodite/Venus (as a child of his environment he almost always calls her Venus *per interpretatione Romana*). Some reflection of almost every detail in this note may be found in *Finnegans Wake*. (Perhaps it is redundant to note that Aphrodite [*Pornê*; *Hetaira*] was patroness of prostitutes.)

Vulcan Vulcanus, Volcanus or Volkanus was an ancient Italian fire-god, associated with volcanic fires. As a native Italian god he was worshipped chiefly to avert fires, but in classical times he was fully identified with the G Hephaestus, to whom the mythology concerning Vulcan is largely to be ascribed. Hephaestus also seems to have been in origin a god of volcanic fire derived from Asia, but the Greeks came to regard him chiefly as god of the smith's fire, and thence as god of smiths and similar craftsmen.

The god is lame (lame men with strong arms in primitive communities would be induced to handicraft rather than farming or warfare) and occupies himself making marvelous works such as the armor of Achilles. He is the maker of Pandora; he is the maker of mankind. In one legend his wife is Aphrodite whom he catches in a net of his own devising while she is in Ares' arms. Here he is ridiculed as a cuckold, but in other legends he is ridiculed for his lameness or ugliness. He keeps his forge under the volcano Aetna.

The cuckolded and ridiculous aspect of Vulcan, probably, recommended him to Joyce as a parallel to Leopold Bloom and HCE. Like

Joyce himself, he was a ridiculed craftsman. His particular associations with Mars and Venus are also, of course, of significance.

Zeus See *Jupiter.*

APPENDIX B

Some Recurrent Words and Phrases

ab ovo usque ad mala   This phrase, literally "from the egg to the apples," is a L adage meaning "from the beginning to the end." The phrase in whole or in part, and in various deformations, is fairly frequent in *Finnegans Wake*. The phrase *ab ovo*, used in English, is often misunderstood as signifying "from the original source, from the kernel, from the seed, from the germ." The L phrase is not so metaphysical. A conventional Roman dinner opened with an egg course, concluded with apples, so "from the egg to the apples" corresponds to "from soup to nuts," and just means "from start to finish."

Ad Majorem Dei Gloriam   "To the Greater Glory of God," the motto of the Society of Jesus, is a phrase very well known, particularly in the form of its initial letters—A.M.D.G.—to every schoolboy taught by Jesuits. It was (and no doubt still is) customary to affix the letters at the head of school exercises and examination papers. In the United States, at least, the letters, or the motto written in full, are often to be found printed on the covers of student notebooks and examination bluebooks.

bella, pia et pura   The ambiguity afforded by the L word *bella* yields Joyce endless confusion in *Finnegans Wake*. As a noun, it is plural of neuter *bellum*, "war"—i.e., it means "wars." As a feminine singular adjective it means "pretty" or "nice." In conjunction with the name of Anna Livia and the feminine singular adjectives *pura* and *pia*, *bella* would seem to form part of a string of attributes of the Blessed Virgin, or a woman like her—*pia, pura, bella*: "dutiful, chaste, fair."

Ancient etymologists responded to this ambiguity by deriving *bellum*, "war," from *bella* (feminine), "nice," by the process *kat' antiphrasin* ("according to the opposite"): "*bellum, quod res bella non sit*"—"war (*bellum*), because it would not be a nice (*bella*) thing."

But Joyce's source for the manifold uses of the phrase is not a pious medieval formula, rather it is Vico's prescription for the establishment of civilized hierarchical society: *pia et pura bella*, "pious and pure wars." As usual, he is able to make words contradict themselves.

bona fides   Although the phrase *bona fides,* "good faith," is perfectly correct L, its reference in *Finnegans Wake* is to little or nothing pertaining to the classical world. In Ireland until very recently the public houses and ordinary drinking places closed nightly, by law, at hours varying between 10:30 and 11:30 p.m. The ordinary hapless drinker was then required to go home, if his home was easily attainable. But the law took account of the unhappy wanderer far from home at the dread hour, and certain establishments were licensed to cater to genuine travelers—*bona fide* travelers—for extended periods after closing time. Such houses were known as *bona fide* houses, and were highly regarded by the drinking fraternity, who were readily transformed into *bona fide* travelers, since the stipulation of the law, drawn up in days of pedestrian or horse-borne transportation, was that a *bona fide* traveler was anyone who at closing time had put a distance of at least five miles between himself and the spot where he had slept the previous night. In the sizeable city of Dublin, well furnished with public and private transportation, it became no trick at all for respectable citizens to drink at night in suburban pubs five miles or more from the beds in which they had spent the previous night and would also spend the ensuing night, when the charms of *bona fide* drinking palled. Presumably HCE's pub was a *bona fide* house: Chapelizod was an ideal location for travelers from north-east and south-east regions of Dublin to venture to for licit late drinking. That delightful legal oddity is alas no more, an unsentimental government having recently extended the regular licensing hours and eliminated the special privilege of night-foundered thirsty travelers.

et tu, Brute?   *Et tu, brute, mi fili,* "And even you, Brutus, my son," is the L translation of what is purported to be Caesar's last utterance as he fell under the daggers of his assassins at the foot of the statue of Pompey in the Roman Senate (for the sources report that his actual dying words were spoken in G). The phrase has become famous as the ultimate response to unexpected and unearned treachery on the part of one loved or trusted. According to the Joyce legend the infant writer composed a denunciation of Tim Healy's betrayal of Parnell (see Appendix A, *Heliopolis*) under the title *Et tu, Healy.* The legend also asserts that Joyce's father had the effusion printed as a broadside or pamphlet, but no copy has survived.

ex nihilo nihil fit   "Nothing can be made out of nothing" is a dictum of the schools that Joyce probably ran across in his attempt to adapt Aquinas to his needs. *Finnegans Wake* contains several variations on the phrase, often with a moral bearing.

ex quovis ligno non fit Mercurius   We have found only two occurrences of this L proverbial equivalent to "You can't make a silk purse out of a sow's ear" in *Finnegans Wake,* and both times mangled almost beyond recognition. Are there other occurrences we have failed to find?

The point of the proverb—"A Mercury is not made out of just any piece of wood you like" (see Appendix A, *Mercurius*)—may not be very persuasive to readers conditioned by Old Testament ridicule of idols, but presumably an ideal herm must have shown a certain aptness for its purpose even before the carver went to work on it. A herm was a sturdy stump of wood topped with a carved human head and made distinctive by a phallus half-way up. Perhaps a good herm-log already showed a knob suitable for the head and had a projecting branch to be shaped into the phallus. Why Joyce uses this proverb, and why he so mangles it, we leave to the reader.

felix culpa   *O felix culpa*—"O happy sin," "O lucky fault"—is the title of a medieval hymn that celebrates the paradox that although the Fall of Adam was the direst misfortune to befall mankind, and the most reprehensible sin ever committed, it yet produced for mankind an entirely unexpected boon and grace, the demonstration of God's infinite love through which came about the Incarnation of God in Man, and the Redemption through the crucifixion, death and resurrection of Christ. The theme much fascinated writers on the theme of the Fall and the Atonement, and is fundamental to Milton's epic, *Paradise Lost.* In Book XII of *Paradise Lost* the fallen but repentant Adam is shown a vision of the future including the redemptive mission of Christ which provokes him to an ecstatic outburst of joy and wonder:

O goodness infinite, goodness immense!
That all this good of evil shall produce,
And evil turn to good; more wonderful
Than that which by creation first brought forth
Light out of darkness! full of doubt I stand,
Whether I should repent me now of sin
By mee done and occasion'd, or rejoice

Much more, that much more good thereof shall spring,
To God more glory, more good will to Men
From God, and over wrath grace shall abound.
(*PL*, XII , 469–478)
For discussion of this theme the finest source is A. O. Lovejoy's
famous article, "Milton and the Paradox of the Fortunate Fall," *ELH*,
IV (1937), 161-79.

A stimulus for continued interest in the paradox was that to wish the
Fall had not happened seemed somewhat impious, for it implied wish-
ing away the Incarnation of Christ. A less doctrinal fortunate result
of Adam's fall not usually adduced in the *felix culpa* tradition is the
fact that it provided Milton with the topic of the greatest poem in the
English language. Similarly, *Finnegans Wake* depends for its existence
on the fall of Tim Finnegan from his ladder, as it does on the recurrent
falls of all the other phoenix culprits who wake again at the *Wake*.

FERT   The L word *fert* is the 3rd person singular present indicative
active form of the verb *fero*, and means "he [she, it] bears *or* carries."
The word we are here dealing with no doubt means "he carries," for
it is a device of the Knights of the Order of the Hospital of St. John
of Jerusalem, and is in fact an acronym of the motto of that Order,
Fortitudo Ejus Rhodum Tenuit.

Fortitudo Ejus Rhodum Tenuit   "His Strength Has Held Rhodes," the
motto of the Order of the Hospital of St. John of Jerusalem, celebrates
the heroic defense of Rhodes by the Order against a determined and
numerically superior Turkish onslaught in 1480. The "he" in question
is either God or St. John. The Order arose in Jerusalem during the
Crusades, and conducted fighting retreats from the Holy Land to
Cyprus, and from Cyprus to Rhodes. In 1523 it was finally forced to
surrender Rhodes to the Turks, and was granted Malta as its base by
the Emperor Charles V, whence it is sometimes called the Order of the
Knights of Malta. In the vicissitudes of modern history the Order
survives, split into Catholic and Protestant divisions. The Catholic part
of the Order became a preserve for the extremely blue-blooded conti-
nental nobility and presumably has shared their fortunes. The principal
Protestant branch became in 19th-century England a charitable organization, which runs the St. John's Ambulance Association. In the
early 20th century ambulances in Dublin were operated by the St.

John's Association, and it was no doubt on O'Connell Street that Joyce encountered first the remnant of the organization that has had so colorful a history and bears so romantically evocative a badge.

Hic, Haec, Hoc   To make a note on *hic, haec, hoc* may be redundant, but Joyce alludes to the paradigm at least a dozen times. *Hic*, etc., translated "this" and sometimes "here," is the L demonstrative pronoun for the First Person. Students learning L have for countless generations learned the paradigm of this pronoun, reciting first the Nominative singular forms for masculine, feminine, and neuter, then the Genitive forms (identical in all genders), then the Dative forms (likewise identical), then the three Accusative forms, etc.: *hic, haec, hoc; huius, huius, huius; huic, huic, huic; hunc, hanc, hoc.* . . . The metronymic effect is hypnotic and rather reminiscent of a religious chant in a sacred language. The echo remains forever in any mind subjected to the old learning process, and remained so rooted in the mind of Joyce that he has coined "hickeryhockery" (160.13) as a name for L.

Laus Deo Semper   "Praise to God Forever" is a Jesuit slogan used as a sort of antiphon to *Ad Majorem Dei Gloriam*, and the initials are often written at the bottom of a paper that is headed A.M.D.G. Joyce found the initials L.D.S. irresistibly alterable into L.S.D. (l.s.d., standing for *libri, solidi, denarii*), the symbols, prior to decimalization, for Pounds, Shillings and Pence. The rearrangement *Laus Semper Deo* continues to make quite acceptable L, but in this form also suggests the mercenary side of a Church that sold Ireland to an English king for Peter's Pence (see Appendix A, *Laudabiliter*).

Obedientia Civium Urbis Felicitas   "The Obedience of the Citizens is the Happiness of the City" is the implausible and no doubt intentionally tendentious motto on the Arms of the City of Dublin. For most of its long history Dublin's citizens were obedient to their foreign masters, who made the city the center of their domination of Ireland, and received in return very little urban felicity. Nobody bothers to note what the slogan may mean now in a parliamentary republic. Joyce uses the formula as a leit-motif for Dublin that occurs at least eleven times in *Finnegans Wake*.

Rhaeda / Rhoda   The enigmatic doublet rhaeda/rhoda, under various spellings, occurs at least four times in *Finnegans Wake (081.09,*

327.11, 434.07, 478.13) and probably oftener. We are quite at a loss
to say what the combination means. *Rhaeda* (spelled various ways,
properly without an h) is a L word borrowed from Celtic, which was
the name of a kind of four-wheeled carriage. *Rhoda* is a G word, plural
of *rhodon*, "a rose," and also the name of a feast day when graves were
decked with roses. Probably this odd doublet is associated some way
with the similar doublet Romulus/Remus (see Appendix A, *Romulus*)
but we confess we are baffled in trying to ascertain its significance.

Securus iudicat orbis terrarum   "Untroubled, the world [*literally*, the
circle of the lands] judges"—this sentiment, under several ingenious
disguises, occurs at least six times in *Finnegans Wake*. Joyce had used
this sentence, received at second hand, much earlier in his career in the
paper called "Drama and Life" that he read before the Literary and
Historical Society of University College, Dublin, on January 20, 1900.
He picked up the phrase—a quotation from St. Augustine (*Contra
Epistolam Parmeniani* ["Against the Letter of Parmenianus"], III ,
24)—from the *Apologia* of Cardinal Newman (Ch. III). Ellmann,
James Joyce, p. 74, gives details, but fails to note that Newman was
also quoting at second hand. Newman had read the sentence (in effect,
"The whole world gives its calm judgment")— a remark directed by
Augustine against the Donatist heresy—in an article by Cardinal Wiseman on "The Anglican Claim." Wiseman's employment of this remark, Newman relates, was the specific impetus to his own abandon-
ment of Anglicanism for Roman Catholicism. Joyce's distortions of
this crucial sentence are perverse and impudent (*Finnegans Wake*
076.07–08, 096.33, 263.27–28, 306.R2, 513.01–02 and 593.13–14).

Thalatta! Thalatta!   "Sea! Sea!" was the cry of the leading elements
of Xenophon's Ten Thousand as they came through the mountain
passes above Trebizond and saw the Black Sea below them in the
distance. The moment is unforgettable in one of the most vividly
written accounts of a military campaign ever recounted, the so-called
Anabasis of Xenophon. Xenophon, exiled from Athens, had gone
virtually as the guest of a Spartan friend along with a contingent of
10,000 Greek mercenaries who had been hired by Cyrus, brother of the
king of Persia, to help him in a revolt against his brother. When, deep
inside Persia, Cyrus was killed in battle, his Persian forces dissolved
leaving the Greeks isolated. The leading officers of the mercenaries,

invited to negotiate with the king's officials, were treacherously massacred, leaving the Ten Thousand without generals. Xenophon with some others took command and led the Greek force northward (their retreat westward to the Mediterranean being blocked) through the mountains of Armenia toward the Black Sea. After dreadful hardship and constant harassment by savage tribesmen in the snow-covered mountains, they finally reached the sea. The excited cry *Thalatta! Thalatta!* rippled back through the ragged ranks of the army.

The word *thalatta* is the Attic form of the more general G word *thalassa*. Joyce uses both forms, in which he is technically correct. Xenophon was an Athenian, but the Ten Thousand included Greeks of all dialects. (The expedition lasted from 401 to 399 b.c.)

Unde gentium festines   "Whence in the world are you hurrying?," "Where among the nations are you hurrying from?" is a question that occurs at least three times in *Finnegans Wake*. By whom? To whom? Why?

Veni, Vidi, Vici   "I came, I saw, I won"—usually rendered "I came, I saw, I conquered"—was Caesar's laconic boast after he had defeated King Pharnaces II of Bosporus at the battle of Zela, in Asia Minor, in 47 b.c., one of the final battles in his successful civil war against Pompey. Laconic once, it has become a verbosity by repetition—at least six times in *Finnegans Wake*.

APPENDIX C

Manducanda at Triv and Quad

306.L2—306.15

Cato: Duty, the daughter of discipline   Perhaps discipline is the daughter of Duty; either opinion would accord with the spirit of the great Censor, who is perhaps less well known for his insistence on public and private moral austerity than for his unremitting insistence on Rome's duty to herself to destroy Carthage: *Carthago delenda est.*

306.L3—306.15-16

Nero: the Great Fire at the South City Markets   In July, 64 a.d., two-thirds of Rome burned down while Nero recited verses about the burning of Troy (the origin of the popular notion about his playing the fiddle). Many blamed the fire on Nero, but he found a convenient scapegoat in the Christians, of whom large numbers were burned to death and killed in other cruel manners.

306.L5—306.17-18

Aristotle: A Place for Everything and Everything in its Place   The topic describes Aristotle's natural intellectual urge. He was the first thinker to work out a theory of reasoning which has survived as deductive logic. His treatises on logic include *Categories*, *Prior Analytics*, and *Posterior Analytics*. He seems in his life's work to have planned to investigate systematically all fields of knowledge and to have projected an Encyclopedia of Philosophy.

306.L6—306.18-19

Julius Caesar: Is the Pen Mightier than the Sword?   In nine years' campaigning Caesar subjugated Gaul completely to Roman rule; in a four-year Civil War he subjected Rome completely to his own rule. Thereupon he wrote *Commentaries* on each war which remain major sources of historical information about them.

306.L7—306.19-20

Pericles: A Successful Career in the Civil Service   Pericles rose rapidly to power as leader of the popular (democratic) party. He increased Athens' naval strength; tried to create a Hellenic Confederation to put an end to Greek internecine wars. He spent public funds to build the Parthenon, the Propylaea, the Odeum, and other noteworthy buildings for which Athens is still famous. He encouraged the drama, which attained its ancient pinnacle during his regime.

306.18—306.20-21

Ovid: The Voice of Nature in the Forest   The Voice of Nature may be Love, subject of many of Ovid's poems, but the reference is probably to his best known and most influential work, *Metamorphoses* in 16 books. For the sake of love, or as victims of lust, large numbers of persons turn into trees, flowers, streams, birds, and beasts—nature in the forest. Many of them recur in *Finnegans Wake*: Hyacinthus, Narcissus, Philomela, and Procne.

306.L10—306.22

Domitian: On the Benefits of Recreation   This topic possibly refers to the fact that Domitian's repression of public immorality accorded very ill with his personal sensuality and solidified the aristocratic opposition that evoked the reign of terror of his last years, which in turn provoked his wife to collaborate with his assassins.

306.L11—306.22-23

Edipus: If Standing Stones Could Speak   . . . they would do well to speak unambiguously. The tragedy of Oedipus was precipitated by the misleading if accurate advice that both he and his father, Laios, received from the Delphic Oracle. Delphi itself was a sort of standing stone, in that it contained the original standing stone that was the navel of the world (the *Omphalos*) and several artistic copies of it. Delphi also treasured the authentic stone that Kronos was induced to swallow in place of the baby Zeus. Another stony dimension of the story is that the name *Laios*, whatever its true etymology, could be construed to mean "stone" (*laas*, Gen. *laos*, pl. *laes*, [G]: "stone").

306.L12—306.23-24

Socrates: Devotion to the Feast of the Indulgence of Portioncula When Socrates was condemned to death, execution was postponed for thirty days because of a sacred mission being sent by Athens to Delos. His friends contrived means for his escape, but he refused to break the law, and devotedly remained to drink his little portion of hemlock on the appointed day.

306.L13—306.24-25

Ajax: The Dublin Metropolitan Police Sports at Ballsbridge   Ajax is recorded to have stood head and shoulders above his contemporaries. Immensely strong, he was a blunt, stolid man, slow of speech, of unshakable courage. His epithet in Homer is "bulwark of the Achaeans." In a word, he would have been a prime recruit as a constable in the late Dublin Metropolitan Police. In the *Iliad* he fought Hector in a duel, of which he had rather the better, and at the funeral "Sports" for the dead Patroclus he wrestled Odysseus in a match billed as brains against brawn. The result was a draw, tie-score.

306.L14—306.25-27

Homer: Describe in Homely Anglian Monosyllables the Wreck of the Hesperus   Although Homer's great poems emerge from the dawn of Greek history, and describe a primitive heroic society, his language is neither homely nor monosyllabic (there may be a send-up here of certain cultural assumptions from the nineteenth century). The reference here is to the *Odyssey*, wherein the hero, Odysseus, because of the wrath of Poseidon his followers have provoked, is shipwrecked every time he tries to sail home to Ithaca. Most of his adventures take place in the western Mediterranean, from Italy to Gibraltar, in waters remote and fabulous to Homer's generation of Greeks (*Hesperos* means "the West").

306.L15—306.27-28

Marcus Aurelius: What Morals, if any, can be drawn from Diarmuid and Grania?   [For Diarmuid and Grania see *A Gaelic Lexicon*, Supplementary Notes, "Toraidheacht Dhiarmada agus Ghráinne," p. 412] 1. Aurelius was fond of drawing morals as his volumes of *Meditations* attest. 2. Diarmuid eloped with Grania, daughter of his king and betrothed of his admired superior, and came to a tragic end. Aurelius legally married Faustina, daughter of his emperor, Antoninus Pius, with the latter's blessing and approval. Antoninus was also Aurelius's admired superior, whom he served loyally for 23 years; Antoninus reciprocated by adopting Aurelius as his son. When Antoninus passed peacefully away at the age of 75, the 40-year-old Aurelius succeeded him as emperor. Morals may be drawn from the comparison.

306.L16—306.28-30

Alcibiades: Do you Approve of our Existing Parliamentary System? Alcibiades did not. Raised in the household of Pericles, befriended by Socrates, his career under diverse governmental systems was brilliant but inevitably disastrous. During the Peloponnesian War, which he had fomented, he was indicted for public sacrilege and fled to Sparta, the enemy, which he aided. Incurring Spartan distrust, he fled to Persia, whence he abetted conspiracies to overthrow the Athenian democracy. Oligarchy being established in Athens, he could find no place in the new system, and led the counter-revolutionary democratic forces against it. Returned to democratic Athens in triumph, he provoked further suspicion and was forced into exile again, and was murdered abroad, either by Athenians or by Spartans. Disapproval was always mutual between Alcibiades and any existing governmental system.

306.L7—306.30

Lucretius: The Uses and Abuses of Insects   Titus Lucretius Carus (99-55 b.c.) was said to have died mad from the effects of a love-potion given to him by his wife. If the love-potion was constituted out of Spanish fly, the episode would instance the use and abuse of insects. In his lucid moments Lucretius wrote a poem, *De Natura rerum*, expounding the philosophy that all Being, including the soul, is made of temporary congeries of atoms, and a Latinization of his terminology could also lead to an abuse of insects. The proper use of the L noun *insectum/insecta* is to regard it as prefixed by intensive *in-* or prepositional *in-*, and as therefore denoting a thing *cut into*, or segmented—i.e., an insect—and as a word corresponding in structure with G *entomon/entoma*, with the same etymological meaning and denotation: an insect. Abuse of the L noun *insectum* would be to regard it as prefixed by privative *in-*, "not-," and therefore meaning a thing *not cuttable*—i.e., infinitely small—and therefore a word corresponding in structure and etymology, but not denotation, with G *atomon*, "an atom."
Book 5 of *De Natura rerum* deals, in passing, with insects, but does not confound them with atoms.

307.L1—307.01

Plato: Clubs   Plato did belong to a number of antidemocratic clubs in Athens, but the word "Clubs" immediately calls to mind the dialogue *Symposium*, which records the discussion at a banquet held by a social group to which Socrates belonged (as did Alcibiades, who was present at the Symposium; *see 306.L16—306.28-30*). The *Phaedo* and other dialogues also record Socrates and his friends gathered in convivial groups. Joyce may also be associating the womanless and faintly homosexual atmosphere of Socratic-Platonic social life with the similar atmosphere in English upperclass club life.

307.L3—307.01-02

Horace: Advantages of the Penny Post   Noteworthy among Horace's poems, and his own invention, so to speak, are his *Epistles*. These are two books of poems, each poem addressed to a friend or acquaintance in the form of a familiar letter, written in the epic meter but in relaxed colloquial language. Book I contains nineteen letters written to various friends, plus a poem addressed to the book of Epistles itself. Book II contains only three letters, all longer and somewhat more formal than those of Book I, and all dealing in one way or another with poetry and criticism; the first is addressed to Augustus and the third is often called simply "The Art of Poetry."

307.L5—307.03-04

Tiresias: Is the Co-Education of Animus and Anima Wholly Desirable?
     Tiresias having one day encountered a pair of snakes copulating was, for some reason profoundly Freudian or Jungian or otherwise, thereupon changed into a woman. A similar experience at a later date reversed the process, setting up Tiresias to be the victim of a dispute between Zeus and Hera as to whether men or women receive the greater sexual gratification; his considered and experienced opinion that women did so angered Hera that she blinded him. Zeus, to compensate him, gave him long life, the power of prophecy, and wisdom so intense that it could survive his bodily death. *Animus* and *Anima* do not actually mean "Male Soul" and "Female Soul" as their respective genders might suggest, but rather "Intellectual Principle" and "Vital Principle." Tiresias received a one-person co-education of male and female, and his educated *Animus* survived with his *Anima* into the netherworld of Shades, but whether he or

anyone else would regard the experience as wholly desirable remains an open question.

307.L6—307.04-05

Marius: What Happened at Clontarf?   With a re-organized army, better trained than any previously produced in the country, he defeated Germanic invaders from the North and saved his country from their ravages. He attained great power by unprecedented constitutional irregularities, and died at an advanced age leaving the country in turmoil, beset by rival military leaders eager to emulate his career. —*The foregoing is a thumbnail biography of* Gaius Marius *or of* Brian Boru. *The defeated Germanic enemies were respectively the* Teutones and Cimbri *and the* Vikings; *the battles were* Aquae Sextiae (102 b.c.), Campi Raudii *(101 b.c.) and* Clontarf (a.d. 1014). [For Brian Boru and Clontarf see *A Gaelic Lexicon*, Supplementary Notes, "Brian Boru," pp. 366-371].

307.L7—307.05-06

Diogenes: Since our Brother Johnathan Signed the Pledge   *Diogenês* means "Zeus-born" or "Born of [i.e., through the favor of] Zeus." *Jonathan* means "Jehovah has given," and *John* [contracted from *Jochanan*], means "Jehovah is gracious." Perhaps "*Johnathan*" may be highhandedly construed to suggest that "Jehovah has graciously given." *Mutatis mutandis*, then, "Diogenes" and "Johnathan" are operative synonyms. Diogenes-Johnathan "signed the pledge" when he determined that happiness is to be attained by satisfying only natural needs and set about to train his body to have as few needs as possible. Giving up alcoholic beverages was the least of the privations this entailed: he lived in an abandoned tub and ate discarded scraps. Another aspect to the regimen practiced by Diogenes of satisfying natural needs in the cheapest and easiest way was to relieve himself when and where the urge arose. From this life-style came his nickname *ho Kynikos*, "the Doglike," which in English is disguised as the *Cynic* philosopher.

307.L8—307.06-07

Procne, Philomela: the Meditations of Two Young Spinsters   Although only Philomela was a spinster in the modern sense of an unmarried woman, both sisters were literally spinsters in that they spun and wove yarn. Philomela wove into a piece of embroidery the story of her maltreatment by Tereus and managed to have it conveyed to Procne, who thus learned of the outrage and set about to concoct in her kitchen a revenge even more distasteful than the crime. The outcome of the sisters' meditations makes their tenor explicit.

307.L10—307.08

Nestor: Hengler's Circus Entertainment   As the "old man" of the Homeric poems, wise no doubt but also somewhat fatuous and garrulous, Nestor is the only person on this list to be identified with HCE. "Sandy Pylos," of which he was king, was famous for raising horses, and Nestor himself is given the epithet *hippodamos*, "horse-tamer," by Homer (*Odyssey* III .17 and elsewhere). Hengler's Circus, like every circus, entertained spectators with trained horses.

307.L11—307.08-09

Cincinnatus: On Thrift   When the messengers came to summon Cincinnatus from his farm to serve the state as dictator, they found him plowing. Upon his resignation after his successful sixteen-day term of office, he returned at once to his farm work: no waste of time, no waste of state funds, minimal diversion from agricultural diligence.

307.L12—307.09-10

Leonidas: The Kettle-Griffith-Moynihan Scheme for a New Electricity Supply
Kettle: *Thermopylae*, "Hot Gates" because of boiling springs there
Griffith: a griffin [see *A Gaelic Lexicon*], a *lionlike* creature: *Leonidas*
Moynihan: "Munsterman" [see *A Gaelic Lexicon*]. Munster is the southernmost province of Ireland, Lakonia (capital, Sparta) is the southernmost province of Greece. "Munsterman" = Spartan.
Electricity Supply: Leonidas and his Spartans *dammed* a pass, a common feature of hydroelectric schemes.

307.L14—307.11

Theocritus: American Lake Poetry   Theocritus, of Syracuse in Sicily, invented the *Idyll* or pastoral poem—a lyric poem presenting a single rural or countrified scene, written in epic meter.
Syracuse, New York, is situated in the Finger-lake region, near Lake Oneida.
English "Lake Poetry" is not pastoral in the technical sense, but it is rural in setting; Wordsworth titled one poem, "Michael: A Pastoral."

307.L16—307.13

Fabius: Circumspection   Fabius Cunctator demonstrated the virtue of circumspection in his cautious approach to Hannibal's superior armies.

307.L19—307.14-16

Esop: Tell a Friend in a Chatty Letter the Fable of the Grasshopper and the Ant   Since Aesop is credited with inventing the fable featuring talking beasts, the allusion is self-evident. As might be expected, however, "The Ant and the Grasshopper" is not by Aesop but by LaFontaine.

307.L20—307.16

Prometheus: Santa Claus   Prometheus gave mankind the immeasurably valuable gift of fire that he stole from heaven, but gift-giving is not his sole connection with Santa Claus. Without fire there would be no fireplaces, without fireplaces there would be no chimneys; without chimneys how could Santa Claus make his deliveries?

307.L22—307.17-18

Pompeius Magnus: The Roman Pontiffs and the Orthodox Churches   Pompey the Great was co-ruler of the Roman world and extended its power to the East. He instituted legislation to end political corruption and was noted for the integrity, chasteness, and gravity of his private life. *In these regards he may be seen as both a Roman pontiff dealing with the East, and as personally orthodox.*
Pompey was not himself Pontifex Maximus at Rome; that office was held by Julius Caesar. In the Civil War between Caesar and Pompey, Caesar held Rome and the West, Pompey held the East. *In these regards Pompey may be seen as equivalent to the Orthodox Eastern Churches, battling the autocracy vested in the Roman pontiff, Caesar.*

307.L22—307.17-18

Miltiades Strategos: The Roman Pontiffs and the Orthodox Churches   *Strategos* was not a part of Miltiades' name, though certainly he was a general and is appropriately called *Miltiadês Stratêgos*, General Miltiades. Perhaps Joyce supplied him with the dignity to balance Pompey's *Magnus*. Miltiades had no associations with Rome, but he was himself a Westerner with an Eastern Policy. His East was Persia. He decisively defeated the first Persian invasion at Marathon. Thereafter he worked up support for a naval expedition against Paros, and when it failed he was convicted of having misled the state, and fined 50 talents (an immense sum, equal to 4,054.5 lbs. or 1,843 kg. of gold: find the current price of gold *per ounce*), but he had been severely wounded at Paros and died of his injuries. His career roughly paralleled that of Pompey: smashing successes in the East, reverses, domestic enemies and death at the nadir of his fortunes.

307.L23—307.18-19

Solon: The Thirty Hour Week   Solon's legal reforms included the freeing of all persons enslaved because of debt, thereby effectively abolishing debt-peonage and serfdom. Specific hours of the work-week were not legislated by Solon, but he has a rather remote connection with the number Thirty. Almost two hundred years after Solon's establishment of the democracy in Athens a junta of Thirty (known to history as "The Thirty" or "The Thirty Tyrants") seized absolute power in the state and held it for about a year (404-403 b.c.) during which they executed about 1,500 men as opponents of the regime. After the counter-revolution the remnants of the Thirty were themselves exterminated.

307.L24—307.19-20

Castor, Pollux: Compare the Fistic Styles of Jimmy Wilde and Jack Sharkey   Although Castor and Pollux are notable battlers they do not fight one the other. Nevertheless, when one is up the other is down: according to some versions of their legend, they share enough immortality for one, so that on alternate days one is alive, one dead, or one with Hades and one in Heaven.

307.L25—307.20-21

Dionysius: How to Understand the Deaf   The allusions here are tangential: 1. Dionysius wrote bad plays, which were criticized and ridiculed by grammarians for misuse of words. Yet his tragedy, *Ransom of Hector*, won first prize at the Athenian Lenaea, before an audience so sensitive to language that Demosthenes is alleged to have deliberately elicited groans and hisses at appropriate parts of his orations by false accentuation. Dionysius was deaf to good Greek, but the Athenians understood his power politically.
2. Dionysius's Ear was the name of a cave in which the slightest whisper was clearly audible; *see 070.36*.

307.L26—307.21-22

Sappho: Should Ladies learn Music or Mathematics?   This question is more than a general one elicited by consideration of Sappho's career; it is one she dealt with herself. If the question is disjunctive, she would perhaps refuse the disjunction, but would opt for music if the choice were forced. Fragment 58 of Sappho consists of lines addressed in contempt to an uneducated woman and asserts that song confers immortality.

307.L29—307.24

Catilina: The Value of Circumstantial Evidence   Catiline's plot to kill the Consuls was leaked to Cicero, who promptly fortified his house against attack and the following day denounced Catiline in a famous speech to the Senate [*see 395.06*]. Catiline fled but his co-conspirators were caught and on the testimony of slaves convicted and executed. The most circumstantial evidence against Catiline was his ultimate insurrection and the battle against the Republic's forces in which he lost his life.

307.L30—307.25

Cadmus: Should Spelling?   If the balance of the question is "be reformed?" the answer for the Greeks who adopted the "Cadmean letters" of the North Semitic alphabet was "Yes." The borrowed alphabet had no vowels; the Greeks specialized the functions of five letters to make A E I O Y. In time several letters were dropped and new ones added until the present form was attained about 400 b.c.

307.L33-307.26

Themistocles: Eu   The point of this association may be eluding us. The word *eu* in G occurs chiefly as an adverb meaning "well; thoroughly, competently; morally well, kindly; fortunately, happily; in good case; safely; right." As a substantive it means "the right, the good; the Good; perfection, the ideal." Although there is little difficulty in identifying competence, good fortune, and moral uprightness in the career of Themistocles, such perfection is not uniquely his. Themistocles earned his historical renown chiefly by masterminding the Greek naval victory over the Persians at Salamis in 480 b.c. Seven years after achieving his glory he was ostracized by the jealous democracy of Athens, was forced to flee to Persia, and ended his days as a resident of Magnesia, in Persian territory. The curve of his career thus stated looks like a medieval tragedy —glory followed by downfall. From Themistocles' own point of view, as

Plutarch relates his life, the graph may have seemed more like a steady ascent, for Plutarch's "Life of Themistocles" is the story of a man for whom disadvantages always turned into advantages. That perhaps is the basis of the essay-topic on Themistocles in Triv & Quad.

The first of a series of disabilities recounted by Plutarch that Themistocles allegedly turned to his own advantage, was the legal restriction in his youth, because his mother was a non-Athenian, confining his gymnastic exercises to one gymnasium set aside for such semi-aliens. Themistocles induced the fashionable youth of Athens to frequent that gymnasium, so that Themistocles' own attendance there, instead of being a social stigma was of the highest social prestige. From an undistinguished background he rose by wit, social aplomb, and political craft to preeminence in the city. As a politician he induced the Athenians to build a navy, playing on their commercial cupidity by suggesting the navy's utility in allowing Athens to seize the carrying-trade among the islands, although historians credit him with foreseeing the need for a defensive navy against a future Persian invasion. When Xerxes did invade Greece, Themistocles had a navy ready, but had to induce the Athenians to abandon their city, indefensible against the Persian hordes, and take to their ships. Omens and oracles received at the time were generally interpreted as unfavorable, but Themistocles managed to construe them all as good, and seems to have cajoled the priesthood into agreeing with him. At Salamis the Athenian fleet was accompanied by a numerically smaller fleet from Sparta and other cities of the Peloponnesus. To weld the allies to him, Themistocles allowed a Spartan nominal command of the joint fleet.

When this Spartan admiral sought to lead the fleet to the safety of the Peloponnesus, Themistocles sent word of the move to Xerxes, so the Persian fleet was able to trap the Greeks in the strait of Salamis. Themistocles courted this apparent disadvantage because he knew conditions of currents and winds favored the Greek ships. In the engagement the allied Greek fleet utterly destroyed a Persian fleet many times superior in numbers, and Themistocles was universally accorded the glory. Had the Greeks lost, and had Themistocles' machinations become known, he would surely have been condemned as a traitor.

Later, when public opinion had been turned against Themistocles (partly because of his unconcealed self-esteem), he continued to turn bad luck to good. After his ostracism from Athens he was accused of treasonable communication with the Persians, his property was confiscated, and a price was put on his head. From the ever-present threat of assassination by bounty-hunters in the Greek cities, Themistocles fled to Persian territory, although the Persian king had previously set a bounty of 200 talents on him. He had himself smuggled to the Persian court, and by adding some adroit religious politicking to the astonishment at his effrontery, was admitted to audience. The king thereupon awarded to Themistocles himself the 200 talents reward for his own apprehension.

Themistocles was highly honored by the Persians and was not required to live at court. He became a leading citizen of Magnesia, in the Hellenic part of the empire. On the occasion of a festival held in his honor, when he was loaded with wealth by the Persians, he made a remark to his children, which is clumsily translated "We would have been undone if we had not been undone"—the purport of which seems to be "If I had not been stripped of my Athenian citizenship and property, I could never have become a Magnesian patrician and millionaire." This is Themistocles' most clearly recorded expression of his own sense that everything he became involved in, however seemingly disadvantageous, would turn out well—*eu*.

One of the many anecdotes concerning both the wit and the self-regard shown by Themistocles that Plutarch relates may be hinted at in the polite exchange contained in the footnote to the occurrence of the word *Eu* in the text of *Finnegans Wake* (307.F8). Accosted once by a man from Seriphos (a place that was in antiquity a by-word for insignificance) who complained that Themistocles owed his eminence to his being an Athenian, Themistocles responded, "True, had I been a Seriphian I would never have become distinguished, and neither would you have, had you been an Athenian" (*Alêthê legeis . . . all' out' an egô Seriphios ôn egenomên endoxos oute su Athênaios*). This reply does not contain the word *eu*, to be sure, but it is framed with the balanced negatives (*out' an . . . oute*) of the footnote (Où . . . Nenni No).

307.L34—307.26-27

Vitellius: Proper and Regular Diet Necessity For   Vitellius arrived in Rome in June a.d. 69, the third new emperor of the year (the suicide Nero had been succeeded by Galba, overthrown in turn by Otho, who then lost his nerve on Vitellius' approach and killed himself), and made himself at once notorious for gluttony, thereby alienating some potential supporters. Toward the end of the year Vespasian's brother revolted in Rome, and in the fighting the Capitol was burned. Vespasian's troops entered the city in December, dragged Vitellius through the streets and murdered him. Vitellius's defeat by Vespasian (aided by Otho's troops) was from the first inevitable, and at one point Vespasian's brother had almost persuaded him to abdicate peacefully, but Vitellius backed out of the agreement. The name *Vitellius* can be construed to mean either "veal" or "egg-yolk".

307.L35—305.27

Darius: If You Do It Do It Now   When attacking Athens Darius landed a large force at Marathon; a defense force of 10,000 Athenians and 1,000 Plataeans, immensely outnumbered, instead of waiting prudently for expected Spartan reinforcements fought the Persians at once and beat them. The Greeks then hurried back to Athens ahead of a Persian naval attack on the city, and drove that, too, off. On both occasions the Athenians "did it now" and the Persians hesitated and failed.

308.L1—308.01

Xenophon: Delays are Dangerous   Xenophon served with Greek mercenaries attached to Cyrus's rebellion against his brother Artaxerxes, king of Persia. After Cyrus's defeat and death at Cunaxa, 10,000 Greeks were isolated inside Persia. At the invitation of the Persians they encamped while their senior officers went to parley with the Persian commanders. The parley was a trap and the Greek officers were cut down and slaughtered. Together with the Spartan, Chirisophus, Xenophon then led a retreat of the 10,000 northwestwards across the mountains to the Black Sea. Indecision and delay had cost them their senior officers; constant movement and fighting got them away safely to the sea in one of the most heroic marches recorded in history.

Supplementary Notes

Digamma

Digamma is the name given by Classical grammarians to what had been the sixth letter of the oldest G alphabets. In the Ionic and Attic dialects, from which developed the *koinê* or common G of the Roman Empire, the sound, and with it the letter, had dropped out of the language before the time of the earliest inscriptions. In some of the other dialects, however, the letter persisted in writing until the Second Century b.c., and the pronunciation of the sound persisted still longer.

The letter represented a consonant, pronounced like the English consonant W, and the name of the letter, when it was still in use, was apparently *wau* (ϝαυ). Although the written letter occurred in several different forms, the best-known (ϝ) resembled a double *gamma* (Γ) or one gamma on top of another. From this appearance the name *digamma* ("double-gamma") was derived.

Although the letter also appears in the form Ⅽ and later as ς, it is clear that the form that evoked the name *digamma* was also the form of the letter that occurred in the version of the G alphabet from which the Etruscan and ultimately the Roman alphabet developed, for the sixth letter of the Roman alphabet is still F. The Romans, however, applied the letter to the representation of a different consonant (#*Labials*).

Historically the sound (and letter) *digamma* was lost in G in initial prevocalic positions in many words the L cognates of which began with V (representing the same consonant as ϝ— i.e., English W). Obvious examples are L *vinum*, G *oinos*, formerly *woinos* (ϝοῖνος), English *wine*; and L *vicus* (see *Finnegans Wake* 003.02) for G *oikos*, formerly *woikos* (οἶκος, ϝοῖκος).

Awareness of the fortunes of this letter gives Joyce several separate opportunities for play—he can drop off W or add it on to the beginnings of words; he can play with those very numerous topsy-turvy versions of the letter F (*Finnegans Wake* p. 18); and he can substitute F for W (*Finnegans Wake* 172.25, "Fireless" for "Wireless"). Whenever we have suspected play with, or allusions to, *digamma*, we have called attention to the fact. The note #*Labials* puts the letter *digamma* in a somewhat wider context.

G-toL: Greek to Latin and Latin to Greek

The heading G-to-L embraces two different but related sets of phenomena:

1. The regular distinctive pattern of correspondences (predictable similarities and differences) between phonetic, syntactical, and lexical features of G and L attributable to their being cognate Indo-European languages at a parallel state of evolution from the common parent;

2. the conventions, in part based on accurate understanding of the genuine patterns of correspondence mentioned in (1.), in part purely formal, that G and L writers habitually employed in transferring elements—i.e., words and concepts—from one language to the other. Although the direction of transfer in most instances is from G-to-L, as the form of our rubric acknowledges, yet during the Roman Empire G absorbed from L a considerable stock of words chiefly having to do with the Roman government and the rulers. But most of the traffic between G and L consisted of the enrichment of the relatively crude primitive L by absorption of the terminology of intellectual and cultural sophistication from G.

Cognate Correspondences

One of the clearest patterns of inherent resemblance between the two languages is their common possession of similar declensions of nouns. Of masculine nouns G has a class with Nom. sing. ending -*os*, Acc. sing. ending -*on*, and Nom. pl. ending -*oi*. Corresponding to these L has a similar class of masculine nouns in which the endings for the same cases occur as respectively -*us*, -*um*, and -*i*. Both languages also have a similar class of neuter nouns, in which both Nom. and Acc. sing. in G end -*on*, in L -*um*. The plural Nom. and Acc. of these nouns end in both languages -*a*. Likewise both languages share a class of feminine nouns ending -*a* in the Nom. sing. (in G sometimes -ê), of which the Gen. sing. and Nom. pl. is -*ai* in G, -*ae* in L. Thus are a number of rule-of-thumb correspondences set up: i.e., -*os* G = -*us* L; -*on* G = -*um* L; -*oi* G = -*i* L; -*a* or -ê G = -*a* L; -*ai* G = -*ae* L.

In these endings the digraphs *ai* (G) and *ae* (L) are phonetically identical, and so establish the principle that G words with -*ai*- in any position will be rendered into L with -*ae*-, and vice-versa. Thus G *Phaidra* becomes L *Phaedra*, and L *Caesar* becomes G *Kaisar* (for *c* L = *k* G, see below). G *oi* and L *i* (as in masc. pl. Nom. of nouns) were not, however, phonetically identical, so that to represent the digraph -*oi*- in G loanwords, L developed (on the analogy of *ai* G = *ae* L) the digraph -*oe*-, whereby G *Phoinix*, for instance, became L *Phoenix*.

The three classes of nouns instanced above that are shared by both languages by no means exhaust either language's complement of nouns. G, for one example, has *neuter* nouns ending -*a* in the Nom. sing., pl. -*ata*. L has *feminine* nouns ending -*io* in the Nom. sing. of which the oblique stem (*in all other cases of the noun*), ends -*ion*. Thus, for example, *natio*, Gen. sing. *nationis*, Acc. sing. *nationem*, Nom. pl. *nationes*, etc., and like words, appear only with the -*ion* stem in the daughter Romance languages (and English), thus Italian *nazione*, Spanish *nación*, French (and English) *nation*; L *unio* by the same process yields French and English *union*. Deliberate confusion [N.B. from L *confusio*] of the L-derived -*ion* ending with G -*on* is the source of some Joycean play, as is also confusion among the feminine and neuter sing. -*a* ending and the neuter pl. -*a* ending.

Examples of Joyce's play with these facts:

(a) a pseudo-word like *chrismon* (*Finnegans Wake* 119.17) is created by assuming that *chrisma* is a G neuter pl., of which *chrismon* would be the regular sing. In fact *chrisma* is a G. neuter sing., of which the plural is *chrismata*.

(b) a pseudo-word like *unium* (*Finnegans Wake* 317.29) is created by assuming that *union* (English or French) is a G neuter Nom./Acc. or a G masculine Acc. sing., and so can be rendered into pseudo-L by altering G -*on* to L -*um*. Of course the word is really of L origin, deriving from the oblique cases of the L feminine *unio*.

A more intriguing pattern of relationships between G and L is seen in the correspondence of certain consonants. Of these correspondences, those most fruitful for Joyce are those of G *h*- to L *s*- and of G *p* and *t* to L *qu*. The first of these equations yields such pairs as G *hyper* = L *super*, G *hypo* = L *sub*, G *hexa*, *hepta* = L *sex*, *septem*, G *herpes* = L *serpes* The second gives for *t* = *qu* the G *tis*, *ti* and *te* = L *quis*, *qui* and *que*, for G *tettara* L *quattuor*; for *p* = *qu* the G *pou* = L *quo*. Both *p* and *t* = *qu* are shown in the pair G *pente* = L *quinque*. The doublet G *hepomai* = L *sequor* shows both h = s and p = qu. In this deponent verb (= "I follow") the G -*mai* and L -*r* are merely inflectional endings which, when removed, leave G *hepo* = L *sequo*.

Joyce employs both of these sets of correspondences. Frequently in *Finnegans Wake* initial *h*- is a pseudo-G rendering of a word properly beginning *s*-; e.g., *hister* (528.11) is a false hellenization of *sister*. The correspondence between G *p* and L *qu* (*c*, *k*), however, is one Joyce employs ceaselessly; see #*P/K Split.*

Classical Conventions

Of the conventions employed by classical writers to transform G into L or vice-versa, few seem to be used consciously and deliberately by Joyce. Since his acquaintance with classical G appears to have been minimal, however, his G vocabulary often appears in latinate disguise, frequently derived from ML. A signal instance is his Dedalus from L Daedalus from G Daidalos. Consequently it may be useful here to list the more usual conventional equivalents, both to clarify Joyce's manipulation of G and to make easier the recognition of the real G underlying some of his latinate constructions:

G	L	Illustrations
ai	ae, e	*kaino-, Klutaimnêstra* G; *caeno-, Clytaemnestra, Clytemnestra* L
ê	a, e	*Athênai, mêtêr* G; *Athenae, mater* L
ei	i	*eidôlon* G; *idolum* L
k	c	*Klutaimnêstra, Kaisar* G; *Clytemnestra, Caesar* L
oi	oe, e, i	*Phoibos, oikonomikos, [w]oinos* G; *Phoebus, oeconomicus, vinum* L
-ôn	-o	*Platôn, Phaidôn* G; *Plato, Phaedo* L
-on	-um	*êlektron, Kênaion* G; *electrum, Cenaeum* L
-os	-us	*Ptolemaios* G; *Ptolemaeus* L
ou	u	*Mousa, Mousaios* G; *Musa, Musaeus* L
u	y	*Psuchê* G; *Psyche* L

Labials

Labial consonants are those produced by employing the two lips (bilabials) or the lower lip and the upper teeth (labiodentals). Twelve hypothetical consonants might be produced in these positions, but at no historical stage did either L or G make use of more than 6 at a time of these 12 potential consonants, and Classical G made do with as few as 4. The specific selection in use, however, has varied at different times, with consequent alteration in the phonetic values of the written symbols (letters or graphs) used to represent them. The variation in the denotations of these consonantal graphs is the basis for spelling games that Joyce plays throughout *Finnegans Wake*. This note will attempt to make those games intelligible.

The *bilabial* position allows for the formation of *stops, aspirates,* and *spirants;* the *labiodental* position conveniently only for *spirants.* Positing an *unvoiced,* a *voiced,* and a *nasal* variant for each of those four formations produces the total of 12 potential labial consonants. Designating each consonantal position by coordinates—a letter for each formation and a number for each variant within the formation—we arrive at a schematic distribution thus:

		unvoiced	*voiced*	*nasal*
Bilabial:	Stop	A1	A2	A3
	Aspirate	B1	B2	B3
	Spirant	C1	C2	C3
Labiodental:	Spirant	D1	D2	D3

Some of these potential consonants are never realized in L, G, or English. None of these languages has at any time featured e.g. a labiodental spirant nasal (D3). As a start to understanding this chart, note that modern English makes regular use of 5 (or 6) of these labial consonants—A1, A2, A3, D1 and D2—represented respectively by the graphs P, B, M, F (and PH), and V. If consonantal W is allowed to occupy position C1, as an unvoiced bilabial spirant, English has 6 labials. The *sound* of position B1 occurs fortuitously in such English words as "u*ph*ill," but English makes no phonemic use of aspirates, and the digraph PH usually represents the same unvoiced labiodental spirant (D1) also represented by F. English also, we should note, makes no use of bilabial spirants, and English speakers consequently often have difficulty in hearing them correctly (witness "buckaroo" for Spanish *vaquero*—initial consonant C2).

The distribution of these consonants in the Classical languages occurs approximately as follows:

I. Greek

A. *Pre-Classical G (OG)* may have had 5 labials: A1, A2, A3, B1 and C1, represented by the symbols π, β, μ, φ and ϝ *(digamma).* (See #*Digamma.*)

B. *Classical G (G)* was reduced to only 4 of these consonants. The sound of C1 being lost, the [Attic] alphabet dropped the letter *digamma* (ϝ).

C. *Post-Classical G* underwent a shift in consonants: B1 was replaced by D1, and A2 by C2. The same symbols continued to be used for the new sounds, however, so that φ now represented D1 instead of B1, and β now represented C2 instead of A2 (=English B).

D. *Modern G (MG)* has displaced C2 by D2, still using the symbol β (now = English V). but in loan words Mod. G has re-acquired the sound of A2 (English B), and in order to write it combines the symbols for the nasal (A3) and unvoiced (A1) homorganics—$\mu\pi$ (= MP)—so that the borrowed Italian word *bomba* ("bomb") must be spelled $\mu\pi o\mu\pi a$ (= MPOMPA).

II . Latin

A. *Pre-Classical L (OL)* like pre-classical G employed 5 labials: A1, A2, A3, C1 and D1, represented by the symbols P, B, M, V, and F. L had developed the letter V for the C1 sound previously written in G by *digamma* ($\mathcal{F}$), but in the D1 position had a sound for which G had no equivalent, and consequently no letter. L accordingly borrowed for this sound the discarded and now redundant *digamma*, in the form F.

B. *Classical L (L)* retained the 5 labial consonants of OL, but to them added the unvoiced aspirate B1 in words borrowed from G. The G letter ϕ was rendered in L by PH. This digraph did *not* then represent the D1 labiodental spirant F, but rather the aspirate P in English "uphill." At this point L had 6 labial consonants, which seems to be the maximum acceptable at one time to any of these languages.

C. *Post-Classical L (LL & ML)*, like post-classical G underwent a disturbance of consonants, in which B1 shifted to D1 (but was still represented by the digraph PH). The C1 sound was voiced, thereby shifting to C2, at the same time the voiced stop A2 in intervocalic position opened to the spirant C2. Consequently the new voiced bilabial spirant C2 was represented by both B and V (the latter no longer retaining its C1 unvoiced sound). Subsequently the C2 sound retracted to the labiodental position, carrying with it the symbol V (whence the modern English value of that consonant). Medieval L (ML) had thus 5 labials: A1, A2, A3, D1, and D2, represented by the graphs P, B, M, F (and PH), and V.

From this conspectus it may be seen that in the Classical languages alone at least 8 of the 12 potential labial consonants were realized at one stage or another, the same symbols carrying different values at different times, viz.:

	1	2	3
A	π, P	β, B	μ, M
B	ϕ, PH	—	—
C	$\mathcal{F}$, V	β, B, V	—
D	F, ϕ, PH	β, V	—

Although our concern here is properly with the Classical languages, which offer in their successive stages such a variety of permutations among the labial consonants, to restrict ourselves to those languages would underestimate the possibilities exploited in *Finnegans Wake.* If we add to the consideration three other languages Joyce knew and used in *Finnegans Wake*— English, German, and Irish—the dimensions of possibility somewhat expand. English makes use of the C1 sound, as we have noted, for which it employs the letter W, yielding another labial graph to play with. In German, however, the same symbol denotes the D2 consonant, and V, which English uses in the D2 position, represents the sound of D1 (=English F).

Still further, in Old Irish we find A2 sometimes represented by the graph P, and C2 by the graph B. Also, unlike the other languages we have been examining, Old Irish realized the consonant possible at C3—a bilabial nasal spirant—which it represented by the symbol M. But in Middle Irish this consonant lost its nasal quality and fell together with C2, which thus came to be represented indifferently by the graphs B and M.

As a final fillip let us add a language we have no direct evidence that Joyce knew anything about—Scottish Gaidhlig. In the orthography of that language the graph B generally stands for the A1 consonant (English P), and the graph P for the aspirate B1 (G ɸ; L PH). Therefore a full chart of the labial consonants in all these languages (transliterating G letters into the Roman alphabet) gives this spread:

	1	2	3
A	P, B	B, P, MP	M
B	PH, P	—	—
C	F, V, W	B, V, M	M
D	F, PH, V	V, B, W	—

According to this chart, then, the graph B, for instance, may be variously equated with the graphs P, MP, V or M; and the graph V may be replaced by F, W, PH, B, or M. If to this astonishing situation is applied the logical theorem that any two things equal to the same third thing must be equal to one another, we are led to the conclusion that *all* of these graphs are interchangeable. Joycean acceptance of this sort of formal logic therefore allows the optional interchange of any of these consonants or digraphs: B,

F, M, MP, P, PH, V, W. Whenever we have noticed the author doing so, we have flagged the place with the lemma #Labials.

L/R Interchange

The phenomena in *Finnegans Wake* that may be characterized as L/R Interchange have been noted in the *Gaelic Lexicon* (pp. 392-393) because they occur so frequently in the book in Irish contexts. As noted in that place, however, the interchange of l and r is a virtually universal linguistic phenomenon. It is appropriate here, therefore, to illustrate this interchange in a classical context, for whatever light it may further shed on Joyce's manipulations.

An equivalence of l and r is sometimes a specific differentiation between G and L, as, for instance, G *leirion* = L *lilium*, G *barbaros* = L *balbus* (#G-to-L). Sometimes this distinction has arisen out of an internal development within L. Thus for G *astêr* L has *stella*. But the first -l- in *stella* comes from assimilation to the second -l-. The word originally in L was *sterula* (preserving the *ster-* root as in G *astêr*, German *Stern*, English *star*) which by L/R Interchange became **stelula* and thence *stella*. Another doublet in L (or apparent doublet: the words may in fact come from quite different originals) consists of *terra* and *tellus*, words virtually identical in meaning.

In the later history of L we at times find -r- replacing -l- instead of the other way round as with *sterula/stella*. The L word *capitulum*, for instance, on its way to becoming French (and English) replaced the -l- with -r-, so yielding *chapitre* and *chapter*.

By combining L/R Interchange with his favorite P/K Split, Joyce on at least one occasion makes a L word out of a non-cognate G word, changing its associations from democratic to aristocratic. The word is *pathoricks* (027.02), in context obviously suggesting Patrick, the L form of whose name, *Patricius* (from *pater*, "father") means "of the rank *or* dignity of the *patres*; belonging to the patricians, patrician, noble." By invoking both P/K Split and L/R Interchange, however, we can restore this word to *catholicks*, from G *katholikos*, an adjective meaning "general, universal," or the adverb *katholikôs*, "generally, in the majority of cases."

P/K Split

A discussion of the linguistic split between p and k (c, qu, q) is included in the Supplementary Notes to the *Gaelic Lexicon* (pp. 403-405) because the distinction between initial p- and initial c- is a differentiating characteristic of the Celtic languages, separating them into so-called P-Celtic (Welsh, Cornish, Breton) and Q-Celtic (Irish, Scottish, Manx). A similar distinction may be noted, however, among the Classical languages, and so it has seemed proper to present the phenomenon again here, in a Classical context. Whether Joyce bases himself specifically on the Celtic languages or on the Classical languages in this regard is not easy to determine, but certainly he seems endlessly fascinated by this linguistic distinction.

With regard to the Classical languages the situation may be stated with relatively little complication. An original Indo-European initial *kw- produced in OL an initial k- sound, usually spelled c-; in L this k had often redeveloped a following semivowel, and occurs in spelling as q-, cu-, and qu-. The same Indo-European initial in G became k- or t- or p-. As between L and G, the P/K Split therefore pertains to those Indo-European words which in L begin qu-, in G p-. Sufficient examples are L *quinque, equos, sequor,* G *pente* (or *pempe*), *hippos, hepô*(mai). This split between L and G does not, however, exhaust the permeations of the P/K Split in the Classical languages.

In G, as we have noted, Indo-European initial *kw- sometimes became t- rather than p-, and words in which this change took place might seem to be outside the survey of the P/K division. It happens however that in Oscan, a once-widespread Italic language fairly closely related to L, the original words that in G developed t-initials instead developed p- initials. So that where the P/K Split fails to operate per se in distinguishing L from G, it remains a characteristic distinction between L and Oscan. Examples to illustrate this point are the G words *tis, ti, te,* for which the L equivalents are *quis, qui, que.* But the L words are distinguished from their Oscan cognates precisely on a P/K Split, the Oscan equivalents being *pis, pi, pe.*

Occasionally, it should be noted, a distinction along the line of a P/K Split arises within L itself. For instance, beside the word *columba/columbus,* "dove, pigeon," L has a separate word, *palumbes* or *palumba* meaning "wood-pigeon, ring-dove." The words are obviously etymological doublets, distinguished by the initial c- and p-. Peculiarly enough, in this case G makes no alteration to the original initial and preserves the word as *kolumbos.*

Joyce's manipulation of the P/K Split in *Finnegans Wake*, regardless of the source of authority to which he may be assumed to appeal, makes no attempt to be either etymologically or historically correct. He is extremely given to interchanging initial p's and k's, and will regard any phonetic k as replaceable by p regardless of its spelling or etymology. Thus at 484.32 he produces *Prestopher* out of, presumably, an initial k spelled ch-, i.e., **Chrestopher* (though ML **Crestafer* for L **Cristafer* is probably also here). In any case, the employment of this device is so omnipresent in *Finnegans Wake* the reader might do well to substitute an initial k for any initial p in the book, and vice-versa, just on the chance Joyce may have another joker up his sleeve.

Reduplication

Reduplication is a process in G and L verbs by which the initial consonant of the stem plus its following vowel are prefixed to the stem of the verb. The process is flectional, and primarily denotes the perfect tense. In G all verbs are subject to reduplication in the perfect, and the process also occurs widely throughout the passive forms of the verb. In L the process is much less widespread, but is still significantly visible in the perfect construction of several verbs.

The process of reduplication appears to have been prevalent in the primitive state of the entire Indo-European linguistic stock, and to have taken originally the form of prefixing to the affected form of the verb the entire initial consonant or consonant-group plus the exact following vowel. Paradoxically, L, which has to a much greater extent than G discarded entirely the system of reduplication, preserves much better than does G the reduplicated vowels. G, which employs reduplication very widely in the flection of its verbs, reduces reduplicated vowels usually to -e- or -i-.

Examples of reduplication in G: *pauô*, "I stop," perfect *pepauka*, "I have stopped"; *leipô*, "I leave," *leloipa*, "I have left"; *graphô*, "I write," *gegrapha*, "I have written."

Examples of reduplication in L: *do*, "I give," *dedi*, "I have given"; *spondeo*, "I pledge," *spospondi*, later *spopondi*, "I have pledged"; *tango*, "I touch," *tetigi*, "I have touched"; *tundo*, "I strike," *tutudi*, "I have struck"; etc.

Reduplication is also employed in both languages to alter the signification of a stem, usually in order to create a transitive verb. E.g., the L verb *sto*, "I stand" (intransitive meaning), by reduplication becomes *sisto*, "I set, I cause to stand, I stand (transitive)." Likewise the stem *gen-* common to both languages produces by reduplication the verb *gignomai* (G) and *gigno* (L), "I beget."

Joyce in *Finnegans Wake* pays particular attention to the reduplicating

L verbs *tango* and *pango* and their reduplicated perfects *tetigi* and *pepigi* (pp. 574-576) alerting his reader to his interest in reduplication. We have therefore assumed in such locutions as "Cawcaught" (*Finnegans Wake* 329.13) that reduplication is being utilized in a perfective sense, and have so marked the occurrence. At times, doubtless, reduplication of an initial syllable is primarily designed to reproduce HCE's guilty stammer, but Joyce is never averse to achieving two or more effects at the cost of one, so we have called atlention to most such occurrences as examples of G and L perfective, transitive or passive reduplication.

Rhotacism

Rhotacism (from G *rho*, the letter R) is the name given to the regular process in L by which an etymological -s- is changed into -r-. The commonest situation in which it occurs is that of third-declension nouns with sibilant stems, in which the final -s of the stem becomes -r- in the stem of the oblique cases (the cases of the noun other than the nominative singular). Examples are: *mas, maris*; *Ceres, Cereris*; *cucumis, cucumeris*; *Venus, Veneris*; *flos, floris*; *corpus, corporis*; *Ligus, Liguris*; *genus, generis*. English derivatives from several of these words are from the rhotacized oblique form, e.g., cucumber from *cucumeris*, venereal from *Veneris*, floral from *floris*, corporal and corporeal from *corporis*, Ligurian from *Liguris* and generic from *generis*.

The L third declension of nouns also contains some sets of doublets, in which two forms of the same noun coexist, one ending -s the other -r: *arbos, colos, honos, lepus, labos*, etc., beside *arbor, color, honor, lepur, labor* etc. It will be noticed that here also it is the rhotacized forms that have come down into our modern languages. Other words in L were early rhotacized, so that their -r- forms are more frequent in the classical period than their -s- forms, and in some instances the -s- forms were ousted completely. Examples of such words are: *asa, lases, plusima, meliosem, foedesum, Fusius, Papisius, Valesius, fusvos, janitos*, all of which became respectively *ara, lares, plurima, meliorem, foederum, Furius, Papirius, Valerius, furvus, janitor*. Other doublets that persisted side by side include *quaeso/quaero, nasus/naris* and *pulvis/pulver*. In all but the double *nasus/naris* (English *nasal*, etc.) it is the rhotacized form that we have inherited.

On a few occasions in *Finnegans Wake* we have suspected Joyce of rhotacizing an etymological -s- in one of the words he is maltreating. We have indicated such places by reference to this present note.